Brief Edition **The**
AMERICAN
PEOPLE

BRIEF EDITION
VOLUME I ~ to 1877

The AMERICAN PEOPLE

Creating a Nation and a Society

Gary B. Nash
University of California, Los Angeles

Julie Roy Jeffrey
Goucher College

John R. Howe
University of Minnesota

Peter J. Frederick
Wabash College

Allen F. Davis
Temple University

Allan M. Winkler
Miami University

HarperCollinsPublishers

Executive Editor: Bruce Borland
Development Editor: Kathleen Dolan
Project Coordination: Hockett Editorial Service
Text and Cover Design: Marsha Cohen, Parallelogram
Cover Illustration: "La Crosse Playing Among the Sioux," by
  Seth Eastman, in the collection of The Corcoran Gallery of
  Art
Photo Researcher: Leslie Coopersmith
Production Manager: Michael Weinstein
Compositor: Graphic Sciences Corporation
Printer and Binder: Arcata Graphics / Kingsport
Cover Printer: The Lehigh Press, Inc.

For permission to use copyrighted material, grateful acknowledgment is made to the copyright holders on p. C-1, which is hereby made part of this copyright page.

The American People: Creating a Nation and a Society, Brief Edition, Volume I to 1877
Copyright © 1992 by HarperCollins Publishers Inc.

Library of Congress Cataloging-in-Publication Data

The American people: creating a nation and a society / Gary B. Nash
  . . . [et al.]. — Brief ed.
     p.   cm.
  Volume I to 1877
  Includes bibliographical references and index.
  ISBN 0-06-500262-8 (Volume I)
  ISBN 0-06-500263-6 (Volume II)
  1. United States — History.   I. Nash, Gary B.
  E178.1.A4932   1992
  973 — dc20   91-26634
                                              CIP

91 92 93 94 9 8 7 6 5 4 3 2 1

Brief Contents

Detailed Contents   vii

Maps/Charts   x

Preface   xi

About the Authors   xvi

PART ONE   A COLONIZING PEOPLE, 1492–1776   1

Chapter 1   Three Worlds Meet   2

Chapter 2   Colonizing a Continent   22

Chapter 3   Mastering the New World   44

Chapter 4   The Maturing of Colonial Society   62

Chapter 5   Bursting the Colonial Bonds   88

PART TWO   A REVOLUTIONARY PEOPLE, 1775–1828   109

Chapter 6   A People in Revolution   110

Chapter 7   Consolidating the Revolution   138

Chapter 8   Creating a Nation   154

Chapter 9   Politics and Society in the Early Republic   170

Chapter 10   The Preindustrial Republic   191

PART THREE   AN EXPANDING PEOPLE, 1820–1877   211

Chapter 11   Currents of Change in the Northeast and the Old Northwest   212

Chapter 12   Slavery and the Old South   232

Chapter 13   Shaping America in the Antebellum Age   251

Chapter 14   Moving West   272

Chapter 15   The Union in Peril   292

Chapter 16   The Union Severed   310

Chapter 17   The Union Reconstructed   331

Appendix   A–1

Credits   C–1

Index   I–1

Detailed Contents

Maps/Charts   x
Preface   xi
About the Authors   xvi

PART ONE   A COLONIZING PEOPLE, 1492–1776   1

1   Three Worlds Meet   2
    The People of America Before Columbus   3
    Africa on the Eve of Contact   8
    Europe in the Age of Exploration   10
    The Iberian Conquest of America   14
    England Looks West   17
    Conclusion : Converging Worlds   20

2   Colonizing a Continent   22
    The Chesapeake Tobacco Coast   23
    Massachusetts and Its Offspring   27
    From the St. Lawrence to the Hudson   34
    Proprietary Carolina : A Restoration Reward   35
    The Quakers' Peaceable Kingdom   38
    Conclusion : The Achievement of New Societies   42

3   Mastering the New World   44
    Black Bondage   45
    Slave Culture   49
    The Struggle for Land   52
    An Era of Instability   54
    Contending for a Continent   58
    Conclusion : Controlling the New Environment   60

4   The Maturing of Colonial Society   62
    America's First Population Explosion   63
    Beyond the Appalachians   65
    A Land of Family Farms   69
    The Plantation South   72
    The Urban World of Commerce and Ideas   74
    The Great Awakening   77
    Political Life   81
    Conclusion : America in 1750   86

5   Bursting the Colonial Bonds   88
    The Climactic Seven Years' War   89
    The Crisis with England   93
    The Ideology of Revolutionary Republicanism   100
    The Turmoil of Revolutionary Society   103
    Conclusion : Forging a Revolution   106

PART TWO   A REVOLUTIONARY PEOPLE, 1775–1828   109

6   *A People in Revolution*   110
     The War for American Independence   112
     The Experience of War   119
     The Revolution and the Economy   125
     The Ferment of Revolutionary Politics   127
     Revolutionary Politics in the States   131
     Conclusion : The Crucible of Revolution   136

7   *Consolidating the Revolution*   138
     Struggling with the Peacetime Agenda   139
     Political Tumult in the States   143
     Toward a New National Government   146
     Conclusion : Completing the Revolution   153

8   *Creating a Nation*   154
     Launching the National Republic   155
     The Republic in a Threatening World   161
     Federalists versus Jeffersonians   163
     Conclusion : Toward the Nineteenth Century   168

9   *Politics and Society in the Early Republic*   170
     Restoring Republican Liberty   171
     Building an Agrarian Republic   174
     Indian-White Relations in the Early Republic   177
     A Foreign Policy for the Agrarian Republic   182
     Culture and Politics in Transition   186
     Conclusion : The Passing of an Era   189

10   *The Preindustrial Republic*   191
     The Preindustrial Economy   192
     The Nature of Preindustrial Society   199
     Perfecting Republican Society   204
     Conclusion : Between Two Worlds   209

PART THREE   AN EXPANDING PEOPLE, 1820–1877   211

11   *Currents of Change in the Northeast and the Old Northwest*   212
     Economic Growth   213
     Early Manufacturing   218
     Urban Life   222
     Rural Communities   227
     Conclusion : The Character of Progress   229

12   *Slavery and the Old South*   232
     Building the Cotton Kingdom   233
     Morning : Master in the Big House   239
     Noon : Slaves in House and Fields   241
     Night : Slaves in Their Quarters   244

Resistance and Freedom   246
Conclusion : Douglass's Dream of Freedom   249

13 *Shaping America in the Antebellum Age*   251
The Political Response to Change   252
Religious Revival and Reform   259
Utopian Communitarianism   260
Reforming Society   262
Abolitionism and Women's Rights   265
Conclusion : Perfecting America   269

14 *Moving West*   272
Probing the Trans-Mississippi West   273
Winning the Trans-Mississippi West   274
Going West   279
Living on the Frontier   282
Cultures in Conflict   286
Conclusion : Fruits of Manifest Destiny   290

15 *The Union in Peril*   292
Slavery in the Territories   293
Political Disintegration   297
Kansas and the Two Cultures   300
Polarization and the Road to War   302
The Divided House Falls   305
Conclusion : The "Irrepressible Conflict"   307

16 *The Union Severed*   310
Organizing for War   311
Clashing on the Battlefield, 1861–1862   314
The Tide Turns, 1863–1865   319
Changes Wrought by War   323
Conclusion : An Uncertain Future   329

17 *The Union Reconstructed*   331
The Bittersweet Aftermath of War   332
National Reconstruction   336
Life After Slavery   340
Reconstruction in the States   343
Conclusion : A Mixed Legacy   348

Appendix   A–1
Declaration of Independence in Congress, July 4, 1776   A–1
Constitution of the United States of America   A–3
Presidential Elections   A–15

Credits   **C–1**

Index   **I–1**

Maps/Charts

Indian Tribes During the Period of Early European Settlement 7
West African Cultures and Slaving Forts 10
Oceanic Exploration in the Fifteenth and Sixteenth Centuries 12
Early Chesapeake Settlement 26
Early New England 31
Restoration Colonies: New York, the Jerseys, Pennsylvania, and the Carolinas 36
Origins and Destinations of African Slaves, 1526–1810 47
German Settlements, 1775 64
Scots-Irish Settlements, 1775 64
Population of European Colonies in North America, 1680–1770 65
France's Inland Empire, 1600–1720 68
Colonial Foundations of the American Political System 82
British Exports to North America, 1756–1775 97
Western Land Claims Ceded by the States, 1782–1802 113
Military Operations in the North, 1776–1780 115
Military Operations in the South, 1778–1781 116
Exports and Imports, 1768–1783 125
Areas of White Settlement and Frontier in 1787 141
British and Spanish Possessions in Eastern North America, 1783 143
Federalist and Anti-Federalist Areas, 1787–1788 151
Presidential Election of 1800 166
Exploring the Trans-Mississippi West, 1804–1807 177
Indian Land Cessions, 1750–1830 178
Missouri Compromise of 1820 188
Important Routes Westward 198
Growth of the Railroads, 1850–1860 214
Southern Cotton Production, 1821–1859 235
Concentration of Slavery, 1820–1860 237
Religion, Reform, and Utopian Activity, 1830–1850 263
United States Territorial Expansion by 1860 275
The Mexican War, 1846–1848 277
Overland Trails to the West 281
Indian Tribes in 1840 288
The Compromise of 1850 295
"Bleeding Kansas" 301
Major Causes and Events Leading to the Civil War 306
Secession of the Southern States 311
Eastern Theater of the Civil War, 1861–1862 315
Trans-Mississippi Campaign of the Civil War 317
The Tide Turns, 1863–1865 322
The United States in 1865: Crisis at the End of the Civil War 333
Reconstruction Amendments 339
Return to the Union During Reconstruction 345

Preface

The Yoruba people of West Africa have an old saying, "However far the stream flows, it never forgets its source." Why, we wonder, do such ancient societies as the Yoruba find history so important, while modern American students question its relevance? This book aims to end such skepticism about the usefulness of history.

When we study our own history, that of the American people, we see a rich and extraordinarily complex human story. This country, whose written history began with a convergence of Native Americans, Europeans, and Africans, has always been a nation of diverse peoples — a magnificent mosaic of cultures, religions, and skin shades. This book explores how American society assumed its present shape and developed its present forms of government; how as a nation we have conducted our foreign affairs and managed our economy; how as individuals and in groups we have lived, worked, loved, married, raised families, voted, argued, protested, and struggled to fulfill our dreams and the noble ideals of the sacred texts of the American experiment.

Several ways of making the past understandable distinguish this book from most textbooks written in the last twenty years. The coverage of public events like presidential elections, diplomatic treaties, and economic legislation is integrated with the private human stories that pervade them. Within a chronological framework we have woven together our history as a nation, as a people, and as a society. When, for example, national political events are discussed, we analyze their impact on social and economic life at the state and local level. Wars are described not only as they unfolded on the battlefields and in the salons of diplomats, but also on the home front, where they are history's greatest motor of social change. The interaction of ordinary Americans with extraordinary events runs as a theme throughout the book.

Above all, we have tried to show the "humanness" of our history as it is revealed in people's everyday lives. The authors have often used the words of ordinary Americans to capture the authentic human voices of those who participated in and responded to epic events such as war, slavery, industrialization, and reform movements.

Goals and Themes of the Book

Our primary goal is to provide students with a rich, balanced, and thought-provoking treatment of the American past. By this we mean a history that treats the lives and experiences of Americans of all national origins and cultural backgrounds, at all levels of society, and in all regions of the country. It also means a history that seeks connections between the many factors — political, economic, technological, social, religious, intellectual, and biological — that have molded and remolded American society over four centuries. And finally it means a history that encourages students to think about how we have all inherited a complex past filled with both notable achievements and thorny problems. The only history befitting a democratic nation is one that inspires students to initiate a frank and searching dialogue with their past.

To speak of a dialogue about the past presumes that history is interpretive. Students should understand that historians are continually reinterpreting the past. New interpretations are often based on the discovery of new evidence, but more often new interpretations emerge because historians reevaluate old evidence in the light of new ideas that spring from the times in which they write and from their personal views of the world.

Through this book, we also hope to promote class discussions, which can be organized around eight questions that we see as basic to the American historical experience:

1. How have Americans developed a stable political system consistent with the fundamen-

tal principles of our nation's founding and flexible enough to address the extraordinary changes that have occurred in the last two centuries? To what degree have they fashioned a national democratic order consistent with those principles?

2. What forms has the tension between idealism — a sense of the special virtue of the American people and the importance of the common good — and individual self-interest, as expressed in the struggle for material gain and personal advancement, taken in the past?

3. What are the competing claims of liberty and authority — in families, schools, workplaces, communities, and nation? How have Americans argued and negotiated over the ways in which power and authority are justified, limited, and rightfully distributed?

4. What has been the character of the sporadic but recurring reform impulse in American society? To what extent has reform in the last two centuries been directed at more fully realizing the ideals of liberty, equality, and social justice in racial, gender, and social relations?

5. What has been the role of our nation in the world, and how has it expressed the tension between mission-oriented expansionism and isolationism?

6. In what ways have economic and technological changes affected the daily lives, work, family structure, leisure habits, and community relations of all Americans?

7. What has been the experience of the country's original inhabitants and newly arrived immigrant groups as they confronted the dominant culture, which often seemed to threaten their ethnic, racial, and religious heritage?

8. In what ways have Americans struggled for social unity and national identity amid cultural diversity and conflict?

In writing a history that revolves around these themes, we have tried to convey two dynamics that operate in all societies. First, we observe people continuously adjusting to new developments, such as industrialization and urbanization, over which they seemingly have little control; yet we realize that people are not paralyzed by history but are the fundamental creators of it. They retain the ability, individually and collectively, to shape the world in which they live and thus in considerable degree to control their own lives.

Second, we emphasize the connections that always exist among social, political, economic, and cultural events. Just as our individual lives are never neatly parceled into separate spheres of activity, the life of a society is made up of a complicated and often messy mixture of forces, events, and accidental occurrences. In this text, political and economic, technological and cultural factors are intertwined like strands in a rope.

Part Organization

The chapters of this book are grouped into six parts relating to major periods in American history. Each part begins with a brief *introductory essay* that outlines how the eight organizing questions described above are developed in the subsequent chapters.

Chapter Structure

Every chapter begins with a *personal story* recalling the experience of an ordinary or lesser-known American. Chapter 1, for example, is introduced with the tragic account of Opechancanough, a Powhattan tribesman whose entire life of nearly ninety years was consumed by a struggle against the land, hunger, and alien values brought by Spanish and English newcomers. This brief anecdote serves several purposes. First, it introduces the overarching themes and major concepts of the chapter, in this case the meeting of three societies — Native American, European, and African — in the North American wilderness, each with different cultural values, life-styles, and aspirations. Second, the personal story launches the chapter in a way that facilitates learning — by engaging the student with a human account. Last, the personal story suggests that history was shaped by ordinary as well as extraordinary people. At the end of the personal story a *brief overview* links the biographical sketch to the chapter by elaborating the major themes of the chapter.

We aim to facilitate the learning process for students in other ways as well. Every chapter ends with pedagogical features to reinforce and expand the presentation. A *conclusion* briefly summarizes the main concepts and developments elaborated in the chapter and serves as a bridge to the following chapter. An annotated list of *recommended readings* provides supplementary sources for further study or research; novels contemporary to the period are often included. Finally, a *timeline* reviews the major events and developments covered in the chapter. Each graph, map, and illustration has been chosen to relate clearly to the narrative.

The Brief Edition

This text is a Brief Edition of the very successful second edition of *The American People*. This shorter volume — approximately half the length of the complete version — will be particularly useful in one semester courses and those courses which assign wide readings in primary sources, monographs, or articles in addition to the main text.

The foremost goal of the abridgement was to preserve the distinctive character of the complete text. The balance of political, social, economic, and cultural history remains the same, revolving around the same central, organizing themes described above. The structure and organization of the text — parts, chapters, sections and subsections — are unchanged. Deletions have been made on a careful line-by-line basis. All important topics are in place, as are the interpretive connections between the many factors molding our society. We have eliminated only detail, extra examples, and illustrative material within sections. While it might have been easier

to delete more of the "humanness" of history, leaving room for facts and more facts, we have been careful to retain our focus on history as it is revealed through the lives of ordinary Americans, and the interplay of social and political factors.

Supplemental Teaching and Learning Aids

Several companion volumes for both teachers and students enhance this comprehensive presentation of American history.

- **Teaching the American People : A Guide for Instructors** by Julie Roy Jeffrey and Peter J. Frederick. Drawing on ideas from their teaching workshops, this comprehensive resource guide offers helpful suggestions on using the text in the classroom, as well as ways in which lively class discussion and active learning among students can be encouraged. The manual also provides a file of exam questions and lists of audio-visual resources.

- **Two-volume Study Guide** by Julie Roy Jeffrey and Peter J. Frederick. This class-tested, two-volume study guide contains chapter outlines with important themes, highlights, and learning goals, in addition to a glossary of terms, learning enrichment ideas, sample test questions, exercises for identification and interpretation, and geography exercises corresponding to maps in the text.

- **Discovering American History Through Maps and Views,** by Gerald A. Danzer, University of Illinois, Chicago. This exciting collection of map transparencies contains 140 full-color cartographic and pictorial maps, views, plans, and photos including urban plans, building diagrams, works of art and classic maps. Each map is accompanied by an instructional outline explaining what can be learned from the map and its historical significance. Assembled in a convenient three-ring binder, this innovative transparency program is free to adopters.

- **Mapping American History: A Guide For Beginning Students,** by Gerald A. Danzer, University of Illinois, Chicago. This *free* student map workbook builds students' geographical literacy while providing opportunities to interpret maps as historical documents.
- **Harper Audio History Cassette: "Oral History: American Voices"; "Great Speeches: Words that Made History".** These cassettes feature voices from America's past as recorded in diaries, letters, interviews, and speeches. They cover a broad range, from interviews by Studs Terkel to the journals of pioneer women, to political speeches.
- **SuperShell II Software.** This computerized study guide includes comprehensive chapter outlines, self-tests with multiple-choice, true-false, and completion quizzes, flash cards for terminology and identification.
- **Test Bank,** by Charles Cook, Houston Community College, and J.B. Smallwood, North Texas State University. This test bank contains approximately 50 questions per text chapter, coded for difficulty level and cognitive type.
- **TestMaster.** This test-generation software offers a menu-driven program that enables instructors to add, delete, edit, and scramble test items. Also has a graphics function. Available for IBM-PC and Macintosh computers.
- **Transparencies.** Over 50 full color transparency acetates of maps, charts, and graphs from the text help sharpen students' analytical and geographical skills and provide useful lecture references.
- **TimeLink Atlas of American History** by William Hamblin of Brigham Young University. This highly graphic, Hypercard-based tutorial is an interactive computer-assisted learning tool on historical geography designed for introductory students. Students can go backward and forward in time and revisit key events in American history.
- **Grades** Classroom Management Software records quiz and exam scores for up to 200 students.

- **Visual Archives of American History,** a new laser disk, provides over 500 stills, including a "portrait gallery" of fine art and photos, and 29 minutes of full-motion film clips from major events in American history. The broadcast quality images, crisp detail and instant remote control access make **Visual Archives** ideally suited for large lecture halls.
- **HarperCollins History Readers** bring your students fresh insights on a variety of thought-provoking subjects. They include:
  Cary / Weinberg: *The Social Fabric,* 6 / e
  Garraty: *History Viewpoints: Notable Articles from American Heritage,* 6 / e
  Gorn / Roberts / Bilhartz: *Constructing the American Past*
  Nash / Graves: *From These Beginnings: A Biographical Approach to American History,* 4 / e
  Nash / Schultz: *Retracing the Past: Readings in the History of the American People,* 2 / e
  Cords / Gerster: *Myth and the American Experience,* 3 / e
  Hewitt: *Women, Families, and Communities*
  Perman: *Perspectives on the American Past: Readings and Commentary on Issues in American History*
  Youngs: *American Realities: Historical Episodes,* 2 / e
  Roberts / Olson: *American Experiences: Readings in American History,* 2 / e

Our aim has been to write a balanced and vivid history of the development of the American nation and its society. We have also tried to provide the support materials necessary to make teaching and learning enjoyable and rewarding. The reader will be the judge of our success. The authors and HarperCollins welcome your comments.

Acknowledgments

Over the years, as the first, second, and brief editions of this text were being developed, many of our colleagues read and criticized the various drafts of the manuscript, or participated in focus groups. For their thoughtful evaluations and constructive suggestions, the authors wish to express their gratitude to the following reviewers:

John K. Alexander, University of Cincinnati
Roberta Sue Alexander, University of Dayton
Kenneth G. Alfers, Mountain View College
Harry Baker, University of Arkansas at Little Rock
Michael Batinski, Southern Illinois University
Gary Bell, Sam Houston State University
Spencer Bennett, Siena Heights College
James Bradford, Texas A&M University
Jeffrey P. Brown, New Mexico State University
Professor David Brundage, University of California at Santa Cruz
Colin Calloway, University of Wyoming
D'Ann Campbell, Indiana University
Neil Clough, North Seattle Community College
Bruce Dierenfield, Canisius College
John Dittmer, DePauw University
Gordon Dodds, Portland State University
Richard Donley, Eastern Washington University
E.J. Fabyan, Vincennes University
Bernard Friedman, Indiana University — Purdue University at Indianapolis
Bruce Glasrud, California State University, Hayward
Professor Richard Griswold-Castillo, San Diego State University
Colonel Williams L. Harris, The Citadel Military College
Robert Haws, University of Mississippi
Frederick Hoxie, McNickle Center for Study of American Indians, Newberry Library
John S. Hughes, University of Texas — Austin
Donald M. Jacobs, Northeastern University
Delores Janiewski, University of Idaho, Mt. Holyoke
David Johnson, Portland State University
Monte Lewis, Cisco Junior College
William Link, University of North Carolina — Greensboro

Vern Mattson, University of Nevada at Las Vegas
John McCormick, Delaware County Community College
Sylvia McGrath, Stephen F. Austin University
Norma Mitchell, Troy State University
William Morris, Midland College
Marian Morton, John Carroll University
Roger Nichols, University of Arizona
Paul Palmer, Texas A&I University
Al Parker, Riverside City College
Neva Peters, Tarrant County Junior College
Ronald A. Petrin, Oklahoma State University
James Prickett, Santa Monica College
Noel Pugash, University of New Mexico
Juan Gomez-Quinones, University of California, Los Angeles
George Rable, Anderson College
Leonard Riforgiato, Pennsylvania State University
Randy Roberts, Purdue University
Mary Robertson, Armstrong State University
David Robson, John Carroll University
Sylvia Sebesta, San Antonio College
Herbert Shapiro, University of Cincinnati
David R. Shibley, Santa Monica College
Kathryn Sklar, Stanford University
James Smith, Virginia State University
John Snetsinger, California Polytechnic State University
Stephen F. Strausberg, University of Arkansas
Tom Tefft, Citrus College
John Trickell, Richland College
Donna Van Raaphorst, Cuyahoga Community College
Morris Vogel, Temple University
Jackie Walker, James Madison University

Gary B. Nash
Julie Roy Jeffrey
John R. Howe
Peter J. Frederick
Allen F. Davis
Allan M. Winkler

About the Authors

Gary B. Nash received his Ph.D. from Princeton University in 1964. He is currently Associate Director of the National Center for History in the Schools at the University of California, Los Angeles, where he teaches colonial and revolutionary American history. Among the books Nash has authored are *Quakers and Politics: Pennsylvania, 1681–1726* (1968); *Red, White, and Black: The Peoples of Early America* (1974, 1982, 1991); *The Urban Crucible: Social Change, Political Consciousness, and the Origins of the American Revolution* (1979); and *Forging Freedom: The Black Urban Experience in Philadelphia, 1720–1840* (1988). His scholarship is especially concerned with the role of common people in the making of history. He wrote Part One of this book.

Julie Roy Jeffrey earned her Ph.D. in history from Rice University in 1972. Since then she has taught at Goucher College, offering the American history survey and historic preservation courses. Honored as an outstanding teacher, Jeffrey has been involved in faculty development activities and curriculum evaluation. Jeffrey's major publications include *Education for Children of the Poor* (1978); *Frontier Women: The Trans-Mississippi West, 1840–1880* (1979); and many articles on the lives and perceptions of nineteenth-century women. She wrote Parts Three and Four in collaboration with Peter Frederick.

John R. Howe received his Ph.D. from Yale University in 1962. At the University of Minnesota his teaching interests include early American politics and relations between Native Americans and whites. His major publications include *The Changing Political Thought of John Adams* (1966) and *From the Revolution Through the Age of Jackson* (1973). His major research currently involves a manuscript entitled "The Transforma-

tion of Public Life in Revolutionary America." Howe wrote Part Two of this book.

Peter J. Frederick received his Ph.D. in history from the University of California at Berkeley in 1966. The innovative teaching of American history has been the focus of his career at San Francisco State College and California State College at Hayward, and since 1970 at Wabash College. His areas of research interest include nineteenth-century American social and intellectual history as well as black and Native American history. Frederick has written *Knights of the Golden Rule: The Intellectual as Christian Social Reformer in the 1890's*. He coauthored Parts Three and Four of this book.

Allen F. Davis earned his Ph.D. at the University of Wisconsin in 1959. He is a professor at Temple University where he is the codirector of the Center for Public History. Davis is the author of *Spearheads for Reform: The Social Settlement and the Progressive Movement* and *American Heroine: The Life and Legend of Jane Addams* and coauthor of *Generations: Your Family in Modern American History*. Most recently he wrote *Philadelphia Stories*, and *One Hundred Years at Hull-House*. Davis wrote Part Five of this book.

Allan M. Winkler received his Ph.D. from Yale in 1974. He is presently teaching at Miami University of Ohio, where he chairs the History Department. His books include *The Politics of Propaganda: The Office of War Information, 1942–1945* (1978); *Modern America: The United States from the Second World War to the Present* (1985); and *Home Front U.S.A.: America during World War II* (1986). His research centers on the connections between public policy and popular mood in modern American history. He is currently studying American atomic energy policy. Winkler wrote Part Six of this book.

PART ONE

A COLONIZING PEOPLE

1492–1776

America has always been a nation of immigrants, an elaborate cultural mosaic created out of the unending streams of people who for four centuries have flocked to its shores from every corner of the world. This intermingling began with the convergence of people from the three continents of North America, Europe, and Africa. We examine the mingling of their values, institutions, and lifeways during the fifteenth and sixteenth centuries in Chapter 1, "Three Worlds Meet." Chapter 2, "Colonizing a Continent," explores five regions of settlement along the Atlantic seaboard.

Chapter 3, "Mastering the New World," explores how colonists struggled against Native Americans to expand their land base and turned to slave labor in the southern colonies. The colonists also had to deal with social and political tensions among themselves at the end of the seventeenth century. At the same time, French territorial ambitions in North America threatened another kind of conflict.

Chapter 4, "The Maturing of Colonial Society," traces the development of the colonies of England, Spain, and France in the first half of the eighteenth century. It shows how economic growth, religious revival, and political maturation prepared the English colonists by 1750 for the epic events that would follow. Chapter 5, "Bursting the Colonial Bonds," describes the coming of the American Revolution.

1

Three Worlds Meet

In the late 1550s, a few years after Catholic King Philip II and Protestant Queen Elizabeth assumed the throne in Spain and England, respectively, Opechancanough was born in Tsenacommacah. In the Algonquian language, the word Tsenacommacah meant "densely inhabited land." Later English colonizers would rename this place Virginia after their monarch, the virgin Queen Elizabeth. Before he died in the 1640s, in the ninth decade of his life, Opechancanough had seen light-skinned, swarthy, and black-skinned newcomers from a half dozen European nations and African kingdoms swarm into his land.

Opechancanough was only an infant when Europeans first reached the Chesapeake Bay region. A small party of Spanish had explored the area in 1561, but they found neither gold nor silver nor anything else of value. Upon departing, they left behind something of unparalleled importance in the history of contact between the peoples of Europe and the Americas : a bacterial infection that spread like wildfire through a population that had no immunity against it. Many members of Opechancanough's tribe died.

In 1570, when Opechancanough was young, the Spanish returned and established a Jesuit mission near the York River. Violence occurred, and before the Spanish abandoned the Chesapeake in 1572, they put to death a number of captured Indians, including a chief who was Opechancanough's relative.

Opechancanough was in his forties when three ships of fair-skinned settlers disembarked in 1607 to begin the first permanent English settlement in the New World. As relations with the whites worsened, his half brother Powhatan, high chief of several dozen loosely confederated tribes in the region, sent him to capture the English leader John Smith and escort him to the Indians' main village. Smith was put through a mock execution but then released. He later got the best of Opechancanough, threatening him with a pistol, humiliating him in front of his warriors, and assaulting one of his sons.

Opechancanough saw English settlements slowly spread in the Chesapeake region. Then, in 1617, he assumed leadership of the Powhatan Confederacy. Five years later, Opechancanough led a determined assault on the English plantations that lay along the rivers and streams emptying into the bay. The Indians killed nearly one-third of the intruders. But they paid dearly in the retaliatory raids that the colonists mounted in succeeding years.

2

As he watched the land-hungry settlers swarm in during the next two decades, Opechancanough's patience failed him. Finally, in 1644, now in his eighties, he galvanized a new generation of warriors and led a final desperate assault on the English. It was a suicidal attempt, but the "great general" of the Powhatan Confederacy, faithful to the tradition of his people, counseled death over enslavement and humiliation. Though the warriors inflicted heavy casualties, they could not overwhelm the colonizers, who vastly outnumbered them. For two years, Opechancanough was kept prisoner by the Virginians. Nearly blind and "so decrepit that he was not able to walk alone," he was fatally shot in the back by an English guard in 1646.

• • •

Over a long lifetime, Opechancanough painfully experienced the meeting of people from three continents. The nature of this violent intermingling of Europeans, Africans, and Native Americans on Chesapeake Bay is an essential part of early American history. But to understand how the destinies of red, white, and black people became intertwined in Opechancanough's land, we must look at the precontact history and cultural foundations of life in the homelands of each of them.

The People of America Before Columbus

The history of humankind in North America began thousands of years ago, as nomadic hunters from Siberia migrated across a land bridge connecting northeastern Asia with Alaska. Paleoanthropologists remain divided on the exact timing, but the main migration apparently occurred either about 12,000 to 14,000 or 25,000 to 28,000 years ago.

Hunters and Farmers

For thousands of years, these early hunters trekked southward and eastward, following vegetation and game. In time, they reached the tip of South America and the eastern edge of North America.

Archaeological evidence suggests that as centuries passed and population increased, the earliest inhabitants evolved into separate cultures, adjusting to a variety of environments in distinct ways. By the 1500s, as Europeans began to explore the New World, the "Indians" of the Americas were enormously diverse in the size and complexity of their societies, the languages they spoke, and their forms of social organization.

The first phase of "Native American" history, the long Beringian epoch, ended about 14,000 years ago. A rich archaeological record from that time indicates that the hunters had developed a new technology. Big game hunters now flaked hard stones into spear points and chose "kill sites" where they slew whole herds of Pleistocene mammals. This more reliable food source allowed population growth, and nomadism began to give way to settled habitations or local migration within limited territories.

In the Archaic era, from about 10,000 to 2,500 years ago, human populations adapted to a warmer climate as the glaciers retreated. The Pleistocene mammals could not survive, but the people learned to exploit new sources of food, especially plant life. In time a second technological breakthrough, the "agricultural revolution," occurred.

When Native Americans learned to "domesticate" plant life, they began the long process of transforming their relationship to the physical world. To learn how to harvest, plant, and nurture a seed was to gain partial control over natural forces that before had been ungovernable. Over the millennia, humans progressed from doorside planting of a few wild seeds to systematic clearing and planting of bean and maize fields. Sedentary village life began to replace a nomadic hunting and gathering existence. The increase in food supply brought about by agriculture triggered the growth of larger populations and greater social and political complexity. Many societies empowered religious figures, who organized the common followers, directed their work, exacted tribute, and undertook to protect the community from hostile forces.

Regional trading networks carried commodities such as salt, obsidian rock for projectile points, and copper for jewelry. Technology, religious ideas, and agricultural practices were also transmitted. By the end of the Archaic period (about 500 B.C.), hundreds of independent, kin-based groups, like people in other parts of the world, had learned to exploit the resources of their particular area and to trade with other groups in their region.

Native Americans in 1600

The last epoch of pre-Columbian development, the post-Archaic phase, occurred during the 2,000 years before contact with Europeans. It involved a complex process of growth and environmental adaptation among many distinct societies — and crisis in some of them. In the American Southwest, the ancestors of the present-day Hopi and Zuni developed carefully planned villages composed of large terraced buildings, each with many rooms. By the time the Spanish reached the American Southwest in

the 1540s, the indigenous Pueblo people were using irrigation canals, check dams, and hillside terracing to bring water to their arid maize fields.

Far to the east were the mound-building societies of the Mississippi and Ohio valleys. These societies declined about 1,000 years before Europeans reached the continent, perhaps because of attacks from other tribes or severe climatic changes that undermined agriculture. Several centuries later, another culture, based on intensive cultivation of beans, maize, and squash, began to flourish in the Mississippi valley. Its center, a city of perhaps 40,000, called Cahokia, stood near present-day St. Louis and included a temple that rose in four terraces to a height of 100 feet. This was the urban center of a far-flung "Mississippi" culture that encompassed thousands of villages from Wisconsin to Louisiana and from Oklahoma to Tennessee.

The influence of the Mound Builders passed eastward to transform the woodlands societies along the Atlantic coastal plain. The numerous small tribes that settled from Nova Scotia to Florida had added limited agriculture to their skill in exploiting natural plants for food, medicine, dyes, and flavoring and had developed food procurement strategies that used all the resources around them — cleared land, forests, streams, shore, and ocean.

Most of the eastern woodlands tribes lived in waterside villages. Locating their fields of maize near fishing grounds, they often migrated seasonally between inland and coastal village sites or situated themselves astride two ecological zones.

As European exploration of the Americas drew near, the continent north of the Rio Grande contained perhaps four million people, of whom perhaps 500,000 lived along the eastern coastal plain and in the piedmont region accessible to the early European settlers. The colonizers were not coming to a "virgin wilderness," as they often described it, but to a land inhabited for thousands of years by people whose village existence in many ways resembled that of the arriving Europeans.

A reconstructed view of Cahokia, the largest town in North America before European arrival; painted by William R. Iseminger.

Contrasting World Views

Colonizing Europeans called themselves "civilized" and typically described the people they met in the Americas as "savage," "heathen," or "barbarian." But the gulf separating people in Europe and North America was not defined so much by their material cultures as by how they viewed their relationship to the environment and defined social relations in their communities. In these areas, a wide difference in values existed.

In the view of Europeans, the natural world was a resource designed for man's use. Native Americans, in contrast, were "contented with Nature as they find her," as one colonist phrased it. In their ethos, every part of the natural environment was sacred. Rocks, trees, and animals all possessed spiritual power, and all were linked to form a sacred whole. To injure the environment, by overfishing or abusing it in any way, was to offend the spiritual power present throughout nature and hence to risk spiritual retaliation.

Regarding the soil as a resource to be exploited for man's benefit, Europeans believed that land should be privately possessed. Their social structure directly mirrored patterns of land ownership, with a land-wealthy elite at the apex of the social pyramid and a mass of propertyless individuals forming the broad base.

Native Americans also had concepts of property, and tribes recognized territorial boundaries. But they believed that land was invested with sacred qualities and should be held in common. Observing the Iroquois of the eastern woodlands in 1657, a French Jesuit noted with surprise that they had no almshouses because "their kindness, humanity and courtesy not only makes them liberal with what they have, but causes them to possess hardly anything except in common. A whole village must be without corn, before any individual can be obliged to endure privation." Not all Europeans were acquisitive, competitive individuals. The majority were peasants scratching a subsistence living from the soil, living in kin-centered villages with little contact with the outside world, and exchanging goods and labor through barter. But in Europe's urban centers a wealth-conscious, striving individual who celebrated wider choices and greater opportunities to enhance personal status was coming to the fore. In contrast, Native American traditions stressed the group rather than the individual. Holding land and other resources in common, Indian societies were usually more egalitarian and their members more concerned with personal valor than personal wealth.

The European newcomers to North America encountered a people whose cultural values differed strikingly from theirs. They also found disturbing the matrilineal organization of many tribal societies. Family membership among the Iroquois, for example, was determined through the female line. A typical family consisted of an old woman, her daughters with their husbands and children, and her unmarried granddaughters and grandsons. When a son or grandson married, he moved from this female-headed household to one headed by the matriarch of his wife's family. Divorce was also the woman's prerogative. If she desired it, she merely set her husband's possessions outside their dwelling door. Clans were composed of several matrilineal kin groups related by a blood connection on the mother's side.

European women, with rare exceptions, were entirely excluded from political affairs. By contrast, in Native American villages, again to

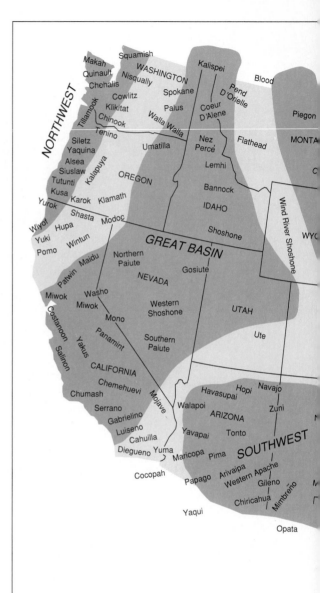

Indian Tribes During the Period of Early European Settlement

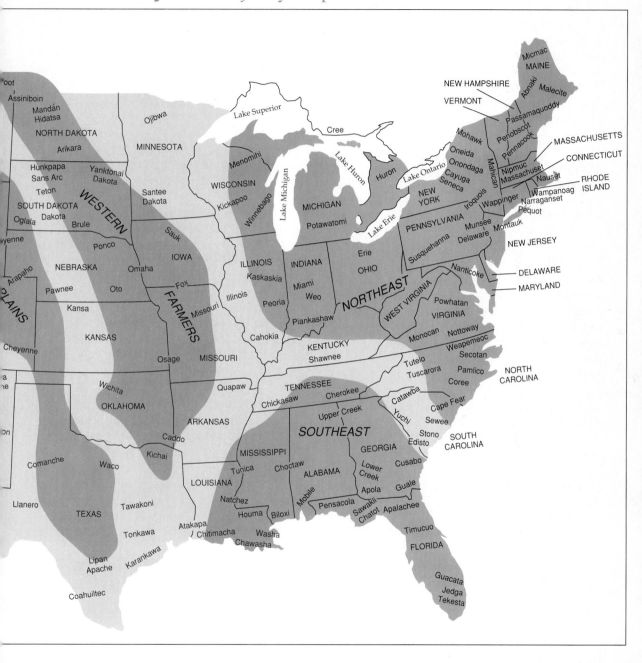

take the Iroquois example, designated men sat in a circle to deliberate and make decisions, but the senior women of the village stood behind them, lobbying and instructing. The village chiefs were male, but they were named to their positions by the elder women of their clans. If they moved too far from the will of the women who appointed them, these chiefs were removed — or "dehorned."

In the tribal economy, men were responsible for hunting, fishing, and clearing land, but women controlled the cultivation, harvest, and distribution of food. When the men were away on hunting expeditions, women directed village life. Europeans perceived such a degree of sexual equality as another mark of the uncivilized nature of tribal society.

In the religious beliefs of Native Americans, the English saw a final cultural defect. Europeans built their religious life around the belief in a single god, written scriptures, an organized clergy, and churches. Most Native American societies believed in a spirit power dwelling throughout nature (polytheism).

Africa on the Eve of Contact

Half a century before Columbus reached the Americas, a Portuguese sea captain, Antam Gonçalves, made the first European landing on the west coast of sub-Saharan Africa. If he had been able to travel the length and breadth of the immense continent, he would have encountered a rich variety of African peoples and cultures. The notion of African "backwardness" and cultural impoverishment was a myth perpetuated after the slave trade had begun transporting millions of Africans to the New World. During the period of early contact with Europeans, Africa, like pre-Columbian America, was recognized as a diverse continent with a long history of cultural evolution.

The Kingdoms of Africa

The peoples of Africa, estimated at about 50 million in the fifteenth century when Europeans began making extensive contact with them, lived in vast deserts, grasslands, and tropical forests. As in Europe and the Americas at that time, most people tilled the soil. Part of their skill in farming derived from the development of iron production, which may have begun in West Africa while Europe was still in the Stone Age. More efficient iron implements increased agricultural productivity, which in turn spurred population growth.

By the time Europeans reached the west coast of Africa, a number of large empires had risen there. The first was the kingdom of Ghana, embracing an immense territory between the Sahara and the Gulf of Guinea and from the Atlantic Ocean to the Niger River. The development of large towns, skillfully designed buildings, elaborate sculpture and metalwork depicting humans and animals, long-distance commerce, and a complex political structure marked the Ghanaian kingdom from the sixth to eleventh centuries.

An invasion of North African Muslim people beginning in the eleventh century introduced a period of religious strife that eventually destroyed the kingdom of Ghana. But in the same region arose the Islamic kingdom of Mali, which flourished until the fifteenth century. Its city of Timbuktu contained a distinguished faculty of scholars with whom North Africans and even southern Europeans came to study. Lesser kingdoms such as Kongo, Songhay, and Benin had also been growing for centuries before Europeans reached Africa by water.

The African Ethos

The peoples of Africa had a rich diversity of cultures, but most of them shared certain ways of life that differentiated them from Europeans. As in Europe, the family was the basic unit of social organization. In many African societies, as in many Native American ones, the family was matrilineal. Property rights and political inheritance descended through the mother rather than the father. It was not the son of a chief who inherited his father's position but the son of the chief's sister. When a man married, he left his family to join that of his bride.

West Africans believed in a supreme creator of the cosmos, an assortment of lesser deities associated with natural forces such as rain, fertility, and animal life, and spirits that dwelt in trees, rocks, and rivers. Ancestors were also worshiped, for they mediated between the Creator and the living of the earth.

Social organization in much of West Africa by the time Europeans arrived was as elaborate as in fifteenth-century Europe. At the top of society stood the nobility and the priests, usually men of advanced age. Beneath them were the great masses of people. Most of them were farmers, but some worked as craftsmen, traders, teachers, and artists. At the bottom of society resided slaves. As in ancient Greece and Rome, they were "outsiders" — war captives, criminals, or sometimes persons who sold themselves into servitude to satisfy a debt. Slaves were entitled to protection under the law and allowed the privileges of education, marriage, and parenthood. Their servile condition was not permanent, nor was it automatically fastened onto their children, as would be the fate of Africans enslaved in the Americas.

The art of sixteenth-century West Africa, much of it ceremonial, shows a high degree of aesthetic development. On the left is Gou, god of war, a metal sculpture from the Fon culture in Dahomey; on the right is a pair of antelope headdresses (worn by running a cord through holes in the base and tying them atop the head) carved of wood by the Bambara tribe of Senegambia.

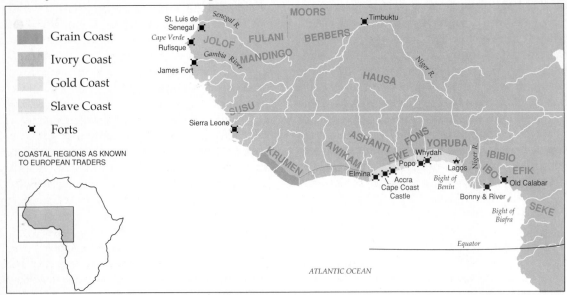

Europe in the Age of Exploration

In the ninth century, about the time that the Mound Builders of the Mississippi valley were constructing their urban center at Cahokia and the kingdom of Ghana was rising in West Africa, western Europe was an economic and cultural backwater. It was overshadowed by Christian Byzantium, which controlled Asia Minor, the Balkans, and parts of Italy, and by the Muslim culture of the Middle East, which had spilled across North Africa and penetrated Spain and West Africa south of the Sahara. Over the next six centuries, an epic revitalization of western Europe occurred, creating the conditions that enabled its leading maritime nations vastly to extend their oceanic frontiers. Thence began a 400-year epoch of the militant expansion of European peoples and European culture into other continents.

The Rise of Europe

The rebirth of western Europe, which began around A.D. 1000, owed much to a revival of long-distance trading from Italian ports on the Mediterranean. Venice, Genoa, Pisa, and other Italian ports grew wealthy and gradually evolved into merchant-dominated city-states that freed themselves from the rule of feudal lords in control of the surrounding countryside.

While merchants led the emerging city-states, western Europe's feudal system was gradually weakening. In the thirteenth and fourteenth centuries, kings began to reassert their political authority and to undertake efforts to unify their realms.

Early developments in England led to a distinctive political system. In 1215, the English aristocracy curbed the powers of the king when they forced him to accept the Magna Charta. On the basis of this charter, a parliament composed of elective and hereditary members eventually gained the right to meet regularly to pass money bills. Parliament was thus in a position to act as a check on the Crown, an arrangement unknown on the Continent. During the sixteenth century, the Crown and Parliament worked toward a more unified state, with the English kings wielding less political power than their European counterparts.

Economic changes of great significance also occurred in England during the sixteenth century. Members of the landed class began to combine their estates in order to practice more intensive and profitable agriculture. In this process, they threw peasant farmers off their plots, turning many of them into wage laborers. The formation of this working class was the crucial first step toward industrial development.

Continental Europe lagged behind England in two respects. First, it was far less affected by the move to consolidate, or "enclose," land. Part of the explanation lies in the values of continental aristocrats, who regarded the maximization of profit as unworthy of gentlemen. French nobles could lose their titles for commercial activities. Second, continental rulers were less successful in engaging the interests of their nobilities, and these nobles never shared governance with their king, as did English aristocrats through their participation in Parliament. The continental monarchs would thus warmly embrace doctrines of royal absolutism developed in the sixteenth century.

The New Monarchies and the Expansionist Impulse

In the second half of the fifteenth century, ambitious monarchs coming to power in France, England, and Spain sought social order and political stability in their kingdoms. Louis XI in France, Henry VII in England, Isabella of Castile, and Ferdinand of Aragon all created strong armies and bureaucratic state machinery. In these countries, and in Portugal as well, economic revival and Renaissance culture, with its secular emphasis on human abilities, nourished the impulse to expand beyond known frontiers. The exploratory urge had two initial objectives : to circumvent Muslim traders by finding an eastward oceanic route to Asia and to tap at its source the African gold trade.

Portugal launched Europe's age of exploration at the end of the fifteenth century. Led by Prince Henry the Navigator, for whom trade was

secondary to the conquest of the Muslim world, Portugal breached the geographical unknown. In the 1420s, Henry began dispatching Portuguese mariners to probe the unknown Atlantic "sea of darkness." His intrepid sailors were aided by important improvements in navigation, mapmaking, and ship design, all promoted by the prince.

By the 1430s, Prince Henry's captains had reached Madeira, the Canaries, and the Azores, lying off the coasts of Portugal and northwestern Africa. These were soon developed as the first European agricultural plantations located on the Continent's periphery. From there, the Portuguese sea captains pushed farther south.

By the time of Prince Henry's death in 1460, Portuguese mariners had reached the west coast of Africa, where they began a profitable trade in ivory, slaves, and especially gold. By 1500, they had captured control of the African gold trade monopolized for centuries by North African Muslims. In 1497, Vasco da Gama became the first European to sail around the Cape of Africa, allowing the Portuguese to colonize the Indian Ocean and to establish trade concessions as far east as the Spice Islands and Canton by 1513.

Reaching the Americas

The marriage of Ferdinand and Isabella in 1469 united the independent states of Aragon and Castile and launched the Spanish nation into its golden age. Leading the way for Spain was an Italian sailor, Christopher Columbus. The son of a poor Genoese weaver, Columbus had married into a prominent family of Lisbon merchants and thus made important contacts at court.

Like many sailors, Columbus had listened to sea tales about lands to the west. He believed that ships could reach the Indies by sailing west across the Atlantic, but for nearly ten years he failed to secure financial backing and royal sanction in Portugal for exploratory voyages. Finally, in 1492, Queen Isabella of Spain commissioned him, and he sailed west with three tiny ships manned by about 90 men.

Oceanic Exploration in the Fifteenth and Sixteenth Centuries

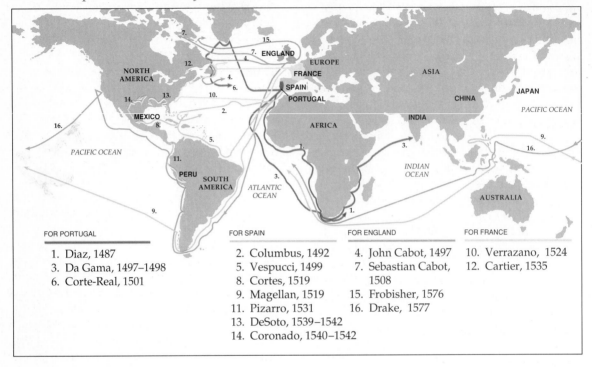

FOR PORTUGAL
1. Diaz, 1487
3. Da Gama, 1497–1498
6. Corte-Real, 1501

FOR SPAIN
2. Columbus, 1492
5. Vespucci, 1499
8. Cortes, 1519
9. Magellan, 1519
11. Pizarro, 1531
13. DeSoto, 1539–1542
14. Coronado, 1540–1542

FOR ENGLAND
4. John Cabot, 1497
7. Sebastian Cabot, 1508
15. Frobisher, 1576
16. Drake, 1577

FOR FRANCE
10. Verrazano, 1524
12. Cartier, 1535

Strong winds, lasting ten days, blew the ships far into the Atlantic. There they were becalmed. In the fifth week at sea — longer than any European sailors had been out of the sight of land — mutinous rumblings swept through the crews. But Columbus pressed on. On the seventieth day, long after Columbus had calculated he would reach Japan, a lookout sighted land. On October 12, 1492, the sailors clambered ashore on a tiny island in the Bahamas, which Columbus named San Salvador (Holy Savior). Grateful sailors "rendered thanks to Our Lord, kneeling on the ground, embracing it with tears of joy."

Believing he had reached Asia, Columbus explored the island-speckled Caribbean for ten weeks, landing on heavily populated islands that he named Hispaniola (shared today by Haiti and the Dominican Republic) and Cuba (which he thought was the Asian mainland). While homeward bound, he penned a report of his discoveries, still convinced that he had reached Asia.

Quickly printed and distributed throughout Europe, Columbus's report of his discoveries brought him financing for three much larger expeditions to explore the newfound lands. Though he led Spain to the threshold of a mighty empire, he reaped few rewards, dying unnoticed and penniless in 1506. To the end he believed that he had found the water route to Asia.

The expansion of Spain and Portugal into new areas of the world profoundly affected patterns of economic activity in Europe. Its commercial center now shifted away from the ports of the Mediterranean to the Atlantic ports facing the New World.

The New World also beckoned as a field of religious conquest. The heavily populated Americas offered millions of potential Christian converts. But the Catholic-Protestant division within

Christianity complicated Christian dreams of converting a "heathen" continent. The people of western Europe, at precisely the time they were unlocking the secrets of the new worlds to the east and west in the sixteenth century, were being torn by religious schisms that magnified the era's national rivalries.

Religious Conflict During the Reformation

At the heart of Europe's religious strife was a continental movement to cleanse the Christian church of corrupt practices and return it to the purer ways of "primitive" Christianity, as practiced by the early Christians. While criticism of the worldliness of the Catholic church mounted during the Renaissance, a German monk, Martin Luther, became the first to break successfully with Rome and initiate a Protestant reformation of theology and practice. As Protestant sects multiplied, a Catholic Reformation grew up within the church, and the two groups began a long battle for the souls of Europeans.

Luther, an Augustinian monk, lost faith in the power of the age-old rituals of the church — prayer, the Mass, confession, pilgrimages to holy places, even crusades against Muslim infidels. He reasoned that salvation came through an inward faith, or "grace," that God conferred on those he chose. Good works, Luther believed, did not earn grace but were only the external evidence of grace won through faith. Luther had taken the revolutionary step of rejecting the church's elaborate hierarchy of officials, who presided over the rituals intended to guide individuals along the path toward salvation. The spread of printing, invented less than 70 years before, allowed the rapid circulation of his ideas.

Luther urged people to seek faith individually by reading the Bible, which he translated into German and made widely available for the first time in printed form. He also called on the German princes to assume control over religion in their states, directly challenging the authority of Rome.

Building on Luther's redefinition of Christianity, John Calvin, a Frenchman, brought new intensity and meaning to the Protestant Reformation. In 1536, at age 26, he published a ringing appeal to every Christian to form a direct, personal relationship with God. By Calvin's doctrine, God had saved a few souls at random before Creation and damned the rest. Human beings were too depraved to know or alter this predestination, but good Christians must struggle to believe in their hearts that they were saved. Without mediation of ritual or priest but by "straight-walking," one was to behave as one of God's elect, the "saints." This radical theology spread among elements in all classes throughout Europe.

Calvin proposed reformed Christian communities structured around the elect few. Communities of "saints" must control the state, rather than the other way around. Elected bodies of ministers and dedicated laymen, called presbyteries, were to govern the church, directing the affairs of society down to the last detail so that all, whether saved or damned, would work for God's ends.

The Reformation, sparked by Martin Luther's protest, brought sweeping changes to western Europe in the sixteenth century and eventually played a part in migrations across the Atlantic. Lucas Cranach the Younger commemorates the Reformation's leaders in his *Epitaph of the Burgomeisters of Myenburg.*

Calvin's radical program converted large numbers of people to Protestantism throughout Europe. Sixteenth-century monarchs regarded attacks on the Catholic church with horror. But many local princes adopted some version of the reformed faith. The most important monarch to break with Catholicism was Henry VIII of England. When Pope Clement VII refused him permission to divorce and remarry, Henry declared himself head of a Protestant (Anglican) church.

The countries most affected by the Reformation — England, Holland, and France — were slow in trying to colonize the New World, so Protestantism did not gain an early foothold in the Americas. Catholicism in Spain and Portugal remained almost immune from the Protestant Reformation. So even while under attack, it swept across the Atlantic almost unchallenged during the century after Columbus's voyages.

The Iberian Conquest of America

From 1492 to 1518, Spanish and Portuguese explorers opened up vast parts of Asia and the Americas to European knowledge. At first, only modest attempts at settlement were made, mostly by the Spanish on Caribbean islands. The three decades after 1518, however, became an age of conquest. In some of the bloodiest chapters in recorded history, the Spanish nearly exterminated the native peoples of the Caribbean islands, toppled and plundered the great inland empires of the Aztecs and Incas in Mexico and Peru, discovered fabulous silver mines, and built a westward oceanic trade of enormous importance to all of Europe. The consequences of this short era of conquest proved to be immense for the entire world.

Portugal, meanwhile, restricted by one of the most significant lines ever drawn on a map, concentrated mostly on building an eastward oceanic trade to southeastern Asia. In 1493, to settle a dispute, the pope had demarcated Spanish and Portuguese spheres of exploration in the Atlantic. Drawing a north-south line 100 leagues

(about 300 miles) west of the Azores, the pope confined Portugal to the European side of the line. One year later, in the Treaty of Tordesillas, Portugal obtained Spanish agreement to move the line 270 leagues farther west. Nobody knew at the time that a large part of South America, as yet undiscovered by Europeans, bulged east of the new demarcation line and therefore fell within the Portuguese sphere. In time, Portugal would develop this region, called Brazil, into one of the most profitable areas of the New World.

The Spanish Onslaught

Within a single generation of Columbus's death in 1506, Spanish conquistadores explored, claimed, and conquered most of South America (except Brazil), Central America, and the southern parts of North America from Florida to California. They were motivated by religion, growing pride of nation, and dreams of personal enrichment. "We came here," explained one Spanish footsoldier in Cortés's legion, "to serve God and the king, and also to get rich."

In two bold and bloody strokes, the Spanish overwhelmed the ancient civilizations of the Aztecs and Incas. In 1519, Hernando Cortés set out with 600 soldiers from coastal Veracruz and marched over rugged mountains to attack Tenochtitlán (modern-day Mexico City), the capital of Montezuma's Aztec empire. In 1521, following two years of tense relations between the Spanish and Aztecs, it fell before Cortés's assault. From the Valley of Mexico, the Spanish extended their dominion over the Mayan people of the Yucatán and Guatemala in the next few decades.

In the second conquest, the intrepid Francisco Pizarro, marching from Panama through the jungles of Ecuador and into the towering mountains of Peru with a mere 168 men, most of them not even soldiers, toppled the Inca empire. Like the Aztecs, the populous Incas lived in a highly organized social system. But also like the Aztecs, violent internal divisions had weakened them. Pizarro captured their capital at Cuzco in 1533. From there, Spanish soldiers marched far-

Before the arrival of Cortés in 1519, Tenochtitlán was the capital and showplace of Montezuma's Aztec empire. The Spanish were astounded to see such a magnificent city, larger than any in Spain at the time. This modern rendering is based on archaeological evidence.

ther afield, plundering other gold- and silver-rich Inca cities. Further expeditions into Chile, New Granada (Colombia), Argentina, and Bolivia in the 1530s and 1540s brought under Spanish control an empire larger than any in the Western world since the fall of Rome.

By 1550, Spain had overwhelmed the major centers of native population throughout the Caribbean, Mexico, Central America, and the west coast of South America. Spanish ships carried gold, silver, dyewoods, and sugar east across the Atlantic and transported African slaves, colonizers, and finished goods west. In a brief half century, Spain had brought into harsh but profitable contact with each other the people of three continents and established the triracial character of the Americas.

For nearly a century after Columbus's voyages, Spain enjoyed almost unchallenged dominion over the fabulous hemisphere newly revealed to Europeans. Only Portugal, which staked out important claims in Brazil in the 1520s, challenged Spanish domination of the New World.

The Great Dying

Spanish contacts with the natives of the Caribbean basin, central Mexico, and Peru in the early sixteenth century triggered the most dramatic and disastrous population decline ever recorded. The population of the Americas on the eve of European arrival had grown to an estimated 50 million or more. Europeans were members of a population that for centuries had been exposed to nearly every lethal parasite that infects humans on an epidemic scale in the temperate zone. Over the centuries, Europeans had built up immunities to these diseases. Such biological defenses did not eliminate smallpox, measles, diphtheria, and other afflictions, but they limited their deadly power. In contrast, the people of the Americas had been geographically isolated from these diseases and had no immunity whatsoever.

The results were catastrophic. On Hispaniola, a population of about one million that had existed when Columbus arrived had only a few thousand survivors by 1530. Of some 25 million inhabitants of the Aztec empire prior to Cortés's arrival, about 90 percent were felled by disease within a half century. Demographic disaster also struck the populous Inca peoples of the Peruvian Andes. Smallpox "spread over the people as great destruction," an old Indian told a Spanish priest in the 1520s. "There was great havoc. Very many died of it. They could not stir, they could not change position, nor lie on one side, nor face down, nor on their backs. And if they stirred, much did they cry out. . . . And very many starved ; there was death from hunger, [for] none could take care of [the sick]."In most areas where Europeans intruded in the hemisphere for the next three centuries, the catastrophe repeated itself. In Spanish territories, the enslavement and brutal treatment of the native people intensified the lethal effects of European diseases. After their spectacular conquests of the Incas and Aztecs, the Spanish enslaved thousands of native people and assigned them work regimens that severely weakened their resistance to disease.

Silver, Sugar, and Their Consequences

Though Europeans looked for gold in the New World, more than three centuries would pass before they found it in windfall quantities on the North American Pacific slope and in the Yukon. Silver, however, proved abundant. Bonanza strikes were made in Bolivia in 1545 and in northern Mexico in the next decade, and much of Spain's New World enterprise focused on its extraction. The Spanish empire in America, for most of the sixteenth century, was a vast mining community.

Native people, along with some African slaves, provided the labor supply for the mines. At Potosí, in Bolivia, 58,000 workers labored at elevations of up to 13,000 feet to extract the precious metal from a fabulous sugarloaf "mountain of silver." The town's population reached 120,000 by 1570, making it larger than any in Spain at the time. Thousands of other workers toiled in the mines of Zacatecas, Taxco, and Guanajuato.

The massive flow of bullion from the Americas to Europe triggered profound changes. It financed further conquests and settlement in Spain's American empire, spurred long-distance trading in luxury items such as silks and spices from the Far East, and capitalized agricultural development in the New World of sugar, coffee, cacao, and indigo.

The enormous increase of silver in circulation in Europe after the mid-sixteenth century also caused a "price revolution." Between 1550 and 1600, prices doubled in many parts of Europe and then rose another 50 percent in the next half century. Landowning farmers got more for their produce, and merchants thrived on the increased circulation of goods. But artisans, laborers, and landless agricultural workers (the vast majority of the population) suffered because their wages did not keep pace with rising prices. The price revolution increased the number of people in western Europe living at the margins of society and thus built up the pressure to emigrate to the Americas.

While the Spaniards concentrated on the extraction of silver from the highlands of Mexico and Peru, the Portuguese staked their future on sugar production in the lowlands of Brazil. Adapting techniques of cultivation worked out earlier on their Atlantic islands, the Portuguese produced sugar for the export market. Whereas the Spanish mining operations used primarily Indian labor, the lowland Portuguese sugar planters scattered the indigenous people and replaced them with platoons of African slaves. By the 1630s this regimented work force was producing 32 million pounds of sugar annually. High in calories but low in protein, the sweet "drug food" revolutionized the tastes of millions of Europeans and caused the oceanic transport of millions of African slaves to the coast of Brazil and later to Colombia, Ecuador, and Peru.

From Brazil, sugar production jumped to the island-specked Caribbean. Here, in the early seventeenth century, England, Holland, and France challenged Spain for the riches of the New World. Once they secured a foothold in the West Indies, Spain's enemies stood at the gates of the Hispanic New World empire. In the seventeenth century they gradually sapped the strength of the first European empire outside of Europe.

Spain's Northern Frontier

The crown jewels of Spain's New World empire were silver-rich Mexico and Peru, with the islands and coastal fringes of the Caribbean representing lesser, yet valuable, gemstones. Distinctly third in importance were the northern borderlands of New Spain — the present-day Sun Belt of the United States. The early Spanish influence in Florida, the Gulf region, Texas, New Mexico, Arizona, and California indelibly marked the history of the United States.

Spanish explorers began charting the southeastern region of North America in the early sixteenth century, beginning with Juan Ponce de León's expeditions to Florida in 1515 and 1521. For the next half century, Spaniards planted small settlements there, and Franciscan priests attempted to gather the local tribes into mission villages and convert them to Catholicism.

The Spanish made several attempts to bring the entire Gulf of Mexico region under their control. From 1539 to 1542, Hernando de Soto, a veteran of Pizarro's conquest of the Incas, led an expedition deep into the homelands of the Creeks and explored westward across the Mississippi to Arkansas. In 1559, Spaniards marched northward from Mexico in an attempt to establish their authority in the lower Gulf region. Everywhere they went, they enslaved Indians and used them as provision carriers. In 1565, they built a fort at St. Augustine in Florida. They held Florida for more than two centuries.

The Southwest became the second region of Spanish activity in North America. Francisco Vásquez de Coronado explored the region from 1540 to 1542, never finding the legendary Seven Cities of Cíbola, but opening much of Arizona, New Mexico, and Colorado to eventual Spanish control.

The Southwest, like Florida, proved empty of the fabled golden cities. Hence, in the seventeenth century, the region chiefly interested Jesuit and Franciscan missionaries. The Catholic mission became the primary institution of the Spanish borderlands. The Spanish missions operated differently, depending on the Indian cultures encountered. In Florida and California, where the native people lived in small, often seminomadic tribes, the Spanish used persuasion mixed with force to gather them within the sound of the mission bell. Setting the Indians to agricultural labor, the Spanish attempted slowly to convert them to European ways of life.

In New Mexico, however, the natives had lived in settled villages and practiced agriculture for centuries, so here the Spanish aimed to graft Catholicism onto Pueblo culture by building churches on the edges of ancient native villages. When they attempted to do more than overlay Indian culture with a veneer of Catholicism, they encountered fierce resistance. Such was the case in Popé's revolt in 1680. For five years, the Spanish padres had tried to root out traditional Pueblo religious practices. In response, a Pueblo leader named Popé led an Indian uprising that destroyed most of the churches in New Mexico and for more than a decade drove the Spanish from the region. Spaniards and Indians declared a kind of cultural truce : The Spaniards agreed to allow certain Pueblo rituals in return for nominal acceptance of Christianity.

England Looks West

By the time England awoke to the promise of the New World, the two Iberian powers were firmly entrenched there. But between 1604 and 1640 the English planted several small colonies in the Caribbean. Few guessed that some relatively unproductive settlements also being planted on the North American mainland would in time be among England's most prized possessions.

England Challenges Spain

England was the most backward of the European nations facing the Atlantic in exploring and colonizing the New World. Only the voyages of John Cabot (the Genoa-born Giovanni Caboto) gave England any claim in the New World sweepstakes. But Cabot's voyages to Newfoundland and Nova Scotia a few years after Columbus's first voyage — the first northern crossing of the Atlantic since the Vikings — were never followed up.

At first, England's interest centered primarily on the rich fishing grounds of the Newfoundland Banks. Exploratory voyages along the eastern coast of North America hardly interested them. It was for the French that Cartier and Verrazano sailed between 1524 and 1535. Looking for straits westward to India, through the northern landmass, which was still thought to be a large island, they made contact with many Indian tribes and charted the coastline from the St. Lawrence River to the Carolinas.

Changes occurred in the late sixteenth century that propelled the English overseas. The rising production of woolen cloth, a mainstay of the English economy, had sent merchants scurrying for new markets after 1550. Their success in establishing trading companies in Russia, Scandinavia, the Middle East, and India vastly widened England's commercial orbit and raised hopes that still other spheres could be developed. At the same time, population growth and rising prices depressed the existence of ordinary people and made them look to the transoceanic frontier for new opportunities.

Queen Elizabeth, who ruled from 1558 to 1603, followed a cautious policy that did not include the promotion of overseas colonies. Ambitious and talented, she had to contend with Philip II, king of Spain and her fervently Catholic brother-in-law, whose long reign nearly coincided with hers. Regarding Elizabeth as a Protes-

tant heretic, Philip plotted incessantly against her.

The smoldering conflict between Catholic Spain and Protestant England broke into open flames. Elizabeth had been providing covert aid to the Protestant Dutch revolt against Catholic rule. Philip vowed to crush the rebellion and decided as well to launch an attack on England in order to wipe out this growing center of Protestant power. In 1585 Elizabeth sent 6,000 English troops to aid the Dutch Protestants. Three years later, Philip dispatched a Spanish armada of 130 ships, sails blazing with crusader's crosses, to conquer Elizabeth's England. For two weeks in the summer of 1588, a sea battle raged off the English coast. A motley collection of smaller English ships, with the colorful sea dog Francis Drake in the lead, defeated the Armada, sinking many of the lumbering Spanish galleons and then retiring as the legendary "Protestant wind" blew the crippled Armada into the North Sea. With Spanish naval power checked, both the English and the Dutch found the seas more open to their rising maritime and commercial interests.

The Westward Fever

In the last decades of the sixteenth century, the idea of overseas expansion captured the imagination of important elements of English society. Urging them on were two Richard Hakluyts, uncle and nephew. In the 1580s and 1590s, they devoted themselves to advertising the advantages of colonizing on the far side of the Atlantic. The New World offered land, opportunities for commerce, and heathen people in need of salvation. The Hakluyts publicized the idea that the time was ripe for England to break the Iberian monopoly on the riches of the New World.

England mounted its first attempts at colonizing, however, in Ireland. In the 1560s and 1570s, the English gradually extended their control over the country through brutal military conquest. Many of the leaders first involved in New World colonizing had served in Ireland, and many of their ideas of how to deal with a "savage" and "barbaric" people stemmed from their Irish experience.

The first English attempts at overseas settlement were small, feeble, and ill-fated. Beginning in 1583, they mounted several unsuccessful attempts to settle Newfoundland. Other settlers, organized by Walter Raleigh, planted a settlement from 1585 to 1588 at Roanoke Island, off the North Carolina coast. They apparently perished in attacks by a local tribe after killing a tribal leader and displaying his head on a pike. Small groups of men sent out to establish a tiny colony in Guiana, off the South American coast, failed in 1604 and 1609, and another group that set down in Maine in 1607 lasted only a year. Even the colonies founded in Virginia in 1607 and Bermuda in 1612, although they would flourish in time, floundered badly for several decades.

English merchants, sometimes supported by gentry investors, undertook these first tentative efforts. They risked their capital and had little backing from the government, in subsidies, ships, or naval protection, though they had the blessing of their queen. The Spanish and Portuguese colonizing efforts, by contrast, were national enterprises, sanctioned, capitalized, and coordinated by the Crown.

Not until these first merchant adventures solicited the wealth and support of the prospering middle class of English society could colonization succeed. This support grew steadily in the first half of the seventeenth century, but even then, investors were drawn far more to the quick profits promised in West Indian tobacco production than to the uncertainties of mixed farming, lumbering, and fishing on the North American mainland. In the 1620s and 1630s, most of the English capital invested overseas went into establishing tobacco colonies in the flyspeck Caribbean islands of St. Christopher (1624), Barbados (1627), Nevis (1628), Montserrat (1632), and Antigua (1632).

Apart from the considerable financing required, the vital element in launching a colony was a suitable body of colonists. About 80,000 streamed out of England between 1600 and 1640, as economic, political, and religious developments pushed them from their homeland at the same time that dreams of opportunity and adventure pulled them westward. In the next 20 years, another 80,000 departed.

Economic difficulties in England prompted many to try their luck in the New World. Probably half the households in England lived on the edge of poverty in the early seventeenth century. "This land grows weary of her inhabitants," wrote John Winthrop of East Anglia, "so as a man, which is the most precious of all creatures, is near more vile among us than a horse or a sheep."

Religious persecution and political considerations intensified the pressure to emigrate from England in the early seventeenth century. The largest number of emigrants went to the West Indies. The North American mainland colonies attracted perhaps half as many, and the Irish plantations in Ulster and Munster still fewer.

Anticipating North America

The early English settlers in North America were far from uninformed about the indigenous people of the New World. Beginning with Columbus's first description of the New World, published in several European cities in 1493 and 1494, reports and promotional accounts circulated among the participants in early voyages of discovery, trade, and settlement.

Colonists who read or listened to these accounts probably held a split image of the native people. On the one hand, the Indians were depicted by Columbus and Verrazano as a gentle people who eagerly received Europeans. The natives, graceful of limb and tawny-colored, Verrazano related in 1524, "came toward us joyfully uttering loud cries of wonderment, and showing us the safest place to beach the boat."

This positive image of the Native Americans reflected both the friendly reception that Europeans often actually enjoyed and the European vision of the New World as an earthly paradise where war-torn, impoverished, or persecuted people could build a new life. The strong desire to trade with the native people also encouraged a favorable view because only a friendly Indian could become a suitable partner in commercial exchange.

A counterimage, of a savage, hostile Indian, however, also entered the minds of settlers coming to North America. As early as 1502, Sebastian Cabot had paraded in England three Eskimos he had kidnapped on an Arctic voyage. They were described as flesh-eating savages and "brute beasts" who "spake such speech that no man could understand them." Many other accounts portrayed the New World natives as crafty, brutal, loathsome half-men, who lived, as Amerigo Vespucci put it, without "law, religion, rulers, immortality of the soul, and private property."

The English were also aware of the Spanish experience in the Caribbean, Mexico, and Peru — and the story was not pretty. Many books described in gory detail the wholesale violence that occurred when Spaniard met Mayan, Aztec, or Inca. Immigrants embarking for North America wondered if similar violent confrontations did not await them.

Another factor nourishing negative images of the Indian stemmed from the Indians' possession of the land necessary for settlement. For Englishmen, rooted in a tradition of the private ownership of property, this presented moral and legal, as well as practical, problems. As early as the 1580s, George Peckham, an early promoter of colonization, had admitted that the English doubted their right to take the land of others. But many argued that in return for land, the settlers would offer the natives the advantages of a more advanced culture and, most important, the Christian religion.

A more ominous argument arose to justify English rights to native soil. By denying the humanity of the Indians, the English, like other Europeans, claimed that the native possessors of the land were disqualified from rightful ownership of it. Defining the Native Americans as "savage" and "brutish" gave the settlers moral justification for taking their land. For their part, people like Opechancanough probably perceived the arriving Europeans as impractical, irreligious, aggressive, and strangely intent on accumulating material wealth.

CONCLUSION
Converging Worlds

The English migrants who began arriving on the eastern edge of North America in the late sixteenth century came late to a New World that other Europeans had been colonizing for more than a century. The first English arrivals, the immigrants to Roanoke, were but a small advance wave of the large, varied, and determined fragment of English society that would flock to the western Atlantic frontier during the next few generations. We turn now to the diversity of founding experiences of the English colonizers of the seventeenth century.

RECOMMENDED READING

The rich pre-Columbian history of the Americas is surveyed in Dean Snow, *The Archaeology of North America : American Indians and Their Origins* (1980). Another fascinating analysis is Marshall Sahlins, *Stone Age Economics* (1972).

Excellent introductions to early African history include Basil Davidson, *The African Genius (1969)*, and J. D. Fage, *A History of West Africa*, 4th ed. (1969).

Europe in the Age of Exploration can be studied in Ralph Davis, *The Rise of the Atlantic Economies* (1973) ; and Eric Wolf, *The People Without History* (1983).

A fine corrective to the much romanticized and often distorted story of the Spanish and Portuguese conquest of the Americas is James Lockhart and Stuart B. Schwartz, *Early Latin America* (1983). Also valuable is C. R. Boxer, *The Portuguese Seaborne Empire, 1415–1825* (1972).

The shape of English society as overseas colonization began is detailed in Carl Bridenbaugh, *Vexed and Troubled Englishmen, 1500–1642* (1968) ; and Peter Laslett, *The World We Have Lost* (1971). England's belated intervention in the Americas is followed in Nicholas P. Canny, *The Elizabethan Conquest of Ireland* (1976) ; David B. Quinn, *England and the Discovery of America, 1481–1620* (1974) ; and David B. Quinn, *North America from Earliest Discovery to First Settlements* (1977).

Time Line

	Pre-Columbian epochs	**1513**	Portuguese explorers reach China
12,000 B.C.	Beringian epoch ends	**1515–1565**	Spanish explore Florida and southern part of North America
6,000 B.C.	Paleo-Indian phase ends	**1520s**	Luther attacks Catholicism
500 B.C.	Archaic era ends	**1521**	Cortés conquers the Aztecs
500 B.C.–A.D.	Post-Archaic era in North America	**1530s**	Calvin calls for religious reform
		1533	Pizarro conquers the Incas
1500	Kingdoms of Ghana, Mali, Songhay in Africa	**1540–1542**	Coronado explores the Southwest
1420s	Portuguese sailors explore west coast of Africa	**1558**	Elizabeth I crowned queen of England
1492	Christopher Columbus lands on Caribbean islands Spanish expel Moors (Muslims)	**1585**	Roanoke Island settlement
		1588	English defeat the Spanish armada
1494	Treaty of Tordesillas	**1603**	James I succeeds Elizabeth I
1497–1585	French and English explore northern part of the Americas	**1607**	English begin settlement at Jamestown, Virginia
1498	Vasco da Gama reaches India after sailing around Africa	**1680**	Popé's revolt in New Mexico

2

Colonizing a Continent

John Mason had emigrated from southeastern England as part of the flock of John Warham, a Puritan minister from the village of Dorchester. In Massachusetts, the group commemorated their origins by giving the name Dorchester to the area assigned to them.

Four years later, in the fall of 1636, Mason followed many of his Dorchester friends out of Massachusetts to the Connecticut River, 100 miles to the west. At their journey's end, they founded the town of Windsor, on the west bank of the Connecticut.

Six months later, when his new village was no more than a collection of crude lean-tos, militia captain John Mason marched south against the Pequots. He commanded several hundred men whom the fledgling Connecticut River towns had dispatched to drive the Pequots from the area. In the years before the English arrival, the powerful Pequots had formed a network of tributary tribes. Finding it impossible to placate the English as they swarmed into the Connecticut River valley, the Pequots chose resistance.

At dawn on May 26, 1637, Captain Mason and his troops approached a Pequot village on the Mystic River. Supported by Narragansett allies, the English slipped into the town and torched the Pequot wigwams. Then they rushed from the fortified village. As flames engulfed the huts, the Pequots fled the inferno, only to be cut down with musket and sword by the English soldiers, who had ringed the community. Most of the terrified victims were noncombatants — old men, women, and children — for the Pequot warriors were preparing for war at another village about five miles away. Before the sun rose, a major portion of the Pequot tribe had been exterminated. Mason wrote that God had "laughed at his enemies and the enemies of his people, . . . making them as a fiery oven."

• • •

Captain John Mason's actions at the Mystic River testify that the European colonization of America involved a violent confrontation of two cultures. We often speak of the "discovery" and "settlement" of North America by English and other

22

European colonists. But the penetration of the eastern edge of what today is the United States might more accurately be called "the invasion of America."

Yet mixed with violence was utopian idealism. The New World was a place to rescue humankind from the ruins of the Old World. This chapter reconstructs the manner of settlement and the character of immigrant life in five areas of early colonization: the Chesapeake Bay, southern New England, the St. Lawrence to the Hudson rivers, the Carolinas, and Pennsylvania.

The Chesapeake Tobacco Coast

England gained a foothold in North America when Walter Raleigh tried to establish a colony on Roanoke Island off the Carolina coast in the 1580s. The colony was too small and poorly financed to succeed. It served only as a token of England's rising challenge to Spain in the western hemisphere and as a source of valuable information for colonists later settling the area.

The Roanoke colony also failed resoundingly as the first sustained contact between English and Native American peoples. Although one member of the first expedition reported that "we found the people most gentle, loving, and faithful, void of all guile and treason," relations with the local tribes quickly soured and then turned violent. In 1591, when a relief expedition reached Roanoke, none of the settlers could be found. It is likely that in spite of their Iron Age weaponry, these "lost colonists" of Roanoke succumbed to Indian attacks. It was an ominous beginning for England's overseas ambitions.

Jamestown

In 1607, a generation after the first Roanoke expedition, a group of merchants established the first permanent colony in North America at Jamestown, Virginia. Under a charter from James I, they operated as a joint-stock company,

As seen in this sixteenth-century watercolor by John White, a member of the expedition to Roanoke Island, the natives who inhabited the village of Secotan lived much like English or Irish peasants.

an early form of a modern corporation that allowed them to sell shares of stock in their company and use the pooled investment capital to outfit and supply overseas expeditions. Although the king's charter to the Virginia Company of London began with a concern for bringing Christian religion to native people, most of the settlers probably agreed with Captain John Smith, who described the company as "making religion their colour, when all their aim was profit."

Profits in the early years proved elusive, however. Most of the early Virginia colonists died miserably of dysentery, malaria, and malnutrition. More than 900 settlers, mostly men, arrived in the colony between 1607 and 1609; only 60 survived. Moreover, one-third of the first three groups of immigrants were gold-seeking adventurers with unroughened hands. Others were unskilled servants, some with criminal backgrounds, who "never did knowe what a days work was," observed John Smith. Both types adapted poorly to wilderness conditions, leaving Smith begging for "but thirty carpenters, husbandmen, gardeners, fishermen, and blacksmiths" rather than "a thousand such gallants as were sent to me, . . ."

The Jamestown colony was also hampered by the common assumption that Englishmen could exploit the Indians of the region as the Spanish had done in Mexico and Peru. But in the Chesapeake the English found that the indigenous peoples were not densely settled and could not easily be subjugated. Relations with some 40 small tribes, grouped into a confederacy led by the able Powhatan, turned bitter almost from the beginning. Powhatan brought supplies of corn to the sick and starving Jamestown colony during the first autumn. However, John Smith, whose military experience in eastern Europe had schooled him in dealing with people he regarded as "barbarians," raided Indian corn supplies and tried to cow the local tribes by shows of force. In response, Powhatan withdrew from trade with the English and sniped at their flanks. Many settlers died in the "starving times" of the first years.

Despite these early failures, merchants of the Virginia Company of London poured more money and settlers into the venture. Understanding the need for ordinary farmers who could raise the food necessary to sustain the colony, they reorganized the company in 1609, promising free land to settlers at the end of seven years' labor for the company. In 1618, they sweetened the terms by offering 50 acres of land outright to anyone journeying to Virginia. More than 9,000 voyaged to Virginia between 1610 and 1622, but only 2,000 remained alive at the end of that period. "Instead of a plantation," wrote one English critic, "Virginia will shortly get the name of a slaughter house."

Sot Weed and Indentured Servants

The promise of free land lured a steady stream of settlers to Virginia, even though the colony proved a burial ground for most immigrants within a few years of arrival. Also crucial to the continued growth of the colony was the discovery that tobacco grew splendidly in Chesapeake soil. Tobacco proved to be Virginia's salvation. The planters shipped the first crop in 1617. By 1624, Virginia was exporting 200,000 pounds of the "stinking weed"; by 1638, though the price had plummeted, the crop exceeded three million pounds. Tobacco became to Virginia in the 1620s what sugar was to the West Indies and silver to Mexico and Peru. In London, men gibed that Virginia was built on smoke.

The cultivation of tobacco obliged Virginia's planters to find a reliable supply of cheap labor. The "sot weed" required intensive care through the various stages of planting, weeding, thinning, suckering, worming, cutting, curing, and packing. To fill their need, planters recruited immigrants in England and Ireland and a scattering from Sweden, Portugal, Spain, Germany, and even Turkey and Poland. Such people, called indentured servants, willingly sold a portion of their working lives in exchange for free passage across the Atlantic. About four of every five seventeenth-century immigrants to Virginia — and later Maryland — came in this status.

Tobacco production involved indentured servants and slaves in a multistage work process as they planted, topped, suckered, cut, cured, stripped, and prized (packed into hogsheads) the leaf. Some of the stages are pictured here in a London book, The Culture of Tobacco.

Nearly three-quarters of them were male, and most of them were between 15 and 24 years old.

Few servants survived long enough to achieve their freedom. If malarial fevers or dysentery did not quickly kill them, they often succumbed to the brutal work routine harsh masters imposed. Masters bought and sold their servants as property, gambled for them at cards, and worked them to death since there was little motive for keeping them alive beyond their term of labor. When servants neared the end of their contract, masters found ways to add time and were backed by courts controlled by the planter class.

Contrary to English custom, masters often put women servants to work at the hoe. Sexual abuse by masters was common. Servant women paid dearly for illegitimate pregnancies. The courts fined them heavily and ordered them to serve an extra year or two to repay the time lost during pregnancy and childbirth. They also deprived mothers of their illegitimate children, indenturing them out at an early age. For many servant women, marriage was the best release from this hard life. Many willingly accepted the purchase of their indenture by any man who suggested marriage.

Expansion and Indian War

As Virginia's population increased, violence mounted between white colonizers and the Powhatan tribes. In 1614, the sporadic hostility ended temporarily with the arranged marriage of Powhatan's daughter, the fabled Pocahontas, to planter John Rolfe. However, the profitable cultivation of tobacco created an intense demand for land, and more and more settlers pushed up the rivers that flowed into Chesapeake Bay.

In 1617, when Powhatan retired, the leadership of the Chesapeake tribes fell to Opechancanough, who began building military strength for an all-out attack on his English enemies. The English murder of Nemattanew, a Powhatan war captain and religious prophet, triggered a fierce Indian assault on Good Friday in 1622 that dealt Virginia a staggering blow. More than one-quarter of the white population fell before the marauding tribesmen; the casualties in cattle, crops, and buildings were equally severe.

The devastating attack led to the bankruptcy of the Virginia Company. As a result, the king annulled its charter in 1624, and established a royal government, which allowed the elected legislative body established in 1619 to

Early Chesapeake Settlement

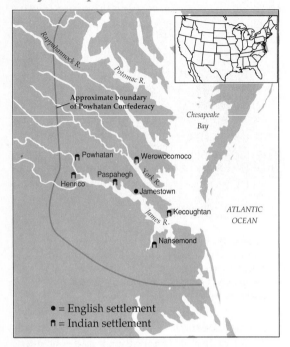

Rappahannock R.

Potomac R.

Approximate boundary
of Powhatan Confederacy

Chesapeake
Bay

⋔ Powhatan   ⋔ Werowocomoco

⋔ Paspahegh
Henrico   ⋔
              ● Jamestown

York R.

James R.   ⋔ Kecoughtan   ATLANTIC
                                OCEAN

⋔ Nansemond

• = English settlement
⋔ = Indian settlement

continue lawmaking in concert with the royal governor and his council.

The Indian assault of 1622 fortified the determination of the surviving planters to pursue a ruthless new Indian policy of "perpetual enmity." The Virginians sent annual military expeditions against the native villages west and north of the settled areas. Population growth after 1630 and the recurrent need for fresh acreage by settlers who planted soil-exhausting tobacco intensified the pressure on Indian land. The tough, ambitious planters soon encroached on Indian territories, provoking war in 1644 and again in 1675, reducing the native population of Virginia to less than 1,000 by 1680. The Chesapeake tribes, Virginians came to believe, had little to contribute to the goals of English colonization; they were merely obstacles to be removed from the path of English settlement.

Proprietary Maryland

By the time Virginia had achieved commercial success in the 1630s, another colony on the Chesapeake took root. Rather than hoping for profit, George Calvert sought to establish in Maryland a religious refuge for Catholics and a New World version of the English manorial countryside.

Catholics were an oppressed minority in England, and Calvert, Lord Baltimore, planned his colony as a place where they could start anew without fear of harassment. But knowing that he needed more than a small band of Catholic settlers, the proprietor planned to invite others as well. Catholics would never form a majority in his colony. They were quickly numerically overwhelmed by Protestants who jumped at the offer of free land with only a modest yearly fee to the proprietary family (a "quitrent") of two shillings per 100 acres.

Calvert died in 1632, leaving his 26-year-old son, Cecilius, to carry out his plans. The charter guaranteed the proprietor control over all branches of government and designated large estates for Calvert's relatives. Neither of these arrangements proved workable. Arriving in 1634, immigrants blithely ignored his plans, took up free land, imported as many indentured servants as they could afford, maintained generally peaceful relations with local Indian tribes, began to grow tobacco on scattered riverfront plantations like their Virginia neighbors, and governed themselves locally as much as possible. Although Maryland grew slowly at first, by 1700, its population of 33,000 was half that of Virginia's.

Daily Life on the Chesapeake

Though immigrants to the Chesapeake Bay region dreamed of bettering the life they had known in England, existence for most of them was dismally difficult. Only a minority could expect to marry and raise a family because marriage had to be deferred until after the indenture was completed, and there were three times more men than women. Once made, marriages were fragile. Either husband or wife was likely to succumb to disease within about seven years. The vulnerability of pregnant women to malaria frequently terminated marriages in the first few years, and death claimed half the children born before they reached adulthood. Few children could expect to have both parents alive while growing up. Grandparents were almost unknown. In a society so numerically dominated by men, widowed women were prized and remarried quickly. Such conditions produced complex families, full of stepchildren and stepparents, half sisters and half brothers.

The household of Robert Beverley of Middlesex County illustrates the tangled family relationships in this death-filled society. Between 1666 and 1687, Beverley had married in succession two widows who bore him nine children and had been stepfather to the eight children his two wives had produced with previous husbands. Not one of these 17 children, from an interlocking set of four marriages, reached adulthood with both a living mother and father.

Plagued by such mortality, the Chesapeake remained, for most of the seventeenth century, a land of immigrants rather than a land of settled families. Social institutions such as churches and schools took root very slowly amid such fluidity. The large number of indentured servants further increased the instability of community life.

The fragility of life showed clearly in the region's architecture. As in most New World colonies, the settlers at first erected only primitive huts and shanties, hardly more than windbreaks. After establishing crops, planters improved their habitats but still built ramshackle, one-room dwellings. "Their houses," it was observed in 1623, "stand scattered one from another, and are only made of wood . . . so as a firebrand is sufficient to consume them all." Even as Virginia and Maryland matured, cheaply built and cramped houses, usually no larger than 16 by 24 feet, remained the norm. Life was too uncertain, the tobacco economy too volatile, and the desire to invest every available shilling in field labor too great for men to build grandly.

The crudity of life also showed in the household possessions of the Chesapeake colonists. Struggling farmers and tenants were likely to own only a straw mattress, a simple storage

We think of the churches of the colonial South as handsome, steepled, red brick buildings, but this clapboard church is typical of the rudimentary buildings erected by early colonists in the Chesapeake region.

chest, and the tools necessary for food preparation and eating — a mortar and pestle to grind corn, knives for butchering, a pot or two for cooking stews and porridges, wooden trenchers and spoons for eating. Most ordinary settlers owned no chairs, no dressers, no plates or silverware. Among middling planters the standard of living was raised only by possession of a flock mattress, coarse earthenware for milk and butter, a few pewter plates and porringers, a frying pan or two, and a few rough tables and chairs. Even one of Virginia's wealthiest planters, the prominent Robert Beverley, had "nothing in and about his house but what was necessary . . . good beds . . . but no curtains, and instead of cane chairs, he hath stools made of wood."

Massachusetts and Its Offspring

While some English settlers in the reign of James I (1603–1625) scrambled for wealth on the Chesapeake, others in England were seized by the spirit of religion. They looked to the wilds of North America as a place to build a tabernacle to God, a society dedicated to reforming the corrupt world. American Puritanism nurtured a belief in America's special mission in the world. But it also sought to banish diversity on a continent where the arrival of streams of immigrants from around the globe was destined to become a primary phenomenon.

Puritanism in England

England had been officially Protestant since 1558. Many English in the late sixteenth century, however, thought the Church of England was still ridden with Catholic elements. Because they wished to purify the Church of England, they were dubbed Puritans.

The Puritan movement attracted men and women who hoped to find in religion an antidote to the changes sweeping over English society. Many feared for the future as they witnessed the growth of turbulent cities, the increase of wandering poor, rising prices, and accelerating commercial activity. In general, they disapproved of the growing freedom from the restraints of gentry-dominated medieval institutions such as the church, guilds, and local government. The concept of the individual operating as freely as possible, maximizing both opportunities and personal potential, is at the core of our modern system of beliefs and behavior. But many in England cringed at the crumbling of traditional restraints of individual action. They worried that individualistic behavior would undermine the notion of community — the belief that people were bound together by reciprocal rights, obligations, and responsibilities. Especially they decried the "degeneracy of the times," which they saw in the defiling of the Sabbath by maypole dancing, card playing, fiddling, and bowling. Puritans vowed not only to purify the Church of England but to reform society as well.

One part of their plan was a social ethic stressing work as a primary way of serving God. The "work ethic" would banish idleness and impart discipline throughout the community. Second, Puritans organized themselves into religious congregations where each member hoped for personal salvation but also supported all others in their quest. Third, Puritans assumed responsibility for the "unconverted" people around them, who might have to be controlled. Religious reform and social vision were in this way interlocked.

When King James VI of Scotland succeeded the childless Elizabeth as James I of England in 1603, he spoke stridently for the divine right of the monarch and his own role as head of the church. He deplored the rising power of the Puritans, who had occupied the pulpits in hundreds of churches, gained control of several colleges at Oxford and Cambridge, and obtained many seats in Parliament. James promised to "harry them out of the land, or else do worse."

When Charles I succeeded to the throne in 1625, the situation worsened for Puritans. Determined to strengthen the monarchy and stifle dissent, the king adjourned Parliament in 1629. He then appointed William Laud, the bishop of London, to high office and turned him loose on the Puritans, whom Laud called "wasps" and "the most dangerous enemies of the state."

By 1629, many Puritans were turning their eyes outward to Northern Ireland, Holland, the Caribbean islands, and especially North America. The depression in the cloth trades, most severe in Puritan strongholds, was an added motivation to emigrate. To some distant shore, many Puritans decided, they would transport a fragment of English society and carry out the completion of the Protestant Reformation. As they understood history, God had assigned them a special task in his plan for the redemption of humankind.

Puritan Predecessors in New England

Puritans were not the first Europeans to reach the shores of New England. No permanent settlement took root, however, until the Pilgrims arrived in Plymouth in 1620. Unlike the Puritans who followed, these humble Protestant farmers did not expect to convert a sinful world. They only wanted to be left alone to realize their radical vision of a pure and primitive life. Rather than reform the Church of England, they left it and hence were called Separatists. They had first fled from England to Holland in 1608, then in 1620 to North America.

For two generations, the Pilgrims tilled the soil and fished while trying to keep intact their religious vision. But with the much larger Puritan migration that began in 1630, the Pilgrim villages nestled on the shores of Cape Cod Bay became a backwater of the thriving, populous Massachusetts Bay Colony, which absorbed them in 1691.

Errand into the Wilderness

In 11 ships, 1,000 Puritans set out from England in 1630 for the Promised Land. They were the vanguard of a movement that by 1642 had brought about 18,000 colonizers to New England's shores. Led by John Winthrop, they operated under a charter from the king to the Puritan-controlled Massachusetts Bay Company. The Puritans set about building their utopia with the characteristic fervor of people convinced they are carrying out a divine task.

Their intention was to establish communities of pure Christians who collectively swore a covenant with God to work for his ends. To accomplish this, the Puritan leaders agreed to employ severe means. Their historic mission was too important, they believed, to allow the luxury of diversity of opinion in religious matters. Likewise, participation in government would be limited to church members. Civil and religious transgressors would be rooted out and severely punished.

To realize their utopian goals, the Puritans willingly gave up freedoms that their compatriots sought. An ideology of rebellion in England, Puritanism in America became an ideology of control. Much was at stake, for as Winthrop reminded the first settlers, "We shall be as a city

John Winthrop was one of the lesser gentry who joined the Puritan movement and in the 1620s looked westward for a new life. Always searching himself as well as others for signs of weakness, Winthrop was one of the Massachusetts Bay Colony's main leaders for many years.

upon a hill [and] the eyes of all people are upon us." That visionary sense of mission would help to shape a distinctive American self-image in future generations.

As in Plymouth and Virginia, the first winter tested the strongest souls. More than 200 of the first 700 settlers perished, but Puritans kept coming. They "hived out" along the Back Bay of Boston, along the rivers that emptied into the bay, south into what became Connecticut and Rhode Island a few years later, and north along the rocky Massachusetts coast.

Motivated by their militant work ethic and sense of mission, led by men experienced in local government, law, and the uses of exhortation, the Puritans thrived almost from the beginning. Most of the ordinary settlers came as freemen in families. Trained artisans and farmers, they established tightknit communities in which, from the outset, the brutal exploitation of labor rampant in the Chesapeake had no place.

An Elusive Utopia

The Puritans built a sound economy based on agriculture, fishing, timbering, and trading for beaver furs with local Indians. Even before leaving England, the directors of the Massachusetts Bay Company transformed their commercial charter into a rudimentary government and transferred the charter to New England. Once there, they laid the foundations of self-government. Free male church members annually elected a governor and deputies from each town who formed one house of a colonial legislature. The other house was composed of the governor's assistants, later to be called councillors. Consent of both houses was required to pass laws.

The Puritans established the first printing press in the English colonies and planted the seed of a university, Harvard College, which opened its doors in 1636 for the training of prospective clergymen. They also organized elementary and secondary schools, open to all.

In spite of these accomplishments, the Puritan colony experienced internal tensions and proved unable to reach a peaceful accommodation with the Native Americans, whose lands some colonists coveted. Others agitated for broader political rights and even briefly ousted Winthrop as governor in 1635.

Winthrop's troubles multiplied in 1633 when Salem's Puritan minister, Roger Williams, began to voice disturbing opinions on church and government policies. The visionary young man argued that the Massachusetts Puritans were not truly pure because they would not completely separate themselves from the polluted Church of England (which most Puritans still hoped to reform). He denounced mandatory worship, and argued that government officials should not interfere with religious matters but confine themselves to civil affairs. Later to be

celebrated as the earliest spokesman for the separation of church and state, Williams seemed in 1633 to strike at the heart of the Bible commonwealth, whose leaders regarded civil and religious affairs as inseparable. Williams also charged the Puritans with illegally intruding on Indian land.

In 1635, under threat of deportation to England, Williams fled southward through winter snow with a small band of followers to found Providence, a settlement on Narragansett Bay in what would become Rhode Island.

Even as they were driving Williams out, the Puritan authorities confronted another threat. Anne Hutchinson, who had arrived in 1634 with her husband and seven children, gained great respect among Boston's women as a practiced midwife, healer, and spiritual counselor. She soon began to discuss religion, suggesting that the "holy spirit" was absent in the preaching of some ministers. Before long Hutchinson was leading a movement labeled antinomianism, an interpretation of Puritan doctrine that stressed the mystical nature of God's free gift of grace while discounting the efforts the individual could make to gain salvation.

By 1636, Boston was dividing into two camps, those who followed the male clergy and those who cleaved to the theological views of a gifted though untrained woman with no official standing. Hutchinson doubly offended the male leaders of the colony because she boldly stepped outside the subordinate position expected of women. "The weaker sex" set her up as "a priest" and "thronged" after her, wrote one male leader.

In 1636 Hutchinson was tried and convicted of sedition and contempt and banished from the colony. Six months later, the Boston church excommunicated her for preaching 82 erroneous theological opinions. In the last month of her eighth pregnancy, Hutchinson, with a band of supporters, followed the route of Roger Williams to Rhode Island, the catch basin for Massachusetts Bay's dissidents.

But ideas proved harder to banish than people. The magistrates could never enforce

Early New England

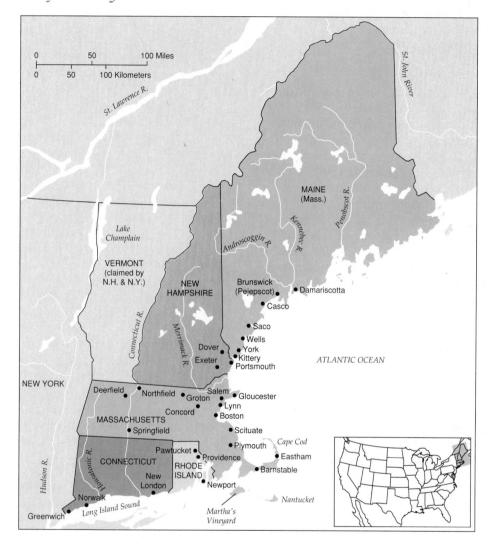

uniformity of belief. Neither could they curb the appetite for land. Growth, geographic expansion, and commerce with the outside world all eroded the ideal of integrated, self-contained communities filled with religious piety. By 1636, groups of Puritans had swarmed not only to Rhode Island but also to Hartford and New Haven, where Thomas Hooker and John Davenport led new Puritan settlements in what became Connecticut.

New Englanders and Indians

The charter of the Massachusetts Bay Company proclaimed the goal of converting the natives to the Christian faith. But the instructions that Governor John Winthrop carried from England reveal other Puritan thoughts about the native inhabitants. According to Winthrop's orders, all men were to receive training in the use of firearms, Indians were prohibited from entering

Puritan towns, and any colonist selling arms to an Indian or instructing one in their use was to be deported.

Only sporadic conflict with local tribes occurred at first because disease had catastrophically struck the Native American population of southern New England, which may have numbered as many as 125,000 in 1600, and left much of their land vacant. The settler pressure for new land, however, soon reached into areas untouched by disease. When land hunger mingled with the Puritan sense of mission, it proved an explosive mix. To a people charged with messianic zeal, the heathen Indians represented a mocking challenge to the building of a religious commonwealth that would "shine as a beacon" back to decadent England.

Making the "savages" of New England strictly accountable to the ordinances that governed white behavior was part of this quest for fulfilling their mission. In this the Puritans succeeded with the smaller, disease-ravaged tribes of eastern Massachusetts. But their attempts to control the stronger Pequots led to the bloody war in 1637 in which John Mason was a leader. The Puritan victory in that war removed the last obstacle to expansion into the Connecticut River valley. Missionary work, led by John Eliot, began among the remnant tribes in the 1640s. After a decade of effort, about 1,000 Indians had been settled in four "praying villages," learning to live according to the white man's ways.

The Web of Village Life

The village was the vital center of Puritan life. Unlike the Chesapeake tobacco planters, who dispersed along the streams and rivers of their area, the Puritans established small, tightly settled villages. Most pursued "open field" agriculture, trudging out from the village each morning to farm narrow strips of land that radiated out from the town. They grazed their cattle on common meadow and cut firewood on common woodland. Such a system recreated agricultural life in many parts of England.

In other towns, Puritans employed the "closed field" system of self-contained farms that they had known at home. But in either system, families lived close together in compact towns built around a common, where the meetinghouse and tavern were located. These small, communal villages kept families in close touch and perfectly served the need for moral surveillance, or "holy watching" among neighbors. Puritans also prohibited single men and women from living by themselves, for this would put individuals beyond patriarchal authority and group observation.

At the center of every Puritan village stood the meetinghouse. These plain wooden structures, sometimes called "Lord's barns," gathered within them every soul in the village twice a week — on the Lord's day and during mid-week as well. The minister was the spiritual leader in these small, family-based, community-oriented settlements, which viewed life as a Christian pilgrimage.

The unique Puritan mixture of strict authority and incipient democracy, of hierarchy and equality, can be seen in the way the Massachusetts town distributed land and devised local government. Each town was founded by a grant of the colony's General Court, sitting in Boston. Only groups of Puritans who had signed a compact signifying their unity of purpose received settlement grants.

After receiving a grant, townsmen met to parcel out land. They awarded individual grants according to the size of a man's household, his wealth, and his usefulness to the church and town. Such a system perpetuated existing differences in wealth and status. But Puritans also believed that every family should have enough land to sustain it, and prospering men were expected to use their wealth for the community's benefit, not for conspicuous consumption. Repairing the meeting-house, building a school, aiding a widowed neighbor — such were the proper uses of wealth.

Having felt the sting of centralized power in church and state, Puritans emphasized local exercise of authority. Until 1684, only male church members could vote, and as the proportion of males who were church members declined, so did the proportion of men who could vote. These voters elected selectmen, who allocated land, passed local taxes, and settled disputes. Once a year, all townsmen gathered for the town meeting, at which they selected town officers for the next year and decided matters large and small: Should the playing of football in the streets be prohibited? Might Widow Thomas be allowed £10 for a kidney stone operation for her son? What salary should the schoolteacher be paid?

The predominance of families also lent cohesiveness to Puritan village life. Strengthening this family orientation was the remarkably healthy environment of the Puritans' "New Israel." While the germs carried by English colonizers devastated neighboring Indian societies, the effect on the newcomers of entering the new environment was the opposite because the low density of settlement prevented infectious diseases from spreading.

The result was a spectacular natural increase in the population and a life span unknown in Europe. The difference was not a higher birthrate. The crucial factor was that chances for survival after birth were far greater than in England because of the healthier climate and better diet. In New England, nearly 90 percent of the infants born in the seventeenth century survived to marriageable age, and life expectancy exceeded 60 years — longer than for the American population as a whole at any time until the early twentieth century. About 25,000 people immigrated to New England in the seventeenth century, but by 1700 they had produced a population of 100,000. By contrast, some 75,000 immigrants to the Chesapeake colonies had yielded a population of about 70,000 by the end of the century.

Women played a vital role in this family-centered society. In the household economies of the Puritan villages, the woman was not only wife, mother, and housekeeper but also custo-dian of the vegetable garden; processor of salted and smoked meats, dairy products, and preserved vegetables; and spinner, weaver, and clothesmaker.

The presence of women and a stable family life strongly affected New England's regional architecture. Well-constructed one-room houses with sleeping lofts quickly replaced the early "wigwams, huts, and hovels." Families then added parlors and lean-to kitchens as soon as they could. Within a half century, New England immigrants accomplished a general rebuilding of their living structures, while the Chesapeake lagged far behind.

A final binding element in Puritan communities was the stress on literacy and education, eventually to become a hallmark of American society. Placing religion at the center of their lives, Puritans emphasized the ability to read catechisms, psalm-books, and especially the Bible.

An event in England in 1642 affected the future development of the New England colonies. King Charles I pushed his people into revolution by violating the country's customary constitution and trying to continue the reformation in the Anglican church. The ensuing civil war climaxed with the trial and beheading of the king in 1649. Thereafter, during the so-called Commonwealth period (1649–1660), Puritans had the opportunity to complete the reform of English religion and society. Migration to New England abruptly ceased.

The 20,000 English immigrants who had come to New England by 1649 were scattered from Maine to Long Island. To combat dispersion, Puritan leaders established a broad intercolony political structure in 1643 called the Confederation of New England. This first American attempt at federalism functioned fitfully for a generation, though Massachusetts, the strongest and largest member, often refused to abide by group decisions when they ran counter to its objectives.

Although the Puritans fashioned stable communities and effective government, their leaders, as early as the 1640s, complained that the founding vision of Massachusetts Bay was faltering. Material concerns seemed to transcend religious commitment; the individual prevailed over the community. A generation later Puritans rarely mentioned the work of salvaging western Protestantism by example. Instead, they concentrated on keeping their children on the straight and narrow road.

Frequent complaints about moral laxness notwithstanding, New England had achieved economic success and political stability by the end of the seventeenth century. If social diversity increased and the religious zeal of the founding generation waned, that was only to be expected. One second-generation Bay colonist put the matter bluntly. His minister had noticed his absence in church and found him late that day at the docks, unloading a boatload of cod. "Why were you not in church this morning?" asked the clergyman. Back came the reply: "My father came here for religion, but I came for fish."

From the St. Lawrence to the Hudson

The New Englanders were not the only European settlers in the northern region, for both France and Holland created colonies there. At the same time that Jamestown was founded, the French repeated their attempt to settle Canada, more successfully than in the 1540s. French explorer Samuel de Champlain established a small settlement in Port Royal, Acadia (later Nova Scotia), in 1604, and another at what would become the capital of New France, Quebec, in 1608. The primary interest of the French was the fur trade. The holders of the fur monopoly in France did not encourage emigration to the colony because settlement would reduce the forests from which the furs were harvested. New France therefore remained so lightly populated that English marauders easily seized and held Quebec from 1629 to 1632.

In 1609, Champlain allied with the Algonquian Indians of the St. Lawrence region in attacking their enemies the Iroquois to the south, earning their eternal enmity. The Iroquois traded furs to the Dutch on the Hudson River for European goods, and when they exhausted the furs of their own territory, they turned north, determined to destroy the French-allied Hurons of the Great Lakes region and seize their rich forests. In the 1640s and 1650s, the Iroquois smashed the Hurons and the French Jesuit missions among them. That ended all commerce in New France for a time and menaced Quebec and Montreal. The bitterness bred in these years colored future colonial warfare, driving the Iroquois to ally with the English against the French. But for the time being, in the mid-seventeenth century, the English remained free of pressure from the beleaguered French colonists, who numbered only about 400.

By the mid-seventeenth century, the Chesapeake and New England regions each contained about 50,000 settlers. Between them lay the mid-Atlantic area controlled by the Dutch, who had planted a small colony named New Netherland at the mouth of the Hudson River in 1624 and in the next four decades had extended their control to the Connecticut and Delaware river valleys. To the south of the Chesapeake lay a vast territory where only the Spanish, on their mission frontier in Florida, challenged the power of Native American tribes.

These two areas, north and south of the Chesapeake, became strategic zones of English colonizing activity after the end of England's civil war in 1660 brought the reinstallation of the English monarchy.

England Challenges the Mighty Dutch

Although for generations they had been the Protestant bulwarks in a mostly Catholic Europe, England and Holland became bitter commercial rivals in the mid-seventeenth century. By the time the Puritans arrived in New England, the Dutch had become the mightiest carriers of seaborne commerce in western Europe. By one contemporary estimate, Holland owned 16,000 of Europe's 20,000 merchant ships. By 1650, the Dutch had temporarily overwhelmed the Portuguese in Brazil, and soon their vast trading empire reached the East Indies, Ceylon, India, and Formosa.

In North America, the Dutch West India Company's New Netherland colony was small but profitable. Agents fanned out from Fort Orange (Albany) and New Amsterdam (New York City) into the Hudson, Connecticut, and Delaware river valleys. There they established a lucrative fur trade with local tribes by hooking into the sophisticated trading network of the Iroquois Confederacy, which stretched to the Great Lakes. At Albany, the center of the Dutch-Iroquois trade, relations remained peaceful and profitable for several generations because both peoples admirably served each other's needs.

By 1650, England was ready to challenge Dutch maritime supremacy. Three times between 1652 and 1675, war broke out between the two Protestant competitors for control of the emerging worldwide capitalist economy. In the second and third wars, the Dutch colony on the Hudson River became an easy target for the English. They captured it in 1664, lost it to the Dutch in 1673, and recaptured it almost immediately. By 1675, the Dutch had been permanently dislodged from the North American mainland. But they remained mighty commercial competitors of the English in Europe, Africa, the Far East, and the Caribbean.

New Netherland, where from the beginning Dutch, French Huguenots, Walloons from present-day Belgium, Swedes, Portuguese, Finns, English, refugee Portuguese Jews from Brazil, and Africans had commingled in a babel of languages and religions, now became New York, named for James, duke of York, brother of the king and heir to the English throne. Under English rule, gradual intermarriage between the Dutch, the Huguenots, and the English — the three main groups — diluted eth-nic loyalties. But New York retained its polyglot, religiously tolerant character.

Proprietary Carolina: A Restoration Reward

In 1663, three years after he was restored to the throne taken from his father, Charles II granted a vast territory named Carolina to a group of men who had supported him when he was in exile. Its boundaries extended from ocean to ocean and from Virginia to central Florida. Within this miniature empire, eight proprietors, including several involved in Barbados sugar plantations, gained large powers of government and semifeudal rights to the land. To lure settlers, they promised religious freedom and offered land free for the asking. Onto this generous land offer they grafted plans for a semimedieval government that provided themselves, their deputies, and a small number of noblemen with a monopoly of political power. A hereditary aristocracy of wealthy manor lords, they thought, would check boisterous small landholders.

However, the reality of settlement in Carolina bore faint resemblance to what the planners envisaged. The rugged sugar and tobacco planters who streamed in from Barbados and Virginia ignored proprietary regulations about settling in compact rectangular patterns and reserving two-fifths of every county for an appointed nobility. Meeting in assembly for the first time in 1670, they refused to accept the proprietors' Fundamental Constitutions of 1667 and ignored the orders of the governor appointed in London. In shaping local government, the planters were guided mostly by their experience in the slave society of Barbados, whence most of them had come.

The Indian Debacle

The proprietors in London had anticipated a well-regulated Indian trade limited to their ap-

Restoration Colonies: New York, the Jerseys, Pennsylvania, and the Carolinas

pointed Carolina agents. But the aggressive settlers from the West Indies and the Chesapeake openly flouted proprietary policy. Those from Barbados, accustomed to exploiting African slave labor, saw that if the major tribes of the Southeast — the Cherokees, Creeks, and Choctaws — could be drawn into trade, the planters might reap vast wealth.

It was not the beaver that beckoned in the Indian trade, as in the North, but the deerskin, much desired in Europe for making warm and durable clothing. But what began as a trade for the skins of deer soon became a trade for the skins of Indians. To the consternation of the London proprietors, capturing Indians for sale in New England and the West Indies became the cornerstone of commerce in Carolina in the early years.

The Indian slave trade plunged Carolina into a series of wars. Local planters and merchants selected a tribe, armed it, and rewarded it handsomely for bringing in captives from another tribe. Even strong tribes that allied for trade with the Carolinians found that after they had used English guns to enslave their weaker neighbors, they themselves were sometimes scheduled for elimination. By the early eighteenth century, the two main tribes of the coastal plain, the Westos and the Savannahs, were nearly extinct.

Early Carolina Society

Carolina's fertile land and warm climate convinced many that it was "a second Paradize." Into the country came Barbadians, Swiss, Scots, Irish, French Huguenots, English, and even migrants from New England and New York. But far from creating paradise, this ethnically and religiously diverse people clashed abrasively in an atmosphere of fierce competition, brutal race relations, and stunted social institutions.

Settlements spread as the Indian population of the coastal region fell sharply. Planters experimented with a variety of exotic crops, including sugar, indigo, tropical fruits, tobacco, and rice. It was this last that proved to be the staple crop upon which a flourishing economy could be built.

The cultivation of rice required backbreaking labor to drain the swampy lowlands, build dams and levees, and hoe, weed, cut, thresh, and husk the crop. Since many of the early settlers had experience with African slaves in Barbados, their early reliance on slave labor came naturally to them. By 1720, when the colony's population had grown to 18,000, blacks outnumbered whites two to one.

As in Virginia and Maryland, the low-lying areas of coastal Carolina were so disease-ridden with malaria and yellow fever that population grew only slowly in the early years. In the

This painting of Mulberry Plantation in South Carolina shows the mansion house, built in 1708, and rows of slave huts constructed in an African style.

healthier northern part of Carolina, mostly pine barrens along a sandy coast, a family-oriented society emerged. Populated largely by small tobacco farmers from Virginia seeking free land, the Albemarle region developed a mixed economy of livestock grazing, tobacco and food production, and the mining of the pine forests for naval stores — turpentine, resin, pitch, tar, and lumber. In 1701, North and South Carolina became separate colonies, but their distinctiveness had emerged before that. Slavery took root only slowly in North Carolina, which was still 85 percent white in 1720.

But in both North and South Carolina, several factors inhibited the growth of a strong corporate identity : the pattern of settlement, the ethnic and religious diversity, and the lack of shared assumptions about social and religious goals.

The Quakers' Peaceable Kingdom

Of all the utopian dreams imposed on the North American landscape in the seventeenth century, the most remarkable was that of the Quakers. During the English civil war, the Society of Friends, as the Quakers called themselves, had sprung forth as one of the many radical sects searching for a more just society and a purer religion. Their visionary ideas and their defiance of civil authority cost them dearly in fines, brutal punishment, and imprisonment. After Charles II and Parliament stifled radical dissent in the 1660s, they too sent many converts across the Atlantic. The society they founded in Pennsylvania foreshadowed more than any other colony the future religious and ethnic pluralism of the United States.

The Early Friends

Like their Puritan cousins, the Quakers regarded the English Protestant church (called the Church of England) as corrupt and renounced its formalities and rituals, which smacked of Catholicism.

They also foreswore all church officials and institutions, persuaded that every believer could find grace through their own "inward light." By discarding the ideas of original sin and eternal predestination, the Quakers offered a radically liberating alternative to the reigning Calvinist doctrine. And their egalitarian doctrine of the light within elevated all lay persons to the position of the clergy and denied the primary place accorded the Scriptures.

Garbing themselves in plain black cloth and practicing civil disobedience, the Quakers presented a threat to social hierarchy and order. They refused to observe the customary marks of deference, such as doffing one's hat to a superior, believing that in God's sight no social distinctions existed. They used the familiar *thee* and *thou* instead of the formal and deferential *you*, they resisted taxes supporting the Church of England, and they refused to sign witnesses' oaths on the Bible, regarding this as profane. They also renounced the use of force in human affairs and refused to perform militia service.

Quakers also affronted traditional views when they insisted on the spiritual equality of the sexes and the right of women to participate in church matters on an equal, if usually separate, footing with men. Quaker leaders urged women to preach and to establish separate women's meetings. Among Quakers who fanned out from England to preach the doctrine of the "inward light," 26 of the first 59 to cross the Atlantic were women. All but four of them were unmarried or without their husbands and therefore living, traveling, and ministering outside the bounds of male authority.

Intensely committed to converting the rest of the world to their beliefs, the Quakers ranged westward to North America and the Caribbean in the 1650s and 1660s. Nearly everywhere they were reviled, mutilated, imprisoned, and deported. Puritan Massachusetts warned them that their liberty in that colony consisted of "free liberty to keep away from us and such as will come to be gone as fast as they can, the sooner the better." The Bay Colony magistrates hanged several Quakers to show they meant business.

Early Quaker Designs

By the 1670s, the English Quakers were looking for a place in the New World to carry out their millennial dreams. Emerging as their leader in this dark period was William Penn, the son of Admiral Sir William Penn, who had captured Jamaica from the Spanish in 1654. Young William had been groomed for life in the English aristocracy, but he rebelled against his parents' designs for him. At age 23, he was converted by a spellbinding speech about the power of the Quaker inward light. After joining the Society of Friends in 1666, Penn devoted himself to their cause.

In 1674, Penn joined other Friends in establishing their own colony on former Dutch territory between the Hudson and Delaware rivers. They purchased the rights to the land, known as West Jersey, from Lord John Berkeley. Penn now helped fashion an extraordinarily liberal constitution for the budding Quaker colony. Legislative power and the authority to constitute courts were vested in an assembly chosen annually by virtually all free males in the colony. Election of justices of the peace and local officeholders was also mandated. Settlers were guaranteed freedom of religion and trial by jury. As Penn and the other trustees of the colony explained, "We lay a foundation for [later] ages to understand their liberty as men and Christians, that they may not be brought in bondage, but by their own consent; for we put the power in the people." Nowhere in the English world did ordinary citizens, especially those who owned no land, enjoy such extensive privileges.

Despite these idealistic plans, West Jersey sputtered at first. Only 1,500 immigrants arrived in the first five years. The focus of Quaker hopes lay across the Delaware River, where in 1681 Charles II granted William Penn a vast territory, almost as large as England itself, in payment of a large royal debt to Penn's father. To the Quakers' great fortune, the territory granted to Penn, the last unassigned segment of the eastern coast of North America, was also one of the most fertile.

Pacifism in a Militant World: Quakers and Indians

On the day Penn received his royal charter for Pennsylvania, he wrote a friend, "My God that has given it to me will, I believe, bless and make it the seed of a nation." The nation that Penn envisioned was unique among colonizing schemes. Penn intended to make his colony an asylum for the persecuted, a refuge from arbitrary state power. Puritans strove to nurture social homogeneity and religious uniformity, excluding all not of like mind. In the Chesapeake and Carolina colonies, aggressive, unidealistic men sought to exploit the region's resources. But Penn dreamed of inviting to his sylvan colony people of all religions and national backgrounds and blending them together in peaceful coexistence. His state would claim no authority over the consciences of its citizens nor demand military service of them.

The Quakers who began streaming into Pennsylvania in 1682 quickly absorbed earlier Dutch, Finnish, and Swedish settlers. Primarily farmers, they fanned out from the capital city of Philadelphia, purchasing land from Penn at reasonable rates.

Even before arriving, Penn laid the foundation for peaceful relations with the Delaware tribe inhabiting his colony. He wrote to the Delaware chiefs: "The king of the Country where I live, hath given me a great Province; but I desire to enjoy it with your Love and Consent, that we may always live together as Neighbors and friends." Recognizing the Indians as the rightful owners of the land included in his grant, Penn pledged not to sell one acre until he had first purchased it from local chiefs. He also promised strict regulation of the Indian trade and a ban on the sale of alcohol.

A comparison between Pennsylvania and South Carolina shows the power of pacifism. A quarter century after initial settlement, Pennsylvania had a population of about 20,000 whites. Penn's peaceful policy had so impressed Native American tribes that Indian refugees began migrating into Pennsylvania from all sides. During the same 25 years, South Carolina had grown to

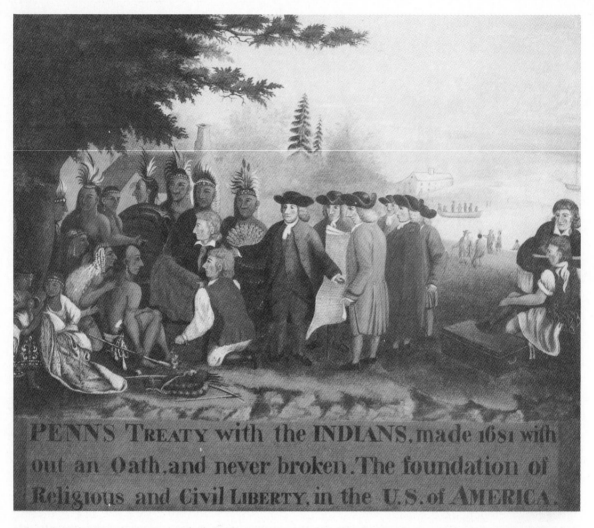

PENN'S TREATY with the INDIANS, made 1681 with out an Oath, and never broken. The foundation of Religious and Civil LIBERTY, in the U.S. of AMERICA.

Edward Hick's Penn's Treaty with the Indians *was painted in the nineteenth century and in a romanticized version of the Treaty of Shackamaxon by which the Lenape Indians ceded the site of Philadelphia to Penn. The treaty was actually made in 1682, but Hicks was correct in implying that the Lenape held Penn in high regard for his fair treatment of them.*

only about 4,000 whites, but the area had become a cauldron of violence. Carolinians spread arms through the region to facilitate slave dealing, shipped some 10,000 members of local tribes off to New England and the West Indies as slaves, and laid waste to the Spanish mission frontier in Florida.

As long as the Quaker philosophy of pacifism and friendly relations with the Delawares and Susquehannocks held sway, interracial relations in the Delaware River valley contrasted sharply with those in other parts of North America. But the Quaker policy of toleration, liberal government, and exemption from military service attracted to the colony, especially in the eighteenth century, thousands of immigrants whose land hunger and disdain for Indians undermined Quaker trust and friendship.

Germans and Scots-Irish flooded in, swelling the population to 31,000 by 1720. Seeking farm land, neither of these groups shared Quaker idealism about racial harmony. They encroached on the lands of the local tribes, sometimes encouraged by the land agents of Penn's heirs. By the mid-eighteenth century, a confrontation of red and white inhabitants was occurring in Pennsylvania.

Building the Peaceable Kingdom

Although Pennsylvania came closer to matching its founder's goals than any other European colony, Penn's dream of a society that banished violence, religious intolerance, and arbitary authority never completely materialized. Nor was he able to convince people to settle in compact villages, which he believed necessary for his "holy experiment." The plain Quaker farmers scattered across the countryside and built simple farmsteads. They created open country networks without any particular centers or boundaries. Yet a sense of common endeavor persisted.

The Quakers maintained their distinctive identity, allowing marriage only within their society, carefully providing land for their offspring, and guarding against too great a population increase (which would cause too rapid a division of farms) by limiting the size of their families.

Pennsylvania's countryside blossomed, and its port capital of Philadelphia also grew rapidly. By 1700, it had overtaken New York City in population, and a half century later it was the largest city in the colonies, bustling with a wide range of artisans, merchants, and professionals.

The Limits of Perfectionism

In spite of commercial success and peace with Native Americans, not all was harmonious in early Pennsylvania. Political affairs were often turbulent, in part because of Pennsylvania's weak leadership. Penn was a much-loved proprietor, but he did not tarry long in his colony to guide its course.

A more important cause of disunity resided in the Quaker attitude toward authority. In England, balking at authority was almost a daily part of Quaker life. To be a Quaker was to refuse to bear arms, to disobey the law prohibiting nonconformists to hold religious services, to deny the Bible as revealed truth, to reject the traditional role assigned women, and to violate social custom obliging inferiors to defer to their superiors. Quakers were bound to each other by decades of persecution.

In Pennsylvania, the absence of persecution eliminated a crucial binding element, and factionalism developed. Their squabbling filled Penn with dismay. Why, he asked, were his settlers so "governmentish, so brutish, so susceptible to scurvy quarrels that break out to the disgrace of the Province?"

Meanwhile, Quaker industriousness and frugality led to such material success that after a generation, social radicalism and religious evangelicalism began to fade. As in other colonies, settlers discovered the door to prosperity wide open and surged across the threshold.

Where Pennsylvania differed from New England and the South was in its relations with Native Americans, at least for the first few generations. It also departed from the Puritan colonies in its immigration policy. Pennsylvania, it is said, was the first community since the Roman Empire to allow people of different national origins and religious persuasions to live together under the same government on terms of near equality. English, Highland Scots, French, Germans, Irish, Welsh, Swedes, Finns, and Swiss all settled in Pennsylvania. This ethnic mosaic was further complicated by a medley of religious groups, including Mennonites, Lutherans, Dutch Reformed, Quakers, Baptists, Anglicans, Presbyterians, Catholics, Jews, and a sprinkling of mystics. Their relations may not always have been friendly, but few attempts were made to discriminate against dissenting groups. Pennsylvanians thereby laid the foundations for the pluralism that was to become the hallmark of American society.

CONCLUSION
The Achievement of New Societies

Nearly 200,000 immigrants reached the coast of North America in the seventeenth century. Coming from a variety of social backgrounds, they represented the rootstock of distinctive societies that would mature in the North American colonies of England, France, Holland, and Spain. For three generations, North America served as a social laboratory for religious and social visionaries, political theorists, fortune seekers, social outcasts, and most of all, ordinary men and women seeking a better life than they had known in their European homelands.

Nearly three-quarters of them came to the Chesapeake and Carolina colonies. Most of them found this a region of disease and death rather than an arena of opportunity. In the northern colonies, to which the fewest immigrants came, life was more secure. Organized around family and community, favored by a healthier climate, and motivated by religion and social vision, the Puritan and Quaker societies thrived, even though utopian expectations were never completely fulfilled.

RECOMMENDED READING

The early settlement of the Chesapeake is the subject of much exciting recent research. Newer works include Edmund S. Morgan, *American Slavery, American Freedom : The Ordeal of Colonial Virginia* (1975) ; Gloria L. Main, *Tobacco Colony : Life in Early Maryland* (1982) ; and Darrett B. Rutman and Anita H. Rutman, *A Place in Time : Middlesex County, Virginia, 1650–1750* (1984).

A good introduction to English Puritanism is Christopher Hill, *Society and Puritanism in Pre-Revolutionary England*, 2d ed. (1967). For information on the Puritans in their early New England communities, consult David G. Allen, *In English Ways* (1981) ; Philip Greven, Jr., *Four Generations* (1970) ; and Stephen Innes, *Labor in a New Land* (1983). Illuminating biographies of early Puritan leaders are Edmund S. Morgan, *The Puritan Dilemma : The Story of John*

Winthrop (1958) ; and Robert Middlekauff, *The Mathers* (1971). For rich analyses of Puritan-Indian relations, see Neal Salisbury, *Manitou and Providence* (1982) ; William Cronon, *Changes in the Land : Indians, Colonists, and the Ecology of New England* (1983) ; and James Axtell, *The Invasion Within* (1985).

Proprietary New York and Carolina are treated in Robert C. Ritchie, *The Duke's Province* (1977) ; Michael Kammen, *Colonial New York* (1975) ; M. Eugene Sirmans, *Colonial South Carolina* (1966) ; and Robert M. Weir, *Colonial South Carolina* (1983).

Quaker Pennsylvania is the subject of Gary B. Nash, *Quakers and Politics* (1968).

On indentured servitude, see David Galenson, *White Servitude in Colonial America* (1981), and Sharon V. Salinger, *"To Serve Well and Faithfully" : Labor and Indentured Servitude in Pennsylvania* (1987).

Time Line

1590	Roanoke Island colony fails	**1635**	Roger Williams banished to Rhode Island
1607	Jamestown settled	**1636**	Anne Hutchinson exiled to Rhode Island
1616–1621	Native American population in New England decimated by European diseases	**1637**	New England wages war against the Pequot tribe
1617	First tobacco crop shipped from Virginia	**1642–1649**	English Civil War ends great migration to New England
1619	First Africans arrive in Jamestown	**1643**	Confederation of New England
1620	Pilgrims land at Plymouth	**1659**	Two Quaker men hanged on Boston Common
1622	Powhatan tribes attack Virginia settlements	**1660**	Restoration of King Charles II in England
1624	Dutch colonize mouth of Hudson River	**1663**	Carolina charter granted to eight proprietors
1630	Puritan migration to Massachusetts Bay	**1664**	English capture New Netherland and rename it New York
1632	Maryland grant to Lord Baltimore (George Calvert)		Royal grant of the Jersey lands to proprietors
1633–1634	Native Americans in New England again struck by European diseases	**1681**	William Penn receives Pennsylvania grant

3

Mastering the New World

Anthony Johnson, an African, arrived in Virginia in 1621 with only the name "Antonio." Caught as a young man in the Portuguese slave-trading net, he was purchased by Richard Bennett and sent to work at Bennett's tobacco plantation situated on the James River. On March 22, 1622, the Powhatan tribes of tidewater Virginia fell upon the white colonizers in a determined attempt to drive them from the land. Of the 57 persons on the Bennett plantation, only black Antonio and four others survived.

Antonio — anglicized to Anthony — labored on the Bennett plantation for some 20 years, slave in fact if not in law, for legally defined bondage was still in the formative stage. During this time he married Mary, another African, and fathered four children. In the 1640s, Anthony and Mary Johnson gained their freedom and at some point adopted their surname. Already past middle age, the Johnsons settled on Virginia's eastern shore. By 1650, they owned 250 acres, a small herd of cattle, and two black servants. By the late 1650s, however, as the lines of racial slavery tightened, the customs of the country began closing in on Virginia's free blacks.

In 1664, convinced that ill winds were blowing away the chances for their children and grandchildren in Virginia, the Johnsons began selling their land to white neighbors. The following spring, most of the clan moved north to Maryland, where they rented land and again took up farming and cattle raising. Five years later, Anthony Johnson died, leaving four children and his wife. A jury of white men in Virginia declared that because Johnson "was a Negroe and by consequence an alien," the 50 acres he had deeded to his son Richard before moving to Maryland should be awarded to a local white planter.

Johnson's children and grandchildren, born in America, could not duplicate the modest success of the African-born patriarch. By the late seventeenth century, people of color faced much greater difficulties. Anthony's sons never rose higher than tenant farmer or small freeholder. John Johnson moved farther north into Delaware in the 1680s. Members of his family married local Indians and became part of a triracial community that has survived to the present day. Richard Johnson stayed behind in Virginia. His four sons became tenant farmers and hired servants. By

44

• • •

now, in the early eighteenth century, slave ships were pouring Africans into Virginia and Maryland to replace white indentured servants, the backbone of the labor force for four generations. To be black had at first been a handicap. Now it became a fatal disability, an indelible mark of degradation and bondage.

• • •

Anthony and Mary Johnson and their children lived in a time of unrest and growing inequality. This chapter surveys the fluid, conflict-filled era from 1675 to 1715, a time when five overlapping struggles for mastery occurred. First, in determining to build a slave labor force, the colonists struggled to establish their mastery over resistant African captives. Second, the settlers sought mastery over Native American tribes. Third, the colonists resisted the attempts of English imperial administrators to bring them into a more dependent relationship. Fourth, within colonial societies, emerging elites struggled to establish their claims to political and social authority. Finally, the colonizers, aided by England, strove for mastery over French, Dutch, and Spanish contenders in North America.

Black Bondage

For almost four centuries after Columbus's voyages to the New World, European colonizers forcibly transported Africans out of their homelands and used their labor to produce wealth in their colonies. Estimates vary widely, but the number of Africans brought to the New World was probably not less than 12 million. Of all the people who populated the New World between the fifteenth and eighteenth centuries, the Africans were by far the most numerous, probably outnumbering Europeans two to one.

Slave traders took most Africans to the West Indies, Brazil, and Spanish America. Yet those who came to the American colonies, about 10,000 in the seventeenth century and 350,000 in the eighteenth, profoundly affected the destiny of American society. In a prolonged period of labor scarcity, their labor and skills were indispensable to colonial economic development. Their African culture mixed continuously with that of their European masters. And the race relations that grew out of slavery so deeply marked society that the problem of race has continued ever since to be the "American dilemma."

The Slave Trade

The African slave trade began as an attempt to fill a labor shortage in the Mediterranean world in the eighth century. Seven centuries later, Portuguese merchants reached the west coast of Africa by water and began buying slaves captured by other Africans and transporting them home by ship. These slaves were mostly criminals consigned to bondage in their own society or unfortunate individuals captured in tribal wars.

More than anything else, sugar transformed the African slave trade. By the seventeenth century, with Europeans developing a taste for sugar almost as insatiable as their craving for tobacco, they vied fiercely for possession of the tiny islands dotting the Caribbean and for control of the trading forts on the West African coast. African kingdoms, eager for European trade goods, warred against each other in order to supply the "black gold" demanded by white ship captains.

Many European nations competed for trading rights on the West African coast. In the seventeenth century, when about one million Africans were brought to the New World, the Dutch

One out of every seven captive Africans did not survive the horrors of the Transatlantic journey on the slave ships.

replaced the Portuguese as the major supplier. But by the 1790s, the English were the foremost slave-trading nation in Europe. All in all, in the eighteenth century, European traders carried at least six million Africans to the Americas, probably the greatest forced migration in history.

Even the most vivid accounts of the slave trade cannot convey the pain and demoralization that accompanied the capture and subsequent treatment of slaves. Olaudah Equiano, an eighteenth-century Ibo from what is now Nigeria, described how raiders from another tribe kidnapped him and his younger sister when he was only 11 years old. He passed from one trader to another while being marched to the coast. Many slaves attempted suicide or died from exhaustion or hunger on these forced marches. But Equiano survived. Reaching the

coast, he and others were confined in barracoons, fortified enclosures on the beach, where a surgeon from an English slave ship inspected him. Equiano was terrified by the light skins, language, and long hair of the English and was convinced that he "had got into a world of bad spirits and that they were going to kill me."

More cruelties followed. Some slaves were branded with a hot iron. Then the slaves were ferried in large canoes to the ships anchored in the harbor. An English captain recounted the desperation of the captives : "The Negroes are so loath to leave their own country, that they have often leaped out of the canoes, boat and ship, into the sea, and kept under the water till they were drowned."

Conditions aboard the slave ships were miserable. Equiano recounted the scene below

Origins and Destinations of African Slaves, 1526-1810

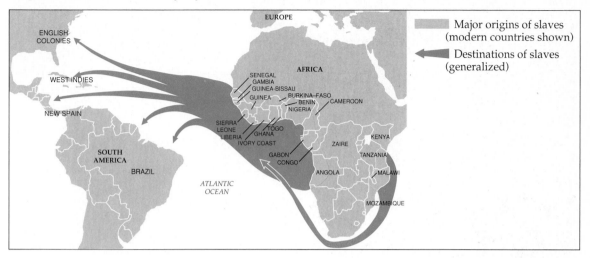

decks, where manacled slaves crowded together like corpses in coffins. "With the loathsomeness of the stench, and crying together, I became so sick and low that I was not able to eat, nor had I the least desire to taste anything." The refusal to

Diagrams such as this, useful to captains wishing to take advantage of "tight packing," were printed as late as the nineteenth century.

take food was so common that ship captains devised special techniques to force feed resistant Africans.

The Atlantic passage usually took four to eight weeks. It was so physically depleting and psychologically wrenching that one of every seven captives died en route. Many others arrived in the Americas deranged or near death. In all, the relocation of any African may have averaged about six months from the time of capture to the time of arrival at the plantation of a colonial buyer. During this protracted personal crisis, the slave was completely cut off from the moorings of a previous life — language, family and friends, tribal religion, familiar geography, and status in a local community.

The Southern Transition to Black Labor

English colonists on the mainland of North America turned only slowly to Africa to solve their labor problem. Indentured white labor proved the best way to meet the demand for labor during most of the seventeenth century. Beginning in 1619, a small number of Africans were brought to Virginia and Maryland to labor in the tobacco fields alongside white servants.

But as late as 1671, when some 30,000 slaves toiled in English Barbados, fewer than 3,000 served in Virginia. They were still outnumbered there at least three to one by white indentured servants.

The transformation of the southern labor force from mostly white to mostly black began in the last quarter of the seventeenth century. Three reasons explain this shift. First, the rising commercial power of England, at the expense of the Spanish and Dutch, swelled English participation in the African slave trade. Beginning in the 1680s, southern planters could purchase slaves more readily and cheaply than before. Second, the supply of white servants from England began drying up. Those who did arrive fanned out among a growing number of colonies. Finally, white servant unrest and a growing population of ex-servants who were landless, discontented, and potential challengers to established white planters led the southern elite to welcome a more pliable labor force. Consequently, by the 1730s, the number of white indentured servants had dwindled to insignificance.

Slavery in the Northern Colonies

Slavery never became the foundation of the northern colonial work force, for labor-intensive crops such as sugar and rice would not grow in colder climates. On the smaller family farms, household labor and occasional hired hands sufficed. Only in the cities, where slaves worked as artisans and domestic servants, and in a few scattered rural areas did slavery take substantial root.

Although the northern colonists employed few slaves, their economies were becoming enmeshed in the commercial network of the Atlantic basin, which depended on slavery and the slave trade. New England's merchant ships pursued profits in the slave trade as early as the 1640s. In New York and Philadelphia, building and outfitting slave vessels proved profitable. New England's seaports became centers for the distilling of rum, which was made from West In-

dian sugar and traded for slaves on the African coast. As the number of slaves in the Caribbean multiplied, the West Indies became a favorite market for codfish from New England, wheat from the middle colonies, and barrel staves and hoops from North Carolina. Thus, every North American colony participated in the racial exploitation in some way.

The System of Bondage

The first Africans brought to the American colonies came as bound servants. They served for a number of years; then, like Anthony and Mary Johnson, many of them eventually gained their freedom. Gradually during the seventeenth century, Chesapeake planters began to draw tighter lines around the activities of black servants. By the 1640s, Virginia forbade blacks, free or bound, to carry firearms. In the 1660s, marriages between white women and black servants were called "shameful matches" and "the disgrace of our Nation." Bit by bit, white settlers strengthened the association between black skin and slave status.

By the mid-seventeenth century, most white colonists were determined to fasten perpetual bondage on their black servants. In this dehumanization of Africans, which the English largely copied from their colonial rivals, the key step was instituting hereditary lifetime service. Once servitude became perpetual, relieved only by death, the elimination of all other privileges followed quickly. When the slave condition of the mother legally fell upon the black infant (not the case in other forms of slavery, such as in Africa), slavery became self-perpetuating, passing automatically from one generation to the next.

Slavery existed not only as a system of forced labor but also as a pattern of human relationships eventually legitimated by law. By the early eighteenth century, most provincial legislatures were enacting laws for controlling black rights and activities, known as "black codes." Slaves were forbidden to testify in court, engage in commercial activity, hold property, participate in the political process, congregate in public, travel without permission, or engage in legal marriage or parenthood. Nearly stripped of human status, they became defined as a form of property.

Eliminating all slave rights had both pragmatic and psychological dimensions. Every black man and woman in chains was a potential rebel. So the rapid increase in the slave population brought anxious demands to bring slaves under strict control. The desire to stifle black rebelliousness mingled with a need to justify brutal behavior toward slaves by defining them as less than human. "The planters," wrote one Englishman in Jamaica, "do not want to be told that their Negroes are human creatures. If they believe them to be of human kind, they cannot regard them as no better than dogs or horses."

Slave Culture

Slave owners could set the external boundaries of existence for their slaves, controlling physical location, work roles, diet, and shelter. But the authority of the master class impinged far less on how slaves established friendships, fell in love, formed kin groups, raised children, worshiped their gods, buried their dead, and organized their leisure time.

In these aspects of daily life, slaves in America drew on their African heritage to shape their existence to some degree. In doing so, they laid the foundations for an Afro-American culture. At first, this culture had many variations because slaves came from many areas in Africa and lived under different conditions in the colonies. But common elements emerged, led by developments in the South, where about 90 percent of American slaves labored in the colonial period.

The Growth of Slavery

In contrast to other areas of the New World, in North America Africans reached a relatively healthy environment. In the southern colonies, where the ghastly mortality of the early decades had subsided by the time Africans were arriving

in large numbers, their chances for survival were much better than in the West Indies or South America. This environmental advantage, combined with a more even sex ratio, led to a natural increase in the North American slave population that was unparalleled elsewhere.

In 1675, about 4,000 slaves were scattered across Virginia and Maryland. Most were men. A half century later, with the decline of white servitude, 45,000 slaves labored on Chesapeake plantations. By 1760, when their number exceeded 185,000, the Chesapeake plantations relied almost entirely on black labor.

Although slave codes severely restricted the lives of slaves, the possibility for family life increased as the southern colonies matured. Larger plantations employed dozens and even hundreds of slaves, and the growth of roads and market towns permitted them greater opportunities to forge relationships beyond their own plantation. By the 1740s, a growing proportion of Chesapeake slaves were American-born, had established families, and lived in plantation outbuildings where from sundown to sunup they could fashion lives of their own.

In South Carolina, African slaves worked mostly on large plantations in swampy lowlands, and their knowledge of rice cultivation gave the colony a solid economic base. In the coastal low country they outnumbered whites three to one by 1760 and hence were able to maintain more of their African culture than slaves in the Chesapeake. Many slaves spoke Gullah, a "pidgin," or mixture, of several African languages. They often gave African names to their children, names like Cudjoe, Cuffe, Quashey, and Phibbi. And they kept alive their African religious customs.

In the northern colonies, slaves made up less than 10 percent of the population. Living in the same house as the master, slaves adapted to European ways much faster than in the South. Slavery was also less repressive in the North than in the South.

Slavery spread more extensively in the northern ports than across the countryside. Artisans, ship captains, and an emerging urban elite

This eighteenth-century watercolor depicts slaves in South Carolina dancing the "juba," a West African dance. The gourdlike banjo and the twisted leather drumsticks are of African design, reflecting the cultural heritage of Africa transplanted to the American colonies.

of merchants, lawyers, and landlords displayed their wealth and status by employing slaves. By the beginning of the eighteenth century, more than 40 percent of New York City's households owned slaves.

Resistance and Rebellion

While struggling to adapt to bondage in various regions of British America, slaves also rebelled in ways that constantly reminded their masters that slavery's price was eternal vigilance. "Saltwater" Africans fresh from their homelands often resisted slavery fiercely. "You would really be surprised at their perseverance," wrote one observer. "They often die before they can be conquered." Commonly this initial resistance

took the form of escaping to the frontier to begin renegade settlements, to Indian tribes in the interior that sometimes offered refuge, or to Spanish Florida. Open rebellions, such as those in New York City in 1712 and at Stono, South Carolina, in 1739, mostly involved newly arrived slaves. There was no North American parallel, however, for the massive slave uprisings that erupted periodically in the West Indies and Brazil, where the slaves vastly outnumbered their masters.

In North America, slaves rarely outnumbered whites except in South Carolina, and the master class tried to cultivate tension between local Indians and slaves so that they would be "a check upon each other," as one worried planter explained. When rebellion did occur, white colonizers stopped at nothing to quell it. They tried to intimidate all slaves by torturing, hanging, dismembering, and even burning captured rebels at the stake.

Open rebelliousness often gave way to more subtle forms of resistance, such as dragging out the job, shamming illness, pretending ignorance, and breaking tools. Slaves also resisted through truancy, arson, crop destruction, pilfering to supplement their food supply, and direct assaults on masters, overseers, and drivers. In 1732, one South Carolina planter drove his slaves late into the night cleaning and barreling a rice crop. When he awoke in the morning, he found his barn, with the entire harvest in it, reduced to ashes.

Black Religion and Family

Afro-Americans struggled to find meaning and worth in their harsh existence. In this quest, religion and family played a central role — one destined to continue far into the post-slavery period.

Africans brought a complex religious heritage to the New World. No amount of desolation or physical abuse could wipe out these deeply rooted beliefs. Coming from cultures where the division between sacred and secular activities was less clear than in Europe, slaves made religion central to their existence. The black Christianity that emerged in the eighteenth century blended African religious practices with the religion of the master class. It laid the foundations for the black church that later became the central institution in Afro-American life.

The religious revival that began in the 1720s in the northern colonies and thereafter spread southward made important contributions to Afro-American religion. Evangelicalism stressed personal rebirth, used music and body motion, and caught individuals up in an intense emotional experience. The dancing, shouting, rhythmic clapping, and singing that came to characterize slaves' religious expression represented a creative mingling of West African and Christian religions.

Besides religion, the slaves' greatest refuge

from their dreadful fate lay in their families. In West Africa, all social relations were centered in kinship lines, which stretched backward to include dead ancestors. Torn from their native societies, slaves placed great importance on rebuilding extended kin groups.

Most English colonies prohibited slave marriages. But in practice, domestic life was an area in which slaves and masters struck a bargain. Masters found that slaves would work harder if they were allowed to form families. Moreover, family ties stood in the way of escape or rebellion.

Slaves fashioned a family life only with difficulty, however. At first males outnumbered females, but as natural increase swelled the slave population in the eighteenth century, the sex ratio became more even.

The sale of either husband or wife could abruptly sever their fragile union. Young children usually stayed with their mothers until about age 8; then they were frequently torn from their families through sale, often to small planters needing only a hand or two. Few slaves escaped separation from family members at some time during their lives.

White male exploitation of black women represented another assault on family life. How many black women were coerced or lured with favors into sexual relations with white masters and overseers cannot be known. But the sizable mulatto (racially mixed) population at the end of the eighteenth century indicates that the number was large.

Not all interracial relationships were cruel. In some cases, black women sought the liaison to gain advantages for themselves or their children. These unions nonetheless threatened both the slave community and the white plantation ideal of separate racial categories.

While slave men struggled to preserve their family role, many black women assumed a position in the family that differed from that of white women. Plantation mistresses usually worked hard in helping to manage estates, but nonetheless the ideal grew that the should remain in the house to guard white virtue and set the standards for white culture. In contrast, the black woman remained indispensable to both the work of the plantation and the functioning of the slave quarters. She toiled in the fields and worked in the slave cabins. Paradoxically, black women's roles, which required constant labor, made them more equal to men than was the case of women in white society.

Above all, slavery was a set of power relationships designed to extract the maximum labor from its victims. Hence it regularly involved cruelties that filled family life with tribulation and uncertainty.

The Struggle for Land

In the same period that slavery gained a permanent foothold in North America, both New England and Virginia fought major wars against Native Americans. The desire for land, a cause of both wars, produced a similar conflict somewhat later in South Carolina. The conflicts brought widespread destruction to the towns of both colonizers and Indians, inflicted heavy human casualties, and left a legacy of bitterness on both sides. For the coastal tribes, it was a disastrous time of defeat and decline.

King Philip's War in New England

Following the Pequot War of 1637 in New England, the Wampanoags and Narragansetts, whose fertile land lay within the boundaries of Plymouth and Rhode Island, attempted to maintain their distance from the New England colonists. But the New Englanders coveted Indian territories and gradually reduced the Indians' land base.

By the 1670s, when New England's population had grown to about 50,000, younger Indians began brooding over their situation. Their leader, Metacomet (named King Philip by the English), was the son of Massasoit, the Wampanoag who had allied himself with the first Plymouth settlers in 1620. As the Wampanoag leader, Metacomet faced one hu-

miliating challenge after another. In 1671, for example, Plymouth forced Metacomet to surrender a large stock of guns and accept a treaty of submission acknowledging Wampanoag subjection to English law. Convinced that more setbacks would follow and humiliated by the discriminatory treatment of Indians brought before English courts, Metacomet began recruiting for a resistance movement.

The execution of three tribesmen in June 1675 was the catalyst for King Philip's War, but the root cause was the rising anger of the young Wampanoag males. As would happen repeatedly in the next two centuries as Americans pushed westward, these younger Native Americans refused to imitate their fathers, who had watched the colonizers erode their land base and compromise their sovereignty. Instead, they attempted a pan-Indian offensive against an intruder with far greater numbers and a much larger arsenal of weapons.

In the summer of 1675, the Wampanoags unleashed daring hit-and-run attacks on villages in the Plymouth colony. By autumn, many New England tribes, including the powerful Narragansetts, had joined King Philip's warriors. Towns all along the frontier reeled under Indian attacks. By the time the first snow fell in November, mobile Indian warriors had laid waste to the entire upper Connecticut River valley.

King Philip's offensive faltered in the spring of 1676. Food shortages and disease sapped Indian strength, and the powerful Mohawks refused to support the New England tribes. By summer, groups of Indians were surrendering, while some moved westward seeking shelter among other tribes. King Philip fell in battle. His head was carried triumphantly back to Plymouth, where it remained on display for 25 years.

At war's end, several thousand colonists and perhaps twice as many Indians lay dead. Of some 90 Puritan towns, 52 had been attacked and 13 completely destroyed. Not for 40 years would the frontier advance beyond the line it had reached in 1675. Indian towns were devastated even more completely. Many of the survivors, including Metacomet's wife and son, were sold into slavery in the West Indies.

Bacon's Rebellion Engulfs Virginia

While New Englanders fought local tribes in 1675 and 1676, the Chesapeake colonies became locked in a struggle involving both a war between the red and white populations and civil war within the colonizers' society. This deeply tangled conflict was called Bacon's Rebellion after the headstrong Cambridge-educated planter Nathaniel Bacon, who arrived in Virginia at age 28.

Bacon and many other amibitious young planters detested the Indian policy of Virginia's royal governor, Sir William Berkeley. In 1646, at the end of the second Indian uprising against the Virginians, the Powhatan tribes had accepted a treaty granting them exclusive rights to territory north of the York River, beyond the limits of white settlement. Stable Indian relations suited the established planters, some of whom traded profitably with the Indians, but became obnoxious to new settlers arriving in the 1650s and 1660s. Nor did it please the white indentured servants who had served their time and were hoping to find cheap frontier land.

In the summer of 1675, a gorup of frontiersmen used an incident with a local tribe as an excuse to attack the Susquehannocks, whose rich land they coveted. Governor Berkeley denounced the attack, but few supported his position. He faced, he said, "a people where six parts of seven at least are poor, indebted, discontented, and armed."

Although badley outnumbered, the Susquehannocks prepared for war. They attacked during the winter of 1675–1676 and killed 36 Virginians. That spring, the hot-blooded Nathaniel Bacon became the frontiersmen's leader. Joined by hundreds of runaway servants and some slaves, he launched a campaign of indiscriminate warfare on friendly and hostile Indians alike. When Governor Berkeley declared Bacon a rebel and sent out 300 militiamen to drag him to Jamestown for trial, Bacon headed into the wilderness and recruited more followers, including many substantial planters. Frontier skirmishes with Indians had turned into civil war.

In the summer of 1676, Bacon and his followers captured the capital at Jamestown and put Governor Berkeley to flight across Chesapeake Bay.

Virginians at all levels had chafed under Berkeley's rule. High taxes, an increase in the governor's powers at the expense of local officials, and the monopoly that Berkeley and his friends held on the Indian trade were especially unpopular. Berkeley tried to rally public support by holding new assembly elections and extending the vote to all freemen, whether they owned property or not. The new assembly promptly turned on the governor, passing a set of reform laws intended to make government more responsive to the common people and to end rapacious officeholding. The assembly also made legal the enslavement of Native Americans.

Time was on the governor's side, however. Having crushed the Indians, Bacon's followers began drifting home to tend their crops. Meanwhile, Berkeley's reports of the rebellion brought the dispatch of 1,100 royal troops from England. By the time they arrived, in January 1677, Nathaniel Bacon lay dead of swamp fever and most of his followers had melted back into the frontier. After Bacon's death in October 1676, Berkeley rounded up 23 rebel leaders and hanged them without benefit of civil trial. Royal investigators who arrived in 1677 remarked on the genocidal mentality of Bacon's followers, whom they denounced as the "inconsiderate sort of men who so rashly and causelessly cry up a war and seem to wish and aim at an utter extirpation of the Indians."

The hatred of Indians did not die with the end of the rebellion. A generation later, in 1711, the Virginia legislature voted military appropriations of £20,000 "for extirpating all Indians without distinction of Friends or Enemys." The remnants of the once populous Powhatan Confederacy lost their last struggle for the world they had known. Now they moved farther west or submitted to a life on the margins of white society as tenant farmers, day laborers, or domestic servants.

After Bacon's Rebellion, an emerging planter aristocracy annulled most of the reform laws of 1676. But the war relieved much of the social tension among white Virginians. Newly available Indian land created fresh opportunities for small planters and former servants. Equally important, Virginians with capital to invest were turning to West Africa to supply their labor needs. A racial consensus, uniting whites of different ranks in the common pursuit of a prosperous, slave-based economy, began to take shape.

North and south of Virginia, Bacon's Rebellion caused insurrectionary rumblings. A dissident group in North Carolina's Albemarle County drove the governor from office and briefly seized the reins of power.

In Maryland, Protestant settlers chafed under high taxes, quitrents, and officeholders regarded as venal, Catholic, or both. Declining tobacco prices and a fear of Indian attacks increased their touchiness. A month after Bacon razed Jamestown, insurgent small planters tried to seize the Maryland government. Two of their leaders were hanged for the attempt. In 1681, another abortive uprising took place.

In all three southern colonies, the volatility of late-seventeenth-century life owed much to the region's peculiar social development. Where family formation was retarded by imbalanced sex ratios and fearsome mortality, and where geographic mobility was high, little social cohesion or attachment to community could grow. Missing in the southern colonies were mature local institutions, a vision of a larger purpose, and experienced and responsive political leaders.

An Era of Instability

A dozen years after the major Indian wars in New England and Virginia, a series of insurrections and a major witchcraft incident rumbled through colonial society. The rebellions were triggered by the Revolution of 1688, known to Protestants in England thereafter as the Glorious Revolution because it ended forever the notion that kings ruled by a God-given "divine right" and marked the last serious Catholic challenge to Protestant supremacy. But these colonial disruptions also signified a struggle for social and political dominance in the expanding colonies, as did the Salem witchcraft trials in Massachusetts.

Organizing the Empire

From the earliest attempts at colonization, the English assumed that overseas settlements existed to promote the national interest at home. According to this mercantilist theory, colonies served as outlets for English manufactured goods, provided foodstuffs and raw materials, stimulated trade (and hence promoted a larger merchant navy), and contributed to the royal coffers by paying duties on exported commodities such as sugar and tobacco. Colonies benefited by the military protection and guaranteed markets provided from England.

England proceeded slowly in the seventeenth century to regulate its colonies accordingly. In 1621, the king's council forbade tobacco growers to export their crop to anywhere but England. Three years later, when the Virginia Company of London plunged into bankruptcy, the crown made Virginia a royal colony, the first of many. In 1651, Parliament passed a navigation act requiring that English or colonial ships, manned by English or colonial sailors, carry all goods entering England, Ireland, and the colonies, no matter where those goods originated.

In 1660, after the monarchy was restored, Parliament passed a more comprehensive navigation act that listed colonial products (tobacco, sugar, indigo, dyewoods, cotton) that could be shipped only to England or to other English colonies. Like its predecessor, the act took dead aim at Holland's domination of Atlantic commerce while increasing England's revenues by imposing duties on the enumerated articles. In the following decades, other navigation acts closed loopholes in the 1660 law and added other enumerated articles. Nevertheless, this regulation bore lightly on the colonists because the laws lacked enforcement mechanisms.

After 1675, England tightened imperial control. That year marked the establishment of the Lords of Trade, a committee of the king's privy council vested with power to make and enforce decisions regarding the management of the colonies. Chief among their goals was the creation of more uniform governments in North America and the West Indies that would answer to the Crown's will. England was becoming the shipper of the world, and its state-regulated policy of economic nationalism, duplicating that of the Dutch, was essential to this rise to commercial greatness.

The Glorious Revolution in New England

When Charles II died in 1685, his brother, the duke of York, assumed the throne as James II. This set in motion a train of events that nearly led to civil war. Like his brother, James II professed the Catholic faith. But unlike Charles II, who had disclosed this only on his deathbed, the new king announced his faith immediately upon assuming the throne. Consternation ensued. James proceeded to favor Catholics in various ways. When his wife gave birth to a son in 1688, a Catholic succession loomed.

Convinced that James was trying to seize absolute power and fearing a Catholic conspiracy, a group of Protestant leaders secretly plotted the king's downfall. In 1688, led by the earl of Shaftesbury, they invited William of Orange, a prince of the Netherlands, to invade England and take the throne with his wife, Mary, James's Protestant daughter. James abdicated rather than fight. It was a bloodless victory for Protestantism, for parliamentary power and the limitation of kingly prerogatives, and for the propertied merchants and gentry of England who stood behind the revolt.

The response of New Englanders to these events stemmed from their previous experience with royal authority and their fear of "papists." New England became a prime target for reform when the administrative reorganization of the empire began in 1675. In 1684, Charles II had annulled the Massachusetts charter. Two years later, James II appointed Sir Edmund Andros, former governor of New York, to rule over the newly created Dominion of New England that soon gathered under one government the colonies of New Hampshire, Massachusetts, Connecticut, Plymouth, Rhode Island, New York, New Jersey, and part of Maine. Puritans were now forced to swallow the bitter fact that they were subjects of London bureaucrats who cared more about shaping a disciplined empire than about the special religious vision of one group of overseas subjects.

At first, New Englanders accepted Andros, but he soon earned their hatred. He imposed taxes without legislative consent, ended trial by jury, abolished the General Court of Massachusetts (which had met annually since 1630), muzzled Boston's town meeting, and challenged the validity of all land titles. He converted a Boston Puritan church into an Anglican chapel and rejected the Puritan practice of suppressing religious dissent.

When news reached Boston in April 1689 that William of Orange had landed in England, ending James II's hated Catholic regime, Bostonians streamed into the streets to the beat of drums. They imprisoned Andros, a suspected papist, and an interim government ruled Massachusetts for three years while the Bay colonists awaited a new charter and a royal governor.

Leisler's Rebellion in New York

In New York, the Glorious Revolution was similarly bloodless at first but far more disruptive. When news arrived of James II's abdication, a local militia captain, the German-born Jacob Leisler, appeared at Fort James at the lower tip of Manhattan. Governor Francis Nicholson made only a token show of resistance before quietly stepping down. Leisler established an interim government and ruled with an elected Committee of Safety for 13 months until a governor appointed by King William arrived.

Leisler's government enjoyed popularity among small landowners and urban laboring people. Most of the upper echelon, however, regarded him as an upstart commoner who had leapfrogged into the merchant class by marrying a wealthy widow. Leislerians were often labeled as people of "mean birth, and sordid education and desperate fortunes."

Much of this antipathy originated in the smoldering resentment lower- and middle-class Dutch inhabitants felt toward the town's English elite. Many Dutch merchants had readily adjusted to the English conquest of New Netherland in 1664, and many incoming English merchants had married into Dutch families. But beneath the upper class, incidents of Anglo-Dutch hostility were common. The feeling rose in the 1670s and 1680s among ordinary Dutch families that the English were crowding them out of the society they had built.

Leisler shared Dutch hostility toward New York's English elite, and his sympathy for the common people, mostly Dutch, earned him the hatred of the city's oligarchy. Leisler freed imprisoned debtors, planned a town-meeting system of government for New York City, and replaced merchants with artisans in important official posts. By the autumn of 1689, Leislerian mobs were attacking the property of some of New York's wealthiest merchants.

When a new English governor arrived in 1691, the anti-Leislerians embraced him and charged Leisler and seven of his assistants with treason for assuming the government without royal instructions. In the ensuing trial, Leisler and Jacob Milbourne, his son-in-law and chief lieutenant, were convicted of treason by an all-English jury and hanged. Leisler's popularity among the artisans of the city was evident when his wealthy opponents could find no carpenter in the city who would furnish a ladder to use at the scaffold. After his execution, peace gradually returned to New York, but for years provincial and city politics reflected the deep rift between Leislerians and anti-Leislerians.

Southern Rumblings

The Glorious Revolution also focused dissatisfactions in several southern colonies. Since Maryland was ruled by a Catholic proprietary family, the Protestant majority predictably seized on word of the Glorious Revolution and used it for their own purposes. Leading officials and planters formed a Protestant Association. Seizing control of the government in July 1689, they vowed to cleanse Maryland of its popish hue and to reform a corrupt customs service, cut taxes and fees, and extend the rights of the representative assembly. John Coode, formerly a fiery Anglican minister who had been involved in a brief rebellion in 1681, assumed the reins of government and held them until the arrival of Maryland's first royal governor in 1692.

In neighboring Virginia, the Catholic governor, Lord Howard of Effingham, had installed a number of Catholic officials. News of the revolution in England led a group of planters to attempt an overthrow of the governor. The uprising quickly faded when the governor's council asserted itself and took its own measures to remove Catholics from positions of authority.

The Glorious Revolution brought political changes to several colonies. The Dominion of New England was shattered. While Connecticut and Rhode Island were allowed to elect their own governors, Massachusetts and New Hampshire became royal colonies with governors appointed by the king. In Massachusetts, a new royal charter in 1691 eliminated church membership as a voting requirement. The Maryland proprietorship was abolished (to be restored in 1715 when the Baltimore family became Protestant), and Catholics were barred from office. Everywhere the liberties of Protestant Englishmen were celebrated.

The Social Basis of Politics

The colonial insurrections associated with the Glorious Revolution revealed social and political tensions in the immature societies. The colonial elite tried, of course, to foster social and political stability. The best insurance of this, they believed, was the maintenance of a stratified society where children were subordinate to parents, women to men, servants to masters, and the poor to the rich. In every settlement, leaders tried to maintain a system of social gradations and subordination. Puritans, for example, did not file into church on Sundays and occupy the pews in random fashion. Rather, the seats were "doomed," or assigned according to customary yardsticks of respectability — age, parentage, social position, wealth, and occupation.

This social ideal proved difficult to maintain on North American soil, however. Regardless of previous rank, settlers rubbed elbows so frequently and faced such raw conditions together that those without pedigrees often saw little reason to defer to men of superior rank. "In Virginia," explained John Smith, "a plain soldier that can use a pickaxe and spade is better than five knights." Colonists everywhere learned that basic lesson. They gave respect not to those who claimed it by birth but to those who earned it by deed.

Ambitious men on the rise, such as Nathaniel Bacon and Jacob Leisler, rose up against the constituted authorities. When they gained power during the Glorious Revolution, in every case only briefly, the leaders of these uprisings linked themselves with a tradition of English struggle against tyranny and oligarchical power. They vowed to make government more responsive to the ordinary people, who composed most of their societies.

Witchcraft in Salem

The greatest internal conflict of the late seventeenth century did not come as a part of the Glorious Revolution in America but was indirectly nourished by the governmental instability associated with it. In Massachusetts, the deposing of Andros left the colony in political limbo for three years, and this allowed what might have been a brief outbreak of witchcraft in the little community of Salem to escalate into a bitter and bloody battle to which the provincial government, caught in transition, reacted only belatedly.

On a winter's day in 1692, 9-year-old Betty Parris and her 11-year-old cousin Abigail Williams began to play at magic in the kitchen of a small house in Salem, Massachusetts. They enlisted the aid of Tituba, the slave of Betty's father, Samuel Parris, the minister of the small community. Tituba told voodoo tales handed down from her African past and baked "witch cakes." The girls soon became seized with fits and began making wild gestures and speeches. Soon other young girls in the village were behaving strangely. Village elders extracted confessions that they were being tormented by Tituba and two other women, one a decrepit pauper, the other a disagreeable hag.

What began as the innocent play of young girls turned into a ghastly rending of a farm community capped by the execution of 20 villagers accused of witchcraft. In the seventeenth century, people still took literally the biblical injunction "Thou shalt not suffer a witch to live." In Massachusetts, more than 100 people, mostly older women, had been accused of witchcraft before 1692, and more than a dozen had been hanged.

In Salem, the initial accusations against three older women quickly multiplied. Within a matter of weeks, dozens had been charged with witchcraft, including several prominent members of the community. But formal prosecution of the accused witches could not proceed because neither the new royal charter of 1691 nor the royal governor to rule the colony had yet arrived. When Governor William Phips arrived from England in May 1692, he ordered a special court to try the accused, but by now events had careened out of control. All through the summer the court listened to testimony. By September it had condemned about two dozen villagers. The authorities hanged 19 of them on barren "Witches Hill" outside the town, and 80-year-old Giles Corey was crushed to death under heavy stones. The trials rolled on into 1693, but by then colonial leaders, including many of the clergy, recognized that a feverish fear of one's neighbors, rather than witchcraft itself, had possessed the little village of Salem.

Many factors contributed to the hysteria. Among them were generational strife, old family animosities, tensions between agricultural Salem Village and the nearby commercial center called Salem Town, and even an outbreak of food poisoning that may have caused hallucinogenic behavior. Probably nobody will ever fully understand the underlying causes, but the fact that the accusations of witchcraft kept spreading suggests the anxiety of this tumultuous era, marked by war, economic disruption, the political takeover of the colony by Andros and then his overthrow, and the erosion of the early generation's utopian vision.

Contending for a Continent

At the end of the seventeenth century, following an era of Indian wars and internal upheaval, the colonists for the first time confronted an extended period of international war. The struggle for mastery of the New World among four contending European powers — Holland, Spain, France, and England — now became more overt, marking the beginning of nearly 100 years of conflict.

Anglo-French Rivalry

In 1661, the French king, Louis XIV, determined to make his country the most powerful in Europe, regarded North America and the Caribbean with renewed interest. New France's timber resources would build the royal navy, its fish would feed the growing mass of slaves in the French West Indies, and its fur trade, if greatly expanded, would fill the royal coffers.

Under the leadership of able governors such as Count Frontenac, New France grew in population, economic strength, and ambition in the late seventeenth century. In the 1670s, Louis Jolliet and Father Jacques Marquette, a Jesuit priest, explored an immense territory wa-

tered by the Mississippi and Missouri rivers, previously unknown to Europeans. A decade later, military engineers and priests began building forts and missions, one complementing the other, throughout the Great Lakes region and the Mississippi valley. In 1682, René Robert de La Salle canoed down the Mississippi all the way to the Gulf of Mexico.

The growth of French strength and ambitions brought New England and New France into deadly conflict for a generation, beginning in the late seventeenth century. Religious hostility overlaid commercial rivalry. Protestant New Englanders regarded Catholic New France as a satanic challenge to their divinely sanctioned mission. When the European wars began in 1689, armed conflict between England and France quickly extended into every overseas theater where the two powers had colonies. In North America, the battle zone was New York, New England, and eastern Canada.

In two wars, from 1689 to 1697 and 1702 to 1713, the English and French, while fighting in Europe, also sought to oust each other from the New World. The zone of greatest importance was the Caribbean, where slaves produced huge sugar fortunes. In the North American zone, problems of weather, disease, transport, and supply were so great that only irregular warfare was possible.

The English struck three times at the centers of French power. In 1690, during King William's War (1689–1697), their small flotilla captured Port Royal, the hub of Acadia (which was returned to France at the end of the war). The English assault on Quebec, however, failed disastrously. In Queen Anne's War (1702–1713), New England attacked Port Royal three times before finally capturing it in 1710. A year later, when England sent a flotilla of 60 ships and 5,000 men to conquer Canada, the land and sea operations foundered before reaching their destinations.

When European-style warfare failed miserably in America, both England and France attempted to subcontract military tasks to their Indian allies. This policy occasionally succeeded, especially with the French, who gladly sent their own troops into the fray alongside Indian partners. The French and Indians wiped out the frontier outpost of Schenectady, New York, in 1690; razed Wells, Maine, and Deerfield, Massachusetts, in 1703; and battered other towns along the New England frontier during both wars. In retaliation, the Iroquois, supplied by the English, stung several French settlements. Too powerful to be dictated to by either France or England, the Iroquois sat out the second war in the early eighteenth century.

The Results of War

The Peace of Utrecht in 1713, which ended the war, capped the century-long rise of England and the decline of Spain in the rivalry for the sources of wealth outside Europe. England, the big winner, received Newfoundland and Acadia (renamed Nova Scotia), and France recognized English sovereignty over the fur-rich Hudson Bay territory. France retained Cape Breton Island, controlling the entrance to the St. Lawrence River. In the Caribbean, France yielded St. Kitts and Nevis to England. In Europe, Spain lost its provinces in Italy and the last of its holdings in the Netherlands to the Austrian Hapsburgs. Spain also surrendered Gibraltar and Minorca to the English and awarded England the lucrative privilege of supplying the Spanish empire in America with African slaves, a favor formerly enjoyed by the French Senegal Company.

The French were the big losers in these wars, but they did not abandon their ambitions in the New World. Soon after Louis XIV died in 1715, the Regency government of the duke of Orleans tried to regain lost time in America by mounting a huge expedition to settle Louisiana. Because of mismanagement, however, this plan produced little result. French colonies expanded only in the Caribbean, where by 1750 the islands of Hispaniola, Martinique, and Guadeloupe counted 46,000 whites and 250,000 slaves.

At the Peace of Utrecht, Spain retained a vast empire in America. When France decided in 1762 that Louisiana was not worth the expense, Spain gladly accepted it and tried to make it a buffer against the British Americans migrating westward toward New Spain.

A seventeenth-century French engraving depicts a frontier settlement in what is now Texas. Note the military presence, always strong in French Louisiana.

Though England had rebuffed France after a generation of war, New England suffered grievously. Massachusetts bore the brunt of the burden. Probably one-fifth of all able-bodied males in the colony participated in the Canadian campaigns, and of these about one-quarter never lived to tell of the terrors of New England's first major experience with international warfare. At the end of the first war in 1697, one leader bemoaned that Massachusetts was left "quite exhausted and ready to sink under the calamities and fatigue of a tedious consuming war." The war debt was £50,000 sterling in Massachusetts alone, a greater per capita burden than the national debt today. At the end of the second conflict in 1713, war widows were so numerous that the Bay Colony faced its first serious poverty problem.

The colonies south of New England were also affected by the wars. In Queen Anne's War, New York lost one of its best grain markets when Spain, allied with France, outlawed American foodstuffs in its West Indian colonies. The French navy plucked off nearly 30 New York merchant vessels, about one-quarter of the port's fleet, and disrupted the vital sea lanes between the mainland and the Caribbean, also to the detriment of Philadelphia's grain merchants.

One lesson of war, to be repeated many times in succeeding generations, was that the burdens and rewards fell unevenly on the participants. Some lowborn men could rise spectacularly. William Phips, the twenty-sixth child in his family, rose from sheep farmer and ship's carpenter in Maine to governor of Massachusetts in 1691. Other men, already rich, multiplied their wealth. Andrew Belcher of Boston, who had grown wealthy on provisioning contracts during King Philip's War in 1675 and 1676, combined patriotism with profit in King William's and Queen Anne's Wars by supplying warships and outfitting the New England expeditions to Canada. However, most men, especially those who did the fighting, gained little, and many lost all.

CONCLUSION
Controlling the New Environment

By the second decade of the eighteenth century, the 12 English colonies on the eastern edge of North America had erected the basic scaffolding of colonial life. With the aid of England, they had ousted the Dutch, fought the French to a draw, and held their own against the Spanish. The coastal Indian tribes were reeling from disease and war. The settlers had overcome a scarcity of labor by copying the other European colonists in the hemisphere and importing slaves. Finally, the colonists had rebelled against what they viewed as arbitrary and tainted governments imposed by England.

Physically isolated from Europe, the colonists developed a large measure of self-reliance. Slowly, they began to identify themselves as the permanent inhabitants of a new land rather than transplanted English, Dutch, or Scots-Irish. The new land was a puzzling mixture of unpredictable opportunity and sudden turbulence, unprecedented freedom and debilitating wars, racial intermingling and racial separation. It was a New World in much more than a geographic sense, for the people of three cultures who now inhabited it had remade it ; and, while doing so, they were remaking themselves.

RECOMMENDED READING

The Atlantic slave trade is explored in Philip Curtin, *The Atlantic Slave Trade* (1969); and Martin Kilson and Robert I. Rotberg, eds., *The African Diaspora* (1976).

The origins and early history of slavery in the Americas are studied in H. Hoetink, *Slavery and Race Relations in the Americas* (1973); and Richard S. Dunn, *Sugar and Slaves* (1972).

For slavery in the American colonies, see Ira Berlin, "Time, Space, and the Evolution of Afro-American Society in British Mainland America," *American Historical Review* 85 (1980); Peter H. Wood, *Black Majority* (1974); and Daniel C. Littlefield, *Rice and Slaves* (1981).

Relations between colonizers and Native Americans after the founding period are examined in James Axtell, *The European and the Indian* (1981); Francis Jennings, *The Invasion of America* (1975), and *The Ambiguous Iroquois Empire* (1984); J. Leitch Wright, *The Only Land They Knew: The Tragic Story of the American Indians in the Old South* (1981); and Gary B. Nash, *Red, White, and Black* (1974, 1982).

For the Glorious Revolution in America and the era of instability at the end of the seventeenth century, consult David Lovejoy, *The Glorious Revolution in America* (1972), and Carol F. Karlsen, *The Devil in The Shape of a Woman* (1987).

Time Line

1600–1700	Dutch monopolize slave trade		1682	La Salle sails down Mississippi River and claims Louisiana for France
1619	First Africans imported to Virginia		1684	Massachusetts charter recalled
1637	Pequot War in New England		1686	Dominion of New England
1640s	New England merchants enter slave trade		1688	Glorious Revolution in England, followed by accession of William and Mary
	Virginia forbids blacks to carry firearms			
1650–1670	Judicial and legislative decisions in Chesapeake colonies solidify racial lines		1689	Overthrow of Governor Andros in New England
				Leisler's Rebellion in New York
1660	Parliament passes first Navigation Act		1689–1697	King William's War
1664	English conquer New Netherland		1690s	Transition from white indentured to black slave labor begins in Chesapeake
1673–1685	French expand into Mississippi valley			
1675–1676	King Philip's War in New England		1692	Witchcraft hysteria in Salem
			1702–1713	Queen Anne's War
1676	Bacon's Rebellion in Virginia			
			1713	Peace of Utrecht

4

The Maturing of Colonial Society

evereaux Jarratt was born in 1733 on the Virginia frontier, the third son of an immigrant yeoman farmer. In New Kent County, where Jarratt grew up, a farmer's "whole dress and apparel," he recalled later, "consisted in a pair of coarse breeches, one or two shirts, a pair of shoes and stockings, an old felt hat, and a bear skin coat." In a maturing colonial society that was six generations old by the mid-eighteenth century, such simple folk stepped aside and tipped their hats when prosperous neighbors went by.

As the colonies grew rapidly after 1700, economic development brought handsome gains for some, opened modest opportunities for many, but produced disappointment and privation for others. Jarratt was among those who advanced. His huge appetite for learning earned him some schooling. But at age 8, when his parents died, he had to take his place behind the plow alongside his brothers. Then, at 19, Jarratt was "called from the ax to the quill" by a neighboring planter's timely offer of a job tutoring his children.

Tutoring put Jarratt in touch with the world of wealth and status. Gradually he advanced to positions in the households of wealthy Virginia planters. His modest success also introduced him to the world of evangelical religion. In the eighteenth century, an explosion of religious fervor dramatically reversed the growing secularism of the settlers. Jarratt first encountered evangelicalism in the published sermons of George Whitefield, an English clergyman.

Later, at the plantation of John Cannon, he personally experienced conversion under the influence of Cannon's wife. Jarratt later became a clergyman in the Anglican church, but he never lost his religious zeal and desire to carry religion to the common people. In this, he was part of the first mass religious movement to occur in colonial society.

• • •

Colonial North America in the first half of the eighteenth century was a thriving, changing set of regional societies that had developed from turbulent

62

seventeenth-century beginnings. New England, the mid-Atlantic colonies, the Upper and Lower South, New France, and the northern frontier of New Spain were all distinct regions. Even within regions, diversity increased in the eighteenth century as newcomers, mostly from Africa, Germany, Ireland, and France added new pieces to the emerging American mosaic.

Despite their bewildering diversity and lack of cohesion, the colonies along the Atlantic seaboard were affected similarly by population growth and economic development. Everywhere except on the frontier, class differences grew. A commercial orientation spread from north to south, especially in the towns, as local economies matured and forged links with the network of trade in the Atlantic basin. The exercise of political power of elected legislative assemblies and local bodies produced seasoned leaders, a tradition of local autonomy, and a widespread belief in a political ideology stressing the liberties that freeborn Englishmen should enjoy. All regions experienced a deep-running religious awakening that was itself connected to secular changes. All of these themes will be explored as we follow the way that scattered frontier settlements developed into mature provincial societies.

America's First Population Explosion

In 1680, some 150,000 colonizers clung to the eastern edge of North America. By 1750, they had swelled sevenfold to top one million. This growth rate, never experienced in Europe, staggered English policymakers. The population boom was fed from both internal and external sources. Natural increase accounted for much of the growth in all the colonies and nearly all of it in New England, where immigrants arrived only in a trickle in the eighteenth century. The black population also began to increase naturally by the 1720s. American-born slaves soon began to outnumber slaves born in Africa.

The Newcomers

While expanding through natural increase, the colonial population also received waves of newcomers. The eighteenth-century arrivals, who far outnumbered those who came before 1700, came overwhelmingly from Germany, Switzerland, Ireland, and Africa, and they were mostly indentured servants and slaves. Of all the groups arriving in the eighteenth century, the Africans were the largest. Numbering about 15,000 in 1690, they grew to 80,000 in 1730 and 325,000 in 1760.

German-speaking settlers, about 90,000 strong, flocked to the colonies in the eighteenth century. Most settled between New York and South Carolina, with Pennsylvania claiming the largest number of them.

Outnumbering the Germans were the Protestant Scots-Irish. Several thousand from Northern Ireland arrived each year after the Peace of Utrecht in 1713 reopened the Atlantic sea lanes. Mostly poor farmers, they streamed into the same backcountry areas where Germans were settling, though more of them followed the mountain valleys south into the Carolinas and Georgia. They washed over the ridges of Appalachia until their appetite for land brought them face to face with the ancient occupiers of the land. No major Indian wars occurred between 1715 and 1754, but the frontier

German Settlements, 1775

Scots-Irish Settlements, 1775

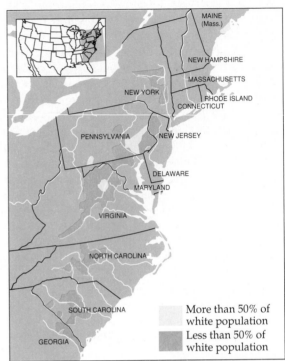

bristled with tension as the new settlers pushed westward.

In the enormous population growth occurring after 1715, New England nearly tripled in population, but the middle and southern colonies quadrupled, though in the South the fast-growing slave population accounted for much more of the growth than in the mid-Atlantic.

New Classes of Newcomers

The social background of these new European immigrants differed substantially from that of their seventeenth-century predecessors. The early settlers included a number of men from the upper levels of the English social pyramid: university-trained Puritan ministers, sons of wealthy gentry, and merchants. The earlier immigrants had also included many from the middle rungs of the English social ladder — yeomen farmers, skilled craftsmen, and shopkeepers. But

slaves and indentured servants made up most of the incoming human tide after 1713. The traffic in servants became a regular part of the commerce linking Europe and America.

Shipboard conditions for servants worsened in the eighteenth century and were hardly better than aboard the slave ships. Crammed between decks in stifling air, servants suffered from smallpox and fevers, rotten food, impure water, cold, and lice. "Children between the ages of one and seven seldom survive the sea voyage," bemoaned one German immigrant, "and parents must often watch their offspring suffer miserably, die, and be thrown into the ocean." The shipboard mortality rate of about 15 percent in the colonial era made this the most unhealthy of all times to seek American shores.

Like indentured servants in the seventeenth century, the servant immigrants who poured ashore after 1715 came mostly from the lower ranks of society. As earlier, some were petty

Population of European Colonies in North America, 1680-1770

English   French   Spanish
*France's North American colonies in Canada and Louisiana ceded to England and Spain, respectively, in 1763.

criminals, political prisoners, and the castoffs of the cities. Yet, as one Englishman commented, "Men who emigrate are from the nature of their circumstances, the most active, hardy, daring, bold and resolute spirits, and probably the most mischievous also."

A Land of Opportunity?

Once ashore, most indentured servants, especially males, found the labor system harsh. Merchants sold them, one shocked Britisher reported in 1773, "as they do their horses, and advertise them as they do their beef and oatmeal." Facing cruel treatment, thousands of servants ran away. Advertisements for them filled the colonial newspapers alongside notices for escaped slaves.

The goal of every servant was to secure a foothold on the ladder of opportunity. "The hope of buying land in America," a New Yorker noted, "is what chiefly induces people into America." However, many servants died before serving out their time. Others won freedom only to toil for years as poor day laborers and tenant farmers. Only a small proportion achieved the dream of becoming independent landholders. The chief beneficiaries of the system of bound white labor were not the laborers but their masters.

Africans in Chains

Among the thousands of ships crossing the Atlantic in the eighteenth century, the ones fitted out as seagoing dungeons for slaves were the most numerous. After the Peace of Utrecht, the slave trade to the southern colonies expanded sharply. The generation after 1730 witnessed the largest influx of African slaves in the colonial period, averaging about 5,000 a year. In the entire period from 1700 to 1775, more than 350,000 African slaves entered the American colonies.

Even as the traffic in slaves peaked, religious and humanitarian opposition to slavery arose. A few individuals, mostly Quaker, had objected to slavery on moral grounds since the late seventeenth century. But the idea grew in the 1750s that slavery contradicted the Christian concept of brotherhood and the Enlightenment notion of the natural equality of all humans. John Woolman, a Quaker tailor from New Jersey, dedicated his life in the 1750s to a crusade against slavery and planted the seeds of abolitionism.

Beyond the Appalachians

By the mid-eighteenth century, the American colonists, though increasing rapidly in number, still occupied only a narrow strip of coastal plain in eastern North America. Of about 1.2 million settlers and slaves in 1750, only a tiny fraction lived farther than 100 miles from the shores of the Atlantic. Beginning in the 1750s, westward-moving colonists in pursuit of more land would encounter four other groups

The commonalistic Moravian immigrants who came to Pennsylvania in the 1740s dedicated themselves, like the Quakers, to peaceful relations with the Indians. The Prussian John Jacob Schmick and his Norwegian wife Johanna were missionaries to the Delaware tribe.

already established to their west: the populous interior Native American tribes, and smaller groups of French-Americans, Spanish-Americans, and Afro-Americans. Changes already

occurring among these groups would affect settlers breaching the Appalachian barrier and, in the third quarter of the eighteenth century, would even reach eastward to the original British settlements.

Cultural Changes Among Interior Tribes

During the first half of the eighteenth century, the inland tribes began to be affected by extensive contact with the French, Spanish, and English. The introduction of European trade goods, especially iron implements, textiles, firearms and ammunition, and alcohol, inescapably changed Indian lifeways. Subsistence hunting, limited to satisfying tribal food requirements, turned into commercial hunting, restricted only by the quantity of trade goods desired. Indian males spent far more time away from the villages trapping and hunting, and the increased importance of this activity to tribal life undermined the matrilineal basis of society. Women were also drawn into the new economic activities, helping to skin the beaver, marten, and fox, scrape and trim the pelts, and sew them into robes. Among some tribes, the trapping, preparation, and transporting of skins became so time-consuming that they had to procure food resources from other tribes.

Involvement in the fur trade altered the traditional Native American belief that the destinies of humans and animals were closely linked. In addition, the fur trade heightened intertribal tensions, often to the point of war. When a tribe depleted the furs in their hunting grounds, they could maintain their trade only by conquering more remote tribes with fertile hunting grounds or by forcibly intercepting the furs of other tribes as they were carried to European trading posts. The introduction of European weaponry, which Indians quickly mastered, further intensified intertribal conflict.

Tribal political organization among the interior tribes also changed in the eighteenth century. Most tribes had earlier been loose confederations of villages and clans, each exercising local autonomy. The Creek, Cherokee, and Iroquois gave primary loyalty to the village, not to the tribe or confederacy. But trade, diplomatic contact, and war with Europeans required more coordinated policies. To deal effectively with traders and officials, the villages gradually adjusted to more centralized leadership.

By 1750, the Cherokee, for example, had formed a more centralized tribal "priest state." When this proved inadequate, warriors began to assume the dominant role in tribal councils, replacing the civil chiefs. By this process the Cherokee reorganized their political structure so that dozens of scattered villages could amalgamate their strength.

While incorporating trade goods into their material culture and adapting their economies and political structures to new situations, the interior tribes held fast to tradition in many ways. They saw little reason to adopt the colonists' systems of law and justice, religion, education, family organization, or child rearing. Their refusal to accept the superiority of white culture frustrated English missionaries, eager to win Native Americans from "savage" ways. But a Carolinian admitted that "they are really better to us than we are to them. We look upon them with scorn and disdain, and think them little better than beasts in human shape, though if well examined, we shall find that, for all our religion and education, we possess more moral deformities and evils than these savages do."

Despite maintaining many cultural practices, the interior Indian tribes suffered from the contact with the British colonizers. Decade by decade, the fur trade spread epidemic diseases, raised the level of warfare, depleted their lands of game animals, and drew the Native Americans into a market economy where their trading partners gradually became trading masters.

France's Inland Empire

While the powerful Iroquois, Cherokee, Creek, and Choctaw tribes interacted with British colonists to their east, they also dealt with a growing French presence to their west. Between 1699 and 1754, the French developed a system of small forts, trading posts, and agricultural villages throughout the central area of the continent from French Canada to the Gulf of Mexico. The Indians retained sovereignty over the land but gradually succumbed to French diseases, French arms, and French-promoted intertribal wars. At the same time, however, because France's interior empire was organized primarily as a military and trading operation, soldiers, fur traders, and other men arriving without wives often exploited or married Indian women. French Louisiana had more mixed-race children and more white and black men who lived with Native Americans than any Anglo-American colony.

In 1718, France settled New Orleans at great cost by transporting almost 7,000 whites and 5,000 African slaves to the mouth of the Mississippi River. Disease rapidly whittled down these numbers, and an uprising of the powerful Natchez tribe in 1729 discouraged further French immigration. Most of the survivors settled around the little town of New Orleans and raised indigo, rice, and other crops.

In its economy and society, New Orleans much resembled early Charleston, South Carolina. What distinguished the people of New Orleans from those of Charleston, however, was that the French knew nothing of representative political institutions. Ruled by a governor, a commissary and chief judge, and a small appointed council, the people had no elections or assembly, no newspapers or taxes.

From its first introduction in Louisiana in 1719, French plantation slavery grew so that by 1765, blacks outnumbered whites. Most slaves and a majority of whites lived in the New Orleans area. The conditions of life for slaves differed little from the southern English colonies. But the French had a paternalistic black legal code that gave slaves some protection in courts. When the Spanish took over the colony in 1769, they instituted their law guaranteeing slaves the right to buy freedom with money earned in their free time. Soon a large free black class emerged, headed by substantial people like Simon Colfat, who ran various enterprises,

France's Inland Empire, 1600-1720

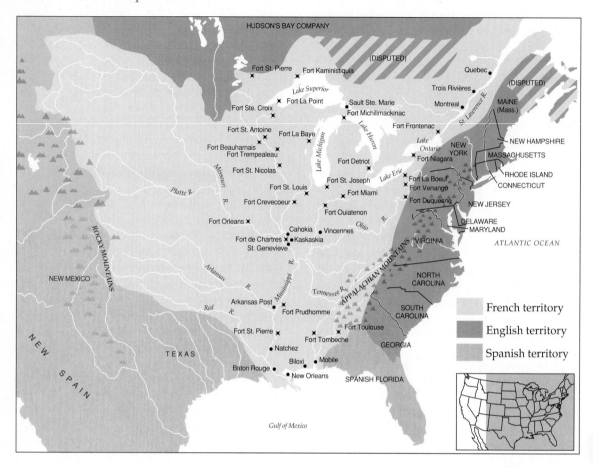

helped other slaves pay for their freedom, and headed the company of free black militia. When Americans acquired the colony in 1803, they suppressed freedom purchase and discouraged manumission.

Spain's America

In the first half of the eighteenth century, the Spanish still possessed by far the largest American empire. Even as Spanish power declined in Europe, it spread in America. Spain strengthened its Florida military posts to challenge English settlement of the Carolinas and French settlement of the Mississippi valley. Also to counter the French, the Spanish established permanent

military posts in Texas and New Mexico for the first time. At the end of the eighteenth century, however, fewer than 50,000 Spanish and Hispanicized people of color inhabited Texas, New Mexico, and California.

As in New France, racial intermixture and social fluidity were more extensive in New Spain than in the English colonies. The Spanish never defined racial groups as distinctly as the English. The word *Spaniard* on a census might mean a white immigrant from Mexico or a part-Indian person who "lived like a Spaniard." Social mobility was considerable because the Crown was willing to raise even a common person to the status of *hidalgo* (minor nobleman) as an inducement to settle in New Spain's remote norther frontier. Most of the immigrants became small ranchers, producing livestock, corn, and wheat for export to other Spanish provinces to the south.

The Native Americans of New Mexico were more successful in resisting Spanish domination than the tribes of California. In the 1770s, the Spanish rapidly completed their western land and sea routes from San Diego to the new port of Yerba Buena (San Francisco) to block Russian settlement south of their base in northern California. The Spanish pioneers were Franciscan missionaries, accompanied by soldiers provided by the Crown. The priests established missions and induced local Indians to settle nearby. These "mission" Indians lived under an increasingly harsh regimen until they were reduced to a condition of virtual slavery.

A Land of Family Farms

Population growth and economic development gradually transformed the landscape of eighteenth-century British America. Three distinct variations of colonial society emerged: the farming society of the North, the plantation society of the South, and the urban society of the seaboard commerical towns.

Northern Agricultural Society

In the northern colonies, especially New England, tightknit farming families, organized in communities of several thousand people, dotted the landscape by the mid-eighteenth century. They based their mixed economy on timber, fish, cultivation, and livestock.

The farmers of the middle colonies — Pennsylvania, Delaware, New Jersey, and New York — set their wooden plows to much richer soils than New Englanders did. They enjoyed the additional advantage of settling an area cleared by Native Americans who had relied more on agriculture than New England tribes. Thus favored, mid-Atlantic farm families produced modest surpluses of corn, wheat, beef,

and pork, which were sold not only to the West Indies, but also to areas that could no longer feed themselves — England, Spain, Portugal, and even New England.

In the North, the broad ownership of land distinguished farming society from every other agricultural region of the Western world. In most communities before 1750, the truly rich and abjectly poor were few and the gap between them small compared to European society. Most men other than indentured servants lived to purchase or inherit a farm of at least 50 acres. Settlers valued land highly, for freehold tenure ordinarily guaranteed both economic independence and political rights.

Amid widespread property ownership, a rising population pressed against a limited land supply by the eighteenth century, especially in New England. Family farms could not be divided and subdivided indefinitely, for it took at least 50 acres (of which only a quarter could usually be cultivated) to support a single family. The decreasing fertility of the soil compounded the problem of dwindling farm size. When land had been plentiful, farmers planted crops in the same field for three years and then let it lie fallow in pasturage seven years or more until it regained its fertility. But on the smaller farms of the eighteenth century, farmers had reduced fallow time to only a year or two. Inevitably, such intense use of the soil reduced crop yields.

The diminishing size and productivity of family farms forced many New Englanders in the eighteenth century to move to the frontier or out of the area altogether. Some drifted south to New York and Pennsylvania. Others sought opportunities as artisans in the coastal towns or took to the sea. More headed for the colony's western frontier or north into New Hampshire and the eastern frontier of Maine. Several thousand New England families migrated even farther north, to the Annapolis valley of Nova Scotia.

Wherever they took up farming, northern cultivators engaged in agricultural work routines that were far less intense than in the South. The growing season was much shorter, and the cultivation of cereal crops required incessant labor only during spring planting and autumn harvesting. This less burdensome work rhythm led many northern cultivators to fill out their calendars with intermittent work as clockmakers, shoemakers, carpenters, and weavers.

Changing Values

On April 29, 1695, an unusually severe hailstorm struck Boston. Merchant Samuel Sewall dined that evening with Cotton Mather, New England's most prominent Puritan clergyman. As Mather wondered why "more ministers houses than others proportionately had been smitten with lightning," hailstones began to shatter the windows of Sewall's house. Sewall and Mather fell to their knees and broke into prayer together "after this awful Providence."

As these two third-generation Massachusetts Puritans understood it, God was angry with them as leaders of a people whose piety and moral rectitude were being overtaken by worldliness. The people of Massachusetts had become "sermon-proof," as one dejected minister put it.

In other parts of the North, the expansive environment and the Protestant emphasis on self-discipline and hard work were also breeding qualities that would become hallmarks of American culture : an ambitious outlook, individualistic behavior, and a love of material things. In Europe, most tillers of the soil expected little from life. In America, one colonist remarked, "Every man expects one day or another to be upon a footing with his wealthiest neighbor."

Commitment to religion, family, and community did not disappear in the eighteenth century. But fewer men and women saw daily existence as a preparation for the afterlife. A slender almanac, written by the twelfth child of a poor Boston candlemaker, captured the new outlook with wit and charm. Born in 1706, Benjamin Franklin had abandoned a declining Boston for a rising Philadelphia. By age 23, he had learned the printer's trade and was publishing the *Pennsylvania Gazette*. Three years later, he began *Poor Richard's Almanack,* next to the Bible the most widely read book in the colonies.

Franklin spiced his annual almanac — the ordinary person's guide to weather and useful information — with quips, adages, and homespun philosophy. Eventually this homely material added up to a primer for success published in 1747 as *The Way to Wealth.* "The sleeping fox gathers no poultry" and "Lost time is never found again," advised Poor Richard, emphasizing that time is money. "It costs more to maintain one vice than to raise two children," he counseled, advocating not morality but practicality. Ever cocky, Franklin caught the spirit of the rising secularism of the eighteenth century. He embodied the growing utilitarian doctrine that the good is whatever is useful and the notion that the community is best served through individual self-improvement and accomplishment.

Women in Northern Colonial Society

In 1662, Elnathan Chauncy, a Massachusetts schoolboy, copied into his writing book that "the soul consists of two portions, inferior and superior ; the superior is masculine and eternal ; the feminine inferior and mortal." This lesson had been taught for generations on both sides of the Atlantic. It was part of a larger conception of a world, of God's design, that assigned degrees of status and stations in life to all persons. In such a world, the place of women was, by definition, subordinate to that of men. As daughters they were subject to their fathers, as wives, to their husbands.

European women usually accepted these narrowly circumscribed roles. Few complained, at least openly, that their work was generally limited to housewifery and midwifery. They remained silent about exclusion from the early public schools and laws that transferred to their husbands any property or income they brought into a marriage. Nor could women speak in their churches or participate in governing them, and they had no legal voice in political affairs. Most

Childbirth was an oft-repeated event in the lives of most colonial wives. In this portrait of the Cheney family, the older woman is a nanny or mother-in-law ; the younger woman holding a baby is Mr. Cheney's second wife.

women did not expect to choose a husband for love ; parental guidance prevailed in a society in which producing legal heirs was the means of transmitting property. Once wed, women expected to remain so until death, for they could rarely obtain a divorce.

On the colonial frontier, women's lives changed in modest ways. In Europe, about one of ten women did not marry. But in the colonies, where men outnumbered women for the first century, a spinster was almost unheard of, and widows remarried with astounding speed. *Woman* and *wife* thus became nearly synonymous.

A second difference concerned property rights. Single women and widows in the colonies, as in England, could make contracts, hold and convey property, represent themselves in court, and conduct business. Under English common law, a woman forfeited these rights, as well as all property, when she married. In the colonies, however, legislatures and courts gave

wives more control over property brought into marriage or left at their husbands' death. In addition, young colonial women slowly gained the right of consenting to a marriage partner — a right that came by default to the thousands of female indentured servants who completed their labor contracts and had no parents within 3,000 miles to dictate to them.

Women had limited career choices in colonial society, but the work spaces and daily routines of husband and wife overlapped and intersected far more than today. A farm wife helped with planting and harvesting, milked cows, made candles and soap, butter and cheese, smoked meat, made cloth, and sometimes marketed farm products. A merchant's wife kept shop, handled accounts when her husband voyaged abroad, and helped supervise the servants and apprentices. "Deputy husbands" and "yoke mates" were revealing terms used by New Englanders to describe eighteenth-century wives.

Women held vital responsibilities as midwives. Until the late eighteenth century, the "obstetrick art" was almost entirely in women's hands. Midwives counseled pregnant women, delivered babies, supervised postpartum recovery, and participated in ceremonies of infant baptism and burial. Mrs. Phillips, an immigrant to Boston in 1719, delivered more than 3,000 infants in her 42-year career. Because childbirth was a recurring and dangerous crisis, the circle of female friends and relatives who attended childbirth created strong networks of mutual assistance.

In her role as wife and mother, the eighteenth-century northern colonial woman differed somewhat from her English counterpart. American women married earlier and produced more children (on average seven, two of whom died in infancy). But gradually, as the coastal plain filled up in the eighteenth century, marriage age crept up and the number of children per family inched down.

Northern child rearing patterns differed considerably. In the seventeenth century, stern fathers dominated Puritan family life, and few were reluctant to punish unruly children. "Better whip'd than damn'd," advised Cotton Mather. In Quaker families, however, mothers played a more active role in child rearing. More permissive, they relied on tenderness and love rather than guilt to mold their children. Attitudes toward choosing a marriage partner also separated early Puritan and Quaker approaches to family life. Puritan parents usually arranged their children's marriages but allowed them the right to veto. Young Quaker men and women made their own matches, subject to parental veto.

Despite this initial diversity in child rearing, the father-dominated family of New England gradually declined in the eighteenth century. In its place rose the mother-centered family, in which affectionate parents encouraged self-expression and independence in their children. This "modern" approach was closer to the parenting methods of the coastal Native Americans, who initially had been widely disparaged for their lax methods of rearing their young.

The Plantation South

Between 1680 and 1750, the white tidewater settlements of the southern colonies made the transition from a frontier society marked by a high immigration rate, a surplus of males, and an unstable social organization to a settled society composed mostly of native-born families. Between the piedmont region and the ocean, a mature southern culture took form.

The Tobacco Coast

Tobacco production in Virginia and Maryland expanded rapidly in the seventeenth century, but war in Europe and the Americas for the two decades bridging the turn of the century drove up transportation costs and dampened the demand for tobacco. Stagnation in the tobacco market lasted from the mid-1680s until about 1715.

Yet it was in this period that the Upper South underwent a profound social transformation. First, slaves replaced indentured servants so rapidly that by 1730 the unfree labor force was overwhelmingly black. Second, the planters responded to the dull tobacco market by diversifying their crops. They shifted some of their tobacco fields to grain, hemp, and flax; increased their herds of cattle and swine; and became more self-sufficient by developing local industries to produce iron, leather, and textiles. By the 1720s, when a profitable tobacco trade with France created a new period of prosperity, their economy was much more diverse and resilient than a generation before.

Third, the structure of the population changed rapidly. Black slaves grew from about seven percent to 35 percent of the region's population between 1690 and 1750, and the drastic imbalance between white men and women disappeared.

Notwithstanding the influx of Africans, slave-owning was far from universal. As late as 1750, a majority of families owned no slaves at all. Among slave owners, fewer than one-tenth held more than 20 slaves. Nonetheless, the common goal was the large plantation where black slaves made the earth yield up profits to support an aristocratic life for their masters.

The Chesapeake planters who acquired the best land and accumulated enough capital to invest heavily in slaves created a gentry life style that set them apart from ordinary farmers such as Devereaux Jarratt's father. Men such as Charles Carroll of Maryland and Robert "King" Carter and William Byrd of Virginia counted their slaves by the hundreds, their acres by the thousands, and their fortunes by the tens of thousands of pounds.

Ritual display of wealth marked southern gentry life. Racing thoroughbred horses and gambling on them recklessly became common sport for young gentlemen, who had often been educated in England. Planters began to construct stately brick Georgian mansions and fill them with imported furniture.

The emerging Chesapeake planter elite controlled the county courts, officered the local militia, ruled the parish vestries of the Anglican church, and made law in their legislative assemblies. To their sons they passed the mantle of political and social leadership.

For all their social display, southern planter squires were essentially agrarian businessmen. They spent their days obtaining credit, dealing in land and slaves, scheduling planting and harvesting routines, conferring with overseers, disciplining slaves, and arranging leases with tenants. A planter's reputation rose and fell with the quality of his crop. His wife also shouldered many responsibilities. She superintended cloth production and the processing and preparation of food while ruling over a household crowded with children, slaves, and visitors. The farms were often so isolated from each other that planter families lived a "solitary and unsociable existence," as one phrased it.

The Rice Coast

The plantation economy of the Lower South in the eighteenth century rested on the production of rice and indigo. Rice exports surpassed 1.5

million pounds per year by 1710 and reached 80 million pounds by the eve of the Revolution. Indigo, a blue dye obtained from plants for use in textiles, became a staple crop in the 1740s after Eliza Lucas Pinckney, a wealthy South Carolina planter's wife, experimented successfully with its cultivation. Within a generation, indigo production had spread into Georgia. It soon ranked among the leading colonial exports.

The expansion of rice production transformed the swampy coastal lowlands. In the rice-producing region radiating out from Charleston, planters imported thousands of slaves after 1720; by 1740, they composed nearly 90 percent of the region's inhabitants. White population declined as wealthy planters left their estates in the hands of resident overseers. At midcentury, a shocked New England visitor described local society as one "divided into opulent and lordly planters, poor and spiritless peasants, and vile slaves."

Throughout the plantation South, the court-house became a central gathering place. Court day brought together people of all classes. They came to settle debts, dispute land boundaries, sue and be sued. When court was over, a multitude lingered on, drinking, gossiping, and staging horse races, cockfights, wrestling matches, footraces, and fiddling contests. Competition and assertiveness lay at the heart of all these demonstrations of male personal prowess.

The Backcountry

While the southern gentry matured along the tobacco and rice coasts, settlers poured into the upland backcountry. Thousands of land-hungry German and Scots-Irish settlers spilled into the interior valleys running along the eastern side of the Appalachians. Their enclaves of small farms remained isolated from the coastal region for several generations, which helped these pioneers cling fiercely to the folkways they had known on the other side of the Atlantic.

The crudity of backcountry life appalled many visitors from the more refined seaboard.

In 1733, William Byrd described a large Virginia frontier plantation as "a poor, dirty hovel, with hardly anything in it but children that wallowed about like so many pigs." Charles Woodmason, a stiff-necked Anglican minister who spent three years tramping between settlements in the Carolina upcountry, wrote: "Many hundreds live in concubinage — swopping their wives as cattle and living in a state of nature more irregularly and unchastely than the Indians."

What Byrd and Woodmason were really observing was the poverty of frontier life and the lack of schools, churches, and towns. Most families lived in rough-hewn log cabins and planted their corn, beans, and wheat between the stumps of trees they had felled. Women toiled alongside men, in the fields, forest, and homestead. For a generation, these settlers endured a poor diet, endless work, and meager rewards.

By the 1760s, the southern backcountry began to emerge from the frontier stage. Small marketing towns became centers of craft activity, church life, and local government. Farms began producing surpluses for shipment east. Density of settlement increased. Class distinctions remained narrow compared with the older seaboard settlements, but many backcountry settlements acquired the look of permanence.

Family Life in the South

As the South emerged from the early era of withering mortality and stunted families, male and female roles gradually became more physically and functionally separated. In most areas, the white gender ratio reached parity by the 1720s. Women lost the leverage in the marriage market that scarcity had provided earlier. With the growth of slavery, the work role of white women also changed. The wealthy planter's wife became the domestic manager in the "great house."

The balanced sex ratio and the growth of slavery also brought changes for southern white males. The planter's son had always been trained in horsemanship, the use of a gun, and the rhythms of agricultural life. Ordering and

disciplining slaves also became a part of his education. Bred to command, southern planters' sons also developed a self-confidence and authority that propelled many of them into leadership roles during the American Revolution.

On the small farms of the tidewater region and throughout the backcountry settlements, women's roles closely resembled those of northern women. Women labored in the fields alongside their menfolk. "She is a very civil woman," noted an observer of a southern frontierswoman," and shows nothing of ruggedness or immodesty in her carriage; yet she will carry a gun in the woods and kill deer and turkeys, shoot down wild cattle, catch and tie hogs, knock down beeves with an ax, and perform the most manful exercises as well as most men in those parts."

Marriage and family life were also more informal in the backcountry. With vast areas unattended by ministers of any religion and courthouses out of reach, most couples married or "took up" with each other in matches unsanctioned by state or church until an itinerant clergyman passed through the area.

The Urban World of Commerce and Ideas

Only about five percent of the colonists lived in towns as large as 2,500, and none of the commercial centers boasted a population greater than 16,000 in 1750 or 30,000 in 1775. Yet the urban societies were at the leading edge of social change. Almost all the alterations associated with the advent of "modern" life occurred first in the seaport towns and radiated outward to the hinterland. In the seaboard centers, the transition first occurred from a barter to a commercial economy, from a social order based on assigned status to one based on achievement, from rank-conscious and deferential politics to participatory and contentious politics, and from small-scale craftsmanship to factory production. In addition, the cities were the centers of intellectual life and the conduits through which European ideas flowed into the colonies.

Sinews of Trade

In the half century after 1690, Boston, New York, and Philadelphia blossomed from urban villages into thriving commercial centers. This urban growth accompanied the development of the agricultural interior, to which the seaports were closely linked. Through the trade centers flowed colonial export staples such as tobacco, rice, wheat, timber products, and fish as well as the imported goods that colonists needed. The imports included manufactured and luxury goods from England such as glass, paper, iron implements, and cloth ; wine, spices, coffee, tea, and sugar from other parts of the world ; and the human cargo to fill the labor gap.

By the eighteenth century, the American economy was integrated into an Atlantic basin trading system that connected Great Britain, western Europe, Africa, the West Indies, and Newfoundland. In the commercial seaports, the pivotal figure was the merchant. Frequently engaged in both retail and wholesale trade, the merchant was also moneylender (for no banks yet existed), shipbuilder, insurance agent, land developer, and often coordinator of artisan production.

The colonists could never produce enough exportable raw materials to pay for the imported goods they craved, so they had to earn credits in England by supplying the West Indies and other areas with foodstuffs and timber products. They also accumulated credit by providing shipping and distributional services. New Englanders became the most ambitious participants in the carrying trade, sailing along the Atlantic seaboard, the Caribbean, and across the Atlantic.

The Artisan's World

Though merchants stood first in wealth and prestige in the colonial towns, artisans were far more numerous. About two-thirds of urban adult males, slaves excluded, labored at handi-

crafts. These "leather apron men" included not only the proverbial butcher, baker, and candlestick maker but also carpenters and coopers (who made barrels) ; shoemakers and tailors ; silver-, gold-, pewter-, and blacksmiths ; mast and sail makers ; masons, plasterers, weavers, potters ; and many more. They worked with hand tools, usually in small shops.

Work patterns for artisans were irregular, dictated by weather, hours of daylight, erratic delivery of raw materials, and shifting consumer demand. When ice blocked northern harbors, mariners and dockworkers endured slack time. If prolonged rain delayed the slaughter of cows in the country or made impassable the rutted roads into the city, the tanner and the shoemaker laid their tools aside.

Urban artisans took fierce pride in their crafts. "Our professions rendered us useful and necessary members of our community," the Philadelphia shoemakers asserted. "Proud of that rank, we aspired to no higher." Yet the upper-class tended to view artisans as mere mechanics, part of the "vulgar herd."

In striving for respectability, artisans placed a premium on achieving economic independence. Every craftsman began as an apprentice, spending five or more teenage years learning the "mysteries of the craft" in the shop of a master "mechanick." After fulfilling his contract, the young artisan became a "journeyman." He sold his labor to a master craftsman and frequently lived in his house, ate at his table, and sometimes married his daughter. The journeyman hoped to complete within a few years the three-step climb from servitude to self-employment. After setting up his own shop, he could control his work hours and acquire the respect that came from economic independence. In trades requiring greater organization and capital, such as distilling and shipbuilding, the rise from journeyman to master proved impossible for many artisans. Nonetheless, the ideal of the independent craftsman prevailed.

In good times, urban artisans fared well. They expected to earn "a decent competency" and eventually to purchase a small house. But success was far from automatic, even for those following all of Poor Richard's advice about hard work and frugal living. An advantageous marriage, luck in avoiding illness, and the size of an inheritance were often the critical factors in whether an artisan moved up or down the ladder of success.

Urban Social Structure

Population growth, economic development, and a series of wars that punctuated the period from 1690 to 1765 altered the urban social structure. Stately townhouses rose as testimony to the fortunes acquired in trade, shipbuilding, war contracting, and urban land development. This last may have been the most profitable of all. "It is almost a proverb," a Philadelphian observed in the 1760s, "that every great fortune made here within these 50 years has been by land." By the late colonial era, some commercial titans had become America's first millionaires by accumulating estates of £10,000 to £20,000 sterling.

Alongside urban wealth grew urban poverty. From the beginning, every city had its disabled, orphaned, and widowed who required aid. But after 1720, poverty marred the lives of many more city dwellers. Boston was hit especially hard in the 1740s. The overseers of the poor groaned that their relief expenditures were double the outlays of any town of equal size "upon the face of the whole earth."

Burdened with mounting poor taxes, cities devised new ways of helping the needy. Rather than support the impoverished in their homes with "outrelief" payments, officials built large almshouses where the poor could be housed and fed more economically. Many of the indigent preferred "to starve in their homes."

The increasing gap between the wealthy and the poor in the colonial cities was recorded in the eighteenth-century tax lists. The top five percent of taxpayers increased their share of the cities' taxable assets between 1690 and 1770, while the bottom half of the taxable inhabitants saw their share of the wealth shrink. The urban

middle classes, except in Boston, continued to make gains. But the growth of princely fortunes amid increasing poverty made some urban dwellers reflect that the conditions of the Old World seemed to be reappearing in the New.

The Entrepreneurial Ethos

As the cities grew, new values took hold. In the older, medieval, "corporate" view of society, economic life ideally operated according to what was equitable, not what was profitable. Citizens usually agreed that government should provide for the general welfare by regulating prices and wages, setting quality controls, licensing providers of service such as tavernkeepers and ferrymen, and supervising public markets where all food was sold. Such regulation seemed natural because a community was defined not as a collection of individuals, each entitled to pursue separate interests, but as a single body of interrelated parts where individual rights and responsibilities formed a seamless web.

In America, as in Europe, new ideas about economic life gathered support. The subordination of private interests to the commonweal became viewed as a lofty but unrealistic ideal. According to the new view, people should be allowed to pursue their own material desires competitively. The resulting impersonal market of producers and consumers would operate to everyone's advantage.

As the colonial port towns took their places in the Atlantic world of commerce, merchants became accustomed to making decisions according to the emerging commercial ethic that rejected traditional restraints on entrepreneurial activity. The underlying tension between the new economic freedom and the older concern for the public good erupted only with food shortages or galloping inflation.

Such a moment struck in Boston during Queen Anne's War. Merchant Andrew Belcher contracted to ship large quantities of wheat to the Caribbean, where higher prices would yield greater profit than in Boston. Ordinary neighbors, threatened with a bread shortage and angered that a townsman would put profit ahead of community needs, attacked one of Belcher's grain-laden ships in 1710. They sawed through the rudder and tried to run the vessel aground in order to seize the grain. Invoking the older ethic that the public welfare outweighed private interests, they took the law into their own hands. Even the grand jury, composed of substantial members of the community, hinted its approval of the violent action against Belcher by refusing to indict the rioters.

The two conceptions of community and economic life rubbed against each other for many decades. But by the mid-eighteenth century, the pursuit of a profitable livelihood, not the social compact of the community, animated most city dwellers.

The American Enlightenment

Ideas about not only economic life but also the nature of the universe and improving the human condition reached across the Atlantic to the colonies. In the eighteenth century, an American version of the European intellectual movement called the Enlightenment occurred, and the cities became centers for disseminating these new ideas.

European thinkers, in what is called the Age of Reason, rejected the pessimistic Calvinist concept of innate human depravity, replacing it with the optimistic notion that a benevolent God had blessed humankind with the supreme gift of reason. Thinkers like John Locke, in his influential *Essay Concerning Human Understanding* (1689), argued that God had not predetermined the content of the human mind but furnished it with the capacity to acquire knowledge. All Enlightenment thinkers prized this acquisition of knowledge, for it allowed humankind to improve its condition. As the great scientific thinker Isaac Newton demonstrated, systematic investigation could unlock the secrets of the physical universe. Moreover, scientific knowledge could be applied to human institutions in order to improve society.

Though only a small number of educated colonists read the Enlightenment authors, they began in the eighteenth century to make significant contributions to the advancement of science. Standing above them all was Benjamin Franklin, whose spectacular (and dangerous) experiments with electricity, the properties of which were just becoming known, earned him an international reputation. Franklin's true genius as a figure of the Enlightenment came in his practical application of scientific knowledge. Among his inventions were the lightning rod, bifocal spectacles, and an iron stove that heated rooms far more efficiently than the open fireplace commonly used. Franklin also played a leading role in founding America's first circulating library in 1731, an artisans' debating club for "mutual improvement" through discussion of the latest ideas from Europe, and an intercolonial scientific association that would emerge in 1769 as the American Philosophical Society.

The Great Awakening

Many of the social, economic, and political changes occurring in the eighteenth-century colonies converged in the Great Awakening, the first of many religious revivals that would sweep American society during the next two centuries. This quest for spiritual renewal challenged old sources of authority and produced patterns of thought and behavior that helped fuel a revolutionary movement in the next generation.

Fading Faith

Colonial America in the early eighteenth century remained an overwhelmingly Protestant culture. The Puritan, or Congregational, church dominated all of New England except Rhode Island. Anglicanism held sway in much of New York and throughout the South except the backcountry. In the mid-Atlantic and in the back settlements, a polyglot of German Mennonites, Dunkers, Moravians, and Lutherans; Scots-Irish

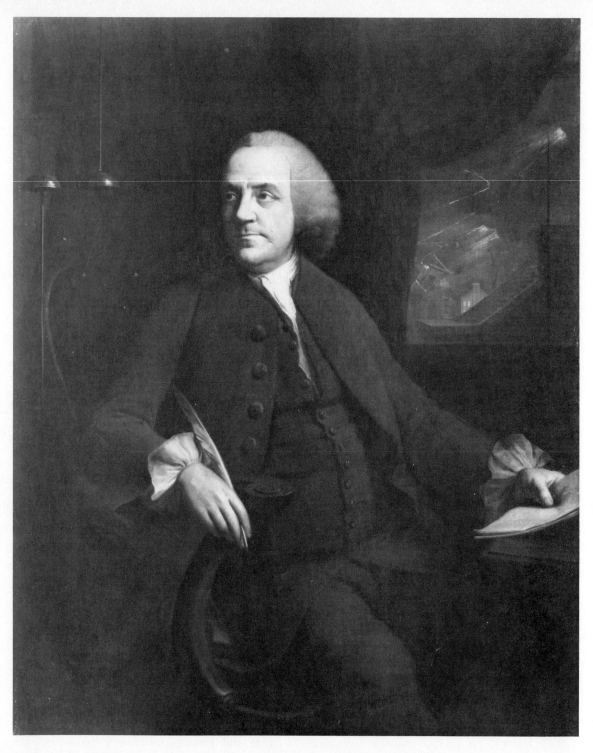

Benjamin Franklin, 1762. Franklin installed the pair of bells, shown at left, in his study, the upper one connected to a lightning rod atop his house, the lower one grounded. During a lightning storm they would ring, to the delight of Franklin's guests.

Presbyterians ; and English Baptists and Quakers mingled.

Yet these diverse groups commanded the allegiance of only about one-third of the colonists. Those who went to no church at all remained the majority. In many areas, ministers and churches were simply unavailable. In Virginia, the most populous colony, only 60 clergymen in 1761 served a population of 350,000 — one parson for every 5,800 people.

In the eighteenth century, most colonial churches were voluntary or gathered ("congregated") groups, formed for reasons of conscience, not because of government compulsion. Catholics, Jews, and nonbelievers could not vote or hold office. But the persecution of Quakers and Catholics had largely passed, and some dissenting groups had gained the right by 1720 to use long-obligatory church taxes to support their own congregations.

The clergy often administered their congregations with difficulty. For example, Anglican ministers had to be ordained in England and make regular reports to the bishop of London. But once installed in Chesapeake parishes, Anglican priests faced wealthy planters who controlled the vestry (the local church's governing body), set the minister's salary, and drove out ministers who challenged them too forcefully.

Though governing their churches frustrated many clergymen, religious apathy was a far more pressing problem in the early eighteenth century. As early as 1662, the Congregational clergy of New England had attempted to return wandering sheep to the fold by adopting the Half-Way Covenant. It specified that children of church members, if they adhered to the "forms of godliness," might join the church even if they could not demonstrate that they had undergone a conversion experience. But despite compromises and innovations, most church leaders saw creeping religious apathy when they surveyed their towns.

The Awakeners' Message

The Great Awakening was not a unified movement but rather a series of revivals that swept different regions between 1720 and 1760 with varying degrees of intensity. The first stirrings came in the 1720s in New Jersey and Pennsylvania. Theodore Frelinghuysen, a Dutch Reformed minister, excited his congregation through emotional preaching. Avoiding theological abstractions, he concentrated on arousing a need to be "saved" among his parishioners. A neighboring Presbyterian, Gilbert Tennent, soon took up the Dutchman's techniques, with similar success.

From New Jersey the Awakening spread to Pennsylvania in the 1730s, especially among Presbyterians, and then broke out in the Connecticut River valley. There it was led by Jonathan Edwards, pastor in Northampton. Edwards later became a philosophical giant in the colonies. But as a young man, he gained renown by lambasting his parishioners : "Are there not some here that have debased themselves below the dignity of human nature, by wallowing in sensual filthiness, as swine in the mire . . . ?" Edwards paraded one sin after another before his trembling congregants : "God and your own consciences know what abominable lasciviousness you have practised in things not fit to be named, when you have been alone ; when you ought to have been reading, or meditating, or on your knees before God in secret prayer."

After cataloging his parishioners' sins, Edwards drew such graphic pictures of the hell awaiting the unrepentant that his Northampton neighbors were soon preparing frantically for the conversion experience by which they would be "born again."

In 1739, these regional brushfires of evangelicalism began to spread. Instrumental in drawing together the separate local revivals and in inspiring a more scorching religious enthusiasm was George Whitefield, a 24-year-old Anglican priest from England. Whitefield made seven barnstorming tours along the American seaboard, the first in 1739 and 1740. Thousands turned out to see him, and with each success his fame and influence grew. In Boston, Whitefield preached to 19,000 in three days. Then, at a farewell sermon, he left 25,000 writhing in fear of damnation. In his wake came American preachers, mostly young men like Devereaux Jarratt, whom he had inspired.

The Awakeners preached that the established, college-trained clergy was too intellectual and tradition-bound to bring faith and piety to a new generation. Congregations were dead, Whitefield declared, "because dead men preach to them." "The sapless discourses of such dead drones," cried another Awakener, were worthless. The fires of Protestant belief could be reignited only if individuals assumed responsibility for their own conversion.

An important form of individual participation was "lay exhorting." In this personal religious testimony, any person — young or old, female or male, black or white — might spontaneously recount a conversion experience and preach "the Lord's truth." This horrified most established clergymen. Lay exhorting shattered the trained clergy's monopoly on religious discourse and permitted ordinary men and women, and even children, servants, and slaves to defy traditionally assigned roles.

How religion, social change, and politics became interwoven in the Great Awakening can be seen by examining two regions swept by revivalism. Both Boston, the heartland of Puritanism, and interior Virginia, a land of struggling small planters and slave-rich aristocrats, experienced the Great Awakening, but in different ways and at different times.

The Urban North

In Boston, revivalism ignited in the midst of political controversy about remedies for the severe depreciation of the province's paper currency. Paper bills had been issued for years to finance military expeditions against French Canada. The English government insisted that Massachusetts retire all paper money by 1741. Searching for a substitute circulating medium, one group proposed a land bank to issue private bills of credit backed by land. Another group proposed a silver bank to distribute bills of credit backed by silver. Large merchants preferred the fiscally conservative silver bank, while local traders, artisans, and the laboring poor preferred the land bank.

Whitefield's arrival in Boston coincided with the currency furor. At first, Boston's elite applauded Whitefield's ability to call the masses to worship. The master evangelist, it seemed, might restore social harmony by redirecting people from earthly matters such as the currency dispute to concerns of the soul.

When Whitefield left Boston in 1740, he was succeeded by others who were more critical of the "unconverted" clergy and the self-indulgent accumulation of wealth. Among them was James Davenport, who arrived in 1742. Finding every church closed to him, Davenport preached daily on Boston Common, aroused religious ecstasy among thousands, and stirred up feeling against Boston's leading figures. Respectable people grew convinced that revivalism had gotten out of hand, for by this time ordinary people were verbally attacking opponents of the land bank in the streets as "carnal wretches, hypocrites, fighters against God, children of the devil, cursed Pharisees." A revival that had begun as a return to religion now threatened polite culture.

The Rural South

The Great Awakening was ebbing in New England and the middle colonies by 1744, although aftershocks continued for years. But in Virginia, the movement rippled through society from the mid-1740s onward. As in Boston, the Awakeners challenged and disturbed the gentry-led social order.

Whitefield stirred some religious fervor during his early trips through Virginia. Traveling "New Light" preachers, led by the brilliant orator Samuel Davies, were soon gathering large crowds both in the backcountry and in the traditionally Anglican parishes of the older settled areas. By 1747, worried Anglican clergymen persuaded the governor to issue a proclamation restraining "strolling preachers." As one critic put it in 1745, the wandering preachers "have turned the world upside down."

New Light Presbyterianism, which challenged the religious monopoly of the gentry-dominated Anglican church, continued to spread in the 1750s. The evangelical cause advanced further with the rise of the Baptists in the 1760s. Renouncing finery and addressing each other as "brother" and "sister," the Baptists reached out to thousands of unchurched people. Like northern revivalists, they focused on the conversion experience. Many of their preachers were uneducated farmers and artisans who called themselves "Christ's poor." They stressed equality in human affairs, and their message penetrated deeply among Virginia's 140,000 slaves and other poor. As in New England, social changes had weakened the cultural authority of the upper class and, in the context of religious revival, produced a vision of a society drawn along more equal lines.

Legacy of the Awakening

By the time George Whitefield returned to America for his third tour in 1745, the revival had burned out in the North. Its effects, however, were long-lasting. The Awakening promoted religious pluralism and nourished the idea that all denominations were equally legitimate ; none had a monopoly on the truth. The Great Awakening gave competing Protestant churches a theory for living together in relative harmony. From this framework of denominationalism came a second change — the separation of church and state. Once a variety of churches gained legitimacy, it was impossible for any one church to claim special privileges. This undermining of the church-state tie would be completed during the Revolutionary era.

A third effect of the revival was to bolster the view that diversity within communities, for better or worse, could not be prevented. Almost from the beginning. Rhode Island, the Carolinas, and the middle colonies had recognized this. But in Massachusetts and Connecticut, people learned through church schism caused by the Awakening that the fabric of community could be woven from threads of many hues.

New eighteenth-century colonial colleges reflected the religious pluralism symbolized by the Great Awakening. Before 1740 there existed only three. Puritans had fought Harvard in 1636 and Yale in 1701 to provide New England with educated ministers, and Anglicans had chartered William and Mary in 1693. To these small seats of higher education were added six new colleges between 1746 and 1769. But none of the new colleges were controlled by an established church, all had governing bodies composed of men of different faiths, and all admitted students regardless of religion.

Last, the Awakening nurtured a subtle change in values that crossed over into politics and daily life. Especially for ordinary people, the revival experience created a new feeling of self-worth. People assumed new responsibilities in religious affairs and became skeptical of dogma and authority. By learning to oppose authority and to take part in the creation of new churches, thousands of colonists unknowingly rehearsed for revolution.

Political Life

"Were it not for government, the world would soon run into all manner of disorders and confusions," wrote a Massachusetts clergyman early in the eighteenth century. Few colonists, wherever they lived, would have disagreed. A much less easily resolved matter was how political power should be divided within each colony. American colonists naturally drew heavily on inherited political ideas and institutions. These were almost entirely English because English charters sanctioned settlement, English governors ruled the colonies, and English common law governed the courts. But in a new environment, where they met unexpected circumstances, the colonists modified familiar political forms to suit their needs.

Structuring Colonial Governments

In England, the notion of the God-given supreme authority of the monarch was crumbling even before the planting of the colonies. In its place arose the belief that stable and enlightened government depended on balancing the interests of monarchy, aristocracy, and democracy.

The Revolution of 1688 in England, by thwarting the king's pretensions to greater power, seemed to most colonists a vindication and strengthening of a carefully balanced political system.

In colonial governments, political balance was achieved somewhat differently. The governor was the king's agent or, in proprietary colonies, the agent of the king's delegated authority. The council, composed of wealthy appointees of the governor in most colonies, was a pale equivalent of the English House of Lords. The assembly, elected by white male freeholders, functioned as a replica of the House of Commons.

Bicameral legislatures developed in most of the colonies in the seventeenth century. The lower houses, or assemblies, represented the local interests of the people at large. The upper houses, or councils (which usually also sat as the highest courts), represented the nascent aristocracy. Except in Rhode Island and Connecticut, every statute required the governor's assent, and all colonial laws required final approval from the king's privy council. But during the months it took to receive such approval, the laws set down in the colonies took force.

Behind the formal structure of politics stood the rules governing who could participate in the political process. In England since the fifteenth century, the ownership of land had largely defined electoral participation (women and non-Christians were uniformly excluded). Only those with property sufficient to produce an annual rental income of 40 shillings could vote or hold office. The colonists usually followed this principle closely, except in Massachusetts,

Colonial Foundations of the American Political System

1606	Virginia companies of London and Plymouth granted patents to settle lands in North America.
1619	First elected colonial legislature meets in Virginia.
1634	Under a charter granted in 1632, Maryland's proprietor is given all the authority "as any bishop of Durham" ever held — more than the king possessed in England.
1635	The council in Virginia deports Governor John Harvey for exceeding his power, thus asserting the rights of local magistrates to contest authority of royally appointed governors.
1643	The colonies of Massachusetts, Plymouth, Connecticut, and New Haven draw up articles of confederation and form the first intercolonial union, the United Colonies of New England.
1647	Under a charter granted in 1644, elected freemen from the Providence Plantations draft a constitution establishing freedom of conscience, separating church and state, and authorizing referenda by the towns on laws passed by the assembly.
1677	The Laws, Concessions and Agreements for West New Jersey provide for a legislature elected annually by virtually all free males, secret voting, liberty of conscience, election of justices of the peace and local officeholders, and trial by jury in public so that "justice may not be done in a corner."
1689	James II deposed in England in the Glorious Revolution, and royal governors, accused of abusing their authority, ousted in Massachusetts, New York, and Maryland.
1701	First colonial unicameral legislature meets in Pennsylvania under the Frame of Government of 1701.
1735	John Peter Zenger, a New York printer, acquitted of seditious libel for printing attacks on the royal governor and his faction, thus widening the freedom of the press.
1754	First congress of all the colonies meets at Albany (with seven colonies sending delegates) and agrees on a Plan of Union (which is rejected by the colonies and the English government).
1765	The Stamp Act Congress, the first intercolonial convention called outside England's authority, meets in New York.

where it took until 1691 to break the requirement of church membership for suffrage.

Whereas in England the 40-shilling freehold requirement was intended to restrict the size of the electorate, in the colonies, because of the cheapness of land, it conferred the vote on a large proportion of adult males. Between 50 and 75 percent of the adult free males could vote in most colonies. As the proportion of landless colonists increased in the eighteenth century, however, the franchise slowly became more limited.

Though voting rights were broadly based, the upper class assumed that only the wealthy and socially prominent were entitled to hold positions of political power. Lesser men, it was held, ought to defer to their betters. Balancing this elitist conception of politics, however, was the notion that the entire electorate should periodically judge the performance of those they entrusted with political power and reject those who represented them inadequately. Unlike the members of the English House of Commons, who by the seventeenth century thought of themselves as representing the entire nation, the colonial representatives were expected to reflect the views of those who elected them locally. Believing this, their constituents judged them accordingly. The people also felt justified in badgering their leaders, protesting openly, and, in extreme cases of abuse of power, assuming control.

The Crowd in Action

What gave special power to the common people when they assembled to protest oppressive authority was the general absence of effective police power. In the countryside, where most colonists lived, only the county sheriff, with an occasional deputy, insulated civil leaders from angry farmers. In the towns, police forces were still unknown. Only the sheriff, backed up by the night watch, safeguarded public order. Under these conditions, crowd action, frequently effective, gradually achieved a kind of

legitimacy. The assembled people came to be perceived as the watchdog of government, ready to chastise or drive from office those who violated the collective sense of what was right and proper.

Boston's impressment riot of 1747 vividly illustrates the people's readiness to fight oppression. It began when Commodore Charles Knowles brought his Royal Navy ships to Boston for provisioning — and to replenish the ranks of mariners thinned by desertion. When Knowles sent press gangs out on a chill November evening with orders to fill the crew vacancies from Boston's waterfront population, they scooped up artisans, laborers, servants, and slaves, as well as merchant seamen from ships riding at anchor in the harbor.

But before the press gangs could hustle their victims back to the British men-of-war, a crowd of angry Bostonians seized several British officers, surrounded the governor's house, and demanded the release of their townsmen. When the sheriff and his deputies attempted to intervene, the crowd mauled them. The militia, called to arms by the governor, refused to respond. By dusk, a crowd of several thousand defied the governor's orders to disperse, stoned the windows of the governor's house, and dragged a royal barge from one of the British ships into the courtyard of his house, where they burned it amid cheers. After several days of negotiations amid further tumult, Knowles released the impressed Bostonians.

The Growing Power of the Assemblies

Incidents such as the impressment riot of 1747 demonstrated the touchiness of England's colonial subjects. But a more gradual and restrained change — the growing ambition and power of the legislative assemblies — was far more important. For most of the seventeenth century, royal and proprietary governors had exercised greater power in relation to the elected legisla-

When frontier farmers marched on Philadelphia in 1763 to demand more protection on the frontier, a miniature civil war almost broke out. Philadelphia had little use for the "Paxton Boys," who had murdered 20 harmless Christian Indians in retaliation for frontier raids.

tures than did the king in relation to Parliament. The governors could dissolve the lower houses and delay their sitting, control the election of their speakers, and in most colonies initiate legislation with their appointed councils. Colonial governors also had authority to appoint and dismiss judges at all levels of the judiciary and to create chancery courts, which sat without juries. Governors also controlled the expenditure of public monies and had authority to grant land to individuals and groups, which they sometimes used to confer vast estates on their favorites.

In the seventeenth century, Virginia, Massachusetts, and New York had become royal colonies, with governors appointed by the Crown. By the 1730s, royal governments had replaced many of the proprietary governments, including New Jersey (1702), South Carolina (1719), and North Carolina (1729). Some of the royal governors were competent military officers or bureaucrats, but most were mediocre.

In the eighteenth century, elected colonial legislatures challenged the swollen executive powers of these colonial governors. Bit by bit, the representative assemblies won new rights — to initiate legislation, to elect their own speakers, to settle contested elections, to discipline their membership, and to nominate provincial treasurers who controlled the disbursement of public funds. The most important gain of all was acquiring the "power of the purse" — the authority to initiate money bills, which specified how much money should be raised by taxes and how it should be spent. Originally thought of as advisory bodies, the elected assemblies gradually transformed themselves into governing bodies reflecting the interests of the electorate.

Local Politics

Binding elected officeholders to their constituents became an important feature of the colonial political system. In England, the House of Commons was filled with representatives from "rotten boroughs," ancient places left virtually uninhabited by population shifts, and with men whose vote was in the pocket of the ministry because they had accepted Crown appointments, contracts, or gifts. The American assemblies, by contrast, contained mostly representatives sent by voters who often instructed them on particular issues and held them accountable for serving local interests. The voters mostly sent merchants, lawyers, and substantial planters and farmers to represent them in the lower houses, and by the mid-eighteenth century in most colonies, these men had formed political elites.

Local government was usually more important to the colonists than provincial government. In the North, local political authority generally rested in the towns. The New England town meeting decided a wide range of matters, striving for consensus, searching and arguing until it could express itself as a single unit. "By general agreement" and "by the free and united consent of the whole" were phrases denoting a decision-making process that sought participatory assent rather than a democratic competition among differing interests and points of view.

In the South, the county constituted the primary unit of government. No equivalent of the town meeting existed for placing local decisions before the populace. The planter gentry ruled the county courts and the legislature, while substantial farmers served in minor offices such as road surveyor and deputy sheriff. At court sessions, usually convened four times a year, deeds were read aloud and then recorded, juries impaneled and justice dispensed, elections held, licenses issued, and proclamations read aloud. On election days, gentlemen treated their neighbors (on whom they depended for votes) to "bumbo," "kill devil," and other alcoholic treats. By the mid-eighteenth century, a landed squire-archy of third-and fourth-generation families had achieved political dominance.

The Spread of Whig Ideology

Whether in local or provincial affairs, a political ideology called Whig or "republican" had spread widely by the mid-eighteenth century. The canons of this body of thought, inherited from England, flowed from the belief that concentrated power was historically the enemy of liberty and that too much power lodged in any person or group inevitably produced corruption and tyranny. The best defenses against concentrated power were balanced government, elected legislatures adept at checking executive authority, prohibition of standing armies (almost always controlled by tyrannical monarchs to oppress the people), and vigilance by the people for telltale signs of corruption in their leaders.

Much of this Whig ideology reached the people through the newspapers that began appearing in the seaboard towns in the early eighteenth century. The first was the *Boston News-Letter,* founded in 1704. By the 1730s, newspapers had become an important conduit of Whig political thought.

The new importance of the press was vividly illustrated in the Zenger case in New York. Young John Peter Zenger, a printer's apprentice, had been hired in 1733 by the antigovernment faction of Lewis Morris to start a newspaper that would publicize the tyrannical actions of Governor William Cosby. In Zenger's *New-York Weekly Journal,* the Morris faction fired salvos at Cosby's interference with the courts and his alleged corruption in giving important offices to his henchmen.

These charges led to Zenger's arrest for seditious libel. He was brilliantly defended by Andrew Hamilton, a Philadelphia lawyer. Although the jury acquitted Zenger, the libel laws remained very restrictive. But the acquittal did reinforce the notion that the government was the people's servant, and it brought home the point that public criticism could keep people with political authority responsible to the people they ruled. Such ideas about liberty and corruption, raised in the context of local politics, would shortly achieve a much broader significance.

CONCLUSION
America in 1750

The American colonies, robust and expanding, matured rapidly between 1700 and 1750. Churches, schools, and towns — the visible marks of the receding frontier — appeared everywhere. A balanced sex ratio and stable family life had been achieved throughout the colonies. Seasoned political leaders and familiar political institutions functioned from Maine to Georgia.

Yet the sinew, bone, and muscle of American society had not yet fully knit together. One-fifth of the population was bound in chattel slavery and the Native American component was still unassimilated and uneasily situated on the frontier. Full of strength yet marked by awkward incongruities, colonial Americans in 1750 approached an era of strife and momentous decisions.

RECOMMENDED READING

James A. Henretta and Gregory Nobles provide a good introduction to the growth and development of eighteenth-century colonial society in *Evolution and Revolution : American Society : 1620–1820* (1986). On immigration and immigration groups, see Jon Butler, *The Huguenots in Colonial America* (1983); Ned Landsman, *Scotland and its First American Colony* (1985); and Bernard Bailyn, *Voyagers to the West* (1986).

On the development of the northern colonies, rich material can be found in Laurel T. Ulrich, *Good Wives* (1982); and Sung Bok Kim, *Landlord and Tenant in the Colony of New York* (1976).

The transformation of eighteenth-century southern society is the subject of Allan Kulikoff, *Tobacco and Slaves* (1986); T. H. Breen, *Tobacco Culture : The Mentality of the Great Tidewater Planters on the Eve of the Revolution* (1985); and Mechal Sobel, *The World*

They Made Together : Black and White Values in Eighteenth-Century Virginia (1987).

Much can be learned about commercial and intellectual life in the cities from Gary M. Walton and James F. Shepherd, *The Economic Rise of Early America* (1979); and Gary B. Nash, *The Urban Crucible* (1979). Henry May addresses the American Enlightenment in *The American Enlightenment* (1976).

Excellent treatments of religious life and the Great Awakening include Harry S. Stout, *The New England Soul : Preaching and Religious Life in Colonial New England* (1986); and Patricia Bonomi, *Under the Cope of Heaven : Religion, Society, and Politics in Colonial America* (1986).

On the maturing colonial political systems, see Bernard Bailyn, *The Origins of American Politics* (1968); Edward M. Cook, Jr., *The Fathers of the Towns* (1976); and Patricia Bonomi, *A Factious People : Politics and Society in Colonial New York* (1977).

Time Line

1662	Half-Way Covenant in New England
1685– 1715	Stagnation in tobacco market
1704	*Boston News-Letter,* first regular colonial newspaper, published
1713	Beginning of Scots-Irish and German immigration
1715– 1730	Volume of slave trade doubles
1718	French settle New Orleans
1720s	Black population begins to increase naturally
1734– 1736	Great Awakening begins in Northampton, Massachusetts
1735	Zenger acquitted of seditious libel in New York
1739– 1740	Whitefield's first American tour spreads Great Awakening Slaves compose 90 percent of population on Carolina rice coast
1740s	Indigo becomes staple crop in Lower South
1747	Benjamin Franklin publishes first *Poor Richard's Almanack* Impressment riot in Boston
1760	Africans compose 20 percent of American population
1760s– 1770s	Spanish establish California mission system
1769	American Philosophical Society founded at Philadelphia

5

Bursting the Colonial Bonds

n 1758, when he was 21 years old, Ebenezer MacIntosh of Boston laid down his shoemaker's awl and enlisted in the Massachusetts expedition against the French on Lake Champlain. He contributed his mite to the climactic Anglo-American struggle that drove the French from North America.

But a greater role lay ahead for the poor Boston shoemaker. Two years after the Peace of Paris ended the Seven Years' War in 1763, England imposed a stamp tax on the American colonists. In the massive protests that followed, MacIntosh emerged as the street leader of the Boston crowd. In two nights of violent attacks on private property, a Boston crowd nearly destroyed the houses of two of the colony's most important officials. On August 14, they tore through the house of Andrew Oliver, a wealthy merchant and the appointed distributor of stamps for Massachusetts. Twelve days later, MacIntosh led the crowd in attacking the mansion of Thomas Hutchinson, a wealthy merchant who served as lieutenant governor and chief justice of Massachusetts. "The mob was so general," wrote the governor, "and so supported that all civil power ceased in an instant."

On November 5, 2,000 townsmen followed MacIntosh in an orderly march through the crooked streets of Boston to demonstrate their solidarity in resisting the hated stamps. Five weeks later, a crowd forced stamp distributor Oliver to announce his resignation publicly at the "Liberty Tree," which had become a symbol of resistance to England's new colonial policies. Few colonists in 1750 wanted to break the connection with England. Yet in a whirlwind of events, two million colonists moved haltingly toward a showdown with mighty England. Little-known men like Ebenezer MacIntosh as well as historically celebrated Samuel Adams, John Hancock, and John Adams were part of the struggle. Collectively, ordinary persons such as MacIntosh influenced — and in fact sometimes even dictated — the revolutionary movement in the colonies. Though we read and speak mostly of a small group of "founding fathers," the wellsprings of the American Revolution can be fully discovered only among a variety of people from different social groups, occupations, regions, and religions.

• • •

This chapter addresses the tensions in late colonial society, the imperial crisis that followed the Seven Years' War (in the colonies often called the French and Indian War), and the tumultuous decade that led to the "shots heard around the world" fired at Concord Bridge in April 1775. It portrays the origins of a dual American Revolution. Ebenezer MacIntosh, in leading the Boston mob against Crown officers and their colonial collaborators, helped set in motion a revolutionary movement to restore ancient liberties thought by the Americans to be under deliberate attack in England. This movement eventually escalated into the War of American Independence.

But MacIntosh's Boston followers were also venting years of resentment at the accumulation of wealth and power by Boston's aristocratic elite. Calls for the reform of a colonial society that had become corrupt, self-indulgent, and elite-dominated thus accompanied the movement to sever the colonial bond. As distinguished from the War for Independence, this was the American Revolution.

The Climactic Seven Years' War

After a brief period of peace following King George's War (1744–1748), France and England fought the fourth, largest, and by far most significant of the wars for empire that had begun in the late seventeenth century. Known variously as the Seven Years' War, the French and Indian War, and the Great War for Empire, this global conflict in part represented a showdown for control of North America between the Atlantic Ocean and the Mississippi River. In North America, the Anglo-American forces ultimately prevailed, and their victory dramatically affected the lives of the great variety of people living in the huge region east of the Mississippi.

War and the Management of Empire

After the Glorious Revolution of 1688, England began constructing a more coherent imperial administration. In 1696, a professional Board of Trade replaced the old Lords of Trade ; the Treasury strengthened the customs service ; and Parliament created overseas vice-admiralty courts, which functioned without juries to prosecute smugglers who evaded the trade regulations set forth in the Navigation Acts. Royal governors received greater powers and more detailed instructions and came under more insistent demands from the Board of Trade to enforce British policies. England was quietly installing the machinery of imperial management and a corps of colonial bureaucrats.

The best test of an effectively organized state was its ability to wage war. Four times between 1689 and 1763, England matched its strength against France, its archrival in North America and the Caribbean. During this period, the English king and Parliament also increased their control over colonial affairs.

Parliament added new articles such as furs, copper, hemp, tar, and turpentine to the list of items produced in North America that had to be shipped to England before being exported to another country. Parliament also curtailed colonial production of articles important to England's economy : woolen cloth in 1699, beaver hats in 1732, finished iron products in 1750. Most important, Parliament passed the Molasses Act in 1733. Attempting to stop the trade between New England and the French West Indies, where Yankee traders exchanged fish, beef, and pork for molasses to convert into rum, Parliament imposed a prohibitive duty of six pence per gallon on molasses imported from the French islands. This turned many of New England's largest merchants, distillers, and ship captains and crews into smugglers.

The generation of peace ended abruptly in 1739 when England declared war on Spain. The cause of the war was England's determination to continue its drive toward commercial domination of the Atlantic basin. Five years after the war with Spain began in 1739, it merged into a much larger conflict between England and France, in Europe called The War of Austrian Succession, that lasted until 1748. The scale of King George's War (1744–1748) far exceeded previous conflicts. As military priorities became paramount, England pressed for increased discipline within the empire and larger colonial revenues. England asked its West Indian and American colonies to share in the costs of defending — and extending — the empire and to tailor their behavior to the needs of the home country.

Outbreak of Hostilities

The tension between English and French colonists in North America was intensified by the spectacular growth of the English colonies : from 0.25 million in 1700 to 1.25 million in 1750 and to 1.75 million in the next decade. Three-quarters of the increase came in the colonies south of New York. Such growth propelled thousands of land-hungry settlers toward the mountain gaps in the Appalachians in search of farmland.

Promoting this westward rush were eastern fur traders and speculators. But the farther west the settlement line moved, the closer it came to the western trading empire of the French and their Indian allies. Colonial penetration of the Ohio valley in the 1740s established the first English outposts in the continental heartland. This challenged the French where their interest was vital. While the English controlled most of the eastern coastal plain of North America, the French had nearly encircled them to the west by building a chain of trading posts and forts along the St. Lawrence River, through the Great Lakes, and southward into the Ohio and Mississippi valleys all the way to New Orleans. The French attempted to block further English expansion by constructing new forts in the Ohio valley and by prying some tribes loose from their new English connections.

By 1755, the French had driven the English traders out of the Ohio valley and established forts as far east as the forks of the Ohio River, near present-day Pittsburgh. It was there, at Fort Duquesne, that the French smartly rebuffed an ambitious young Virginia militia colonel named George Washington, dispatched by his colony's government to expel them from the region.

Men in the capitals of Europe, not in the colonies, made the decision to force a showdown in the interior of North America. Urged on by England's powerful merchants, who were eager to destroy French overseas trade, the English ministry ordered several thousand troops to America in 1754 ; in France, 3,000 regulars embarked to meet the English challenge.

With war looming, the colonial governments attempted to coordinate their efforts. Representatives of seven colonies met with 150 Iroquois chiefs at Albany, New York, in June 1754. The twin goals were to woo the powerful Iroquois out of their neutrality and to perfect a plan of colonial union. Both failed. "Everyone cries a union is necessary," sighed Benjamin Franklin, "but when they come to the manner and form of the union, their weak noodles are perfectly distracted."

With his British army and hundreds of American recruits, General Edward Braddock slogged his way across Virginia in the summer of 1755, cutting a road through forests and across mountains at a few miles a day. A headstrong professional soldier, Braddock had contempt for the woods-wise French regiments and their stealthy Indian allies.

As Braddock neared Fort Duquesne, the entire French force and the British suddenly surprised one another in the forest. The French had 218 soldiers and militiamen and 637 Indian allies, while Braddock commanded twice that many men but few Indians. After an initial standoff, the French redeployed their Indian allies along both sides of the road in the trees. Unseen, the Indians poured murderous fire into Braddock's tidy lines of men. Braddock was mortally wounded, and two-thirds of his forces were killed or wounded. The Anglo-American force beat a hasty, ignominious retreat.

Throughout the summer, French-supplied Indian raiders put the torch to the Virginia and Pennsylvania backcountry. "The roads are full of starved, naked, indigent multitudes," observed one officer. One French triumph followed another during the next two years, and almost every tribe north of the Ohio River joined the French side.

The turning point in the war came after the energetic William Pitt became England's prime minister in 1757. Proclaiming "I believe that I can save this nation and that no one else can," he abandoned Europe as the main theater of action against the French and threw his nation's military might into the American campaign. About 23,000 British troops landed in America in 1757 and 1758, and the huge naval fleet that arrived in the latter year included 14,000 mariners. But even forces of this magnitude, when asked to engage the enemy in the forests of North America, were not necessarily sufficient to the task without Indian support, or at least neutrality.

Tribal Strategies

Anglo-American leaders knew that in a war fought mainly in the northern colonies, the support of the Iroquois Confederacy and their tributary tribes was crucial. Iroquois allegiance could be secured in only two ways, through purchase or by a demonstration of power that would convince the tribes that the English would prevail with or without their assistance. The Iroquois

understood that their interest lay in playing off one European power against the other.

In 1758, the huge English military buildup began to produce victories. After a failed British and American assault on Fort Ticonderoga on Lake Champlain in June 1758, the tide turned. Troops under Sir Jeffrey Amherst captured Louisbourg, on Cape Breton Island, and Fort Duquesne fell to an army of 6,000 led by General John Forbes. The resolute Pitt had mobilized the fighting power of the English nation and put more men in the field than existed in all of New France. The colonists, in turn, had put aside intramural squabbling long enough to overwhelm the badly outnumbered French.

The victories of 1758 finally moved the Iroquois to join the Anglo-American side. In the South, however, back country skirmishes with the Cherokee from Virginia to South Carolina turned into a costly war from 1759 to 1761.

Other Anglo-American victories in 1759, the "year of miracles," decided the outcome of the bloodiest war yet known in the New World. The culminating stroke came with a dramatic victory at Quebec. Led by 32-year-old General James Wolfe, 5,000 troops scaled a rocky cliff and overcame the French on the Plains of Abraham. The capture of Montreal late in 1760 completed the shattering of French power in North America. The theater of operations shifted to the Caribbean, where fighting continued, as in Europe, for three years longer. But in the American colonies, the "Gallic menace" was gone.

Consequences of War

For the interior Indian tribes, the Treaty of Paris ending the Seven Years' War in 1763 dealt a harsh blow. Unlike the coastal Native Americans, whose population and independence had ebbed rapidly through contact with the colonizers, the inland tribes had maintained their strength and sometimes even grown more unified through relations with settlers. Although they came to depend on European trade goods, Native Americans had turned this commercial connection to their advantage so long as more than one source of trade goods existed.

The Indian play-off system ended with the French defeat. By the terms of the Treaty of Paris, France ceded Canada and all territory east of the Mississippi, except for New Orleans, to England. To Spain went New Orleans and France's trans-Mississippi empire. Spain yielded Florida to England. For the interior tribes, only one source of trade goods remained. Two centuries of European rivalry for control of eastern North America ended abruptly. Iroquois, Cherokee, Creek, and other interior peoples were now forced to adjust to this reality.

After concluding peace with the French, the English government launched a new policy in North America designed to separate Native Americans and colonizers by creating a racial boundary roughly following the crestline of the Appalachian Mountains from Maine to Georgia. The Proclamation of 1763 ordered the colonial governors to reserve all land west of the line for Indian nations. White settlers already living beyond the Appalachians were charged to withdraw to the east.

Though well intended, this attempt to legislate interracial accord failed completely. Even before the proclamation was issued, the Ottawa chief Pontiac was organizing a pan-Indian movement to drive the British out of the Ohio valley. Although his plan collapsed in 1764, it served notice that the interior tribes would fight for their lands.

The English government could not enforce its racial separation policy. Staggering under an immense wartime debt, England decided to maintain only small army garrisons in America to regulate the interior. Nor could royal governors stop land speculators and settlers from privately purchasing land from trans-Appalachian tribes or from simply encroaching on their land. Under such circumstances, the western frontier seethed with tension after 1763.

While the Seven Years' War marked an epic victory of Anglo-American arms over the French and redrew the map of North America, it also had important social and economic effects on colonial society. The war convinced the colonists of their growing strength, yet left them debt-ridden and weakened in manpower. The wartime economy spurred economic development and poured British capital into the colonies, yet rendered them more vulnerable to cyclic fluctuations in the British economy.

Military contracts, for example, brought prosperity to most colonies during the war years. Huge orders for ships, arms, uniforms, and provisions enriched northern merchants and provided good prices for farmers as well.

The war, however, required heavy taxes and took a huge human toll. The magnitude of the human losses in Boston indicates the war's impact. The wartime muster lists show that nearly every working-class Bostonian tasted military service at some point during the long war. When peace came, Boston had a deficit of almost 700 men in a town of about 2,000 families. The high rate of war widowhood produced a feminization of poverty and required expanded poor relief for the maintenance of husbandless women and fatherless children.

Peace ended the casualties but also brought depression. After the British forces left the American theater in 1760, the economy slumped badly, especially in the coastal towns. The greatest hardships fell on laboring people, although even some wealthy merchants went bankrupt. In Philadelphia, many poor people, unable to pay their property taxes, were "disposing of their huts and lots to others more wealthy than themselves." A New York artisan expressed a common lament in 1762. Although he still had employment, he had fallen into poverty and found it "beyond my ability to support my family . . . [which] can scarcely appear with decency or have necessaries to subsist." His situation, he added, "is really the case with many of the inhabitants of this city."

In spite of its heavy casualties and economic repercussions, the Seven Years' War paved the way for a far larger conflict in the next generation. The legislative assemblies, for example, which had been flexing their muscles at the expense of the governors in earlier decades, accelerated their bid for political power. During wartime, knowing that their governors must obtain military appropriations, they extracted concessions as the price for raising revenues. The war also trained a new group of military and political leaders. In carrying out military operations on a scale unknown in the colonies and in shouldering heavier political responsibilities, men such as George Washington, Samuel Adams, Benjamin Franklin, Patrick Henry, and Christopher Gadsden acquired the experience that would serve them well in the future.

The Seven Years' War, in spite of the severe costs, left many of the colonists with a sense of buoyancy. New Englanders rejoiced at the final victory over the "Papist enemy of the North." Frontiersmen, fur traders, and land speculators also celebrated the French withdrawal, for the West now appeared open for exploitation. The colonists also felt a new sense of their identity after the war. Surveying a world free of French and Spanish threats, they could not help but reassess the advantages and disadvantages of subordination to England.

The Crisis with England

George Grenville became the chief minister of England's 25-year-old king, George III, at the end of the Seven Years' War. Struggling to reduce the large national debt, Grenville proposed new taxes in England and others in North America, where the colonists were asked to bear their share of running the empire. Grenville's particular concern was financing the 10,000 British regulars left in North America after 1763 to police French-speaking Canada and the frontier. His revenue program initiated a rift between England and its colonies that a dozen years later would culminate in revolution.

Sugar, Currency, and Stamps

In 1764, Grenville pushed through Parliament several bills that in combination pressed hard against the economic system of the colonies.

First came the Revenue Act (or Sugar Act) of 1764. While reducing the tax on imported French molasses from six to three pence per gallon, it added a number of colonial products to the list of commodities that could be sent only to England. It also required American shippers to post bonds guaranteeing observance of the trade regulations before loading their cargoes. Finally, it strengthened the vice-admiralty courts, where violators of the trade acts were prosecuted.

Many of the colonial legislatures grumbled about the Sugar Act, but only New York objected that *any* tax by Parliament to raise revenue (rather than to control trade) violated the rights of overseas English subjects who were unrepresented in Parliament. On the heels of the Sugar Act came the Currency Act, which forbade the colonies to issue paper money as legal tender. In a colonial economy chronically short of hard cash, this constricted trade.

The move to tighten up the machinery of empire confused the colonists because many of the new regulations came from Parliament, which had heretofore been content to allow the king, his ministers, and the Board of Trade to run overseas affairs. In a world where history taught that power and liberty were perpetually at war, generations of colonists had viewed Parliament as a bastion of English liberty, the bulwark against despotic political rule. The Parliament on which colonial legislatures had modeled themselves now began to seem like a violator of colonial rights.

After Parliament passed the Sugar Act in 1764, Grenville announced his intention to extend to America the stamp duties that had already been imposed in England. However, he gave the colonies a year to suggest alternative ways of raising revenue. The colonies objected strenuously to the proposed stamp tax, but none provided another plan. The Stamp Act, effective November 1765, required revenue stamps on every newspaper, pamphlet, almanac, legal document, liquor license, college diploma, pack of playing cards, and pair of dice.

Colonial reaction to the Stamp Act ranged from disgruntled submission to mass defiance.

In many cases, resistance involved not only discontent over England's tightening of the screws on the American colonies but also internal resentments born out of the play of local events. Especially in the cities, the defiance of authority and destruction of property by people from the middle and lower ranks redefined the dynamics of politics, setting the stage for a ten-year internal struggle for control among the various social elements alarmed by the new English policies.

Stamp Act Riots

The Virginia House of Burgesses was the first legislature to react to the news of the Stamp Act, which arrived in April 1765. In May, led by 29-year-old Patrick Henry, a fiery lawyer newly elected from a frontier county, the House of Burgesses debated seven strongly worded resolutions. Old-guard burgesses regarded some of them as treasonable. The legislature finally adopted the four more moderate resolves, including one proclaiming Virginia's right to impose taxes. They rejected the other resolves, which declared it "illegal, unconstitutional, and unjust" for anybody outside Virginia to lay taxes, asserted that Virginians did not have to obey any externally imposed tax law, and labeled as "an enemy to this, his Majesty's colony," anyone denying Virginia's exclusive right to tax its inhabitants. But within a month, all seven resolutions were broadcast in the newspapers of other colonies.

Governor Francis Bernard of Massachusetts called the Virginia resolves "an alarm bell for the disaffected." The events in Boston in August 1765 amply confirmed his view. On August 14, Bostonians reduced the luxurious mansion of stamp distributor Andrew Oliver to a shambles. Twelve days later, the shoemaker Ebenezer MacIntosh led the crowd again in attacks on the handsomely appointed homes of two British officials and Lieutenant-Governor Thomas Hutchinson. Military men "who have seen towns sacked by the enemy," one observer reported, "declare they never before saw an instance of such fury."

In attacking the property of men associated with the stamp tax, the Boston crowd demonstrated its opposition to parliamentary policy. But the crowd was also expressing hostility toward a local elite that for years had disdained lower-class political participation and had publicly denounced the working poor for their supposed lack of industry and frugality. For decades, ordinary Bostonians had aligned politically with the Boston "caucus," which led the colony's "popular party" against conservative aristocrats such as Hutchinson and Oliver. But the "rage-intoxicated rabble" had suddenly broken away from the leaders of the popular party and gone farther than they had intended. The more cautious political leaders knew that they would have to struggle to regain control of the protest movement.

Violent protest against the Stamp Act also wracked New York and Newport, Rhode Island. Leading the resistance were groups calling themselves the Sons of Liberty, composed mostly of artisans, shopkeepers, and ordinary citizens. Protest took a more dignified form at the Stamp Act Congress, called by Massachusetts and attended by representatives of nine colonies, who met in New York in October 1765. The delegates formulated 12 restrained resolutions that accepted Parliament's right to legislate for the colonies but denied its right to tax them directly unless they had representation in the law-making body.

All over America by late 1765, effigy-burning crowds had convinced stamp distributors to resign their commissions. The colonists defied English authority even more directly by forcing most customs officers and court officials to open the ports and courts for business after November 1 without using the hated stamps required after that date. In March 1766, Parliament bowed to expediency and repealed the hated Stamp Act. The crisis had passed, yet nothing was really solved.

In the course of challenging parliamentary authority, the Stamp Act resisters politicized their communities as never before. The established leaders, generally cautious in their pro-

From the time of his election to the Virginia House of Burgesses at the age of 29, Patrick Henry was an outspoken proponent of American rights. In this portrait, he pleads a case at a county courthouse crowded with local planters.

tests, were often displaced by those beneath them on the social ladder. Scribbled John Adams in his diary : "The people have become more attentive to their liberties, . . . and more determined to defend them."

An Uncertain Interlude

Ministerial instability in England hampered the quest for a coherent, workable American policy. Attempting to be a strong king, George III chose ministers who commanded little respect in Parliament. This led to strife between Parliament and the king's chief ministers ; that in turn led to a shuffling of chief ministers and to a chaotic political situation at the very time that the king was attempting to overhaul the administration of the empire.

To manage the colonies more effectively, the Pitt-Grafton ministry that the king appointed in 1767 obtained new laws to reorganize the customs service, establish a secretary of state for American affairs, and install three new vice-admiralty courts in the port cities. Still hard pressed for revenue, the ministry also pushed through Parliament the Townshend duties on paper, lead, painters' colors, and tea. A final law suspended New York's assembly until that body ceased its noncompliance with the Quartering Act of 1765, which required public funds for support of British troops garrisoned in the colony since the end of the Seven Years' War.

Colonial reaction to the Townshend Acts, centered in Massachusetts, was more restrained than in 1765. New York buckled under to the Quartering Act rather than see its assembly suspended. But the Massachusetts House of Representatives sent a circular letter to each colony objecting to the new Townshend duties, small though they were. Written by Samuel Adams, the letter attacked as unconstitutional the plan to underwrite salaries for royal officials in America from customs duties. "The Americans have made a discovery," declared Edmund Burke before Parliament, "that we mean to oppress them ; we have made a discovery that they intend to raise a rebellion. We do not know how to advance ; they do not know how to retreat."

While most of the colonists only grumbled and petitioned, Bostonians protested angrily. In the summer of 1768, after customs officials seized a sloop owned by John Hancock for a violation of the trade regulations, an angry crowd mobbed them. They fled to a British warship in Boston harbor and remained there for months. The newspapers warned of new measures designed "to suck the life blood" from the people and predicted that troops would be sent "to dragoon us into passive obedience."

Troops indeed came. The attack on the customs officials brought a resolute response from England. The ministry dispatched two regiments from England and two more from Nova Scotia. On October 1, 1768, red-coated troops marched into Boston without resistance.

After the troops occupied Boston, the colonists' main tactic of protest against the Townshend Acts became economic boycott. First in Boston and then in New York and Philadelphia, merchants and consumers adopted nonimportation and nonconsumption agreements. They pledged neither to import nor to use British articles. These measures promised to bring the politically influential English merchants to their aid, for half of British shipping was engaged in commerce with the colonies, and one-quarter of all English exports were consumed there.

Many colonial merchants, however, did not wish to support the boycott and had to be persuaded to comply by street brigades. Crowd action welled up again in the seaports, as determined patriot bands attacked the homes and warehouses of offending merchants and "rescued" incoming contraband goods seized by zealous customs officials. When the southern colonies also adopted nonimportation agreements in 1768, a new step toward intercolonial union had been taken.

England's attempts to discipline its American colonies and oblige them to share the costs of governing an empire lay in shambles by the end of the 1760s. The Townshend duties had failed miserably, yielding less than £21,000 by 1770 while costing British business £700,000 through the colonial nonimportation movement.

In London, on March 5, 1770, Parliament repealed all the Townshend duties except the one on tea. On that same evening in Boston, British troops fired on an unruly crowd of heckling citizens. When the smoke cleared, five bloody bodies, including that of Ebenezer MacIntosh's brother-in-law, lay dead in the snow-covered street. Bowing to furious popular reaction, Thomas Hutchinson, recently appointed governor, ordered the British troops out of town and arrested the commanding officer and the soldiers involved. They were later acquitted, with two young local lawyers, John Adams and Josiah Quincy, Jr., providing a brilliant defense.

The Growing Rift

After the "Boston massacre," opposition to English policies subsided for a time. From 1770 to 1772, relative quiet descended over the colonies. Not until June 1772 did England provide another inflammatory issue. Then, by announcing that it would pay the salaries of the royal governor and superior court judges in Massachusetts rather than allow the provincial legislature to continue supporting these positions, the Crown created a new furor. Even though the measure saved the colony money, it was seen as a dangerous innovation because it undermined a right set forth in the colony's charter. Judges paid from London, it was assumed, would respond to London.

Boston's town meeting protested loudly and created a Committee of Correspondence "to state the rights of the colonists . . . and to communicate and publish the same to the several towns and to the world." Crown supporters called the committee "the foulest, subtlest, and most venomous serpent ever issued from the egg of sedition." By the end of 1772, another 80 towns in Massachusetts had created committees. In the next year, all but three colonies established Committees of Correspondence in their legislatures.

Samuel Adams was by now the leader of the Boston radicals. A man with deep roots among the laboring people despite his Harvard degree, he organized the working ranks through the taverns, clubs, and volunteer fire companies and also secured the support of wealthy merchants such as John Hancock. In England, Adams became known as one of the most dangerous firebrands in America.

In 1772, a band of Rhode Island colonists gave Adams new material to work with when they attacked a royal warship. The British commander of the *Gaspee* was roundly hated for hounding the fishermen and small traders of Narragansett Bay. When his ship ran aground, Rhode Islanders boarded the stranded vessel and burned it to the water's edge. A Rhode Island court then convicted the Gaspee's captain of illegally seizing what he was convinced was smuggled sugar and rum. The government in London reacted with cries of high treason. Finding the lips of Rhode Islanders sealed regarding the identity of the arsonists, an investigating committee could do little. The event was tailor-made for Samuel Adams, who used it to "awaken the American colonies, which have been too long dozing upon the brink of ruin."

In early 1773, Parliament's passage of the Tea Act precipitated the final plunge into revolution. The act allowed the East India Company, which was on the verge of bankruptcy, to ship its tea directly to America. By eliminating English middlemen and English import taxes, this provided Americans with the opportunity to buy their tea cheaply from the company's agents in the colonies. Even with the small tax to be paid in the colonies, Indian tea would now undersell smuggled Dutch tea.

Parliament monumentally miscalculated the American response. For several years, merchants in Philadelphia and New York had been flagrantly smuggling Dutch tea. As a consequence, imports of English tea plummeted. The merchants bitterly denounced the new act for giving the East India Company a monopoly on the North American tea market. The colonists also objected that the government was shrewdly trying to gain implicit acceptance of Parliament's taxing power by offering tea at a new reduced rate. When Americans drank the taxed tea, they

British Exports to North America, 1756-1775

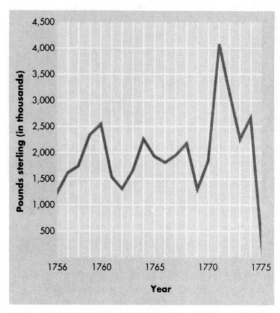

Source: U.S. Bureau of the Census.

would also be swallowing the English right to impose taxes. Mass meetings in the port towns soon forced the resignation of the East India Company's agents, and citizens vowed to stop the obnoxious tea at the water's edge.

Governor Hutchinson of Massachusetts brought the tea crisis to a climax. The popular party led by Samuel Adams wanted to send the tea back to England, but Hutchinson refused to grant the tea ships clearance papers to return to England with their cargoes. Finally, a band of Bostonians, dressed as Indians, boarded the tea ships at nightfall, broke open the chests of tea, and flung £10,000 worth of the East India Company's property into Boston harbor. Lord North, the king's chief minister, now argued that the dispute was no longer about taxes but about whether England had any authority at all over the colonies.

Thoroughly aroused by the Boston Tea Party, Parliament passed the Coercive Acts, which Bostonians promptly labeled the "Intolerable Acts." The acts closed the port of Boston to all shipping until the colony paid for the destroyed tea. They declared British soldiers and officials immune from local court trials for acts committed while suppressing civil disturbances. Parliament amended the Massachusetts charter to transform the council from an upper legislative chamber, elected by the lower house, to a body appointed by the governor. The acts also authorized the governor to prohibit all town meetings except for one annual meeting in each town to elect local officers of government. Finally, General Thomas Gage, commander in chief of British forces in America, replaced Thomas Hutchinson as governor. The Americans now found their maneuvering room severely narrowed.

When the Intolerable Acts arrived in May 1774, Boston's town meeting reacted belligerently. It dispatched a circular letter to all the colonies urging an end to trade with England. This met with faint support. But a second call, for a meeting in Philadelphia of delegates from all colonies, received a better response. The Continental Congress, as it was called, now began to

Public sentiment against the importation of tea and other British goods often found expression in a coat of tar and feathers applied to the bare skin of the offending importer. Note the symbols in The Bostonians Paying the Excise-Man: *the Liberty Tree with a hangman's noose and the overturned copy of the Stamp Act. In the background, Bostonians dump chests of tea into the harbor.*

transform a ten-year debate on constitutional rights conducted by separate colonies into a unified American cause.

Fifty-five delegates from all the colonies except Georgia converged on Carpenter's Hall in Philadelphia in September 1774. The discussions centered not on how to prepare for a war that many sensed was inevitable, but on how to resolve differences that most delegates feared were irreconcilable.

Some delegates, led by cousins Samuel and John Adams from Massachusetts and Richard Henry Lee and Patrick Henry of Virginia, argued for outright resistance to Parliament's Coercive Acts. Moderate delegates from the middle colonies, led by Joseph Galloway of Pennsylvania and James Duane of New York, urged restraint and further attempts at reconciliation. After weeks of debate, the delegates agreed to issue a restrained Declaration of Rights and Resolves, which attempted to define American grievances and to justify the colonists' defiance. More concrete was the Congress's agreement on a plan of resistance. If England did not rescind the Intolerable Acts by December 1, 1774, a ban on all imports and exports between the colonies and Great Britain, Ireland, and the British West Indies would take effect. Some exceptions were made for the export of southern staple commodities in order to keep reluctant southern colonies in the fold.

By the time the Congress adjourned in late October. Boston's cause had been transformed into a national movement. Patrick Henry declared, "The distinctions between Virginians, Pennsylvanians, New Yorkers, and New Englanders are no more. I am not a Virginian, but an American." Many of Henry's fellow delegates were more bound to their provincial identities, but in adjourning, the Congress agreed to reconvene in May 1775.

Even before the Second Continental Congress met, the fabric of government had been badly torn in most colonies. Revolutionary committees, conventions, and congresses, entirely unauthorized by law, were replacing legal governing bodies. Assuming authority in defiance of royal governors, these extralegal bodies created and armed militia units, promoted observance of boycotts, levied taxes, operated the courts, and obstructed the work of English customs officials. By the end of 1774, all but three colonies defied their own charters by appointing provincial assemblies without royal authority. In the next year, this independently created power became evident in the nearly complete cessation of trade with England.

The Final Rupture

The final spark to the revolutionary powder keg was struck in early 1775. General Thomas Gage had assumed the governorship of Massachusetts 11 months earlier and occupied Boston with 4,000 troops — one for every adult male in the town. Ordered to arrest the leaders of the Boston insurrection, Gage sent 700 redcoats under cover of night to seize colonial arms and ammunition in nearby Concord. But Americans learned of the plan. When the troops reached Lexington at dawn, 70 "Minutemen" — townsmen available on a minute's notice — occupied the village green. In the skirmish that ensued, 18 Massachusetts farmers fell, 8 of them mortally wounded.

Marching six miles west, the British entered Concord, where another firefight broke out. Withdrawing, the redcoats made their way back to Boston, harassed by militiamen firing from farmhouses and barns and from behind stone walls. Before the bloody day ended, 273 British and 95 Americans lay dead or wounded. News of the bloodshed swept through the colonies. Within weeks, thousands of men besieged the British troops in Boston. One colonist reported that wherever one traveled, "you see the inhabitants training, making firelocks, casting mortars, shells, and shot."

The outbreak of fighting vastly altered the debates of the Second Continental Congress, which assembled in Philadelphia in May 1775. New delegates included Boston's wealthy merchant, John Hancock, a tall, young planter-lawyer from Virginia, Thomas Jefferson, and the much-applauded Benjamin Franklin, who had arrived from London only four days before the Congress convened.

The Congress had no power to legislate or command; it could only request and recommend. But setting to work, it authorized a continental army of 20,000 and chose George Washington as commander in chief. It issued a "Declaration of Causes of Taking-up Arms," sent the king an "Olive Branch Petition" humbly begging him to remove the obstacles to reconciliation, made moves to secure the neutrality of the interior Indian tribes, issued paper money, erected a postal system, and approved plans for a military hospital.

While debate continued over whether the colonies ought to declare themselves independent, military action grew hotter. The hotheaded Ethan Allen and his Green Mountain boys from eastern New York captured Fort Ticonderoga, controlling the Champlain valley, in May 1775. On New Year's Day in 1776, the British shelled Norfolk, Virginia. In March 1776, Washington's army forced the British to evacuate Boston. Hope for reconciliation with England crumbled at the end of 1775 when news arrived that the king, rejecting the Olive Branch Petition, had dispatched 20,000 additional British troops to quell the American insurrection and had proclaimed the colonies in "open and avowed rebellion." Those fatal words made all the Congress's actions treasonable and turned all who obeyed them into traitors.

By the time Thomas Paine's hard-hitting pamphlet *Common Sense* appeared in Philadelphia on January 9, 1776, members of the Congress were talking less gingerly about independence. Paine's blunt words and compelling rhetoric smashed through the remaining reserve. "O ye that love mankind! Ye that dare oppose not only the tyranny, but also the tyrant, stand forth!" wrote Paine. Within weeks the pamphlet was in bookstalls all over the colonies. "The public sentiment which a few weeks before had shuddered at the tremendous obstacles, with which independence was envisioned," declared Edmund Randolph of Virginia, now "overleaped every barrier."

The Continental Congress continued to debate independence during the spring of 1776, even as the war became bloodier. When an American assault on Quebec failed in May 1776, England embargoed all trade to the colonies and ordered the seizure of American ships. That convinced the Congress to declare its ports open to all countries. "Nothing is left now," Joseph Hewes of North Carolina admitted, "but to fight it out." On June 9 the Congress ordered a committee chaired by Jefferson to begin drafting a declaration of independence.

The declaration was not a highly original statement. It drew heavily on the addresses that the Congress had been issuing to justify American resistance, and it presented a theory of government that was embedded in the scores of pamphlets that had issued from the colonial presses over the previous decade. Jefferson's committee brought its handiwork before the Congress on June 28. On July 2, twelve delegations voted for the declaration, with New York's abstaining, thus allowing the Congress to say that the vote for independence was unanimous. Two days more were spent cutting and polishing the document. On July 4, Congress sent the Declaration of Independence to the printer.

The Ideology of Revolutionary Republicanism

In the years after 1763, the colonists pieced together a political ideology, borrowed partly from English political thought, partly from the theories of the Enlightenment, and partly from their own experiences. Historians call this new ideology "revolutionary republicanism." But it is important to understand that because the colonists varied widely in interests and experiences, there was never a single coherent ideology to which they all subscribed.

A Plot Against Liberty

Many American colonists subscribed to the notion advanced by earlier English Whig writers that corrupt and power-hungry men were slowly extinguishing the lamp of liberty in England. The so-called "country" party represented by these Whig pamphleteers proclaimed itself the guardian of the true principles of the English constitution and opposed the "court" party representing the king and his appointees.

Every ministerial policy and parliamentary act in the decade after the Stamp Act appeared as a subversion of English liberties. The belief that England was carrying out "a deep-laid and desperate plan of imperial despotism . . . for the extinction of all civil liberty," as the Boston town meeting expressed it in 1770, spread rapidly in the next few years. By 1774, John Adams was writing of "the conspiracy against the public liberty [that] was first regularly formed and begun to be executed in 1763 and 1764." From London, America's favorite writer, Benjamin Franklin, described the "extreme corruption prevalent among all orders of men in this old rotten state."

Among many Americans, especially merchants, the attack on constitutional rights blended closely with the threats to their economic interests contained in the tough new trade policies. Merchants perceived a coordinated attack on their "lives, liberties, and property," as

they frequently phrased it. Others saw in revolution an opportunity to revitalize American society to a state of civic virtue, spartan living, and godly purpose.

The fervent support of the patriot movement by much of the colonial clergy, especially in New England, helped give a high-toned moral character to colonial protest. The notion of moral regeneration through battle against a corrupt enemy ennobled the cause.

The growth of a revolutionary spirit among common people also owed much to the plain style of polemical writers such as Thomas Paine and Patrick Henry. Paine's *Common Sense* attacked the idea of monarchy itself. Its astounding popularity — it sold more copies than any

In *Common Sense*, Thomas Paine dared to articulate, in plain but muscular language, the thoughts of rebellion and independence that others had only alluded to.

printed piece in colonial history — stemmed not only from its argument but also from its style. Paine wrote for the common people, using plain language and assuming their knowledge of nothing more than the Bible. He appealed to millennial yearnings: "We have it in our power to begin the world over again," if only the Americans would stand up for liberty, the goddess whom "Europe regards . . . like a stranger, and England hath given . . . warning to depart." Many Whig leaders denounced Paine as "crackbrained," but thousands who read or listened to *Common Sense* were radicalized by it.

Rejecting Monarchy

The rejection of monarchy was one basic component of the republican faith that emerged in the prerevolutionary decade. But the American people did not easily turn away from the English monarchy. Only at the very end of the imperial crisis, after they had already repudiated Parliamentary authority, did the colonists attack the king. It was Paine's unsparing rejection of monarchy, his denial that it was in any way compatible with liberty, that made his pamphlet *Common Sense* so radical. "Of more worth is one honest man to society, and in the sight of God," he scoffed, "than all the crowned ruffians that ever lived."

In rejecting monarchy, the American people also rejected the system of hierarchical authority on which the monarchy was based. They set aside the belief that political authority grew out of governmental power and the doctrine that in return for the king's protection, the people owed him loyalty and obedience. Therein lay much of the true radicalism of their republican faith.

Balancing Liberty and Power

Revolutionary republicanism emphasized not the benefits of governmental power but its dangers. Political power — the ability to influence and control others — was understood to entice people and ultimately to corrupt them. Those possessing power inevitably used it for their own advantage rather than for the general good.

In the republican world view, liberty was seen as the opposite of power: freedom from the controlling influence of others and the ability to govern one's own life. The Revolutionary generation believed that this tension between power and liberty was the central theme of human history. Their recent experience with England burned the lesson indelibly into their minds. Thus their overriding concern in thinking about politics and government was to find ways of controlling power and maximizing liberty.

Given the dangers of governmental power and the need to limit it, how could political order be maintained? The Revolutionary generation chose republicanism. Order was not to be imposed from above through such traditional agencies of control as monarchies, centralized governments, or standing armies. In republican systems, political order flowed upward from the responsible, self-regulated behavior of the people, especially from their willingness to put the public good before their own private interests. In a republic, explained one pamphleteer, "each individual gives up all private interest that is not consistent with the general good." The term for this extraordinary self-denial was "public virtue." It formed the core of the Revolution's republican faith.

In placing responsibility for political order with the people and counting on them to act for the good of the whole, Americans made a revolutionary change in the location of authority. It was an extraordinarily hopeful but risk-filled undertaking.

Republicanism posed another problem for the Revolutionary generation. Republics, given their lack of strong, central government, were understood to be vulnerable to internal decay and external attack. The concern over internal decay centered on the problem of "faction," or organized political interests. History taught that internal divisions had destroyed every republic in the past. Factional conflict, once begun, could easily spin out of control.

The only way to master the demon was to avoid its causes, and that was possible only where societies were small and homogeneous, free of serious economic, social, or religious conflicts. It was impossible to measure exactly how much internal division a republic could tolerate. Some people worried that the larger colonies, such as New York and Pennsylvania, were already too diverse, but most assumed that the familiar colonial boundaries could safely be used to separate one republican state from another. Few Americans during the early years of independence believed that a single, unified continental republic was possible. The nation would have to be organized differently, as a confederation of individual republican states. The problem of faction and its control would trouble American politics throughout the years of the nation's founding.

Debate Over Political Equality

Political equality was the other great principle at the heart of the nation's republican faith. No doctrine was more fundamental — or, as events soon proved, more controversial. The belief that republican citizens must watch over their governments meant that every citizen must have a political voice.

As the Revolution approached, some Americans took the principle literally, arguing that no one should have more political power than anyone else. This position found its greatest support among groups largely outside the political process — farmers and tenants in the interior, workers and artisans in the coastal towns and cities.

Republican equality, however, meant something quite different to other revolutionaries. More cautious patriots talked about order as well as liberty and emphasized the importance of what they called an "aristocracy of talent" — that is, of ability, wisdom, and public virtue. That argument was voiced most frequently by individuals and groups who already enjoyed political power — merchants, planters, large commercial farmers. They saw no need to alter radically the existing political system.

The Turmoil of Revolutionary Society

The long struggle with England over colonial rights between 1764 and 1776 did not occur in a unified society. Social and economic change, which accelerated in the late colonial period, brought deep unrest and calls for reform from many quarters.

As agitation against English policy intensified, previously acquiescent people took a more active interest in politics. Groups emerged — slaves, urban laboring people, backcountry farmers, evangelicals, women — who enunciated goals of their own that were sometimes only loosely connected to the struggle with England. The stridency and potential power of these groups raised for many upper-class leaders the frightening specter of a radically changed society. Losing control of the protests they had initially led, many of them would abandon the resistance movement against England.

Urban People

Although the cities contained only about 5 percent of the colonial population, they formed the vital cores of revolutionary agitation. They led the way in protesting English policy, and they soon contained the most politicized citizens in America. Local politics could be rapidly transformed as the struggle against England became enmeshed with calls for internal reform.

In Philadelphia, for example, economic difficulties in the 1760s and 1770s led craftsmen to band together within their craft and their community. Artisans played a central role in forging a nonimportation agreement in 1768, calling public meetings, publishing newspaper appeals, organizing secondary boycotts against foot-dragging merchants, and ferreting out and tarring and feathering opponents to their policies.

By 1772, artisans were filling elected municipal positions, and insisting on their right to participate equally with their social superiors in nominating assemblymen and other important officeholders.

By 1774, working-class intermeddling in state affairs had taken a bold new step — the de facto assumption of governmental powers by committees called into being by the people at large. Craftsmen had first clothed themselves in such extralegal authority in policing the nonimportation agreement in 1769. Five years later, in response to the Intolerable Acts, they put forward a radical slate of candidates for a committee to enforce a new economic boycott. Their ticket drubbed one nominated by the city's conservative merchants.

The political mobilization of laboring Philadelphians continued as the impasse with England reached a climax in 1775. Many pacifist Quaker leaders of the city had abandoned politics by this time, and other conservative merchants had also concluded that mob rule had triumphed. Into the leadership vacuum stepped a group of radicals from the middling ranks: the fiery Scots-Irish doctor, Thomas Young, who had agitated in Boston and Albany before migrating to Philadelphia; Timothy Matlack, a hardware retailer who was popular with the lower class for matching his prize bantam cocks against those of New York's aristocratic James Delancy; James Cannon, a young schoolteacher; Benjamin Rush, whose new medical practice took him into the garrets and cramped rooms of the city's poor; and Thomas Paine, a recent immigrant seeking something better in America than he had found as an ill-paid excise officer in England.

The political support of the new radical leaders was centered in the 31 companies of the Philadelphia militia, composed mostly of laboring men, and in the extralegal committees now controlling the city's economic life. Their leadership helped to overcome the conservatism of the regularly elected Pennsylvania legislature, which was resisting the movement of the Continental Congress toward independence. In addition, the new radical leaders demanded internal reforms: opening up opportunity; curbing the accumulation of wealth by "our great merchants" who were "making immense fortunes at the expense of the people"; abolishing the property requirement for voting; allowing militiamen to elect their officers; and imposing stiff fines, to be used for the support of the families of poor militiamen, on men who refused militia service.

Mobilization among artisans, laborers, and mariners, in other cities as well as Philadelphia, became part of the chain of events that led toward independence. Whereas most of the patriot elite fought only to change English colonial policy, the populace of the cities also struggled for internal reforms and raised notions of how an independent American society might be reorganized.

Women also played a vital role in the urban crucibles of revolutionary activity. They facilitated the economic boycott of English goods, especially textiles and tea. From Georgia to Maine, women and children began spinning yarn and weaving cloth. "Was not every fireside, indeed a theatre of politics?" John Adams remembered after the war. After the Tea Act in 1773, patriotic women boycotted their favorite drink. Newspapers carried recipes for tea substitutes and recommendations for herbal teas. Many women could agree with one Rachel Wells: "I have done as much to carry on the war as many that set now at the helm of government."

Protesting Farmers

In most of the agricultural areas of the colonies, where many settlers made their livelihoods, passions concerning English policies were aroused only slowly. After about 1740, farmers had benefited from a sharp rise in the demand for foodstuffs in England, southern Europe, and the West Indies. Living far from harping English customs officers, impressment gangs, and occupying armies, the colonists of the interior had to be drawn gradually into the resistance movement by their urban cousins. Even in Concord,

As marketgoers and consumers, urban women played a crucial role in applying economic pressure on England during the pre-Revolutionary decade. This British cartoon, published in 1775, derisively depicts a group of North Carolina ladies signing an antitea agreement.

Massachusetts, only a dozen miles from the center of colonial agitation, townspeople found little to protest in English policies until England closed the port of Boston in 1774.

Yet some parts of rural America seethed with social tension in the prewar era. The dynamics of conflict, shaped by the social development of particular regions, eventually became part of the momentum for revolution. In three western counties of North Carolina and in the Hudson River valley of New York, for example, widespread civil disorder marked the pre-Revolutionary decades. The militant rhetoric and tactics small farmers used to combat exploitation formed rivulets that fed the main stream of revolutionary consciousness.

For years, the small farmers of western North Carolina had suffered exploitation by corrupt county court officials appointed by the governor and a legislature dominated by eastern planter interests. Sheriffs and justices, allied with land speculators and lawyers, seized property when farmers could not pay their taxes and sold it, often at a fraction of its worth, to their cronies. In the mid-1760s, frustrated at getting no satisfaction from legal forms of protest, the farmers formed associations of so-called Regulators, that forcibly closed the courts, attacked the property of their enemies, and whipped and publicly humiliated judges and lawyers. When their leaders were arrested, the Regulators stormed the jails and released them.

In 1768 and again in 1771, Governor William Tryon led troops against the Regulators, who were finally defeated. Seven leaders were executed in the ensuing trials. Though the Regulators lost on the field of battle, their protest against the self-interested behavior of a wealthy elite became part of the larger revolutionary struggle.

Rural insurgency in New York flared up in the 1750s and again in 1766 over land rights. The Hudson River valley had long been controlled by a few wealthy families with enormous landholdings, which they leased to small tenant farmers. The Van Rensselaer manor totaled a million acres, the Phillipses' manor nearly half as much. When tenants resisted rent increases or purchased land from Indians who swore that manor lords had extended the boundaries of their manors by fraud, the landlords began evicting their leaseholders.

The landlords had the power of govern- ment, including control of the courts, on their side, so the tenants, like the Carolina Regulators, went outside the law. By 1766, while New York City was absorbed in the Stamp Act furor, tenants led by William Prendergast began resisting sheriffs who tried to evict tenants from lands they claimed. The militant tenants threatened landlords with death and broke open jails to rescue their friends. British troops from New York were used to break the tenant rebellion. Prendergast was tried and sentenced to be hanged, beheaded, and quartered. Although he was pardoned, the bitterness of the Hudson River tenants endured through the Revolution, when most of them, unlike the Carolina Regulators, fought with the British because their landlords had joined the patriot cause.

CONCLUSION
Forging a Revolution

The Seven Years' War nurtured the colonists' sense of separate identity. Yet it left them with difficult economic adjustments, heavy debts, and growing social divisions. The Treaty of Paris in 1763 led to a reorganization of England's triumphant yet debt-torn empire that had profound repercussions in North America.

In the pre-Revolutionary decade, a dual disillusionment penetrated ever deeper into the colonial consciousness. Pervasive doubt arose concerning both the colonies' role, as assigned by England, in the economic life of the empire and the sensitivity of the government in London to the colonists' needs. At the same time, the colonists began to perceive British policies — instituted by Parliament, the king, and his advisers — as a systematic attack on the fundamental liberties and natural rights of British subjects in America.

The fluidity and diversity of colonial society and the differing experiences of Americans during and after the Seven Years' War evoked varying responses to the disruption that accompanied the English reorganization of the empire. In the course of resisting English policy, many previously inactive groups entered public life to challenge gentry control of political affairs. Often occupying the most radical ground in the opposition to England, they simultaneously challenged the growing concentration of economic and political power in their own communities.

When the Congress turned the 15-month undeclared war into a formally declared struggle for national liberation in July 1776, it steered its compatriots onto turbulent and unknown seas.

RECOMMENDED READING

Further knowledge of the long, exhausting wars of empire that embroiled the colonies for four generations before 1763 can be derived from Douglas E. Leach, *Arms for Empire* (1973); and William Eccles, *The Canadian Frontier*, rev. ed. (1983).

The administration of the British Empire and

the advent of the Seven Years' War are addressed in Michael Kammen, *Empire and Interest* (1970); and Francis Jennings, *Empire of Fortune: Crown, Colonies, and Tribes in the Seven Years' War in America* (1988).

For different points of view on the origins of the American Revolution, see Bernard Bailyn, *The Ideological Origins of the American Revolution* (1967); Gary B. Nash, *The Urban Crucible* (1979); Joseph A. Ernst, *Money and Politics in America, 1755–1775* (1973); David Ammerman, *In the Common Cause* (1974); and Pauline Maier, *From Resistance to Rebellion* (1972).

Rich local studies of the Revolutionary crisis include Dirk Hoerder, *Crowd Action in Revolutionary Massachusetts* (1977); and Edward Countryman, *A People in Revolution* (1981); Excellent essays on various aspects of the coming of the Revolution can be found in Alfred F. Young, ed., *The American Revolution* (1976); and Jeffrey J. Crow and Larry E. Tise, eds., *The Southern Experience in the American Revolution* (1978).

Time Line

1696	Parliament establishes Board of Trade	**1764**	Sugar and Currency acts Pontiac's Rebellion in Ohio valley
1701	Iroquois set policy of neutrality	**1765**	Colonists resist Stamp Act Virginia House of Burgesses issues Stamp Act resolutions
1702–1713	Queen Anne's War		
1713	Peace of Utrecht	**1766**	Declaratory Act Tenant rent war in New York Slave insurrections in South Carolina
1733	Molasses Act		
1744–1748	King George's War	**1767**	Townshend duties imposed
1754	Albany conference	**1768**	British troops occupy Boston
1755	Braddock defeated by French and Indian allies	**1770**	"Boston Massacre" Townshend duties repealed (except on tea)
1756–1763	Seven Years' War		
1759	Wolfe defeats the French at Quebec	**1771**	North Carolina Regulators defeated
1759–1761	Cherokee War against the English	**1772**	*Gaspee* incident in Rhode Island
		1773	Tea Act provokes Boston Tea Party
1760s	Economic slump	**1774**	"Intolerable Acts" First Continental Congress meets
1763	Treaty of Paris ends Seven Years' War Proclamation line limits westward expansion	**1775**	Second Continental Congress meets Battles of Lexington and Concord
		1776	Thomas Paine publishes *Common Sense* Declaration of Independence

PART TWO

A REVOLUTIONARY PEOPLE
1775–1828

The American Revolution not only marked an epic military victory over the powerful mother country but also set the course of national development in ways that still affect American society. Members of the Revolutionary generation were inspired by the idea of building a model society based on principles of freedom and equality. Their attempt to construct a *novus ordo seclorum*, a new order of the ages, continued beyond the Revolutionary era and continues yet today.

Chapter 6, "A People in Revolution," traces the impact of the Revolutionary call to arms on the various groups — male and female, white, black, and Native American — that made up American society and traces the exhilarating yet divisive efforts to fashion a new, republican political order. Chapter 7, "Consolidating the Revolution," examines the critical years of the 1780s, when the new nation struggled to forge national unity following the Revolutionary War and to find security in a hostile Atlantic world. Out of that struggle and the continuing competition for political power in the states emerged a great debate over the new nation's government. That debate led to the replacement of the Articles of Confederation with a new constitution. Learning to live under the new constitution during the 1790s is the focus for Chapter 8, "Creating a Nation."

Chapters 9 and 10, overlapping in time, should be considered as a pair. Chapter 9, "Politics and Society in the Early Republic," delves into the political and diplomatic developments of the first three decades of the nineteenth century. Chapter 10, "The Preindustrial Republic," examines the underlying social and economic changes occurring in the early years of the republic.

6

A People in Revolution

Among the Americans wounded and captured at the Battle of Bunker Hill in the spring of 1775 was Lieutenant William Scott of Peterborough, New Hampshire. Asked by his captors how he had come to be a rebel, "Long Bill" Scott replied:

The case was this Sir! I lived in a Country Town; I was a Shoemaker, & got [my] living by my labor. When this rebellion came on, I saw some of my neighbors get into commission, who were no better than myself. . . . I was asked to enlist, as a private soldier. My ambition was too great for so low a rank. I offered to enlist upon having a lieutenant's commission, which was granted. I imagined my self now in a way of promotion. If I was killed in battle, there would be an end of me, but if my Captain was killed, I should rise in rank, & should still have a chance to rise higher. These Sir! were the only motives of my entering into the service. For as to the dispute between Great Britain & the colonies, I know nothing of it; neither am I capable of judging whether it is right or wrong.

People fought in America's Revolutionary War for many reasons: fear, ambition, principle. We have no way of knowing whether Long Bill Scott's motives were typical. Certainly many Americans knew more than he about the colonies' struggle with England. But many did not.

In the spring of 1775, the Revolutionary War had just begun. So, as it turned out, had Long Bill's adventures. When the British evacuated Boston a year later, they transported Scott as a prisoner to Halifax, Nova Scotia. After more than a year's captivity, he managed to escape and make his way home to fight once more. He was recaptured near New York City when its garrison fell to a surprise British assault. Again Scott escaped, this time by swimming the Hudson River at night with his sword tied around his neck and his watch pinned to his hat.

During the winter of 1777, he returned to New Hampshire to recruit his own militia company. It included two of his sons. In the fall, he joined in the defeat of Burgoyne's army near Saratoga, New York, and later took part in the fighting around Newport, Rhode Island. In early 1778, Scott's health broke, and he was permitted to resign from the army. After only a few months, however, he was at it again. During the last year of the war, he served as a volunteer on a navy frigate.

110

For seven years, the war held Scott in its harsh grasp. Scott's oldest son died of camp fever after six years of service. In 1777, Long Bill sold his New Hampshire farm to meet family expenses. The note he took in exchange turned into a scrap of paper when the dollar of 1777 became worth less than two cents by 1780. He lost a second farm, in Massachusetts, when his military pay depreciated similarly. After his wife died, he helplessly turned their younger children over to his oldest son and set off to beg a pension or job from the government. He was employed by the government as a surveyor when he died of a fever in 1796, near Sandusky in the Ohio country.

• • •

The Revolutionary War, which was so hard on Long Bill Scott, transformed the lives of countless Americans. The war lasted for seven years, longer than any other of America's wars until Vietnam nearly two centuries later, and it was fought on American soil, among the American people. It called men by the thousands from shops and fields, disrupted families, killed civilians, spread diseases, and made a shambles of the economy.

While carrying on this struggle for independence, the American people also mounted a political revolution of profound importance. Politics, government, and elections were transformed in keeping with republican principles and the rapidly changing circumstances of political life. What did republican liberty mean? How was governmental power to be organized and controlled? How democratic should American politics be? These were among the fundamental questions with which the American people wrestled at the nation's beginning.

As people turned increasingly to politics to solve their problems and achieve their goals, they clashed repeatedly over such explosive issues as slavery, the separation of church and state, paper money and debt relief, the regulation of prices, and the toleration of political dissent. They argued as well over the design of new state constitutions and the shape of a new national government. Seldom has America's political agenda been fuller or more troubled.

The American Revolution dominated the lives of all who lived through it. But it had different consequences for men than for women, for black slaves than for their white masters, for Native Americans than for frontier settlers, for overseas merchants than for urban workers, for northern businessmen than for southern planters. Our understanding of the Revolutionary experience out of which the American nation emerged must begin with the Revolutionary War, for independence came at a high cost.

The War for American Independence

On October 19, 1781, near the Virginia hamlet of Yorktown, Lord Charles Cornwallis, commander of His Majesty's army in the southern states, surrendered to General George Washington. Learning the news of Yorktown a month later, Lord North, the king's chief minister, exclaimed, "Oh, God! It is all over." In Philadelphia, citizens poured into the streets to celebrate while the Congress assembled for a solemn ceremony of thanksgiving. Sporadic fighting continued for another year; not until November 1782 were the preliminary articles of peace signed. But everyone knew after Yorktown that the war was over. Americans had won their independence.

Creating an Independent Government

America's military victory over mighty England was all the more remarkable given the weak national government that directed the war effort. For six years, the American cause depended on the inadequately empowered Continental Congress. It operated under a document called the Articles of Confederation that was not ratified until the war was almost over.

Prior to independence, the colonies had repeatedly quarreled over territory, settlers, control of the fur trade, and commercial advantage within the British Empire. The crisis with England, however, forced them together, and the Continental Congress was the first embodiment of that union. The First Continental Congress sent resolutions of protest to England and functioned as a temporary assembly.

The Second Continental Congress, however, meeting in May 1775, in the midst of a war crisis, began to exercise some of the most basic responsibilities of a sovereign government: raising an army and conducting diplomatic relations. Its powers, though, were unclear, its legiti-macy uncertain. As independence and the prospects of an extended war loomed, pressure grew to establish the Congress on a sounder footing. On June 20, 1776, shortly before independence was declared, Congress appointed a committee, chaired by John Dickinson of Pennsylvania, to draw up a plan of perpetual union. It was called the Articles of Confederation. While the war erupted around them, the delegates struggled with the new and difficult problem of creating a permanent government. They clashed over whether to form a strong, consolidated regime or a loosely joined confederation of sovereign states.

The final "Articles of Confederation" represented a compromise. Article 9 gave the Congress sole authority to regulate foreign affairs, declare war, mediate boundary disputes between the states, manage the post office, and administer relations with Indians living outside state boundaries. The Articles also stipulated that the citizens of each state were to enjoy "the privileges and immunities" of the citizens of every other state. Embedded in that clause was the basis for national, as distinguished from state, citizenship.

At the same time, the Articles sharply limited what the Congress could do and reserved broad governing powers to the states. For example, the Congress could not raise troops or levy taxes on its own authority. Perhaps most important, Article 2 stipulated that each of the states was to "retain its sovereignty, freedom and independence, and every power, jurisdiction, and right which is not by this confederation expressly delegated to the United States in Congress assembled."

Though the Congress sent the Articles to the states for approval in November 1777, they were not ratified until March 1781. This was primarily because of disputes over the control of lands west of the Appalachian Mountains between states such as Virginia, South Carolina, and New York, which had western claims tracing back to their colonial charters, and states such as Maryland and New Jersey, which had none.

Western Land Claims Ceded by the States, 1782-1802

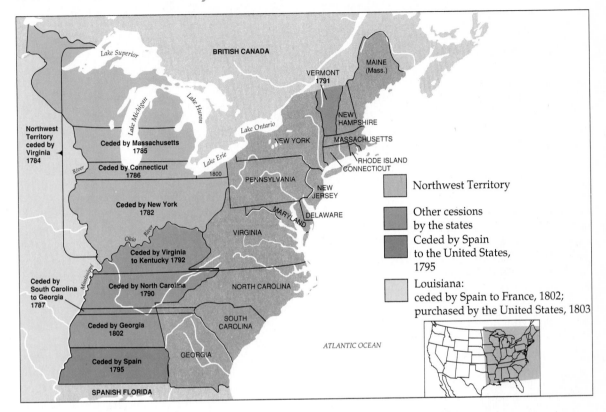

For several years, ratification hung in the balance while politicians and speculators jockeyed for advantage. A breakthrough finally came in 1780, when New York and Virginia agreed to transfer their western lands to the Congress. In early 1781, Maryland became the final state to approve the Articles and their ratification was assured.

The war did not wait during the struggle over ratification. The Congress did the best it could, using the unratified Articles as a guide. Events, however, quickly proved the inadequacy of the powers allotted to the Congress, since it could do little more than pass resolutions and ask the states for support. If they refused, as they frequently did, the Congress could only protest and urge cooperation. Its ability to function was further limited by the stipulation that each state's delegation cast but one vote. On a

number of occasions, disagreements within state delegations prevented them from voting at all. That could paralyze the Congress, since most important decisions required a nine-state majority.

During the war, Washington repeatedly criticized the Congress for its failure to support the army adequately. In 1778, acknowledging its own ineffectiveness, the body temporarily granted Washington extraordinary powers and asked him to manage the war on his own.

The War in the North

As we know, the war began in Massachusetts in 1775. Within a year, the center of fighting shifted to the middle states. After 1779, the South was the primary theater. Why did this geographic pattern develop?

At first, British officials thought of launching forays out from Boston into the surrounding countryside. They soon reconsidered, however, for the growing size of the continental army and the absence of significant Loyalist strength in the New England region urged caution. Even more important, the Americans' successful emplacement of artillery on the strategic Dorchester Heights overlooking the city made its continued occupation untenable. On March 7, 1776, the British commander, General William Howe, decided to evacuate.

For a half dozen years after Boston's evacuation, British ships prowled the New England coast, attacking American commerce, confiscating supplies, and destroying towns. Yet away from the coast there was little fighting at all. Most New Englanders had reason to be thankful for their good fortune.

After evacuating Boston, British officials established their military headquarters in New York City, which offered important advantages over Boston. New York was more centrally located, and its spacious harbor lay at the mouth of the Hudson River, the major water route northward into the interior. Control of New York would, in addition, ensure access to the abundant grain and livestock of the Middle Atlantic states. Finally, Loyalist sentiment ran wide and deep among the inhabitants of the city and its environs.

In the summer of 1776, Washington tried to challenge the British for control of Manhattan, but he was outmaneuvered and badly outnumbered. By late October, the city was firmly in British hands. It would remain so until the war's end.

In the fall of 1776, King George III instructed his military commanders in North America to make one last effort at reconciliation with the colonists. When the British demanded that Congress revoke the Declaration of Independence, however, the negotiations collapsed.

For the next two years, the war swept back and forth across New Jersey and Pennsylvania. Reinforced by German mercenaries hired in Europe, the British moved virtually at will. Neither the state militias nor the continental army offered serious opposition. At Trenton in December 1776 and again at Princeton the following month, Washington surprised the British and scored victories that prevented the Americans' collapse. For the rebels, however, survival remained the primary goal.

American efforts during the first year of the war to invade Canada and bring that British colony into the rebellion also fared badly. In November 1775, American forces under General Richard Montgomery had taken Montreal. But the subsequent assault against Quebec ended with almost 100 Americans killed or wounded and more than 300 taken prisoner. The American cause could not survive many such losses.

At New York, Washington had learned the painful lesson that his troops were no match for the British in frontal combat. Thus he adopted a strategy of caution and delay. He would harass the British but avoid major battles. For the remainder of the war, Washington's posture was primarily defensive and reactive.

As a consequence, the war's middle years turned into a deadly chase that neither side proved able to win. In September 1777, the British took Philadelphia, sending the Congress fleeing into the countryside, but then failed to press their advantage. In October, the Americans won a victory at Saratoga, New York, where General Burgoyne surrendered with 5,700 British soldiers.

The War Moves South

As the war in the North bogged down in a costly stalemate, British officials adopted another strategy: invasion and pacification of the South. Royal officials in the South encouraged the idea with the promise that thousands of Loyalists would rally to the British standard. The southern coastline with its numerous rivers, moreover, offered maximum advantage to British naval strength. Then there were the slaves, that vast but imponderable force in southern society. If they could be lured to the British side, the balance might tip in Britain's favor. Persuaded by

Military Operations in the North, 1776-1780

× Forts
← American movements
← British movements
✶ American victory
✦ British victory

these arguments, British policymakers made the southern states the primary theater of military operations during the final years of the war.

In December 1778, the British took Savannah, Georgia's major port, and on May 12, 1780, they occupied Charleston, South Carolina, after a month's siege. At a cost of only 225 casualties, the British captured the entire 5,400-man American garrison. It was the costliest American defeat of the war. The British then quickly extended their control north and south along the Carolina coast.

Their successes, however, proved deceptive, for British officers quickly learned the difficulty of extending their control into the interior. The distances were too large, the problems of supply too great, the reliability of Loyalist troops too problematic, and support for the Revolutionary cause among the people too strong.

In October 1780, Washington sent Nathanael Greene south to lead the continental forces. Greene knew the region and the kind of war that had to be fought. Dividing his army into small, mobile bands, he employed what today would be called guerrilla tactics, harassing the British and their Loyalist allies at every opportunity, striking by surprise and then disappearing into the interior. Bands of private marauders, roving the land and seizing advan-

tage from the war's confusion, compounded the escalating violence.

In time, the tide began to turn. At Cowpens, South Carolina, in early 1781, American troops under General Daniel Morgan won a decisive victory. In April 1781, convinced that British authority could not be restored in the Carolinas while Virginia remained a supply and staging area for the rebels, British Commander Cornwallis moved north out of the Carolinas. With a force of 7,500, he raided deep into Virginia. In June, his forces sent Governor Jefferson and the Virginia legislature fleeing from Charlottesville

Military Operations in the South, 1778-1781

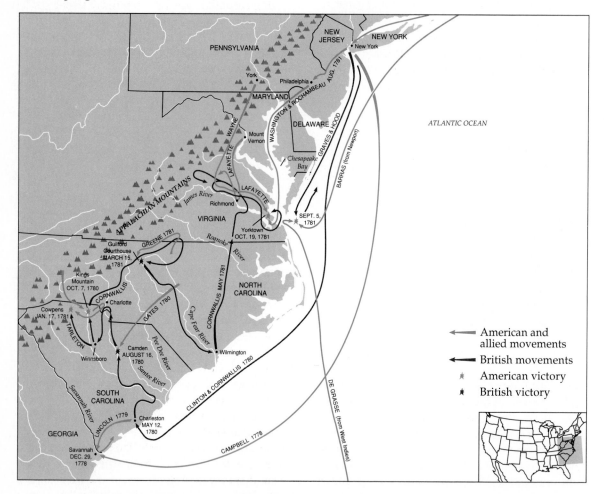

into the mountains. But again Cornwallis had to turn toward the coast for protection and resupply. His goal was Yorktown, where he arrived on August 1.

As long as the British fleet controlled the waters of Chesapeake Bay, his position was secure. That advantage, however, did not last. In 1778, the French government, still smarting from its defeat by England in the Seven Years' War and buoyed by the American victory at Saratoga in 1777, had signed a treaty of alliance with the American Congress, promising to send its naval forces into the war. On August 30, 1781, the French admiral, Comte de Grasse, arrived off Yorktown. Reinforced by a second French squadron from the North, De Grasse established naval superiority in the region. Cut off from the sea and caught on a peninsula between the York and James rivers by 17,000 French and American troops, Cornwallis's fate was sealed. On October 17, 1781, he opened negotiations for surrender.

Native Americans in the Revolution

The Revolutionary War involved more than Englishmen and colonists, for it drew in countless Native Americans as well. It could hardly have been otherwise, for the lives of all three peoples had been intimately connected since the first white settlements more than a century and a half before.

By the time of the Revolution, the coastal tribes were mostly gone, victims of white settlement and the ravages of European diseases. Between the Appalachian Mountains and the Mississippi River, however, powerful tribes remained. The Iroquois Six Nations, formed into a confederation numbering 15,000 people, controlled the area from Albany, New York, to the Ohio country and dominated the "western" tribes of the Ohio valley — the Shawnee, Delaware, Wyandotte, and Miami. In the Southeast, five tribes — the Choctaw, Chickasaw, Seminole, Creek, and Cherokee, together numbering 60,000 people, occupied the interior.

When the Revolutionary War began, British and American officials urged neutrality on the Indians. But by the spring of 1776, both sides were actively seeking Indian alliances. Recognizing their immense stake in the Anglo-colonial conflict, Native Americans up and down the interior debated their options. Alarmed by the westward advance of white settlement and eager to take advantage of the colonists' troubles, a band of Cherokee, led by the warrior Dragging Canoe, launched a series of raids in July 1776 against white settlements in what is today eastern Tennessee. In a quick and devastating response, the Virginia and Carolina militias laid waste a group of Cherokee towns.

During the winter of 1780–1781, American militias again attacked the Cherokees. Though the Cherokees raided sporadically throughout the war, they never again mounted a sustained military effort against the patriots. Seeing what had become of their neighbors, the Creek stayed aloof. Their time for resistance would come decades later, when white settlers began to push aggressively onto their lands.

The Devastation of the Iroquois

To the northeast, a similar but even more deadly scenario unfolded. A council of the Iroquois Six Nations at first opted for neutrality, but as the war spread throughout the Northeast and American troops raided deep into Mohawk territory west of Albany in the summer of 1777, most of the Iroquois abandoned neutrality and joined the struggle against the Americans. They did so at the urging of Joseph Brant, a Mohawk warrior who had visited England several years before and argued England's value as an ally against American expansion.

It was a fateful decision for Indians and whites alike. Over the next several years, the Iroquois and their English allies devastated large areas in central New York and Pennsylvania. The Americans' revenge came swiftly. During

Mohawk chief Joseph Brant (Tayadaneega) played a major role in the Iroquois's decision to enter the war on the side of Britain.

the summer of 1779, General John Sullivan led a series of raids into Iroquois country, burning the Iroquois villages, killing men, women, and children, and destroying fields of corn. The Iroquois recovered sufficiently to conduct punishing counter-raids during the final years of the war, but their losses in human lives and property were great.

At the peace talks that ended the Revolutionary War, the British entirely ignored the interests of their Indian allies. They received neither compensation for their losses nor any guarantees of their land, for the boundary of the United States was set far to the west, at the Mississippi River.

Negotiating Peace

In September 1781, formal peace negotiations began in Paris between the British commissioner and the American emissaries, Benjamin Frank-

lin, John Adams, and John Jay. The negotiations were complicated by the fact that several European countries, seeking opportunity to weaken Great Britain, had become involved. France had entered the war in February 1778. Eight months later, Spain declared war on England, though it declined to recognize American independence. Between 1780 and 1782, Russia, the Netherlands, and six other European countries joined in a League of Armed Neutrality aimed at protecting their maritime trade against British efforts to control it. America's Revolutionary War had quickly become internationalized.

Dependent on French economic and military support, the Congress instructed the American commissioners to follow the advice of Vergennes, the French foreign minister. As the treaty talks began, the Americans learned to their distress that Vergennes was prepared to let the exhausting war continue in order to weaken England further and tighten America's dependence on France.

In the end, the American commissioners ignored their instructions and, without a word to Vergennes, arranged a provisional peace agreement with the British emissaries. In the Treaty of Paris, signed in September 1783, England agreed to recognize American independence. Moreover, Britain promised that U.S. fishermen would have the "right" to fish the waters off Newfoundland and that British forces would evacuate American territory "with all convenient speed" once hostilities had ceased. In return, the Congress agreed to recommend that the states restore the rights and property of the Loyalists. Both sides agreed that prewar debts owed the citizens of one country by the citizens of the other would remain valid. Each of these issues would trouble Anglo-American relations in the decades ahead, but for the moment it seemed a splendid outcome to a long and difficult struggle.

The Ingredients of Victory

How were the weak and disunited American states able to defeat Great Britain, the most powerful nation in the Atlantic world? Certainly the

Dutch and French loans, war supplies, and military forces were crucially important. More decisive, though, was the American people's determination not to submit. Often the Americans were disorganized and uncooperative. As the war progressed, however, the people's estrangement from England and their commitment to the "glorious cause" increased. To subdue the colonies, England would have had to occupy the entire eastern third of the continent, and that it could not do.

The American victory also owed much to the administrative and organizational talents of Washington. Against massive odds, he held the continental army together, often by the sheer force of his will. Had he failed, the Americans could not possibly have defeated the British.

In the end, however, it is as accurate to say that Britain lost the war as that the United States won it. With vast economic and military resources, Britain enjoyed clear military superiority over the American states, and, until the closing months of the contest, naval superiority as well.

Britain had difficulty, however, extending its command structures and supply routes across several thousand miles of ocean. Because information flowed erratically back and forth across the water, strategic decisions made in London were often based on faulty or outdated intelligence. Given the difficulties of supply over such distances, British troops often had to live off the land. This reduced their mobility and antagonized the Americans whose crops and animals they commandeered. Faced with these circumstances, British leaders were often overly cautious.

British commanders also generally failed to adapt their battlefield tactics to the realities of the American war. They continued to fight in the European style, during specified times of the year and using set formations of troops deployed in formal battlefield maneuvers. Much of the American terrain, however, was rough and wooded and thus better suited to the use of smaller units and irregular troops. Washington and Greene were more flexible, often employing a patient strategy of raiding, harassment, and strategic retreat. Over time the costs of continuing the war became greater than the British government could bear. As a much later American war in Vietnam would also reveal, a guerrilla force can win if it does not lose ; a regular army loses if it does not consistently win.

The Experience of War

In terms of loss of life and destruction of property, the Revolutionary War pales by comparison with America's more recent wars. How destructive, we might ask, could a war have been in which Benjamin Franklin urged the widespread use of bows and arrows? "Nothing terrifies enemies more," Franklin explained, "than the deadly silent flight of a volley of arrows."Yet modern comparisons are misleading, for the War for American Independence was terrifying to the people caught up in it and destructive of lives and property.

Recruiting an Army

Estimates vary, but on the American side as many as 250,000 men may at one time or another have borne arms. That would amount to about one out of every two or three adult males.

Tens of thousands served in the state militias. At the time of independence, however, the militia in most of the states was not an effective fighting force. This was especially true in the South, where Nathanael Greene complained that the men came "from home with all the tender feelings of domestic life" and were not "sufficiently fortified . . . to stand the shocking scenes of war, to march over dead men, [or] to hear without concern the groans of the wounded."

The militia did serve as a convenient recruiting system. Given its grounding in local community life, it also served to secure people's commitment to the Revolutionary cause. What better way to separate the Patriots (those who supported the cause of independence) from the Loyalists (those who supported England) than by mustering the local militia company and seeing who turned out?

During the first year of the war, when enthusiasm ran high, men of all ranks — rich and middle-class as well as poor — volunteered to fight the British. But as the war progressed, it gradually became a battle by conscripts. Eventually it was transformed, as wars so often are, into a poor man's fight. Middle- and upper-class men increasingly hired substitutes to replace them, and communities filled their militia quotas with strangers lured by the promise of enlistment bonuses. This social transformation was even more evident in the continental army, where terms were longer, discipline stiffer, and battlefields more distant from the soldiers' homes.

For the poor and the jobless, whose ranks the war rapidly expanded, bonus payments and the promise of board and keep proved attractive. But often the bonuses failed to materialize, and pay was long overdue. Moreover, life in the camps was harsh, and soldiers frequently heard from their wives about their families' distress at home. Faced with such trials, soldiers often became disgruntled and insubordinate. As the war progressed, Washington imposed harsher discipline on the continental troops in an effort to hold them in line.

Throughout the war, soldiers suffered from severe shortages of supplies. At Valley Forge during the terrible winter of 1777–1778, men hobbled about without shoes or coats. "I am sick, discontented, and out of humour," declared one despairing soul. "Poor food, hard lodging, cold weather, fatigue, nasty cloathes, nasty cookery, vomit half my time, smoked out of my senses. The Devil's in't, I can't Endure it. Why are we sent here to starve and freeze?"

The states possessed food and clothing enough but were often reluctant to strip their own people of wagons and livestock, blankets and shoes for use elsewhere. Moreover, mismanagement and difficulties in transportation stood in the way. Wagon transport was slow and costly, and the presence of the British fleet made water transportation along the coast perilous. Though many individuals served honorably as supply officers, others took advantage of the army's distress. Washington commented bitterly on the "speculators, various tribes of money makers, and stock-jobbers of all denominations" whose "avarice and thirst for gain" threatened the country's ruin.

The Casualties of Combat

Medical treatment, whether for wounds or diseases such as smallpox, dysentery, and typhus that raged through the camps, did little to help. Casualties poured into hospitals, overcrowding them beyond capacity. Dr. Jonathan Potts, the attending physician at Fort George in New York, reported that "we have at present upwards of one thousand sick crowded into sheds & labouring under the various and cruel disorders of dysentaries, bilious putrid fevers and the effects of a confluent smallpox: to attend to this large number we have four seniors and four mates, exclusive of myself."

Surgeons, operating without anesthetics and with the crudest of instruments, as readily threatened life as preserved it. Doctoring consisted mostly of bleeding, blistering, vomiting, and laxatives. Mercury, a highly toxic chemical, was a commonly administered drug.

How many soldiers actually died we do not know, but the most conservative estimate runs to over 25,000, a higher percentage of the total population than for any other American conflict except the Civil War. About 12 percent of American soldiers died of wounds or disease, a rate virtually the equivalent of the Civil War and higher than any of America's other conflicts.

The death that soldiers dispensed to each other on the battlefield was intensely personal. Because the effective range of muskets was little more than 100 yards, combat was typically at close quarters. According to eighteenth-century military conventions, armies formed on the battlefield in ranks and fired in unison. After massed volleys, the lines often closed for hand-to-hand combat with knives and bayonets. The partisan warfare in the South, with its emphasis on ambush and small group actions, shocked British officers used to more distanced and dispassionate styles of warfare. One attributed to the American troops "a sort of implacable ardor and revenge."

The Americans' fervor in battle may be explained by the fact that this was in part a civil war. As many as 50,000 colonists fought for the king and engaged in some of the war's bitterest encounters. They figured importantly in Burgoyne's invasion from Canada and in the attacks on Savannah and Charleston. Benedict Arnold led a force of Loyalists on raids through the Connecticut and James river valleys, and Loyalist militia joined Indian allies in destructive sweeps through the Carolina backcountry. Throughout America, communities and families were divided against each other. The war's violent temper reflected this civil conflict.

Moreover, the war was fought in the midst of American society. Soldiers often found themselves fighting for the survival of their family and community. Finally, Americans believed fervently in the Revolutionary cause. The struggle, as they understood it, was for their own liberty. In such a crusade, against such a foe, nothing was to be spared that might bring victory.

Civilians and the War

Noncombatants also suffered, most of all in the densely settled areas along the coast, where England focused its military efforts. At one time or another, British troops occupied every major port — Boston, New York, Philadelphia, Charleston, and Savannah. The resulting disruptions of urban life were profound.

The chaos in New York was typical. In September 1776, a fire consumed 500 houses, nearly a quarter of the city's dwellings. About half the town's inhabitants fled when the British occupation began and were replaced by an al-most equal number of Loyalists who streamed in from the surrounding countryside. Ten thousand British and German troops added to the crowding. The growing numbers of poor erected makeshift shelters of sailcloth and timbers.

In Philadelphia, the occupation was shorter and the disruptions were less severe, but the shock of invasion was no less real. Elizabeth Drinker, living alone after local Patriots had exiled her Quaker husband, found herself the unwilling landlady of a British officer, Major Crammond, and his friends. Constantly anxious, she confided to her journal that "I often feel afraid to go to Bed." During the occupation, British soldiers frequently took what they wanted, tore down fences for their campfires, and confiscated food to supplement their own tedious fare. Even the Loyalists commented on the "dreadful consequences" of occupation.

Along the entire coastal plain, British landing parties descended without warning to capture supplies or terrorize inhabitants. In 1780 and 1781, the British mounted a sustained attack along the Connecticut coast. Over 200 buildings in Fairfield were burned, and much of nearby Norwalk was destroyed.

The southern coast, with its broad rivers, was even more vulnerable. In December 1780, Benedict Arnold ravaged the James River valley, uprooting tobacco, confiscating slaves, and creating panic among the white population. Similar devastation befell the coasts of Georgia and the Carolinas. Such punishing attacks sent civilians fleeing into the interior. During the first years of the war, the port cities lost nearly half their population, while inland communities strained to cope with the thousands of migrants who streamed into them.

Not all the traffic was inland, away from the coast. In New York, Pennsylvania, Virginia, and the Carolinas, numerous frontier settlements collapsed in the face of British and Indian assaults. By 1783, the white population along the Mohawk River west of Albany, New York, had declined from 10,000 to 3,500. According to one observer, after nearly five years of warfare in

In September 1776, as American troops fought unsuccessfully for control of New York, nearly a quarter of the city was destroyed by fire. Not until the war ended did reconstruction and cleanup of the ruins begin.

Tryon County, 12,000 farms had been abandoned, 700 buildings burned, hundreds of thousands of bushels of grain destroyed, nearly 400 women widowed, and perhaps 2,000 children orphaned.

Wherever the armies went, they generated a swirl of refugees, who spread vivid tales of the war. This refugee traffic, added to the constant movement of soldiers back and forth between army and civilian life, brought the war home even to people who did not experience it at first hand.

Disease followed the armies like an avenging angel, ravaging civilians and soldiers alike. And wherever they went, the armies lived off the land, commandeering the supplies they needed. During the desperate winter of 1777–1778, in an effort to protect the surrounding population, Washington issued an order prohib-

iting his troops from roaming more than a half mile from camp. In New Jersey, Britain's German mercenaries generated special fears among the citizenry. The Patriot press was filled with lurid stories of attacks on American civilians, especially women.

The Loyalists

None among the American people suffered greater losses than those who remained loyal to the crown. On September 8, 1783, Thomas Danforth, formerly a lawyer from Cambridge, Massachusetts, appeared in London before the King's Commission of Enquiry into the Losses and Services of the American Loyalists. Danforth was there to seek compensation for losses he had suffered at the hands of the American Revolutionaries. He explained that

... now he finds himself near his fortieth year, banished under pain of death, to a distant country, where he has not the most remote family connection ... cut off from his profession — from every hope of importance in life, and in a great degree from social enjoyments.

The commission's response is unknown, but few of the several thousand Loyalists who appeared before it were reimbursed for more than one-third of their losses.

Though no count of the colonists who remained loyal to England can be exact, as many as 80,000 men, women, and children may have departed from the new nation, while several hundred thousand more remained in the United States. These are substantial numbers when set against the total American population, black and white, of about 2.5 million. The incidence of loyalism differed dramatically from region to region. There were fewest Loyalists in New England and most in and around New York City, where British authority was most stable.

Why did so many Americans remain loyal, often at the cost of personal danger and loss? Customs officers, members of the governors' councils, and Anglican clergymen — all appointed to office in the King's name — often remained with the Crown. Loyalism was common as well among groups dependent on British authority — for example, settlers on the Carolina frontier who believed themselves mistreated by the planter elite along the coast; ethnic minorities, such as the Germans in the middle states, who feared domination by the Anglo-American majority; or tenants on some of the large estates along the Hudson River, who had struggled for years with their landlords over the terms of their leaseholds.

For many Loyalists, the prospect of confronting English military power proved sufficiently daunting. Others doubted the ability of a new, weak nation to survive in an Atlantic world dominated by competing empires, even if independence could be won.

William Eddis wondered what kind of society independence would bring when Revolu-

tionary crowds showed no respect for the rights of Loyalist dissenters such as he. "If I differ in opinion from the multitude," he asked, "must I therefore be deprived of my character, and the confidence of my fellow-citizens; when in every station of life I discharge my duty with fidelity and honour?"

Whatever their motives, the Loyalists believed themselves advocates of reason and the rule of law in the midst of revolutionary passion. Tens of thousands of Americans believed strongly enough in their position to sacrifice home, community, and personal safety on its behalf.

Many who faced exile successfully established new lives in other parts of the empire. The majority settled in the Maritime Provinces of Canada. But even under the best of circumstances, forced resettlement was traumatic.

Loyalists came from all social classes but were most numerous among the upper and middle ranks of society, where individuals were most likely to have direct political and social connections with English officials and to fear the social consequences of revolution. Given their adherence to monarchical government and its values of hierarchy and subordination, their loss weakened the forces of social conservatism in America and facilitated the progress of revolutionary reform.

Blacks and the Revolution

American blacks were deeply involved in the Revolution. Once the war was under way, they found a variety of ways to turn events to their own advantage. For some, this meant applying Revolutionary principles to their own lives and calling for their personal freedom. For others, it meant seeking liberty behind English lines or in the continent's interior.

During the pre-Revolutionary decade, as their white masters talked excitedly about liberty, increasing numbers of black Americans questioned their own oppression. In the North, some slaves petitioned legislatures to set them free. In the South, pockets of insurrection appeared. In 1765, more than 100 South Carolina slaves fled to the interior, where they tried to establish a colony of their own. The next year, slaves paraded through the streets of Charleston, chanting, "Liberty, liberty!"

In November 1775, Lord Dunmore issued a proclamation offering freedom to all Virginia slaves and servants, "able and willing to bear arms," who would leave their masters and join the British forces in Norfolk. Within weeks, 500 to 600 slaves had responded. Among them was Thomas Peters, from Wilmington, North Carolina.

Kidnapped from the Yoruba tribe in what is now Nigeria and brought to America by a French slave trader, Peters had been first purchased in Louisiana about 1760. He resisted enslavement so fiercely that his master sold him into the English colonies. By 1770, Peters belonged to William Campbell, an immigrant Scots planter on North Carolina's Cape Fear River, where he toiled while the storm brewed between England and the colonies. Four months after Dunmore issued his dramatic proclamation, Thomas Peters escaped and joined the British-officered Black Pioneers.

How many American blacks such as Peters sought liberty behind British lines is unknown, but as many as 20 percent may have done so. In contrast to their white masters, blacks saw in England the promise of freedom, not tyranny. From the Virginia slaves who responded to Dunmore's proclamation, a regiment of black soldiers was formed and marched into battle, their chests covered with sashes on which was emblazoned "Liberty to Slaves." At the war's end, several thousand former slaves were evacuated with the British to Nova Scotia, where they established their own settlements. Their reception by the white inhabitants there, however, was generally hostile. By the end of the century, most had left Canada to found the free black colony of Sierra Leone on the west coast of Africa. Thomas Peters was a leader among them.

During the Revolutionary War, James Armistead Lafayette, a Virginia slave, served as a spy against the British for the French general, Lafayette. In recognition of his service, the Virginia General Assembly granted him his freedom in 1786.

Many of the slaves who fled behind English lines never won their freedom. In keeping with the terms of the peace treaty, hundreds were returned to their American owners. Several thousand others were transported to the West Indies and the harsher slavery of the sugar plantations.

Other blacks took advantage of the war's confusion to drift away in pursuit of a new life. Some sought refuge among the Indians. The Seminoles of Georgia and Florida generally welcomed them. Their reception by the Cherokees and Creeks, however, was more uncertain. Some were taken in, but others were returned to their white owners in return for bounties, while still others were held in slavelike conditions by new Indian masters. Numerous blacks made their way north, following rumors that slavery had been abolished there. Whatever their destination, thousands of American blacks acted to throw off the bonds of slavery.

Fewer blacks fought on the American side than on England's, because the Americans were not eager to see blacks armed. Of the blacks who served the Patriot cause, many received the freedom they were promised. The patriotism of countless others, however, went unrewarded.

The Revolution and the Economy

The Revolutionary War altered people's lives in ways that reached beyond the sights and sounds of battle. Before the war was over, major sectors of the American economy fell into disarray. The colonial economies had developed within England's imperial system. Independence broke those historic ties, leaving the new nation to face the daunting challenge of surviving on its own.

The American people experienced the economic shocks of warfare as well — destruction of property, loss of human life, diversion of productive labor into the army, rampant inflation, and collapse of the monetary system. No other American war has been more economically disruptive.

The Interruption of Trade

Waterborne commerce had long been the lifeblood of the colonial economy. It carried away America's agricultural exports and brought back manufactured goods, while providing jobs for sailors and ship captains, carpenters and sailmakers, lumbermen and provisioners. During the imperial crisis, nonimportation had temporarily interrupted this trade. Independence and the war halted it.

Gone after 1776 were the familiar overseas markets in England and the British West Indies for such staple exports as New England fish, Pennsylvania wheat, and Chesapeake tobacco. Gone were most of the English manufactured goods that had dominated American imports. Gone were the business connections with English bankers, wholesalers, and insurance brokers who had supported American commerce. Gone as well was the protection of the British fleet, for it was now the enemy blockading the coast, attacking coastal towns, and sweeping American merchantmen from the sea.

A certain amount of trade with England actually continued during the war, because Ameri-

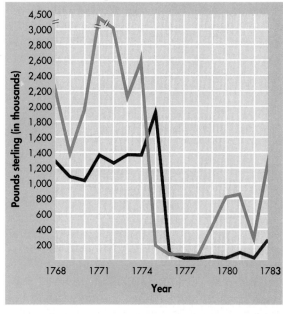

Exports and Imports 1768-1783

Imports   Exports

Source: U.S. Bureau of the Census.

can buyers could always be found for English goods. For some merchants, this illicit trade proved highly profitable. In addition, some merchants and ship captains found profit in privateering, the chartering of private vessels by state or Congress to prey on English merchantmen. Elias Derby of Salem, Massachusetts, became one of New England's richest merchants in this way. The risks, however, were high, and the majority of ventures did not return a profit.

Up and down the coast, communities whose livelihoods depended on the sea felt the war's impact. New England's fishing industry was decimated. As a consequence, countless laborers and artisans, sailors and dock-workers were cut adrift.

Boom and Depression in Agriculture

The majority of Americans worked the land for their living. Independence and the war also wreaked havoc on their lives. No area was harder hit than the Chesapeake. With the loss of English markets, tobacco production dropped precipitously, and a deep depression settled over the region. Not until 1790 would tobacco exports regain their prewar level. South Carolina's rice continued to command a good price in Europe when it could be slipped through the British blockade. The production of indigo, however, the state's second most valuable export commodity, virtually ceased. To the north, Pennsylvania and New England farmers staggered under the loss of their overseas trade.

Armies and navies have to eat, of course. British and French as well as American troops sharply increased the demand for agricultural produce. As a consequence, farmers often prospered while the armies were nearby. As the war went on, however, farmers often received payment in continental dollars that depreciated before they could be spent, or in other kinds of governmental IOUs that carried only the most distant prospect of redemption. When things got truly difficult, military commanders simply seized the corn, hay, livestock, and wagons they needed.

Agricultural productivity declined as well. The cost of agricultural labor escalated as men were called into the army and as large numbers of southern slaves slipped behind British lines or ran away. During the war, crop acreage decreased.

Farm women increased their already essential contributions to family incomes by making shirts, blankets, and other goods. In spite of their best efforts, however, the average real worth per farm, as measured by the combined value of farm implements, livestock, and crops, also declined. For agriculturalists everywhere, independence and the war took a heavy toll.

Manufacturing and Wartime Profits

The war's impact on American manufacturing was uneven. New England shipbuilding was hardest hit. On the eve of independence, New England's booming shipyards had constructed nearly half the merchant tonnage carrying cargo within England's Atlantic empire. During the war, shipbuilding virtually ceased. For the ropemakers, shipwrights, blacksmiths, and sailors in towns like Boston and Newburyport, Massachusetts, the results were disastrous.

At the same time, the war stimulated other manufactures. With British goods excluded, American producers moved to take up the slack. Wearing homespun signified commitment to the Revolutionary cause. Women spun more thread, wove more cloth, and fashioned it into clothing appropriate for republican citizens.

It was hard to increase production, however, for artisans and craftsmen fabricated virtually everything by hand. In Pennsylvania, skilled gunsmiths could produce no more than 50 muskets a year, for each part had to be made and fitted individually.

There were, of course, profits to be made, especially by opportunistic merchants with the right political connections. The largest returns came from government contracting. Too often the search for profits shaded over into outright profiteering. Then as now, the boundaries between individuals' private interests and their public responsibilities were often hazy. Silas Deane capitalized on his position as congressional purchasing agent in France by using public money to arrange lucrative trading ventures of his own. The Congress finally called the unscrupulous Deane to account, but many others acted much the same while charting their courses more carefully.

Robert Morris, an eminent Philadelphia merchant, insisted on his right to continue his private ventures after he became treasurer of the Congress, and the Congress agreed. Explained Morris to one of his associates, "There never has been so fair an oppert'y of making a large fortune since I have been conversant in the world." At the same time, the public benefited immeasurably from Morris's services, for he worked mightily to stabilize congressional finances and at several critical moments committed his own sizable fortune to support the Congress's tottering credit.

When peace returned in 1783, America's manufacturing boom collapsed as the demand for war material dropped and long-excluded English goods again flooded the market, driving the cruder American goods from the stores. American merchants welcomed the renewal of English trade but artisans, who found their livelihoods endangered by English competition, were alarmed.

Financial Chaos

The Revolution left American finances in a state of chaos that would take more than a decade to repair. The war required unprecedented governmental expenditures, and Congress and the states responded by printing money. In the first year of the war, they together issued more than $400 million in various kinds of paper. By war's end, they had pumped additional millions into the economy. The result was a headlong collapse of the currency's value. Congressional bills of credit that in 1776 were pegged against gold at the ratio of 1.5 to 1 had slipped five years later to 147 to 1. State currencies depreciated even more alarmingly.

For countless Americans the flood of depreciated paper proved disastrous. What was one to do when goods and wages had no consistent value, and when even the incentive to work disappeared? James Lovell observed uneasily that "sailors with clubs parade" the streets of Boston "instead of working for paper." In Boston, a crowd of women, angered by the escalating costs of food and other necessities, tossed a merchant suspected of monopolizing commodities into a cart and dragged him through the city's streets while "a large concourse of men stood amazed."

With property values in disarray, it seemed at times as if the very foundations of society were coming unhinged. John Witherspoon remarked to a friend that his son-in-law had sold his furniture before leaving Virginia to come to Philadelphia. The continental bills of credit that he received for it soon depreciated to nothing. His loss was virtually complete.

The poor suffered most, but farmers and merchants, planters and artisans also faced increasing debt and uncertainty. Rarely has the American economy been in such disarray as at the nation's founding.

The Ferment of Revolutionary Politics

The Revolution also transformed the content of American political thought, patterns of political behavior, and the structure and operations of government. The result was a new political order independent of British authority, struggling to define the republican principles on which it was based and driven by the clash of social and economic interests.

Politicizing the People

Under the pressure of Revolutionary events, politics absorbed people's attention and energies as never before. The intense politicization was evident in the flood of printed material that streamed from American presses. Newspapers multiplied in number, and between 1750 and 1783, more than 1,500 pamphlets joined the debate. Declared one contemporary in amazement, "Never ... were [political pamphlets] ... so cheap, so universally diffused, so easy of access." Pulpits rocked with political exhortations as well. Religion and politics had never been sharply separated in colonial America, but the Revolution drew them more tightly together. Some believed that God intended America as the place of Christ's Second Coming and that independence foretold that glorious day. Others thought of America as a New Israel, a covenanted people specially chosen by God to preserve liberty in a threatening world. Samuel Adams called on Bostonians to create a society that would be a "Christian Sparta."

The belief that God sanctioned their Revolution strengthened the resolve of Americans. It also encouraged them to equate national interest with divine intent and thus offered justification for whatever they believed necessary to do. This

In celebration of American independence, Patriots and their slaves toppled the statue of King George III that stood at Bowling Green in New York City.

was not the last time that Americans would make that dangerous equation.

Loyalist Anglican clergy, such as Maryland's Jonathan Boucher, called upon parishioners to support the king as head of the church. During the months preceding independence, as the local Committee of Safety interrupted worship to harass him, Boucher carried a loaded pistol into the pulpit while he preached obedience and submission to royal authority.

Belief in the momentous importance of what they were doing intensified politics for the Revolutionary generation. John Adams, writing to his wife, Abigail, as the Congress moved toward its fateful declaration, exalted independence as "the greatest question . . . which ever was debated in America, and a greater, perhaps, never has nor will be debated among men."

As independence was declared, people in towns and hamlets throughout the land raised

toasts to the great event: "Liberty to those who have the spirit to preserve it." They called themselves the Patriots of '76. Inspired by the searing experience of rebellion, war, and nation building, they believed themselves accountable for the fate of human liberty. Small wonder that they took politics so seriously.

Mobilizing the People

As political life intensified, more voters cast ballots and elections were more frequently contested. Archibald Stuart of Virginia observed disapprovingly that "competition for seats in the House runs higher than ever it did under the old government." In addition, an array of extralegal committees formed, and spontaneous gatherings erupted across the states during the 1770s and 1780s.

Earlier in the imperial crisis, people had frequently gathered "out of doors" to organize protests against measures like the Stamp Act (see Chapter 5). That practice accelerated as people formed committees and held meetings to enforce nonimportation, regulate prices and wages, intimidate Loyalists, levy taxes, administer justice, and, as one individual protested, even direct "what we shall eat, drink, wear, speak, and think" — all on behalf of the Revolution.

More radical republicans celebrated such activity as the most legitimate expression of the popular will. More conservative republicans, however, believed that such behavior threatened political stability. Even Thomas Paine was concerned. "It is time to have done with tarring and feathering," he wrote in 1777. "I never did and never would encourage what may properly be called a mob, when any legal mode of redress can be had."

This dramatic expansion of popular politics resulted naturally from the momentous process of rebellion and war. Artisans, workingmen, and farmers, people formerly on the margins of political life, took seriously all the talk about liberty, natural rights, and government by consent and applied those principles to their own lives, demanding more access to the political process.

The expanded activities of the new state governments also stimulated political participation. The war forced the states to tax and spend on an unprecedented scale, raise troops, control the Tories, regulate prices and wages, establish a stable money supply, and deal with the powerful issues of slavery and the relationship between church and state. It was a large, explosive political agenda that would dominate political debate for years to come.

The Limits of Citizenship

Revolutionary politics, however, was not open to everyone, for republican citizenship excluded blacks and Native Americans.

Most Native Americans lived outside the boundaries of white society and politics. The Revolution did nothing to change that. By the standards of white society, Native Americans continued to be regarded as "uncivilized" and "savage." Moreover, most Native Americans supported England in the great struggle.

The Revolutionary generation admired Native Americans' reputation for bravery and their image as uncorrupted "children of nature." The Indian woman became the earliest model for Columbia, the figure devised to represent the new American republic. However, the tribes occupied interior lands that the American people coveted. Obtaining that land would be easier if Indians could be dealt with as separate, dependent nations and excluded from political life.

Nor did the Revolutionary generation seriously consider incorporating blacks into the political community. Black slaves lacked the most essential attributes of republican citizenship — personal autonomy and political independence. Freedom and liberty, the watchwords of republicanism, had no relevance for people who were legally enslaved.

But what of the growing number of free blacks in the northern states and the Chesapeake area? Unlike Native Americans, most free blacks lived within the boundaries of white society and were subject to the actions of state governments. In Pennsylvania, New York, and North Carolina, blacks did occasionally vote. When the first draft of the Massachusetts constitution explicitly excluded blacks and mulattoes from the vote, Reverend William Gordon voiced his protest "Would it not be ridiculous, inconsistent and unjust to exclude freemen from voting . . . though otherwise qualified, because their skins are black, tawny or reddish? Why not [be] disqualified for being long-nosed, short-faced, or higher or lower than five feet nine?" In the end, Massachusett's constitution made no mention of race, and during the 1780s a few blacks did cast ballots.

If black participation in the North was scattered and temporary, in the South it was altogether absent. Nor could blacks count on such basic rights of citizenship as protection of their persons and property before the law. No matter that most state constitutions explicitly guaranteed such rights. Blacks remained almost entirely without political voice, except in the petitions against slavery and mistreatment that they frequently pressed upon the state regimes.

Republican Women

The boundaries of republican politics were not even broad enough to include all white Americans. Only persons with property could vote. Most states reduced property requirements for the franchise, but nowhere were they abolished altogether.

Even more significant, republican citizenship did not encompass women. Except on scattered occasions, women had neither voted nor held public office during the colonial period. Nor, with rare exceptions, did they do so in Revolutionary America. The New Jersey constitution of 1776 opened the franchise to property-owning women, but the experiment did not last long. Declared one political leader : "It is evident that women, generally, are neither by nature, nor habit, nor education ... fitted to perform this duty with credit to themselves, or advantage to the public." In 1807, the New Jersey assembly passed a bill specifically disenfranchising women. Its author, John Condict, had several years earlier narrowly escaped defeat when a number of women voted for his opponent. In no other state did women even temporarily secure the vote.

Most women did not press for political equality, for the idea flew in the face of long-standing social convention, and its advocacy often exposed a person to public ridicule. Some women did make the case, most often with each other or their husbands. "I cannot say, that I think you are very generous to the ladies," Abigail Adams chided her husband John. "For whilst you are proclaiming peace and good will to men, emancipating all nations, you insist upon retaining an absolute power over all wives."

Prior to independence, most women had accepted the principle that political debate fell outside the feminine sphere, but the Revolution changed that. Women felt the urgency of the Revolutionary crisis as much as men. "How shall

Abigail Adams, like many women of the Revolutionary generation, protested the contradiction in men's subordination of women while they extolled the principles of liberty and equality.

I impose a silence upon myself," wondered Anne Emlen in 1777, "when the subject is so very interesting, so much engrossing conversation — & what every member of the community is more or less concerned in ?" With increasing frequency, women wrote and spoke to each other about public events, especially as they affected their own lives.

As the war progressed, increasing numbers of women ventured their opinions publicly. A few, such as Esther DeBerdt Reed of Philadelphia, published essays explaining women's urgent need to contribute to the Patriot cause. In her 1780 broadside, "The Sentiments of an American Woman," she called on women to renounce "vain ornament" as they had earlier renounced tea and English finery. The money no longer spent on clothing and hairstyles would be "the offering of the Ladies" to Washington's army. In Philadelphia, women responded by collecting $300,000 in continental currency from over 1,600 individuals. Refusing Washington's proposal that the money be mixed with general funds in the national treasury, they insisted on using it to purchase materials for shirts so that each soldier might know he had received a contribution specifically from the women.

In the Revolutionary context, traditional female roles took on new political meanings. With English imports cut off and the army badly in need of clothing, spinning and weaving assumed increased importance. Often coming together as Daughters of Liberty, women made shirts, stockings, and other items of clothing. Charity Clarke, a New York teenager who knitted "stockens" for the soldiers, acknowledged that she "felt Nationaly."

Finally, the most traditional of female roles, the care and nurture of children, also took on political overtones during the Revolutionary era. How could the republic be sustained once independence had been won? Only by a rising generation of republican citizens schooled in the principles of public virtue and ready to assume the task. How would they be prepared? During their earliest years by their republican mothers, the women of the Revolution.

In a variety of ways, women developed new connections with the public realm during the Revolutionary years. Those connections remained limited, for the assumption that politics and government belonged to men did not die easily. But challenges to that assumption would come, and when they did, women found guidance in the principles that the women of the Revolution had helped to define.

Revolutionary Politics in the States

While the struggle for independence continued, revolutionary politics centered in the states, for the state governments were most active in people's lives. The Congress, lacking both authority and the power to govern effectively, and elected indirectly by state legislatures rather than directly by the people, seemed remote and largely irrelevant to most Americans. Not until a new central government began to operate under the national constitution of 1788 would popular politics begin to develop at the national level.

Revolutionary politics took different forms in different states. In Pennsylvania and Vermont, political change ran deep, while in other states, such as Connecticut and Virginia, change was more muted. Everywhere, though, citizens struggled with a bewildering and often intractable array of issues. Defining republican liberty, controlling governmental power, deciding who would share political power, finding a balance between individual liberty and public order— these were the problems with which people wrestled. Nothing revealed more clearly the clash of ideology and interest than the struggle over new state constitutions.

Creating Republican Governments

With their English ties dissolved, the Revolutionaries set about the difficult task of creating new state governments. Connecticut and Rhode Island continued under their colonial charters, simply deleting all references to the British Crown. The other 11 states, however, set their charters aside and started anew. Within two years, all but Massachusetts had completed the task. By 1780, it had done so as well.

The work was not easy, for the American people had no experience with government making on such a scale; they were embroiled in war, and they were sharply divided over the kind of government they wished to create.

Given the promptings of republican theory and their own recent experience with England, the Revolutionary generation began with two overriding concerns: to limit the powers of government and to hold government officials accountable. The only certain way of accomplishing these goals was by creating a fundamental law, in the form of a written constitution, that could serve as a standard for regulating governmental behavior.

In most states, the provincial congresses, extralegal successors to the defunct colonial assemblies, wrote the first constitutions. As the process went along, however, people became increasingly uneasy. Constitutions were intended to define and control government, but if governmental bodies wrote the documents, they could change them as well. If they could do that, what would guarantee against the abuse of governmental power? Some way had to be found of grounding the constitutions directly in the people's sovereign will.

Massachusetts was the first state to perfect the new procedures. In 1779, its citizens formed a special convention for the sole purpose of preparing a new constitution. The convention did its work, and the resulting constitution was returned to the people for ratification.

Through trial and argumentation, the Revolutionary generation worked out a practical understanding of what a constitution was and how it should be developed. In the process, it established some of the most basic doctrines of American constitutionalism: that sovereignty resides in the people; that written constitutions, produced by specially elected conventions and then ratified by the people, embody their sovereign will; and that government functions within constitutional limits. No doctrines have been more important to the preservation of American liberty.

The new state constitutions redefined American government in fundamental and lasting ways. For one thing, the new governments were considerably more democratic than the colonial regimes had been. Most officials were now elected, many of them annually rather than every two or three years as before.

Most of the new constitutions also sharply reduced the governors' powers and increased the powers of the assemblies. Above all, the documents sharply reduced the governors' powers of appointment. "He who has the giving of . . . places in the government," went the common refrain, "will always be master."

The assemblies absorbed most of the powers stripped from the governors. Not only were the assemblies more powerful, but they were larger and more representative as well. Reflecting the spirit of republican reform as well as the demands of farmers and artisans for a larger voice in public affairs, the assemblies grew in size by half or more.

The Revolution also transformed the relationship between rulers and ruled. Inspired by republican beliefs and concerned increasingly about governmental power, people came to view their representatives not as independent agents acting on their behalf but as direct extensions of the people's will. Vigilance, even outright suspicion of officials' behavior, became the hallmark of the true republican.

Different Paths to the Republican Goal

Constitution making generated considerable controversy, for there was strong disagreement about how democratic the new governments should be. In Pennsylvania, a coalition of western farmers, Philadelphia artisans, and radical leaders such as Thomas Paine, Timothy Matlack, and Thomas Young pushed through the most democratic state constitution of all. Drafted less than three months after independence, during the most intense period of republican reform, it rejected the familiar English model of two legislative houses and an independent executive. Instead, the constitution provided for a single, all-powerful legislative house, its members annually elected, its debates open to the public. There was to be no governor. Legislative committees would assume executive duties. A truly radical assumption underlay this design: that only the "common interest of society" and not "separate and jarring private interests" should be represented in public affairs. Property-holding requirements for public office were abolished, and the franchise was opened to every male over 21 who paid taxes. The bill of rights introducing the document guaranteed every citizen religious freedom, trial by jury, and freedom of speech.

The most radical proposal of all called for the redistribution of property within the state, a step described as essential to preserving republican liberty. This was narrowly defeated.

Debate over the constitution divided the state deeply. Men of wealth led the opposition, but in 1776, the radicals had their way. The Pennsylvania constitution — together with its counterparts in Vermont and Georgia — represented the most radical thrust of Revolutionary republicanism. Its guiding principle, declared Thomas Young, one of the constitution's most ardent supporters, was that "the people at large [are] the true proprietors of governmental power." The struggle for control of the Revolution in Pennsylvania was not over, for in 1790 a new and more moderate constitution would be approved. For the moment, however, the lines of political power had been decisively redrawn in Pennsylvania.

In Massachusetts, constitution making followed a more cautious course. There, the disruptions of the war were less severe and the continuity of political leadership was much greater. The main architect of the constitution, John Adams, readily admitted that the new government must be firmly grounded in the people. No principle was more fundamental to America's new republican faith. Yet Adams saw danger in reckless experimentation. A balance between two legislative houses and an independent executive was essential to preserve liberty, he believed, for "power must be opposed to power, force to force, . . . interest to interest, . . . and passion to passion."

Adams thought that society was inescapably divided between "democratic" and "aristocratic" forces. Believing that each was dangerous if dominant, he sought to isolate them in separate legislative houses where they could guard against each other. The lower house or assembly, he explained, should be "an exact portrait, in miniature" of the people ; it should "think, feel, act, and reason" like them. The senate, by contrast, should constitute a "natural aristocracy" of wealth, talent, and good sense. Following Adams's advice, the Massachusetts convention provided for a popular, annually elected assembly and a senate apportioned according to the

amount of taxes paid in special senatorial districts. The Massachusetts constitution also provided for an independent governor with the power to veto legislation, make appointments, serve as commander in chief of the militia, and oversee state expenditures.

On March 2, 1780, the convention sent the document to the town meetings for approval. Farmers of the interior and artisans in Boston attacked it as too "aristocratic," too much like the old colonial regime. The citizens of Richmond feared that the property requirement for the franchise would "exclude many good members of society." Despite these and other objections, when the convention reconvened in June 1780, it declared the constitution approved, and the document went into effect four months later.

Separating Church and State

Another issue generating political controversy was the explosive question of the proper relationship between church and state in a republican order. In most of the colonies prior to the Revolution, one religious group had enjoyed the benefits of endorsement by the government and public tax support for its clergy. At the time of independence, however, "dissenting" groups such as the Methodists and the Baptists were growing in numbers, especially among the lower classes of city and countryside and were grudgingly tolerated by colonial authorities.

With independence, pressure built for severing church and state completely. Even before independence, Rhode Island, New Jersey, Pennsylvania, and Delaware had established full religious liberty. In five additional states, the Anglican church collapsed when English support was withdrawn.

In Massachusetts, Connecticut, and New Hampshire, the Congregationalists fought to retain their long-established privileges. Isaac Backus, the most outspoken of the New England Baptists, protested that "many, who are filling the nation with the cry of *liberty* and against oppressors are at the same time themselves violating that dearest of all rights, *liberty of conscience.*"

Massachusetts's new constitution guaranteed everyone the right to worship God "in the manner and season most agreeable to the dictates of his own conscience." But as Backus pointed out, it also empowered the legislature to require towns to lay taxes for "the public worship of *God*, and for the support and maintenance of public protestant teachers of piety, religion, and morality." During the decades following independence, New England's Congregational establishment continued to weaken. But not until the early nineteenth century — in Massachusetts not until 1833 — were the laws linking church and state finally repealed.

In Virginia, the Baptists pressed their cause against the Protestant Episcopal church, successor to the Church of England. In 1786, the adoption of Thomas Jefferson's Bill for Establishing Religious Freedom, rejecting all connections between church and state and removing all religious tests for public office, finally settled the issue. Three years later, that statute served as a model for the First Amendment to the new federal Constitution.

Legal disestablishment did not end religious discrimination. But it did implant firmly the principle of religious liberty in American constitutional law.

Loyalists and the Public Safety

Emotions ran high between Patriots and Loyalists in Revolutionary America. "The rage of civil discord," lamented one individual, "hath advanced among us with an astonishing rapidity. The son is armed against the father, the brother against the brother, family against family." The security, perhaps the very survival, of the republic required stern measures against counterrevolutionaries. Security, however, was not the only motive at work, for the Patriots were also determined to exact revenge on those whose "disloyalty" threatened the Revolutionary cause.

During the war, each of the states passed a series of laws designed to deprive Loyalists of the vote, confiscate their property, and banish them from their homes. In 1776, the Connecticut assembly passed a remarkably punitive law threatening anyone who criticized either the assembly or the Continental Congress with immediate fine and imprisonment. Probably not more than a few dozen Tories died at the hands of the Revolutionary regimes, but many others died in combat, and thousands found their livelihoods destroyed, their families ostracized, and themselves subject to physical attack.

Punishing Loyalists — or persons accused of loyalism — was a popular activity, especially since Loyalists were most numerous among the upper classes. Yet many of the more conservative Patriots wondered how safe their property was if others' property could be confiscated and sold.

Caught up in the Revolution's turmoil, many argued that the Loyalists had put themselves outside the protection of American law. Others worried about the implications of setting aside the protections of the law, even for Loyalists. Republics, after all, were supposed to be "governments of law, and not of men." Once that distinction disappeared, no one would be safe.

After the war ended and passions cooled, most states repealed their anti-Tory legislation. In the midst of the Revolution, however, no issue raised more clearly the troubling question of how to balance individual liberty against the needs of public security.

Slavery Under Attack

The place of human slavery in a republican society also vexed the Revolutionary generation. During the several decades preceding the imperial crisis, the trade in human chattels had flourished. Though several northern colonies abolished the slave trade, the 1760s witnessed the largest importations of slaves in colonial history.

The Revolution halted that trade almost completely. Once the war ended, southern planters sought to replace their lost slaves. But revolutionary principles, a reduced need for fieldhands in the depressed tobacco economy, continuing natural increase in the slave population, and post-Revolutionary anxiety over black rebelliousness argued for the slave trade's extinction. By 1790, every state except South Carolina and Georgia had outlawed slave importations.

Termination of the slave trade reduced the infusion of new Africans into the black population. This meant that over time an ever higher proportion of blacks were American-born, thus speeding the process of cultural transformation by which Africans became African Americans.

The institution of slavery itself also came under attack during the Revolutionary era. Public criticism of slavery began even before independence. As the crisis with England heated up, catchwords such as *liberty* and *tyranny*, employed by colonists protesting British policies, reminded citizens that one-fifth of the colonial population was in chains. Samuel Hopkins, a New England clergyman, chided his compatriots for "making a vain parade of being advocates for the liberties of mankind, while . . . you at the same time are continuing this lawless, cruel, inhuman, and abominable practice of enslaving your fellow creatures." Independence brought intensified attacks.

In South Carolina and Georgia, where blacks outnumbered whites more than two to one, slavery escaped significant challenge. In Virginia and Maryland, by contrast, whites argued openly over slavery's incompatibility with republicanism, and change did occur. The depression in the tobacco economy made the debate easier. Though neither state abolished slavery, both passed laws making it easier for owners to free their slaves. Moreover, increasing numbers of blacks petitioned for their own freedom, purchased it from their masters, or simply fled. By 1800, more than one of every ten blacks in the Chesapeake region was free, a dramatic increase over 30 years before. For many blacks in the Chesapeake region, the conditions of life slowly changed for the better.

The most dramatic breakthroughs occurred in the North. There slavery was either abolished or put on the road to extinction. Abolition was easier in the North because there were fewer slaves. In most areas, they constituted no more than 4 percent of the population.

Northern blacks joined in the attack on slavery. Following independence, they frequently petitioned state assemblies for their freedom. "Every Principle from which America has acted in the course of their unhappy difficulties with Great Britain," declared one group of Philadelphia blacks, "pleads stronger than a thousand arguments in favor of our petition." In 1780, the Pennsylvania assembly passed a law stipulating that all newborn blacks were to be free when they reached age 28. It was a cautious but decisive step. In the following decades, other northern states adopted similar policies of gradual emancipation.

Freed blacks continued to encounter pervasive discrimination. Still, remarkable progress had been made. Prior to the Revolution, slavery had been an accepted fact of northern life; after the Revolution, it no longer was. In addition, there now existed a coherent and publicly proclaimed antislavery argument, one closely linked in Americans' minds with the nation's founding. The first antislavery organizations had been created as well. Although another half century would pass before antislavery became a force in national political life, the groundwork for slavery's final abolition had been laid.

Politics and the Economy

Revolutionary politics also had to deal with the economic disruptions of independence and war, including price and wage inflation, skyrocketing taxation, and mushrooming private and public debt. Heated debates centered on whether the states' war debts should be funded at face value or at some reduced rate. In support of full value were the states' creditors — merchants and other persons of wealth — who had loaned the states money and had bought up large amounts of securities at deep discounts. Opposed were common folk, angered at the large profits often reaped by these speculators.

The issue of taxation, seared into Americans' consciousness by their troubles with England, generated even more heated controversy. As the costs of the war mounted, so did the tax burden. Taxes, complained one anguished soul in Massachusetts, equaled nearly one-third of the inhabitants' incomes. Massachusetts was not unique.

Farmers, artisans, and others of modest means argued that taxes should be payable in depreciated paper money or government securities rather than only in specie, as some state laws required. Most of them had no gold or silver coin and thus faced the prospect of having their property foreclosed when they could not meet their tax obligations. Government officials protested that to allow payment in depreciated paper was to deprive the governments of badly needed revenue.

In the New York assembly, men of property urged continuing dependence on the poll tax, a uniform assessment levied on all males 16 years of age and older. Working people, however, argued that taxes should be levied on property because that bore some relationship to people's ability to pay. The debate was bitterly contested.

Controversy swirled around the states' efforts to control soaring prices as well. Each state experimented with price controls at one time or another. Seldom were such efforts effective; always they generated political storms.

In general, the poor and those not yet integrated into the market economy supported price controls. Faced with escalating prices, they had difficulty simply making ends meet. They also believed that goods should be sold for a "just price," one deemed fair to buyer and seller alike. In keeping with these principles, a crowd in New Windsor, New York, in 1777 seized a shipment of tea bound for Albany and sold it for what they deemed a fair price.

Merchants, shopkeepers, and others caught up in the commercial economy, however, believed that economic transactions should be controlled by the laws of supply and demand. "It is contrary to the nature of commerce," declared Benjamin Franklin, "for government to interfere in the prices of commodities." Attempts to regulate prices only created a disincentive to labor, which was "the principal part of the wealth of every country."

There were no ready solutions to the problems of debt, taxation, and price control. Thus they continued on the public agenda through the 1780s, heightening political tensions.

CONCLUSION
The Crucible of Revolution

Independence and war redrew the contours of American life and changed the destinies of the American people. Though the Revolutionary War ended in victory, independence had its costs. Lives were lost, property was destroyed, local economies were deranged. The war changed relationships between Indians and whites, for it left the Iroquois and Cherokee severely weakened and opened the floodgates of western expansion. For black Americans, the Revolution had paradoxical results. It produced an ideology that decried slavery of all sorts and marked the first general debate over abolishing the oppressive institution. Yet the Revolutionary generation took steps to eradicate slavery only where it was least important, in the North, while preserving it in the South, where it was most important.

By 1783, a new nation had come into being, a nation based on the doctrines of republican liberty. That was the greatest change of all. The years immediately ahead would determine whether the republican experiment, launched with such hopefulness in 1776, would succeed.

RECOMMENDED READING

Standard accounts of the Revolutionary War can be found in Don Higginbotham, *The War of American Independence* (1971); and Robert Middlekauff, *The Glorious Cause* (1982). Charles Royster, *A Revolutionary People at War* (1979), explains how the continental army embodied the Revolution's social and ideological goals. Jonathan Dull, *A Diplomatic History of the American Revolution* (1985), offers skillful discussion of Revolutionary War diplomacy.

The most vivid description of Native American involvement in the Revolution can be found in Anthony Wallace, *The Death and Rebirth of the Seneca* (1969). James O'Donnell discusses the situation in the Southeast in *Southern Indians in the American Revolution* (1973). Books that deal with the tangled history of slavery, race, and the Revolution include Duncan MacLeod, *Slavery, Race, and the American Revolution* (1974); and Ira Berlin and Ronald Hoffman, eds., *Slavery and Freedom in the Age of the American Revolution* (1983).

Linda Kerber, *Women of the Republic* (1980) examines the Revolutionary experience of women. Robert Calhoon, *The Loyalists in Revolutionary America, 1760–1781* (1973), deals with the experiences of Loyalist Americans. On daily life in the period, see Robert Gross, *The Minutemen and Their World* (1976); Jeffrey Crow and Larry Tise, eds., *The Southern Experience in the American Revolution* (1987); and Barbara Smith, *After the Revolution: The History of Everyday Life in the Eighteenth Century* (1985). Thomas Doerflinger, *A Vigorous Spirit of Enterprise* (1986), describes the Revolution's economic impact on Philadelphia.

For further information about the ideology of Revolutionary republicanism, see Bernard Bailyn, *The Ideological Origins of American Revolution* (1967).

State constitution making is discussed in Gordon Wood, *The Creation of the American Republic, 1776–1787* (1969). On Revolutionary state politics *see* Ronald Hoffman, *A Spirit of Dissension: Economics, Politics and the Revolution in Maryland* (1987); and Eric Foner, *Tom Paine and Revolutionary America* (1976).

Among many readable biographical accounts are Pauline Maier, *The Old Revolutionaries: Political Lives in the Age of Samuel Adams* (1980); Fawn Brodie, *Thomas Jefferson: An Intimate History* (1974); Claude Lopez and Eugenia Herbert, *The Private Franklin: The Man and His Family* (1975); and Marcus Cunliffe, *George Washington: Man and Monument* (1958).

Time Line

1775 Lord Dunmore's proclamation to slaves and servants in Virginia
Iroquois Six Nations pledge neutrality
Continental Congress urges "states" to establish new governments

1776 British evacuate Boston and seize New York City
Declaration of Independence
Eight states draft constitutions
Cherokee raids and American retaliation

1777 British occupy Philadelphia
Most Iroquois join the British
Americans win victory at Saratoga
Washington's army winters at Valley Forge

1778 War shifts to the South
Savannah falls to British
French treaty of alliance and commerce

1779 Massachusetts state constitutional convention
Sullivan destroys Iroquois villages in New York

1780 Massachusetts constitution ratified
Charleston surrenders to British
Pennsylvania begins gradual abolition of slavery

1780s Virginia and Maryland debate abolition of slavery
Destruction of Iroquois Confederacy

1781 Cornwallis surrenders at Yorktown
Articles of Confederation ratified by states

1783 Peace Treaty with England signed in Paris
Massachusetts Supreme Court abolishes slavery
King's Commission on American Loyalists begins work

7

Consolidating the
Revolution

Timothy Bloodworth of New Hanover County, North Carolina, knew what the American Revolution was about, for he had experienced it firsthand. A man of humble origins, Bloodworth had worked hard as an innkeeper and ferry pilot, self-styled preacher and farmer. By the mid-1770s, he owned nine slaves and 4,200 acres of land, considerably more than most of his neighbors.

His unpretentious manner and commitment to political equality earned Bloodworth the confidence of his community. In 1758, at the age of 22, he was elected to the North Carolina colonial assembly. Over the next three decades, he remained deeply involved in North Carolina's political life.

When the colonies' troubles with England drew toward a crisis, Bloodworth spoke ardently of American rights and mobilized support for independence. In 1784, shortly after the war ended, the North Carolina assembly named Bloodworth one of the state's delegates to the Confederation Congress. There he learned for the first time about the problems of governing a new nation. As the Congress struggled through the middle years of the 1780s, Bloodworth shared the growing conviction that the Articles of Confederation were too weak. He supported the Congress's call for a special convention to meet in Philadelphia in May 1787 to address this problem.

Like thousands of Americans, Bloodworth eagerly awaited the convention's work, but he was stunned by the result, for the proposed constitution seemed to him designed not to preserve republican liberty but to endanger it. Once again sniffing political tyranny on the breeze, he resigned his congressional seat in August 1787 and hurried back to North Carolina where, over the next several years, he worked tirelessly to prevent its ratification.

A national government as strong as the one described in the proposed constitution, Bloodworth feared, would gobble up the states and destroy individual liberties. Alarmed by the provisions giving Congress the power of taxation as well as by the absence of explicit guarantees of trial by jury, Bloodworth demanded the addition of a federal bill of rights to protect individual liberties.

Bloodworth also feared the sweeping authority Congress would have "to make all laws which shall be necessary and proper for carrying into execution . . . all other powers vested . . . in the government of the United States." That language, he insisted, threatened the integrity of the states.

In North Carolina, the arguments of Bloodworth and his Anti-Federalist colleagues carried the day. By a vote of 184 to 84, the state ratifying convention declared that a bill of rights "asserting and securing from encroachment the great Principles of civil and religious Liberty, and the unalienable rights of the People" must be approved before North Carolina would concur. Not until November 1789 — well after the new government had gotten under way and Congress had forwarded a national bill of rights to the states for approval — did North Carolina enter the new union.

• • •

As a member of the Confederation Congress, Timothy Bloodworth confronted the continuing vestiges of colonialism — the patronizing attitudes of England and France, their continuing imperial ambitions in North America, and the republic's ongoing economic dependence on Europe. He also observed the Congress's inability to reduce the war debt, open foreign ports to American commerce, and persuade the states to cooperate in solving the new nation's problems.

By 1786, Bloodworth, like countless other Americans, was caught up in the escalating debate between the Federalists, who believed that the Articles of Confederation were fatally deficient, and the Anti-Federalists, committed to retaining America's traditional localism and still deeply impressed by the dangers posed to individual liberties by consolidated power.

That debate came to a focus in the momentous Philadelphia convention of 1787, which produced not reform but revolutionary change in the national government and opened a portentous new chapter in the history of the American people.

Struggling with the Peacetime Agenda

As the war ended, difficult problems of demobilization and adjustment to the conditions of independence troubled the new nation. Whether the Confederation Congress could effectively deal with the problems of the postwar era remained unclear.

Demobilizing the Army

Demobilizing the army presented the Confederation government with some difficult moments, for when the fighting stopped, many of the troops refused to disband and go home until the Congress redressed their grievances. Trouble first arose in January 1783, when officers at the continental army camp in Newburgh, New York, sent a delegation to the Congress to complain about arrears in pay and other promised benefits. The Congress responded by calling for the army to be decommissioned. Almost immediately, an anonymous address circulated among the officers, attacking the "coldness and severity" of the Congress, and hinting darkly at direct action if their grievances were not met. Washington urged the officers not to tarnish the victory they had so recently won. His efforts succeeded, for the officers reaffirmed their confidence in the Congress and agreed to disband.

In June, several hundred disgruntled continental soldiers and Pennsylvania militiamen gathered to express their frustrations in front of Independence Hall, causing Congress to flee to Princeton, New Jersey. Again, the crisis was eventually smoothed over, but the Congress's authority had been seriously challenged. During the mid-1780s, the Congress shuffled between Princeton and Annapolis, Trenton and New York, its transiency visible evidence of its steadily eroding position.

Opening the West

The Congress was not without important accomplishments during the postwar years. Most notable were the two great land ordinances of 1785 and 1787. The first provided for the systematic survey and sale of the region west of New York and Pennsylvania and north of the Ohio River. The area was to be laid out in townships six miles square, which were in turn to be subdivided into lots of 640 acres each. Thus began the rectangular grid pattern of land survey and settlement that to this day characterizes the nation's midwest and distinguishes it so markedly from the irregular settlement patterns of the older colonial areas to the east.

Two years later, the Congress passed the Northwest Ordinance. It provided for the political organization of the same interior region, first with congressionally appointed officials, then with popularly elected assemblies, and ultimately as new states to be incorporated into the Union "on an equal footing with the original states in all respects whatsoever." Together these two pieces of legislation provided the legal mechanism for the nation's dramatic territorial expansion during the nineteenth century.

Despite its success in providing the legal framework for settlement of the trans-Appalachian frontier, however, Congress could neither secure removal of the British troops from the western posts after 1783 nor guarantee free navigation of the Mississippi. Nor could it clear the tribes of the Ohio region out of the white settlers' way.

During the immediate postwar years, the Congress operated as if the Native Americans of the interior were "conquered" peoples. The Treaty of Paris, American officials insisted, gave the United States political sovereignty over the tribes east of the Mississippi as well as ownership of their land.

For a few years the conquest strategy seemed to work. During the mid-1780s, the Congress negotiated several important land treaties with the interior tribes. At the Treaty of Fort Stanwix in 1784, the first congressional treaty with an Indian tribe, the Iroquois Six Nations made peace, ceded much of their land to the United States, and retreated to small reservations where they struggled for survival against disease and poverty, their traditional lifeways gone, their self-confidence broken.

The Iroquois were not the only tribes to lose their land. In January 1785, representatives of the Wyandotte, Chippewa, Delaware, and Ottawa tribes relinquished claim to most of present-day Ohio. The treaties with the Indians, however, were often exacted under the threat of force and generated widespread resentment. At Fort Stanwix, for example, negotiations were held at gunpoint, and hostages were taken to coerce the Indian delegates. Two years later, the Iroquois openly repudiated the treaty, asserting that they were still sovereigns of their own soil and "equally free as . . . any nation under the sun."

The Revolution, moreover, left behind a legacy of bitterness for both Indians and whites: for Indians because they had suffered betrayal and defeat, for white Americans because the Indians had sided with England and thus threatened the success of the Revolutionary cause. This bitterness would trouble Indian-white relations for years to come.

By the mid-1780s, tribal groups both above and below the Ohio River were actively resisting white expansion onto their land. In the summer of 1786, the Creek resumed hostilities in the

Areas of White Settlement and Frontier in 1787

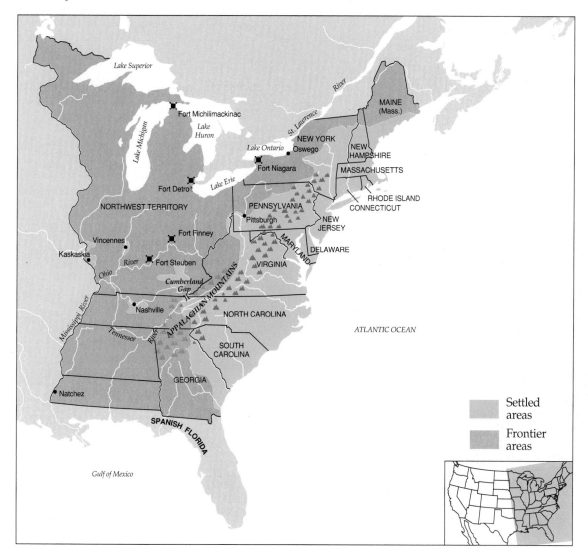

backcountry of Georgia, while north of the Ohio, the Shawnee, Delaware, Wyandotte, and Miami moved to strengthen their Western Confederacy, reject the conquest theory, and prepare for the defense of their common homeland. When white settlers continued to press into the region, Native Americans launched a series of devastating raids, virtually halting white settlement. By 1786, the entire region from the Great Lakes to the Gulf of Mexico was embroiled in warfare. With the continental army disbanded and the nation in no position to raise a new one, there was little that Congress could do.

Settling the interior also involved relations with other nations, and here, too, the Congress proved ineffective. In June 1784, Spain — still in possession of Florida, the Gulf Coast, and the trans-Mississippi West — closed the outlet of the Mississippi River at New Orleans to American shipping. Spain's action raised a storm of pro-

The symbolic figure of Columbia, often presented in the form of an Indian maiden embodying the innocence and freedom of the new republic, first became popular during the Revolution. This began to change as Americans moved west across the Appalachians. By the time this French engraving appeared in the early nineteenth century, Columbia was usually garbed in classical attire and had lost her Indian headdress.

test, especially among settlers in the West, who counted on the interior river system to float their produce downstream to outside markets. Land speculators from Virginia to South Carolina were aroused as well, for closure of the Mississippi would discourage development of the southern backcountry. Rumors spread that Spanish agents were urging backcountry American settlers to break away and seek affiliation with Spain. When Foreign Secretary John Jay offered to relinquish American claims to free transit of the Mississippi in return for a new commercial treaty opening Spanish ports to American shipping, the northern states supported the

bargain. The southern states, however, angry at Jay's betrayal of their interests, refused. Thus stalemated, the Congress could take no action at all.

Wrestling with the National Debt

The Congress's inability to deal effectively with the massive war debt offered further evidence of the Confederation government's weakness. The public debt stood at about $35 million, much of it held abroad by French and Dutch bankers. Not only was the Congress unable to make regular payment against the loan's principal, but it had to borrow additional money abroad simply to pay the accumulating interest.

At home, things were no better. In response to the incessant demands of its creditors, the government could only delay and try to borrow more. Lacking the power to tax, the Congress continued to depend on the states' willingness to honor their obligations. This arrangement proved unworkable. By 1786, total federal revenue amounted to no more than $370,000 a year, not a sufficient amount, as one official lamented, to provide for "the bare maintenance of the federal government [even] on the most economical establishment, and in a time of profound peace."

Not all Americans were alarmed. Some pointed out approvingly that several state governments were beginning to assume responsibility for portions of the national debt. Others saw that as additional evidence of the Congress's weakening condition and wondered how a government unable to maintain its credit could long endure.

Surviving in a Hostile World

The Congress's difficulties in countering Spain's decision to close the Mississippi River to American commerce and in dealing with its creditors overseas pointed to a broader problem in American foreign relations. Even after the United States had formally won independence, England, France, and Spain continued to harbor imperial ambitions in North America. France had lost its North American possessions following the Seven Years' War, but before the century was over, it would gain title to most of the continent west of the Mississippi River. England's Union Jack continued to fly over eastern Canada, while English troops retained possession of strategic outposts on American soil — at Detroit, Michilimackinac, and Niagara. As the Jay-Gardoqui affair made evident, Spain still conjured up grim memories of past New World conquests. The reason for America's diplomatic troubles was clear : The country was new, weak, and republican in a world dominated by monarchical governments and divided into warring empires.

Nothing revealed more starkly the difficulties of national survival than the Congress's largely futile efforts to rebuild America's over-

British and Spanish Possessions in Eastern North America, 1783

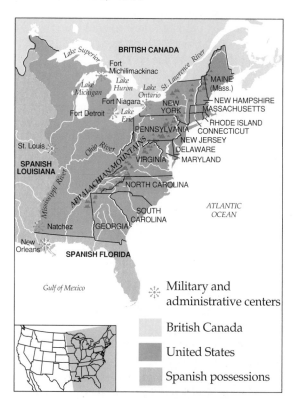

Military and administrative centers

British Canada

United States

Spanish possessions

seas commerce. A flourishing overseas trade, across the Atlantic to markets in England and down the coast to the Caribbean, had been the foundation of colonial economic prosperity. Once the war was over, American traders sought eagerly to rebuild this trade. It proved a difficult task because the Congress could give them little support.

When the war ended, familiar English goods flooded American markets. Few American goods, however, flowed the other way, for English officials could command American markets without needing to grant trade concessions in return. Meanwhile, France and Spain gradually withdrew the special war-time trading privileges they had extended and returned to their policy of mercantile restrictions.

In an effort to rebuild American commerce, the Congress tried to secure the states' cooperation in a program of economic recovery. In 1784, however, it failed to obtain authorization from the states to regulate foreign commerce ; each state wanted to channel its own trade for its own advantage. As a result, the Congress was unable to negotiate satisfactory commercial agreements abroad, and overseas trade continued to languish.

By the late 1780s, the per capita value of American exports had fallen a startling 30 percent from two decades earlier. In an Atlantic world divided into exclusive, imperial trading spheres, the United States stood outside and alone, lacking both the political unity and the economic power to protect its interests.

Political Tumult in the States

As the Confederation Congress struggled to chart the nation's postwar course, controversy again embroiled state politics. Two issues carried over from the Revolutionary agenda came together with particularly explosive force : problems of debt relief and paper money on the one hand, and continuing arguments over political equality and the sharing of political power on the other.

The Limits of Republican Experimentation

In a pattern that would frequently recur in American history, the postwar era witnessed growing social and political conservatism. Popular voting declined, while leadership in the state governments fell increasingly to people convinced that republican experimentation had gone too far, that order had to balance liberty, and that the "better sort" of men, not democratic newcomers, should be in charge. The repeal of anti-Loyalist legislation and the occasional reappearance of Loyalists in public life provided evidence of the changing political climate.

In 1790, Pennsylvania replaced its radical constitution of 1776 with a more conservative document that provided for a strong governor with power to veto legislation and control the militia and a senate intended to balance the more democratic assembly. Gaining a majority in the assembly as early as 1786, the conservatives dismantled much of the radicals' program, repealing the revolutionary test oaths and thus reenfranchising thousands of conservatives, stopping the issuance of paper money, and rechartering the Bank of North America.

Shays's Rebellion

In other states, popular opposition to hard money and high-tax policies, problems still festering from the Revolution, provoked vigorous protest. The controversy that erupted in Massachusetts in 1786 echoed strongly of equal rights and popular consent, staples of the rhetoric of 1776.

The war vastly expanded the burden of debt among Massachusetts' citizens. By the mid-1780s, increasing numbers of people had to borrow money just to pay their taxes or support their families, while others borrowed to speculate in western land or government securities. Because there were no commercial banks in the state, people borrowed from each other in a complicated and vulnerable pyramid of credit and debt.

A crisis began to build shortly after the war's end. As English goods once again flooded the American market, American importers borrowed heavily in England to expand their purchases, which they sold to local retailers at a handsome profit. Some of those profits they loaned back to the retailers so they could sell even more goods. The retailers in turn extended credit to their customers.

In time the flood of English goods glutted the American market and forced prices down. By 1785, a number of English banking houses, heavily overcommitted in the American trade, were in trouble. When they called in their American loans, American merchants in turn tried to collect the debts due them, sending a credit crisis surging through the economy.

The crisis was most acute among the small farmers and laboring people of country and town. Caught in a tightening bind, they turned to their state governments for "stay laws" suspending the collection of private debts. If not granted relief, they faced foreclosure and the loss of shops and farms. They also pressed for new issues of paper money so that they would have something with which to pay both private debts and public taxes.

The largest creditors, however, most of whom lived in commercial areas along the coast, fought these relief proposals, because they wanted to collect sums owed them in hard currency.

By 1786, Massachusetts farmers, made desperate by private debt and a lingering agricultural depression, petitioned the Massachusetts assembly for relief. Peter Wood, tax collector for the town of Marlborough, reported that "there was not . . . the money in possession or at command among the people . . . to discharge taxes." Between 1784 and 1786, fully 29 towns declared themselves unable to meet their tax payments. The farmers' appeals, however, fell on deaf ears, for commercial and creditor interests now controlled the government.

As frustrated citizens had done before and would do again when the law proved unresponsive to their needs, Massachusetts farmers stepped outside the law and took matters into their own hands. A Hampshire County convention of 50 towns condemned the state senate, lawyers, court fees, and the tax system. It advised against violence, but crowds soon began to form.

The county courts drew much of the farmers' wrath because they issued the writs of property foreclosure that state and private creditors demanded. On August 31, 1786, armed men prevented the county court from sitting at Northampton, and on September 5, angry citizens closed down the court at Worcester. When farmers threatened similar actions elsewhere, an alarmed Governor James Bowdoin dispatched 600 militiamen to protect the Supreme Court, then on circuit at Springfield.

About 500 insurgents had gathered near there under the leadership of Daniel Shays, a popular Revolutionary War captain recently fallen on hard times. Most of the men who gathered around Shays were also debtors and veter-

ans. Worried about a possible raid on the federal arsenal at Springfield, the Continental Congress authorized 1,300 troops to be readied for use against Shays and his rebels. For a few weeks, Massachusetts seemed poised on the brink of civil war.

In late November, the insurrection collapsed in eastern Massachusetts, but things were far from over in the west. When several insurgent groups refused to disband at Governor Bowdoin's command, he called out a force of 4,400 men, financed and led by worried eastern merchants. On January 26, 1787, Shays led 1,200 men toward the federal arsenal. Frightened by the siege, its defenders opened fire, killing four of the attackers and sending the Shaysites into retreat.

Over the next several weeks, the militia chased the remnants of Shays's followers across the state and sent Shays himself fleeing into Vermont for safety. By the end of February, the rebellion was over. In March, the legislature par-

An unknown artist provided in 1787 the only contemporary image of General Daniel Shays and Colonel Jacob Shattuck, leaders of the Massachusetts farmers' rebellion against foreclosures and heavy taxes.

doned all but Shays and three other leaders ; in another year, they too had been forgiven.

Similar challenges to public authority, fired by personal troubles and frustration over unresponsive government, erupted in South Carolina in May 1785, in Maryland in June 1786, and in several other states. Across the nation, state politics was in turmoil.

Toward a New National Government

By 1786, belief was spreading among members of the Congress and other political leaders that the nation was in crisis. Attention focused increasingly on the inadequacies of the Articles of Confederation. Within two years, following a raucous political struggle, a new and far more powerful constitution replaced the Articles. That outcome would change forever the course of American history.

The Rise of Federalism

The supporters of a stronger national government called themselves Federalists (leading their opponents to adopt the name Anti-Federalists). Led by men such as Washington, Hamilton, Madison, and Jay, they believed that the nation was in the midst of a social and political crisis that threatened its very survival. Such men had never been comfortable with the more radical impulses of the Revolution. While supporting the principles of moderate republicanism, they continued to believe in an aristocracy of talent and to place high value on social order and the rights of property.

They were now persuaded that social and political change had carried too far. The Revolution, Jay lamented, "laid open a wide field for the operation of ambition," especially for "men raised from low degrees to high stations and rendered giddy by elevation." It was time, he insisted, to find better ways of protecting "the worthy against the licentious." In 1776, American liberty had needed protection against English power. Danger now, however, came from too much liberty threatening to degenerate into license. "We have probably had too good an opinion of human nature," wrote Washington. "Experience has taught us, that men will not adopt and carry into execution measures the best calculated for their own good, without the intervention of a coercive power." In the Federalists' minds, America needed "a strong government, ably administered" by the "better sort."

Congressional inability to handle the national debt, establish public credit, and restore overseas trade also troubled the Federalists. They stressed the need for a new national government capable of extending American trade, spurring economic recovery, and protecting national interests against Anglo-European designs.

Beyond that, the Federalists shared a vision of an expanding commercial republic, its people spreading across the rich lands of the interior, its merchant ships connecting America with the markets of Europe and beyond. That vision, so rich in national promise, seemed also at risk.

The Grand Convention

The first step toward governmental reform came in September 1786, when delegates of five states, who had gathered in Annapolis, Maryland, to discuss interstate commerce, prepared an address to all 13 states. Written by the ardent nationalist Alexander Hamilton, it called for a new convention to gather in Philadelphia in May 1787. In February, the Confederation Congress cautiously endorsed the idea of a convention to revise the Articles of Confederation. Before long, however, it became clear that more dramatic changes were in store.

During May, delegates representing every state except Rhode Island began assembling in Philadelphia. Eventually 55 delegates would participate in the convention's work, though daily attendance was usually between 30 and 40. The city bustled with excitement as they gathered, for the Grand Convention's roster read like an honor roll of the Revolution. From Virginia came the distinguished lawyer George

Mason, chief author of Virginia's trailblazing bill of rights, and the already legendary George Washington. James Madison was there as well. No one, with perhaps the single exception of Alexander Hamilton, was more committed to nationalist reform. Madison brought to Philadelphia his own design for a new national government. That design, presented in the convention as the Virginia Plan, would serve as the basis for the new constitution. Nor did anyone rival the diminutive Madison's contributions to the convention's work. Tirelessly he took the convention floor to argue the nationalist cause or buttonhole wavering delegates to strengthen their resolve. In addition, he somehow found the energy to keep extensive notes in his personal shorthand. Those notes constitute our essential record of the convention's proceedings.

Two distinguished Virginians were conspicuously absent. Thomas Jefferson was abroad serving as minister to France, while the old pa-

James Madison of Virginia worked tirelessly between 1786 and 1788 to replace the Articles of Confederation with a new and more effective national constitution.

triot Patrick Henry, an ardent champion of state supremacy, wanted no part of the convention.

Other distinguished delegates included the venerable Franklin, the erudite lawyer James Wilson and the wealthy Robert Morris from Pennsylvania; Elbridge Gerry and Rufus King from Massachusetts; John Rutledge and Charles Pinckney from South Carolina; and Roger Sherman from Connecticut.

The New York assembly sent a deeply divided delegation that included Alexander Hamilton. Determined to protect New York's autonomy and his own political power, Governor George Clinton saw to it that several Anti-Federalist skeptics also made the trip to Philadelphia. They were no match for Hamilton, whose immense intelligence and ingratiating charm had enabled him to rise rapidly in the world. In 1777, while still in his early twenties, he became Washington's wartime aide-de-camp. That relationship served Hamilton well for the next 20 years. Returning from the war, Hamilton wooed and won the wealthy Elizabeth Schuyler, thereby securing his personal fortune and strengthening his political support. At Philadelphia, he was determined to drive his own nationalist vision ahead.

Meeting in Independence Hall, where the Declaration of Independence had been proclaimed little more than a decade before, the convention elected Washington its presiding officer, adopted rules of procedure, and, after spirited debate, voted to close the doors and conduct the convention's business in secret.

Debate focused first on Madison's Virginia Plan, which outlined a powerful national government and effectively set the convention's agenda. According to its provisions, there would be a bicameral congress, with the lower house elected by the people and the upper house, or senate, elected by the lower house from nominees proposed by the state legislatures. The plan also called for a president to be chosen by the congress, a national judiciary, and a council of revision, whose task was to review the constitutionality of legislation.

This painting by Thomas Rossiter, done in the early nineteenth century, provides an imaginative portrayal of the Philadelphia convention, with George Washington presiding and a rising sun, symbolic of the new nation, in the background.

The smaller states quickly objected to the Virginia Plan's provision for proportional rather than equal representation. On June 15, William Paterson introduced a counterproposal, the New Jersey Plan, which would retain the Articles of Confederation while granting Congress the powers to tax and regulate both foreign and interstate commerce. After three days of heated debate, by a vote of seven states to three, the delegates adopted the Virginia Plan as the basis for further discussions. It was now clear that the convention would set aside the Articles for a much stronger national government. Over the next four months, the convention struggled to shape that new government.

At times it seemed that the Grand Convention would collapse under the weight of its own disagreements and the oppressive summer heat as delegates wrestled over the sharply conflicting interests of large and small states, the balance of power between national and state governments, and the volatile issue of slavery. By early July, with tempers frayed and frustrated over the apparent deadlock, the delegates agreed to recess, ostensibly in recognition of Independence Day but actually to enable Franklin, Roger Sherman, and others to mount a final effort at compromise. All agreed that only a bold stroke could save the convention from collapse.

That stroke came on July 12, as part of what has become known as the Great Compromise. The reassembled delegates agreed that representation in the lower house should be based on the total of each state's white population plus three-fifths of its black population. Though blacks were not accorded citizenship and could not vote, the southern delegates argued that they should be fully counted for this purpose. Delegates from the northern states, where relatively few blacks lived, did not want them counted at all, but the bargain was struck. As part of this compromise, the convention agreed that direct taxes would also be apportioned on the basis of population and that blacks would be counted similarly in that calculation as well. On July 16, the convention accepted the principle that each state should have an equal vote in the senate.

The compromise thus accommodated the interests of both large and small states.

The convention then submitted its work to a committee of detail for drafting in proper constitutional form. That group reported on August 6, and for the next month the delegates hammered out the exact language of the document's seven articles.

Determined to give the new government the stability the state governments lacked, the delegates created an electoral process designed to bring only persons of standing and experience into national office. An electoral college of wise and experienced leaders would meet to choose the president. The process functioned exactly that way during the first several presidential elections.

Selection of the new Senate would be similarly indirect, for its members were to be named by the state legislatures. (Not until 1913, when the Seventeenth Amendment to the Constitution was ratified, would the people elect their senators.) Even the House of Representatives, the only popularly elected branch of the new government, was to be filled with persons of standing and wealth, for the Federalists were confident that only experienced and well-known leaders would be able to attract the necessary votes.

The delegates' final set of compromises touched the fate of black Americans. At the insistence of southerners, the convention agreed that the slave trade would not formally end for another 20 years. The delegates never used the words *slavery* or *slave trade* but spoke more vaguely about not prohibiting "the migration or importation of such persons as any of the states now existing shall think proper to admit." Their meaning, however, was clear.

More than that, they guaranteed slavery's protection, writing in Section 2 of Article 4 of the Constitution: "No person held to service or labour in one state, . . . [and] escaping into another, shall, in consequence of any law . . . therein, be discharged from such service, but shall be delivered up on claim of the party to whom such service or labour may be due." The delegates thus provided federal sanction for the capture and return of runaway slaves. This fugitive slave clause would return to haunt northern consciences in the years ahead, but at the time it seemed a small price to pay for sectional harmony and a new government. Northern accommodation to the demands of the southern delegates was eased, however, by knowledge that southerners in the Confederation Congress had recently agreed to prohibit the entry of new slaves into the Northwest Territory.

The document that emerged from the Philadelphia Convention, then, represented compromises between large states and small, as well as between North and South. Some of those compromises came at the expense of black Americans, who had no voice in the Constitution's drafting or ratification.

The Constitution decisively strengthened the national government, for Congress would now have authority to levy and collect taxes, regulate commerce, devise uniform rules for naturalization, and control the federal district in which it would eventually be located. Conspicuously missing was any statement reserving to the states all powers not explicitly conferred on the central government, which had been a crippling limitation of the Articles. On the contrary, the Constitution contained a number of clauses bestowing general grants of power on the new government. A final measure of the Federalists' determination to make the new government supreme over the states was the assertion in Article 6 that the Constitution and all laws passed under it were to be regarded as "the supreme Law of the Land."

When the convention had finished its business, 3 of the 42 remaining delegates refused to sign the document. The other 39, however, affixed their names and forwarded it to the Confederation Congress along with their request that it be sent on to the states for approval. On September 17, the Grand Convention adjourned.

Federalists versus Anti-Federalists

Ratification presented the Federalists with more difficult problems than they had faced at Philadelphia. Now the debate shifted to the states, where sentiment was sharply divided and the situation was more difficult to control. Recognizing the unlikelihood of gaining quick agreement from all 13 states, the Federalists provided that the Constitution should go into effect when any nine agreed to it. Other states could then enter the Union as they were ready. They arranged for ratification by specially elected conventions rather than the state assemblies, since under the Constitution the assemblies would lose substantial amounts of power. Ratification by convention was also more constitutionally sound, since it would give the new government its own grounding in the people and free it from dependence on the state governments.

Word of the dramatic changes being proposed spread rapidly. In each state, Federalists and Anti-Federalists prepared to debate the new articles of government. Some critics feared that a stronger central government would threaten state interests or their own political power. Others, like Timothy Bloodworth, charged the Federalists with betraying Revolutionary republicanism. Like all "vigorous" and "energetic" governments, they warned, the new one would be corrupted by its own power.

The Anti-Federalists were aghast at the Federalists' vision of an expanding "republican empire." "The idea of . . . [a] republic, on an average of 1000 miles in length, and 800 in breadth, and containing 6 millions of white inhabitants all reduced to the same standards of morals, . . . habits . . . [and] laws," exclaimed one critic incredulously, "is itself an absurdity, and contrary to the whole experience of mankind." Such an attempt would guarantee factional conflict and disorder. Nor did the Anti-Federalists believe that the proposed separation of executive, legislative, and judicial powers or the balancing of state and national governments would prevent power's abuse.

Federalist spokesmen moved quickly to counter the criticism. The Federalists' most important effort was a series of essays penned by James Madison, Alexander Hamilton, and John Jay and published in New York under the pseudonym "Publius." Madison, Hamilton, and Jay moved systematically through the proposed constitution, explaining its virtues and responding to the Anti-Federalists' attacks. In the process, they described a political vision fundamentally different from that of their Anti-Federalist opponents.

Power, the Federalists now argued, was not the enemy of liberty but its guarantor. Nothing was more dangerous than the "mischievous effects of unstable government." Where government was not "energetic" and "efficient" (these were favorite Federalist words), demagogues and disorganizers did their work.

The *Federalist Papers* also countered the Anti-Federalists' warning that a single, extended republic encompassing the country's economic and social diversity would lead inevitably to factional warfare and the end of republican liberty. Factional divisions, they explained, could never be avoided, even in the smallest societies, because they were the inevitable by-products of economic and social development. Faction, moreover, was the necessary accompaniment of human liberty. Wrote Madison in *Federalist* No. 10 : "Liberty is to faction what air is to fire, an aliment without which it instantly expires." To suppress faction would be to destroy liberty itself. Out of the clash and accommodation of social and economic interests would emerge public order and the best possible approximation of the public good.

The Federalists' arguments left the Anti-Federalists sputtering in amazement. What would become of public virtue in a system built on the notion of competing factional interests ? They also accused their opponents of elitism, of wishing to join the government to wealth and privilege. Not all the Antis were democrats, but they were more consistently sympathetic to democratic principles than were their Federalist opponents. Certainly they believed more firmly that for government to be safe, it must be tied intimately to the people.

As the ratification debate revealed, the Federalists and Anti-Federalists held sharply contrasting visions of the new republic. The Antis remained much closer to the original republicanism of 1776, with its suspicion of power and wealth, its emphasis on the primacy of local government, and its fears of centralization. The Federalists, arguing that America's situation had changed dramatically since 1776, embraced the idea of nationhood and looked forward with anticipation to the development of a rising "republican empire" based on commercial development and led by men of wealth and talent. Both Federalists and Anti-Federalists claimed to be heirs of

the Revolution, yet they differed dramatically on what the Revolution had meant.

The Struggle for Ratification

No one knows with certainty what most Americans thought of the proposed constitution. No national plebiscite on the Constitution was ever taken. A majority of the people probably opposed the document, either out of indifference

Federalist and Anti-Federalist Areas, 1787-1788

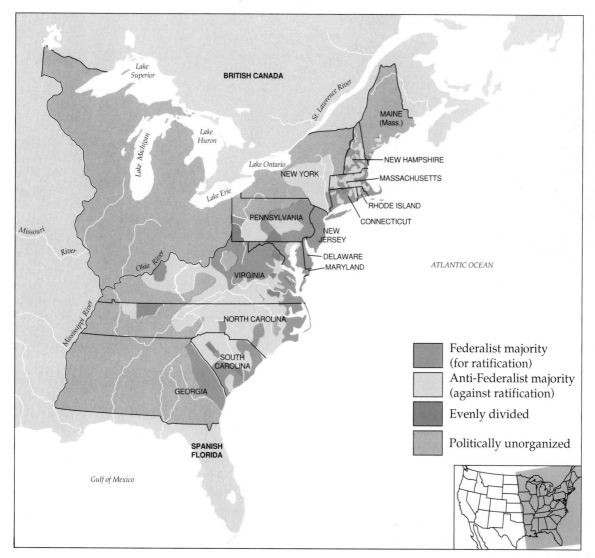

Federalist majority (for ratification)

Anti-Federalist majority (against ratification)

Evenly divided

Politically unorganized

or alarm. Fortunately for the Federalists, they did not have to persuade most Americans; they needed only secure majorities in nine of the state ratifying conventions, a much less formidable task.

It took less than a year from the time the document left Congress to secure approval of the necessary nine states. Delaware, Pennsylvania, and New Jersey ratified first, in December 1787. Approval came a month later in Georgia and Connecticut. Massachusetts was next to ratify, but only after Federalist leaders forwarded a set of amendments outlining a federal "bill of rights" along with notice of ratification. Maryland and South Carolina were the seventh and eighth states to approve. The honor of being ninth and putting the Constitution over the top went to New Hampshire, which ratified on June 21.

Two massive gaps in the new Union remained — Virginia and New York. Clearly, the nation could not endure without them. In Virginia, careful politicking by Madison and other Federalist leaders made the difference. On June 25, the Virginia convention voted to ratify by the narrow margin of ten votes.

The New York convention met on June 17 at Poughkeepsie, with the Anti-Federalist followers of Governor Clinton firmly in command. Hamilton worked for delay, hoping that news of the results in New Hampshire and Virginia would turn the tide. For several weeks, approval hung in the balance while the two sides maneuvered for support. On July 27, approval squeaked through, 30 to 27. That left two states still uncommitted. North Carolina (with Timothy Bloodworth's cautious approval) finally ratified in November 1789. The final state, Rhode Island, did not enter the Union until May 1790, more than a year after the new government had gotten under way.

The Social Geography of Ratification

A glance at the geographic pattern of Federalist and Anti-Federalist strength indicates their dif-

ferent sources of political support. Federalist strength was concentrated along the coast and navigable rivers and was strongest in cities and towns. The centers of Anti-Federalist support lay away from the coast, in the interior of New England, upstate New York, the Virginia piedmont and southside, and the western regions of the Carolinas.

Merchants and businessmen supported the Constitution most ardently. Enthusiasm also ran high among urban laborers, artisans, and shopkeepers, who believed that a stronger government could better promote the overseas trade on which their prosperity depended and protect American artisans from foreign competition. The Constitution also found support in the countryside, especially among commercial farmers and southern planters eager for profit and anxious about overseas markets. But Federalist enthusiasm waned and Anti-Federalist sentiment increased in the interior. Among most ordinary farmers living outside the market economy and immersed in their own localities, the republicanism of 1776 outweighed their interests in national affairs. They found the Federalist vision of an "American empire" both strange and alarming.

Why were the Federalists finally successful? Their task was simplified by the widespread perception that the Articles needed strengthening. In light of the obvious troubles of the Confederation, the Federalists could argue that the Revolution was doomed to failure unless dramatic action was taken.

Most of all, however, the Federalists succeeded because of their determination and political skill. Most of the Revolution's major leaders were Federalists. Time and again these heroes spoke out for the Constitution in the state ratifying debates, and time and again their support proved decisive. Their experience as army officers and as members of the Continental and Confederation congresses caused them to identify with the nation and what it might become. They brought their vision to the ratification process and asked others to share it. With their success, the Federalists turned the American republic in a new and fateful direction.

CONCLUSION
Completing the Revolution

Only five years had passed between England's acknowledgment of American independence in 1783 and ratification of the new national Constitution, yet to many Americans it seemed far longer. By war's end, the difficulties of sustaining American liberty were evident. The experience of the next half decade added to them. Americans continued to argue about their experiment in republicanism and to wonder whether it would actually work.

At the same time, the American people retained an immense reservoir of optimism about the future. Much would depend, of course, on their new constitution and the government soon to be created under it. As the ratification debate subsided and Congress prepared for the transition, the American people looked eagerly and anxiously ahead.

RECOMMENDED READING

Among the major works dealing with the Articles of Confederation and the 1780s are Jack Rakove, *The Beginnings of National Politics : An Interpretive History of the Continental Congress* (1979) ; and Peter Onuf, *The Origins of the Federal Republic* (1983).

On the Philadelphia convention see Richard Morris, *Witnesses at the Creation : Hamilton, Madison, Jay and the Constitution* (1985) ; Christopher Collier and James Collier, *Decision in Philadelphia* (1986) ; and J. Jackson Barlow et al., *The American Founding : Essays on the Formation of the Constitution* (1988). Robert Rutland's *James Madison, the Founding Father* (1987) is a readable biography of the most important constitution maker.

For postwar political and economic problems, see Ronald Hoffman and Peter Albert, eds., *Sovereign States in an Age of Uncertainty* (1918) ; and David Szatmary, *Shays's Rebellion : The Making of an Agrarian Rebellion* (1980).

Though several decades old, Jackson Main, *The Anti-Federalists : Critics of the Constitution, 1781–1788* (1961), is still important for an understanding of the Anti-Federalist opposition. See also Steven Boyd, *The Politics of Opposition : Antifederalists and the Acceptance of the Constitution* (1979). Dumas Malone et al., *Rhetoric and the Founding* (1987), examines the relationship between language and meaning in the constitutional debates.

Time Line

1784	Treaty of Fort Stanwix with the Iroquois
	Spain closes Mississippi River to American navigation
1785	Treaty of Hopewell with the Cherokee
	Land Ordinance for the Northwest Territory
	Jay-Gardoqui negotiations
1786	Virginia adopts "Bill for Establishing Religious Freedom"
	Annapolis convention calls for revision of the Articles of Confederation
1786–1787	Shays's Rebellion
1787	Northwest Ordinance
	Constitutional Convention
	Federalist Papers published by Hamilton, Jay, and Madison
1788	Constitution ratified

8

Creating a Nation

In October 1789, David Brown arrived in Dedham, Massachusetts. Born about 50 years before in Bethlehem, Connecticut, Brown served in the Revolutionary army and after the war shipped out on an American merchantman to see the world. His travels, as he later reported, took him to "nineteen different . . . Kingdoms in Europe, and nearly all the United States."

Though Brown had little formal schooling, he was a man with powerful opinions and considerable natural ability. His reading and personal experience had persuaded him that government was a conspiracy of the rich to exploit farmers, artisans, and other common folk, and he was quick to make his opinions known. "The occupation of government," Brown declared bluntly in one of his numerous pamphlets, "is to plunder and steal." The object of his wrath was the central government recently established under the new national constitution. The leaders of government, he charged, were engrossing the nation's western lands for themselves. "Five hundred [people] out of the union of five millions receive all the benefit of public property and live upon the ruins of the rest of the community."

In the highly charged political climate of the 1790s, Brown's attacks on the new government's leaders brought a sharp response. In 1798, John Davis, the federal district attorney in Boston, issued a warrant for Brown's arrest on charges of sedition. Brown fled to Salem on the Massachusetts coast, but was caught and charged with intent to defame the government and aid the country's enemies. For want of $400 bail, he was clapped in prison.

In June 1799, Brown came before the U.S. Circuit Court, Justice Samuel Chase presiding. Determined to make Brown an example of what criticism of the government would bring, Chase sentenced him to a fine of $480 and 18 months in jail. For nearly two years, Brown languished in prison. Not until the Federalist party was defeated in the election of 1800 and the Jeffersonian Republicans had taken office, was he freed.

• • •

David Brown discovered how easy it was for critics of the government to get into trouble during the 1790s, a decade of extraordinary political controversy. Even though the Revolutionary War was long past, the debate over Revolutionary principles and the struggle to create a republican political order continued. As Benjamin

Rush, Philadelphia physician and Revolutionary patriot, explained : "The American War is over, but this is far from being the case with the American revolution. On the contrary, nothing but the first act of the great drama is closed. It remains . . . to establish and perfect our new forms of government."

As we have seen, the contest for ratification of the new Constitution had generated fierce debate over the familiar concerns about power, political equality, and the proper role of the central government in a republican society. As the new government got under way during the 1790s, that debate heated up once again, catching countless people like David Brown in its toils.

As the decade proceeded and the political debate escalated, Americans divided into two opposing political camps. The Federalists supported the presidential administrations of George Washington and John Adams ; the Jeffersonian Republicans were the Federalists' increasingly vocal critics. Seldom has American political discourse been so virulent, and rarely has the survival of the republic seemed to hang more clearly in the balance.

In this chapter, we examine the new government's beginnings, and the domestic and foreign issues that polarized political divisions between Federalists and Jeffersonian Republicans during the administration of John Adams. The chapter ends with the election of 1800, which brought Federalist defeat and Thomas Jefferson's election to the presidency.

Launching the National Republic

Once ratification of the Constitution was achieved, many Anti-Federalists seemed ready to give the new experiment a chance. They determined, however, to watch it closely and raise the alarm at the first sign of danger. It was not many months before those alarms were sounded.

Beginning the New Government

On April 16, 1789, George Washington started north from Virginia toward New York City to be inaugurated as the first president of the United States. The first electoral college had convened under the Constitution and unanimously elected him to the nation's highest office. His feelings were mixed as he set forth. "I bade adieu to Mount Vernon, to private life, and to domestic felicity," he confided to his diary, "and with a mind oppressed with more anxious and painful sensations than I have words to express, set out for New York ... with the best disposition to render service to my country in obedience to its call, but with less hope of answering its expectations."

Washington's journey through the countryside resembled a royal procession, for he was the object of constant adulation along the way. When he reached New York City, throngs of citizens and newly elected members of Congress greeted the weary traveler. Over the streets of the city stretched gaily decorated arches. During the parade uptown to the governor's mansion, young women in white flowing robes preceded him, strewing flowers in his path. That night, bonfires illuminated the city.

Already the transition from the old Confed-

This imaginative scene of president-elect Washington's reception in Trenton, New Jersey, during his trip from Virginia to New York City for his first inauguration depicts the popular adulation that surrounded him as well as the sharply different political roles of men and women.

eration Congress to the new government was under way. On October 10, the old Congress adjourned *sine die* after setting March 4, 1789, as the day for the new Congress to assemble.

Inaugural day was April 30. Shortly after noon, on a small balcony overlooking a Wall Street thronged with people, Washington took the oath of office. With the crowd roaring approval and 13 guns booming in the harbor, the president bowed his way off the balcony and into Federal Hall. The rest of the day and late into the night, celebrations filled the air.

The Bill of Rights

Among the new government's first items of business were the amendments that several states had made conditions of their ratification. After considerable debate, Congress reached agreement on 12 amendments and sent them on to the states, which ratified ten of them. These ten became the Bill of Rights. Among other things, they guaranteed freedom of speech, press, and religion; pledged the right of trial by jury, the right to bear arms, and the right to due process of law; forbade "unreasonable searches and seizures"; and protected individuals against

self-incrimination in criminal cases. These constitutional amendments have protected individuals' basic rights throughout the nation's history.

During its first months in office, Washington's administration enjoyed almost universal support, both in Congress and among the people. The honeymoon, however, did not last long. Within a year, criticism began and by the middle of the decade, opposition groups came together in a political coalition known as the Jeffersonian Republicans. By 1800, the Jeffersonians had gained control of the government. The political conflict of this first decade revealed the fragility but also the resilience of this new government.

The People Divide

Disagreement began in January 1790, when Secretary of the Treasury Alexander Hamilton submitted the first of several major policy statements, the "Report on the Public Credit," to Congress. Seldom in the nation's history has a single official so dominated public affairs as Hamilton did during these years. A man of extraordinary intelligence and ambition, Hamilton was both a nationalist and a proponent of America's economic development. Perhaps more clearly than anyone else among the nation's founders, he foresaw the country's future strength and was determined to promote its growth. The United States, he was fond of saying, was "a Hercules in the cradle."

He believed that the proper role of the new government was to promote economic enterprise. The people he most admired were men of wealth, ambitious entrepreneurs eager to tie their own fortunes to America's rising empire. Hamilton regarded a close alliance between these people and government officials as essential to achieving American greatness.

If Hamilton's economic policies were liberal in looking forward to enhanced economic opportunity, his politics were profoundly conservative. He distrusted the people and doubted their wisdom. "The people," he asserted, "are turbulent and changing; they seldom judge or

*Alexander Hamilton used both the office of
secretary of the treasury and his personal
relationship with President Washington to shape
national policy during the early 1790s.*

determine right." That stark belief guided much of what he did.

With the Constitution now in place, Hamilton set about to give it proper direction. His opportunity came when Washington named him secretary of the treasury. Hamilton had five objectives: stabilize the government's finances and establish its credit, build and demonstrate its power, tie the interests of the rich and well-born to the national government, promote the country's commercial expansion overseas and its economic development at home, and anchor the nation's foreign relations in a commercial and diplomatic alliance with England. All were essential to the nation's survival; each, he believed, was closely tied to the others.

In his first "Report on the Public Credit," Hamilton recommended funding the remaining Revolutionary War debt by encouraging the government's creditors to exchange their badly depreciated securities at full face value for new interest-bearing government bonds. The foreign debt, held chiefly in France and the Netherlands, Hamilton set at $11.7 million. The domestic debt, including back interest, he fixed at $40.4 million. Second, he proposed that the federal government assume responsibility for the $21.5 million in remaining state war debts. By these actions, he hoped to revive confidence in the government at home and abroad and tie business and commercial interests, which held most of the outstanding securities, firmly to the new government.

The proposal to fund the foreign debt aroused little controversy, but Hamilton's plans for handling the government's domestic obligations generated immediate opposition. In the House of Representatives, James Madison protested the unfairness of funding depreciated securities at their face value, especially since speculators, anticipating Hamilton's proposals, had acquired most of them at a fraction of their initial worth. In addition, Madison and many of his southern colleagues knew that northern businessmen held most of the securities and that funding would little benefit the South. After a bit of grumbling, Congress endorsed the funding plan.

Federal assumption of the remaining state debts aroused even greater criticism. States with the largest remaining unpaid obligations, such as Massachusetts, thought assumption a splendid idea. But others, such as Virginia and Pennsylvania, which had already retired much of their debt, were opposed. Critics also pointed out that assumption would strengthen the central government at the expense of the states, for wealthy individuals would now look to it rather than the states for a return on their investments. Moreover, with its increased need for revenue, the federal government would now have reason to exercise its newly acquired power of taxation. That was exactly what Hamilton intended.

Once again, Congress supported Hamilton's bill. Both Madison and Jefferson approved it as part of an agreement to move the seat of government from New York, first to Philadelphia and then, after 1800, to a special federal district on the Potomac River.

While the southern states continued to complain about the funding and assumption schemes, Hamilton introduced the second phase of his financial program in December 1790. He proposed a national bank capable of handling the government's financial affairs and pooling private investment capital for economic development. Though he was careful not to mention it publicly, he had the example of the Bank of England and its ties with the royal government clearly in mind.

Congressional opposition to the bank came almost entirely from the South. It seemed obvious that the bank would serve the needs of northern merchants and manufacturers far bet-

ter than of southern agrarians. Still, in February 1791, Congress approved the bank bill.

Before signing it, Washington asked his cabinet for advice. Following the constitutional doctrine of "implied powers" — the principle that the government possessed the authority to make any laws "necessary and proper" for exercising the powers specifically granted to it — Hamilton argued that Congress could charter such a bank under its power to collect taxes and regulate trade. Secretary of State Jefferson disagreed, maintaining that since the Constitution said nothing at all about chartering banks, the bill was unconstitutional and should be rejected.

Jefferson also opposed the bank because he feared it would promote a commercial republic filled with merchants and a dependent laboring class. He sought instead an agrarian republic

Overcoming opposition by Secretary of State Jefferson, Hamilton secured congressional approval of a national bank in 1791. The first bank building was erected in Philadelphia four years later.

populated by yeoman farmers committed to economic and political equality. To Jefferson's distress, Washington followed Hamilton's advice and signed the bank bill into law.

In December 1790, in his second "Report on the Public Credit," Hamilton broached the issue of federal taxation. He proposed a series of excise taxes, including one on the manufacture of distilled liquor. The power to tax and spend, Hamilton knew, was the power to govern. The Whiskey Tax became law in March 1791.

Finally, in his "Report on Manufactures," issued in December 1791, Hamilton called for a system of protective tariffs for American industry, bounties to encourage the expansion of commercial agriculture, and a network of federally sponsored internal improvements such as roadways and lighthouses. Neither the agrarian South nor northern seaport districts, however, wanted tariffs that might reduce trade and raise the cost of living. As a result, Congress never endorsed this report.

All the while, criticism of Hamilton's policies continued to grow, reaching a climax in January 1793 when Representative William Branch Giles of Virginia introduced a series of resolutions calling for an inquiry into the condition of the Treasury and urging censure of the secretary's conduct. None of Giles's accusations passed the House, but the debate was now spreading beyond the circle of governing officials in Philadelphia to ordinary people in the towns and countryside.

The Whiskey Rebellion

The farmers of western Pennsylvania provided the most dramatic expression of popular discontent with government policies. Their anger focused on the Whiskey Tax, for their livelihood depended on their ability to transport surplus grain eastward across the mountains to market. To ship it in bulk was prohibitively expensive, so they distilled the grain and moved it in the more cost-efficient form of whiskey. Hamilton's tax threatened to make this practice unprofitable.

He knew that but cared little what the farmers thought.

Trouble was brewing by the summer of 1792 as angry farmers and their supporters gathered in mass meetings across western Pennsylvania. In August, a convention at Pittsburgh drew up a series of resolutions denouncing the tax and declaring that the people would prevent its collection. The convention's pronouncements echoed the Anti-Federalists' warnings against the centralizing and taxing tendencies of a national government. Like opponents of the Stamp Act in 1765, they decided that repression would follow if resistance did not soon begin.

Alarmed by the convention's resolutions, Washington quickly issued a proclamation warning against such "unlawful" gatherings and insisting on the enforcement of the excise. In July 1794, federal marshal David Lennox, in company with John Neville, a local excise inspector, attempted to serve papers on several western farmers, commanding their appearance in court at Philadelphia. An angry crowd gathered and stood in the way. Soon 500 armed men surrounded Neville's home just outside Pittsburgh and demanded his resignation. Learning that Neville had left, they ordered the dozen soldiers trapped in the house to lay down their arms and come out. The soldiers refused, and for several hours the two sides exchanged rifle fire. After several men had been wounded, the soldiers finally surrendered, whereupon Neville's house was put to the torch. Similar episodes involving angry crowds and the erection of Liberty Poles reminiscent of the Revolution erupted across the state. At Parkinson's Ferry, a convention of over 200 delegates debated both armed resistance and secession from the United States.

Alarmed that the protests might spread through the entire whiskey-producing backcountry from New York to Georgia, Washington ordered the insurgents home and called out troops from eastern Pennsylvania and surrounding states to restore order. Hamilton viewed the insurrection not as evidence of an unjust policy needing change but as a test of the

President Washington and Treasury Secretary Hamilton led a federal army of nearly 13,000 troops into the whiskey-producing region of western Pennsylvania in 1794. Rebelling farmers, protesting the government's excise tax on whiskey, dispersed as the army approached.

administration's ability to govern. Suppressing the rebellion, Hamilton explained, "will . . . add to the solidity of everything in this country." He eagerly volunteered to accompany a federal army west.

In late August, a force of nearly 13,000 men, larger than the average strength of the continental army during the Revolutionary War, moved toward western Pennsylvania. At its center was Colonel William McPherson's "Pennsylvania Blues," an upper-class and strongly Federalist cavalry regiment. At its head rode the president of the United States and the secretary of the treasury. Washington soon returned to Philadelphia, persuaded by his aides of the danger to his safety, but Hamilton pressed ahead. The battle that Hamilton had anticipated, never materialized for as the federal army approached,

the "Whiskey Rebels" dispersed. The army managed to take 20 prisoners, two of whom were convicted of high treason and sentenced to death. Later, in a calmer mood, Washington pardoned them both.

As people quickly realized, the "Whiskey Rebellion" had never threatened the government's safety. Even as ardent a Federalist as Fisher Ames was uneasy at the sight of federal troops marching against American citizens. Though a government "by overcoming an unsuccessful insurrection becomes stronger," he noted, "elective rulers can scarcely ever employ the physical force of a democracy without turning the moral force, or the power of public opinion, against the government." Americans would soon have additional reason to ponder Ames's warning.

The Republic in a Threatening World

Because the nation was so new and the outside world so threatening, issues of foreign policy during the 1790s generated extraordinary excitement. In the arguments over the French Revolution and its implications for the new American republic, the American people revealed once again how sharply they differed in values and beliefs.

The Promise and Peril of the French Revolution

France's revolution began in 1789 as an effort to reform an arbitrary monarchy weakened by debt and administrative decay. Pent-up demands for social justice, however, quickly outran the initial attempts at moderate, constitutional reform. By the early 1790s, France was embroiled in a radical social revolution. In January 1793, the monarch, Louis XVI, was beheaded. While the rest of Europe watched in horror and fascination, the forces of revolution and reaction struggled for the nation's soul.

As the revolution grew, the forces of conservatism across the Continent gathered in opposition. In response, France's revolutionary government launched a series of military thrusts into Belgium and Prussia. By the end of 1793, Europe was locked in a deadly war between revolutionary France and a counterrevolutionary coalition led by Prussia and Great Britain.

For more than a decade, the French Revolution dominated European affairs. It also cut like a ploughshare through the surface of American politics, dividing Americans more deeply against each other.

The outbreak of European war posed a number of thorny problems for Washington's administration. Both England and France wanted America's raw materials and each was determined to prevent them from reaching the other. Both nations attempted to control American trade for their own advantage by stopping American ships headed for the other's ports and confiscating American cargoes.

America's relations with England were further complicated by its practice of impressing American sailors into service aboard ships of the Royal Navy to meet its growing demand for seamen. Washington faced the problem of upholding the country's neutral rights and protecting its citizens without getting drawn into the European war.

The old French alliance of 1778 compounded the government's dilemma. If still in effect, it seemed to require the United States to aid France, much as France had assisted the American states a decade and a half before. But some insisted that the old treaty had been dissolved when the French monarchy collapsed.

The American people's intense reaction to the European drama further complicated the situation. At first, virtually everyone supported the French Revolution, viewing it as an extension of their own struggle for liberty. Even the swing toward social revolution did not immediately dampen American enthusiasm.

By the mid-1790s, however, especially after France's revolutionary regime launched its attacks on organized Christianity, many Americans pulled back in alarm. This certainly did not resemble their own revolution. What connection could there possibly be between the principles of 1776 and the chaos of revolutionary France? "There is a difference between the French and the American Revolution," insisted the *Gazette of the United States*, a Federalist newspaper. "In America no barbarities were perpetrated — no men's heads were stuck upon poles — no mangled ladies bodies were carried thro' the streets in triumph. . . . Whatever blood was shed, flowed gallantly in the field." The writer ignored the violence meted out by the supporters of monarchy in France and betrayed a selective memory of America's own revolution. But the differences were indeed profound.

For the Federalists, revolutionary France now symbolized social anarchy. With increasing vigor, they castigated the revolution and championed England as the defender of European stability and civilization.

Many Americans, however, continued to support France. While decrying the revolution's excesses, they believed that republican liberty would ultimately emerge from the turmoil. Jefferson wrote that although he regretted the shedding of innocent blood, he believed it necessary if true liberty were to be achieved.

Citizen Genêt and the Democratic-Republican Societies

Popular associations known as the Democratic-Republican societies provided the most vocal support for revolutionary France. As early as 1792, ordinary citizens began to establish "constitutional societies" dedicated to "watching over the rights of the people, and giving an early alarm in case of governmental encroachments." During the government's first years, several dozen such societies, modeled after the Sons of Liberty of 30 years before, formed to oppose Hamilton's financial program.

It was the French Revolution, however, that kindled democratic enthusiasm and stimulated the societies' growth. The arrival in April 1793 of Citizen Edmund Genêt, minister from the French republic to the United States, provided the spark. Genêt landed first at Charleston, South Carolina, to a tumultuous reception. His instructions were to woo public support and negotiate a commercial treaty with Washington's administration. However, he soon began commissioning American privateers to prey on British shipping in the Caribbean and enlisting American seamen for expeditions against Spanish Florida, both clear violations of American neutrality.

Later, despite a warning by Secretary of State Jefferson, Genêt, in open defiance of diplomatic protocol, urged Congress to reject Washington's recently issued neutrality proclamation and side with revolutionary France. That was the final straw. On August 2, the president de-manded Genêt's recall, charging that his conduct threatened "war abroad and anarchy at home."

If Genêt had little success as a diplomat, he did fan popular enthusiasm for revolutionary France. In June 1793, with his open encouragement, the largest and most influential of the new societies, the Democratic Society of Pennsylvania, was founded in Philadelphia. About 40 similar organizations scattered from Maine to Georgia sprang up during the next several years. Working people — mechanics, artisans, and laborers in the cities, small farmers and tenants in the countryside — provided the bulk of membership. The leaders, however, were doctors, lawyers, tradesmen, and landowners. All were united by a common dedication to what they called the "principles of '76" and a determination to preserve those principles against the "royalizing" tendencies of Washington's administration. They labeled Washington's proclamation of neutrality a "pusillanimous truckling to Britain." Declared the New York society : "We firmly believe that he who is an enemy to the French revolution cannot be a firm republican ; and therefore ... ought not to be entrusted with the guidance of any part of the machine of government." Several of the societies openly urged the United States to enter the war on France's behalf.

In western areas, local societies agitated against the continuing British occupation of the frontier posts around the Great Lakes and berated Spain for closing the Mississippi. In the East, they castigated England for its "piracy" against American shipping. In the Carolinas, they demanded fuller representation for the growing backcountry in the state's assembly. And almost to a person they protested the Excise Tax, opposed the administration's overtures to England, and demanded that public officials, state and federal alike, attend to the people's wishes. Finally, they campaigned for a press free from the political control of Federalist "aristocrats." "The greater part of the American newspapers," they protested, "seem to be lock, stock, and barrel in the hands of the anti-democrats."

President Washington and his supporters were incensed by the societies' support of Genêt and their criticism of the government's domestic program. The "real design" of the societies, thundered the staunch Federalist Fisher Ames, was "to involve the country in war, to assume the reins of government and tyrannize over the people." Writing in the *Virginia Chronicle* of January 17, 1794, "Xantippe" berated Kentucky's Democratic Society as "that horrible sink of treason, that hateful synagogue of anarchy, that odious conclave of tumult, that frightful cathedral of discord, that poisonous garden of conspiracy, that hellish school of rebellion and opposition to all regular and well-balanced authority!" Such polemics illustrated how inflamed public discourse had become.

Jay's Controversial Treaty

Controversy over Jay's Treaty with England further heightened tensions at mid-decade. Alarmed by the worsening relations with England, Washington sent Chief Justice John Jay to London in the spring of 1794 with instructions to negotiate on a wide range of troublesome issues, including continued British occupation of the western posts, British interference with American neutral shipping, and impressment of American seamen.

Early in 1795, Jay returned home with a treaty that resolved almost none of America's grievances. England finally agreed to vacate the western posts, but not for another year and then only if it had uninterrupted access to the fur trade on American soil south of the Great Lakes. Jay failed to secure compensation for American slaves carried off by the British at the end of the Revolution. Nor would the British foreign minister offer guarantees against the future impressment of American seamen, compromise on the issue of neutral rights, or open the British West Indies to American shipping.

When the terms of the treaty were made public, they triggered an explosion of protest. Southern planters were angry because the agreement brought no compensation for their slaves. Westerners complained that the British were not evacuating the posts, while merchants and sailors railed against Jay's capitulation on the West Indies trade and impressment. After a long and acrimonious debate, however, the Senate ratified the treaty by the narrowest of margins.

The administration made better progress on the still volatile issue of free transit out the mouth of the Mississippi River. In the Treaty of San Lorenzo, negotiated by Thomas Pinckney in 1795, Spain for the first time recognized the United States' boundaries under the peace treaty of 1783, and thus gave up all claim to U.S. territory. Spain also granted free navigation of the Mississippi and the right of American merchants to unload their goods on shore for transshipment for the next three years.

By mid-decade, political harmony had disappeared, and the American people stood sharply divided on almost every significant issue of foreign and domestic policy. Increasingly estranged from administration policy, Jefferson resigned as secretary of state in July 1793 and soon joined politicians such as Madison and Albert Gallatin of Pennsylvania in open opposition to the Federalist administration.

In September 1796, Washington announced that he would not accept a third term. He had long been contemplating retirement, for he was now 64 and was exhausted by the political controversy swirling about him.

Federalists versus Jeffersonians

By 1796, bitter controversy surrounded the national government. That controversy intensified during the last half of the 1790s until it seemed to threaten the very stability of the country.

The Election of 1796

The presidential election of 1796 reflected the political storms buffeting the nation. In 1792, Washington and Adams had been reelected without significant opposition. Four years later, the situation was vastly different.

With Washington out of the picture, the presidential contest quickly narrowed to John Adams and Thomas Jefferson. Both were now elder statesmen. Both had played distinguished roles during the Revolution, when they had become friends and earned each other's respect. Though they had worked closely together, Adams and Jefferson differed in many ways. Short, round, and self-consciously neat, Adams contrasted sharply in physical appearance with the tall and frequently disheveled Jefferson. Intensely ambitious, Adams struggled self-consciously with his public career. Jefferson, by contrast, charted his course more quietly and repeatedly sought the solace of private life.

They differed in intellect and vision as well. Jefferson's mind was more expansive and his interests far more encompassing. Politician and political theorist, he was also an avid naturalist, architect, and philosopher. Adams's interests were more tightly focused on legal and constitutional affairs. By the mid-1790s, they differed as well in their visions of the new republic.

Adams, a committed Federalist, was appalled by the French Revolution, and longed for political and social order. Jefferson, while firmly supporting the constitution, was alarmed by Hamilton's financial program, viewed France's revolution as a logical if chaotic extension of America's struggle for freedom, and sought to expand political democracy. By 1796, he had become the vocal leader of an increasingly articulate political opposition, the Jeffersonian Republicans.

The election of that year bound Jefferson and Adams in a strained alliance. With Washington gone, Adams became the Federalists' candidate. He received 71 electoral votes and was declared president. Jefferson came in second with 68 and therefore, as specified in the Constitution, became vice-president. The narrowness of Adams's majority gave indication of the Federalists' weakness and the growing strength of the Jeffersonians.

The War Crisis with France

Adams had no sooner taken office than he confronted a deepening crisis with France. Hoping to ease diplomatic relations between the two countries, he sent off a three-person commission to try to negotiate an accord.

When the commissioners arrived in Paris, agents of the French foreign minister, Talleyrand, visited them and made it clear that the success of the negotiations depended on a prior loan to the French government and a $240,000 gratuity for them. The two staunchly Federalist commissioners, John Marshall and Charles Pinckney, indignantly rejected the demands and sailed home. The third commissioner, Elbridge Gerry, stayed behind, still hoping for an accommodation and alarmed by Talleyrand's intimation that if all three Americans left, France would declare war.

When Adams submitted a report to Congress on this so-called XYZ affair, Americans were outraged. Federalist congressmen thundered against the insult to American honor and demanded action. "Millions for defense, but not one cent for tribute" became their rallying cry. Adams now found himself an unexpected hero. Caught up in the anti-French furor, the president lashed out at "enemies" at home and abroad. "In the last extremity," he declared, "we shall find traitors who will unite with the invading enemy and fly within their lines."

For the moment, the Republicans were in disarray. Publicly they deplored the French government's behavior and pledged to uphold the nation's honor. But among themselves they talked with alarm about the Federalists' intentions. They had good reason for concern, because the Federalists quickly mounted a crash program to repel foreign invaders and roust out traitors in the country's midst.

The Alien and Sedition Acts

In May 1798, Congress created the Navy Department and called for the rapid development of a naval force to defend the American coast against French attack. In July, Congress unilaterally repealed the treaty of 1778, thus moving closer to an open breach with France, and then approved a 10,000-man army. The army's stated mission was to defend the country against an expected French invasion. The Jeffersonians, however, feared otherwise, for they remembered the speed with which the Federalists had used force against the Whiskey Rebels.

As criticism of the army bill mounted, Adams had second thoughts. He was still enough of a revolutionary to worry about the domestic dangers of standing armies. "This damned army," he burst out, "will be the ruin of the country." To the dismay of hard-line Federalists, he issued only a few of the officers' commissions that Congress had authorized. Without officers, the troops could not be mobilized.

Fearful of foreign subversion and aware that French immigrants were active in the Jeffersonian opposition, the Federalist-dominated Congress moved in the summer of 1798 to curb the flow of aliens into the country. The Naturalization Act extended from 5 to 14 years the residence requirement for citizenship, and the Alien Act authorized the president to expel "all such aliens as he shall judge dangerous to the peace and safety of the United States." Another bill, the Alien Enemies Act, empowered the president in time of war to arrest, imprison, or banish the subjects of any hostile nation without specifying charges against them or providing opportunity for appeal.

The implications of these acts for basic political liberties were ominous enough, but the Federalists had not yet finished. In July 1798, Congress passed the Sedition Act, aimed directly at the Jeffersonian opposition. The bill made it a high misdemeanor, punishable by fine and imprisonment, for anyone, citizen or alien, to conspire in opposition to "any measure or measures of the government" or to aid "any insurrection, riot, unlawful assembly, or combination." Fines and imprisonment were provided as well for persons who "write, print, utter, or publish . . . any false, scandalous and malicious writing" bringing the government, Congress, or the president into disrepute. The Federalists now equated preservation of their own political power with national survival. The Federalist moves stunned the Jeffersonians, for they threatened to smother political opposition.

Under the terms of the Alien Act, Secretary of State Pickering launched investigations intended to force the registration of all foreigners. The act's chilling effects were widespread. In July, Pickering noted approvingly that large numbers of aliens, especially persons of French ancestry, were leaving the country. Prosecutions under the Sedition Act were numerous. Twenty-five people, including David Brown of Dedham, were arrested and charged with violating the act. Fifteen were indicted, and ten were ultimately convicted, the majority of them Jeffersonian printers and editors.

Passage of the Alien and Sedition acts generated a firestorm of protest. The Virginia and Kentucky assemblies directly challenged the Federalist laws. The Kentucky Resolutions, drafted by Jefferson and passed on November 16, 1798, declared that the national government had violated the Bill of Rights. Faced with the arbitrary exercise of federal power, the resolutions continued, each state "has an equal right to judge by itself . . . infractions . . . [and] the mode and measure of redress." Nullification (declaring a law invalid within a state's borders) was the "rightful remedy" for unconstitutional laws. The Virginia Resolutions, written by Madison and passed the following month, asserted that when the central government threatened the people's liberties, the states "have the right and are in duty bound to interpose for arresting the progress of the evil." It would not be the last time that state leaders would claim authority to set aside a federal law.

The Kentucky and Virginia resolutions received little support elsewhere, but they indicated the depth of popular opposition to the

Federalists' program. In Philadelphia, armed Federalist patrols walked the streets to protect government officials from angry crowds. As 1799 began, the country seemed on the brink of upheaval.

Within a year, however, the cycle turned again, this time decisively against the Federalists. The break came with Adams's dramatic decision to send a new emissary to France. From Europe, Adams's son, John Quincy Adams, sent assurances that Talleyrand was ready to negotiate an honorable accord. The President seized the opening, fearing that war with France "would convulse the attachments of the country." "The end of war is peace," Adams explained, "and peace was offered me." Moreover, he had concluded that his only chance of reelection lay in fashioning a peace coalition out of both parties.

Adams's cabinet strongly disapproved, for the entire Federalist war program depended on the credibility of the French crisis. But by year's end, the president's emissaries had secured an agreement providing for the restoration of peaceful relations between the two nations.

The "Revolution of 1800"

As the election of 1800 approached, the Federalists were bitterly divided. The Hamiltonians were furious at Adams's "betrayal" and demanded that he not seek reelection. When Adams did not withdraw, the Hamiltonians plotted his defeat.

Both sides believed that the republic's survival hung in the balance. Jefferson declared that this election would "fix our national character" and "determine whether republicanism or aristocracy" would prevail. The Federalists saw the choice as between republicanism and "anarchy." In Virginia, rumors of a slave insurrection briefly interrupted the feuding. But the scare passed quickly, and Federalists and Jeffersonians were soon at each others' throats once again.

Though election day was tense throughout the nation, it passed without serious interruption. As the results were tallied, it became clear

Presidential Election of 1800

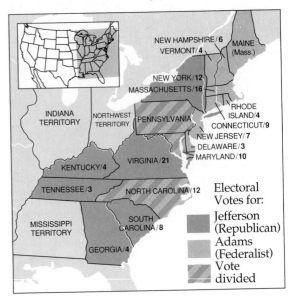

that the Jeffersonians had handed the Federalists a decisive defeat. Jefferson, the Republicans' preferred candidate for president, and Aaron Burr, their other nominee, each had 73 votes. Adams followed with 65.

Because of the tie vote, the election was thrown into the House of Representatives, where a deadlock quickly developed. After a bitter struggle, the House finally elected Jefferson, ten states to four, on the thirty-sixth ballot. (Seeking to prevent a recurrence of such a crisis, the new Congress soon passed, and the states ratified, the Twelfth Amendment, providing for separate electoral college ballots for president and vice-president.) The magnitude of the Federalists' defeat was even more evident in the congressional elections, where they lost their majorities in both House and Senate.

The election's outcome revealed the strong sectional divisions now evident in the country's politics. The Federalists remained dominant in New England because of regional loyalty to Adams, the importance of the area's commercial ties with England, and fears that the Jeffersonians intended to import social revolution. From Maryland south, Jeffersonian control was almost as complete. In South Carolina, whites' fears of the black majority smothered every tendency toward political division, and the Federalists remained solidly in control. But elsewhere, loyalty to Jefferson, strong anti-British and pro-French sentiment, and suspicion of the commercially oriented Federalists kept power in the hands of the Jeffersonians.

In the middle states, Federalists and Jeffersonians were more evenly balanced and the election was more fiercely contested because economic and social differences were greater and issues of foreign and domestic policy cut across society in more complicated ways. This sectional pattern would continue to shape American politics.

The distinctions between the Federalists and Jeffersonians were grounded in socioeconomic divisions as well. The Federalists were strongest among merchants, manufacturers, and commercial farmers located within easy reach of the coast — groups that had supported the Constitution in 1787 and 1788. In both New York City and Philadelphia, the Federalists' main strength was in the wards where assessments were highest and addresses most fashionable.

By contrast, the Jeffersonians included most of the old Anti-Federalists, agriculturalists in both North and South, and countless urban workers and artisans who resented Federalist arrogance. They also attracted people such as Irish and French immigrants and religious minorities — Baptists, Jews, and Catholics — restive under the lingering religious establishments.

By 1800, presidential elections were generating increased popular interest, as evidenced by this textile banner celebrating Jefferson's victory.

The political alignment of 1800 resembled but did not duplicate the Federalist — Anti-Federalist division of 1786–1788. The Jeffersonian coalition was much broader than the Anti-Federalists' had been, for it included countless individuals, from urban workers to leaders such as Madison and Jefferson, who had supported the Constitution and helped set the new government on its feet. Unlike the Anti-Federalists, the Jeffersonians were ardent supporters of the Constitution who called for the new government to be grounded in the principles of liberty, political equality, and a strong dependence on state authority. Nationally, the Jeffersonians now enjoyed a clear political majority. Their coalition would dominate American politics well into the nineteenth century.

CONCLUSION
Toward the Nineteenth Century

The election of 1800 provided a remarkable outcome to more than a decade of political crisis. The series of events had begun in the late 1780s with the intensifying debate over the Articles of Confederation and the movement toward a stronger central government. Under the new Constitution, divisions began to form, first in Congress, then, increasingly, among the people. Hamilton's domestic policies first generated opposition, but it was foreign affairs — the French Revolution, the European war, Jay's Treaty, and the prospect of a war with France — that galvanized political energies and set the Federalists and Jeffersonians against each other.

After the election of 1800, control of the federal government passed for the first time from one political party to another, not easily but peacefully and legally. The Jeffersonians called it "The Revolution of 1800." The future would show whether the Jeffersonians were correct.

RECOMMENDED READING

On politics in the states during the 1790s see Richard Beeman, *The Old Dominion and the New Nation, 1788–1801* (1972); Norman Risjord, *Chesapeake Politics, 1781–1800* (1978); and Charles Steffen, *The Mechanics of Baltimore : Workers and Politics in the Age of Revolution, 1763–1812* (1984).

For cogent discussions of the ideological debates between Federalists and Jeffersonians, see Joyce Appleby, *Capitalism and a New Social Order : The Republican Vision of the 1790s* (1984); and Lance Banning, *The Jeffersonian Persuasion : The Evolution of a Party Ideology* (1978).

Party development during the 1790s can be followed in John Hoadley, *Origins of American Political Parties, 1789–1803* (1986); and Merrill Peterson, *Thomas Jefferson and the New Nation* (1970).

The Bill of Rights and the problem of civil liberties are treated by Bernard Schwartz, *The Great Rights of Mankind* (1977); and Leonard Levy, *Legacy of Suppression : Freedom of Speech and Press in Early American History* (1960).

For a fuller understanding of foreign policy issues, turn to Harry Ammon, *The Genêt Mission* (1973); Jerald Combs, *The Jay Treaty* (1970); and Daniel Lang, *Foreign Policy in the Early Republic* (1985).

Thomas Slaughter explains the character of backwoods revolt in *The Whiskey Rebellion : Frontier Epilogue to the American Revolution* (1986). Aleine Austin, *Matthew Lyon : "New Man" of the Democratic Revolution, 1749–1822* (1981), traces the meaning of political equality in the life of an ardent Jeffersonian.

Time Line

1789	George Washington inaugurated as first president
	Outbreak of French Revolution
1790	Slave trade outlawed in all states except Georgia and South Carolina
	Hamilton's "Reports on the Public Credit"
1791	Bill of Rights ratified
	Whiskey tax and national bank established
	Hamilton's "Report on Manufactures"
1792	Washington reelected
1793	Outbreak of war in Europe
	Washington's Neutrality Proclamation
	Jefferson resigns from cabinet
	Controversy over Citizen Genêt's visit
1794	Whiskey Rebellion in Pennsylvania
1795	Controversy over Jay's Treaty with England
1796	Washington's Farewell Address
	John Adams elected president
1797	XYZ affair in France
1798	Naturalization Act; Alien and Sedition Acts
	Virginia and Kentucky Resolutions
1798–1800	Undeclared naval war with France
1801	Jefferson elected president by House of Representatives

9

Politics and Society
in the Early Republic

I n June 1799, a middle-aged Seneca named Handsome Lake, living on a cramped reservation in western New York, began to preach a message of hope and redemption to his people. Like so many of his tribe, Handsome Lake had been beaten down by the experiences of the preceding 30 years. As a young warrior, he had joined England in the fight against American independence. Wounded on several occasions, his spirit broken by the American victory, he had watched helplessly as the Senecas' land was taken and his people were confined on reservations. Handsome Lake's own life had crumbled as well. On several occasions, alcohol and depression brought him close to death.

As he lay on his bunk, scarcely breathing, Handsome Lake experienced a vision. In that vision and others, the Great Spirit gave him two "gospels" to share with his people. In the first, or apocalyptic gospel, Handsome Lake preached the imminence of the world's destruction, the dangers of spiritual sins such as witchcraft, abortion, and drunkenness, and the promise of salvation through the rituals of *Gaiwiio*, a new form of worship combining Christian elements with the great ceremonies of the Senecas' traditional religious calendar.

Handsome Lake also preached a social gospel, offering guidance for the reconstruction of Seneca life. Here again he called for a mingling of old ways and new, but he emphasized the importance of temperance, peace, land retention, acculturation, and domestic morality.

Though in time his dictatorial manner alienated many supporters, his message inspired a dramatic revitalization of the Seneca nation. In 1800, the Seneca people were hungering for leadership, and Handsome Lake offered them hope and renewed pride. His gospels, moreover, originated in a vision transmitted by the Great Spirit. In Seneca culture, no source of truth was more powerful or certain. He also commanded the attention of his people because he had shared with them the humiliation of defeat and the poverty of reservation life. Finally, his gospels had effect because they were supported by other tribal leaders, especially his half sister Gayantgogwus, who spoke for the tribal women before the Great Council, and Cornplanter, political leader of the community and Handsome Lake's half brother.

• • •

Revitalization was one strategy of survival Native Americans followed during the early nineteenth century. There were others, including armed resistance. Indians' relations with white settlers and with state and national governments reveal much about the nation's early history.

Other changes as well transformed American life between 1800 and 1828. After their victory over the Federalists in 1800, the Jeffersonian Republicans reshaped the national government, reconstructed America's diplomatic relations with Europe and the rest of the Western Hemisphere, and worked to create a new cultural identity consistent with their republican values.

American politics continued to evolve during the years of Jeffersonian ascendency. At the local level, this meant the increasing democratization of political life. Nationally, these years brought the collapse of the Federalist-Jeffersonian party system of the 1790s and set the stage for the dramatically new political era that Andrew Jackson's election to the presidency in 1828 would usher in.

Restoring Republican Liberty

The Jeffersonians entered office in March 1801 with several objectives in mind : calming the political storms that had threatened to rend the country, consolidating their recent victory, purging the government of Federalist holdovers, and setting it on a proper republican course.

The Jeffersonian Republicans Take Control

The government had moved from Philadelphia to the new capital in the District of Columbia in November 1800, while John Adams was still president. When the politicians arrived in Washington, they were stunned by its primitiveness and isolation, for the new capital was little more than a swampy clearing, holding about 5,000 residents, on the banks of the Potomac River.

In keeping with his desire to rid the government of Federalist embellishments, Jefferson planned a simple inauguration. Shortly before noon on March 4, the president-elect walked to the Capitol from his temporary lodgings at a nearby boardinghouse. "His dress," noted one observer, "was, as usual, that of a plain citizen, without any distinctive badge of office." Chief Justice John Marshall, a Virginian but a staunch Federalist as well, administered the oath of office, and a company of militia fired a 16-gun salute.

Though simple, the inauguration was filled with significance. This was the first time in the nation's brief history that control of the government had shifted from one political party to another. Mrs. Samuel Harrison Smith, Washington resident and political observer, described the occasion's drama : "I have this morning witnessed one of the most interesting scenes a free people can ever witness," she wrote a friend. "The changes of administration, which in every . . . age have most generally been epochs of confusion, villainy, and bloodshed, in this our happy country take place without any species of distraction or disorder." Many Americans shared her sense of relief and pride.

In his inaugural speech, Jefferson enumerated "the essential principles of republican government" that would guide his administration : "equal and exact justice to all," support of the

Washington boasted few of the comforts to be found in the nation's earlier capitals of New York City and Philadelphia. This view of Georgetown, a neighboring settlement, in 1800, gives a vivid impression of the area's newness.

states as "the surest bulwarks against anti-republican tendencies," "absolute acquiescence" in the decisions of the majority, supremacy of civil over military authority, reduction of government spending, "honest payment" of the public debt, freedom of the press, and "freedom of the person under the protection of the *habeas corpus*." Though Jefferson never mentioned the Federalists by name, his litany of principles reverberated with the dark experience of the 1790s.

The president spoke also of political reconciliation. "Every difference of opinion," he explained, "is not a difference of principle. We have called by different names brethren of the same principles. We are all republicans — we are all federalists."

Not all his followers welcomed that final flourish, for many were eager to root out the Federalists and scatter them to the political winds. Jefferson's goal, however, was to absorb

the moderate Federalists, isolate the extremists, and destroy the Federalist party as a political force. His strategy worked, for never again did the Federalists regain control of the national government.

Cleansing the Government

Having swept both houses of Congress as well as the presidency in 1800, the Jeffersonians claimed a mandate to rid the government of Federalist officeholders. They were especially outraged by a flurry of last-minute appointments President Adams had pushed through the lame-duck Federalist Congress during the closing days of his administration in an effort to reward party loyalists and deny the Jeffersonians full control of the government.

Under pressure from party supporters, Jefferson agreed that "a general sweep" of Federalist officeholders was necessary. By the time

Jefferson left office in 1808, virtually all government personnel were solid Republicans.

The Judiciary and the Principle of Judicial Review

Late in Adams's administration, the Federalists had introduced a new Judiciary Act calling for more circuit courts and judges with their attendant array of federal marshals, attorneys, and clerks. Congress passed the bill in February 1801, just before adjourning. This blatant effort to pack the judiciary aroused the Jeffersonians' wrath.

A Federalist judiciary was especially obnoxious because during the 1790s Federalist judges continued to base their decisions on English common law. The Jeffersonians protested that the common law was a product of monarchic government and was incompatible with republican liberty. "The revolution [of 1800]," declared Representative William Branch Giles, "is incomplete so long as that strong fortress [the judiciary] is in possession of the enemy." Something had to be done. In January 1802, Senator John Breckenridge of Kentucky introduced a bill calling for repeal of the Judiciary Act of 1801.

In addition to political patronage and the inappropriateness of English common law, the controversy centered on issues of judicial review, the doctrine that it was the federal courts' responsibility to judge the constitutionality of laws and executive behavior, and freedom of the courts from political attack. Gouverneur Morris, Federalist senator from New York, declared that an independent judiciary was necessary "to save the people from their most dangerous enemy, themselves." The Jeffersonians argued that each branch of the government — executive and legislative as well as judicial — must have the right to decide on the validity of an act. Congressional debate over repeal of the Judiciary Act drew wide public attention, for it offered a vivid contrast between Federalist and Jeffersonian notions of republican government. In February 1802, by a strict party vote, Congress repealed the Judiciary Act.

The Jeffersonians also sought to purge several highly partisan Federalist judges from the bench. In March 1803, the House of Representatives voted to impeach federal District Judge John Pickering of New Hampshire. The grounds were not "high crimes and misdemeanors" as the constitution required, but the Federalist diatribes with which Pickering regularly assaulted defendants and juries. The Senate convicted Pickering, by a strict party vote.

Spurred on by success, the Jeffersonians brought impeachment charges against Supreme Court Justice Samuel Chase, one of the most notorious Republican baiters. The trial, however, revealed that Chase had committed no impeachable offense. He was acquitted on every count and returned triumphantly to the bench.

After that defeat, the Jeffersonians pulled back, content to allow time and the regular turnover of personnel to cleanse the courts of Federalist control.

Repeal of the Judiciary Act did not settle the issue of judicial review. That came in several trail-blazing Supreme Court decisions. In *Marbury* v. *Madison* (1803), Chief Justice Marshall laid down the principle in unmistakable terms. "It is emphatically the province and duty of the judicial department," he declared, "to say what the law is." In another landmark decision, *McCulloch* v. *Maryland* (1819), the court struck down as unconstitutional a Maryland law taxing the Baltimore branch of the Second Bank of the United States. No state, explained Chief Justice Marshall, possessed the right to tax a nationally chartered bank, for "the power to tax involves the power to destroy." In the *McCulloch* decision, Marshall also affirmed the constitutionality of the bank's congressional charter and laid down the constitutional argument for broad congressional authority. Let congressional intent "be within the scope of the Constitution," he wrote, "and all means which are appropriate . . . which are not prohibited, but consist with the letter and spirit of the Constitution, are constitutional." These two decisions established some of the most fundamental principles of American constitutional law.

Dismantling the Federalist War Program

The Jeffersonians had regarded the Federalists' war program as a threat to republican liberty, so they moved quickly to dismantle it. Jefferson stopped prosecutions under the hated Sedition Act and freed its victims. In 1802, the act silently lapsed. The Jeffersonians, though not thorough-going civil libertarians, never duplicated the Federalists' campaign to stifle dissent.

Jefferson handled the Alien acts similarly, not bothering to seek their repeal but disman-tling the Federalists' inspection system and al-lowing enforcement to lapse. In 1802, Congress passed a new and more liberal naturalization law, restoring the requirement of 5 rather than 14 years of residence for citizenship. The Feder-alists' provisional army was also reduced by 1802, to only 3,400. No longer would federal troops intimidate American citizens. The excise tax was left in place until it expired in 1802.

Finally, the Jeffersonians sought ways to re-duce the size and operations of the federal gov-ernment. The central government, Jefferson de-clared in his first message to Congress in 1801, was "charged with the external and mutual rela-tions only of these states. The principal care of our persons, our property, and our reputation, constituting the great field of human concerns," should be left to the states because they were more closely attuned to the people's needs and could be held more closely accountable.

In terms of domestic policy, the federal gov-ernment did little more than deliver the mail, deal with Native Americans, and administer the public lands. As the nation grew, however, so did pressures for a federal program of internal im-provements. That reflected in part the growing political influence of the West, for the new states forming beyond the Appalachians sought closer ties of trade and communication with the East. The government responded by launching con-struction of several western routes, including the National Road (in 1811) connecting Cumber-land, Maryland, with Wheeling on the Ohio River. The states, however, carried the major re-sponsibility for internal improvements.

The Jeffersonians also reduced the na-tional debt. In spite of the extraordinary costs of the Louisiana Purchase (1803), the debt dropped from $83 million in 1801 to $57 mil-lion a decade later. Though the Jeffersonians may not have "revolutionized" the government as they claimed, they clearly changed its char-acter and direction.

Building an Agrarian Republic

The Jeffersonians worked vigorously to im-plement their vision of an expanding, agrar-ian republic. That vision was mixed and inconsistent, for the Jeffersonian party was an amalgam of different and often conflicting groups: southern patricians determined to maintain a privileged, slavery-based agrarian order; lower- and middle-class southern whites generally committed to black slavery though re-sentful of the patricians' social pretensions, and ardent proponents of political equality; north-ern artisans dedicated to honest toil, political au-tonomy, and their own economic interests; and western farmers devoted to working the land and living free. In time, this diversity would splinter the Jeffersonian coalition. For the mo-ment, however, these groups found unity not only against their common Federalist enemies but also in a set of broadly shared principles. Those principles guided Jeffersonian policies for over two decades, through the presidential administrations of Jefferson (1801–1808), James Madison (1809–1816), and James Monroe (1817–1824).

The Jeffersonian Vision

Political liberty, the Jeffersonians believed, could survive only under conditions of broad eco-nomic and social equality. The central task of Jeffersonian statecraft was thus to maintain an open and roughly equal society. The task was believed difficult because as societies grew in wealth and power, equality eroded and liberty was snuffed out. England's efforts to destroy colonial liberties had offered ample evidence of that.

The Jeffersonians, however, continued to believe that America, if properly guided, could escape England's fate. Their strategy centered on the independent yeoman farmer — self-reliant, secure in person and possessions, industrious and yet filled with concern for the public good. Such people exemplified the qualities essential to republican citizenship.

The Jeffersonian vision threatened to become clouded, however, because industriousness generated wealth, and wealth bred inequality. In short, economic and social development threatened to destroy the social bases of republicanism.

The solution to the problem of economic and social development, the Jeffersonians believed, lay in rapid territorial expansion. Land, constantly expanding and readily available to the nation's yeoman citizens, would offer opportunity to a restless people, draw them out of the cities and off the crowded lands of the East, and preserve the social equality that republican liberty required. The republic's growth across the North American continent would delay, perhaps even prevent, the cyclic process of growth, maturity, and decay through which all past societies had traveled.

Calls for expanding America's land base were strengthened by the arguments of an English clergyman and political economist named Thomas Malthus. In 1798, Malthus published an essay that jolted Europeans and Americans alike. Given the remarkable fecundity of human beings, Malthus argued, population increased more rapidly than agricultural production. Enlightenment notions of the steadily improving quality of human life, he warned, were a delusion, for the future would be filled with increasing misery and exploitation as population outran food. The future was most clear in Europe, where land was limited and poverty widespread, but the same fate awaited America.

Jefferson believed that America's vast reservoir of land would enable its people to escape Europe's fate. Rapid and continuing national expansion was thus indispensable to the Jeffer-

sonian vision of the agrarian republic. Occupation of the West was also essential to secure America's borders against continuing threats from England, France, and Spain. The rapid sale of new public lands would in addition provide revenue for reducing the national debt. Finally, the Jeffersonians calculated that the creation of new western states would strengthen their political control and assure the Federalists' demise.

The Windfall Louisiana Purchase

Efforts to secure the agrarian republic by rapid territorial expansion explain Jefferson's most dramatic accomplishment, his purchase of the Louisiana Territory in 1803.

In 1800, Spain ceded the vast trans-Mississippi region known as Louisiana to France. When Jefferson learned of the secret agreement in 1801, he was profoundly disturbed. Especially upsetting were rumors that Spain would soon transfer New Orleans, the major outlet for western agricultural produce, to France.

In January 1803, the president sent his young associate James Monroe to Paris with instructions to purchase New Orleans and West Florida, which contained Mobile, the only good harbor on the Gulf Coast, and the mouths of several rivers that drained the southern interior.

When Monroe arrived, he found French Foreign Minister Talleyrand ready to sell all of Louisiana. The black rebellion against the French in Haiti and the threat of renewed war with England at any moment made Napoleon eager to concentrate French troops in Europe. In addition, he feared American designs on Louisiana and knew he would not be able to keep American settlers away. In an effort to cut his losses, Napoleon decided to get what he could from the eager Americans and vacate North America.

In April, the deal was struck. For $15 million, the United States obtained all of Louisiana, nearly 830,000 square miles, in one stroke doubling the nation's size. The public's response was overwhelmingly favorable, and Congress readily approved the purchase.

The Federalists, however, reacted with alarm to the acquisition. They feared that the new states to be carved from Louisiana would be staunchly Jeffersonian and that rapid expansion of the frontier would "decivilize" the nation. In New England, Federalist extremists talked briefly of forming a northern confederacy and seceding from the Union.

The nation's expansion did not stop with Louisiana. In 1810, American adventurers fomented a revolt in Spanish West Florida, captured the fort at Baton Rouge, proclaimed an independent republic, and sought annexation by the United States. In May 1812, over vigorous Spanish objections, Congress formally annexed West Florida. In 1819, pressured by American expansionists and facing a rising tide of rebellion throughout its Latin American colonies, Spain ceded East Florida as well in the Adams-Onis treaty. As part of that agreement, the United States also extended its territorial claims beyond Louisiana to include the Pacific Northwest. This impressive accomplishment set the stage for the final surge of continental expansion during the 1840s.

Exploring and Opening the Trans-Mississippi West

If America's vast new domain was to serve the needs of the agrarian republic, it would have to be explored and made ready for settlement. In the summer of 1803, Jefferson dispatched an expedition led by his personal secretary, Meriwether Lewis, and William Clark, a young army officer, to explore the Far Northwest, make contact with the Native Americans there, and bring back scientific information about the area. For nearly 2½ years, the intrepid band of explorers, assisted by the Shoshoni woman Sacajawea, made its way across thousands of miles of unmapped and hostile terrain — up the Missouri River, through the Rockies via the Bitterroot Valley and Lolo Pass, down the Columbia to the Pacific coast, and back again, finally

reemerging at St. Louis in September 1806. Lewis and Clark's reports of their journey fanned American interest in the trans-Mississippi West, established an American presence in the region, and demonstrated the feasibility of an overland route to the Pacific.

In 1805 and 1806, Lieutenant Zebulon Pike explored the sources of the Mississippi as far as Leech Lake in northern Minnesota. He followed that trek with an equally bold venture into New Mexico and Colorado, where he explored and named the peak that bears his name. In the decade after 1815, the government established a string of military posts from Fort Snelling, at the confluence of the Minnesota and Mississippi rivers, to Fort Atkinson on the Missouri and Fort Smith on the Arkansas. They were intended to secure the American frontier, promote the fur trade, and support white settlement.

The Jeffersonians' agrarian vision also guided changes in land policy. The primary objective of Federalist land policy had been to produce government revenue. The Jeffersonians were more interested in settling people on the land.

The Land Act of 1801 reduced the minimum purchase of federal land to 320 acres, established a four-year credit system, and provided 8 percent discounts for cash sales. Over the next year and a half, settlers, speculators, and land companies purchased nearly 400,000 acres of federal land, more than four times as much as during the entire 1790s. The amounts increased geometrically in the following decade.

During the 1820s, several additional principles were added to federal land policy: preemption, which for the first time enabled squatters to secure title to land, and pricing graduation, whereby lands that did not readily sell were offered at less than the established price or were even given away. All were efforts to speed the transfer of public land into private hands.

Northeastern Federalists, anxious about the West's growing political power and concerned that labor costs would rise as eastern workers sought new opportunities beyond the mountains, opposed these policies, but to no avail.

Exploring the Trans-Mississippi West, 1804-1807

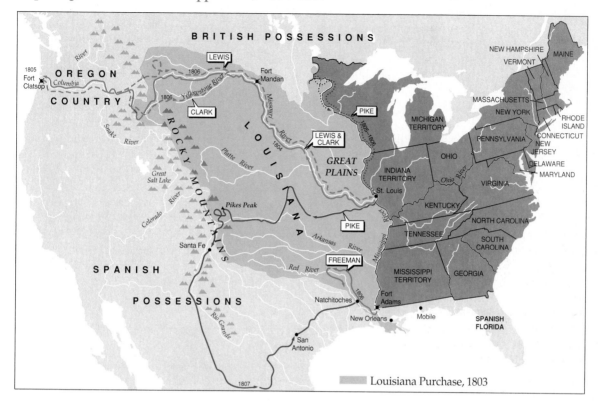

Louisiana Purchase, 1803

Indian-White Relations in the Early Republic

As white settlers surged across the interior, they found a land already occupied by Native American peoples. By 1800, white settlement, disease, and warfare had decimated Native Americans along the Atlantic coast. Powerful tribes, however, still controlled much of the trans-Appalachian interior. North of the Ohio River, the Shawnee, Delaware, Miami, and Potawatomi were allied in a Western confederacy capable of mustering several thousand warriors. South of the Ohio lived five major tribal groups : the Cherokee, Creek, Choctaw, Chickasaw, and Seminole. Together these southern tribes totaled nearly 60,000 people.

The years from 1790 to the 1820s brought a decisive shift in Indian-white relations through-

out the trans-Appalachian interior. As the pressures of white expansion increased, tribal groups devised various strategies of resistance and survival. Handsome Lake led the Seneca toward cultural revitalization. The Cherokee followed a path of peaceful accommodation. Others, like the Shawnee and the Creek, rose in armed resistance. None of the strategies was altogether successful, for by the 1820s the balance of power in the interior had shifted, and the Indians faced a bleak future of continued acculturation, military defeat, or forced migration to lands west of the Mississippi.

Land and Trade

Between 1790 and 1820, federal policymakers attempted to protect Native Americans from exploitation by unscrupulous whites and to

Christianize and civilize them in preparation for their admission into white society. Yet the goal of territorial expansion and officials' sensitivity to the demands of western settlers for Indian land made the acquisition of Native American land the main objective of federal Indian policy. By 1790, the government had given up its earlier "conquest" theory, recognized Indian rights to the soil, and declared that land transfers would henceforth be accomplished through treaty agreements.

Responsibility for the management of Indian affairs rested with the War Department. Henry Knox, Washington's first secretary of war, laid out the government's basic positions in 1789. The Indians, he said, "being the prior occupants of the soil, possess the right of the soil." It should not be taken from them "unless by their

free consent, or by the right of conquest in case of just war." Few of the land treaties negotiated after 1789 represented the "free consent" of Native American people. Still, Knox had established a new, more humane principle, the acquisition of Native American land by formal treaty agreement.

The new treaty-based strategy was effective. Native American leaders were frequently willing to cede land in return for trade goods, yearly annuity payments, and assurances that no further demands would be made on them. When tribal leaders proved reluctant, they could often be persuaded to cooperate by warnings about the inevitable spread of white settlement, or more tractable chieftains could be found. In these ways, state and national governments gained title to vast areas of tribal land through-

Indian Land Cessions, 1750-1830

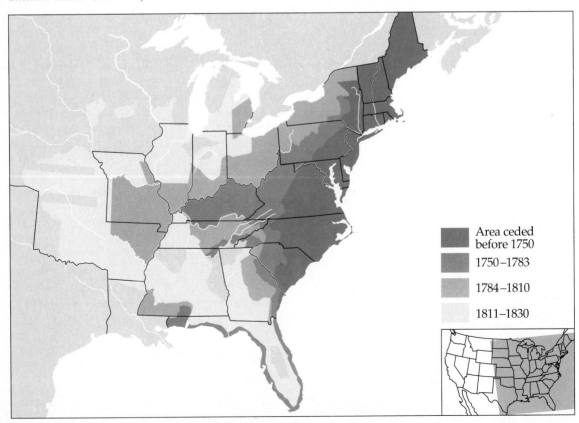

Area ceded before 1750
1750–1783
1784–1810
1811–1830

out the trans-Appalachian interior. The continuing loss of land disastrously affected Native Americans, altering the balance of tribal power and forcing many to migrate west.

The fur trade was also a major concern of federal Indian policy. By 1790, most trans-Appalachian tribes served as intermediaries for hunters farther to the west. Both Native Americans and whites entered willingly into the trade. In return for furs, which they had in abundance, the Indians secured highly valued goods such as blankets, guns, rum, and ironware. White traders acquired valuable furs in exchange for relatively inexpensive trade items. Both sides also used the trade to cement diplomatic relations with each other.

The fur trade served white society very well. It had severe costs, however, for Native Americans, who fell victim to deadly diseases such as smallpox and measles, and became dependent on renewed supplies of rum, firearms, and other goods. As the demand for furs and pelts increased, moreover, Native Americans over-trapped their hunting grounds, forcing them to reach farther west for fresh sources of supply. That process disturbed long-standing tribal patterns of trade and diplomatic relations.

Remaking Indian Culture

A third objective of federal Indian policy was to civilize and Christianize the Native Americans and ultimately assimilate them into white society. In the trans-Appalachian West, where whites and Native Americans struggled openly for survival, most people believed that Indians would always remain "savage" and regarded them as impediments to be moved out of white settlement's way. Different attitudes, however, were evident in the East, where clergymen and government officials, newspaper editors and ordinary citizens displayed greater sympathy for the Native Americans' well-being.

A policy of assimilation seemed to offer hope for the Indians' survival in the face of continuing warfare, disease, and white expansion. Although the assimilationists cared deeply about the physical and spiritual fate of Native American people, they had little sympathy for Indian culture, for they demanded that Native Americans cease being Indian and adopt the ways of white society instead. Assimilation or continuing destruction were the alternatives posed by even the most benevolent whites.

Education and Christianization were the major instruments of assimilationist policy. Together Moravian, Quaker, Baptist, Congregationalist, and Dutch Reformed churches sent scores of missionaries to live among the Indians, preach the gospel, and teach the benefits of white civilization. Baptist missionary Isaac McCoy ministered to the Shawnee tribe in Indiana from 1817 to 1829. John Stewart, a freeborn mulatto who was part Indian, preached to the Wyandotte near Sandusky, Ohio, from 1815 to his death in 1821. Among the most selfless were the Quaker missionaries who labored with the Iroquois in New York.

The missionaries' greatest success occurred where Indians had succumbed to white control or when missionaries blended Indian beliefs with the basic tenets of Christianity. Even so, most Native Americans remained aloof, for the chasm between Christianity and their own religions was wide (see Chapter 1), and the missionaries' denigration of Indian culture was obvious.

Education was the other weapon of the assimilationists. In 1793, Congress appropriated $20,000 to promote literacy, agriculture, and vocational instruction. Church groups established schools as well, and in 1819, the government handed over to the churches full responsibility for Indian education. Because federal officials thought that Christianity and civilization went hand in hand, they encouraged missionaries to teach their Indian students religious doctrine as well as reading, writing, and vocational skills.

Strategies of Survival: The Cherokee

Faced with the steady loss of land and autonomy, the Cherokee sought to combine white and

Few government officials or other white Americans saw any reason to understand Native American customs, such as the Choctaw ceremonial dance shown in this painting by George Catlin.

Native American ways in a distinctive strategy of survival.

As the nineteenth century began, the Cherokee still controlled millions of acres in Tennessee, Georgia, and the western Carolinas. Their land base, however, was shrinking. Already, more than 40 Cherokee towns had disappeared, and over two-thirds of all Cherokee families had been forced to move into the increasingly crowded settlements that remained.

In 1801, the Tennessee legislature unilaterally expanded the boundaries of several counties to include Cherokee land and then claimed that the Indians fell under the authority of state law. The Cherokee, declaring that they had their own system of justice and distrusting the state courts with their all-white juries and exclusion of Indian testimony, rejected white demands.

In Cherokee councils, a group of full-blood leaders argued for armed resistance. Others, however, including mixed-bloods such as John Ross, pointed out the futility of fighting and argued that accommodation offered the only hope

for survival. In the early 1800s, following a bitter struggle for tribal control, the accommodationists won out.

Their first goal was to bring the tribe's scattered villages under a common government. In 1808, the Cherokee National Council adopted a written legal code combining elements of white and Indian law, and in July 1827, the Cherokee devised a written constitution patterned after those of nearby states, complete with executive, legislative, and judicial branches of government. They accompanied it with a bold declaration of their standing as an independent nation. In 1829, the Cherokee government formalized the "blood law," making it an offense punishable by death for any tribe member to transfer land to white ownership without the consent of tribal authorities.

Meanwhile, the process of social and cultural accommodation went forward. Missionaries opened a school for Cherokee youth on the Hiwanee River in 1804 and established a boarding school near present-day Chattanooga 12 years later. They stepped up their religious activities as well, baptizing Cherokee into the Christian faith.

As the Cherokee changed from a mixed hunting, gathering, and farming economy to one based predominantly on settled agriculture, many of them moved from traditional town settlements onto individual farmsteads. The majority continued to inhabit crude log cabins and live a hand-to-mouth existence. However, some prospered, especially mixed-bloods who learned English and understood how to deal with white society. A few of the most successful lived as well as upper-class whites. Joseph Vann, known as "Rich Joe," accumulated hundreds of acres of fertile land, scores of black slaves, and an assortment of mills, stores, and river ferries.

Changes in the Cherokee economy altered relations with blacks as well. Since the mid-eighteenth century, the Cherokee had held a few blacks in slavelike conditions. During the early nineteenth century, however, Cherokee slavery expanded and became more harsh. By 1820, there were nearly 1,300 black slaves in the Cherokee nation. Such changes came about primarily because the spread of cotton cultivation increased the demand for slave labor among Cherokee as well as whites.

By 1820, the strategy of peaceful accommodation had brought obvious rewards. Tribal government was stronger, the standard of living higher, and the sense of Cherokee identity reasonably secure. In the end, however, the Cherokee's success proved their undoing, for as their self-confidence grew, so did the hostility of southern whites, who were increasingly impatient to get them out of the way. That hostility would soon erupt in a final campaign to remove the Cherokee from their land forever (see Chapter 13).

Patterns of Armed Resistance: The Shawnee and the Creek

Not all tribes of the interior proved so accommodating to white expansion. Faced with growing threats to their political and cultural survival, the Shawnee and Creek nations rose in armed resistance during the War of 1812.

In the late 1780s, the tribes of the Old Northwest had launched a series of devastating raids across Indiana, Ohio, and western Pennsylvania, creating panic among white settlers. In September 1790, a force of 1,500, dispatched by President Washington to quell the uprising, fell into an ambush in northwestern Ohio, losing nearly 200 men. The following year, another army of 6,000 troops met a similar fate. Buoyed by their victories, the Shawnee and their allies followed up with a furious assault, virtually clearing northern and central Ohio of white settlement.

Faced with two humiliating defeats, Washington determined to smash the Indians' resistance. In the autumn of 1793, General Anthony Wayne led a third army of conquest into the Ohio wilderness. The following year, his army won a complete victory in the decisive Battle of Fallen Timbers. After the smoke of battle had cleared, the assembled chiefs ceded the southern two-thirds of Ohio in return for $20,000 in trade goods and a $10,000 annual annuity. It was the largest single transfer of Indian land yet, and it opened the heart of the Old Northwest to white control.

In subsequent years, additional treaties further reduced the Indians' land base, driving the Shawnee and Delaware, the Miami and Wyandotte more tightly in upon each other. In the early years of the nineteenth century, two Shawnee leaders, the brothers Tecumseh and Elskwatawa, the latter known to whites as "the Prophet," began to forge an alliance of the region's tribes against the invading whites. In 1809, they established headquarters at an ancient Indian town named Kithtippecanoe in northern Indiana.

Between 1809 and 1811, Tecumseh carried his message of Indian nationalism and military resistance south to the Creek and the Cherokee, calling for "a war of extermination against the paleface." The southern tribes refused to join, but by 1811, over 1,000 fighting men had gathered at Kithtippecanoe.

Alarmed by the Indians' growing militancy, the governor of the Indiana Territory, William Henry Harrison, mustering a force of 1,000 soldiers, attacked and burned Kithtippecanoe.

Over the next several months, Tecumseh's followers, taking advantage of the recent outbreak of the War of 1812 between the United States and England, and aided by British troops from Canada, carried out devastating raids across Indiana and southern Michigan. Together they crushed American armies at Detroit and Fort Nelson. At the Battle of the Thames near Detroit, the tide finally turned, for there Harrison inflicted a grievous defeat on a combined British and Indian force. Among those slain was Tecumseh.

The American victory at the Thames signaled the end of Indian resistance in the Old Northwest. Beginning in 1815, American settlers surged once more across Ohio and Indiana and pressed on unimpeded into Illinois and Michigan.

To the south, the Creek challenged white intruders with similar militancy. As the nineteenth century began, white settlers were pushing onto Creek lands in northwestern Georgia and central Alabama. While some Creek leaders urged accommodation, others, called Red Sticks, prepared to fight. The embers of this smoldering conflict were fanned into flame by an aggressive Tennessee militia commander named Andrew Jackson. Citing Creek atrocities, Jackson urged President Jefferson in 1808 to endorse a campaign against the Creek.

Bristling at their treatment by Georgia and Alabama, the Red Sticks carried out a series of violent frontier raids in the spring and summer of 1813. They capped their campaign with an assault on Fort Mims on the Alabama River, where they killed as many as 500 people, women and children among them. News of that tragedy raised bitter cries for revenge. At the head of 5,000 Tennessee and Kentucky militia, augmented by Cherokee, Choctaw, and Chickasaw warriors eager to punish their traditional Creek enemies, Jackson launched his long-awaited attack. As he moved south, the ferocity of the fighting grew.

The climactic battle of the Creek War came in March 1814 at Horseshoe Bend, on the Tallapoosa River in central Alabama. There, in the fortified town of Tohopeka, 1,000 Creek warriors made a futile stand against 1,400 state troops and 600 Indian allies. Over 800 Native Americans died, more than in any other single battle in the history of Indian-white warfare. With no hope left, Red Eagle, one of the few remaining Red Stick leaders, walked alone into Jackson's camp and addressed the American commander:

> General Jackson, I am not afraid of you. . . . for I am a Creek warrior. . . . You can kill me if you desire. But I come to beg you to send for the women and children of the war party, who are now starving in the woods. . . . If I could fight you any longer I would most heartily do so. Send for the women and children. They never did you any harm. But kill me, if the white people want it done.

The war against the Creek was finished, and Jackson allowed Red Eagle to return home.

But the general was not quite done. He built Fort Jackson on the Hickory Ground, the most sacred spot of the Creek nation and seized 22 million acres of land, nearly two-thirds of their domain. Before his Indian-fighting days were over, Jackson would acquire through treaty and military conquest nearly three-fourths of Alabama and Florida, a third of Tennessee, and a fifth of both Georgia and Mississippi.

The Creek's defeat at Horseshoe Bend broke the back of Indian defenses in the South. With all possibility of armed resistance gone, the Native Americans of the Old Southwest gave way before the swelling tide of white settlement.

A Foreign Policy for the Agrarian Republic

During the early decades of the nineteenth century, the Jeffersonians struggled to fashion a foreign policy appropriate for the expanding agrarian republic. They had several major goals: protecting American interests on the high seas, clearing America's western territories of foreign troops and influence, and breaking free from the country's historic dependence on Europe. Those goals were not easily accomplished; yet by the 1820s, aided by changes taking place across the Atlantic, the Jeffersonians had fashioned a new relationship with Europe. In the Monroe Doctrine of 1823, they also projected a momentous new role for the United States within the Americas.

Jeffersonian Principles

Jeffersonian foreign policy was based on the doctrine of "no entangling alliances" with Europe that Washington had articulated in his Farewell Address of 1796. In the Jeffersonians' minds, England was still the prime enemy, but France was now suspect as well. By the time the Jeffersonians took office, the French Revolution had run its course and ended in the consulate of Napoleon. Second, the Jeffersonians emphasized the importance of overseas commerce to the security and prosperity of the agrarian republic, for trade provided markets for America's agricultural produce and fetched back manufactured goods in return. Third, they sought to maintain peace, because they feared war's effects on republican liberty. Not only did war kill people and destroy property but it also inflamed politics, stifled freedom of speech, disrupted the economy, increased the public debt, and expanded governmental power.

The Jeffersonians' handling of the crisis leading into the War of 1812 against Great Britain illustrates how eagerly, and in this case how futilely, they sought to avoid conflict.

Struggling for Neutral Rights

After a brief interlude of peace, European war resumed in 1803. Once again England and France seized American shipping. England's overwhelming naval superiority made its attacks especially serious. British impressment of American seamen and continued occupation of the

Great Lakes posts also increased tension between the two nations.

In response to increasing British seizures of American shipping, in April 1806, Congress passed the Non-Importation Act, prohibiting the importation of English goods that could be produced domestically or acquired elsewhere. On May 16, Britain replied by declaring a full blockade of the European coast. Threatened by Britain's action, Napoleon answered with the Berlin Decree, forbidding all commerce and communication with the British Isles. Americans were further angered by Britain's refusal to deal in good faith on issues of impressment and the reopening of the West Indian trade.

Tension between England and the United States reached the breaking point in June 1807, when the British warship *Leopard* stopped the American frigate *Chesapeake* off the Virginia coast. The British captain claimed that four *Chesapeake* crew members were British deserters and demanded their surrender. When the American commander refused, the *Leopard* opened fire, killing 3 men and wounding 18, and removed the alleged deserters. After the *Chesapeake* limped back into port with the story, cries of outrage rang across the land.

Fearing the approach of war and recognizing that the United States was not prepared to confront England, Jefferson decided to withdraw American ships from the Atlantic. In December 1807, Congress passed the Embargo Act, forbidding all American vessels from sailing for foreign ports. It was one of Jefferson's most ill-fated decisions.

The embargo had relatively little effect on England. British shipping actually profited from the withdrawal of American competition. The embargo's domestic impact, however, was far-reaching. American exports fell 80 percent in a year, and imports dropped by more than half. New England ports were hardest hit, but up and down the coast, communities dependent on overseas commerce openly challenged the embargo. At Plattsburgh, New York, on Lake Champlain, federal officials declared martial law and sent in federal troops in an effort to stop smuggling into Canada. The result was guerrilla skirmishing as local citizens fired on U.S. revenue boats and recaptured confiscated goods. Throughout the largely Federalist Northeast, bitterness threatened to escalate into open rebellion. Connecticut's governor, in words reminiscent of the Virginia and Kentucky resolutions, warned that whenever Congress exceeded its authority, the states were duty-bound "to interpose their protecting shield between the rights and liberties of the people and the assumed power of the general government."

In the election of 1808, the Federalists rebounded after nearly a decade of decline. James Madison handily succeeded Jefferson in the presidency, but the Federalist candidates, C. C. Pinckney and Rufus King, garnered 47 electoral votes. Their party also made gains in Congress and recaptured several state legislatures.

Faced with the embargo's ineffectiveness abroad and its disastrous political consequences at home, Congress repealed the measure in 1809. In that year and the next, Congress tried more limited trade restrictions aimed at reducing English and French attacks on American shipping, but these strategies also failed, and American war fever continued to grow.

The War of 1812

The most vocal calls for war came from the West and the South. The election of 1810 had brought to Congress a new group of western and southern leaders, firmly Republican in their party loyalty but impatient with the administration's bumbling policy and convinced of the need for tougher measures. The War Hawks, they were called, and an impressive group they proved to be: Henry Clay and Richard Johnson of Kentucky, John Calhoun and Langdon Cheves from South Carolina, Felix Grundy of Tennessee, and Peter Porter from western New York.

For too long, the War Hawks cried, the United States had tolerated Britain's presence on American soil, encouragement of Tecumseh's confederation, and attacks on American commerce. Their language echoed as well with talk of territorial expansion north into Canada and

south into Florida. Their overriding goals were to secure the republic from European threats and demonstrate the Republican party's ability to govern.

Responding to the growing pressure, President Madison finally asked Congress for a declaration of war on June 1, 1812. Opposition came entirely from the New England and Middle Atlantic states — ironically, the regions British policies affected most adversely — while the South and West voted solidly for war. Seldom had sectional alignments been sharper.

The war itself was a curious affair, for its causes were uncertain and its goals unclear. England successfully fended off several American forays into Canada. The British navy once again blockaded American coastal waters, while British landing parties launched punishing attacks up and down the East Coast. On August 14, a British force occupied Washington, torched the Capitol and the president's house (which became known as the White House after being repaired and whitewashed), and sent the president, Congress, and a panic-stricken American army fleeing into Virginia. England, however, did not press its advantage, for it was preoccupied with Napoleon's armies in Europe and wanted to end the American quarrel.

On the American side, emotions ran high among both the war's Federalist critics and Republican supporters. In Baltimore, on the night of June 22, 1812, a Republican crowd demolished the printing office of the *Federal-Republican*, a local Federalist newspaper.

In late July, after copies of the *Federal-Republican* again appeared on Baltimore's streets, a thousand men and women once more surrounded the paper's office. This time, 50 armed Federalists were there to defend it. When the Federalist defenders opened fire, the crowd rolled up a cannon and sent a round of grapeshot into the building. Several people lay dead on both sides before the militia finally arrived to cart the Federalists off to the safety of jail.

On the following night, a crowd reassembled in front of the city jail and seized ten prisoners, including James Lingan, an old Revolutionary War general. The enraged mob beat Lingan and several others to death and left the bodies, stripped of their fine clothing, sprawling in the street.

Though the Baltimore riots were not duplicated elsewhere, emotions ran high throughout the country. In Federalist-dominated New England, opposition to the war veered toward outright disloyalty. In December 1814, delegates from the five New England states met at Hartford, Connecticut, to debate proposals for secession. Cooler heads prevailed, but before adjourning, the Hartford Convention asserted the right of a state "to interpose its authority" against "unconstitutional" acts of the government. As the war dragged on, Federalist fortunes soared in the Northeast, while elsewhere bitterness grew over New England's disloyalty.

Before the war ended, American forces won several impressive victories, among them Commander Oliver Hazard Perry's defeat of the British fleet on Lake Erie in 1813. The most dramatic American triumph was Andrew Jackson's smashing victory in 1815 over an attacking British force at New Orleans. It occurred, however, after preliminary terms of peace had already been signed.

The treaty signed on Christmas Eve in 1814, at Ghent, Belgium, resolved almost nothing, for it ignored impressment, blockades, neutral rights, and American access to Canadian fisheries. England did agree to evacuate the western posts, but other than that, the treaty simply ended the conflict, provided for an exchange of prisoners and the restoration of conquered territory, and called for several joint commissions to deal with the remaining disputes.

The war did leave its mark on the American nation. It made Andrew Jackson a military hero and established him as a national political leader of major importance. The American people, moreover, regarded the contest as a "Second War of American Independence," in which they had whipped the British once again. The republic seemed finally secure. No longer would Americans have to worry about the vulnerability of their republican "experiment" to outside attack.

The years following 1815 brought an end to America's colonial-like dependence on Europe and a reorientation toward the tasks of internal development — occupying the continent, industrializing the economy, and reforming American society. At the same time, Europe entered nearly a century free from general conflict. In the past, European wars had involved the American people; in the twentieth century, they would do so again. For the remainder of the nineteenth century, however, that fateful link was missing. Also, the focus of European colonialism was shifting away from the Americas to Africa and Asia. From the 1820s on, Europe left the Americas relatively alone.

The United States and the Americas

While disengaging from Europe, the Jeffersonians fashioned new policies for Latin America that would guide the United States' hemispheric relations for years to come. Although the American people gave little thought to Europe's Latin American colonies prior to 1800, when those colonies began their struggles for independence from Spain and Portugal in 1808, Americans voiced support. In the early 1820s, the United States recognized the new Latin American republics of Colombia, Mexico, Chile, and Argentina.

In November 1822, the Holy Alliance (France, Austria, Russia, and Prussia) talked of a plan to help Spain regain its American colonies, alarming both the United States and Great Britain. The British foreign secretary, George Canning, broached the idea of Anglo-American cooperation to thwart Spain's intentions.

Secretary of State John Quincy Adams opposed the idea. Son of the former Federalist president, Adams had joined the Jeffersonian camp some years before as part of the continuing exodus from the Federalist party. In the new spirit of nationalism so evident following the War of 1812, Adams declared that the United States should not "come in as a cockboat in the wake of the British man-of-war." He urged independent action based on two principles: a sharp separation between the Old World and the New, and the United States' dominance in the Western Hemisphere.

President Monroe soon agreed that the United States should issue its own policy statement. In his annual message of December 1823, he outlined a new Latin American policy. Though known as the Monroe Doctrine, its content was of Adams's devising.

Monroe asserted four basic principles: (1) the American continents were closed to new European colonization, (2) the political systems of the Americas were separate from those of Europe, (3) the United States would consider as dangerous to its peace and safety any attempts to extend Europe's political influence into the Western Hemisphere, and (4) the United States would neither interfere with existing colonies in the New World nor meddle in the internal affairs of Europe.

When Monroe issued his doctrine, the United States had neither the economic nor military power to enforce it. By the end of the nineteenth century, however, when the country's power had increased, it would become clear what a fateful turning point in the history of the Americas Monroe's declaration had been.

Culture and Politics in Transition

The event-filled years of the early republic had important consequences for cultural and political life as well. Americans disagreed over the extent to which Anglo-European or new republican standards of art should prevail in the United States. Jeffersonians and Federalists differed almost as sharply over definitions of republican culture as they did over republican politics.

During the early nineteenth century, American politics also continued to evolve. By the 1820s, the very character of political life was changing.

The Tensions of Republican Culture

Many among the Revolutionary generation had believed that independence would bring an outpouring of cultural creativity. This did not occur, in part because America's commercial spirit and growing preoccupation with the practical tasks of national development drained energy from literature and the arts. In the expanding world of early nineteenth-century America, commerce and technology counted for more than literature or painting. Novelists such as Charles Brockden Brown and Susanna Haswell Rowson found only limited audiences, and painters such as Gilbert Stuart and Thomas Sully turned to portraiture to make a living.

John Quincy Adams, son of John and Abigail Adams and secretary of state under President Monroe, developed the basic principles of the famous Monroe Doctrine.

Focusing on American themes, Jonathan Trumbull created a series of massive canvases depicting the Battle of Bunker Hill, Cornwallis's surrender, and the Declaration of Independence. The poet Joel Barlow confected a sprawling epic poem, *The Vision of Columbus* (1787), while Noah Webster sought in his *Spelling Book* (1783) and *American Dictionary of the English Language* (1828) to standardize American styles of spelling and pronunciation and rid them of English affectations.

Sharp disagreement arose over the continuing suitability of English cultural standards for republican America. Federalist poets and essayists including Timothy Dwight, David Humphries, and Lemuel Hopkins consciously employed English literary styles in their satires on public education, popular religion, and what they called Jeffersonian mob rule. Many Americans, however, rejected English standards and spurned the arts as artifacts of wealth and moral decadence, incompatible with republican simplicity and moral virtue.

Politics in Transition

By the 1820s, the Federalist-Jeffersonian party system was in shambles. The Federalist party, its reputation damaged by charges of disloyalty during the War of 1812 and its continuing antidemocratic image, lay shattered as a national political force. The Jeffersonian Republicans stood triumphant, their ranks swollen by fresh recruits in the East and the admission of new states in the West. The Jeffersonians' success, however, proved their undoing, for no single party could contain the nation's growing diversity of economic and social interests, sectional differences, and individual ambitions.

Following the War of 1812, largely in response to growing pressures from the West and Northeast, the government launched a Federalist-like program of national economic development. Wartime disorganization of the currency demonstrated the need for a new national bank to replace the First Bank of the United States, whose charter had expired in 1811. In March 1816, President Madison signed a bill creating a second bank, intended to stimulate economic expansion and regulate the loose currency-issuing practices of the country's countless state-chartered banks. In his final message to Congress in December 1816, Madison called for a tariff to protect the country's infant industries. Congress responded with the first truly protective tariff in American history, a set of duties on imported woolen and cotton goods, iron, leather, hats, paper, and sugar.

The administration's program of national economic development drew sharp criticism from so-called Old Republicans, a group of southern politicians who regarded themselves as keepers of the Jeffersonian conscience. Thirty-three Old Republicans voted against the bank bill. Over the next decade, their strength dwindled, even as their cries of alarm became increasingly shrill. By the early 1820s, Henry Clay and others, taking up the name National Republicans, were proposing an ambitious "American system" of tariffs and internal improvements.

The Specter of Sectionalism

Sectional tensions added to the growing disorganization of American politics around 1820. While New England's opposition to the War of 1812 continued to fester, the Missouri crisis of 1819–1820 revealed how deep-seated sectional rivalries had become.

Ever since 1789, politicians had labored to keep the explosive issue of slavery safely beneath the surface of political life, for they recognized how quickly it could jeopardize national unity. Their fears were borne out in 1819 when Missouri applied for admission to the Union and raised anew the question of slavery's expansion. In the Northwest Ordinance of 1787, Congress had prohibited slavery north of the Ohio River while allowing its expansion to the south. But what about the vast new territory west of the Mississippi?

Southerners insisted that the trans-Mississippi West should be open to their slave property and were determined to maintain the Senate's balance between slave and free states. Already, the North's more rapidly growing population had given it a 105 to 81 advantage in the House of Representatives. Northerners vowed to keep the trans-Mississippi West open to free labor. That meant closing it to slavery.

For nearly three months, Congress angrily debated the issue. In the end, compromise prevailed. Missouri gained admission as a slave state while Maine came in as a counterbalancing free state, and a line was drawn west from the western border of Missouri at latitude 36° 30' to the Rocky Mountains, dividing the lands that would be open to slavery from those that would not. For the moment, the explosive issue of slavery's expansion had again been put to rest.

A New Style of Politics

By the 1820s, basic patterns of political behavior were changing. Most evident was the surge of voter participation in state and local elections. Women, blacks, and Native Americans continued to be excluded, but white men flocked to the polls in unprecedented numbers. The flood of voters resulted in part from removal of property-holding and taxpaying restrictions on the franchise in some states.

Equally important were the growing strength of democratic beliefs among the people and the appearance of a new generation of political leaders skilled in the techniques of mass, electoral politics.

Collapse of the First Party System

The final collapse of the Federalist-Jeffersonian party system came with the presidential election of John Quincy Adams in 1824. For the first time since 1800, when the "Virginia dynasty" of Jefferson, Madison, and Monroe began, there was competition for the presidency from every

Missouri Compromise of 1820

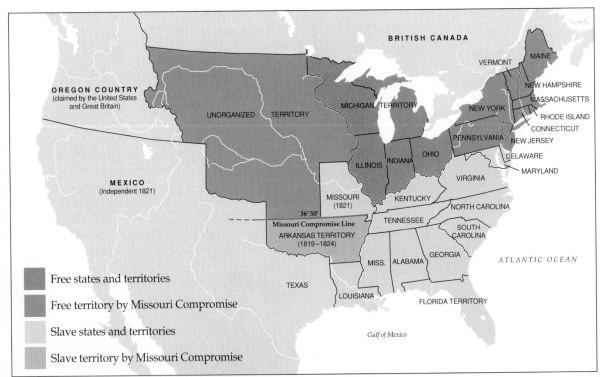

major wing of the Jeffersonian party. Of the five candidates, Adams of Massachusetts and Henry Clay of Kentucky advocated strong federal programs of economic development. William Crawford of Georgia and Andrew Jackson of Tennessee clung to traditional Jeffersonian principles of limited government, agrarianism, and states' rights. In between stood John Calhoun of South Carolina, just beginning his fateful passage from nationalism to southern nullification.

A medical problem eliminated Crawford from the campaign, while Calhoun, attracting limited support, withdrew to become the vice-presidential partner of both Adams and Jackson. When none of the remaining candidates received an electoral majority, the election, as in 1800, moved into the House of Representatives. There, an alliance of Adams and Clay supporters gave the New Englander the election, even though he had trailed Jackson in electoral votes, 84 to 99. The Jacksonians' charges of a "corrupt bargain" gained credence when Adams appointed Clay secretary of state.

Adams's ill-fated administration revealed the disarray in American politics. His stirring calls for federal road and canal building, standardization of weights and measures, establishment of a national university, promotion of commerce and manufacturing, and government support for science and the arts quickly fell victim to sectional conflicts, political factionalism, and his own open scorn for the increasingly democratic politics of the day. Within a year of Adams's inauguration, his administration was floundering. For the rest of his term, politicians jockeyed for position in the political realignment that was under way.

CONCLUSION
The Passing of an Era

During the first quarter of the nineteenth century, Americans saw their nation's territory more than double in size while the Jeffersonians labored to set the government on a proper republican course. They promoted agrarian expansion and transformed the country's relations with Europe and the Americas. They also sought, less successfully, to reconcile Native American rights with national expansion.

The 1820s brought an end to the era of founding, a turning point that was dramatized on July 4, 1826, the fiftieth anniversary of American independence, when two of the remaining Revolutionary patriarchs, John Adams and Thomas Jefferson, died within a few hours of each other. "The sterling virtues of the Revolution are silently passing away," wrote George McDuffie of South Carolina, "and the period is not distant when there will be no living monument to remind us of those glorious days of trial." A new and different era was at hand.

RECOMMENDED READING

Drew McCoy, *The Elusive Republic* (1980), describes the importance of agrarian expansion for the Jeffersonians. For Jeffersonian politics and government, see also Noble Cunningham, *The Process of Government Under Jefferson* (1978); Daniel Jordan, *Political Leadership in Jefferson's Virginia* (1983); and Andrew Cayton, *The Frontier Republic: Ideology and Politics in the Ohio Country, 1780–1825* (1986). Discus-sions of the Federalists can be found in James Broussard, *The Southern Federalists, 1800–1816* (1978); and Linda Kerber, *Federalists in Dissent* (1970). Steven Watts, *The Republic Reborn: War and the Making of Liberal America, 1790–1820* (1987), traces the change from Revolutionary republicanism to liberal capitalism.

Robert Berkhofer discusses white attitudes toward Indians in *The White Man's Indian* (1978). See also William McLoughlin, *Cherokees and Missionaries, 1789–1839* (1984).

Foreign policy issues and the politics surrounding them are portrayed by Reginald Horsman, *The Diplomacy of the New Republic, 1776–1815* (1986); and Ernest May, *The Making of the Monroe Doctrine* (1975).

On politics and the Supreme Court, see Richard Ellis, *The Jeffersonian Crisis: Courts and Politics in the Young Republic* (1971).

Donald Jackson, *Thomas Jefferson and the Stony Mountains: Exploring the West from Monticello* (1981), discusses Jefferson's fascination with the West. For problems of cultural nationalism, see Joseph Ellis, *After the Revolution: Profiles of Early American Culture* (1979); Emory Elliott, *Revolutionary Writers: Literature and Authority in the New Republic, 1725–1810* (1985), and David Simpson, *The Politics of American English* (1986).

Time Line

Year	Event	Year	Event
1789	Treaty of Fort Harmar Knox's reports on Indian affairs	1810	Macon's Bill No. 2
1794	Battle of Fallen Timbers	1811	Battle of Kithtippecanoe
1795	Treaty of Greenville	1812	Madison reelected West Florida annexed War declared against Great Britain
1796	Congress establishes Indian Factory System	1813	Battle of the Thames
1800	Capital moves to Washington	1813–1814	Creek War
1801	Thomas Jefferson elected president Judiciary Act New Land Act	1814	Treaty of Ghent Battle of Horseshoe Bend
1802	Judiciary Act repealed	1814–1815	Hartford Convention
1803	*Marbury* v. *Madison* Louisiana Purchase	1815	Battle of New Orleans U.S. establishes military posts in trans-Mississippi West
1803–1806	Lewis and Clark expedition	1816	James Monroe elected Second United States Bank chartered
1803–1812	Napoleonic Wars resume British impress American sailors	1819	Adams-Onis Treaty with Spain Spain cedes East Florida to U.S. *McCulloch* v. *Maryland*
1804	Jefferson reelected		
1805–1807	Pike explores the West	1820	Land Act Missouri Compromise
1806	Nonimportation Act	1822	Diplomatic recognition of Latin American republics
1807	Embargo Act *Chesapeake-Leopard* affair Congress prohibits slave trade	1823	Monroe Doctrine proclaimed
1808	James Madison elected Cherokee legal code established	1824	John Quincy Adams elected
1809	Tecumseh's confederacy formed Non-Intercourse Act	1827	Cherokee adopt written constitution

10

The Preindustrial Republic

Jn April 1795, Ben Thompson arrived in New York City from Queen Anne's County, Maryland. He first supported himself by common labor on the city's docks, then signed up as a seaman. Sailors were in demand, pay was good, and few questions were asked.

For five years, Ben sailed the seas. Several times his ship narrowly escaped capture by British and French men-of-war. Having enough of travel, he returned to New York.

About the same time, Phyllis Sherman left her home in Norwalk, Connecticut. She also headed for New York, where she took a job as a maid in the household of one of the city's wealthy merchants. As fate would have it, Phyllis and Ben met, fell in love, and, in the spring of 1802, were married.

There is little of note in all this, except that Ben and Phyllis were former slaves and were married in the new African Methodist Episcopal Zion Church. Ben had set aside his slave name, Cato, as a sign of liberation, while Phyllis kept the name her master had given her. Ben was doubly fortunate, for his master had allowed him to buy his freedom and move north just as cotton production was beginning to spread through the Chesapeake region. In another few years, he would have faced greater trouble securing his freedom. Phyllis had been freed as a child when slavery ended in Connecticut. As she grew up, she grew tired of living as a servant with her former owner's family and longed for the companionship of other blacks. She had heard that there were people of color in New York City, and she was correct. In 1800, it contained 6,300 blacks, more than half of them free.

Though life in New York was better than either Ben or Phyllis had known before, it was hardly easy. Along with most blacks, and many white families as well, they struggled just to get along. In 1804, they watched helplessly as yellow fever carried off their daughter and many of their friends. They had to be on guard, moreover, because slave ships still moved in and out of the port, and runaways from the South were pursued in the city's streets.

Still, they persevered. Like other Americans, white and black, they struggled to understand the economic and social forces that placed them in transition between

191

two contrasting ways of life — the rural, preindustrial world of the eighteenth century and the increasingly urban, industrial world of nineteenth-century America.

• • •

By the 1820s, the processes of industrialization, urbanization, large-scale immigration, and westward expansion that would later revolutionize American life were already under way, though they had not yet carried far enough to displace earlier ways of life. In economic and social affairs, as in government and politics, the years of the early republic were years of transition between old ways of life and new. If we are to understand this nineteenth-century transformation, we must first understand the world that was transformed.

In this chapter, we first examine the underlying economic changes that between 1790 and 1828 began to remake American life. We turn next to a discussion of preindustrial society and how people lived in its distinctive regions and local communities. Finally, we examine the new ways in which the American people were beginning to think about their republican society and their first efforts at republican social reform.

The Preindustrial Economy

In early nineteenth-century America, most people earned their livings much like their parents before them. The economy still depended on overseas trade, while agriculture, which occupied over 80 percent of the people, differed little from decades earlier. Change, however, was afoot in commerce, and especially in manufacturing.

The Return of Commercial Prosperity

On August 14, 1801, the merchant ship *Arabella*, Captain Charles Adams in command, left New York bound for Liverpool, England, with a cargo of Pennsylvania flour, Chesapeake tobacco, and sugar from the West Indies. Adams and his crew were uneasy as the American coast dropped out of sight because the North Atlantic was a dangerous as well as profitable place for American merchantmen.

Danger and profit arose from the same circumstance — European war. We saw in Chapter 8 how the outbreak of European war in 1793 had affected American politics. It had equally important consequences for the economy. In 1790, the nation's merchants were still struggling to rebuild overseas trade to its pre-Revolution levels. By the end of the decade, however, American commerce was booming, and the country was in the midst of prosperity undreamed of but a few years before.

In part, the newfound prosperity stemmed from actions taken under the direction of Secretary of the Treasury Hamilton to establish American credit and restore the confidence of investors. Decisions made in the capitals of Europe, rather than in America, however, lay behind the country's surging commercial expansion. England and France, locked in deadly struggle, sought North America's raw materials, especially its foodstuffs and naval stores. Each was anxious to keep American goods out of the hands of the other. As Europe's war-induced demand for American commodities grew, the price

The street bustle created by renewed commercial prosperity is vividly illustrated in this street scene of New York by Francis Guy.

of those goods increased. As prices rose, so did profits and so, in turn, did the willingness of American merchants to risk capture on the high seas.

According to established practice, neutral nations in time of war could trade with the belligerents as long as two conditions were met. First, the goods that were exchanged could not include arms or other war matériel; second, the trade connections must predate the outbreak of hostilities. American commerce met both those conditions. Both England and France, however, sent armed cruisers to prowl the Atlantic and intercept American merchant ships believed to be headed for the other's ports.

For nearly two decades following 1793, England and France continued their desperate struggle. The losses in American ships and cargoes during those years were alarmingly high and included the *Arabella,* which ran afoul of a British cruiser off southern France and was lost to its owners.

The profits waiting for cargoes that got through, however, more than compensated for the risks. And so American exports surged upward, more than tripling in value between 1793 and 1807. American tonnage also increased dramatically. By 1800, American bottoms were carrying an astonishing 92 percent of all commerce between America and Europe. The freight earnings from this expanded fleet added further to the country's newfound prosperity.

The main beneficiaries were the merchants — men such as E. H. Derby of Salem, John Jacob Astor of New York, and Stephen Girard of Philadelphia — who built the ships, gathered the cargoes, and dispatched them to the waiting markets in Europe. But America's booming commerce benefited others as well, especially in the ports, where overseas trade affected nearly everyone. The expansion of commerce stimulated insurance and banking activities and brought the shipbuilding industry out of its long doldrums. Though America's prosperity was most evident in the ports, its effects radiated into the surrounding countryside, where the cargoes of agricultural and forest goods and the provisions required by the ships' crews were produced.

In spite of the prosperity, however, escape from England's empire had not fundamentally changed the realities of American economic life. The export trade continued to depend on European demand for America's raw materials. American consumers, moreover, still preferred English and European manufactured goods to cruder American products. As yet, the United States had insufficient population, investment capital, manufacturing capability, transportation systems, and levels of labor productivity to support its own internally generated economic development. Not until the second quarter of the nineteenth century would it finally escape this colonial-like dependence on Europe.

While commerce continued in its traditional channels, a few merchants began to reap the benefits of new forms of business organization, notably incorporation. A charter of incorporation from a state government often brought legal privileges, such as the exclusive right to carry on certain activities for a number of years or special tax incentives. Corporations, moreover, could sell stock and thus accumulate capital for investment. Between 1776 and 1800, the states chartered some 300 commercial, banking, and manufacturing enterprises. That was a striking change from the earlier practice of reserving charters almost exclusively for towns, colleges, and philanthropic organizations.

Most merchants, however, still operated their businesses individually or in simple partnerships. Even the largest mercantile houses employed no more than a half dozen clerks. Moreover, they usually marketed their goods through personal ties with wholesalers and shopkeepers.

As we shall see, many of the profits generated by the new prosperity would soon be put to new and innovative uses. The commercial activity that produced them, however, remained firmly rooted in the past.

Agriculture in the North

During the early years of the republic, the vast majority of Americans drew their living from the land. In 1800, fully 83 percent of the labor force was engaged in agriculture; as late as 1820, that figure had hardly changed.

During the early nineteenth century, more agriculturalists entered into commercial market exchanges. Along the Hudson River in New York and in southeastern Pennsylvania, access to urban and European markets stimulated production for commercial sale. In New England, where the soil was poor, farmers turned fields into pasture and switched to more profitable dairying and livestock raising.

The commercialization of agriculture, however, remained limited. As late as 1820, no more than 25 percent of agricultural output was available for export. The rest was consumed on the country's farms or used in local exchange. Most farm families still strove for self-reliance. "The great effort," reported a European traveler, "was for every farmer to produce anything he required within his own family; and he was esteemed the best farmer, to use a phrase of the day, 'who did everything within himself.'"

Across much of the country, cash still played only a small part in economic exchanges. "Instead of money going incessantly backwards and forwards into the same hands," declared an

observant Frenchman in 1790, people "supply their needs in the countryside by direct reciprocal exchanges. The tailor and the bootmaker go and do the work of their calling at the home of the farmer . . . who most frequently provides the raw material for it and pays for the work in goods."

Most farms were not large. By 1800, the average size in the longer-settled areas of New England and the Middle Atlantic states was no more than 100 to 150 acres, down substantially from 50 years before. Northern farms were not only small but limited in productivity, even in southeastern Pennsylvania, probably the richest and most productive area in the North. During the eighteenth century, people had called it "the best poor man's country" in America.

As the nineteenth century began, however, economic opportunity was actually declining in southeastern Pennsylvania. The average farm was no larger than 125 acres, barely above the margin of profitability. This resulted from the growing population and the continuing division of farm property from fathers to sons. By 1800, nearly 20 percent of the taxpayers were single freemen, clear evidence that young men were finding it harder to establish themselves on the land before taking a wife. Declining productivity plagued inhabitants as well. Long and continuous cropping had robbed the soil of its fertility, and as population increased, farmers were forced to bring marginal land under cultivation.

Agricultural technology had changed little from a century before. Farmers still worked the land with crude, wooden plows that required several yoke of oxen and two or three men to use. Not until the 1830s did efficient metal plows come into general use.

One mark of increasing commercialization was greater dependence on livestock and dairying. Most farmers, however, owned only a few animals — perhaps several horses, four or five cattle, some pigs, and a flock of chickens. Few farmers knew much about scientific breeding; even fewer practiced it. Animals typically grazed together in common fields or were allowed to forage for themselves in the countryside. Even in winter, many farmers neither sheltered their animals nor provided them with fodder. One observer remarked, "It is a very pitiable sight to go about our country and see the condition of multitudes of cattle and sheep which fill almost every farmer's yard in the spring of the year."

By 1820, Pennsylvania's farmers were producing considerably more than 50 years before, but that was because there were more of them cultivating more land, not because there had been improvements in agricultural productivity.

The South Embraces Cotton

As the eighteenth century ended, southern agriculture was in disarray. Falling prices, wornout lands, and the destruction wrought by the Revolutionary War had left the Chesapeake's tobacco economy in shambles. The extensive loss of slaves added to the region's economic woes.

Even before the Revolution, Virginia and Maryland planters had begun to diversify their crops in an effort to escape dependence on tobacco. Those efforts continued during the 1780s and 1790s.

As the new century began, however, southern planters turned back to single-crop agriculture, only this time the crop was cotton. Planters were most successful in cultivating the long-staple variety. Its silky fibers were highly valued and could easily be separated from the cotton's seeds. The delicate long-staple plant, however, grew only where soil and climate were right — on the sea islands off the coast of Georgia and South Carolina.

There was an alternative — the hardier short-staple variety, which could be successfully cultivated across large areas of the South. Its fibers, though, could be separated from the plant's sticky green seeds only with great difficulty. A slave could clean no more than a pound of short-staple cotton a day.

Demand for cotton of all sorts was growing, especially in England, where new textile factories created an insatiable appetite for the crop. Demand and supply began to come together in 1793 when Eli Whitney, a Yankee schoolteacher

seeking employment in the South, designed a functioning model of what he called a "cotton gin." In conception it was disarmingly simple, nothing more than a box containing a roller, equipped with wire teeth, designed to pull the fibers through a comblike barrier, thus stripping them from the seeds. A hand crank activated the mechanism. With this crude device a slave could clean up to 50 pounds of short-staple cotton per day.

During the next several decades, southern cotton production soared. In 1790, the South produced only 3,135 bales. By 1800, output had grown to 73,145 bales, and by 1820, it had mushroomed to 334,378. The growing demand of England's textile mills provided the stimulus, but a portentous combination of factors made possible the South's dramatic response: wonderfully productive soil; a long and steamy growing season; the availability of ample, well-trained slave labor; and the long experience of southern planters with the production and marketing of staple crops.

The swing to cotton marked a momentous turning point for both the South and the nation. Perhaps most important, it breathed new life into the institution of slavery, for as cotton production increased, so did the value of prime

Although the cotton gin, invented in 1793, simplified one step of cotton processing, much of the work on a plantation continued to be done with rudimentary tools by slave labor. Here Benjamin Latrobe sketches An Overseer Doing His Duty.

fieldhands. Some of the escalating demand for slave labor was met from overseas. In 1803 alone, Georgia and South Carolina imported 20,000 new slaves. Much of the labor demand, however, would be met by natural reproduction and the internal slave trade that moved blacks from the worn-out lands of the Chesapeake to the booming "black belt" of the Deep South.

Preindustrial Manufacturing

Economic change was more noticeable in the manufacturing sector during the early nineteenth century. Merchant capitalists, seeking investment opportunities for profits earned in overseas trade, began to buy into and consolidate industries such as textiles and shoes. Development of the factory system still lay in the future, but the early nineteenth century brought the first steps toward industrialization.

How much of the American work force was involved in manufacturing is difficult to determine, since most people did a variety of jobs. In the rural North, for example, farmers augmented their income by running gristmills, building cabinets, or repairing wagons. Farm women contributed as well by making clothes for sale or exchange with neighbors. "Almost all the farmers of the United States," declared one European visitor, "combine some trade with agriculture."

Manufacturing in preindustrial America was small in scale and widely decentralized. The rural landscape was dotted with small enterprises — grain mills and sawmills, potash works and iron forges — that employed three or four workers and served people in the immediate vicinity. Artisans made goods much as they had for decades — slowly, by hand, and with the simplest of tools. Where more than human power was required, as in milling grain or sawing wood, waterwheels provided it. In the small shops of preindustrial America, labor and management were closely aligned. Artisans occupied both roles, working side by side with their journeymen helpers but also managing the enterprise. They owned their shops, which

were often attached to their houses, hired their help, and made their living from profits rather than wages.

Merchant Capitalism and the Putting-Out System

During the first several decades of the nineteenth century, this decentralized, artisan-based manufacturing system slowly began to change. The explanation for the transformation is to be found, once again, in America's continuing involvement with Europe.

In an attempt to prevent the United States from becoming more deeply embroiled in the ongoing European war, President Jefferson in 1807 declared an embargo, cutting off American trade across the Atlantic (see Chapter 9). In one year, the value of American exports declined nearly 80 percent. When the embargo was lifted in 1809, American trade gradually recovered. In 1812, however, Britain and the United States once again went to war. During the next three years, overseas trade sank to its lowest level in recorded history. Even after the war's end, American commerce languished, largely because England's new Corn Laws prohibited the importation of American grain.

With profits from overseas trade drastically reduced, merchants sought investment opportunities in domestic manufacturing.

Merchants brought organizational skills as well as ambition and surplus capital. Their strategy was to gain control both of the raw materials from which goods were fashioned — leather in the case of shoes; cotton, flax, and wool for textiles — and the arrangements for marketing the finished products. Some steps in the manufacturing process they farmed out to workers in shops and homes, paying them on a piecework basis, a practice that came to be called the "putting-out" system. Other steps they consolidated in their own central shops.

The development of the early shoe industry in Lynn, Massachusetts, illustrates how merchant capitalism worked. During the eighteenth century, Lynn's farmers learned to augment their income by making shoes. By 1800, Lynn had become a center of shoe production, the town's many small shops turning out one pair of shoes for every five people in the country.

At first, individual shopkeepers commissioned shoemakers to fill specific orders. But seeing the vast potential in shoe manufacturing, merchant capitalists soon began to take control of the industry. In the years following 1805, they developed central shops where the leather was cut into pieces and then put out to hundreds of workers, many of them women laboring at home, who sewed the pieces together. The completed uppers were then returned to the central shops, checked, and sent out again, this time to male workers, who attached the soles. The finished shoes were then gathered, inspected, and packed for shipment.

The process was efficient and turned a handsome profit for the merchant capitalists who managed it. It had serious implications, however, for the master craftsmen who had formerly dominated the trade. With manufacturing increasingly under the control of the merchants and focused around the central shops, the masters lost both their own independence and influence over their journeyman apprentices.

A few, such as Chris Robinson, prospered under the new system. In 1818, he made shoes in a 10-foot-long shop attached to the back of his home. Within four years, he was able to build a new shop measuring 16 by 28 feet. A decade later, now with a partner, Robinson erected a wooden factory on one side of the town common. Among artisans, however, Robinson was the exception. Most shoemakers either entered the central shops or continued to work at home, no longer as independent producers but as dependent wage earners. Less and less often did they make important production decisions; those were reserved for the "bosses" who ran the enterprise. Moreover, the workers could be "turned away" for bringing in unsatisfactory work and thus deprived of their livelihood. By the 1820s, shoemaking in Lynn was no longer controlled by individual artisans.

Panic and Depression

Following the end of America's second war with England, consolidation under the limited system of merchant capitalism slowed. British goods again flooded American markets, and the manufacturing boom collapsed. The American shoe industry survived, but hundreds of others did not.

In 1819, the economy suffered a severe financial panic. Caught up in the commercial and manufacturing booms, commercial bank directors extended credit and printed money without retaining sufficient specie (coined money) in their vaults to cover their obligations. It was a financial system waiting to collapse, and in 1819 it did when the Bank of the United States, which had been rechartered by Congress in 1816, forced the state banks to redeem their note issue in specie. Many could not meet the demands, thus triggering a sequence of bank failures and the collapse of credit.

The panic was followed by a depression that generated an unprecedented stream of bankruptcies and shattered fortunes. Across New England and the Middle Atlantic states, businesses failed, unemployment soared, and wages plummeted. William Greene, secretary to the governor of Ohio, reported in 1820 that "the greater part of our mercantile citizens are in a state of bankruptcy," while "the citizens of every class are uniformly delinquent in discharging even the most trifling of debts." In the South, farms and plantations stood abandoned as cotton and tobacco exports fell.

By the early 1820s, however, recovery was under way, and the stage had been set for the second and more dramatic phase of America's epic industrial revolution.

An Ideology of Expectant Capitalism

During the colonial period, circumstances had dampened the economic ambitions of many Americans. English mercantilism had stressed the subordination of colonial to British enterprise. More important, limited opportunities curbed economic incentives for most Americans. While southern tobacco and rice planters and northern merchants accumulated significant wealth, ordinary Americans did not, nor did they expect to.

Attitudes began to change, however, late in the eighteenth century as a newly expansive economic spirit began to take hold. The break with England enhanced Americans' sense of economic freedom and autonomy. Beyond that, they increasingly shared the attitudes toward economic affairs that Adam Smith elevated to an ideology in his *Wealth of Nations.* Published in England in 1776, Smith's tract launched an assault on the restrictive, controlling assumptions of mercantilism. Smith asserted that individual self-interest was the only reliable guide to human behavior and that the public good was best served by the free and unregulated play of individual ambition in the marketplace. Government, Smith explained, should not control eco-

nomic affairs but should act only to guarantee the free working of supply and demand. Smith's doctrines suited the circumstances of the new republic wonderfully. The booming prosperity at the turn of the century also convinced many Americans that economic opportunities were expanding.

The new spirit was fed, finally, by the accelerating pace of westward settlement. In 1790, only 100,000 white settlers lived in the nation's interior beyond the Appalachian Mountains. By 1800, their numbers had swollen to nearly a million; by 1820, to over two million. They traveled by wagon overland and by flatboat down the Ohio River. A traveler in 1797 counted 500 wagons a day on the road west from Albany. "The woods are full of new settlers," wrote an observer near Batavia, New York, in 1805. "Axes are resounding, and the trees literally falling about us as we passed."

Between 1790 and 1820, land companies hawked vast areas of New York, Ohio, Kentucky,

Important Routes Westward

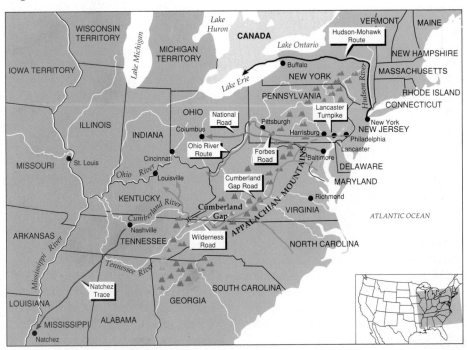

and Alabama to prospective settlers back east. The Holland Land Company, financed by a consortium of Dutch bankers, bought 2.5 million acres of prime land in western New York and another 1.5 million in Pennsylvania. Individual settlers shared in the speculative fever, going into debt to buy extra land so that they might sell it at a premium when population increased and land prices rose.

Even the panic and depression of 1819–1821 failed to dampen for long the exuberance of America's expansionary capitalist faith. By the 1820s, the American economy stood poised at a historic divide. Behind it lay the traditional world of preindustrial America; ahead loomed the emerging industrial world of the future. The details of that new order were not yet clear, but its outlines were coming into view.

The Nature of Preindustrial Society

Just as America's preindustrial economy differed from the later industrial order, so did the preindustrial society of the early republic. During the nineteenth century, the combined forces of industrialization, urban growth, large-scale immigration, and westward expansion would transform American social life. By the 1820s, enough had changed to make clear that a new social order was in the making. At the same time, the traditional social relationships defined by family, community, class, gender, and race were considerably slower to change than ways of producing and marketing goods.

A Nation of Regions

Were we to be transported back to that preindustrial world, nothing would impress us more than the smallness of American communities and the isolation of people from each other. In the early nineteenth century, community and region were more real to most Americans than any sense of nationhood.

The country was divided first by distinct and separate regions. The regional differences between North and South that originated in the colonial period persisted and even increased during the early nineteenth century. The northern states continued down the path of economic diversification, with mixed farming, commerce, fishing, and manufacturing. The South, by contrast, focused increasingly on the cultivation and export of cotton.

As the two regions' economies diverged, so did their societies. In the North, wealth was not equally distributed, but the free-labor system did reward most people for their work. In the South, the slave-labor system produced a dramatically uneven distribution of wealth, for the masters reaped the profit from their slaves' labor. In white society, class differences were expanding. As cotton took hold, people without slaves or with access only to marginal lands fell rapidly behind.

America's regional diversity now included the vast area of Trans-Appalachia as well. During the first years of settlement on that rapidly moving frontier, life was hard as settlers struggled to clear the land and get their first crops in the ground. As population increased, however, and the rich virgin soil began to bloom, Trans-Appalachia began to grow. Above the Ohio, mixed, free-labor agriculture quickly appeared as farmers worked to reproduce the life they had known in Pennsylvania or New England. In short order, towns such as Columbus and Cincinnati emerged to provide services and cultural amenities for the surrounding population.

As people continued to spill into the region, they established churches, courts, and schools. Even so, Trans-Appalachia retained a reputation for its rough and colorful quality of life. Life could be depressingly lonesome for families lost in the hollows of the Cumberland Mountains of eastern Tennessee. In the river towns along the Ohio River, by contrast, boatmen and gamblers, con men and speculators gave civic life a raucous quality; and everywhere the transiency, youthfulness, and predominant maleness of the population kept society unsettled.

No characters were more colorful in popular folklore than westerners like Mike Fink, the mythical riverman, who boasted that he "was half man, half alligator" and could "whip his weight in grizzly bears."

A Nation of Communities

If regional identity was important in Americans' lives, social existence centered even more tightly on communities, for most people spent their lives within the physical and social boundaries of their localities. In the early republic, the social world of most Americans was intimate and self-contained.

The written word was the only means of communicating across space. By 1820, the number of newspapers had risen to 512 but most appeared only once or twice weekly and had small circulations.

The number of post offices and the flow of mail increased more dramatically. When Washington was inaugurated, only 75 post offices existed in the entire nation; 30 years later, there were nearly 8,500. Still, it cost 25 cents to send a letter 30 miles or more. At a time when the daily wage averaged about a dollar, that was prohibitively expensive for most people.

Overland travel improved during these years. In 1800, it took two days to go by horseback or coach from New York to Philadelphia and more than a week to Pittsburgh in western Pennsylvania. By 1820, travel times had been halved, especially north of Virginia and east of the Appalachians, where the roads were better. Beginning in the 1790s, a flurry of turnpike construction began in the Northeast. The first one of any length opened between Philadelphia and Lancaster, Pennsylvania, in 1794. It immediately proved profitable, and soon dozens of similar projects were under way. In 1806, Congress authorized construction of the National Road westward from Cumberland, Maryland. By 1818, it had penetrated as far as Wheeling on the Ohio River and had reduced travel time along its length from eight days to three.

The turnpike system, begun in the 1790s, reduced travel time through the countryside. Tree stumps were cut low enough to clear under a wagon's axles, and log roads were built over streams and swamps. Here an express coach makes its way through the forest.

Even the turnpikes, though, amounted to little more than dirt roadways with the bushes trimmed back along the sides and the tree stumps cut off at 16 inches, just low enough for most wagon axles to clear. The usual pace of travel, whether on foot or horseback, was no more than three or four miles an hour. At that rate, a trip of 25 miles filled a day.

The contrast with modern communications is staggering. When George Washington died in December 1799 in Alexandria, Virginia, it took 5 days for the news to reach Philadelphia, 11 days to get as far as Boston, and over three weeks to penetrate west to Lexington, Kentucky. By contrast, when President Kennedy was assassinated in 1963, fully 68 percent of the American people heard the news *within half an hour.*

By 1810, steamboats were appearing along the Atlantic coast and on the Ohio and Mississippi rivers. In 1807, Robert Fulton launched his 160-ton sidewheeler *Clermont* on the Hudson River and demonstrated the feasibility of steam travel. Within a few decades, steamboats would revolutionize transportation on the nation's vast interior river system. For the moment, however, most westerners still depended on flatboats to carry them downstream and keelboats for the laborious task of poling upriver.

Also missing from America's preindustrial communities were regional and national organizations such as today knit localities together. Churches, schools, fire companies, laboring men's associations, militia companies — all were tightly bounded by the local community and had but tenuous connections with similar groups elsewhere. In the early years of the republic, the organizational as well as informational boundaries of community life were tightly drawn.

Lives of Intimacy and Quietness

Life in preindustrial communities was intimate and highly personal. The vast majority of America's 5.2 million people in 1800 lived on farms and plantations or in villages of no more than a few hundred souls. Only ten places in the entire country were home to as many as 5,000 people. The two largest, New York and Philadelphia, had about 60,000 inhabitants each.

In these rural and small-town settings, people went to church together, shared the joys of birth and the sorrows of death, exchanged goods, and gossiped at village stores. Everyday life consisted of a dense and intensely personal network of social relations.

The accelerating migration westward increased geographic mobility, but the movement of people from countryside to town also contributed to it. This traffic was especially heavy in New England, where young men and women, finding it increasingly difficult to get a start on the crowded and rock-strewn soil, sought opportunity in Boston and emerging mill towns such as Waltham, Lowell, and Pawtucket. But it was evident in the Middle Atlantic states as well. Between 1790 and 1820, the nation's cities grew at a rate nearly twice that of the population as a whole. Most people, however, did not move far or often during their lifetimes. As a result, generational continuity, family stability, and extended kin networks continued to characterize community life.

Life in the communities of preindustrial America was remarkably quiet as well. When the enveloping silence was interrupted, it was by the pealing of church bells or the clopping of horses' hoofs or the unmagnified sounds of human voices conversing. Out in the endless countryside, where most Americans lived, the sounds were nature's own — the wind blowing in the trees, a summer thunderstorm, the lowing of a cow, the call of a catbird seeking its mate.

Work patterns were deliberate and informal. Since most Americans gained their living from the land, they were bound by the unhurried cycle of the seasons. When not tending their crops, men found more than enough to do repairing the barn, shoeing a horse, or rooting out tree stumps from a field. Women also worked long hours cultivating the garden, raising children, preserving food, and making clothes, but the pace was slow, and schedules were almost nonexistent.

Artisans likewise worked when there were orders to fill and closed their shops when there were none. Seldom did either craftsmen or merchants keep regularly scheduled hours, nor did their customers expect that of them.

Indeed, for most Americans, life went on in the absence of clocks and timepieces. Not until the 1830s did they become cheap enough for most families to own. Nor did most communities have public clocks, either on church towers or public buildings. Days, months, and seasons of the year were meaningful measures of human activity; hours and minutes often were not.

Lives of Difficulty and Trial

As modern visitors to the communities of preindustrial America, we would be impressed as well by the rigors of daily life. Though most Americans were better off than their colonial ancestors, their lives were hardly comfortable. The wealthy could afford fine townhouses or elegant plantation mansions, but most Americans could not. For southern slaves, frontier settlers, and the urban poor, housing meant cramped and filthy spaces; dirt floors; small window openings, often lacking glass; and only the most rudimentary furniture.

Even the wealthy depended on fireplaces or stoves for heat and had no indoor plumbing. After dark, people used candles and firelight for illumination. During the winter months, when the sun set early and the nights were cold, evening activities were curtailed and people sought warmth in bed.

People's diet was limited as well. Farm and small-town families enjoyed regular access to fresh fruits and vegetables, dairy products, domestic animals, and wild game. In the cities, many families still maintained small garden plots, a few chickens, perhaps even a cow. But as the cities grew and land values increased, that became increasingly difficult. Ice for refrigeration was often scarce; as a consequence, every city dweller knew the familiar taste of sour milk and the smell of rancid butter. Fresh meats and vegetables, purchased in the town market, were but occasional parts of most urban dwellers' diets. Far more common were bread, potatoes, onions, and salt pork.

Even in the countryside, fresh fruits and vegetables disappeared during the winter months, and people turned to the dried fruits and root vegetables they had stored away. Coffee, sugar, and spices were expensive enough that most people could enjoy them only occasionally.

Alcohol was a central part of the diet. By 1830 American consumption had risen to 5.2 gallons of hard liquor for every man, woman, and child in the nation, nearly triple today's rate. Whiskey was the most popular drink, with hard cider close behind. Not until midcentury, after large numbers of Germans had entered the country and brewing techniques had changed, did the consumption of beer begin to grow.

Then, as now, drinking patterns differed across social boundaries. Among whites, the heaviest drinking was done by young, lower-class males. Drinking rates were also high among the foreign-born and people living in the West.

Women drank less extravagantly than men but still consumed from an eighth to a quarter of the nation's liquor. Eastern upper-class women frequently drank in mixed company at dinner parties, while at frontier dances the whiskey bottle was "passed pretty briskly from mouth to mouth, exempting neither age nor sex." Even infants were often taught to imbibe.

As the consumption of alcohol grew, so did public concern. Washington thought that distilled spirits were "the ruin of half the workmen in this country." Anne Royall, who spent much of her life crisscrossing the country in stage coaches, observed, "When I was in Virginia, it was too much whiskey — in Ohio, too much whiskey — in Tennessee, it is too, too much whiskey!" By the 1830s, concern would change to alarm.

Birth, Death, and Disease

The quality of life in early nineteenth-century America was also affected by the constant presence of disease and death. High infant mortality, the rigors of daily life, limitations of diet, and the risks of medical care resulted in dramatically shorter life spans than we enjoy today. At the turn of the century, only half the people could expect to live to age 45. Unlike today, women on the average died sooner than men, their bodies weakened by the rigors of frequent childbirth. Though birthrates were declining, white women could expect to give birth to four to eight children, and immigrant and black women averaged even more.

Disease constantly threatened human life. Germ theories of infection were still unknown, and hospitals and well-trained physicians were few. Most Americans, especially among the lower classes, depended for health care on home remedies and prayer. That was probably not all bad, considering that the standard medical treatment for most diseases included bleeding, purging, and blistering.

Diseases such as diphtheria and tuberculosis took a steady toll of human life, and epidemics of smallpox and yellow fever periodically raced through the population with devastating results. During the 1790s, yellow fever struck the coastal cities repeatedly. The most devastating attack hit Philadelphia in 1793. Within months, nearly 10 percent of the city's population died.

After the crisis passed, city officials took steps to improve sanitation by cleaning the streets of their usual filth. Garbage, however, continued to litter the streets, animals still roamed freely in the cities, the collection of human excrement remained sporadic, and the wells from which people drank were often polluted. Disease-carrying mosquitoes continued to take their toll. Yellow fever returned to Philadelphia in 1797 and 1798, hitting hard at other seaboard cities as well. Disease and death were regular visitors to community and family life.

Patterns of Wealth and Poverty

One of the defining features of any society is the way in which wealth, power, and status are distributed among its people. During the nineteenth century, class distinctions increased as early industrialization redrew the contours of economic and social life.

As the century began, property was already unequally distributed across gender and racial lines. Women continued to hold far less property than men. The large majority of blacks, moreover, were slaves; for them, ownership of anything more than a few items of personal property was beyond reach. Though the condition of free blacks was better, they too held little of the country's wealth.

Among white males, property was most broadly shared in rural areas of the North, where free-labor and family-farm agriculture

predominated, and least so in the South, where control of slave labor and the best land permitted tobacco, rice, and cotton planters to monopolize the region's wealth.

Class lines were also sharply drawn in the ports, where merchant capitalists controlled the sources of commercial and manufacturing wealth. Small artisans, sailors, and unskilled workers lived at the margins of the economy, their lives taken up almost entirely by a struggle for survival. Perhaps the most even distribution of property existed on the edges of settlement in the trans-Appalachian frontier, but that was an equality of want.

Taking the country as a whole, the pattern of wealth distribution had not changed much from pre-Revolutionary times. In 1800, the top 10 percent of property holders controlled about 42 percent of the nation's wealth, very close to what it had been 50 years before.

When the century opened, not many Americans were truly rich. Even the wealthiest could not match the grandeur of English landed aristocrats or the great London merchants. Neither did America contain a large, destitute underclass such as could be found in the cities and countryside of Europe. By comparison with England and France, property in the United States was broadly distributed.

Poverty, however, existed and was increasing. In the South, it was most evident among slaves and poor whites living on the sandy pine barrens of the backcountry. In the North, the port cities housed growing numbers of the poor.

The commercial recession following Jefferson's embargo in 1807 hit the urban poor with particular force, for they felt the effects of unemployment most directly. Winter seasons regularly brought hard times for many as shipping slowed and jobs disappeared. During the winter of 1814–1815, relief agencies assisted nearly one-fifth of New York City's population.

Even in rural New England and southeastern Pennsylvania, a lower class of transient and propertyless people was growing. The "strolling poor," they were called — landless men, and sometimes women, forced to roam the country-side searching for work.

Three other groups were conspicuous among the nation's poor. One consisted of old Revolutionary War veterans like Long Bill Scott, who had found poverty as well as adventure in the war. The others were women and children. Annual censuses of almshouse residents in New York City from 1816 to 1821 consistently listed more women and children than men.

Nothing more clearly illustrated poverty's grip or the vulnerability of many Americans to economic hard times than the depression of 1819–1821. Hardest hit were the West and South, where land speculation and wildcat banking had been rampant. When the financial bubble burst and depression settled in, a tide of foreclosures swept across the West, destroying the livelihoods of farmers and speculators alike. Residents of the port cities felt the harsh grip of depression as well, as commerce slowed, banks collapsed, and businesses shut down, leaving thousands without employment.

Poverty was a continuing reality in the early nineteenth century. And for every American who actually suffered its effects, there were several others living just beyond its reach, their margin of safety alarmingly thin.

Perfecting Republican Society

During the Revolutionary era, politics had preoccupied the American people. Between 1790 and 1828, Americans turned their thoughts to issues of social change and reform, for if their political experiment was to succeed, society would have to be republicanized as well. Behind their reform efforts lay a cluster of beliefs regarding the unique character of the American people.

The Youthfulness of America

The reform impulse that emerged in the 1790s had roots deep in the colonial past. From the first days of colonial settlement, European immigrants had thought of America as a place free of Old World ills and open to new ways of life. The Revolutionary generation called their new society *novus ordo seclorum*, a new order of the ages. They believed that reason rather than habit or tradition would guide America's development. Americans insisted that their country was a "young" and "rising" republic, a "new nation" taking its place among the "old" and "decadent" empires of Europe.

The Meaning of Social Equality

Equality was the second element of America's new social faith. By this, most people did not mean literal equality of social condition. They meant, first of all, equality of opportunity. In a republican society, social differences should not be based on privilege or inherited position but on ability. For that to be true, society had to provide people with the opportunity to rise as far as abilities and ambition would carry them.

The doctrine of equal opportunity had little relevance for the actual life circumstances of many Americans. Slaves, women, and working-class men understood all too well the limits of opportunity in preindustrial America. But the principle was bold and inspiring for countless others.

Social equality also implied an equality of social worth among individuals, no matter what their wealth or social standing might be. That attitude showed up vividly in an episode that took place in New York City in 1795. Thomas Burke and Timothy Crady, two recent Irish immigrants, operated a ferry across the East River between lower Manhattan and Brooklyn. One day in early November, Gabriel Furman, a merchant and Federalist alderman, arrived on the Brooklyn shore a bit before the scheduled departure time and instructed the ferrymen to leave early. When they refused, he upbraided the "rascals" for their disrespect and threatened to have them arrested. Crady was especially angered by the alderman's arrogance. He and Burke, Crady exploded, "were as good as any buggers." When the ferry landed on the Manhattan shore, Furman had the two arrested.

Both Crady and Burke were eventually hauled before Mayor Varick and three other Federalist aldermen, sitting as the Court of General Sessions. There was no jury. The judges quickly decided to make examples of the two insolent Irishmen. "You rascals, we'll trim you," Varick allegedly said ; "we'll learn you to insult men in office." The magistrates quickly found the two guilty on charges of insulting an alderman and threatening the constable, sentenced them to two months at hard labor, and ordered 25 lashes for Crady as well.

Within a month, the two ferrymen had bolted from jail and disappeared into Pennsylvania, never to be heard from again. The episode, however, was not yet over, for a young Jeffersonian lawyer named William Keteltas took up the case and in time carried it all the way to the New York assembly. In a two-column newspaper account signed "One of the People," he castigated "the tyranny and partiality of the court" and concluded that Burke and Crady had been punished to "gratify the pride, the ambition and insolence of men in office." That, he argued, was intolerable in a republican society. The assembly, he charged, was protecting the mayor to save his reputation. But what of the ruined reputations of the ferrymen ? Were they not just as important ?

Before it was over, the incident generated wide public anger, and Keteltas earned a jail sentence for his efforts. When released, however, he was paraded through the streets by a throng carrying American and French flags and a banner inscribed "What, you rascal, insult your superiors ?" In the early republic, notions of equal social worth spread rapidly.

The Doctrine of Individualism

The doctrine of individualism was the third element in America's new social faith. It asserted that society's basic purpose was to promote the interests of its individual members. That idea had been voiced during the colonial years, but it

had been carefully balanced by the opposing view that individuals existed as parts of a larger social order and must subordinate themselves to the general good, a notion central to revolutionary republicanism. The Revolutionary experience, however, had moved the balance in favor of an emphasis on the primacy of the free and unfettered individual.

Equality of opportunity and moral worth, individualism, and a belief that society could be shaped in ways to increase human liberty all combined to create a dramatically new social vision that Americans carried with them into the nineteenth century.

The Second Great Awakening and Social Reform

The early stages of the Second Great Awakening, a swelling tide of religious revivalism that began sweeping across the nation in the 1790s, added urgency and moral sanction to the idea of social reform. The Awakening's theology, articulated most powerfully by itinerant Methodist and Baptist preachers, was simple and direct. In contrast with the intricate theological arguments of the First Great Awakening a half century before, it emphasized the immediacy of every believer's encounter with God, embraced the notion of universal salvation, and proclaimed the responsibility of each individual for his or her own soul. Such beliefs were fully consistent with popular republicanism.

The Awakening took hold first among ordinary people in the farms and villages of the West. One of the most spectacular outpourings of religious enthusiasm occurred in 1801 at Cane Ridge, Kentucky, where for six frenetic days 10,000 people gathered to exalt God and wrestle with the Devil. With hundreds shouting at once, the uproar could be heard for miles around. "The noise," declared James Finley, an observer and participant, "was like the roar of Niagara." He counted as many as seven ministers preaching at once, while some of the people sang, others prayed, and still others cried out for mercy "in the most pitiable accents."

The popular revivalism of the Second Great Awakening rejected theological subtleties and emphasized the individual's direct and emotional encounter with God. This Anabaptist ceremony of baptism by immersion was painted by the Russian traveler Paul Svinin.

The Awakening reinforced Americans' sense of personal autonomy and new beginnings, and rekindled broad millennialist hopes that America would become the perfect place for Christ's Second Coming. The Awakening's theology, moreover, emphasized human equality before God and stressed the duty of Christian believers to demonstrate their faith by doing good works in the world.

Alleviating Poverty and Distress

It was a heady brew, this new combination of social and religious beliefs that underlay early nineteenth-century social reform.

The alleviation of poverty was one goal of the early social reformers. Benjamin Rush of Philadelphia believed that poverty could be reduced permanently and proposed programs of education for the poor designed to achieve that end. Many Americans, however, continued to believe that poverty was inevitable, that its primary causes were hard drink and moral indolence, and that the most that could be done was to offer selective relief to deserving individuals.

Most of the more than 100 charitable and relief agencies in New York City focused their ef-

forts on the "worthy poor," respectable folk who were victims of circumstance and merited assistance, and turned their backs on the "idle" or "vicious poor," who lacked character and thus deserved their fate. New Yorkers had not yet connected pauperism with the changing conditions of urban, commercial life.

Educating the Republic's Children

A virtuous republic required an educated citizenry. As Noah Webster explained, educating the "rising generation" of young Americans involved not just the three R's, but "an acquaintance with ethics and . . . the general principles of law, commerce, money and government" — in other words, the basic doctrines of republican society.

Except in New England, which had a long tradition of public schooling, education in the colonial era had been largely left to the family. Typically that meant that only the children of the well-to-do, who could pay the costs of tutors or academies, received even the most rudimentary education.

Following the Revolution, however, state legislatures, led by Massachusetts in 1789, began to appropriate tax revenues for the support of free public education. New York followed suit in the 1790s. Tax-shy legislatures and deep-seated devotion to local control often frustrated the efforts of educational reformers, but the new principle that the state had an obligation to educate its citizens had been established. In the meantime, free charity schools, financed by churches and private philanthropists, took up some of the slack.

Colleges were also affected by the new attention to education. When the Revolution began, only nine colleges existed in the colonies. By 1800, that number had increased to 25 — including the first state universities in North Carolina (1789), Georgia (1801), and Virginia (1819) — and by 1820, to more than twice that many. In most of them, traditional education, based on classical languages and theology, designed primarily for training clergymen, was broadened to include geography, natural sciences, and European languages, subjects deemed more useful for republican leaders.

Women in Republican Society

Though women's lives did not change markedly during these early years, changes that helped set the stage for later, more dramatic breakthroughs did occur.

Divorce was one area where women achieved more equal treatment. When a neighbor asked John Backus, a silversmith in Great Barrington, Massachusetts, why he kicked and struck his wife, John replied that it was partly owing to his education, for his father often treated his mother in the same manner. We do not know whether John's mother tolerated such abuse, but his wife did not. She complained of cruelty, desertion, and adultery and obtained a divorce. Her reaction was not unique, for around the turn of the nineteenth century, more and more women followed her example.

The process was not easy, for most states allowed divorce only on the ground of adultery, and South Carolina did not permit it at all. Moreover, women typically had to present detailed evidence of their husbands' infidelities and face the discomfort of an all-male court, while a wife's transgressions could be more easily established and might include disobedience as well as more serious offenses. Still, divorce was becoming more available to women. In Massachusetts during the decade after independence, 50 percent more women than men filed for divorce, with almost exactly the same rate of success. These figures suggest that women shared the new notions of individualism and social equality and from them developed rising expectations of marriage. They also reveal that women's complaints were being taken more seriously.

Changes also occurred in women's education. This was part of the general enthusiasm for educational reform, but it reflected a special concern for women's place in the new republic. Given women's role as keepers of public morality and nurturers of future citizens, their education was a subject of general concern. If the republic was to fulfill its destiny, young women would have to prepare for the responsibilities that motherhood would bring. During the 1790s, Judith Sargeant Murray published a series of essays, gathered under the title *The Gleaner*, in which she criticized parents who "pointed their daughters" toward marriage and dependence. "I would give my daughters every accomplishment which I thought proper," Murray wrote. "They should be enabled to procure for themselves the necessaries of life; independence should be placed within their grasp."

Between 1790 and 1820, a number of female academies were established, most of them in northeastern cities. Timothy Dwight, the future president of Yale, opened his academy at Greenfield Hill in Connecticut to girls and taught them the same subjects he taught boys, at the same time and in the same room; but he was the exception. Benjamin Rush, in his essay "Thoughts upon Female Education" (1787), prescribed bookkeeping, reading, grammar, penmanship, geography, natural philosophy, vocal music ("because it soothes cares and is good for the lungs"), and history. Traditionalists such as the Boston minister John Gardiner were decidedly less sympathetic. "Women of masculine minds," he warned, "have generally masculine manners, and a robustness of person ill calculated to inspire the tender passions."

The prediction that intellect would unsex women was accompanied by the warning that educated women would abandon their proper sphere as mothers and wives. Even the most ardent supporters of female learning insisted that they seek education so that they might function more effectively within their traditional sphere.

The Limits of Reform: Race and Slavery

Early nineteenth-century reform made only limited progress in ameliorating the twin evils of slavery and racism. In spite of Ben Thompson's experience, manumission of individual slaves by private owners slowed as well. The reasons were several. The gradual abolition of slavery in the North soothed many consciences, while in the

South, the spread of cotton increased the value of slave labor. Equally important in shaping white attitudes, however, were two slave rebellions, one bloody and successful on the Caribbean island of Hispaniola during the 1790s, the other, smaller and unsuccessful but alarming nevertheless, near Richmond, Virginia, in 1800.

Panic-stricken whites fleeing Hispaniola for their lives carried word to the North American mainland of the black Haitians' successful rebellion against a French colonial army of 25,000. The news spread terror, especially through the South, where southern whites immediately tightened their black codes, cut the importation of new slaves from the Caribbean, and quizzed their slaves in an effort to root out suspected Haitian revolutionaries. The bloody rebellion and the prospect of a nearby island nation governed by blacks frightened northern whites as well.

A second shock followed in the summer of 1800, when another rebellion, this time just outside Richmond, was nipped in the bud. Gabriel Prosser, a 24-year-old free black, had devised a plan to arm 1,000 slaves for an assault on Richmond. Betrayed by several black house servants, Prosser's plan failed. No white lives were lost, but scores of slaves and free blacks were arrested, and 25 suspects, including Prosser, were hanged at the personal order of Governor James Monroe.

In the early nineteenth century, antislavery appeals all but disappeared from the South, while proslavery arguments increased.

In the North, antislavery attitudes were increasingly conciliatory toward slave owners and unsympathetic toward blacks. Most of slavery's critics assumed that private manumission was the only safe approach, that it should be gradual so as to avoid social turmoil, and that freed blacks should be relocated to colonies in Africa. The American Colonization Society, founded in 1816, typified these attitudes. The Society never sent many blacks abroad, but it did express white anxieties.

Nor did free blacks living in the North find their lives much improved by the first stirrings of republican reform. During the half century following independence, strong and growing black communities appeared in the northern ports, notably in Boston, New York, Philadelphia, and Baltimore. Their growth was fed by people like Phyllis Sherman coming in from the northern countryside and Ben Thompson making his way up from the South. On the eve of independence, 4,000 slaves and a few hundred free blacks had called the four port cities home; 50 years later, more than 30,000 free blacks did so.

The men who came sought employment as laborers or sailors, the women as domestics. They sought as well the companionship of other people of color. The development of black neighborhoods was a result both of white discrimination and the black desire for community. In rural areas, free blacks lived in relative isolation and were largely defenseless against white hostility. In the cities, however, numbers provided some protection and greatly improved the chances of finding a marriage partner, establishing a family, and participating in community activities. Family formation was eased by the fact that many of the migrants were women, thus correcting a long-standing gender imbalance.

As their numbers increased, blacks organized community institutions. In 1794, Richard Allen and Absalom Jones founded the first two black churches in Philadelphia. By 1813, the two congregations had over 1,800 members. "African" schools, mutual-aid societies, and fraternal associations followed, first in Philadelphia and Boston, more slowly in New York and Baltimore, where slavery lingered longer.

By 1820, a rich institutional and cultural life had taken root in the black neighborhoods of the port cities. White hostility, however, remained. Slavery's abolition actually increased rather than diminished white enmity in the North, in part because it pitted free blacks more directly against white laborers for employment and cheap housing. Race, as well as gender and class, continued to separate Americans from each other and reveal the limits of America's new social faith.

CONCLUSION
Between Two Worlds

The years between 1790 and 1828 were years of transition between preindustrial America and the industrializing world of the nineteenth century. Northern agriculture remained largely unchanged, but the continuing spread of commercial agriculture would soon launch a revolution in farm productivity. Staple agriculture still dominated the South, but cotton would transform the region and powerfully affect the entire nation. Perhaps most important, a newly exuberant spirit of economic opportunity began to dominate the land.

Region and locality still shaped people's lives, while conditions of race, class, and gender remained largely unchanged.

And yet new attitudes were forming as an emphasis on youthfulness and change, social equality and individualism, fanned by republican idealism and the Second Great Awakening, shaped Americans' attitudes toward social reform. Life in the early republic still echoed the past but pointed unmistakably toward the future.

RECOMMENDED READING

Valuable information on America's preindustrial economy can be found in Stuart Bruchey, *The Roots of American Economic Growth*, 1607–1861 (1965).

For illuminating discussions of merchant capitalism and early industrialization, see Jonathan Prude, *The Coming of Industrial Order : Town and Factory Life in Rural Massachusetts, 1810–1860* (1983); Howard Rock, *Artisans of the New Republic : The Tradesmen of New York City in the Age of Jefferson* (1979); and Bruce Laurie, *Working People of Philadelphia, 1800–1850* (1980). Early nineteenth-century agriculture is examined in James Lemon, *The Best Poor Man's Country : A Geographical Study of Early Southeastern Pennsylvania* (1972).

Important information on the trans-Appalachian West can be found in Malcolm Rohrbough, *The Trans-Appalachian Frontier : People, Societies, and Institutions, 1775–1850* (1978). Changes in transportation and communication are traced in Alan Pred, *Urban Growth and the Circulation of Information : The United States System of Cities, 1790–1840* (1973).

On the Great Awakening, see John Bole, *The Great Revival, 1787–1805* (1972) and Donald Mathews, *Religion in the Old South* (1977).

Themes of class and wealth are dealt with in Sean Wilentz, *Chants Democratic : New York City and the Rise of the American Working Class, 1788–1850* (1984); and Robert Doherty, *Society and Power : Five New England Towns, 1800–1860* (1977).

Among important works on women are Lee Chambers-Schiller, *Liberty, a Better Husband* (1984); and Joan Jensen, *Loosening the Bonds : Mid-Atlantic Farm Women, 1750–1850* (1987). On race and slavery, see Gerald Mullin, *Flight and Rebellion* (1972); and Gary B. Nash, *Forging Freedom : The Formation of Philadelphia's Black Community, 1720–1840* (1988).

On early education see Carl Kaestle, *Pillars of the Republic : Common Schools and American Society, 1780–1860* (1983).

Two recent volumes provide splendid overviews of American society in the early republic : Jack Larkin, *Reshaping Everyday Life, 1790–1840* (1988), and Barbara Clark Smith, *After the Revolution : The Smithsonian History of Everyday Life in the Eighteenth Century* (1987).

Time Line

1776	Adam Smith publishes *Wealth of Nations*
1790s	Turnpike construction in Northeast
	Yellow fever epidemics in cities
	Female academies founded
	Cotton production booms in the South
	Second Great Awakening begins
1791	Black rebellion begins in Haiti
1793	Eli Whitney invents the cotton gin
	Europe embroiled in war
1794	First Afro-American churches founded
1800	Gabriel Prosser's Rebellion in Virginia
1807	Robert Fulton launches first steamboat
	Cast-iron plow patented
	U.S. slave trade ends
1807–1809	Trade embargo
1811	Successful steamboat trip from Ohio River to New Orleans
1812–1814	War with Great Britain
	American Colonization Society formed
1819–1821	Depression

PART THREE

AN EXPANDING
PEOPLE

1820 – 1877

During the first half of the nineteenth century, the young nation expanded rapidly. As Americans surged west, and, in the 1840s, pushed on to the Pacific coast, the population soared and became more diverse. Expansion also sharpened regional differences, particularly between the North and the South, and the period ended with the most devastating conflict the nation has ever experienced.

Chapters 11, 12, and 13 cover roughly the same time period. Chapter 11, "Currents of Change in the Northeast and the Old Northwest," investigates the economic and social transformations that affected everyday life in these two regions. Chapter 12, "Slavery and the Old South," considers the South's distinctive economic and social system, which, based as it was on slavery, raised questions about the special virtue of the nation and the meaning of justice and equality.

In Chapter 13, "Shaping America in the Antebellum Age," we focus on economic and social changes that sharpened the familiar tension between narrowly defined self-interest and social concerns. The election of Andrew Jackson as president marked the advent of the second American party system and of a lively political culture firmly rooted in new economic and social conditions.

Chapter 14, "Moving West," shows the power of American expansionism and the limited meaning many Americans gave to terms like *liberty* and *equality*. During the 1840s, as settlers to new frontiers sought to re-create familiar institutions and patterns, the earlier inhabitants, mostly Mexicans and Native Americans, found themselves excluded from most of the promises of American life.

The expansion of slavery into the West threatened the political balance of power between the North and the South and raised the question of where power and authority lay to decide the future of the West.

Chapter 15, "The Union In Peril," traces the disintegration of the second party system and the eruption of civil war in Kansas. Secession and civil war soon followed. Chapter 16, "The Union Severed," examines the Civil War and the unanticipated results of the conflict. Chapter 17, "The Union Reconstructed," explores how Americans tried to resolve the many dilemmas of the postwar period.

11

Currents of Change in the Northeast and the Old Northwest

I n the fall of 1845, 15-year-old Mary Paul informed her father that she had decided to leave northern Vermont for employment in the Lowell textile mills. Mary had already held a job as a domestic servant for a farming family near her hometown of Barnard. But she disliked the position. Her mistress, Mrs. Angell, was difficult and sometimes refused to speak to her.

Lowell, with its thousands of jobs and bustling economy, offered Mary both the chance to escape haughty mistresses and "degrading" housework and the opportunity to be economically independent. Lowell also represented a sophisticated city life that the country-bred girl found alluring. As she explained to her father, she "could earn more to begin with [in Lowell] than I can anywhere about here. I am in need of clothes which I cannot get if I stay about here and for that reason I want to go to Lowell."

By November, Mary was settled in the mill town, living in "a very good boarding place" and working in a spinning room under a "first rate" overseer. Her situation pleased her, and she planned to stay "a year certain, if not more."

Over the next few years, Mary worked intermittently in Lowell. Though she kept returning to the mills, her later experiences were not as positive as her initial encounter. In 1848, after a six-month break, she returned to Lowell to discover that all the mills "seem to be very full of help." Finally, she secured a place in the dressing rooms of the Tremont Corporation, where she prepared yarn for the weaving process. "It is *very* hard work indeed," Mary reported, "and sometimes I think I shall not be able to endure it." Not only was the work difficult, but Mary found that the companies were planning to reduce wages.

On the whole, Mary seemed to have benefited from her contact with the new industrial world of work. When she tired of regimented mill life, she returned home to Vermont or tried some new job — making coats in Vermont, housekeeping in

New Hampshire, even joining a utopian community in New Jersey. In 1857, after 12 years of independence, she married Isaac Guild, a marbleworker. She retired from the wage labor work force to live as wife and mother in Lynn, Massachusetts.

• • •

This chapter explores the economic changes in the Northeast and Old Northwest that not only transformed the economy between 1820 and 1860, as Mary Paul discovered, but also shaped social, cultural, and political life. Though most Americans still lived in rural settings rather than in factory towns or cities, economic growth and the new industrial mode of production affected them through the creation of new goods, opportunities, and markets. In urban communities and factory towns, the new economic order ushered in new forms of work, new class arrangements, and new forms of social strife.

After discussing the factors that fueled antebellum growth, the chapter turns to the industrial world, where so many of the new patterns of work and life appeared. An investigation of urbanization reveals shifting class arrangements and values as well as rising social and racial tensions. Finally, an examination of rural communities in the East and on the frontier in the Old Northwest highlights the transformation of these two sections of the country. Between 1840 and 1860, industrialization and economic growth increasingly knit them together.

Economic Growth

Between 1820 and 1860, the American economy moved away from its reliance on agriculture as the major source of growth toward an industrial and technological future. Real per capita output of goods and services grew an average of 2 percent annually between 1820 and 1840 and slightly less between 1840 and 1860. But the economy, though expanding, was also unstable, lurching from periods of boom (1822–1834, mid-1840s–1850s) to periods of bust (1816–1821, 1837–1843). As never before, Americans faced dramatic shifts in the availability of jobs and goods and in prices and wages. Moreover, because regional economies were increasingly linked, problems in one area tended to affect conditions in others.

Expansion and Immigration

What accounted for this new phase of growth and economic development? The United States,

of course, had abundant natural resources, enormously increased by the Louisiana Purchase in 1803. An expanding population, soaring from 9 million in 1820 to over 30 million in 1860, represented the new workers, new households, and new consumers so essential to economic development. Until the 1840s, most of the growth in population came from natural increase. But as the size of American families gradually shrank — in 1800, the average white woman bore seven children; by 1860, the number had declined to five — foreign immigration took up the slack.

Immigration from Europe to the American continent snowballed after 1840. During the 1820s, some 128,502 foreigners came to American shores. In the 1850s, more than 2.8 million migrated to the United States. Most of the newcomers were young European men who represented a cheap pool of labor for American employers.

The Irish were the most numerous of all newcomers to America in the two decades preceding the Civil War. They came to escape famine in Ireland caused by a terrible blight that destroyed the potato crop in 1845. They usually arrived almost penniless in eastern port cities.

Germans, the second largest group of immigrants during this period (1,361,506 arrived between 1840 and 1859), were not fleeing from desperate circumstances in their homeland. Some had sufficient resources to go west and buy land. Others joined the urban working class as shoemakers, cabinetmakers, and tailors. The arrival of so many non-British newcomers made the American work force more diverse than it had ever been.

Transportation: The Critical Factor

Improved transportation was the most important factor behind economic and geographic expansion. Early in the century, high freight rates discouraged production for distant markets, and primitive transportation hindered western settlement. During the 1820s and 1830s, however, canal-building projects revolutionized travel and commerce and made migration much easier. The Erie Canal, completed in 1825, stretched 363 miles between Albany and Buffalo, New York. The canal was

Growth of the Railroads, 1850–1860

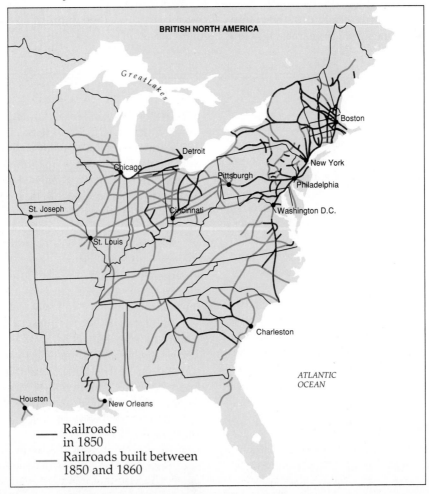

Railroads in 1850
Railroads built between 1850 and 1860

the last link in the chain of waterways binding New York City to the Great Lakes and the Northwest.

The Erie Canal and hundreds of other newly constructed canals provided farmers, merchants, and manufacturers with cheap and reliable access to distant markets and goods. They encouraged Americans to settle the frontier and cultivate virgin lands. Eventually, the strong economic and social ties the waterways fostered between the Northwest and the East led people living in the two regions to share political outlooks.

Politicians, promoters, and others, impressed with Britain's success with railways, also supported the construction of railroads. Only 73 miles of track were laid between 1828 and 1830, but by 1840, there were 3,000 miles of track, most in the Northeast. By the end of the 1850s, total mileage soared to 30,000.

The railroads exerted enormous influence. Their routes could determine whether a city, town, or even homestead survived. In the 1850s, the railroad transformed Chicago from a small settlement into a bustling commercial and transportation center. The dramatic rise in railroad construction in the two decades before the Civil War contributed to faster economic growth and stimulated agricultural expansion and regional specialization.

Capital Investment

Internal improvements, the exploitation of natural resources, and the cultivation of new lands all demanded capital. Much of it came from European investors. Between 1790 and 1861, over $500 million flowed into the United States from Europe. Foreign investors from Europe, adding to funds brought by immigrant families, financed as much as a third of all canal construction and bought about a quarter of all railroad bonds.

American mercantile capital fueled growth as well. As Chapter 10 suggested, the merchant class prospered in the half century after the Revolution. Now merchants invested in schemes ranging from canals to textile factories. Many

ventured into the production of goods and became manufacturers themselves.

Prosperous Americans eagerly sought opportunities to put their capital to work. Two New Yorkers, Arthur Bronson and Charles Butler, made a careful tour of the Northwest in 1833. Despite primitive conditions, both men saw wonderful opportunities. Detroit, Butler concluded, "is destined to be a very great city," while Chicago "presents one of the finest fields in America for industry & enterprise." Each man channeled funds into western projects. Bronson's investments ranged from Ohio banks to farmland in Wisconsin Territory, Illinois, Michigan, Ohio, and Indiana to real estate in Chicago and Detroit, all in addition to his holdings in New York ironworks and banks.

The Role of Government

Local and state government enthusiastically supported economic growth. States often helped new ventures raise capital by passing laws of incorporation, by awarding entrepreneurs special privileges such as tax breaks or monopolistic control, by underwriting bonds for improvement projects, which increased their investment appeal, and by providing loans for internal improvements. New York, Pennsylvania, Ohio, Indiana, Illinois, and Virginia publicly financed almost 75 percent of the canal systems in their states between 1815 and 1860.

The national government assisted some internal improvements such as the National Road linking Maryland and Illinois. Federal tariff policy shielded American products, and the second U.S. Bank provided the financial stability investors required. The line separating the public sector from the private often became unclear.

The law also helped to promote aggressive economic growth. The case of *Palmer* v. *Mulligan*, decided by the New York State Supreme Court in 1805, laid down the principle that property ownership included the right to develop property for business purposes. A series of important Supreme Court decisions between 1819 and 1824 clarified contract law, establishing the basic principle that contracts were binding.

The Innovative Mentality

Economic expansion depends on intangible factors as well as more obvious ones such as improved transportation. The entrepreneurial mentality that encouraged investment, new business ventures, and land speculation was an important component of antebellum economic development. Another factor was American energy and openness to change. As one Frenchman explained in 1834, "All here is circulation, motion, and boiling agitation. Experiment follows experiment; enterprise succeeds to enterprise."

Others described an American mechanical "genius." The American was "a mechanic by nature," one Frenchman insisted. "In Massachusetts and Connecticut, there is not a labourer who had not invented a machine or tool." This observer exaggerated, but Americans did develop a number of efficient and productive tools and machines. The McCormick harvester, the Colt revolver, Goodyear vulcanized rubber products, and the sewing machine were developed, refined, and developed further. Such improvements cut labor costs and increased efficiency.

While the shortage of labor in the United States stimulated technological innovations that replaced humans with machines, the rapid spread of education after 1800 also contributed to innovation and increased productivity. By 1840, most whites were literate. In that year, public schools nationwide were educating 38.4 percent of white children between the ages of 5 and 19.

The belief that education spurred economic growth helped to foster enthusiasm for public education, particularly in the Northeast. Massachusetts moved first toward mass education by mandating in 1827 that taxes pay the whole cost of the state's public schools. At first, the Massachusetts school system did not function well. School buildings were often run-down and even unheated. Because school curricula were virtually nonexistent, students often lounged idly at their desks.

Under the leadership of Horace Mann, the reform of state education for white children began in 1837. Mann advocated graded schools, uniform curricula, teacher training, and reduced the power of local districts over schools. His campaigns made the Massachusetts system a model for reformers everywhere.

Mann believed that education promoted inventiveness. It "had a market value." Businessmen often agreed. Prominent industrialists in the 1840s believed that education produced workers who could handle complex machinery without undue supervision and were superior employees — reliable, punctual, industrious, and sober.

Ambivalence Toward Change

While supporting education as a means to economic growth, many Americans also firmly believed in its social value. Public schools could mold student character and promote "virtuous habits" and "rational self-governing" behavior. Students learned facts by rote because memory work and recitation taught them discipline and concentration. Nineteenth-century schoolbooks reinforced the classroom message. "It is a great sin to be idle," children read in one 1830 text, while another warned "Poverty is the fruit of idleness."

The concern with education and character indicate that as much as Americans welcomed economic progress, they also feared social and economic change. Schools, which taught students to be deferential, obedient, and punctual, could counter the worst by-products of change. Schools served as much as a defense against change as its agents.

The touted virtues of diligence, punctuality, temperance, and thrift probably did assist economic growth, but the success of early nineteenth-century economic ventures frequently depended on the ability to take risks, to think daringly. The emphasis given to the safe but stolid virtues suggests that the fear of social disintegration ran through antebellum society.

The Advance of Industrialization

Significant economic growth between 1820 and 1860 resulted from the reorganization of production. Factory production reorganized work by breaking down the manufacture of an article into discrete steps. At first, manufacturers often relied on the putting-out system (see Chapter 10). Eventually, they centralized all the steps of production under one roof, where hand labor gradually gave way to power-driven machinery such as wooden "spinning jennies." Often they sought the help of British immigrants who had the practical experience and technical know-how no American possessed.

As factory workers replaced artisans and home manufacturers, the volume of goods rose, and prices dropped dramatically. The price of a yard of cotton cloth fell from 18 cents to 2 cents over the 45 years preceding the Civil War.

Between 1820 and 1860, textile manufacturing became the country's leading industry. Textile mills sprang up across the New England and the Middle Atlantic states, regions that contained swift-flowing streams to power the mills, capitalists eager to finance the ventures, children and women to tend the machines, and numerous cities and towns with ready markets for cheap textiles. Early mills were small affairs, containing only the machines for carding and spinning. The thread was then put out to home workers to be woven into cloth. The early mechanization of cloth production did not replace home manufacture but supplemented it.

Already underway in 1813, however, were experiments that would lead to the development of the power loom. Eventually, the loom devised by Francis Cabot Lowell and Paul Moody was installed in a mill at Waltham, Massachusetts.

The most important innovation of the Waltham operation was Lowell's decision to bring all the steps of cotton cloth production together under one roof. By centralizing the entire manufacturing process and work force in one factory, cloth for the mass market could be produced more cheaply and more profitably. In 1823, the Boston Associates expanded their op-

This calico factory, located in Manchester, New Hampshire, produced colorful fabrics for American consumers. In 1854, fully 1,250 of the 2,000 workers were female.

erations to East Chelmsford on the Merrimack River, a town they renamed Lowell.

Most New England mills followed the Lowell system. The cumulative impact of the rise of the textile industry was to supplant the home production of cloth, even though some women would continue to spin and weave for their families for some years to come, and hand-loom weavers would survive for another generation. In the process, Americans were transformed from a people clad in earth-colored homespun into a nation decked out in gayer, more colorful clothing.

Textile mills helped to account for the increasingly industrial character of the Northeast. By 1860, fully 71 percent of all manufacturing workers lived in this region of the country.

Other important manufacturing operations reached west and south from New England. The processing of wheat, timber, and hides using power-driven machinery was common in most communities of 200 families or more. Paper mills were widespread, although a third of them were clustered in Philadelphia. The iron and metalworking industry stretched from Albany, New York, south to Maryland and west to Cincinnati.

Early Manufacturing

Industrialization created a more efficient means of producing more goods at much lower cost than had been possible in the homes and small shops of an earlier day. Philadelphian Samuel Breck's diary reveals some of the new profusion and range of goods. "Went to town principally to see the Exhibition of American Manufactures at the Masonic Hall," he noted in 1833. "More than 700 articles have been sent. Among this great variety, I distinguished the Philadelphia porcelains, beautiful Canton cotton, made at York in this state, soft and capacious blankets, silver plate, . . . chymical drugs, hardware, saddlery, and the most beautiful black broadcloth I ever saw."

The Impact of Industrialization

Two examples illustrate how industrialization transformed American life. Before the nineteenth century, local printing shops depended on manual labor to produce books, newspapers, and journals. The cost of reading material was high enough to make a library a sign of wealth.

Between 1830 and 1850, however, adoption and improvement of British inventions, together with managerial and marketing innovations, revolutionized the printing and publishing industries.

As books and magazines dropped in cost and grew in number, far more people could afford them. No longer dependent solely on the words of the "better sort" for information, people could now form their views on the basis of what they read. The proliferation of printed matter had an enormous impact on people's stock of information, values, tastes, and use of leisure time. It also contributed to the rising literacy rate among white Americans.

Just as printed materials wrought great changes in American life, the making of inexpensive timepieces affected its pace and rhythms. Before the 1830s, when few Americans could afford a clock, it was difficult to make exact plans. But the production of timepieces soared in the 1830s, and by midcentury, inexpensive, mass-produced ones could be found everywhere. Clocks encouraged a more disciplined use of time and undergirded the economic changes taking place. Timepieces, for example, were essential for the successful operation of railroads, which ran on schedules. Clocks also imposed a new rhythm in many workplaces.

A New England Textile Town

To understand the process of industrialization and its impact on work and the work force, let us examine Lowell, the "model" Massachusetts textile town, and Cincinnati, a bustling midwestern industrial center.

Lowell was a new town, planned and built expressly for industrial purposes in the 1820s. Regarded as a model factory community, in 1836, Lowell, with 17,000 inhabitants, aspired to become the "Manchester of America." It was the country's most important textile center.

By 1830, women composed nearly 70 percent of the Lowell textile work force. The women who came to Lowell for jobs were the first American women to labor outside their homes in large numbers. They were also among the first Americans to experience the full impact of the factory system.

Working and Living in a Mill Town

Mary Paul was typical of the young women drawn to work in Lowell and other New England textile towns. As the planners had anticipated, most were unmarried and young. In 1830, more than 63 percent of Lowell's population was female, and most were between the ages of 15 and 29.

These women, from New England's middling rural families, came to the mills for a variety of reasons ranging from the desire for economic independence to the decline of home manufacturing. As Sally Rice from Vermont explained, "I am almost nineteen years old. I must of course have something of my own before many more years have passed over my head. And where is that something coming from if I go home and earn nothing." Mill work paid women relatively well in the 1820s and 1830s. Domestic servants' weekly wages hovered around 75 cents and seamstresses' 90 cents, while in the mid-1830s women could make between $2.40 and $3.20 a week in the mill.

Few of the women considered their decision to come to Lowell a permanent commitment. They came to work for a few years, felt free to go home or to school for a few months, and then returned to mill work. Once married, they left the mill work force forever.

New manufacturing work was regimented and exhausting. The standard schedule was 12 hours a day, six days a week, with only a half hour for breakfast and lunch.

Within the factory, the organization of space facilitated production. In the basement was the waterwheel, the source of power. Above, successive floors were completely open, each containing the machines necessary for the different steps of cloth making: carding, spinning, weaving, and dressing. Elevators moved materials from one floor to another. On a typical floor, rows of machines stretched the length of the low room, tended by operatives who might watch over several machines at the same time. From his elevated desk at the end of the room, the overseer watched the workers.

Involving an adaptation to a completely new work situation, mill work also entailed an entirely new living situation for women operatives. The companies provided substantial quarters for their overseers and housing for male workers and their families. Hoping to attract respectable females to Lowell, the mill owners also constructed company boardinghouses where women workers had to live, usually four to six to a room. Headed by female housekeepers, the boardinghouse maintained strict rules, including a 10 o'clock curfew. Amid such intimate working and living conditions, young women formed close ties with one another and developed a strong sense of community.

Female Responses to Work

Although mill work offered better wages than other occupations open to women, all female workers had limited job mobility, because only men could hold supervisory positions. Most female operatives accepted such sexual discrimination as part of life. But the sense of sisterhood supported open protest when trouble arose.

Trouble broke out when hard times hit Lowell in February 1834. Falling prices, poor sales, and rising inventories prompted managers to announce a 15 percent wage cut. This was their way of protecting profits — at the expense of their employees. The mill workers sprang into

Work in textile mills was often tedious and repetitive. Although women were paid less than men, they often welcomed the opportunity to live independently and to earn their own money.

action. Petitions circulated, threatening a strike. Meetings followed. At one lunchtime gathering, the company agent, hoping to end the protests, fired an apparent ringleader. But, as the agent reported, "she declared that every girl in the room should leave with her," then "made a signal, and . . . they all marched out & few returned the ensuing morning." The strikers roamed the streets appealing to other workers and visited other mills. In all, about a sixth of the town's work force turned out.

Though this work stoppage was brief and failed to prevent the wage reduction, it demonstrated women workers' concern about the impact of industrialization on the labor force. Strikers, taunted as unfeminine for their "amazonian display," refused to agree that workers were inferior to bosses. Pointing out that they were daughters of free men, strikers called the bosses "Tories in disguise" and sought to link their pro-

test to their fathers' and grandfathers' efforts to throw off the bonds of British oppression during the Revolution. Revolutionary rhetoric that once held only political meaning took on economic overtones as Lowell women confronted industrial work.

During the 1830s, wage cuts, long hours, increased work loads, and production speed-ups, mandated by owners' desires to protect profits, constantly reminded Lowell women and other textile workers of the possibility of "wage slavery." In Dover, New Hampshire, 800 women turned out and formed a union in 1834 to protest wage cuts. In the 1840s, women in several New England states agitated for the ten-hour day, while petitions from Lowell prompted the Massachusetts legislature to hold the first government hearing on industrial working conditions.

The Changing Character of the Work Force

Most protest efforts met with limited success. The short tenure of most women mill workers prevented permanent labor organizations. In addition, the waves of immigration that deposited so many penniless foreigners in northeastern cities in the 1840s and 1850s created a new pool of labor. The newcomers were desperate for jobs and would accept lower wages than New England farm girls. Gradually, the Irish began to replace Yankee women in the mills. Representing only 8 percent of the Lowell work force in 1845, the Irish composed nearly half the workers by 1860. As the ethnic makeup of the work force changed, so did its gender composition. More men came to work in the mills. By 1860, some 30 percent of the Lowell workers were male. All these changes made the women expendable and increased the costs of going "against the mill."

Lowell itself changed as the Irish crowded into the city and New England women gradually left the mills. With owners no longer feeling the need to continue paternalistic practices, boardinghouses disappeared. A permanent work force, once a nightmare to owners, had become a reality by 1860, and Lowell's reputation as a model factory town faded away.

Factories on the Frontier

Cincinnati, a small Ohio River settlement of 2,540 in 1810, grew to be the country's third largest industrial center by 1840. With a population of 40,382, it contained a variety of industries at different stages of development. Cincinnati manufacturers who turned out machines, machine parts, hardware, and furniture were quick to mechanize for increased volume and profits. Other trades like carriage making and cigar making moved far more slowly toward mechanization before 1860. Alongside these concerns, artisans like coopers, blacksmiths, and riverboat builders still labored in small shops using traditional hand tools. The new and the old ways coexisted in Cincinnati, as they did in most manufacturing communities.

In 1850, most Cincinnati workers worked in small or medium-size shops, but almost 20 percent labored in factories with over 100 employees. Some craftsmen continued to use a wide array of skills as they produced goods in time-honored ways. Others worked in new factories, performing more specialized and limited tasks. In furniture factories, for example, some artisans worked exclusively as varnishers, others as carpenters, and still others as finishers. No single worker made a chair from start to finish. But all used some of their skills and earned steady wages. Though in the long run machines threatened to replace them, these skilled factory workers often had reason in the short run to praise the factory's opportunities. Less fortunate was the new class of unskilled factory laborers, who received low wages and had little job security.

Many of Cincinnati's female residents were "outworkers" who worked in small shops or at home as seamstresses for the city's growing ready-to-wear clothing industry. Manufacturers purchased the cloth, cut it into basic patterns, and then contracted the work out to be finished.

Paid by the piece, female outworkers were among the most exploited of Cincinnati's work-

ers. The successful marketing of sewing machines in the 1850s contributed to worsening working conditions and lower pay. Since the sewing machine made stitching easier, the pool of potential workers increased and the volume of work that bosses expected grew.

Cincinnati employers claimed that the new industrial order offered great opportunities to most of the city's male citizens. Manufacturing work encouraged the "manly virtues" so necessary to the "republican citizen." Not all Cincinnati workers agreed. Like workers in Lowell and other manufacturing communities, Cincinnati's laborers rose up against their bosses in the decades before the Civil War.

The workingman's plight, as Cincinnati labor leaders analyzed it, stemmed from his loss of independence. The new industrial order was changing the nature of the laboring class itself. A new kind of worker had emerged. Rather than selling the products of his skills, he had only his raw labor to sell. His "wage slavery," or dependence on wages, promised to be lifelong. The reorganization of work signaled the end of the progression from apprentice to journeyman to master and undermined traditional skills. Few workers could expect to rise to the position of independent craftsman. Most would only labor for others, just as slaves labored for their masters. Nor would wages bring to most that other form of independence, the ownership of shop and home. The expression "wage slavery" contained a deep truth about the changed conditions of many American workingmen.

Workers also resented the masters' attempts to control their lives. In the new factories, owners insisted on a steady pace of work and uninterrupted production. Artisans who were used to working in spurts, stopping for a few moments of conversation or a drink, disliked the new routines.

The fact that workers' wages in Cincinnati, as in other cities, rose more slowly than food and housing costs compounded discontent over changing working conditions. The working class sensed it was losing ground at the very time the city's rich were visibly growing richer. In 1817, the top tenth of the city's taxpayers owned over half the wealth, while the bottom half possessed only 10 percent. In 1860, the share of the top tenth had increased to two-thirds, while the bottom half's share had shrunk to 2.4 percent.

In the decades before the Civil War, Cincinnati workers formed unions, turned out for fair wages, and rallied in favor of the ten-hour day. Like the Lowell mill women, they cloaked their protest with the mantle of the Revolution. Striking workers staged parades with fifes and drums and appropriated patriotic symbols to bolster their demands for justice and independence. They insisted that masters were denying them a fair share of profits, thereby dooming them to economic dependency. Since the republic depended on a free and independent citizenry, the male workers warned that their bosses' policies threatened to undermine the republic itself.

Only in the early 1850s did Cincinnati workers begin to suspect that their employers formed a distinct class of parasitic "nonproducers." Although most strikes still revolved around familiar issues of better hours and wages, signs appeared of the more hostile labor relations that would emerge after the Civil War.

As elsewhere, skilled workers were in the forefront of Cincinnati's labor protest and union activities. But Cincinnati workers did not readily unite with them. The uneven pace of industrialization meant that these workers, unlike the Lowell mill women, had no common working experience. Moreover, growing cultural and ethnic diversity compounded differences in the workplace. By 1850, almost half the people in the city were foreign-born, most of them German, compared to 22 percent in 1825. Protestant workers frequently felt that they had more in common with their Protestant bosses than with Catholic Irish or German fellow workers.

These tensions exploded in Cincinnati in the spring of 1855. Americans attacked barricades erected in German neighborhoods, crying out death threats. Their wrath visited the Irish as well. In many cases, labor disunity served economic progress by undermining workers' efforts

for higher pay, shorter hours, and better working conditions, thus favoring businesses.

Urban Life

Americans experienced the impact of economic growth most dramatically in the cities. In the four decades before the Civil War, the rate of urbanization in the United States was faster than ever before or since. In 1820, about 9 percent of the American people lived in cities (defined as areas containing a population of 2,500 or more). Forty years later, almost 20 percent of them did.

The Process of Urbanization

Three distinct types of cities — commercial centers, mill towns, and transportation hubs — emerged during these years of rapid economic growth. Commercial seaports like Boston, Philadelphia, and Baltimore expanded steadily and developed diversified manufacturing to supplement the older functions of importing, exporting, and providing services and credit. New York replaced Philadelphia as the country's largest and most important city. With the completion of the Erie Canal, New York merchants gained control of much of the trade with the West. By 1840, they had also secured the largest share of the country's import and export trade.

Access to waterpower fueled the development of a second kind of city like Lowell, Massachusetts; Trenton, New Jersey; and Wilmington, Delaware. Situated inland along the waterfalls and rapids that provided the power to run their mills, these cities burgeoned in the decades before the Civil War.

West of the Appalachian Mountains, a third type of city arose. Louisville, Cleveland, and St. Louis were typical of cities that had served as transportation service and distribution centers from the earliest days of frontier settlement. Chicago acted as "grand depot, exchange, counting-house, and metropolis" for its hinterlands.

As the number of urban dwellers grew, their needs helped to generate economic growth. Cities provided a growing market for farm products and manufactured goods such as shoes, clothing, furniture, carriages, cast-iron stoves, and building materials.

Until 1840, the people eagerly crowding into cities came mostly from the American countryside. Then a growing number of immigrants arrived in the seaport cities. Many moved on to the interior, but the penniless had little choice but to remain in eastern cities and search for work there. By 1860, fully 20 percent of the people living in the Northeast were immigrants. The Irish, fleeing famine and poverty at home, were the largest foreign group in the Northeast.

A look at Philadelphia reveals the character and tensions of urban life during the antebellum period. An inland port, Philadelphia stood second only to New York. Though William Penn's "green country town" boasted an attractive appearance and an orderly plan, the expanding nineteenth-century city merited little praise. Speculators interested only in profit relied on the grid pattern as the cheapest and most efficient way to divide land for development. They built monotonous miles of new streets, new houses, new alleys, with "not a single acre left for public use, either for pleasure or health," as merchant Samuel Breck observed.

Overwhelmed by rapid growth, city governments provided few of the services we consider essential today, and usually only to those who paid for them. Water is a case in point. Only by paying a special fee could Philadelphians have water brought into their homes, so most of the city's residents went without. An inspection carried out by Mathew Carey in 1837 had pointed to an even more basic problem: 253 persons crowded into 30 tenements without even one privy. The ability to pay for services determined not only comfort but health.

Class Structure in the Cities

The drastic differences in the quality of urban life reflected the growing economic inequality that characterized Philadelphia and other American cities. In sharp contrast to the colonial period, the first half of the nineteenth century witnessed a dramatic rise in the concentration of wealth in the United States. The pattern was most extreme in cities. By the late 1840s, the wealthiest 4 percent of Philadelphia's population (merchants, brokers, lawyers, bankers, and manufacturers) held about two-thirds of the wealth. The economic pattern was similar in other American cities.

This widening gap between the upper class and the working class did not translate into mass suffering because more wealth was being generated. But the growing inequality hardened class lines, nourished social tensions, and contributed to the labor protests of the antebellum period.

Between 1820 and 1860, Philadelphia's working class, like Cincinnati's, was transformed. As preindustrial ways yielded to factory production, some former artisans and skilled workers climbed into the middle class, becoming businessmen, factory owners, mill supervisors, and shopkeepers. But downward occupational mobility also increased. Fed by waves of immigrants, the lower class was growing at an accelerating rate. Moreover, within the working class itself, the percentage of unskilled wage earners living in poverty or on its brink increased.

The Urban Working Class

As with so much else in urban life, housing reflected social and economic divisions. The poorest rented quarters in crowded, flimsily constructed shacks, shanties, and two-room houses. The urban working class faced not just poverty but the transformation of family life. Men could no longer be sure of supporting their wives and children, even when they were employed, and they felt that they had lost much of their authority and power in the family. Some found their wives no longer subservient or seemingly careless with their hard-earned money. Family violence that spilled out onto the streets was not uncommon in working-class quarters.

Middle-Class Life and Ideals

Members of the comfortable middle class profited from the dramatic increase in wealth in antebellum America. The houses of the city's elite were spacious and filled with new conveniences. Samuel Breck's house in 1839 was elegant and luxurious, with "parlours 14 feet high, . . . furnaces, water closet and shower and common bath up stairs, marble mantels and fireplaces in dressing rooms."

For the urban middle and upper class, the rewards of economic success included residential comfort, choice, and stability. But working-class renters moved often, from one cramped lodging to another. This common pattern of repeated mobility made it difficult to create close-knit neighborhoods in urban settings.

As the gap between classes widened, new middle-class norms emerged, nourished by the changing economy. Better transportation, new products, and the rise of factory production and large businesses changed family life. Falling prices for processed and manufactured goods made it unnecessary for women to continue making these items at home. As men increasingly involved themselves in a money economy, women's and children's contributions to the family economy became relatively less significant. Even the rhythm of their lives, oriented to housework rather than the demands of the clock, separated them from the bustling commercial world where their husbands now labored. By 1820, the notion emerged that the sexes occupied separate spheres.

While men pursued success in the public world, what were women's responsibilities? Sarah Hale, editor of the popular magazine *Godey's Lady's Book*, and Catharine Beecher, well-known lecturer and writer, argued that woman's sphere was at home, keeping house and creating a clean, wholesome, and private setting for family life.

Women also served as their families' moral and cultural guardians. Arguing that women had different characters from men, that they were innately pious, virtuous, unselfish, and modest, publicists maintained that mothers

would train future citizens and workers to be obedient, moral, patriotic, and hardworking. Just as important, they would preserve important values in a time of rapid change. As one preacher explained, a wife was the guardian angel who "watches over" her husband's interests, "warns him against dangers, comforts him under trial ; and by . . . pious, assiduous, and attractive deportment, constantly endeavors to render him more virtuous, more useful, more honourable, and more happy."

This view, characterizing women as morally superior to and different from men, had important consequences for many women's lives. The physical separation of the male and female worlds and the shift in women's status often meant that women shared more with one another than with men, even their husbands. Similar social experiences and perspectives made female friendships central for many women, the source of comfort, security, and happiness.

They also experienced both pleasure and frustration in their role as housekeepers. Now that most domestic production had disappeared from the household, the task of creating a comfortable and attractive home became primary. But new standards of cleanliness, order, and beauty were often impossible to achieve. Moreover, efforts to create a perfect home often worked against harmonious family life.

Although the concept of domesticity seemed to confine women to the domestic sphere, it actually prompted women to take on activities in the outside world. If women were the guardians of morality, why should they not carry out their tasks in the public sphere ? This reasoning lay behind the tremendous growth of voluntary female associations in the early decades of the nineteenth century. Initially, most involved religious and charitable activities. In the 1830s, as we shall see in Chapter 13, women added specific moral concerns like the abolition of slavery to their missionary and benevolent efforts, often clashing with men and with social conventions about "woman's place."

Domesticity described norms, not the actual conduct of middle-class women. Obviously not all women were pious, disinterested, selfless, virtuous, cheerful, and loving. But these ideas influenced how women thought of themselves. The new norms, effectively spread by the publishing industry, influenced rural women and urban working women. The insistence on marriage and service to family discouraged married women from entering the work force. Those who had to work often bore a burden of guilt. Though the new feminine ideal may have seemed noble to middle-class women in cities and towns, it created difficult tensions in the lives of working-class women.

As family roles were reformulated, a new view of childhood emerged. Working-class children still worked or scavenged for goods to sell or use at home, but middle-class children were no longer expected to contribute economically to the family. Middle-class parents now came to see childhood as a special stage of life, a period of preparation for adulthood.

Children were to spend their early years learning important values from their mothers and through schooling. Children's fiction also presented dutiful, religious, loving, and industrious youngsters as role models.

The growing publishing industry helped to spread new ideas about family roles and appro-

priate family behavior. Novels, magazines, etiquette and child-rearing manuals, and schoolbooks all carried the message from northern and midwestern centers of publishing to the South, to the West, and to the frontier. Probably few Americans lived up to the new standards established for the model parent or child, but the standards increasingly influenced them.

New notions of family life supported the widespread use of contraception for the first time in American history. Since children required so much loving attention and needed careful preparation for adulthood, many parents desired smaller families. The declining birthrate was evident first in the Northeast, particularly in cities and among the middle class. Contraceptive methods included abortion, which was legal in many states until 1860. This medical procedure terminated perhaps as many as a third of all pregnancies. Other birth control methods included coitus interruptus and abstinence. The success of these methods for family limitation suggests that many men and women adopted the new definitions of the female sex as naturally affectionate but passionless and sexually restrained.

Mounting Urban Tensions

The social and economic changes transforming American cities in the half century before the Civil War produced urban violence on a scale never before witnessed in America, not even during the Revolution. Festering ethnic and racial tensions often triggered mob actions that lasted for days.

Racial tensions contributed to Philadelphia's disorders. An unsavory riot in August 1834 revealed other important sources of social antagonism as well as the inability of its police force to control disorder.

One hot August evening, several hundred white Philadelphians wrecked a building on South Street that contained the "Flying Horses," a merry-go-round patronized by both blacks and whites. A general melee followed. As the *Philadelphia Gazette* reported, "At one time it is supposed that four or five hundred persons were

Erastus Salisbury Field (1805–1900), an accomplished folk artist, painted this middle-class family in Ware, Massachusetts, in 1839. His portrait suggests different family roles and the domestic comfort that characterized middle-class family life.

engaged in the conflict, with clubs, brickbats, paving stones, and the materials of the shed in which the flying horses were kept." Spurred by the taste of blood, the white mob moved into the center of the crowded, racially mixed neighborhood, where they continued their orgy of destruction, looting, and intimidation of black residents.

An investigation following the riots revealed that the white mob had caused at least $4,000 of damage to two black churches and more than 36 private homes. At least one black had been killed, and numerous others had been injured.

Many rioters bragged that they were "hunting the nigs." Riots, however, are complicated events, and this racial explanation does not reveal the range of causes underlying the rampage of violence and destruction.

The mob's composition hints at some of the reasons for participation. Many of the rioters were young and at the bottom of the occupational and economic ladder, competing with blacks for jobs. This was particularly true of the newly arrived Irish immigrants, who were attempting to replace blacks in low-status jobs. Subsequent violence against blacks suggested that economic rivalry was an important component of the riot. "Colored persons, when engaged in their usual vocations," the *Niles Register* observed, "were repeatedly assailed and maltreated. . . . Parties of white men have insisted that no blacks shall be employed in certain departments of labor."

Some rioters were skilled workers who had experienced the negative impact of a changing economic system that was undermining the small-scale mode of production. To them, blacks were scapegoats, but the real but intangible villain was the economic system itself. Trade union organizing and a general strike a year later would highlight the grievances of this group.

Rapid urban expansion also figured as a factor in the racial violence. Most of the rioters lived either in the riot area or nearby. All had experienced the overcrowded and inadequate living conditions caused by the city's rapid growth.

The racial tensions generated by squalid surroundings and social proximity go far to explain the outbreak of violence. The same area would later become the scene of race riots and election trouble and became infamous for harboring criminals and juvenile gangs.

The city's small, newly formed police force proved unable to control the mob, thus prolonging the violence. Philadelphia, like other eastern cities, was in the midst of creating its police force. Only continued rowdiness, violence, and riots would convince residents and city officials in Philadelphia (and in other large cities) to support an expanded, quasi-military, preventive police force in uniforms. By 1855, most sizable eastern cities had established such forces.

Finally, the character of the free black community itself was a factor in producing those gruesome August events. Not only was the community large and visible, but it had also created its own institutions and its own elite. Whites resented "dressy blacks." The mob targeted the solid brick houses of middle-class blacks, robbing them of silver and watches.

The Black Underclass

Events in Philadelphia showed how hazardous life for free blacks could be. Northern whites, like southerners, believed in black inferiority and depravity and feared black competition for jobs and resources. Although northern states had passed gradual abolition acts between 1780 and 1803 and the national government had banned slaves from entering new states to be formed out of the Northwest Territory, nowhere did any government extend equal rights and citizenship or economic opportunities to free blacks in their midst.

For a time in the early nineteenth century, some blacks living in the North were permitted to vote, but they soon lost that right. Beginning in the 1830s, Pennsylvania, Connecticut, and New Jersey disenfranchised blacks. New York allowed only those with three years' residence and property valued at $250 or more to vote. Only the New England states (with the exception of Connecticut), which had tiny black populations, preserved the right to vote regardless of color. By 1840, fully 93 percent of the northern free black population lived in states where law or custom prevented them from voting.

Other black civil rights were also restricted. In five northern states, blacks could not testify against whites or serve on juries. In most states, the two races were thoroughly segregated. Blacks increasingly endured separate and inferior facilities in railway cars, steamboats, hospitals, prisons, and other facilities. They sat in "Negro pews" in churches and took communion only after whites had left the church. Although most Protestant religious denominations in the antebellum period split into northern and southern branches over the issue of slavery, most northern churches were not disposed to welcome blacks as full members.

As the Philadelphia riot revealed, whites were driving blacks from their jobs. In 1839, *The Colored American* blamed the Irish. "These impoverished and destitute beings . . . are crowding themselves into every place of business . . . and driving the poor colored American citizen out." Increasingly after 1837, these "white niggers" became coachmen, stevedores, barbers, cooks, house servants — all occupations blacks had once held.

Educational opportunities for blacks were also severely limited. Only a few school systems admitted blacks, in separate facilities. The case of Prudence Crandall illustrates the lengths to which northern whites would go to maintain racial segregation. In 1833, Crandall, a Quaker schoolmistress in Canterbury, Connecticut, announced that she would admit "young colored ladies and Misses" to her school. The outraged townspeople, unable to persuade her to abandon her project, harassed and insulted students and teachers, and finally demolished the school. Crandall was arrested, and after two trials — in which free blacks were declared to have no citizenship rights — she finally gave up and moved to Illinois.

Crandall would not have found the Old Northwest much more hospitable. The fast-

growing western states were intensely committed to white supremacy and black exclusion. As an Indiana newspaper editor observed in 1854, informal customs made life dangerous for blacks. They were "constantly subject to insults and annoyance in traveling and the daily avocations of life ; [and] are practically excluded from all social privileges, and even from the Christian communion."

Rural Communities

Although the percentage of families involved in farming fell from 72 to 60 percent between 1820 and 1860, Americans remained a rural people. Agriculture persisted as the country's most significant economic activity, and farm products still made up most of the nation's exports. The small family farm still characterized eastern and western agriculture.

Farming remained the dominant way of life, but agriculture changed in the antebellum period. Vast new tracts of land came under cultivation in the West. Railroads, canals, and better roads pulled rural Americans into the orbit of the wider world. Some crops were shipped to regional markets ; others, like grain, hides, and pork, stimulated industrial processing. Manufactured goods, ranging from cloth and tools to books and periodicals, flowed in return to farm families. Commercial farming encouraged different ways of thinking and acting and lessened the isolation so typical before 1820.

Farming in the East

During the antebellum period, economic changes created new rural patterns in the Northeast. Marginal lands in New England, New York, and Pennsylvania, cultivated as more fertile lands ran out, yielded discouraging returns. Gradually after 1830, farmers abandoned these farms, often to move westward. By 1860, almost 40 percent of people who had been born in Vermont had left their native state.

Farmers who did not migrate west had to transform their production. Realizing that they could not compete with western grain, they sought new agricultural opportunities created by better transportation and growing urban markets. One of the demands was for fresh milk. By the 1830s, some eastern cities had grown so large that milk was turning sour before it reached central marketplaces. To meet the desire for milk, several cities, including New York City, started urban dairies. As railroad lines extended into rural areas, however, farmers living as far away as Vermont and upper New York State discovered that they could ship cooled milk to urban centers. City residents had fresher and cheaper milk and drank more of it as a result.

Urban appetites encouraged other farmers to cultivate fruit and vegetables for sale in city markets. With fresh produce in regular supply, cookbooks began to include recipes calling for fresh ingredients.

As northern farmers adopted new crops, they began to consider farming as a scientific endeavor. After 1800, northern farmers started using manure as fertilizer rather than disposing of it as a smelly nuisance. By the 1820s, some farmers were rotating their crops and planting new grasses and clover to restore fertility to the soil. By 1860, American farmers had developed thousands of special varieties of plants for local conditions. Many improvements resulted from experimentation, but farmers also enjoyed more and better information, which they found in new journals like the *New England Farmer,* the *Farmers' Register,* and the *Cultivator.* Following New York's lead in 1819, many states established agricultural agencies to propagate new ideas. A "scientific" farmer in 1850 could often produce two to four times as much per acre as in 1820.

Farmers in the fertile area around Northampton, Massachusetts, illustrate the American farmer's adjustment to new economic conditions. As roads and canals improved, markets became more accessible. Farmers started to cultivate crops "scientifically" in order to increase profits. Farming was becoming a business.

At home, women found themselves freed from many of their traditional tasks. Peddlers brought goods to the door. The onerous duty of making cloth and clothing disappeared with the coming of inexpensive ready-made cloth and even ready-made clothes in the 1820s. Daughters liberated from the chores of home manufacturing went off to the mills or earned money by taking in piecework from local merchants. Cash transactions replaced the exchange of goods. Country stores became more reluctant to accept wood, rye, corn, oats, and butter as payment for goods instead of cash.

Some farmers prospered as they became involved in the market economy; others just got along. Wealth inequality increased near Northampton, as it did elsewhere in the rural Northeast.

Frontier Families

Many people who left the North during these years headed for the Old Northwest, where they raised corn and pork, sending their products down the Ohio and Mississippi rivers to southern buyers. In 1820, less than one-fifth of the American population lived west of the Appalachians; by 1860, almost half did, and Ohio and Illinois had become two of the nation's most populous states.

In 1830, Chicago had only 250 residents. Conditions were often primitive, as Charles Butler and Arthur Bronson discovered during their 1833 trip. Their hotel in Michigan City, Indiana, was "a small log house, a single room, which answered the purpose of drawing room, sitting room, eating room & sleeping room; in this room some eleven or twelve persons lodged in beds & on the floor."

During the 1830s, land sales and settlement boomed in the Old Northwest. Eastern capital contributed to the boom with loans, mortgages, and speculative buying. Internal improvement schemes after 1830 also influenced new settlement patterns and tied the Old Northwest firmly to the East. Erasmus Gest, who as a 17-year-old had worked on canal projects in Indiana, recalled the settlers' enthusiasm for improvements : "We Engineers were favorites with the People wherever we went."

Wheat for the eastern market rather than corn and hogs for the southern market became increasingly important with the transportation links eastward. Between 1840 and 1860, Illinois, southern Wisconsin, and eastern Iowa turned into the country's most rapidly growing grain regions. In the 1850s, these three states accounted for 70 percent of the increase in national wheat production.

Settling in the Old Northwest required hard work and at least some money. Catharine Skinner, who moved from New York to Indiana with her husband when she was 24, wrote to her sister in 1849 : "We have got 80 acres of land in the woods of Indiana, a very level country ; we have got two acres cleared and fenced and four more pirty well under way ; we have got about five acres of wheat in the ground ; we raised corn enough for our use and to fat our pork . . . we have a cow so that we have milk and butter and plenty of corn bread but wheat is hard to be got in account of our not having mony."

The Skinners probably spent $500 to $600 to start farming. They invested perhaps $100 for 80 acres of government land, $300 for basic farming equipment, and another $100 or $150 for livestock. To buy an already "improved" farm cost more. Once farmers moved onto the prairies of Indiana and Illinois, they needed an initial investment of about $1,000 since they had to buy materials for fencing, housing, and expensive steel plows. If farmers invested in the new horse-drawn reapers, they could cultivate more land, but all their costs also increased.

Opportunities in the Old Northwest

It was possible to begin farming with less, however. Some farmers borrowed from relatives, banks, or insurance companies like the Ohio Life Insurance and Trust Company. Others rented land from farmers who had bought more acres than they could manage. Tenants who furnished their own seeds and animals could expect to keep about a third of the yield. Within a few years, some saved enough to buy their own farms. Even those without any capital could work as hired hands. Since labor was scarce, they earned good wages. Probably about a quarter of the western farm population consisted of young men laboring as tenants or hired hands.

Rural communities, unlike the cities, had no growing class of propertyless wage earners, but inequalities nevertheless existed in the Old Northwest. In Butler County, Ohio, for example, 16 percent of people leaving wills in the 1830s held half of the wealth. By 1860, the wealthiest 8 percent held half of the wealth. While wealth was not as concentrated in rural areas as in the cities, a few residents benefited more from rapid economic development than others. Nevertheless, the Northwest offered many American families the chance to become independent producers and to enjoy "a pleasing competence."

CONCLUSION
The Character of Progress

Between 1820 and 1860, the United States experienced tremendous growth and economic development. Visitors constantly remarked on the amazing bustle and rapid pace of American life. The United States was, in the words of one Frenchman, "one gigantic workshop, over the entrance of which there is the blazing inscription 'NO ADMISSION HERE, EXCEPT ON BUSINESS.'"

Although the wonders of American development dazzled foreigners and Americans alike, economic growth had its costs. Expansion was cyclic, and financial panics and depression punctuated the era.

Growing inequality characterized urban and rural life, prompting some labor activists to criticize new economic and social arrangements. But workers, largely still unorganized, did not speak with one voice. Ethnic, racial, and religious diversity divided Americans in new and troubling ways.

During these decades, many also noted that the paths between the East, Northwest, and South seemed to diverge. The rise of King Cotton in the South, where slave rather than free labor formed the foundation of the economy, created a new kind of tension in American life, as the next chapter will show.

RECOMMENDED READING

Two useful introductions to economic change during this period are Stuart Bruchey, *The Roots of American Economic Growth, 1607–1861* (1965), and Albert W. Niemi, *U.S. Economic History: A Survey of the Major Issues* (1975).

Thomas C. Cochran provides an overview of industrial development in *Frontiers of Change: Early Industrialism in America* (1981), while technological innovation is the subject of David J. Jeremy, *Transatlantic Industrial Revolution: The Diffusion of Textile Technology Between Britain and America, 1790–1830* (1981).

On economic change in individual communities, see Thomas Dublin, *Women at Work: The Transformation of Work and Community in Lowell, Massachusetts, 1826–1860* (1979), and (as editor) *Farm to Factory: Women's Letters, 1830–1860* (1981); Allen F. Davis and Mark H. Haller, eds., *The Peoples of Philadelphia: A History of Ethnic Groups and Lower-Class Life, 1790–1940* (1973); and Steven J. Ross, *Workers on the Edge: Work, Leisure, and Politics in Industrializing Cincinnati, 1788–1890* (1985). See also Gary B. Nash, *Forging Freedom: The Formation of Philadelphia's Black Community, 1720–1840* (1988).

Alexis de Tocqueville analyzes American society in the 1830s in *Democracy in America* (1957 ed.). Edward Pessen shows the growth of inequality in four cities in *Riches, Class, and Power Before the Civil War* (1973). Mary P. Ryan focuses on the middle-class family in *Cradle of the Middle Class: The Family in Oneida County, New York, 1790–1865* (1981), while Christine Stansell focuses on lower-class urban women in *City of Women: Sex and Class in New York, 1789–1860* (1986). On family life see also Robert V. Wells, *Revolutions in Americans' Lives: A Demographic Perspective of the History of Americans, Their Families, and Their Society* (1982). Immigrant life is described in Stephan Thernstrom, ed., *Harvard Encyclopedia of American Ethnic Groups* (1980).

On the midwestern frontier, see Clarence Danhof, *Changes in Agriculture: The Northern United States, 1820–1870* (1969); Don H. Doyle, *The Social Order of a Frontier Community: Jacksonville, Illinois, 1825–1870* (1978); and John Mack Faragher, *Sugar Creek: Life on the Illinois Prairies* (1986).

Time Line

1805	*Palmer* v. *Mulligan*
1816	Second U.S. Bank
1817	New York Stock Exchange
1819	*Dartmouth College* v. *Woodward*
1820	Lowell founded by Boston Associates
	Land Act of 1820
	The expression "woman's sphere" becomes current
1824	*Sturges* v. *Crowninshield*
1824–1850	Construction of canals in the Northeast
1825–1856	Construction of canals linking the Ohio, the Mississippi, and the Great Lakes
1828	Baltimore and Ohio Railroad begins operation
1830	Preemption Act
1830s	Boom in the Old Northwest
	Increasing discrimination against free blacks
	Public education movement spreads
1833	Philadelphia establishes small police force
1834	Philadelphia race riots
	Lowell work stoppage
1837	Horace Mann becomes secretary of Massachusetts Board of Education
1837–1844	Financial panic and depression
1840	Agitation for ten-hour day
1840s–1850s	Rising tide of immigration
1841	Distributive-Preemption Act

12

Slavery and the Old South

s a young slave boy, Frederick Douglass was sent by his master to live in Baltimore. When he first met his mistress, Sophia Auld, she appeared to be "a woman of the kindest heart and finest feelings." He was "astonished at her goodness" as she began to teach him to read. Her husband, however, ordered her to stop because Maryland law forbade teaching slaves to read. In the seven years he lived with the Aulds, young Frederick had to use "various strategems" to teach himself to read and write, the key to his later escape to freedom.

Slaves and masters were inextricably bound to each other. After her husband's interference, Sophia Auld, Douglass observed, was transformed from an angel into a demon by the "fatal poison of irresponsible power." Her formerly tender heart turned to "stone" when she ceased teaching him. "Slavery proved as injurious to her," Douglass wrote, "as it did to me."

Such was also the case in Douglass's relationship with Mr. Covey, a slavebreaker to whom he was sent in 1833 to have his will broken. Covey succeeded for a time, Douglass reported, in breaking his "body, soul, and spirit" by brutal hard work and discipline. But one hot August day in 1833, the two men fought a long, grueling battle, which Douglass won. His victory, he said, "rekindled the few expiring embers of freedom, and revived within me a sense of my own manhood." Although it would be four more years before his escape to the North, the young man never again felt like a slave. The key to Douglass's successful resistance to Covey's power was not just his strong will, but rather his knowledge of how to jeopardize Covey's reputation and livelihood as a slavebreaker. The oppressed survive by knowing their oppressors.

As Mrs. Auld and Covey discovered, as long as some people were not free, no one was free. After quarreling with a house servant, one plantation mistress complained that she "exercises dominion over me — or tries to do it. One would have thought . . . that I was the Servant, she the mistress." Many whites lived in constant fear of a slave revolt, sometimes sleeping with "a brace of loaded pistols at their sides."

Slavery, then, was an intricate web of human relationships as well as a labor system. After showing the economic growth and development of the Old South, in which slavery and cotton played vital roles, this chapter will emphasize the daily lives and relationships of masters and slaves who, like Douglass and the Aulds, lived, loved, learned, worked, and struggled with one another in the years before the Civil War.

• • •

Perhaps no issue in American history has generated quite as many interpretations or as much emotional controversy as slavery. As American attitudes toward that institution have changed over the years, three interpretive schools have developed, each adding to our knowledge of the "peculiar institution." The first saw slavery as a relatively humane and reasonable institution in which plantation owners took care of helpless, childlike slaves. The second depicted slavery as a harsh and cruel system of oppressive exploitation. The third, and most recent, interpretation described the slavery experience from the perspective of the slaves, who did indeed suffer brutal treatment in slavery but who also survived with individual self-esteem and a sense of community and culture.

The first and second interpretive schools emphasized workaday interactions among masters and slaves, while the third focused on life in the slave quarters from sundown to sunup. In a unique structure, this chapter follows these masters and slaves through their day, from morning in the Big House through hot afternoon in the fields to the slave cabins at night. But although slavery was the crucial institution in defining the Old South, many other social groups and patterns contributed to the tremendous economic growth of the South from 1820 to 1860. We will look first at these diverse aspects of antebellum southern life.

Building the Cotton Kingdom

The vast region of the antebellum South was not a monolithic society filled only with large cotton plantations worked by hundreds of slaves. The realities of the South and slavery were much more complex. Large-plantation agriculture was dominant, but most southern whites were not even slaveholders, much less large planters. Most southern farmers lived in dark, cramped, two-room cabins. Cotton was a key cash crop in the South, but it was not the only crop grown there. Some masters were kindly, but many were not; some slaves were contented, but most were not.

There were many Souths, encompassing several geographic regions, each with different economic bases and social structures. The older Upper South of Virginia, Maryland, North Carolina, and Kentucky grew different staple crops from those grown in the newer, Lower or "Black Belt" South that stretched from South Carolina to eastern Texas. Within each state, moreover, the economies differed between flat, coastal areas and inland, up-country forests and pine barrens. A still further diversity existed between these areas and the Appalachian highlands of northern Alabama and Georgia, eastern Tennessee and Kentucky, and western Virginia and North Carolina. Finally, the cultural and economic life of New Orleans, Savannah, Charles-

Frederick Douglass, photographed here in about 1855, spent his life working for freedom and improved opportunities for blacks after his own escape to freedom as a young man in 1838.

ton, and Richmond differed dramatically from that of rural areas of the South. But although the South was diverse, agriculture dominated its industry and commerce.

Economic Expansion

In the 20 years preceding the Civil War, the South's economy grew slightly faster than the North's. Personal income in 1860 was 15 percent higher in the South than in the prosperous states of the Old Northwest. The cotton gin was fundamental to this economic growth, wedding the southern economy to cotton production for a century and stimulating the expansion of slavery into vast new territories.

As we learned in Chapter 10, most cotton farmers planted "long staple" cotton prior to the invention of Eli Whitney's cotton gin in 1793. After the cotton gin, the "short staple" variety, which could grow anywhere in the South, predominated. But only large plantation owners could afford to buy gins and purchase the fertile bottomlands of the Gulf states. Thus the planta-

tion system and slavery spread with the rise of cotton.

Although corn was a larger crop than cotton in total acreage, cotton was the largest cash crop and for that reason was called "king." In 1820, the South became the world's largest producer of cotton, and from 1815 to 1860 cotton represented more than half of all American exports. Cotton was not only the mainstay of the southern economy, but also was a crucial link in the national economy.

The supply of cotton from the South grew at an astonishing rate, soaring from 461,000 bales in 1817 to 1.35 million bales in 1840, 2.85 million bales in 1849, and 4.8 million bales in 1860. In the period from 1817 to 1860, cotton production jumped over tenfold. This rapid growth was stimulated by world demand, especially from English textile mills. The availability of new lands, a self-reproducing supply of cheap slave labor, and low-cost steamboat transportation down the Mississippi River to New Orleans helped to keep cotton king.

White and Black Migrations

Southerners migrated southwestward in huge numbers between 1830 and 1860 to grow more and more cotton. They pushed the southeastern Indians and the Mexicans in Texas out of the way and were still moving into Texas as the Civil War began. The migration process made many planters rich.

By the 1830s, the center of cotton production had shifted from South Carolina and Georgia to Alabama and Mississippi. This process continued in the 1850s as southerners forged into Arkansas, Louisiana, and eastern Texas. As they moved, they carried their values and institutions, including slavery, with them.

Not only were these migrating southern families attracted by the pull of fresh land and cheap labor, but they were also pushed westward by worsening economic conditions and other pressures in the older Atlantic states. Beginning in the 1820s, the states of the Upper

Southern Cotton Production, 1821-1859

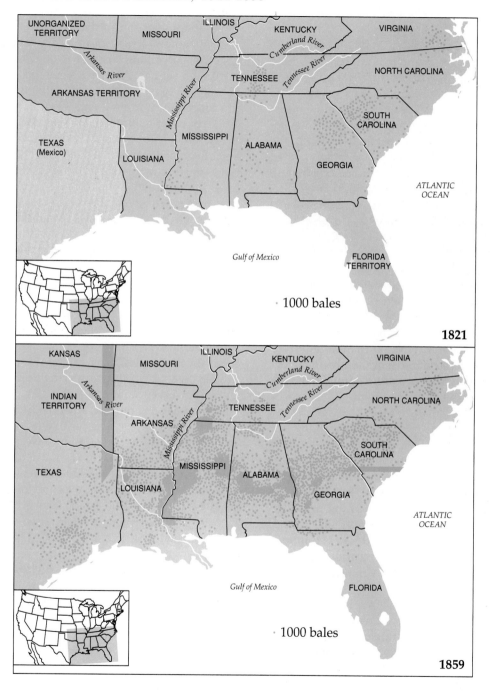

1821

1859

South underwent a long depression affecting tobacco and cotton prices. Moreover, years of constant use had exhausted their lands. Those who stayed in the Upper South continued to shift to grains, mainly corn and wheat. Because these crops required less labor than tobacco, slave owners began to sell some of their slaves.

The internal slave trade from Virginia "down the river" to the Old Southwest thus became a multimillion-dollar "industry" in the 1830s. Between 1830 and 1860, an estimated 300,000 Virginia slaves were transported south for sale. Although most southern states attempted occasionally to outlaw or control the traffic in slaves, these efforts were poorly enforced and usually short-lived. Besides, the reason for outlawing the slave trade was generally not humanitarian but rather originated in a fear of a rapid increase in the slave population, especially of "wicked" slaves sent south because they were considered unmanageable. Alabama, Mississippi, and Louisiana all banned the importation of slaves after the Nat Turner revolt in Virginia in 1831 (described later in this chapter). But all three states permitted the slave trade again during the profitable 1850s.

Congress formally ended the external slave trade on January 1, 1808, the earliest time permitted by the Constitution. Although many thousands of blacks continued to be smuggled to North America until the end of the Civil War, the tremendous increase in the slave population was the result not of this illegal trade but of natural reproduction, often encouraged by slaveowners eager for more laborers and salable human property.

The Dependence on Slavery

The rapid increase in the number of slaves, from 1.5 million in 1820 to 4 million in 1860, paralleled the growth of the southern economy and its dependence on the slave labor system. Economic growth and migration southwestward changed the geographic distribution of slaves, thus hindering the cause of abolition.

Although most slaves worked on plantations and medium-size farms, they could be found in all segments of the southern economy. In 1850, some 75 percent of all slaves were engaged in agricultural labor. The 300,000 slaves in 1850 who were not domestics or agricultural laborers worked as lumberjacks and turpentine producers in Carolina and Georgia forests; gold, coal, and salt miners in Virginia and Kentucky; boiler stokers and deckhands on Mississippi River steamships; toilers on road and railroad construction gangs in Georgia and Louisiana; textile laborers in Alabama cotton mills; dockworkers in Savannah and Charleston; and tobacco and iron workers in Richmond factories.

Slaves were also used in the industrial sector. The Tredegar Iron Company of Richmond decided in 1847 to shift from white labor "almost exclusively" to slave labor in order to destroy the potential power of organized white workers to strike. Tredegar's decision, though local, had enormous future implications. Although black and white workers have sometimes been able to agree on class issues, racial animosities based on white perceptions of threats to their job security by black workers continue to this day.

Whether in iron factories, coal mines, or cotton fields, slavery was profitable to owners. In 1859, the average plantation slave produced $78 in cotton earnings for his master annually while costing only about $32 to be fed, clothed, and housed. Slaves were also a good investment. In 1844, a "prime field hand" sold for $600. A cotton boom beginning in 1849 raised this price by 1860 to $1,800.

The economic growth of the slaveholding South was impressive, but it was limited because of the dependence on slavery. Generally, agricultural growth leads to the rise of cities and industry, facilitating sustained economic growth. In the planter-dominated antebellum South, however, agricultural improvements did not lead to industrialization and urbanization. On the eve of the Civil War, one southerner in 14 was a city dweller, compared to one of every three people in the North. The South would be economically

Concentration of Slavery, 1820-1860

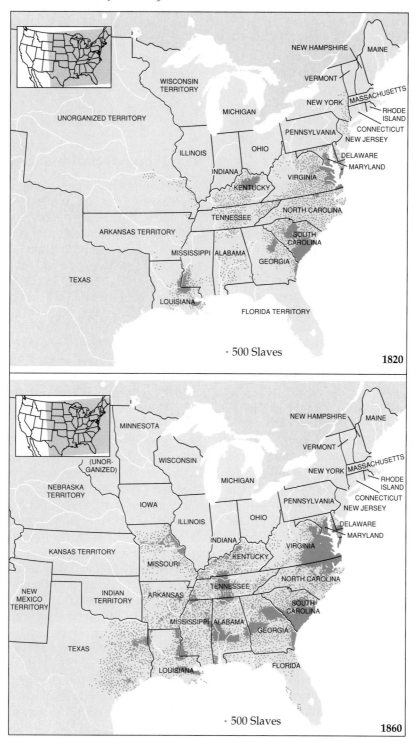

backward as long as the whites with capital insisted on putting all their business energies toward cotton production.

Slavery and Class in the South

Slavery was more than an economic institution, for it also served social purposes. Although the proportion of southern white families that owned slaves slowly declined from 40 to 25 percent as some families sold off their slaves to cotton planters, the ideal of slave ownership still permeated all classes and determined the hierarchical character of the southern social structure. At the top stood the planter aristocracy, much of it new wealth. Some 10,000 rich families owned 50 or more slaves in 1860; about 3,000 of these owned over 100. Below them was a slightly larger group of small planters who held from 10 to 50 slaves. But the largest group, 70 percent of all slaveholders in 1860, comprised 270,000 middle-level farm families with fewer than ten slaves. The typical slaveholder worked a small family farm of about 100 acres with eight or nine slaves, perhaps members of the same family. The typical slave, however, was more likely to be in a group of 20 or more other slaves on a large farm or small plantation.

In 1841, a young, white North Carolinian, John Flintoff, went to Mississippi to fulfil his dream of wealth and prestige. Beginning as an overseer managing an uncle's farm, he bought "a negro boy 7 years old" even before he owned any land. After several years of unrewarding struggle, Flintoff married and returned to North Carolina. There he finally bought 124 acres and a few more cheap, young blacks, and by 1860 he had a modest farm with several slaves growing corn, wheat, and tobacco. Although he never became as prosperous as he had dreamed, his son went to college, and his wife, he reported proudly, "has lived a *Lady*."

Like Flintoff, most southerners supported slavery for reasons of upward economic mobility, social prestige, and political influence. But they also defended the institution because it gave them a sense of superiority over at least one

group and a sense of kinship, if not quite equality, with other whites. Although there was always a small element of southern society that believed in emancipation, most southerners did not. A small Alabama farmer told a northern visitor in the 1850s that if the slaves were given their freedom, "they'd all think themselves just as good as we. . . . How would you like to hev a nigger feelin' just as good as a white man?"

The Nonslaveholding South

Below Flintoff and other middling farmers lived the majority of white southerners, who owned no slaves but were equally, or even more, antiblack. Newton Knight, for example, worked a harsh piece of land cut out of the pines of southern Mississippi. He and his wife lived in a crude log cabin, scratching out their livelihood by growing corn and sweet potatoes and raising chickens and hogs. A staunch Baptist given to fits of violence, Knight had once killed a black.

The 75 percent of southern whites who owned no slaves were scattered throughout the South. Many were Scots-Irish. Most lived in the foothills of the mountains and worked generally poorer land than the large planters. Largely self-sufficient, they raised mostly corn and wheat, hogs, enough cotton for their own clothes and a little cash, and subsistence vegetable crops. They lived in two-room log houses separated by a "dog run." Families gathered at corn huskings and quilting parties, logrolling and wrestling matches, and political stump and revivalist camp meetings. In many ways the yeoman farmers were the solid backbone of the South. Fiercely proud of their independence, they had a share of political power, voting overwhelmingly for Andrew Jackson.

Another little-known group of southern whites were the herdsmen who raised hogs and other livestock. They supplied bacon and pork to local slaveholders (who often thought hog growing was beneath their dignity) and drove herds of hogs to stockyards in Nashville, Louisville, and Savannah. The South raised two-thirds of the nation's hogs. In 1860, the value of southern livestock was $500 million, twice that of cotton. However valuable the total size of the hog business, individual hog herdsmen did not stand very high on the southern social ladder.

Below them were the poor whites of the South, about 10 percent of the population. Often sneeringly called "hillbillies," "dirt eaters," "crackers," or "poor white trash," they eked out a living from the poor soil of pine barrens, sand hills, and marshes. Although they grew a little corn and vegetables, their livelihood came mostly from fishing, hunting small game, and raising a few pigs. Some made corn whiskey, and many hired themselves out as farmhands for an average wage, with board, of about $14 per month. Because of poor diet and bad living conditions, these poor whites often suffered from diseases such as hookworm and malaria.

The poor whites were kept poor in part because the slave system allowed the planter class to accumulate a disproportionate amount of land and political power. High slave prices made entry into the planter class increasingly difficult, thus increasing class tensions within the South. Because the larger planters dominated southern life and owned the most slaves, an understanding of the character of slavery and the relationships between masters and slaves is best accomplished by looking at plantation life during a typical day from morning to night.

Morning: Master in the Big House

It is early morning on the southern plantation. Imagine three scenes. In the first, on the South Carolina plantation of James Hammond, the horn blows an hour before daylight to awaken the slaves for work in the fields. Hammond rises soon after, ever aware that "to continue" as a wealthy master, he must "draw the reign tighter and tighter" to hold his slaves "in complete check." He is as good as his word, recommending that "in general 15 to 20 lashes will be sufficient flogging" for most offenses but

that "in extreme cases" the punishment "must not exceed 100 lashes in one day."

On an Alabama plantation, Hugh Lawson is up early, writing a sorrowful letter to Susanna Clay, telling her of the death of a "devotedly attached and faithful" slave, Jim. "I feel desolate," Hugh writes. "My most devoted friend is gone and *his place* can never be supplied by another." As Lawson pens his letter, a female slave has already awakened and "walked across a frosty field in the early morning and gone to the big house to build a fire" for her mistress. As the mistress wakes up to a warming house, she says to the slave, a grown woman responsible for the welfare of two families, "Well, how's my little nigger today?"

In a third household, this one a medium-size farm in up-country Georgia, not far from Hammond's huge plantation, Charles Brock wakes up at dawn and joins his two sons and four slaves to work his modest acreage of grains and sweet potatoes, while Brock's wife and a female slave tend the cows that provide milk and butter. On small and medium-size family farms with five or fewer slaves, blacks and whites commonly worked together, as one observer noted, with "the axe of master and man [slave] falling with alternate strokes . . . [and] ploughing side by side."

As these scenes suggest, slavery thoroughly permeated the lives of southern whites. For the slaves, morning was a time for getting up and going to work. But for southern whites, morning involved contact with slaves in many ways: as burdens of figuring profit and loss, as objects to be kept obedient and orderly, as intimates and fellow workers, and as ever-present reminders of fear, hate, and uncertainty.

The Burdens of Slaveholding

Robert Francis Withers Allston (1801–1864) was a major rice planter in a low, swampy, mosquito-infested tidal area of South Carolina. It was a perfect spot for growing rice, but so unhealthy that few whites wanted to live there. The death rate among slaves was appallingly high. In 1840, a total of 18,274 slaves toiled in the Georgetown district, but only 2,193 whites, many for only part of the year. By 1860, Allston owned seven plantations along the Peedee River, totaling some 4,000 acres. He held nearly 600 slaves, 236 of whom worked at the home plantation, Chicora Wood. Rich in land and labor, he nevertheless had large mortgages and outstanding debts.

Allston was an educated, talented, public-spirited man. He served in the South Carolina state senate for 24 years and as governor from 1856 to 1858. His political creed, he wrote in 1838, was one of "virtue and purity" based on "the principles of Thomas Jefferson." Allston was active in the Episcopal church and an ardent reformer, advocating liberalization of South Carolina's poor laws; an improved system of public education open to rich and poor alike; humanitarian care of the deaf, blind, insane, and other disabled persons; and the improvement of conditions on the reservations of the Catawba Indians.

In 1832, Allston married Adele Petigru, an equally enlightened and hardworking person. She participated fully in the management of the plantation and ran it while Robert was away on politics. After Robert's death during the Civil War, she assumed control of the Allston plantations, which had been abandoned when Union troops moved through the area.

State politics lured Robert from his land for part of each year, but he was by no means an absentee owner. Managing thousands of acres of rice required careful supervision of both the slaves and an elaborate irrigation system.

Allston's letters frequently expressed the serious burdens of owning slaves. Although he was careful to distribute enough cloth, blankets, and shoes to his slaves and to give them sufficient rest, the sickness and death of slaves, especially young field-workers, headed his list of concerns. "I lost in one year 28 negroes," Allston complained, "22 of whom were task hands." He tried to keep slave families together but sold slaves when necessary.

Other planters shared Allston's concerns, seeing slavery as both a duty and a burden.

An Overseer's Report
W. Sweet to Adele Petigru Allston
N[ightin]gale hall, 14th September, 1864.
DEAR MADAM *I commence my harvest on last saterday on Boath Plantations the weather is very fin for harvest so far I will Bring some Rice in to the Barn yard at N[ightin]gale hall to Day and at ganderloss to morrow. I think that I will make about 2 Barrels of Syrrup on Each Place I finish grinding at ganderloss to Day I will not finish at Nightingale hall until the last of next weeak. litle Dianah was confined with a boy child on the 9 I am very sorry to say to you that one of Prisilia children a boy name July Dide on 12th with fits a[nd] fever I have had a grea[t] deal of fever among the children But not much among the grone negroes. old Rose is Stil quite sick mr Belflowers sent toney to mee on friday last I have concluded to let toney wife stay whare she is for a while as I understand that she is Pregnant and will not Be much survice in the harvest if I am Rong for soe Doing Pleas let mee know. the negroes all sends thare love to you an family my self and family is very un well.*
Source: *The South Carolina Rice Plantation As Revealed in the Papers of Robert F. W. Allston, ed. J. H. Easterby (1945).*

Many planters insisted that they worked harder than their slaves to feed and clothe them and to make their lives "as comfortable as possible." R. L. Dabney of Virginia exclaimed that "there could be no greater curse inflicted on us than to be compelled to manage a parcel of Negroes." Curse or not, Dabney and other planters profited from their burdens, a point they seldom admitted.

Their wives experienced other kinds of burdens. "The mistress of a plantation," wrote Susan Dabney Smedes, "was the most complete slave on it." Plantation mistresses were expected to act as chaste ladies, while their husbands had virtually unrestricted sexual access to slave women. "God forgive us, but ours is a monstrous system," Mary Boykin Chesnut wrote in her diary. "Like the patriarchs of old, our men live all in one house with their wives and their concubines; and the mulattoes one sees in every family partly resemble the white children. Any lady is ready to tell you who is the father of all the mulatto children in everybody's household but her own. Those, she seems to think, drop from the clouds."

Chesnut called the sexual dynamics of slavery "the sorest spot." There were others. Southern white women had to tend to the food, clothing, health, and welfare not just of their husbands and children but of the plantation slave population as well. The plantation mistress, then, served many roles: as a potential humanizing influence on men; as a tough, resourceful, responsible manager of numerous plantation affairs; as a coercer of slaves and perpetuator of the system; and sometimes as a victim herself.

Justifying Slavery

As slavery was increasingly attacked as immoral, slaveholders felt compelled to justify their institution. Until the 1830s, their defense explained slavery as a "necessary evil." After the abolitionists stepped up their attack in that decade, however, the justification shifted to defending slavery, in John C. Calhoun's words, as "a positive good." Various arguments were used: biblical, historical, constitutional, scientific, and sociological.

The biblical justification was based in part (incorrectly) on the curse of Canaan, the son of Ham, who was condemned to eternal servitude because his father had looked on Noah's nakedness. Furthermore, in various places both the Old and New Testaments admonished servants to obey their masters and accept their earthly lot. Southern apologists also cited historical arguments. Slavery had existed throughout history. In fact, the greatest civilizations — Egypt, Greece, and Rome — had all built their strength and grandeur in part on slave labor.

A third argument justified slavery on legal grounds. Southerners pointed out (correctly) that the United States Constitution clearly sanctioned slavery.

A fourth justification was "scientific." Southern ethnologists argued that blacks had been created separately (a theory called "poly-

genesis") and were an inherently inferior race with inferior brains. Therefore, the destiny of the inferior Africans was to serve the superior Caucasians (the "Adamic race") in work.

In a paternalistic defense of slavery based on racism and social control, George Fitzhugh argued that "the Negro is but a grown child and must be governed as a child." Social chaos would result if the slaves were freed. Emancipation, therefore, would be heartless and unthinkable, a burden to both blacks and whites.

Southern apologists for slavery faced the difficult intellectual task of justifying a system that ran counter to the main ideological directions of nineteenth-century American society: the expansion of individual liberty, mobility, economic opportunity, and democratic political participation. Moreover, the southern defense of slavery had to take into account the 75 percent of white families who owned no slaves and who envied those who did. Because of the potential for class antagonisms among whites, wealthy planters developed a justification of slavery that deflected class differences by maintaining that all whites were superior to all blacks but equal to one another. The theory of democratic equality among whites, therefore, was made consistent with racism and the holding of slaves.

As the southern defense of slavery intensified in the 1840s and 1850s, it aroused greater opposition from northerners and from slaves themselves. Although slavery was cruel in many ways, perhaps its worst feature was not physical but psychological: to be enslaved at all and barred from economic advancement in a nation that put a high value on freedom and equality of opportunity.

Noon: Slaves in House and Fields

It is two o'clock on a hot July afternoon on the plantation. The midday lunch break is over, and the slaves are returning to their work in the fields. Lunch was the usual nutritionally deficient fare of cornmeal and pork. Douglass remembered that "we worked all weathers. . . . It was never too hot, or too cold" for toiling in the fields.

Daily Toil

The daily work schedule for most slaves, whether in the fields or the Big House, was long and demanding. Aroused by a bell or horn before daybreak, they worked on an average day 14 hours in the summer and 10 hours in the winter. During harvest time, it was not uncommon to work for 18 hours. Ben Simpson, a Georgia slave, remembered vividly how his master would use a "great, long whip platted out of rawhide" to hit a slave in the work gang who would "fall behind or give out."

Under the task system, each slave had a specific task to complete daily. This system gave slaves the incentive to work hard enough to finish early, but it meant that the quality of their work was scrutinized constantly. An overseer's weekly report to Robert Allston in 1860 noted that he had "flogged for hoeing corn bad Fanny 12 lashes, Sylvia 12, Monday 12, Phoebee 12, Susanna 12, Salina 12, Celia 12, Iris 12."

An average slave was expected to pick 130 to 150 pounds of cotton per day. The work on sugar and rice plantations was even harder. Sugar demanded constant cultivation and the digging of drainage ditches in snake-infested fields. At harvest time, cutting, stripping, and carrying the cane to the sugar house for boiling was exhausting. In addition, huge quantities of firewood had to be cut and carried. Working in the low-country rice fields was worse: Slaves spent long hours standing in water up to their knees.

House slaves, most of them women, had relatively easier assignments than the field slaves, though they were usually called on to help with the harvest. They also ate and dressed better than their fellow slaves in the fields. But house slaves were watched more closely, were on call at all hours of the day and night, and

were more often involved in personality conflicts in the white household. The most feared punishment for a house slave, other than sale to the Deep South, was to be sent to the fields.

Slave Health

Although slave owners had an interest in keeping their slaves healthy by providing adequate care, slaves led sickly lives. Home was a crude, one-room log cabin with a dirt floor. Most cabins had a fireplace for heat and cooking, a table, some stools or boxes to sit on, an iron pot and wooden dishes, and perhaps a bed. The cabins were crowded, with usually more than one family living in each. Slave clothing was shabby and uncomfortable.

Studies on the adequacy of slave diet disagree, some showing that the food most slaves ate was deficient in calories and vitamins, others claiming that the energy value of the slave diet exceeded that of free whites in the general population. Compared to Latin American slaves, American slaves were well fed, receiving weekly rations of cornmeal, salt pork or bacon, molasses, and perhaps sweet potatoes. This bland fare was supplemented for some slaves, with the master's permission, by vegetables grown in a small garden and by fishing or hunting small game.

Most slaves, however, rarely enjoyed fresh meat, dairy products, fruits, or vegetables. To make up for these deficiencies, they sometimes stole from the master's kitchen, gardens, and barnyard. Inadequate diet led some slaves to become dirt eaters, which gave them worms and "swollen shiny skin, puffy eyelids, pale palms and soles." Others suffered regularly from skin disorders, cracked lips, and sore eyes. Many slaves, like poor whites, came down with vitamin deficiency diseases such as rickets, pellagra, beriberi, scurvy, and even mental illness.

Women slaves especially suffered weaknesses caused by vitamin deficiency, hard work, and disease, as well as those associated with the menstrual cycle and childbirth. Women were expected to do the same tasks in the fields as the men, in addition to cooking, sewing, child care, and traditional female jobs in the quarters when the fieldwork was finished. "Pregnant women," the usual rule stated, "should not plough or lift but must be kept at moderate work until the last hour" and were given a three-week recovery period after giving birth. But these guidelines were more often violated than honored. Infant mortality of slave children under 5 years of age was twice as high as for white children.

Life expectancy for American slaves was longer than for those in Latin America and the Caribbean, but not very high for either blacks or whites in the antebellum South (21.4 for blacks and 25.5 for whites in 1850). In part because of poor diet and climate, slaves were highly susceptible to disease. Many died from malaria, yellow fever, cholera, intestinal ailments, and respiratory diseases.

The relatively frequent incidence of whippings and other physical punishments aggravated the poor physical condition of the slaves. The slave William Wells Brown reported that on his plantation the whip was used "very frequently and freely" for inadequate or uncompleted work, stealing, running away, and even insolence and lying. Former slaves described a good owner as one who did not "whip too much" and a bad owner as one who "whipped till he'd bloodied you and blistered you." Other forms of punishment included isolation and confinement in stocks and jails during leisure hours, chains, muzzling, salting lash wounds, branding, burning, and castration.

Slave Law and the Family

Complicating master-slave relationships was the status of slaves as both persons and property, a legal and psychological ambiguity the South never resolved. On the one hand, the slaves had names, personalities, families, and wills of their own. This required dealing with them as fellow humans. On the other hand, they were items of property, purchased and maintained to perform specific profit-making tasks. As a Kentucky court put the problem, "Although the law of this state considers slaves as property, . . . it recognizes their personal existence, and, to a qualified extent, their natural right."

This ambiguity in the laws changed after the challenges to slavery in the early 1830s. As a result of Nat Turner's revolt and William Lloyd Garrison's publication of the abolitionist *Liberator* in 1831 (discussed later), the South tightened up the slave system. Laws prohibiting manumission were passed, but at the same time, laws protecting slaves from overly severe treatment were strengthened, and material conditions generally improved.

But whatever the law said, the practice was always more telling. Treatment varied with individual slaveholders. This was especially true with regard to the slave family. Most planters, like Robert Allston, generally encouraged their slaves to marry and did all they could to keep families intact. They believed that families made black males more docile and less inclined to revolt or run away. But some masters failed to respect slave marriages or broke them up because of financial problems. This tendency was supported by southern courts and legislatures, which did not legally recognize slave marriages or the right to family unity.

Adding to the pain of forced breakup of the slave family was the sexual abuse of black women. Although the frequency of such abuse is unknown, the presence of thousands of mulattoes in the antebellum era is testimony to this practice. White men in the South abused black slave women in several ways: by offering gifts for sexual "favors," by threatening those who refused with physical punishment or the sale of a child or loved one, by purchasing concubines, or by rape. As Frederick Douglass put it, the "slave woman is at the mercy of the fathers, sons or brothers of her master."

Because of the need to obtain cheap additional slaves for the work force, slaveholders encouraged young slave women to bear children, whether married or not. If verbal prodding and inducements such as less work and more rations did not work, masters would choose mates and foist them on slave women. More often, slaves chose their own mates on the basis of mutual attraction during an uneasy courtship complicated by the threat of white interferences. As among poor whites, premarital intercourse was frequent, but promiscuous behavior was rare. Most couples maintained affectionate, lasting relationships.

Although motherhood was the key event in a slave woman's life, bearing children and the double burden of work and family responsibilities challenged her resourcefulness. New mothers often had to choose between taking their babies into the fields to be fed or leaving them with others. Some masters would provide time off for nursing mothers, but the more common practice was for them to work in the fields with their newborn infants lying nearby, wrapped in cloth to protect them from the sun. Women developed networks of mutual support, looking after each other's children, meeting together to sew, quilt, cook, or do laundry, and attending births, caring for the sick and dying, and praying together.

The most traumatic problem for slaves was the separation of families, a haunting fear rarely absent from slave consciousness. The separation of husbands and wives (one-third according to one study of three Deep South states) challenged the couples to maintain contact. When Abream Scriven informed his wife, Dinah, of his sale to a trader in New Orleans, he had no idea where he would be sold but promised to "write and let you know where I am. . . . My Dear Wife for you and my Children my pen cannot Express the griffe I feel to be parted from you all."

There was much basis in fact for the abolitionists' contention that slavery was a harsh, brutal system. Yet, despite the travail of slavery, whether under relatively kind or cruel masters, the slaves endured with dignity, communal sensitivity, and even some joy. If daytime in the fields describes a view of slavery at its worst, nighttime in the quarters, as examined from the black perspective, reveals the slaves' survival

powers and their capacity to mold an African-American culture under slavery.

Night: Slaves in Their Quarters

It is near sundown, and the workday is almost over. Some of the slaves begin singing the gentle spiritual "Steal Away to Jesus," and others join in. Or perhaps they sing, "Dere's a meeting here tonight." To the unwary overseer or master, the humming, soothing sound of the song suggests happy slaves, content with their earthly lot and looking forward to deliverance in heaven, "in the sweet bosom of Jesus." To the slaves, however, the songs are a signal that, as an ex-slave, Wash Wilson, put it, they are to "steal away to Jesus" because "dere gwine be a 'ligious meetin' dat night." When evening arrived on the plantation, after a hard day of work in the hot sun or in the Big House, the slaves returned to their own quarters. There, as Wilson said, "sometimes us sing and pray all night."

In the slave quarters, away from white masters, overseers, and the burdens of daily work, an elaborate black community helped the slaves make sense out of their lives. In family life, religion, song, dance, the playing of musical instruments, and the telling of stories, the slaves both described their experiences and sought release from hardship and suffering. However burdensome their lives from sunup to sundown, after work the slaves experienced enjoyment and a sense of self-worth, hope, and group identity in their quarters.

Black Christianity

As suggested by the scene Wash Wilson described, Christian worship was an indispensable part of slave life in the quarters. The revivals of the early nineteenth century led to an enormous growth of Christianity among black Americans. Some independent black Baptist and Methodist churches, especially in border states and cities,

Religious meetings provided an outlet for emotions hidden all day from the overseer. At the Christmas holidays, music and dancing continued day and night.

served both slaves and free blacks and occasionally even whites. These separate churches had to steer a careful path to maintain their freedom and avoid white interference. But the vast majority of southern blacks were slaves, attending plantation missions set up by their masters.

For the slaveholders, religion often represented a form of social control. Black religious gatherings were usually forbidden unless white observers were present or white preachers led them. Whether in slave or white churches (where blacks sat in the back), preachers often delivered sermons from the text "Servants, obey your masters."

Although some slaves accommodated themselves to the master's brand of Christianity and patiently waited for heavenly deliverance, others rebelled and sought earthly liberty. Douglass had an illegal Sabbath school on one plantation, where he and others risked being whipped while learning about Christianity and how to read. "The work of instructing my dear fellow-slaves," he wrote, "was the sweetest engagement with which I was ever blessed." Sarah Fitzpatrick, an Alabama slave, recalled that the slaves wanted so much to "go to church by de'selves" that they were willing to sit through the "white fo'ks' . . . service in de mornin'." But when evening came, "a'ter dey clean up, wash de dishes, an' look a'ter ever'thing," the slaves would "steal away" to the nearby woods for their own service. Long into the night they would sing, dance, shout, and pray.

Although many of the expressive forms were African, the message reiterated over and over in the slave church was the Christian theme of suffering and deliverance from bondage. Slaves identified with the children of Israel and with the Exodus story, as well as with the suffering of Jesus and the inner turmoil of an unconverted "trebbled spirit." Nothing illustrated both the communal religious experience and these mixed Christian themes of suffering and redemption better than slave spirituals.

The Power of Song

A group of slaves gathers in the dark of night in the woods behind their quarters to sing and shout together.

O brothers, don't get weary
O brothers, don't get weary
O brothers, don't get weary
We're waiting for the Lord.
We'll land on Canaan's shore
We'll land on Canaan's shore
When we land on Canaan's shore
We'll meet forever more.

Music was a crucial form of expression in the slave quarters on both secular and religious occasions. The slaves were adept at creating a song, as one slave woman recalled, "on de spurn of de moment."

Although the spirituals were composed for many purposes, they reiterated one basic Christian theme : A chosen people, the children of God, were held captive in bondage but would be delivered. The titles and lyrics reveal the message : "We Are de People of de Lord," "To the Promised Land I'm Bound to Go," "Go Down, Moses," "Who Will Deliver Po' Me ?" What they meant by "deliverance" was not always clear and often had a double meaning : freedom in heaven and freedom in the North.

"The songs of the slave," Douglass wrote, "represent the sorrows of his heart." Although they often expressed the sadness of broken families and the burdens of work, they also expressed joy, triumph, and deliverance. Slave songs did not always contain hidden meanings. Sometimes slaves gathered simply for music, to play fiddles, drums, and other instruments fashioned by local artists in imitation of West African models. Sacred and secular events such as weddings, funerals, holiday celebrations, family reunions, and a successful harvest were all occasions for a communal gathering, usually with music. So too was news of external events that affected their lives — a crisis in the master's situation, a change in the slave code, the outcome of a battle during the Civil War, or emancipation itself.

The Enduring Family

The role of music in births, weddings, funerals, and other milestones of family life suggests that the family was central to life in the slave quarters. Although the pain of sexual abuse and family separation was a real or potential part of the experience of all slaves, so was the hope for family continuity.

The benefits of family cohesion were those of any group : love, protection, education, moral guidance, the transmission of culture, and the provision of status, role models, and basic support. All of these existed in the slave quarters. As the slaves gathered together at the end of the working day, parents passed on to their children the family story, language patterns and words, recipes, folktales, religious and musical traditions, and strong impressions of strength and beauty. In this way they preserved cultural tradition, which enhanced the identity and self-esteem of parents and children alike. Parents taught their children how to survive in the world and how to cope with life under slavery. As the young ones neared the age when they would work full time in the fields, their parents instructed them in the best ways to pick cotton or corn, how to avoid the overseer's whip, whom to trust and learn from, and ways of fooling the master.

The love and affection that slaves had for each other was sometimes a liability. Many slaves, women especially, were reluctant to run away because they did not want to leave their families. The slave family, though constantly endangered, played a crucial role in helping blacks adapt to slavery and achieve a sense of self-esteem.

Resistance and Freedom

Songs, folktales, and other forms of cultural expression enabled slaves to articulate their resistance to slavery. For example, Old Jim was going on a "journey" to the "kingdom" and, as he invited others to "go 'long" with him, he taunted his owner : "O blow, blow, Ole Massa, blow de cotton horn / Ole Jim'll neber wuck no mo' in de cotton an' de corn." From refusal to work it was a short step to outright revolt. In another song, "Samson," the slaves clearly stated their determination to abolish the house of bondage: "An' if I had-'n my way /I'd tear the buildin' down!/... And now I got my way/ And I'll tear this buildin' down." Every hostile song, story, or event, like Douglass's victory over Covey, was an act of resistance by which the slaves asserted their dignity and gained a measure of freedom. Some escaped slavery altogether to achieve such autonomy as was possible for free blacks in the antebellum South.

Forms of Black Protest

One way slaves protested the burdensome demands of continuous forced labor was in various "day to day" acts of resistance. These ranged from breaking or misplacing tools to burning crops, barns, and houses, from stealing or destroying animals and food to defending fellow slaves from punishment, from self-mutilation to deliberate work slowdowns, and from poisoning masters to feigning illness.

Overseers also suffered from these acts of disobedience, for their job depended on productivity, which in turn depended on the goodwill of the slave workers. No one knew this better than the slaves themselves, who adeptly played on the frequent struggle between overseer and master. Often the conflicts were ended by firing a bad overseer and hiring a more suitable replacement. Many slave-holders eventually resorted to using black drivers rather than overseers, but this created other problems.

The slave drivers were "men between," charged with the tricky job of getting the master's work done without alienating fellow slaves or compromising their own values. Although some drivers were as brutal as white overseers, many became leaders and role models for other slaves. A common practice of the drivers was to appear to punish without really doing so. Solomon Northrup reported that he "learned to handle the whip with marvellous dexterity and precision, throwing the lash within a hair's breadth of the back, the ear, the nose, without, however, touching either of them." As he did this, the "punished" slave would howl in pretended pain

and complain loudly to his master about his harsh treatment.

Another form of resistance was to run away. The typical runaway was a young male, who ran off alone and hid out in a nearby wood or swamp. He left to avoid a whipping or because he had just been whipped, to protest excessive work demands, or, as one master put it, for "no cause" at all. But there was a cause — the need to experience a period of freedom away from the restraints and discipline of the plantation.

Some slaves left again and again. Remus and his wife Patty ran away from their master, James Battle, in Alabama. They were caught and jailed three times, but each time they escaped again. Battle urged the next jailer to "secure Remus well." Some runaways, called "Maroons," hid out for months and years at a time in communities of runaway slaves. Several Maroon colonies were located in the swamps and mountains of the South, especially in Florida, where Seminole and other Indian groups befriended them. In these areas, blacks and Indians, sharing a common hostility to local whites, frequently intermarried, though sometimes Indians were hired to track down runaway slaves.

The underground railroad, organized by abolitionists, was a series of safe houses and stations where runaway slaves could rest, eat, and spend the night before continuing. Harriet Tubman, who led some 300 slaves out of the South on 19 separate trips, was the railroad's most famous "conductor." It is difficult to know exactly how many slaves actually escaped to the North and Canada, but the numbers were not large. One estimate suggests that in 1850 about a thousand slaves (out of over three million) attempted to run away, and most of them were returned. Nightly patrols by white militiamen, an important aspect of southern life, reduced the chances for any slave to escape and probably deterred many slaves from even trying to run away.

Slave Revolts

The ultimate act of resistance, of course, was rebellion. Countless slaves committed individual acts of revolt. In addition, there were hundreds of conspiracies whereby slaves met to plan a group escape and often the massacre of whites. Most of these conspiracies never led to action, either because circumstances changed or the slaves lost the will to follow through or, more often, because some fellow slave— perhaps planted by the master— betrayed the plot. Such spies thwarted the elaborate conspiracies of Gabriel Prosser (Richmond, Virginia, 1800) and Denmark Vesey (Charleston, South Carolina, 1822). Both resulted in severe reprisals by whites, including mass executions of leaders and the random killing of innocent blacks.

Only a few organized revolts, in which slaves threatened white lives and property, ever actually took place. Latin American slaves challenged their masters more often than their North American counterparts. Weaker military control, easier escape to rugged interior areas, the greater imbalance of blacks to whites, and the continued dependence of Latin American slaveholders on the African slave trade for their supply of mostly male workers explain this pattern. The imbalance of males to females (156 to 100 in Cuba in 1860, for example, compared to a near one-to-one ratio in the United States) weakened family restraints on violent revolts.

The most famous slave revolt in North America, led by Nat Turner, occurred in Southampton County, Virginia, in 1831. Turner was an intelligent, skilled, unmarried, religious slave who had experienced many visions of "white spirits and black spirits engaged in battle." He believed that he was "ordained for some great purpose in the hands of the Almighty."

On a hot August night, Turner and a small band of fellow slaves launched their revolt. They intended, as Turner said, "to carry terror and devastation" throughout the country. They crept into the home of Turner's master, Joseph Travis, who Nat said was "a kind master" with "the greatest confidence in me," and killed the entire family. Before the revolt was finally put down, 55 white men, women, and children had been murdered and twice as many blacks killed in the aftermath. Turner hid in a hole in the woods for

two weeks before he was apprehended and executed, but not before dictating a chilling confession to a white lawyer. Rarely thereafter would slaveholders go to sleep without the Southampton revolt in mind.

Free Blacks: Becoming One's Own Master

No matter how well they coped with their bondage, the slaves obviously preferred freedom. As Frederick Douglass said of the slave, "Give him a *bad* master, and he aspires to a *good* master; give him a good master, and he wishes to become his *own* master." Between 1820 and 1860, the number of free blacks in the United States doubled, from 233,500 to 488,000. This rise resulted from natural increase, successful escapes, "passing" as whites, purchasing freedom, and a continuation of some manumissions despite legal restriction in most states after the 1830s.

However freedom was achieved, what was life like for the 11 percent of the total black population who in 1860 were not slaves? More than half the free blacks lived in the South, most (85 percent in 1860) in the Upper South, where the total number of slaves had declined slightly. Free blacks generally lived away from the dense plantation centers, scattered on impoverished rural farmlands and in small towns and cities. One-third of southern free blacks lived in cities such as Baltimore, Richmond, Charleston, and New Orleans. In part because it took a long time to buy their freedom, they tended to be older, more literate, and more skilled than other blacks. A great many were light-skinned women, reflecting the favored privileges these blacks received from slaveholders.

Most southern free blacks were poor, laboring as farmhands, day laborers, or woodcutters. In the cities, they lived in appalling poverty and worked in factories. A few skilled jobs, such as barbering, shoemaking, and plastering, were reserved for black men; they were barred from more than 50 other trades. Women worked as cooks, laundresses, and domestics. The 15 percent of free blacks who lived in the Lower South were divided into two distinct castes. Most were poor. But in New Orleans, Charleston, and other southern cities, a small, mixed-blood class of free blacks emerged as an elite group, closely connected to white society and removed from the mass of poor blacks. A handful even owned land and slaves.

Most free blacks, however, had no such privileges. In most states, they could not vote, bear arms, buy liquor, assemble, speak in public, form societies, or testify against whites in court. In Richmond, efforts were also made to confine the free blacks to certain sections of the city or, increasingly by the 1850s, to compel them to leave the city, county, or state altogether. Those who stayed had trouble finding work, were required to carry licenses and freedom papers to be surrendered on demand, and often needed a white guardian to approve their actions. Nevertheless, free blacks and slaves often worked together in factories and fields, attended the same churches and places of entertainment, and sometimes even married.

The center of urban black community was the church. Martin Delaney wrote to Douglass in 1849 that "among our people . . . the Church is the Alpha and Omega of all things." The church not only performed the usual religious functions but also provided and promoted education, social insurance, fraternal associations, and picnics, concerts, and other forms of recreation. Besides the church, black community identity and

Churches for free blacks, rare before 1800, became a major source of social as well as religious activity by the 1840s.

pride revolved around the African schools and various burial and benevolent societies for self-help and protection against poverty, illness, and other disasters. Like their counterparts among whites, these societies grew and took on a new and significant social importance in the two decades before the Civil War.

Free blacks faced a crisis of extinction in the 1850s, especially when pressures increased late in the decade either to deport the free blacks or to enslave them. In the wake of increasing threats to their already precarious free status, some black leaders not surprisingly began to look more favorably on migration to Africa. That quest was interrupted, however, by the outbreak of the Civil War, rekindling in Douglass and others the "expiring embers of freedom."

CONCLUSION
Douglass's Dream of Freedom

Frederick Douglass won his freedom by forging a free black sailor's pass and escaping through Chesapeake Bay to New York. In a real sense, he wrote himself into freedom. The *Narrative of the Life of Frederick Douglass*, "written by himself" in 1845, was a way both of exposing the many evils of slavery and of creating his own

identity, even to the point of choosing his own name. Ironically, Douglass had learned to value reading and writing, we recall, from his Baltimore masters, the Aulds. This reminds us again of the intricate and subtle ways in which the lives of slaves and masters were tied together in the antebellum South.

In a poignant moment in his *Narrative*, Douglass described his dreams of freedom as he looked out at the boats on the waters of Chesapeake Bay as a boy. As we will see later, southern white planters also bemoaned their lack of freedom relative to the North and made their own plans to achieve independent status through secession. Meanwhile, as that struggle brewed beneath the surface of antebellum life, many other Americans were dismayed by various evil aspects in their society, slavery among them, and sought ways of shaping a better America. We turn to these other dreams in the next chapter.

RECOMMENDED READING

Gavin Wright provides a difficult but thorough analysis of the economic development of the Old South in *The Political Economy of the Cotton South : Households, Markets, and Wealth in the Nineteenth Century* (1978). On the economics of slavery, see Paul David et al., *Reckoning with Slavery : A Critical Study of the Quantitative History of American Negro Slavery* (1976). Nonagricultural slaves are dealt with in Robert Starobin, *Industrial Slavery in the Old South* (1970). The most readable story of the lives of nonslaveholding whites in the South is an old one, Frank Owsley's *Plain Folk in the Old South* (1949).

A brilliant study of racism in America, including excellent chapters on the southern justification of slavery, is George Fredrickson, *The Black Image in the White Mind : The Debate on Afro-American Character and Destiny, 1817–1914* (1971). For a stunning portrayal of female slaves in the plantation South, see Deborah Gray White, *Arn't I a Woman?* (1985). A remarkable new work that treats both white and slave women is Elizabeth Fox-Genovese, *Within the Plantation Household* (1988).

Of the many collections of primary source documents about slavery, the best is Willie Lee Rose, *A Documentary History of Slavery in North America* (1976). Among the best surveys of slavery are Nathan I. Huggins, *Black Odyssey : The Afro-American Ordeal in Slavery* (1977); and John Blassingame, *The Slave Community*, rev. ed. (1979). Slave culture and life in the quarters are treated brilliantly in Charles Joyner, *Down by the Riverside : A South Carolina Slave Community* (1984); and Lawrence Levine, *Black Culture and Black Consciousness : Afro-American Folk Thought from Slavery to Freedom* (1977). Frederick Douglass's experiences are told in three separate autobiographies, including *My Bondage and My Freedom* (1855), and *Life and Times of Frederick Douglass* (1881). A superb recent biography is *Frederick Douglass* (1990) by William S. McFeely.

The definitive work on free blacks in the South is Ira Berlin, *Slaves Without Masters : The Free Negro in the Antebellum South* (1976). Slave resistance and revolt are described in Vincent Harding, *There Is a River : The Black Struggle for Freedom in America* (1981), but a superb way to experience both slavery and the struggle for freedom is by reading an old classic, Harriet Beecher Stowe's *Uncle Tom's Cabin* (1852).

Time Line

1787	Constitution adopted with pro-slavery provisions
1793	Eli Whitney invents cotton gin
1800	Gabriel Prosser conspiracy in Virginia
1808	External slave trade prohibited by Congress
1820	South becomes world's largest cotton producer
1822	Denmark Vesey's conspiracy in Charleston
1830s	Southern justification of slavery changes from a necessary evil to a positive good
1831	Nat Turner's slave revolt in Virginia
1845	*Narrative of the Life of Frederick Douglass* published
1850s	Cotton boom
1851	Indiana state constitution excludes free blacks
1852	Harriet Beecher Stowe publishes best-selling *Uncle Tom's Cabin*
1860	Cotton production and prices peak

13

Shaping America in the Antebellum Age

On November 19, 1836, 30-year-old Marius Robinson and Emily Rakestraw were married near Cincinnati, Ohio. Two months after their wedding, he went on the road to speak against slavery and to organize abolitionist societies throughout Ohio. Emily stayed in Cincinnati to teach in a school for free blacks. During their ten-month separation, they exchanged affectionate letters that reflected their love and work. Marius, who had experienced a series of conversions inspired by the revivalist Charles G. Finney and his abolitionist disciple Theodore Dwight Weld, described the reason for their separation: "God and humanity bleeding and suffering demand our services apart." Thus motivated by a strong religious commitment to serve others, these two young reformers dedicated themselves to several social causes: the abolition of slavery, equal rights and education for free blacks, temperance, and women's rights.

Their commitments cost more than separation. Emily's parents disapproved of Marius and of their reformist activities. Teaching at the school in Cincinnati was demanding, and the white citizens of the city resented the school and the young abolitionists in their midst. But Emily persisted in the work of "our school" while worrying about the health and safety of her husband on the road.

She had good reason for concern, for Marius's letters were full of reports of mob attacks, disrupted meetings, stonings, and narrow escapes. In June, he was dragged from the home of his Quaker host and beaten, tarred, and feathered. Never quite recovering his health, Marius spent half a year in bed, weak and dispirited. For nearly ten years after that, the Robinsons lived quietly on an Ohio farm, only slightly involved in the abolitionist movement. Despite the joyous birth of two daughters, they felt lonely, restless, and guilt-ridden, "tired of days blank of benevolent effort and almost of benevolent desires."

• • •

The work of Emily and Marius Robinson represents one response by the American people to the rapid social and economic changes of the antebellum era described in Chapters 11 and 12. In September 1835, a year before the Robinsons' marriage, the *Niles Register* commented on some 500 recent incidents of mob violence and social upheaval. *"Society seems everywhere unhinged,* and the demon of 'blood and slaughter' has been let loose upon us. . . . [The] character of our countrymen seems suddenly changed." How did Americans adapt to these changes and maintain some sense of control over their lives?

One way was to embrace the changes fully. Thus some Americans became entrepreneurs in new industries; invested in banks, canals, and railroads; bought more land and slaves; and invented new machines. Others went west or to the new textile mills, enrolled in common schools, joined trade unions, specialized their labor both in the workplace and the home, and celebrated the practical benefits that resulted from modernization. Marius Robinson eventually went into life insurance, though he and Emily never fully abandoned their reformist efforts and idealism.

But many Americans were uncomfortable with the character of the new era. Some worried about the unrestrained power and selfish materialism symbolized by the slavemaster's control over his slaves. Others feared that institutions like the U.S. Bank represented a "monied aristocracy" capable of undermining the country's honest producers. Seeking positions of leadership and authority, these critics of the new order tried to shape a nation that retained the benefits of economic change without sacrificing humane principles of liberty, equality of opportunity, and community virtue. This chapter examines four ways in which the American people responded to change by attempting to influence their country's development: party politics, religious revivalism, utopian communitarianism, and social reform.

The Political Response to Change

At the heart of American politics was the concern for the continued health of the republican experiment. As American society changed, so too did the understanding of political measures necessary to maintain that health. The economic dislocations after 1819 and in the late 1830s, and the spirited presidential campaigns of Andrew Jackson helped to create widespread interest in politics in the era between 1820 and 1840.

Changing Political Culture

The presidency of Andrew Jackson was a crucial factor in bringing politics to the center of many Americans' lives. Styling himself as the people's candidate in 1828, Andrew Jackson derided the Adams administration as corrupt and aristocratic and promised a more democratic political system with the interests of the people at its center. Then as today, many Americans believed the campaign rhetoric. Four times more men turned out to vote in the election of 1828 than had gone to the polls four years earlier. They gave Jackson a resounding 56 percent of their ballots. No other president in the century would equal that percentage of popular support.

Despite campaign rhetoric, Jackson was not personally very democratic, nor did the era he symbolized involve any significant redistribution of wealth. Jackson himself owned slaves, defended slavery, and condoned mob attacks on abolitionists like Marius Robinson in the mid-

1830s. And belying promises of widening opportunity, the rich got richer during the Jacksonian era, and most farming and urban laboring families did not prosper.

But the nation's political life had changed in important ways. The old system of politics based on elite coalitions and the deference of voters to their "betters" largely disappeared. In its place emerged a competitive party system, begun early in the republic but now oriented toward widespread voter participation in state and local politics. Political parties sponsored conventions, rallies, and parades. In the North, even women turned out for political rallies and speeches and rode on floats at party parades. Party-subsidized newspapers regularly indulged in scurrilous attacks on political candidates.

Jackson's Path to the White House

Andrew Jackson's personality suited the new era. Orphaned at 14, young Jackson was rowdy, indecisive, and often in trouble. As a law student he was a "most roaring, rollicking, game-cocking, horse-racing, card-playing, mischievous fellow." He passed the bar and set out at the age of 21 to seek his fortune in the West. Settling in the frontier town of Nashville, the tall, red-headed young man built up a successful law practice in Tennessee and went on to become attorney general. Eventually, he became a substantial landowner and a prominent citizen of Nashville.

Jackson's national reputation stemmed mainly from his military exploits against American Indians and from his victory over the British at New Orleans in 1815. Careful political maneuvering in Tennessee in the early 1820s brought him election as U.S. senator and nomination for the presidency in 1824.

In the 1824 election, Jackson won both the popular and electoral votes but lost in the House of Representatives to John Quincy Adams. When Henry Clay threw his support to Adams and was named secretary of state, Jackson condemned this deal as a "corrupt bargain." Jackson's loss convinced him of the importance

of having an effective political organization. He organized his campaign by setting up loyal committees and newspapers in many states and by encouraging efforts to undermine Adams and Clay.

The loose coalition promoting Jackson's candidacy, which began to call itself the Democratic party, was a mixed lot, drawing in politicians of diverse views from all sections of the country. Jackson played down his position on controversial issues, but he made clear his intentions of reforming government by throwing out of office anyone who was incompetent or who failed to represent the will of the people. Democratic newspapers picked up this theme and presented Jackson as a politician who would cleanse government of corruption and privileged interests.

The campaign between Jackson and Adams in 1828 degenerated into a nasty but entertaining contest. Both sides engaged in slanderous personal attacks. Supporters of Adams and Clay, who called themselves National Republicans, claimed that Jackson was "an adulterer, a gambler, a cockfighter, a brawler, a drunkard, and a murderer." The Jacksonians in turn described Adams as a "stingy, undemocratic" aristocrat determined to destroy the people's liberties. Worse yet, Adams was an intellectual, "a man who can write." Jackson, by contrast, was the hero of the Battle of New Orleans, "a man who can fight." The efforts of Jackson and his party paid off as he won an astonishing 647,286 ballots, about 56 percent of the total.

Jackson's inauguration on a mild March 4 horrified many Americans. Washington was packed for the ceremonies. When Jackson appeared on the steps of the Capitol to take the oath of office, wild and unrestrained cheering broke out. After making a short address and taking the oath, Jackson was all but mobbed as he tried to make his way to his horse.

The White House reception soon got completely out of hand. A throng of people poured into the White House with muddy boots to overturn furniture in a rush for food and punch. The inauguration, according to Justice Joseph Story,

As depicted in this Robert Cruickeshank lithograph, All Creation Going to the White House, the first inauguration of Andrew Jackson in 1829 was the scene of wild festivities, a harbinger of the excesses in American life and politics in the ensuing years.

illustrated "the reign of King Mob." Another observer called it "a proud day for the people." These contrasting views on the events of the inauguration captured the essence of the Jackson era. For some they symbolized the excesses of democracy; for others they represented democratic fulfillment.

Old Hickory's Vigorous Presidency

President Jackson's decisions, often controversial, helped to sharpen what it meant to be a Democrat and what it meant to be Democracy's opponent. A few key convictions — the principle of majority rule, the limited power of the national government, the obligation of the national government to defend the interests of the nation's average people against the machinations of the "monied aristocracy" — guided Jackson's political behavior as president. Because he saw himself as the people's most authentic representative (only the president was elected by all the people), Jackson intended to be an effective, vigorous executive. More than any previous

president, Jackson used presidential power in the name of the people and justified his actions by popular appeals to the electorate.

Jackson asserted his power most dramatically through use of the veto. The six preceding presidents had used the veto only nine times, most often against measures that they had believed unconstitutional. Jackson vetoed 12 bills during his eight years in office.

One of the abuses Jackson had promised to correct was what he described as an undemocratic and corrupt system of government officeholding. Too often "unfaithful or incompetent" men held onto their offices for years, making a mockery of the idea of representation. In the first year and a half of his presidency, Jackson removed 919 officeholders of a total of 10,093, fewer than one in ten. Most of these were for good reason — corruption or incompetence. The new Democratic appointees were not much better than their predecessors.

Jackson's similarly controversial Indian policy of forcible removal and relocation westward defined white American practice for the rest of the century. In the opening decades of the nineteenth century, the vast landholdings of the five "civilized nations" of the Southeast (the Cherokee, Choctaw, Chickasaw, Seminole, and Creek) had been seriously eroded by the pressures of land-hungry whites supported by successful military campaigns led by professional Indian fighters such as General Jackson. Land cessions to the government and private sales accounted for huge losses of Indian lands. In his first annual message to Congress in 1829, Jackson urged removal of the southeastern tribes. He argued that because the Indians were "surrounded by the whites with their arts of civilization," it was inevitable that the "resources of the savage" would be destroyed, dooming the Indians to "weakness and decay." Removal was justified, Jackson claimed, by both "humanity and national honor." He also endorsed the paramount right of state laws over the claims of either Indians or the federal government.

With the president's position clear, the crisis soon came to a head in Georgia. In 1829, the

Georgia legislature declared the Cherokee tribal council illegal and its laws null and void in Cherokee territories and announced that the state had jurisdiction over both the tribe and its lands. Without legal recourse on the state level, the Cherokee carried their protests to the Supreme Court. In 1832, Chief Justice Marshall supported their position in *Worcester* v. *Georgia*, holding that the Georgia law was "repugnant to the Constitution" and did not apply to the Cherokee nation.

With Jackson's blessing, however, Georgians defied the Court ruling. By 1835, harassment, intimidation, and bribery had persuaded a minority of chiefs to sign a removal treaty. But most Cherokee refused to leave their lands. Therefore, in 1837 and 1838, the United States Army searched and seized the terrified Indians and gathered them in stockades prior to herding them west to the "Indian Territory" in Oklahoma. An eyewitness described how the Cherokee trek began:

Families at dinner were startled by the sudden gleam of bayonets in the doorway and rose to be driven with blows and oaths along the weary miles of trail that led to the stockade. Men were seized in their fields, or going along the road, women were taken from their [spinning] wheels and children from their play. In many cases, on turning for one last look as they crossed the ridge they saw their homes in flames, fired by the lawless rabble that followed on the heels of the soldiers to loot and pillage.

The removal, the $6 million cost of which was deducted from the $9 million awarded the tribe for its eastern lands, brought death to perhaps a quarter of the 15,000 who set out. The Cherokee remember this event as the "Trail of Tears." Other southern and some northwestern tribes between 1821 and 1840 shared a similar fate. Although both Jackson and the Removal Act of 1830 had promised to protect and forever guarantee the Indian lands in the west, within a generation those promises, like others before and since, would be broken.

Indian removal left the eastern United States open for the enormous economic expansion described in Chapters 11 and 12. On the question of internal improvements to support that expansion, Jackson also imposed his enormous will.

When proposals for federal support for internal improvements seemed to rob local and state authorities of their proper function, Jackson, a firm believer in states' rights, opposed them. But projects of national significance, like the building of lighthouses or river improvements, were different matters. In fact, Jackson supported an annual average of $1.3 million in internal improvements while he was in office.

In a period of rapid economic change, tariffs were a matter of heated debate. New England and the Middle Atlantic states, the center of manufacturing operations, favored protective tariffs. But the South had long opposed such tariffs because they made it more expensive for southerners to buy manufactured goods from the North or abroad. Feelings against the high protective "Tariff of Abominations" were particularly strong in South Carolina, which was suffering from an economic depression.

Vice-President Calhoun, a brilliant political thinker, argued that minority rights could be protected by seeing the nation as "a confederacy of equal and sovereign states." In 1828, the same year as the hateful tariff, Calhoun published an anonymous essay, *Exposition and Protest*, which presented the doctrine of nullification as a means by which southern states could protect themselves from harmful national action. He argued that when federal laws were deemed to overstep the limits of constitutional authority, a state had the right to declare that legislation null and void and to refuse to enforce it.

In 1830, at a Jefferson birthday dinner, President Jackson declared himself on the issue. Despite his support of states' rights, Jackson did not believe that any state had the right to reject the will of the majority or to destroy the Union. He rose for a toast, held high his glass, and said, "Our Union — it must be preserved." Not to be outdone, Calhoun followed with his toast: "The

Union — next to our liberty most dear." The split between them widened, and in 1833 Calhoun resigned as vice-president. Final rupture came in a collision over the tariff and nullification.

In 1832, following Jackson's recommendation of a "middle course" for tariff revisions, Congress modified the tariff of 1828 by retaining high duties on goods such as wool, woolens, iron, and hemp and lowering other rates to an earlier level. Many southerners felt injured. In a special convention later that year in South Carolina, the delegates adopted an Ordinance of Nullification, declaring that the offending tariffs of 1828 and 1832 were null and void in that state. None of the duties would be collected. Furthermore, South Carolina threatened secession if the federal government should try to force the state to comply.

South Carolina's actions represented a direct attack on the concepts of federal union and majority rule. Jackson responded with a proclamation that stated emphatically that "the laws of the United States must be executed.... The Union will be preserved and treason and rebellion promptly put down."

Jackson's proclamation stimulated an outburst of patriotism and popular support all over the country. No other southern states supported nullification, and several state legislatures denounced it. South Carolina stood alone. When Jackson asked Congress for legislation to enforce tariff duties (the Force Bill of 1833), the crisis neared resolution. Tariff revisions, engineered by Henry Clay and supported by Calhoun, called for reductions over a ten-year period. South Carolina quickly repealed its nullification of the tariff laws but saved face by nullifying the Force Bill at the same time, an act that Jackson ignored. The crisis was over, but left unresolved were the constitutional issues it raised.

Jackson's Bank War and "Van Ruin's" Depression

As the people's advocate, Jackson could not ignore the Second Bank of the United States,

which had been chartered for 20 years in 1816. Jackson believed the bank threatened the people's liberties and called it a "monster." But the bank was not as irresponsible as Jacksonians imagined.

Guided since 1823 by the aristocratic Nicholas Biddle, the Philadelphia bank and its 29 branches performed many useful financial services and generally played a responsible economic role in an expansionary period. As the nation's largest commercial bank, the U.S. Bank was able to shift funds to different parts of the country as necessary and to influence state banking activity. It restrained state banks from making unwise loans by insisting that they back their notes with specie (gold or silver coin) and by calling in its own loans to these institutions. The bank accepted federal deposits, made commercial loans, and bought and sold government bonds. Businessmen, state bankers needing credit, and nationalist politicians such as Daniel Webster and Henry Clay, who were on the bank's payroll, all favored the bank.

Other Americans, however, led by the president, distrusted the bank. Jackson had long opposed the bank both for personal reasons (a near financial disaster in his own past) and because he and his advisers believed it was the chief example of a special privilege monopoly that hurt the common man — farmers, craftsmen, and debtors.

Aware of Jackson's persisting hostility, Clay and Webster persuaded Biddle to ask Congress to recharter the bank in 1832, four years ahead of schedule. They reasoned that in an election year, Jackson would not risk a veto. The bill to recharter the bank swept through Congress and landed on the president's desk one hot, muggy day in July. "The bank . . . is trying to kill me," he told Martin Van Buren, *"but I will kill it."*

Jackson determined not only to veto the bill but also to carry his case to the public. His veto message condemned the bank as undemocratic, un-American, and unconstitutional. He denounced the bank as a dangerous monopoly that helped the rich and harmed "the humble members of society."

The furor over the bank helped to clarify party differences. In the election of 1832, the National Republicans, now becoming known as Whigs to show their opposition to "King Andrew," nominated Henry Clay. Democratic campaign rhetoric pitted Jackson, the people, and democracy against Clay, the bank, and aristocracy. The Anti-Masons, the first third party in American political life and the first to hold a nominating convention, revealed real issues more clearly than the two major parties. The anti-Masonic movement, which began in upstate New York, expressed popular resentments against the elitist Masonic order (Jackson was a member) and other secret societies. At a deeper level, anti-Masonry reflected tensions over commercialization as new groups vied with old families for political power.

When the ballots were counted, Jackson had once again won handsomely, garnering 124,000 more popular votes than the combined total for Clay and the Anti-Mason candidate, William Wirt, who said of Jackson, "He may be President for life if he chooses."

Although the election results suggest that the bank issue actually harmed Jackson, he interpreted the election as a victory for his bank policy and made plans to finish his war with Biddle. The bank still had four years before the charter expired, so Jackson and his advisers decided to weaken the bank by transferring $10 million in government funds to state banks. Although two secretaries of the treasury balked at the removal request as financially unsound, Jackson persisted until he found one, Roger Taney, willing to remove the funds. And when Chief Justice John Marshall, a Whig, died in 1835, Jackson replaced him with Taney.

Jackson's war with Biddle and the bank had serious economic consequences. A wave of speculation in western lands and ambitious new state internal improvement schemes in the mid-1830s led to rising land prices and a flood of paper money. Determined to curtail irresponsible economic activity, in July 1836 Jackson issued the Specie Circular, announcing that the government would accept only gold and silver in payment for public lands. Panicky investors rushed to change paper notes into specie, while banks started to call in loans. The result was the Panic of 1837. Although Jackson was blamed for this rapid monetary expansion followed by sudden deflation in the mid-1830s, international trade problems with Britain and China probably contributed more to the panic and to the ensuing seven years of depression than Jackson's erratic policies.

Whatever the primary cause, Jackson stuck his successor, Martin Van Buren, who was elected in 1836 over a trio of Whig opponents, with an economic crisis. Van Buren had barely taken the oath of office in 1837 when banks and businesses began to collapse. His term as president was marked by a depression so severe that it brought him the unfortunate nickname "Martin Van Ruin." As New York banks suspended credit and began calling in loans, an estimated $6 million was lost on defaulted debts.

By the fall of 1837, one-third of America's workers were unemployed, and thousands of others found only sporadic, part-time work. Wages fell, while the price of necessities like flour, pork, and coal nearly doubled.

The pride of workers was damped as soup kitchens and bread lines grew faster than jobs. Moreover, the depression destroyed the trade union movement begun a decade earlier, leaving laboring families isolated and defenseless. In 1842, when Philadelphia textile employers lowered wages below subsistence levels, angry hand-loom weavers broke machinery, destroyed cloth, and wrecked the homes of Irish strike-breakers. Job competition, poverty, and ethnic animosities led to violent clashes in other eastern cities as well, as we saw in Chapter 11.

"How is it," a Philadelphia mechanic asked in 1837, that in a country as rich as the United States so many people were "pinched for the common necessaries of life?" President Van Buren's responses to the social misery behind this question were sympathetic but limited and inadequate. Political participation, as well as church membership, reached new heights during the depression, as Americans sought to alleviate their "gloom and despair."

The Second American Party System

By the mid-1830s, a new two-party system and a lively participatory national political culture had emerged in the United States. Although both parties included wealthy and influential, even despotic leaders, the Democrats had the better claim that they were the party of the common man with strength in all sections of the country.

Whigs represented greater wealth than Democrats and were strongest in New England and in areas settled by New Englanders across the Upper Midwest. Whigs generally favored a national bank, federally supported internal improvements, and tariff protection for industry. Artisans and laborers belonged equally to each party, making it difficult to draw clear regional or class distinctions between Whigs and Democrats.

In the Jeffersonian tradition, the Democrats espoused liberty and local rule. They wanted freedom from legislators of morality, from special privilege, and from too much government. Those who wanted to maintain religious or ethnic traditions found a home in the Democratic party. The Scots-Irish, German, French and Irish Catholic immigrants, as well as free thinkers and labor organizers, tended to be Jacksonians. They were less moralistic than Whigs, especially on matters like temperance and slavery. Democrats sought to keep politics separate from moral issues.

By contrast, for many Whigs the line between reform and politics was hazy. Old-stock New England Yankee Congregationalists and Presbyterians were usually Whigs. So were Quakers and evangelical Protestants, who believed that positive government action could change moral behavior and eradicate sin. Whigs supported a wide variety of reforms, such as temperance, antislavery, public education, and strict observance of the Sabbath, as

well as government action to promote economic development.

The election of 1840 illustrated the new style of political culture. Passing over Henry Clay, the Whigs nominated William Henry Harrison of Indiana, the aging hero of the Battle of Tippecanoe (Kithtippecanoe), fought nearly 30 years earlier. A Virginian, John Tyler, was nominated as vice-president to underline the regional diversity of the party. The Democrats had no choice but to renominate Van Buren, who

In the election of 1840, the Whigs "out-Jacksoned the Jacksonians" by playing to the popular political style of slogans, songs, and cider. They also touted their candidate as a backwoodsy Indian fighter while maligning the Democrat Van Buren as an aristocratic dandy.

conducted a quiet campaign. The Whig campaign, however, featured every form of popularized appeals for votes — barbecues, torchlight parades, songs, and cartoons. Harrison (who lived in a mansion) was depicted in front of a rural log cabin with a barrel of hard cider, while the Whigs labeled Van Buren an aristocratic dandy. Harrison reminded voters of General Jackson and they swept him into office, 234 electoral votes to Van Buren's 60. In one of the largest turnouts in American history, over 80 percent of eligible voters marched to the polls. Commenting on the defeat, a Democratic party journal acknowledged that the Whigs had out-Jacksoned the Jacksonians: "We taught them how to conquer us."

Concern over the new politics outlasted Harrison, who died only a month after taking office. For many Americans, usually Whigs and often women, it was precisely the excesses of Jacksonian politics, most notably intemperance and the inherent violence of slavery, that led them to seek other ways than politics of imposing order and morality on American society. To gain a measure of control over their lives and reshape their changing world, the American people turned also to religion, social reform, and utopianism.

Religious Revival and Reform

When the Frenchman Alexis de Tocqueville visited the United States in 1831 and 1832, he observed that he could find "no country in the whole world in which the Christian religion retains a greater influence over the souls of men than in America." What de Tocqueville was describing was a new and powerful religious enthusiasm among the American people.

Finney and the Second Great Awakening

From the late 1790s until the late 1830s, a wave of religious revivals that matched the intensity of the Great Awakening in the 1730s and 1740s swept through the United States. The camp meeting revivals of the frontier at the turn of the century and the New England revivals sparked by Lyman Beecher took on a new emphasis and location after 1830. Led by the spellbinding Charles G. Finney, revivalism shifted to upstate New York and the Old Northwest. Both areas had been experiencing profound economic and social changes, as the example of Rochester, New York, suggests.

By the 1830s, Rochester, like Lowell and Cincinnati, was a rapidly growing American city. Its location on the recently completed Erie Canal changed Rochester from a sleepy little village of 300 in 1815 to a bustling commercial and milling city of nearly 20,000 inhabitants by 1830. Saloons and unions sprang up in workingmen's neighborhoods, and workers became more transient, following the canal and other opportunities westward.

Prominent Rochester citizens, sensing a widening gulf between laborers and their masters, invited Charles Finney to come to town in 1830 to deliver some sermons. What followed was one of the most successful revivals of the Second Great Awakening. For six months Rochester went through a citywide prayer meeting in which one conversion led to another. The Rochester revival was part of the wave of religious enthusiasm in America that contributed to the tremendous growth of the Methodists, the Baptists, and other evangelical sects in the first half of the nineteenth century.

Most revivalists, especially in the South, sought individual salvation. The Finney revivals, however, were unique in that they nourished collective reform. Finney taught that humans were not passive objects of God's predestined plan but moral free agents who could choose good over evil, convince others to do the same, and thereby eradicate sin from the world. Conversion and salvation were not the end of religious experience but the beginning. Finney's idea of the "utility of benevolence" meant not only individual reformation but also the commitment to reform society. The Bible commanded humans, "Be ye therefore perfect even as your Father in heaven is perfect," and mid-nineteenth-century reformers took the challenge seriously.

Reform and Politics

The reform impulse ultimately involved antebellum activists in the broader politics of the Jacksonian era. Reformers and party politicians, especially Whigs, both faced timeless dilemmas about how best to effect change. Does one, for example, try to change attitudes first and then behavior, or the reverse? Which is more effective, to appeal to people's minds and hearts in order to change bad institutions or to change institutions first, assuming that altered behavior will change hearts and attitudes? Reformers, moreover, have to decide whether to attempt to improve on a partly defective system or tear down the entire system in order to build a utopian new one; whether to use or recommend force; and whether to enter into coalitions with less principled potential allies.

Advocates of change also experience enormous pressures, recriminations, and persecution, as Marius and Emily Robinson learned. Nevertheless, their duty to themselves, their society, and God sustains their commitment.

The Transcendentalists

No one knew this better than Ralph Waldo Emerson, a Concord, Massachusetts, essayist who was the era's foremost intellectual figure. The small but influential group of New England intellectuals who lived near Emerson were called Transcendentalists because of their belief that truth was found beyond experience in intuition. Casting off the European intellectual tradition, Emerson urged Americans to look inward and to nature for self-knowledge, self-reliance, and the spark of divinity burning within all persons. "To acquaint a man with himself," he wrote, would inspire a "reverence" for self and others, which would then lead outward to social reform. "What

is man born for," Emerson wrote, "but to be a Reformer?"

The Transcendentalists questioned not only slavery, an obvious evil, but also the obsessive competitive pace of economic life, the overriding concern for materialism, and the restrictive conformity of social life.

Although not considered Transcendentalists, Nathaniel Hawthorne and Herman Melville, two giants of midcentury American literature, also reflected these concerns in their fiction. In his greatest novel, *The Scarlet Letter* (1850), Hawthorne sympathetically told the story of a courageous Puritan woman's adultery and her eventual loving triumph over the narrowness of both cold intellect and intolerant social conformity.

Herman Melville's epic novel *Moby Dick* (1851), at one level a rousing story of pursuit of the great white whale, was actually an immense allegory of good and evil, bravery and weakness, innocence and experience. Like Emerson, Hawthorne and Melville mirrored the tensions of the age as they explored issues of freedom and control.

When Emerson wrote, "Whoso would be a man, must be a nonconformist," he described his friend Henry David Thoreau. On July 4, 1845, Thoreau went to live in a small hut by Walden Pond, near Concord, to confront "the essential facts of life." When Thoreau left Walden two years later, he protested against slavery and the Mexican War by refusing to pay his taxes. He went to jail briefly and wrote an essay, "On Civil Disobedience" (1849), and a book, *Walden* (1854), which are still considered classic statements of what one person can do to protest unjust laws and wars and live a life of principle.

Utopian Communitarianism

Thoreau tried to lead an ideal solitary life. Other reformers sought to create perfect communities. Emerson noted in 1840 that he hardly met a thinking, reading man who did not have "a draft of a new community in his waistcoat pocket."

Oneida and the Shakers

One such man was John Humphrey Noyes of Putney, Vermont, an instant, if unorthodox, convert of Charles Finney. Noyes believed that the act of final conversion led to absolute perfection and complete release from sin. Among those who were perfect, he argued, all men and women belonged equally to each other. For Noyes, complete sharing in family relationships was a step toward perfect cooperation and shared wealth in socioeconomic relationships. Others called his heretical doctrines "free love" and socialism. Noyes married a loyal follower, and when she delivered four stillborn children within six years, he revised even further his unconventional ideas about sex.

In 1848, Noyes and 51 devoted followers founded a "perfectionist" community at Oneida, New York. Sexual life at the commune was subject to many regulations, including sexual restraint and male continence except under carefully prescribed conditions. In a system of planned reproduction, only certain spiritually advanced males (usually Noyes) were allowed to father children. Other controversial practices included communal child rearing, sexual equality in work, the removal of the competitive spirit from both work and play, and an elaborate program of "mutual criticism" at community meetings presided over by "Father" Noyes.

The Oneida community grew and prospered through manufacturing. Oneida specialized at first in the fabrication of steel animal traps and later diversified into making silverware. Eventually abandoning religion to become a joint-stock company in which individual members held shares, Oneida thrived for many years and continues today as a silverware company.

Noyes greatly admired another group of communitarians, the Shakers, who also believed in perfectionism, the surrender of all worldly property to the community, and the devotion of one's labor and love to bringing about the millennial kingdom of heaven. But unlike the Oneidans, Shakers viewed sexuality as a sin and believed in absolute chastity, trusting in conversions to perpetuate their sect. They believed that God had a dual personality, male and female, and that their founder, Mother Ann Lee, was the female counterpart to the masculine Christ. The Shaker worship service featured frenetic dancing intended to release (or "shake") sin out through the fingertips. Shaker communities, some of which survived long into the twentieth century, were characterized by communal ownership of property, the equality of women and men, simplicity, and beautifully crafted furniture.

Other Utopias

In an era of disruptive economic and social change, over 100 utopian communities like Oneida and the Shaker colonies were founded. Some were religiously motivated; others were secular. Most were small and lasted only a few months or years. All eventually failed.

Pietist German-speaking immigrants founded the earliest utopian communities in America to preserve their language, spirituality, and ascetic life style. The most notable of these were the Ephrata colonists in Pennsylvania, the Harmonists in Indiana, the Zoar community in Ohio, and the Amana Society in Iowa. In 1840, Adin Ballou founded Hopedale in Massachusetts as "a miniature Christian republic" based on the ethical teachings of Jesus. Hopedale's newspaper, *The Practical Christian*, advocated temperance, pacifism, women's rights, and other reforms.

The secular communities responded more directly to the social misery and wretched working conditions accompanying the industrial revolution. They believed that altered environments rather than new morals would eliminate or reduce poverty, ignorance, intemperance, and other ugly by-products of industrialism.

In 1824, Robert Owen, a Scottish industrialist, founded New Harmony in Indiana. But problems rather than harmony prevailed. Overcrowding, lazy and uncooperative members, Owen's frequent absences, splintered goals, and financial mismanagement ruined New Harmony within three years.

Brook Farm, founded by two Concord friends of Emerson, Bronson Alcott and George Ripley, was an experiment in integrating "intellectual and manual labor." Residents would hoe in the fields and shovel manure for a few hours each day and then study literature and recite poetry. The colony lasted less than three years.

Whether secular or religious, the utopian communities all failed for similar reasons. Americans seemed ill-suited to communal living and work responsibilities and were unwilling to share either their property or their spouses with others. Nor was celibacy greeted with much enthusiasm. Other recurring problems included unstable leadership, financial bickering, the hostility of local citizens, the indiscriminate admission of members, and a waning of enthusiasm after initial settlement. Emerson pinned the failure of the communities on their inability to confront the individualistic impulses of human nature. As he said of Brook Farm, "It met every test but life itself." That could serve as an epitaph for all the utopian communities.

Millerites and Mormons

If utopian communities failed to bring about the millennium, an alternative hope was to leap directly past the thousand years of peace and harmony to the Second Coming of Christ. William Miller, a shy farmer from upstate New York, became so absorbed with the idea of the imminent coming of Christ that he figured out mathematically the exact time of the event : 1843, probably in March. A religious sect, the Millerites, gathered around him to prepare for Christ's return and the Day of Judgment. When 1843 passed without the expected end, Miller and his followers recalculated and set a series of alternative dates. Each new disappointment diminished Miller's followers, and he died in 1848 a discredited man.

Other groups that emerged from the same religiously active area of upstate New York were more successful. As Palmyra, New York, was being swept by Finney revivalism, young Joseph Smith, a recent convert, claimed to be visited by the angel Moroni. According to Smith, Moroni led him to golden tablets buried in the ground near his home. On these plates were inscribed more than 500 pages of *The Book of Mormon*, which described the one true church and a "lost tribe of Israel" missing for centuries. The book also predicted the appearance of an American prophet who would establish a new and pure kingdom of Christ in America. Smith published his book in 1830 and soon founded the Church of Jesus Christ of Latter-day Saints.

Smith and a steadily growing band of converts migrated successively to Ohio and Missouri and then back to Illinois. Despite ridicule, persecution, and violence, the Mormons prospered and increased. By the mid-1840s, Nauvoo, Illinois, with a thriving population of nearly 15,000, was the showplace of Mormonism. Smith petitioned Congress for separate territorial status and ran for the presidency in 1844. This was too much for the citizens of nearby towns. Violence escalated and culminated in Smith's trial for treason and his murder by a mob. Under the brilliant leadership of Smith's successor, Brigham Young, the Mormons headed westward in 1846 in their continuing search for the "land of promise."

Reforming Society

Most Americans sought to bring about "the promised land" by focusing in a practical way on a specific social evil rather than by embracing whole new religions or joining utopian colonies.

"We are all a little wild here," Emerson wrote in 1840, "with numberless projects of social reform." The reformers, including thousands of women, created and joined all kinds of societies for social betterment. They addressed such issues as alcohol consumption ; diet and health ;

Religion, Reform, and Utopian Activity, 1830-1850

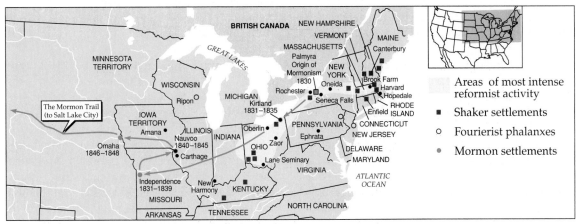

Areas of most intense reformist activity

■ Shaker settlements

○ Fourierist phalanxes

● Mormon settlements

sexuality ; institutional treatment of the mentally ill, the disabled, paupers, and criminals ; education ; the rights of labor ; slavery ; and women's rights.

Temperance

On New Year's Eve in 1831, a Finney disciple, Theodore Dwight Weld, delivered a four-hour temperance lecture in Rochester. In graphic detail he described the awful fate of those who refused to stop drinking and urged his audience not only to cease their tippling but to stop others as well. Several were converted to abstinence on the spot. The next day, Elijah and Albert Smith, the largest providers of whiskey in Rochester, rolled their barrels out onto the sidewalk and smashed them. Cheering Christians applauded as the whiskey ran out into Exchange Street.

Americans in the nineteenth century drank heavily. One man observed that "a house could not be raised, a field of wheat cut down, nor could there be a log rolling, a husking, a quilting, a wedding, or a funeral without the aid of alcohol." The corrosive effects of drinking were obvious : poverty, crime, illness, insanity, battered and broken families, and corrupt politics.

Early efforts at curbing alcohol consumption emphasized moderation. But the American Temperance Society, founded in 1826, was dedicated to total abstinence. Within a few years, thousands of local and state societies had formed, though some refused to prohibit drinking of hard cider and communion wine.

Temperance advocates copied successful revival techniques. Fiery lecturers expounded on the evil consequences of drink and distributed a deluge of graphic and sometimes gory temperance tracts.

By 1840, disagreements over goals and methods split the temperance movement into many separate organizations. The Washington Temperance Society, founded in a Baltimore tavern in 1840, was enormously popular with unemployed young workers and grew to an estimated 600,000 members in three years. The Washingtonians, arguing that alcoholism was a disease rather than moral failure, changed the shape of the temperance movement. They replaced revivalist techniques with those of the new party politics by organizing parades, picnics, melodramas, and festivals to encourage people to take the pledge.

Tactics in the 1840s also shifted away from moral suasion to political action. Temperance societies lobbied for local option laws, which allowed communities to prohibit the sale, manufacture, and consumption of alcohol. The Maine law in 1851 was the first in the nation. Fifteen other states followed with similar laws before the Civil War. Despite weak enforcement, the per capita consumption of alcohol declined dramatically in the 1850s. Interrupted by the Civil War, the movement did not reach its ultimate objective until passage of the Eighteenth Amendment to the Constitution in 1919.

The temperance crusade reveals the many practical motivations that attracted Americans to join reform societies. For some, as in Rochester, temperance provided an opportunity for the Protestant middle classes to exert some control over laborers, immigrants, and Catholics. For perfectionists, abstinence was a way of practicing self-control and reaching moral perfection. For many women, the temperance effort was a respectable way to control the behavior of drunken men who beat wives and daughters. For many young men, especially after the onset of the depression of 1837, a temperance society provided entertainment, fellowship, and contacts to help their careers. In temperance societies as in political parties, Americans found jobs, purpose, support, spouses, and relief from the loneliness and uncertainty of a changing world.

Health and Sexuality

It was a short step from the physical and psychological ravages of drink to other potentially harmful effects on the body. Reformers were quick to attack excessive eating, use of stimulants of any kind, and, above all, the evils of too much sexual activity. Many endorsed a variety of special diets and exercise programs for maintaining good health. Some promoted panaceas for all ailments. One of these was hydropathy : Clients sojourned at one of 70 special resorts for bathing and water purges of the body.

Another movement concerned sexual purity. In 1834, Sylvester Graham, a promoter of proper diet and hygiene, delivered a series of lectures on chastity, later published as a manual of advice. To those "troubled" by sexual desire, the inventor of the Graham cracker recom-

mended taking "more active exercise in the open air" and using "the cold bath under proper circumstances." Women were advised to remain pure and to "have intercourse only for procreation."

The authors of antebellum "health" manuals advocated abstinence from sexual activity as vehemently as they recommended abstinence from alcohol. Semen was to be saved for reproductive purposes and should not be used for pleasure in either masturbation or intercourse. Such use, maintained the manuals on sexual purity, would lead to enervation, disease, insanity, and death. Some argued further that the "expenditure" of sperm meant a loss of needed energy from the economy. One doctor argued that women ought not to be educated because blood needed for the womb would be diverted to the head, thus breeding "puny men."

Humanizing the Asylum

In their effort to restore order to American society, some reformers preferred to work not for private influence over individuals but toward public changes in institutions. They wanted to transform such social institutions as asylums, almshouses, prisons, schools, and even factories. In many ways, Horace Mann, who led the struggle for common schools in Massachusetts (see Chapter 11), was a typical antebellum reformer. He blended dedicated idealism with a canny, practical sense of how to institutionalize educational improvements in one state : teacher training schools, higher teachers' salaries, and compulsory attendance laws.

Other reformers were less successful in achieving their goals. This was especially true of the treatment of society's outcasts. In 1843, Dorothea Dix, a frail New Englander, horrified the Massachusetts legislature with her famous report that imprisoned insane persons in the state were subject to "the extremest state of degradation and misery." They were confined in "cages, closets, stalls, pens ! Chained, naked, beaten with rods, and lashed into obedience ! "

Dix recommended special hospitals or asylums where the insane could be "humanly and properly controlled" by trained attendants.

Many perfectionist reformers like Dix believed that special asylums could reform society's outcasts. But all too often, results were disappointing. Prison reformers believed that a properly built and administered penitentiary could bring a hardened criminal "back to virtue." Some assumed that by putting "penitents" into isolated cells to study the Bible and reflect on their wrongdoing, they would eventually decide to become good citizens. In practice, many criminals simply went mad or committed suicide. The institutions build by well-intentioned reformers became dumping places for society's outcasts. By midcentury, American prisons and mental asylums had become the impersonal, understaffed, overcrowded institutions we know today.

Working-Class Reform

For working-class Americans, the social institution most in need of transformation was the factory. Workers, many of whom were involved in other issues such as temperance, peace, and abolitionism, took it upon themselves to improve their own lives. As labor leader Seth Luther told a meeting of New England mechanics and laborers, "We must take our business into our own hands. Let us awake." And awake they did, forming both trade unions and workingmen's parties as Andrew Jackson neared the presidency.

Between 1828 and 1832, dozens of workingmen's parties were formed, advocating such programs as free, tax-supported schools, free public lands in the West, equal rights for the poor, and the elimination of all monopolistic privilege. Trade union activity began in Philadelphia in 1827 as skilled workers organized journeymen carpenters, plasterers, printers, weavers, tailors, and other tradesmen. That same year, 15 unions combined into a citywide federation, a process followed in other cities. The National Trades Union, founded in 1834,

was the first attempt at a national labor organization.

The trade unions called for shorter hours, wages that would keep pace with rising prices, and ways (such as the closed shop) of warding off the competitive threat of cheap labor. In addition, both workers and their middle-class interlocutors called for the abolition of imprisonment for debt and of compulsory militia duty both of which often cost workers their jobs; free public education; improved living conditions in workers' neighborhoods; and the right to organize.

With union membership of near 300,000, workers struck some 168 times between 1834 and 1836, usually for higher wages. The Panic of 1837 and the ensuing depression dashed the hopes and efforts of American workers. But the organizational work of the 1830s promised that the labor movement would reemerge with greater strength later in the century.

Abolitionism and Women's Rights

As American workers struggled in Lowell and other eastern cities for better wages and hours in 1834, Emily and Marius Robinson arrived in Cincinnati to fight for their causes. They had been attracted there, along with scores of other young idealists, by the newly founded Lane Seminary, a school to train abolitionist leaders. Lane soon became a center of reformist activity. When nervous local residents persuaded President Lyman Beecher to crack down on the students, 40 "Lane rebels," led by Theodore Weld, fled to Oberlin in northern Ohio. As the Robinsons remained in southern Ohio, the group in the north turned Oberlin College into the first institution in the United States open equally to women and men, blacks and whites. Thus the movements to abolish slavery and to grant equal rights to women and free blacks were joined. Whether seeking to eliminate coercion in the cotton fields or in the kitchen, reformers faced the dual challenge of pursuing distant and elusive goals while at the same time achieving practical changes in everyday life.

Tensions Within Antislavery

Although the antislavery movement had a smaller membership than temperance reform, it revealed more clearly the difficulties of trying to achieve significant social change in America. On January 1, 1831, eight months before Nat Turner's revolt, William Lloyd Garrison published the first issue of *The Liberator*, soon to become the leading antislavery journal in the United States. "I am in earnest," he wrote. "I will not equivocate —AND I WILL BE HEARD." After first organizing the New England Anti-Slavery Society with a group of blacks and whites in a church basement in Boston, in 1833 Garrison and 62 others established the American Anti-Slavery Society.

Until Garrison's publication, most people opposed to slavery, other than blacks, had advocated gradual emancipation by individual slave owners and colonization of the freed blacks on the west coast of Africa. Garrison opposed the moderation and gradualism of the colonizationists, declaring that compromise was unthinkable. There would be "no Union with slaveholders," he cried, condemning the Constitution that perpetuated slavery as *a covenant with death, an agreement with Hell.*" The American Anti-Slavery Society called for the immediate and total abolition of slavery. But the abolitionists did not always agree, splitting into factions over ideological differences between colonizationists, gradualists, and immediatists.

Abolitionists also differed over the tactics of ending slavery. Their primary method was moral suasion, by which they sought to convince slaveholders and their supporters that slavery was a sin. In an outpouring of sermons, petitions, resolutions, pamphlets, and speeches, abolitionists tried to overwhelm slaveholders with moral guilt to get them to free their slaves as an act of repentance. In 1839, Weld published

American Slavery As It Is, which described in gory detail every conceivable form of inhumane treatment of the slaves.

Other abolitionists preferred more direct methods. Some brought antislavery petitions before Congress or formed third parties. Another tactic was to boycott goods made by slave labor. A fourth approach, although rare, was to call for slave rebellion, as did two northern blacks, David Walker in a pamphlet in 1829 and Henry Highland Garnet in a speech at a convention of black Americans in 1843.

Disagreement over tactics helped to splinter the abolitionist movement. Class differences and race further divided abolitionists. Northern workers, though fearful of the job competition implications of emancipation, nevertheless saw their "wage slavery" as similar to chattel slavery. Strains between northern labor leaders and middle-class abolitionists, who minimized the seriousness of workingmen's concerns, were similar to those between white and black antislavery forces. Whites like Wendell Phillips decried slavery as a moral blot on American society, while blacks like Douglass were more concerned with the effects of slavery and discrimination on black people. Moreover, white abolitionists tended to see slavery and freedom as absolute moral opposites : A person was either slave or free. Blacks, however, knew that there were degrees of freedom and that discriminatory restrictions on freedom existed for blacks in the North just as did relative degrees of servitude in the South.

Furthermore, black abolitionists themselves experienced prejudice, not just from ordinary northern citizens but also from their white abolitionist colleagues, many of whom refused to hire black workers. One free black described a white abolitionist as one who hated slavery, "especially that slavery which is 1000 to 1500 miles away," but who hated even more "a man who wears a black skin."

The celebrated conflict between Garrison and Douglass reflected these tensions. The famous runaway slave was one of the most effective orators in the movement. But after a while, rather than simply describing his life as a slave, Douglass began skillfully to analyze abolitionist policies. Garrison warned him that audiences would not believe he had ever been a slave, and other whites told him to stick to the facts and let them take care of the philosophy. Douglass gradually moved away from Garrison's views, endorsing political action and sometimes even slave rebellion.

Moving beyond Garrison, a few black nationalists, like the fiery Martin Delany, totally rejected white American society and advocated emigration and a new destiny in Africa. Most blacks, however, agreed with Douglass to work to end slavery and discrimination in the United States, which, for better or worse, was their home. These black leaders organized a National Negro Convention Movement, which began annual meetings in 1830. They met not only to condemn slavery but also to discuss concrete issues of discrimination facing free blacks in the North.

Flood Tide of Abolitionism

Black and white abolitionists, however, agreed more than they disagreed and usually worked together well. They supported each other's publications, stayed in each other's homes when they traveled, and cooperated on the underground railroad.

The two races worked together fighting discrimination as well as slavery. When David Ruggles was dragged from the "white car" of a New Bedford, Massachusetts, railway in 1841, Garrison, Douglass, and 40 other protesters organized what may have been the first successful integrated "sit-in" act of civil disobedience in American history. Blacks and whites also worked harmoniously in protesting segregated schools. In 1855, Massachusetts became the first state to outlaw segregated public education.

White and black abolitionists united in defending themselves against the attacks of people who regarded them as dangerous fanatics. Mob attacks like the one on Marius Robinson in Ohio in 1836 occurred frequently in the mid-1830s.

Abolitionists were stoned, dragged through streets, ousted from their jobs and homes, and reviled by northern mobs, often led or encouraged by leading citizens. Theodore Weld, known as "the most mobbed man in the United States," could hardly finish a speech without disruption. In 1837, an antislavery editor in Illinois, Elijah Lovejoy, was murdered and his printing press destroyed.

Antiabolitionists were as fervid as the abolitionists themselves and equally determined to publicize their cause. "I warn the abolitionists, ignorant and infatuated barbarians as they are," growled one South Carolinian, "that if chance shall throw any of them into our hands, they may expect a felon's death." President Jackson denounced the abolitionists in his annual message in 1835 as "incendiaries" who deserved to have their "unconstitutional and wicked" activities broken up by mobs. The president went on to urge Congress to ban antislavery literature from the U.S. mails. A year later, southern Democratic congressmen, with the crucial support of Van Buren, succeeded in passing a "gag rule," which stopped the flood of abolitionists petitions in Congress until the rule was repealed in 1844.

By the 1840s, many northerners, including many workers otherwise unsympathetic to the goal of ending slavery, decried the mob violence, supported the right of free speech, and denounced the South and its northern defenders as undemocratic. The gag rule, interference with the mails, and the killing of Lovejoy seemed proof of the growing pernicious influence of slave power.

Women's Rights

As a young teacher in Massachusetts in 1836, Abby Kelley circulated petitions for the local antislavery society. She came to reform from revivalism and in 1837 wrote, "'Tis a great joy to see the world grow better. . . . Indeed I think endeavors to improve mankind is the only object worth living for." A year later, she braved the threats of an angry crowd in Philadelphia by delivering an abolitionist speech to a convention of antislavery women. Her speech was so eloquent that Weld told her that if she did not join the movement full time, "God will smite you." Before the convention was over, a mob, incensed by both abolitionists and women speaking in public, attacked with stones and torches and burned the hall to the ground.

After a soul-searching year, Kelley left teaching to devote all her efforts to antislavery and women's rights. When she married Stephen Foster, she retained her own name and went on lecture tours of the West while her husband stayed home to care for their daughter.

Angelina and Sarah Grimké, two demure but outspoken Quaker sisters from Philadelphia who had grown up in slaveholding South Carolina, went to New England in 1837 to lecture to disapproving audiences on behalf of abolitionism and the rights of women. After the tour, Angelina married Theodore Weld and stopped her public speaking to show that she could also be a good wife and mother.

Young couples like Grimké and Weld, the Robinsons, and Kelley and Foster, while pursuing reform, experimented with equal private relationships in an age that assigned distinctly unequal roles to husbands and wives.

Catharine Beecher argued that it was by accepting marriage and the home as woman's sphere and by mastering domestic duties there that women could best achieve moral power and autonomy. In another form of "domestic feminism," American wives exerted considerable control over their own bodies by convincing their husbands to practice abstinence, coitus interruptus, and other forms of birth control. Some women found an outlet for their role as moral guardians by attacking the sexual double standard. They worked to convert prostitutes to evangelical Protestantism and to close houses of prostitution.

Women reformers sought more legally protected equal rights with men. Campaigns to secure married women control of their property and custody of their children involved many women, who discovered striking similarities be-

tween their own oppression and that of slaves. American women "have good cause to be grateful to the slave," Kelley wrote, for in "striving to strike his iron off, we found most surely, that we were manacled *ourselves.*"

Activist antislavery women encountered hostility, especially from clergymen, who quoted the Bible to justify female inferiority and servility. Sarah Grimké struck back in 1837 with a series called *Letters on the Condition of Women and the Equality of the Sexes,* claiming that "men and women were CREATED EQUAL" and that "whatever is *right* for man to do, is *right* for woman."

Male abolitionists were divided about women's rights. At the World Anti-Slavery Convention in 1840, attended by many American abolitionists, the delegates refused to let women participate. Two upstate New Yorkers, Elizabeth Cady Stanton and Lucretia Mott, were compelled to sit behind curtains and not even be seen, much less be permitted to speak. When they returned home, they resolved to "form a society to advocate the rights of women." In 1848, in Seneca Falls, New York, their intentions, though delayed, were fulfilled in one of the most significant protest gatherings of the antebellum era.

In preparing for the meeting, Mott and Stanton drew up a list of women's grievances. They discovered that even though some states had awarded married women control over their property, they still had none over their earnings. Modeling their Declaration of Sentiments on the Declaration of Independence, the women at Seneca Falls proclaimed it a self-evident truth that "all men and women are created equal," and that men had usurped women's freedom and dignity. A man, the Declaration of Sentiments charged, "endeavored in every way he could, to destroy [woman's] confidence in her own powers, to lessen her self-respect, and to make her willing to lead a dependent and abject life." The remedy was expressed in 11 resolutions calling for equal opportunities in education and work, equality before the law, and the right to appear on public platforms. The most controversial res-

Elizabeth Cady Stanton (1815-1902) and Lucretia Mott (1793-1880) were the leaders of the 1848 gathering for women's rights at Seneca Falls, New York.

olution called for women's "sacred right to the elective franchise." The convention approved Mott and Stanton's list of resolutions.

Throughout the 1850s, led by Stanton and Susan B. Anthony, women continued to meet in annual conventions, working by resolution, persuasion, and petition campaign to achieve equal political, legal, and property rights with men. The right to vote, however, was considered the cornerstone of the movement. It remained so for

72 years of struggle until 1920, when passage of the Nineteenth Amendment made woman suffrage part of the Constitution. The Seneca Falls convention was crucial in beginning the campaign for equal public rights. The seeds of gaining psychological autonomy and self-respect, however, were sown in the struggles of countless women like Abby Kelley, Sarah Grimké, and Emily Robinson. The struggle for that kind of liberation continues today.

CONCLUSION
Perfecting America

Advocates for women's rights and temperance, abolitionists, and other reformers carried on very different crusades from those waged by Andrew Jackson against Indians, nullificationists, and the U.S. Bank. In fact, Jacksonian politics and antebellum reform

were often at odds. Most abolitionists and temperance reformers were anti-Jackson Whigs. Jackson and most Democrats repudiated the passionate moralism of reformers.

Yet both sides shared an abiding faith in change

and the idea of progress. Whether inspired by religious revivalism or political party loyalty, both believed that by stamping out evil forces, they could shape a better America.

As the United States neared midcentury, slavery emerged as the most divisive issue. Although both major political parties tried to evade the question, westward expansion and the addition of new territories to the nation would soon make avoidance impossible. Would new states be slave or free? The question increasingly aroused the deepest passions of the American people. For the pioneer family, the driving force behind the westward movement, however, questions involving their fears and dreams seemed more important. We turn to this family and that movement in the next chapter.

RECOMMENDED READING

Richard McCormick, *The Second Party System: Party Formation in the Jacksonian Era* (1966); and Richard Latner, *The Presidency of Andrew Jackson: White House Politics, 1829–1837* (1979), are the definitive works on those topics. See also Richard Ellis, *The Union at Risk: Jacksonian Democracy, States Rights, and The Nullification Crisis* (1987); Ronald Formisano, *The Transformation of Political Culture* (1983); and Jean Baker, *Affairs of Party* (1983). On Jackson's popular appeal, see two books by Robert Remini, *Andrew Jackson and the Course of American Freedom, 1822–1832* (1981), and *Andrew Jackson and the Course of American Democracy* (1984). Jackson's political opponents are best understood by reading biographies of his major rivals: Clement Eaton, *Henry Clay and the Art of American Politics* (1957); Irving H. Bartlett, *Daniel Webster* (1978); and Margaret Coit, *John P. Calhoun: American Portrait* (1950).

The best single volume on antebellum religion and reform is Ronald Walters, *American Reformers, 1815–1860* (1978). A fascinating account of revivalism is William McLoughlin, *Modern Revivalism: From Charles G. Finney to Billy Graham* (1959). Paul Johnson, *A Shopkeeper's Millennium: Society and Revivals in Rochester, New York, 1815–1837* (1978), details the social impact of both economic change and revivalism in one community. To understand the Transcendentalists, read Perry Miller, ed., *The Transcendentalists* (1957), or Thoreau's *Walden*.

The standard work on utopian communities is Arthur Bestor, *Backwoods Utopias* (1950); but John Humphrey Noyes's *History of American Socialisms* (1870) is indispensable.

On the temperance crusade, see Ian Tyrrell, *Sobering Up: From Temperance to Prohibition in Antebellum America, 1800–1860* (1979). The experience of most efforts at institutional reforms is superbly analyzed in David Rothman, *The Discovery of the Asylum: Social Order and Disorder in the New Republic* (1971). Working class reformers are the focus in Edward Pessen, *Most Uncommon Jacksonians: The Radical Leaders of the Early Labor Movement* (1967). On women's suffrage, see Eleanor Flexner, *Century of Struggle: The Woman's Rights Movement in the United States*, rev. ed. (1975).

Time Line

1824	New Harmony established
1825	John Quincy Adams chosen president by the House of Representatives
1826	American Temperance Society founded
1828	Calhoun publishes *Exposition and Protest* Jackson defeats Adams for the presidency Tariff of Abominations
1828–1832	Rise of workingmen's parties
1830	Webster-Hayne debate and Jackson-Calhoun toast Joseph Smith publishes *The Book of Mormon*
1830	Indian Removal Act
1830–1831	Charles Finney's religious revivals
1831	Garrison begins publishing *The Liberator*
1832	Jackson vetoes U.S. Bank charter Jackson reelected *Worcester* v. *Georgia*
1832–1833	Nullification crisis
1832–1836	Removal of funds from U.S. Bank to state banks
1833	Force Bill Compromise tariff Calhoun resigns as vice-president American Anti-Slavery Society founded
1834	New York Female Moral Reform Society founded National Trades Union founded Whig party established
1835–1836	Countless incidents of mob violence

1836	"Gag rule" Specie circular Van Buren elected president
1837	Financial panic and depression Sarah Grimké publishes *Letters on the Equality of the Sexes* Emerson's "American Scholar" address
1837–1838	Cherokee "Trail of Tears"
1840	William Henry Harrison elected president American Anti-Slavery Society splits World Anti-Slavery Convention Ten-hour day for federal employees
1840–1841	Transcendentalists found Hopedale and Brook Farm
1843	Dorothea Dix's report on treatment of the insane
1844	Joseph Smith murdered in Nauvoo, Illinois
1846–1848	Mormon migration to the Great Basin
1847	First issue of Frederick Douglass's *North Star*
1848	Oneida community founded First women's rights convention at Seneca Falls, New York
1850	Nathaniel Hawthorne, *Scarlet Letter*
1851	Maine prohibition law Herman Melville, *Moby Dick*
1853	Children's Aid Society established in New York City
1854	Thoreau publishes *Walden*
1855	Massachusetts bans segregated public schools

14

Moving West

By the 1840s, the frontier was retreating across the Mississippi. As Americans contemplated the lands west of the great river, they debated the question of expansion. Some, like Michigan's senator Lewis Cass, saw the Pacific Ocean as the only limit to territorial expansion. Cass believed that the West represented not only economic opportunity for Americans but political stability for the nation as well. People crowded into cities and confined to limited territories endangered the republic, he told fellow senators in a speech. But if they headed west to convert "the woods and forests into towns and villages and cultivate[d] fields" and to extend "the dominion of civilization and improvement over the domain of nature," they would find rewarding personal opportunities that would ensure political and social harmony.

Thousands of men seconded Cass's sentiments by volunteering to join American forces in the war against Mexico in the summer of 1845. Largely untrained, the companies hurried south. But before long these supporters of expansion saw the ugly side of territorial adventures : insects, bad weather, poor food, unsanitary conditions, and illnesses such as the "black vomit" (yellow fever), dysentery, and diarrhea. As a member of the American occupying army, Henry Judah also experienced the hostility of conquered peoples. In his diary, he reported, "It is dangerous to go out after night . . . Four of our men were stabbed today."

Thomas Gibson, a captain of Indiana volunteers, described a battlefield "still covered with [Mexican] dead" where "the stench is most horrible." Indiana friends had been killed, and Gibson himself had narrowly escaped. His wife, Mary, had not escaped the heady propaganda for national expansion. She had heard that Indiana soldiers had "shode themselves great cowards by retreating during battle," and she disapproved. "We all would rather you had stood like good soldiers," she told her husband.

• • •

Lewis Cass, Henry Judah, Thomas and Mary Gibson, and thousands of other Americans played a part in the nation's expansion into the trans-Mississippi West. The differences and similarities in their perspectives and in their responses to territorial growth unveil the complex nature of the western experience. Lewis Cass's speech illustrates the hold the West had on people's imagination and how some Americans linked expansion to individual opportunity and national progress. Yet his assumption that the West was vacant points to the costs of white expansion for Mexican-Americans and Native Americans.

This chapter concerns movement into the trans-Mississippi West between 1830 and 1865. First, we will consider how and when Americans moved west, by what means the United States acquired the vast territories that in 1840 belonged to other nations, and the meaning of "Manifest Destiny," the slogan used to defend the conquest of the continent west of the Mississippi River. Then, we explore the nature of life on the western farming, mining, and urban frontiers. Finally, the chapter examines responses of Native Americans and Mexican-Americans to expansion and illuminates the ways in which different cultural traditions intersected in the West.

Probing the Trans-Mississippi West

Until the 1840s, most Americans lived east of the Mississippi. The admission of new states between 1815 and 1840 symbolized the steady settlement of the eastern half of the continent. By 1860, some 4.3 million Americans had moved west of the great river.

Foreign Claims and Possessions

With the exception of the Louisiana Territory, Spain held title to most of the trans-Mississippi region in 1815. Spanish holdings stretched south to Mexico and west to the Pacific and included present-day Texas, Arizona, New Mexico, Nevada, Utah, western Colorado, California, and small parts of Wyoming, Kansas, and Oklahoma. When Mexico won its independence from Spain in 1821, it inherited these lands and the 75,000 Spanish-speaking inhabitants and numerous Native Americans living there.

To the north of California was the Oregon country, a vaguely defined area extending from California to Alaska. Both Great Britain and the United States claimed the Oregon country on the basis of explorations in the late eighteenth century and fur trading in the early nineteenth. Joint occupation, agreed on in the Convention of 1818 and the Occupation Treaty of 1827, temporarily deferred settling the boundary question.

Traders, Trappers, and Cotton Farmers

Americans made commercial forays into the trans-Mississippi West long before the migrations of the 1840s and 1850s and became familiar with some of its people and terrains. As early as 1811, Americans engaged in the fur trade in Oregon, and within ten years, fur trappers and traders were exploiting the resources of the Rocky Mountain region. By the mid-1830s, trappers had almost exterminated the beaver, but trade in bison robes prepared by the Plains tribes flourished in the area around the upper Missouri River and its tributaries until after 1860.

With the collapse of the Spanish Empire in 1821, American traders were able to penetrate the Southwest. Each year, caravans from "the States" followed the Santa Fe Trail over the plains and mountains, loaded with weapons, tools, and brightly colored calicoes, which they traded for metals and furs.

To the south, in Texas, land for cotton rather than trade attracted settlers and squatters in the 1820s. By 1835, almost 30,000 Americans were living in Texas, the largest group of Americans living outside the nation's boundaries at that time.

On the Pacific, New England traders acquired California cowhides and tallow in exchange for clothes, boots, hardware, and furniture manufactured in the East.

Among the earliest easterners to settle in the trans-Mississippi West were tribes from the South and the Old Northwest whom the American government forcibly relocated in present-day Oklahoma and Kansas. Ironically, some of these eastern tribes acted as agents of white civilization by introducing cotton, the plantation system, and schools. Other tribes triggered conflicts that weakened the western tribes with whom they came into contact. The Cherokee, Shawnee, and Delaware forced the Osages out of their Missouri and Arkansas hunting grounds, while tribes from the Old Northwest claimed hunting areas long used by Kansas plains tribes. These disruptions foreshadowed white incursions later in the century.

The facts that much of the trans-Mississippi West lay outside U.S. boundaries and that the government had guaranteed Indian tribes permanent possession of some western territories did not curtail American economic activities. By the 1840s, a growing volume of published information fostered dreams of possession. Lansford Hasting's *Emigrants' Guide to Oregon and California* (1845) provided not only the practical information that emigrants would need but also the encouragement that heading for the frontier was the right thing to do.

In his widely read guide, Hastings minimized the importance of Mexican and British sovereignty. His belief that Americans would obtain rights to foreign holdings in the West came true within a decade. In the course of the 1840s, the United States acquired the Southwest and Texas as well as the Oregon country up to the 49th parallel. Later, with the Gadsden Purchase in 1853, the total area of all these new lands amounted to over 1,500,000 square miles.

Manifest Destiny

Bursts of rhetoric accompanied territorial growth, and its slogan, "Manifest Destiny." The phrase, coined in 1845 by the editor of the *Democratic Review,* suggests that the country's superior institutions and culture gave Americans

John Gast's 1872 painting captures the perspective of white emigrants on the meaning of Manifest Destiny and the westward movement.

a God-given right to spread their civilization across the entire continent.

This sense of a unique mission was a legacy of early Puritan utopianism and revolutionary republicanism. By the 1840s, however, an argument for territorial expansion merged with the belief that the United States possessed a unique civilization. States could successfully absorb new territories. Publicists of Manifest Destiny proclaimed that the nation must.

Winning the Trans-Mississippi West

Manifest Destiny justified expansion but did not cause it. Concrete events in Texas triggered the national government's determination to acquire territories west of the Mississippi River.

The Texas question originated in the years when Spain held most of the Southwest. Although some settlements such as Santa Fe, founded in 1609, were almost as old as Jamestown, the Spanish considered the sparsely populated and underdeveloped Southwest primarily a buffer zone for Mexico. In the Adams-Onis treaty with Spain in 1819, the United States accepted a southern border excluding Texas, to which the Americans had vague claims stemming from the Louisiana Purchase.

Annexing Texas, 1845

By the time the treaty was ratified in 1821, Mexico had won its independence from Spain. The new nation inherited the borderlands, their people, and their problems. Mexicans soon had reason to fear American expansionism, after several attempts by the United States to buy Texas and continuing aggressive American statements.

In 1823, the Mexican government determined to strengthen border areas by increasing population. To attract settlers, it offered land in return for token payments and pledges to become Roman Catholics and Mexican citizens.

Stephen F. Austin, who gained rights to bring 300 families into Texas, was among the first of the American *empresarios*, or contractors, to take advantage of this opportunity. By the end of the decade, some 15,000 white Americans and 1,000 slaves lived in Texas, far outnumbering the 5,000 Mexican inhabitants.

Mexican officials soon questioned their invitation. Few American settlers became Catholics, and they remained more American than Mexican. Some of the settlers disliked Mexican laws and customs, and in late 1826, a small group raised the flag of rebellion and declared the Republic of Fredonia. Although settlers like Austin assisted in putting down the brief uprising, American newspapers hailed the rebels as "apostles of democracy" and called Mexico "an alien civilization."

United States Territorial Expansion by 1860

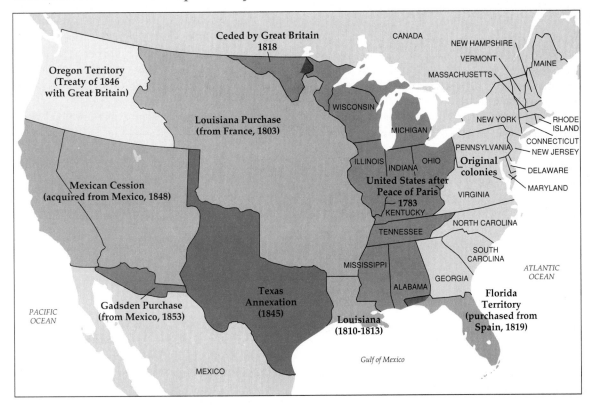

Mexican anxiety grew apace. In 1829, the Mexican government, determined to curb American influence, abolished slavery in Texas. The next year, it forbade further American immigration, and officials began to collect customs duties on goods crossing the Louisiana border. But little changed in Texas. American slave owners freed their slaves and forced them to sign life indenture contracts. Emigrants still crossed the border and continued to outnumber Mexicans.

Tensions escalated to the brink of war. In October 1835, a skirmish between the colonial militia and Mexican forces signaled the beginning of hostilities. Sam Houston, onetime governor of Tennessee and army officer, became commander in chief of the Texas forces.

Mexican dictator and general Antonio López de Santa Anna hurried north to crush the rebellion with an army of 6,000 conscripts. Santa Anna and his men won the initial engagements of the war: the Alamo at San Antonio fell to him, taking Davy Crockett and Jim Bowie with it. So too did the fortress of Goliad, to the southeast.

As he pursued Houston and the Texans toward the San Jacinto River, carelessness proved Santa Anna's undoing. When the Mexican general and his men settled down to their usual siesta on April 21, 1836, without posting an adequate guard, the Americans attacked. With cries of "Remember the Alamo! Remember Goliad!" the Texans overcame the army, captured its commander in his slippers, and won the war within 20 minutes. Their casualties numbered only two, while 630 Mexicans lay dead.

With the victory at San Jacinto, Texas gained its independence. But although Texans immediately sought admission to the Union, their request failed. Many northerners violently opposed annexation of another slave state. The Union was precariously balanced, with 13 free and 13 slave states. Texas would upset that equilibrium in favor of the South.

For the next few years, the Lone Star Republic led a precarious existence. Mexico refused to recognize its independence, and Texans skirmished with Mexican bands. Financial ties with the United States increased, however, as trade grew and many Americans invested in Texas bonds and lands.

Texas became headline news again in 1844, when President John Tyler (who assumed office after Harrison's sudden death) reopened the question of annexation, hoping that Texas would ensure his reelection. The issue exploded, however, bringing to life powerful sectional, national, and political tensions. Southern Democrats insisted that the South's future hinged on the annexation of Texas.

Democrats Lewis Cass, Stephen Douglas of Illinois, and Robert Walker of Mississippi vigorously supported annexation, not because it would expand slavery, a topic they avoided, but because it would spread the benefits of American civilization. Their arguments, classic examples of the tenets of Manifest Destiny, put the question into a national context of expanding American freedom. So successfully did they link Texas to Manifest Destiny and avoid sectional issues that their candidate, James Polk of Tennessee, secured the Democratic nomination in 1844. Polk called for "the reannexation of Texas at the earliest practicable period" and the occupation of the Oregon Territory. Manifest Destiny had come of age.

Polk won a close election in 1844. But by the time Polk took the oath of office in March 1845, Tyler, in his last months in office, had pushed through Congress a joint resolution admitting Texas to the Union. Nine years after its revolution, Texas finally became part of the Union. The agreement gave Texas the unusual right to divide into five states if it chose to do so.

War with Mexico, 1846–1848

When Mexico learned of Texas's annexation, it promptly severed diplomatic ties with the United States. It was easy for Mexicans to interpret the events from the 1820s on as part of a gigantic American plot to steal Texas. Now that the Americans had gained Texas, would they want still more?

Polk, like many other Americans, failed to appreciate how the annexation of Texas humiliated Mexico and increased pressures on its government to respond belligerently. Aware of its weakness, the president anticipated that Mexico would grant his grandiose demands: a Texas bounded by the Rio Grande rather than the Nueces River 150 miles to its north, as well as California and New Mexico.

Even before the Texans could accept the long-awaited invitation to join the Union, rumors of a Mexican invasion were afloat. As a precautionary move, Polk ordered General Zachary Taylor to move "on or near the Rio Grande." By October 1845, Taylor and 3,500 American troops had reached the Nueces River. In November, the president sent his secret agent, John L. Slidell, to Mexico City with instructions to secure the Rio Grande border and to buy Upper California and New Mexico. When the Mexican government refused to receive Slidell, an angry Polk decided to force Mexico into accepting American terms. He ordered Taylor south of the Rio Grande. To the Mexicans, who insisted that the Nueces River was the legitimate boundary, their presence constituted an act of war.

In late April, the Mexican government declared a state of defensive war. Two days later, a skirmish broke out between Mexican and Ameri-

The Mexican War, 1846–1848

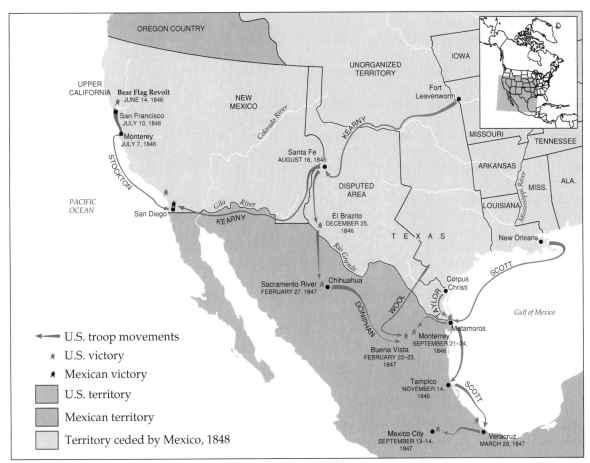

can troops, resulting in 16 American casualties. When Polk received Taylor's report, he quickly drafted a war message for Congress. The president claimed that Mexico had "passed the boundary of the United States . . . invaded our territory and shed American blood upon American soil." "War exists," he claimed, and, he added untruthfully, "notwithstanding all our efforts to avoid it, exists by act of Mexico."

Although Congress declared war, the conflict bitterly divided Americans. Many Whigs, including Abraham Lincoln, questioned the accuracy of Polk's initial account of the events, and their opposition grew more vocal as time passed. In 1847, a month after General Winfield Scott took Mexico City, Philadelphian Joseph Sills wrote in his diary, "There is a widely spread conviction . . . that it is a wicked & disgraceful war."

Yet Polk enjoyed the enthusiastic support of expansionists. Thomas Gibson's men, like most other soldiers, were eager volunteers. Some expansionists even urged permanent occupation of Mexico.

In the end, chance helped draw hostilities to a close. Mexican moderates approached Polk's diplomatic representative, Nicholas Trist, who accompanied the American army in Mexico. In Trist's baggage were detailed, though out-of-date, instructions outlining Polk's requirements: the Rio Grande boundary, Upper California, and New Mexico. Although the president had lost confidence in Trist and had ordered him home in chains, Trist stayed in Mexico to negotiate an end to the war. Having obtained most of Polk's objectives, Trist returned to Washington to an ungrateful president. Apparently Polk had wanted more territory from Mexico for less money. Firing him from his job at the State Department, Polk denounced Trist as an "impudent and unqualified scoundrel."

California and New Mexico

Polk made it clear from the early days of his presidency that California and New Mexico were part of any resolution of the Mexico crisis. Serious American interest in California dated only from the late 1830s. A few Americans had settled in California during the 1820s and 1830s. But gradual recognition of California's fine harbors, its favorable position for the China trade, and the suspicion that other countries, especially Great Britain, had designs on the region nourished the conviction that it must become part of the United States. As more Americans poured into California in the early 1840s, one resident realized, "The American population will soon be sufficiently numerous to play the Texas game."

Polk tried to purchase California, but Santa Anna, who bore the burden of having lost Texas, was in no position to sell. Thus in 1846, a few armed American settlers rose up against Mexican "tyranny" and established the "Bear Flag Republic."

New Mexico was also on Polk's list. Ties with the United States began in the 1820s, when American traders began to bring their goods to Santa Fe. New Mexicans had little desire for annexation, however, and the unsuccessful attempt by the Texans to capture Santa Fe in 1841 and border clashes in the following two years did not enhance the attractiveness of their Anglo neighbors. But standing awkwardly in the path of westward expansion, New Mexico's future as a Mexican province was uncertain.

In June 1846, shortly after the declaration of war with Mexico, the Army of the West, led by Colonel Stephen W. Kearny, left Fort Leavenworth, Kansas, for New Mexico. Two months later, the army took Santa Fe without a shot. New Mexico's upper class, who had already begun to intermarry with American merchants and send some sons to colleges in the United States, readily accepted the new rulers. However, ordinary Mexicans and Pueblo Indians did not take conquest so lightly. After Kearny departed, resistance erupted in New Mexico. Californians also fought the American occupation force. Kearny was wounded, and the first appointed American governor of New Mexico was killed. In the end, however, superior American military strength won the day. By January 1847, both California and New Mexico were firmly in American hands.

The Treaty of Guadalupe Hidalgo, 1848

Negotiated by Trist and signed on February 2, 1848, the Treaty of Guadalupe Hidalgo dictated the fate of most people living in the Southwest. The United States absorbed the region's 75,000 Spanish-speaking inhabitants and its 150,000 Native Americans and increased its territory by 529,017 square miles, almost a third of Mexico's extent. Mexico received $15 million and in 1853 would receive another $10 million for large tracts of land in southern Arizona and New Mexico (the Gadsden Purchase). In the treaty, the United States guaranteed the civil and political rights of former Mexican citizens and their rights to land and also agreed to satisfy all American claims against Mexico. The war had cost the United States 13,000 American lives, lost mostly to diseases such as measles and dysentery, and $97 million expended for military operations.

The Oregon Question, 1844–1846

Belligerence and war secured vast areas of the Southwest and California for the United States. In the Pacific Northwest, the presence of mighty Great Britain rather than the weak, crisis-ridden Mexican government suggested more cautious tactics. There diplomacy became the means for territorial gains.

Despite the disputed nature of claims to the Oregon Territory, Polk assured the inauguration day crowd huddled under umbrellas that "our title to the country of Oregon is 'clear and unquestionable,' . . . already our people are preparing to perfect that title by occupying it with their wives and children." Polk's words reflected American confidence that settlement carried the presumption of possession. But the British did not agree.

Between 1842 and 1845, the number of Americans in Oregon grew from 400 to over 5,000. Most located south of the Columbia River in the Willamette valley. By 1843, these settlers had written a constitution and soon after elected a legislature. At the same time, British interests in the area were declining as the fur trade dwindled.

The Democratic platform and the slogan that had helped elect Polk laid claim to a boundary of 54°40'. In fact, Polk was not willing to go to war with Great Britain for Oregon. Privately, he considered reasonable a boundary at the 49th parallel, which would extend the existing Canadian-American border to the Pacific and secure the harbors of Puget Sound for the United States. But Polk could hardly admit this to his Democratic supporters, who had so enthusiastically shouted "Fifty-four forty or fight" during the recent campaign.

Soon after his inaugural, Polk offered his compromise to Great Britain. But his tone offended the British minister, who rejected the offer at once. However, most Americans did not want to fight for Oregon and preferred to resolve the crisis diplomatically. As war with Mexico loomed, this task became more urgent.

The British, too, were eager to settle. In June 1846, the British agreed to accept the 49th parallel boundary if Vancouver Island remained British. With overwhelming Senate approval, Polk ended the crisis just a few weeks before the declaration of war with Mexico.

As these events show, Manifest Destiny was an idea that supported and justified expansionist policies. It corresponded, at the most basic level, to what Americans believed, that expansion was both necessary and right.

Going West

After diplomacy and war clarified the status of the western territories, Americans lost little time in moving there. A trickle of emigrants became a flood. During the 1840s, 1850s, and 1860s, thousands of Americans left their homes for the frontier. By 1860, California alone had 380,000 settlers.

Some chose to migrate by sea, sailing around South America to the West Coast or taking a ship to Panama, crossing the isthmus by land, and then continuing by sea. Most emigrants, however, chose land routes. In 1843, the first large party succeeded in crossing the plains and mountains to Oregon. More followed. Between 1841 and 1867, some 350,000 traveled over the overland trails to California or to Oregon, while others trekked part of the way to intermediate points like Colorado and Utah.

The Emigrants

Most of the emigrants who headed for the Far West, where slavery was prohibited, were white and American-born. They came from the Midwest and the Upper South. A few free blacks made the trip as well. Pioneer Margaret Frink remembered seeing "a Negro woman . . . tramping along through the heat and dust, carrying a cast iron black stove on her head, with her provisions and a blanket piled on top . . . bravely pushing on for California." Emigrants from the Deep South usually selected Arkansas or Texas as their destination, and many brought their slaves with them. By 1840, over 11,000 slaves toiled in Texas and 20,000 in Arkansas.

The many pioneers who kept journals during the five- to six-month overland trip captured the human dimension of emigrating. One migrant, Lodisa Frizzell, described her feelings of parting in 1852:

> Who is there that does not recollect their first night when started on a long journey, the well known voices of our friends still ring in our ears, the parting kiss feels still warm upon our lips, and that last separating word FAREWELL! sinks deeply into the heart. It may be the last we ever hear from some or all of them, and to those who start . . . there can be no more solemn scene of parting only at death.

Most emigrants traveled with family and relatives. Only during the gold rush years did large numbers, usually young men, travel independently. Migration was a family experience, mostly involving men and women from their late twenties to early forties. A sizeable number of them had recently married, and many had moved before. The difference was the vast distance to this frontier and the seemingly final separation from home.

Migrants' Motives

What led so many Americans to sell most of their possessions and embark on an unknown future thousands of miles away? Many believed that frontier life would offer rich opportunities. Thousands sought riches in the form of gold. Others anticipated making their fortune as merchants, shopkeepers, peddlers, land speculators, or practitioners of law or medicine.

Most migrants dreamed of bettering their life by cultivating the land. Federal and state land policies made the acquisition of land increasingly alluring. Preemption acts during the 1830s and 1840s gave "squatters" the right to settle public lands before the government offered them for sale and then allowed them to purchase these lands at the minimum price once they came on the market. At the same time, the amount of land a family had to buy shrank to only 40 acres. In 1862, the Homestead Act went further by offering 160 acres of government land free to citizens or future citizens over 21 who lived on the property, improved it, and paid a small registration fee. Oregon's land policy, which predated the Homestead Act, was even more generous. It awarded a single man 320 acres of free land and a married man 640 acres provided he occupied his claim for four years and made improvements.

Some emigrants hoped the West would restore them to health. Others pursued religious or cultural missions in the West. Missionary couples like David and Catherine Blaine, who settled in Seattle when it was a frontier outpost, determined to bring Protestantism and education west. Stirred by the stories they had heard of the "deplorable morals" on the frontier, they left the comforts of home to evangelize and educate westerners. Still others, like the Mormons, made the long trek to Utah to establish a society in conformity with their religious beliefs.

Not everyone who dreamed of setting off for the frontier could do so. The trip to the Far

West involved considerable expense. The sea route around Cape Horn came to perhaps $600 per person. For the same sum, four people could make the overland trip. And if the emigrants sold their wagons and oxen at the journey's end, the final expenses might amount to only $220. Clearly, however, the initial financial outlay was considerable enough to rule out the trip for the very poor. Despite increasingly liberal land policies, migration to the Far West (with the exception of group migration to Utah) was a movement of middle-class Americans.

The Overland Trails

The trip started for most emigrants in the late spring, when they left their homes and headed for starting points in Iowa and Missouri : Council Bluffs, Independence, Westport, St. Joseph. There companies of wagons gathered, and when grass was up for the stock, usually by the middle of May, they set out. Emigrant trains first followed the valley of the Platte River. Making only 15 miles a day, they slowly wound their way through the South Pass of the Rockies, heading for destinations in California or Oregon.

Emigrants found the first part of the trip novel and even enjoyable. The Indians, one woman noted, "proved better than represented." Men drove and repaired the wagons, ferried cattle and wagons across rivers, hunted, and stood guard at night. Women labored at domestic chores, caring for children, cooking meals, and washing clothes. Many of the children later remembered the trip as an exciting adventure.

As the trip lengthened, difficulties multiplied. Cholera often took a heavy toll. Conflict with Indians became a problem only in the 1850s and made emigrants jumpy during the second half of the trip. (Between 1840 and 1860, Indians killed about 400 emigrants, most during the second half of the trip ; the emigrants themselves killed at least that many Indians.) Travel-

Overland Trails to the West

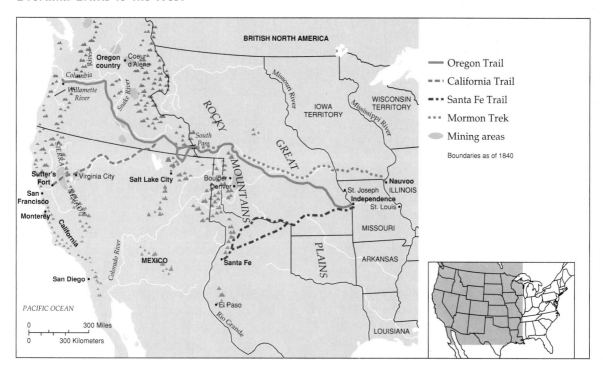

ing grew more arduous as deserts and mountains replaced rolling prairies.

Since emigrants had to cross the final mountain ranges of the Sierras and the Cascades before the first snowfall, there was a pressing need to push ever onward. Animals weakened by constant travel, poor feed, and bad water sickened, collapsed, and often died. As families faced the harsh realities of travel, they had to lighten their wagons by throwing out possessions lovingly brought from home. Food grew scarce.

Finally, five or six months after setting out, emigrants arrived, exhausted and often penniless, in Oregon or California. As one wrote on a September day in 1854, her journey had ended "which for care, fatigue, tediousness, perplexities and dangers of various kinds, can not be excelled."

Living on the Frontier

When emigrants finally reached their destinations and began building a new life, they naturally drew on their experiences back east. "Pioneers though we are, and proud of it, we are not content with the wilds . . . with the idelness of the land, the rudely construct[ed] log cabin," one Oregon settler explained. "Pioneers are not that kind of folks."

The Agricultural Frontier

Pioneer farmers faced the urgent task of establishing their homesteads and beginning farming. First, the family had to locate a suitable claim. Clearing the land and constructing a crude shelter followed. Only then could crops be planted. Since emigrants brought few of their possessions west, their work was more difficult. A young Oregon bride who set up housekeeping in the 1840s with only a stew kettle and three knives was not unusual.

After months of intense interaction with other travelers, families were now alone on their claims. The typical frontier household consisted of parents with one to four children. For several years, isolation was the rule. One pioneer remembered, "We were . . . 'all told,' eleven families within a radius of six or eight miles, widely separated by our holdings and three hundred and twenty acres to each family. In those days anyone residing within twenty miles was considered a neighbor." But the isolation usually ended within a few years as most areas attracted new emigrants and old settlers seeking better claims.

In Oregon, the pioneers set up a political system based on eastern models before the status of the territory was resolved. Before permanent schools or churches existed, men resumed the familiar political rituals of voting, electioneering, and talking politics. They were also going to court to resolve controversies and to ensure law and order. Although modern movies and novels suggest that violence was a part of everyday life on the frontier, this was not true on the farming frontier. Courts, rather than rough-and-ready vigilante groups, usually handled the occasional violence.

The chronic shortage of cash on the frontier retarded the growth of both schools and churches. Until farmers could send their goods to market, they had little cash to spare. Geographic mobility also contributed to institutional instability. Up to three-quarters of the population of a frontier county might vanish within a ten-year period as emigrants left to seek better land. Some farmed in as many as four locations until they found a satisfactory claim. Institutions relying on continuing personal and financial support suffered accordingly.

Yet even if their efforts to re-create familiar institutional life often faltered, settlers did not lose sight of their goals. Newspapers, journals, and books, which circulated early on the frontier, reinforced familiar values and norms and kept determination strong. As more and more settlers arrived, the numbers willing to support educational, religious, and cultural institutions grew. In the end, as one pioneer pointed out, "We have a telegraph line from the East, a daily rail road train, daily mail and I am beginning to feel quite civilized. And here ended my pioneer experience." Only 16 years had passed since she had crossed the Plains.

Although the belief in the frontier's special economic and social opportunities encouraged emigration, the dream was often illusory. The appearance of workers for hire and tenant farmers also pointed to real economic differences and hinted at the difficulties those on the bottom would face as they tried to improve their situation. Their widespread geographic mobility also indicates that many found it difficult to capitalize on the benefits of homesteading. Census data show that those who moved were generally less successful than the core of stable residents.

The Mining Frontier

On the mining frontier, tales of prospectors who had reportedly struck it rich fueled the fantasies of fortune hunters. News of the discovery of gold in 1848 in California swept the country like wildfire. Thousands raced to cash in on the bonanza. Within a year, California's population ballooned from 14,000 to almost 100,000. By 1852, that figure had more than doubled.

The forty-niners were mostly young, unmarried, predominantly male, and heterogeneous. Of those pouring into California in 1849, about 80 percent came from the United States, 8 percent from Mexico, and 5 percent from South America. The rest came from Europe and Asia. Few were as interested in settling the West as they were in extracting its precious metals and returning home rich.

California was the first and most dramatic of the western mining frontiers. Later gold strikes drew prospectors to the Pacific Northwest and British Columbia, Colorado, and Montana in the 1850s and 1860s. In the mid-1870s, yet another discovery of gold, this time in the Black Hills of South Dakota, attracted hordes of fortune seekers.

The discovery of gold or silver spurred immediate, if usually short-lived, growth. Merchants, saloonkeepers, cooks, druggists, gamblers, and prostitutes hurried into boom areas as fast as prospectors. Usually about half of the res-

idents of any mining camp were there to relieve the miners of their profits, not to prospect themselves.

Life in the mining boomtowns was often disorderly. Racial antagonism between American miners and foreigners, whom they labeled "greasers" (Mexicans), "chinks" (Chinese), "keskedees" (Frenchmen), and lesser "breeds," led to ugly riots and lynchings. Fistfights, drunkenness, and murder occurred often enough to become part of the lore of the gold rush. Wrote one woman, "In the short space of twenty four days, we have had murders, fearful accidents, bloody deaths, a mob, whippings, a hanging, an attempt at suicide, and a fatal duel."

Although the lucky few struck it rich or at least made enough money to return home with pride intact, miners' journals and letters reveal that many made only enough to keep going. The problem was that easily mined silver and gold deposits soon ran out. The remaining rich deposits lay deeply embedded in rock or gravel. Extraction required cooperative efforts, capital, technological experience, and expensive machinery. Eventually, mining became a corporate industrial concern, with miners as wage earners. As early as 1852, the changing nature of mining in California had transformed most of the shaggy miners into wage workers.

Probably five percent of early gold rush emigrants to California were women and children. Many of the women also anticipated getting "rich in a hurry." Because there were so few of them, the cooking, nursing, laundry, and hotel services women provided had a high value. Yet it was wearying work, and some wondered if the money compensated for the exhaustion. As Mary Ballou thought it over, she decided, "I would not advise any Lady to come out here and suffer to toil and fatigue I have suffered for the sake of a little gold." As men's profits shrank, so too did those of the women who served them.

Some of the first women to arrive on the mining frontier were prostitutes, who may have comprised as much as 20 percent of California's female population in 1850. During boom days, they made good money and sometimes won a

Although there were only a few women on the early mining frontier, they often found that the predominantly male environment offered them good opportunities to earn money.

recognized place in society. But they were more often the victims of murder and violence than the recipients of courtesy.

The Mexicans, South Americans, Chinese, and small numbers of blacks seeking their fortunes in California soon discovered that racial discrimination flourished vigorously in the land of golden promise. At first, American miners hoped to force foreigners out of the gold fields altogether. But an attempt to declare mining illegal for all foreigners failed. A high tax on foreign miners proved more successful. Thousands of Mexicans and Chinese left the mines. As business stagnated in mining towns, however, white miners had second thoughts about the levy and reduced it. In 1870, the tax was declared unconstitutional.

Black Americans found that color placed them in a situation akin to that of foreigners. Deprived of the vote, forbidden to testify in civil or criminal cases involving whites, excluded from the bounties of the state's homestead law, blacks led a precarious existence. When news arrived of the discovery of gold in British Columbia in the late 1850s, hundreds of blacks as well as thousands of Chinese left the state hoping that the Canadian frontier would be more hospitable than California.

Although men's and women's fantasies of dazzling riches rarely came true, gold had a huge impact on the West as a whole. Between 1848 and 1883, California mines supplied two-thirds

of the country's gold. This gold transformed San Francisco from a sleepy town into a bustling metropolis. It fueled the development of California and Oregon, and it built harbors, railroads, and irrigation systems all over the West.

The Mormon Frontier

In the decades before 1860, many emigrants heading for the Far West stopped to rest and buy supplies in Salt Lake City, the heart of the Mormon state of Deseret. There they encountered a society that seemed familiar and orderly, yet foreign and shocking. Visitors admired the attractively laid out town with its irrigation ditches, gardens, and tidy houses, but they deplored polygamy. They were amazed that so few Mormon women seemed interested in escaping from the bonds of plural marriage.

Violent events had driven the Mormons to the arid Great Basin area. Joseph Smith's murder in 1844 marked no end to the persecution of his followers. By the fall of 1846, angry mobs had chased the last of the "Saints" out of Nauvoo, Illinois. Smith's successor, Brigham Young, realized that flight from the United States represented the best hope for survival.

Young selected the Great Basin area, technically part of Mexico, as the best site for his future kingdom. It was arid and remote, 1,000 miles from its nearest "civilized" neighbors. But if irrigated, Mormon leaders concluded it might prove as fertile as the fields and vineyards of ancient Israel.

In April 1847, Young led an exploratory expedition of 143 men, three women, and two children to this promised land. By September 1847, fully 566 wagons and 1,500 of the Saints had made the arduous trek to Salt Lake City. By 1850, the Mormon frontier had attracted over 11,000 settlers. Missionary efforts in the United States and abroad, especially in Great Britain and Scandinavia, drew thousands of converts to the Great Basin. By the end of the decade, over 30,000 Saints lived in Utah. Though hardship marked these early years, the Mormons thrived. As one early settler remarked, "We have everything around us we could ask."

Non-Mormon or "Gentile" emigrants passing through Utah found much that was recognizable, but also perceived profound differences, for the heart of Mormon society was not the individual farmer living on his own homestead but the cooperative village. Years of persecution had nourished a strong sense of group identity and acceptance of church leadership. Organized by the church leaders, who made the essential decisions, farming became a collective enterprise. All farmers were allotted land. All had irrigation rights, for water did not belong to individuals but to the community. During Sunday services, the local bishop might give farming instructions to his congregation along with his sermon.

The church was omnipresent in Utah; in fact, nothing separated church and state. When it became clear that Utah would become a territory, Mormon leaders drew up a constitution that divided religious and political power. But once in place, powers overlapped. As one Gentile pointed out, "This intimate connection of church and state seems to pervade everything that is done. The supreme power in both being lodged in the hands of the same individuals, it is difficult to separate their two official characters, and to determine whether in any one instance they act as spiritual or merely temporal officers."

The Treaty of Guadalupe Hidalgo officially incorporated Utah into the United States but little affected political and religious arrangements. Brigham Young became territorial governor. Local bishops continued to act as spiritual leaders as well as civil magistrates in Mormon communities.

Other aspects of the Mormon frontier were distinctive. Mormon policy toward the Indian tribes was remarkably enlightened. As one prominent Mormon pointed out, "It has been our habit to shoot Indians with tobacco and bread biscuits rather than with powder and lead, and we are most successful with them." After two expeditions against the Timpanagos and Shoshone in 1850, Mormons concentrated on converting rather than killing Native Americans. Mormon missionaries learned Bannock, Ute, Navajo, and Hopi languages in order to bring the faith to these tribes. They also encouraged Native Americans to ranch and farm.

While most Gentiles could tolerate some of the differences they encountered on the Mormon frontier, few could accept polygamy and the seemingly immoral extended family structure that plural marriage entailed. Although Joseph Smith and other church leaders had secretly practiced polygamy in the early 1840s, Brigham Young only publicly revealed the doctrine in 1852, when the Saints were safely in Utah.

Actually, relatively few families were polygamous. During the 40-year period in which Mormons practiced plural marriage, only 10 to 20 percent of Mormon families were polygamous. Few men had more than two wives. Because of the expense of maintaining several families and the personal strains involved, usually only the most successful and visible Mormon leaders practiced polygamy. To the shock of outsiders, Mormon women defended polygamy to the outside world. Polygamy was preferable to monogamy, which left the single woman without the economic and social protection of family life and forced some of them into prostitution.

Although the Mormon frontier seemed alien to outsiders, it succeeded in terms of its numbers, its growing economic prosperity, and its group unity. Long-term threats loomed for this community, however, once the area became part of the United States. Attacks on Young's power as well as heated verbal denunciations of polygamy proliferated. Efforts began in Congress to outlaw polygamy. In the years before the Civil War, Mormons withstood these assaults on their way of life. But as Utah became more connected to the rest of the country, the tide would turn against them.

The Urban Frontier

Many emigrants went west to settle in cities like San Francisco, Denver, and Portland. There they hoped to find business and professional opportunities or, perhaps, the chance to make a fortune by speculating in town lots.

Cities were an integral part of frontier life and sometimes preceded agricultural settlement. Some communities turned into bustling cities as they catered to the emigrant trade. St. Joseph, Missouri, outfitted families setting out on the overland journey. Salt Lake City offered pioneers headed for California an opportunity to rest and restock. Portland was the destination of many emigrants and became a market and supply center for homesteaders.

Some cities, like San Francisco and Denver, sprang up almost overnight. In a mere 12 years, San Francisco's population zoomed from 812 to 56,802.

Young, single men seeking their fortunes made up a disproportionate share of the urban population. Frontier Portland had more than three men for every woman. Predictably, urban life was often noisy, rowdy, and occasionally violent. Eventually the sex ratio became balanced, but as late as 1880, fully 18 of the 24 largest western cities had more men than women.

Although western cities began with distinctive characters, they soon resembled eastern cities. As a western publication boasted, "Transport a resident of an Eastern city and put him down in the streets of Portland, and he would observe little difference between his new surroundings and those he beheld but a moment before in his native city."

The history of Portland suggests the common pattern of development. In 1845, Portland was only a clearing in the forest. By the early 1850s, it had grown into a small trading center. As farmers poured into Oregon, the city became a regional commercial center. More permanent structures were built, giving the city an "eastern" appearance.

The belief that urban life in the West abounded with special opportunities initially drew many young men to Portland and other western cities. Many of them did not find financial success there. Opportunities were greatest for newcomers who brought assets with them. These residents became the elite of the community.

Cultures in Conflict

Looking at westward expansion through the eyes of white emigrants provides only one view of the frontier experience. An entry from an Oregon Trail journal suggests other perspectives. On May 7, 1864, Mary Warner, a bride of only a few months, described a frightening event. That day, a "fine-looking" Indian had visited the wagon train and tried to buy her. Mary's husband, probably uncertain how to handle the situation, played along, agreeing to trade his wife for two ponies. The Indian generously offered three. "Then," wrote Mary, "he took hold of my shawl to make me understand to get out [of the wagon]. About this time I got frightened and really was so hysterical [that] I began to cry." Everyone laughed at her, she reported, though surely the Indian found the whole incident no more amusing than she had. This ordinary encounter on the overland trail only begins to hint at the social and cultural differences separating white Americans moving west and the peoples with whom they came into contact.

Confronting the Plains Tribes

During the 1840s, white Americans first came into extensive contact with the powerful Plains tribes. Probably a quarter million Native Americans occupied the area from the Rocky Mountains to the Missouri River and from the Platte River to New Mexico. Nearest the Missouri and Iowa frontier lived the "border" tribes — the Pawnee, Omaha, Oto, Ponca, and Kansa. These Indians, unlike other Plains tribes, lived in villages and raised crops, though they supplemented their diet with buffalo meat during the summer months. On the Central Plains lived the Brulé and Oglala Sioux, the Cheyenne, the Shoshone, and the Arapaho, aggressive tribes who followed the buffalo and often raided the border tribes. In the Southwest were the Comanche, Ute, Navajo, and some Apache bands, while the Kiowa, Wichita, Apache, and southern Comanche claimed northern and western Texas as their hunting grounds.

Although there were differences among these tribes, they shared certain characteristics. Most had adopted a nomadic way of life after the introduction of horses in the sixteenth century increased their seasonal mobility from 50 miles to 500 miles. Horses allowed Indian braves to hunt the buffalo with such success that tribes (with the exclusion of the border groups) came to depend on the beasts for food, clothing, fuel, tepee dwellings, and trading purposes. Because women were responsible for processing buffalo products, some men had more than one wife to tan skins for trading.

Mobility also increased tribal contact and conflict. War played a central part in the lives of the Plains tribes. But tribal warfare was not like the warfare of white men. Indians sought not to exterminate their enemies or to claim territory but rather to steal horses and to prove individual prowess. They considered it braver to touch an enemy than to kill or scalp him.

The Plains tribes, though disunified, posed a fearsome obstacle to white expansion. They had signed no treaties with the United States

Artists were fascinated by Plains Indian life, which they captured in sketches and paintings. Most anticipated that native culture would disappear with the coming of whites to the West.

Indian Tribes in 1840

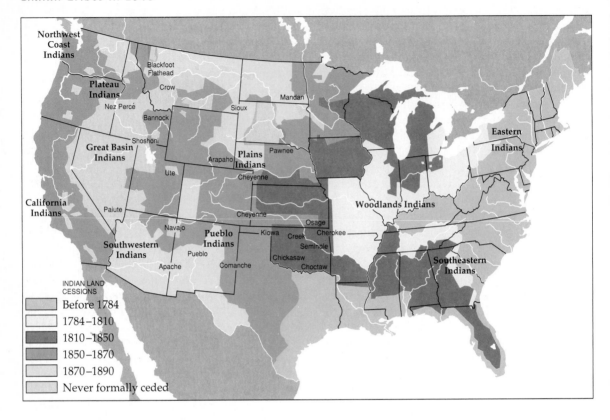

and had few friendly feelings toward whites. Their contact with white society had brought gains through trade in skins, but the trade had also brought alcohol and destructive epidemics.

When the first emigrants drove their wagons across the plains and prairies in the early 1840s, relations between Indians and whites were peaceable. But the intrusion of whites set in motion an environmental cycle that eventually drew the two groups into conflict. Indian tribes depended on the buffalo and slaughtered only what they needed. Whites, however, adopted the "most exciting sport," the buffalo hunt. As the great herds began to shrink, Native American tribes began to battle one another for hunting grounds and food. In an 1846 petition to President Polk, the Sioux requested compensation for damages caused by whites. When the president denied their re-

quest, they tried to extract taxes from the emigrants passing over their lands. Emigrants were outraged.

The discovery of gold in California, which lured over 20,000 across the Plains in 1849 alone, became the catalyst for federal action. The vast numbers of gold seekers and their animals wrought such devastation in the Platte valley that it rapidly became a wasteland for the Indians. The dreaded cholera that whites carried with them spread to the Indians, killing thousands.

To meet the crisis, government officials devised a two-pronged plan. The government would construct a chain of forts to protect emigrants and, simultaneously, call the tribes to a general conference. Officials expected that in return for generous presents, Indians would end tribal warfare and limit their movements to prescribed areas. They instructed tribes to select chiefs to speak for them at the conference.

The Fort Laramie Council, 1851

In 1851, the council convened at Fort Laramie. As many as 10,000 Indians, hopeful of ending the destruction of their way of life and eager for the promised presents, gathered at the fort. Tribal animosities simmered, however. Skirmishes occurred on the way to the fort, and the border tribes, fearful of the Sioux, declined to participate. The Comanche, Kiowa, and Apache also refused to come since their enemies, the Sioux and the Crow, were to be there.

At the conference, whites told the gathered tribes that times had changed. In the past, "you had plenty of buffalo and game . . . and your Great Father well knows that war has always been your favorite amusement and pursuit. He then left the question of peace and war to yourselves. Now, since the settling of the districts West of you by the white men, your condition has changed." There would be compensation for the destruction of their grass, timber, and buffalo and annual payments of goods and services. But in return, the tribes had to give up their rights of free movement. The government drew tribal boundaries, and chiefs made promises to stay within them. In most cases, some tribal lands were sold.

The Fort Laramie Treaty was the first agreement between the Plains tribes and the United States government. It expressed the conviction of whites that Indians must stay in clearly defined areas apart from white civilization.

But ominous signs appeared that more trouble would precede any "resolution" of Indian-white affairs. Sioux chief Black Hawk told whites, "You have split the country and I do not like it." His powerful tribe refused to be restricted to lands north of the Platte. In the following years, it would become evident that Americans and Sioux had conflicting interests south of the Platte. Elsewhere in the trans-Mississippi West, other tribes, like the fierce Navajo of New Mexico, also resisted white attempts to confine them.

Overwhelming the Mexicans

In the Southwest, in Texas, and in California, Americans contended with a Spanish-speaking population. Americans regarded Mexicans as lazy, ignorant, and cunning, the "dregs of society." Although Mexicans easily recognized such cultural arrogance, they lacked the numbers to fend off American aggression.

Although Anglo-Mexican interaction differed from place to place, few Anglos heeded the Treaty of Guadalupe Hidalgo's assurances that Mexicans would have citizens' rights and the "free enjoyment of their liberty and property." The greatest numbers of Spanish-speaking people lived in New Mexico, and, of all former Mexican citizens, they probably fared the best. Most were of mixed blood, living marginally as ranch hands for rich landowners or as farmers and herdsmen in small villages dominated by a *patron* or headman. As the century wore on, Americans produced legal titles and took over lands long occupied by peasant farmers and stock raisers. But despite economic reversals, New Mexicans survived, carrying their rural culture well into the twentieth century.

Light-skinned, upper-class landowners fared better. When the United States annexed New Mexico, this substantial and powerful class contracted strategic marriage and business alliances with the Anglo men who slowly trickled into the territory. During the 1850s, they maintained their influence and prestige and their American connections. Only rarely did they bother with the plight of their poor country-men. Class outweighed ethnic or cultural considerations.

In Texas, the Spanish-speaking residents, only 10 percent of the population in 1840, shrank to a mere 6 percent by 1860. Although the upper class also intermarried with Americans, they lost most of their power as Germans, Irish, French, and Americans poured into the state. Poor, dark-skinned Hispanics clustered in low-paying and largely unskilled jobs.

In California, the discovery of gold radically changed the situation for Hispanic-Americans.

In 1848, there were 7,000 Californios and about twice as many Anglos. By 1860, the Anglo population had ballooned to 360,000. Hispanic-Americans were hard pressed to cope with the rapid influx of outsiders.

In 1851, Congress passed the Gwin Land Law, which forced California landowners to defend what was already theirs and encouraged squatters to settle on land in the hopes that the Californios' titles would prove false. It took an average of 17 years to establish clear title to land. A victory at court often turned into a defeat when legal expenses forced owners to sell their lands to pay debts. In the south, where Anglos judged land less valuable than in the mining north, the process of dispossession was slower. But by the early 1860s, the ranching class there had also lost most of its extensive holdings.

Many working-class Hispanic-Americans lived marginal existences in California's growing towns and cities. Others became cowboys on American ranches or lived on their own small ranches in the backcountry. For them, the coming of the Anglos presented not opportunity but oppression. By 1870, the average Hispanic-American worker's property was worth only about a third of its value of 20 years earlier.

As the career of Tiburcio Vásquez, a notorious *bandido* in southern California, suggests, some Hispanics felt that they could protest events only through violence:

> My career grew out of the circumstances by which I was surrounded. . . . As I grew to manhood I was in the habit of attending balls and parties given by the native Californians, into which the Americans, then beginning to become numerous, would force themselves and shove the native born men aside, monopolizing the dance and the women. This was about 1852. A spirit of hatred and revenge took possession of me. I had numerous fights in defense of my countrywomen. The officers were continually in pursuit of me. I believed we were unjustly and wrongfully deprived of the social rights that belonged to us.

What Anglos called crime, Vásquez called self-defense.

CONCLUSION
Fruits of Manifest Destiny

Like Lewis Cass, many nineteenth-century Americans were convinced that the country had merely gained western territories to which it was entitled. The expanding nation did gain vast natural wealth in the trans-Mississippi West. But only a small fraction of the hopeful emigrants heading for the frontier realized their dreams of success. And the move west had a dark side as Americans clashed with Mexicans and Native Americans in their drive to fulfill their "Manifest Destiny."

RECOMMENDED READING

Ray Allen Billington gives an overview of the move west in *America's Frontier Heritage* (1966). Gilbert C. Fite treats agriculture in *The Farmer's Frontier, 1865–1900* (1966). The cities of the West are the subject of *The Urban West at the End of the Frontier* (1978) by Lawrence H. Larson.

Frederick Merk explores Manifest Destiny in *Manifest Destiny and Mission in American History* (1963). Robert W. Johanssen treats the Mexican War in *To the Halls of Montezuma : The Mexican War in the American Imagination* (1985).

George Pierre Castile treats cultural conflict in *North American Indians : An Introduction to the Chichimeca* (1979). Peter Nabakov has edited a collection of Indian responses, *Native American Testimony : An Anthology of Indian and White Relations* (1978).

Julie Roy Jeffrey compensates for the neglect of women in older frontier studies in *Frontier Women: The Trans-Mississippi West, 1840–1880* (1979). Sandra Myres edited women's diaries in *Ho for California! Women's Overland Diaries from the Huntington Library* (1980). See also John D. Unruh, Jr., *The Plains Across: The Overland Emigrants and the Trans-Mississippi West, 1840–1860* (1979). For details of the mining frontier, consult Rodman W. Paul, *California Gold: The Beginning of Mining in the Far West* (1974). Although there were not many blacks on the frontier, William Loren Katz studies them in *The Black West* (1971). As for the Mormons, see Richard L. Bushman's *Joseph Smith and the Beginnings of Mormonism* (1984). Studies of Mexicans include Leonard Pitt, *The Decline of the Californios: A Social History of the Spanish-Speaking Californians, 1846–1890* (1970); M. S. Meir and Feliciano Rivera, *The Chicanos: A History of Mexican-Americans* (1972); and Alfredo Mirande and Evangeline Enriquez, *La Chicana: The Mexican-American Woman* (1979).

Time Line

1803–1806	Lewis and Clark expedition
1818	Treaty on joint U.S.-British occupation of Oregon
1819	Spain cedes Spanish territory in United States and sets transcontinental boundary of Louisiana Purchase, excluding Texas
1821	Mexican independence Opening of Santa Fe Trail Stephen Austin leads American settlement of Texas
1821–1840	Indian removals
1829	Mexico abolishes slavery in Texas
1836	Texas declares independence Battles of the Alamo and San Jacinto
1840s	Emigrant crossings of Overland Trail
1844	James Polk elected president
1845	"Manifest Destiny" coined United States annexes Texas and sends troops to the Rio Grande Americans attempt to buy Upper California and New Mexico
1846	Mexico declares defensive war United States declares war and takes Santa Fe Resolution of Oregon question
1847	Attacks on Veracruz and Mexico City Mormon migration to Utah begins
1848	Treaty of Guadalupe Hidalgo
1849	California gold rush begins
1850	California admitted to the Union
1851	Fort Laramie Treaty
1853	Gadsden Purchase
1862	Homestead Act

15

The Union in Peril

T he election of 1860 confronted Abraham Lincoln and the American people with the most serious crisis since the founding of the Republic. Feeling deeply "the responsibility that was upon me," Lincoln won an unusual four-party election with only 39 percent of the popular vote. He had appealed almost exclusively to northern voters in a blatantly sectional campaign, defeating his three opponents by carrying every free state except New Jersey.

Other Americans sensed the mood of crisis that fall and faced their own fears and responsibilities. A month before the election, plantation owner Robert Allston wrote his oldest son, Benjamin, that "disastrous consequences" would follow from a Lincoln victory. After the election, Allston corresponded with a southern colleague about the need for "an effective military organization" to resist "Northern and Federal aggression." In this shift from sewing machines to military ones, Robert Allston prepared for what he called the "impending crisis."

Frederick Douglass, however, greeted the election with characteristic optimism. "Slaveholders," he said, "know that the day of their power is over when a Republican President is elected." But no sooner had Lincoln's victory been determined than Douglass's hopes turned sour. He noted that Republican leaders, in their desire to keep southern border states from seceding, sounded more antiabolitionist than antislavery. Slavery would, in fact, Douglass bitterly concluded, "be as safe, and safer" with Lincoln than with a Democrat.

Michael Luark, an Iowa farmer, was not so sure. Born in Virginia, Luark was a typically mobile nineteenth-century American. After growing up in Indiana, he followed the mining booms of the 1850s to Colorado and California before returning to the Midwest to farm. Writing in his diary on the last day of 1860, Luark looked ahead to 1861 with a deep sense of fear. "Startling" political changes would occur, he predicted, perhaps even the "Dissolution of the Union and Civil War with all its train of horrors." Within four months of this diary entry, the guns of the Confederate States of America fired on a federal fort in South Carolina, and the Civil War began.

• • •

Such a calamitous event had numerous causes, large and small. But as Douglass understood, by 1860 it was clear that "slavery is the real issue, the single bone of contention between all parties and sections."

This chapter analyzes how the momentous issue of slavery disrupted the political system and eventually the Union itself. We will look at how four major developments between 1848 and 1861 contributed to the Civil War: first, a sectional dispute over the extension of slavery into the western territories; second, the breakdown of the political party system; third, growing cultural differences in the views and life styles of southerners and northerners; and fourth, intensifying emotional and ideological polarization between the two regions over losing their way of life and sacred republican rights at the hands of the other. The election of Lincoln was the spark that touched off the conflagration.

Slavery in the Territories

The North and the South had managed to contain their differences over slavery, with only occasional difficulties, during the 60 years after the Constitutional Convention. Political compromise in 1787 had resolved the questions of the slave trade and how to count slaves for congressional representation. In 1820, the Missouri Compromise had established a workable way of balancing the admission of free and slave states to the Union and had also defined a geographic line (36° 30′) to determine future decisions. In 1833, compromise had defused South Carolina's nullification of the tariff, and the gag rule in 1836 had kept divisive abolitionist petitions to end slavery off the floor of Congress.

One reason these compromises were temporarily successful was the existence of a two-party system with intersectional membership. Whigs and Democrats lived on both sides of the Mason-Dixon line. This changed in the late 1840s with territorial expansion, and the change would prove catastrophic to the Union.

Free Soil or Constitutional Protection?

When the Mexican War broke out in 1846, it seemed likely that the United States would acquire new territories in the Southwest. Would they be slave or free? To an appropriations bill

to pay for the war, David Wilmot, a congressman from Pennsylvania, added a short amendment declaring that "neither slavery nor involuntary servitude shall ever exist" in any territories acquired from Mexico. The debates in Congress over the Wilmot Proviso were significant because legislators voted not as Whigs and Democrats but as northerners and southerners.

When the Mexican War ended, several solutions were presented to deal with this question of slavery in the territories. The first was the "free soil" idea of preventing any extensions of slavery. Supporters of "free soil" had mixed motives. For some, slavery was a moral evil. But for many northern white farmers looking to move westward, the threat of economic competition with an expanding system of large-scale slave labor was even more serious. Nor did they wish to compete for land with free blacks. As Wilmot put it, his proviso was intended to preserve the area for "the sons of toil, of my own race and own color." Other northerners resented the "insufferable arrogance" of the "spirit and demands of the Slave Power."

Opposed to the free-soil position were the arguments of Senator John C. Calhoun of South Carolina, expressed in several resolutions introduced in the Senate in 1847. Not only did Congress lack the constitutional right to exclude slavery from the territories, Calhoun argued, but it had a positive duty to protect it. The Wilmot Proviso, therefore, was unconstitutional, as was the Missouri Compromise and any other federal act that prevented slaveholders from taking their slave property into the territories of the United States.

Economic, political, and moral considerations stood behind the Calhoun position. Many southerners hungered for new cotton lands in the West and Southwest. Politically, southerners wanted to protect their institutions against destructive abolitionists. Southern leaders saw the Wilmot Proviso as a moral issue that raised questions about basic republican principles. Senator Robert Toombs of Georgia warned that if Congress passed the proviso, he would favor disunion rather than "degradation."

Popular Sovereignty and the Election of 1848

With such divisive potential, it was natural that many Americans sought a compromise solution to keep slavery out of politics. "Popular sovereignty," as promulgated by Senator Lewis Cass, left the decision of whether to permit slavery in a territory to the local territorial legislature. The Democratic party, attracted to the idea that popular sovereignty could mean all things to all people, nominated Cass for president in 1848. He denounced abolitionists and the Wilmot Proviso but otherwise avoided the issue of slavery.

The Whigs found an even better way to evade the slavery issue. They nominated the Mexican War hero, General Zachary Taylor, a Louisiana slaveholder, who compared himself to Washington as a "no party" man above politics. This was nearly the only thing he stood for. Southern Whigs supported Taylor because they thought he might understand the burdens of slave-holding, while northern Whigs were pleased that he took no stand on the Wilmot Proviso.

The evasions of the two major parties disappointed Calhoun, who tried to create a new unified southern party. Threatening secession, Calhoun called for a united effort against further attempts to interfere with the southern right to extend slavery, but his effort failed.

Warnings also issued from the North. Disaffected Democrats in New York and "conscience" Whigs from Massachusetts met in Buffalo, New York, to form the Free-Soil party and nominate Martin Van Buren as president. The platform of the new party, composed of an uneasy mixture of ardent abolitionists and racist opponents of free black mobility into western lands, pledged to fight for "free soil, free speech, free labor and free men."

General Taylor won the election easily, largely because defections from Cass in New York and Pennsylvania to the Free-Soilers cost the Democrats the electoral votes from those states. Although weakened, the two-party system survived, and purely sectional parties were prevented.

The Compromise of 1850

Taylor won the election by avoiding slavery issues, but as president he could no longer do so. As he was inaugurated in 1849, four compelling issues faced the nation. The rush of some 80,000 unruly gold miners to California qualified that territory for admission to the Union. But California's entry as a free state would upset the balance between slave and free states in the Senate that had prevailed since 1820.

The unresolved status of the Mexican cession in the Southwest posed a second problem. The boundary between Texas and the New Mexico Territory was also in dispute, with Texas claiming lands all the way to Santa Fe. This increased northern fears that Texas might be divided into five or six slave states.

The existence of slavery and one of the largest slave markets in North America in the nation's capital was a third problem, especially to abolitionists. Fourth, Southerners resented the lax federal enforcement of the Fugitive Slave Act of 1793. They called for a stronger act that would end the protection northerners gave runaway slaves as they fled along the underground railroad to Canada.

Early in 1850, therefore, the old compromiser, Henry Clay, introduced a series of resolu-

The Compromise of 1850

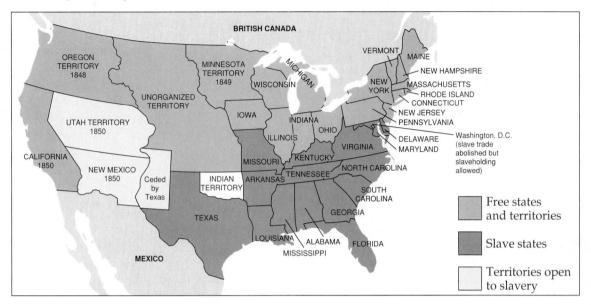

tions in an omnibus package intended to settle these issues once and for all. Despite some 70 speeches on behalf of the compromise, however, the Senate defeated Clay's Omnibus Bill, and the tired and disheartened 73-year-old Clay left Washington. Into the gap stepped a new compromiser, Senator Stephen Douglas of Illinois, who understood that Clay's resolutions had a better chance of passing if voted on individually rather than as a package. Under Douglas's leadership, and with the support of Millard Fillmore, who succeeded to the presidency upon Taylor's untimely death, a series of bills was finally passed.

The so-called Compromise of 1850 put Clay's resolutions, slightly altered, into law. First, California entered the Union as a free state, upsetting the balance of free and slave states, 16 to 15. Second, the territorial governments of New Mexico and Utah were organized by letting the people of those territories decide for themselves whether to permit slavery. The Texas–New Mexico border was settled in a compromise that denied Texas the disputed area. In turn, the federal government compensated

Texas with $10 million to pay off debts owed to Mexico. Third, the slave trade, but not slavery itself, was abolished in the District of Columbia. Fourth, a strengthened Fugitive Slave Act went into effect; it contained many provisions that offended northerners.

Consequences of Compromise

The Compromise of 1850 was the last attempt to keep slavery out of politics. The intersectional party system was severely tested but for a while was preserved. Douglas celebrated the acts of 1850 as a "final settlement" of the slavery question.

The Compromise, however, only delayed more serious sectional conflict. It added two new ingredients to American politics. The first hinted at the realignment of parties along sectional lines. Second, although repudiated by most ordinary citizens, ideas like secessionism, disunion, and a "higher law" than the Constitution entered more and more into political discourse.

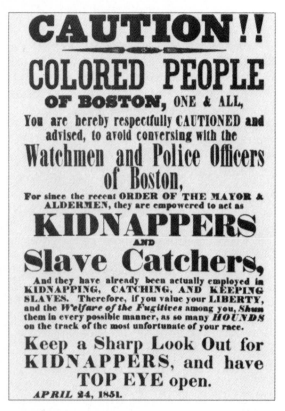

The dangers of the Fugitive Slave Act are evident in this 1851 broadside published by Boston abolitionist Theodore Parker, which alerted the city's black community to the dangers posed by the new law.

The new fugitive slave law angered many northerners because it brought the evils of slavery right into their midst, compelling northerners to turn in runaways. The owners of escaped slaves hired agents, labeled "kidnappers" in the North, to hunt down fugitives. Ralph Waldo Emerson said it was "a filthy law" that he would not obey.

Frederick Douglass would not obey it either. As a runaway slave himself, he was threatened with arrest and return to the South until friends overcame his objections and purchased his freedom. Arguing the "rightfulness of forcible resistance," he urged free blacks to arm themselves and even wondered whether it was justifiable to kill kidnappers. Douglass raised money for black fugitives, hid runaways in his home, and helped

hundreds escape to Canada. Other northerners, white as well as black, increased their work for the underground railroad in response to the fugitive slave law.

Douglass and others also spoke out on the wrongs of slavery. In an Independence Day speech in 1852, Douglass wondered, "What, to the American slave, is your 4th of July?" It was, he said, the day that revealed to the slave "the gross injustice and cruelty to which he is the constant victim." To a slave, the American claims of national greatness were vain and empty; the "shouts of liberty and equality" were "hollow mockery." Douglass's speeches, like those of another ex-slave, Sojourner Truth, took on an increasingly strident tone in the early 1850s.

At a women's rights convention in Akron, Ohio, in 1851, Truth made one of the decade's boldest statements for minority rights. The convention was attended by clergymen, who kept interrupting the proceedings to heckle female speakers. Up stood Sojourner Truth. She pointed to her many years of childbearing and hard, backbreaking work as a slave, crying out in a repetitive refrain, "And ar'n't I a woman?" Referring to Jesus, she asked where he came from: "From God and a woman: Man had nothing to do with Him." Referring to Eve, she concluded, "If the first woman God ever made was strong enough to turn the world upside down all alone, these women together ought to be able to turn it back, and get it right side up again! And now they is asking to do it, the men better let them." Her brief speech silenced the hecklers.

As Truth spoke, another American woman, Harriet Beecher Stowe, was finishing a novel, *Uncle Tom's Cabin.* Stowe's novel gave readers an absorbing indictment of the horrors of slavery and its immoral impact on both northerners and southerners. Published initially in serial form, each month's chapter ended at a nail-biting dramatic moment. Readers throughout the North cheered Eliza's daring escape across the ice floes on the Ohio River, cried over Uncle Tom's humanity and Little Eva's death, suffered under the lash of Simon Legree, and rejoiced in the reuniting of black family members. When published in full in 1852, *Uncle Tom's Cabin* became one of the all-time best-sellers in American history.

Political Disintegration

The response to *Uncle Tom's Cabin* and the Fugitive Slave Act indicated that politicians had congratulated themselves too soon for saving the Republic in 1850. Political developments, not all dealing with slavery, were already weakening the ability of political parties — and ultimately the nation — to withstand the passions slavery aroused.

The Apathetic Election of 1852

Political parties must convince voters that their party stands for moral values and economic policies crucially different from those of the opposition. In the period between 1850 and 1854, these differences were blurred, thereby undermining party loyalty. First, both parties scrambled to convince voters that they had favored the Compromise of 1850. In addition, several states rewrote their constitutions and remodeled their laws in the early 1850s, standardizing many political and economic procedures. One effect of these changes was to reduce the number of patronage jobs available for party victors to dispense. Another effect was to regularize the process, begun in the 1830s, for securing banking, railroad, and other corporate charters, removing the role formerly played by the legislature. Both of these weakened the importance of the party in citizens' lives.

The third development that weakened parties was economic. During the prosperity of the early 1850s, party distinctions over economic policies seemed less important. Economic issues persisted, but the battles were fought at the local rather than national level. Around such issues as temperance, free blacks, taxes for internal improvements, and a ten-hour working day, local politicians formed fleeting alliances. As a Balti-

more businessman said, "The two old parties are fast melting away."

The election of 1852 illustrated the lessening significance of political parties. After 52 ballots, the Whigs nominated General Winfield Scott, another Mexican War hero. Democrats had their own problems deciding on a candidate. After 49 ballots, in which Cass, Douglas, and James Buchanan each held the lead for a time, the party turned to the lackluster Franklin Pierce of New Hampshire as a compromise candidate.

The two parties offered little choice. The Baltimore *Sun* remarked that "there is no issue that much interests the people." Democratic prospects were aided by thousands of new Catholic immigrants from Ireland and Germany. Party officials often bought their votes with bribes and drinks. Internal conflicts and defections seriously weakened the Whigs, and Pierce won easily, 254 to 42 electoral votes.

The Kansas-Nebraska Act

The Whig party's final disintegration came on a February day in 1854 when southern Whigs stood to support Stephen Douglas's Nebraska bill, thus choosing to be more southern than Whig. The Illinois senator had many reasons for introducing a bill organizing the Nebraska Territory (which included Kansas). As an ardent nationalist and chairman of the Committee on Territories, he was concerned for the continuing development of the West. As an Illinoisan in a period of explosive railroad building, he wanted the eastern terminus for a transcontinental railroad in Chicago rather than in rival St. Louis. This meant organizing the lands west of Iowa and Missouri. Douglas also wanted to recapture the party leadership he had held when he led the fight to pass the Compromise of 1850, and he harbored presidential ambitions.

The entire Nebraska Territory lay north of the line where slavery had been prohibited by the Missouri Compromise. But Douglas's bill, introduced early in 1854, recommended using the principle of popular sovereignty in organizing the Kansas and Nebraska territories. This meant that inhabitants could vote slavery in, thereby violating the Missouri Compromise. Douglas reasoned, however, that the climate and soil of the prairies in Kansas and Nebraska would never support slavery-based agriculture, and the people would decide to be a free state. Therefore, he could win the votes he needed for the railroad without also getting slavery.

Douglas miscalculated. Northerners from his own party immediately attacked him and his bill as a "criminal betrayal of precious rights." The outrage among Whigs and abolitionists was even greater.

But Stephen Douglas was a fighter. The more he was attacked, the harder he fought. Eventually his bill passed, but not without seriously damaging the political party system. What began as a railroad measure ended in reopening the question of slavery in the territories that Douglas and others had thought finally settled in 1850. What began as a way of avoiding conflict ended up in violence. What began as a way of strengthening party lines ended up destroying one party (the Whigs), planting deep, irreconcilable divisions in another (the Democrats), and creating two new ones (Know-Nothings and Republicans).

Expansionist "Young America"

The Democratic party was weakened in the early 1850s not only by the Kansas-Nebraska Act but also by an ebullient, expansive energy that led Americans to adventures far beyond Kansas. As republican revolutions erupted in Europe in 1848, Americans greeted them as evidence that the American model of free republican institutions was the wave of the future. Those dedicated to the idea of this continuing national mission, which ironically included the spread of slavery, were called "Young America."

President Pierce's platform in 1852 recalled the successful expansionism of the Polk years, declaring that the Mexican War had been "just and necessary." Many Democrats took their overwhelming victory as a mandate to continue adding territory to the Republic. Pierce's ambas-

sador to Mexico, for example, James Gadsden, tried without success to purchase large parts of Mexico. But he did manage to purchase a strip of desert along the southwest border in order to build a transcontinental railroad linking the Deep South with the Pacific Coast.

The failure to acquire more territory from Mexico legally did not discourage expansionist Americans from pursuing illegal means. During the 1850s, Texans and Californians staged dozens of raids (called "filibusters") into Mexico. The most daring adventurer of the era was William Walker, a 100-pound Tennesseean with a zest for danger and power. After migrating to southern California, Walker made plans to add slave lands to the country. In 1853, he invaded Lower California with fewer than 300 men and declared himself president of the independent Republic of Sonora. Although eventually arrested and tried in the United States, he was acquitted after eight minutes of deliberation. He later took it upon himself to invade Nicaragua. Walker came to a fitting end in 1860 when he was captured and shot by a Honduran firing squad after invading that country.

Undaunted by failures in the Southwest, the Pierce administration looked more seriously to the acquisition of Cuba, a Spanish colony many Americans thought destined to be a part of their country. Secretary of State William Marcy instructed the emissary to Spain, Pierre Soulé, to offer $130 million for Cuba. If that failed, Marcy suggested stronger measures. In 1854, the secretary arranged for Soulé and the American ministers to France and England to meet in Belgium to consider options. The result was the Ostend Manifesto, a document intended to pressure Spain to sell Cuba to the United States.

The manifesto argued that Cuba "belongs naturally" to the United States. Both geographically and economically, the fortunes and interests of Cubans and southerners were so "blended" that they were "one people with one destiny." Trade and commerce in the hemisphere would "never be secure" until Cuba was part of the United States.

If Spain refused to sell the island, the ministers threatened a revolution in Cuba with American support. If that should fail, the manifesto warned, "we should be justified in wresting it from Spain." Even Secretary Marcy was shocked when he received the document from Belgium, and he quickly rejected it. Like the Kansas-Nebraska Act, the Ostend Manifesto was urged most by Democrats who advocated the expansion of slavery. The outraged reaction of northerners in both cases divided and further weakened the Democratic party.

Nativism, Know-Nothings, and Republicans

Foreign immigration damaged an already enfeebled Whig party and created concern among many native-born Americans. To the average, hard-working Protestant American, the foreigners pouring into the cities and following the railroads westward spoke unfamiliar languages, wore funny clothes, drank alcohol freely in grogshops, and increased crime and pauperism. Still worse, they attended Catholic churches, sent children to their own schools, and worked for lower wages in worse conditions than American workers. Perhaps worst of all, these nativists said, the new immigrants corrupted American politics.

Catholic immigrants preferred the Democratic party out of traditional loyalties and because Democrats were less inclined than Whigs to interfere with religion, schooling, drinking, and other aspects of personal behavior. It was mostly former Whigs, therefore, who in 1854 founded the American party to oppose the new immigrants. Members wanted a longer period of naturalization and pledged themselves never to vote for Irish Catholics for public office since it was assumed that their highest loyalty was to the pope in Rome. They also agreed to keep information about their order secret. If asked, they would say, "I know nothing." Hence, they were dubbed the Know-Nothing party.

The Know-Nothings were overwhelmingly a party of the middle and lower classes, workers who worried about their jobs and wages, and farmers and small-town Americans who worried about disruptive new forces in their lives. In the 1854 and 1855 elections, the Know-Nothings gave anti-Catholicism a national political focus for the first time. They did so well that they threatened to replace the Whigs as the second major party.

Meanwhile, a group of ex-Whigs and Free-Soilers met and formed the nucleus of another new party, called the Republican party. Its first challenge was to respond to popular sentiments by mobilizing sectional fears and ethnic and religious concerns.

Composed almost entirely of northerners, former "conscience" Whigs, and disaffected Democrats, the Republican party combined four main elements. The first group sought to prohibit slavery in the territories and to repeal the Fugitive Slave Act. A more moderate and larger group, typified by Abraham Lincoln of Illinois, opposed slavery in the western territories, but indicated they would not interfere with it where it already existed.

A third element of the party was anti-Catholic, reflecting the traditional Whig position. The fourth element wanted the federal government to promote commercial and industrial development and the dignity of labor. This fourth group, which Lincoln was in as well, believed that a system of free labor led to progress. As the Springfield *Republican* said in 1856, the Republican party's strength came from "those who work with their hands, who live and act independently, who hold the stakes of home and family, of farm and workshop, of education and freedom — these as a mass are enrolled in the Republican ranks."

The strengths of the Republican and Know-Nothing (American) parties were tested in 1856. Which party could best oppose the Democrats? The American party nominated Fillmore, who had strong support in the Upper South and border states. The Republicans chose John C. Frémont, a Free-Soiler from Missouri with virtually no political experience. The Democrats nominated James Buchanan of Pennsylvania, commonly known as "a northern man with southern principles." Frémont won several free states, while Fillmore won only Maryland. Buchanan, taking advantage of the divided opposition, won the election, but with only 45 percent of the popular vote. After 1856, the Know-Nothings died out, but nativism did not.

Kansas and the Two Cultures

As slaveholders sought ways of expanding slavery westward across the Plains and south into Cuba in the mid-1850s, Republicans wanted to halt the advance of slavery. In 1854, Lincoln worried that it was slavery that "deprives our republican example of its just influence in the world."

Competing for Kansas

Lincoln was concerned about the passage of the Kansas-Nebraska Act in 1854, which opened the way for proslavery and antislavery forces to meet physically and to compete over whether Kansas would become a slave or free state. No sooner had the bill passed Congress than Eli Thayer founded the Massachusetts Emigrant Aid Society to recruit free-soil settlers to go to Kansas. From New York, Frederick Douglass called for "companies of emigrants from the free states . . . to possess the goodly land." By the summer of 1855, about 1,200 New England colonists had migrated to Kansas.

David Atchison, Democratic senator from Missouri, believed that Congress had an obligation to protect slavery in the territories, thereby permitting Missouri slaveholders to move into Kansas. He described New England migrants as "negro thieves" and "abolition tyrants." He recommended to fellow Missourians that they defend their property and interests "with the *bayonet* and with *blood*" and, if need be, "to kill every God-damned abolitionist in the district."

Under Atchison's inflammatory leadership, secret societies sprang up in the Missouri counties adjacent to Kansas. They vowed to combat the Free-Soilers. Rumors of 20,000 Massachusetts migrants spurred Missourians to action. Thousands poured across the border late in 1854 to vote in the first territorial election. Twice as many ballots were cast as the number of registered voters, and in one polling place only 20 of over 600 voters were legal residents.

In March 1855, a second election was held to select a territorial legislature. The pattern of border crossings, intimidation, and illegal voting was repeated. Atchison himself, drinking "considerable whiskey" along the way, led a band of armed men across the state line to vote and frighten would-be Free-Soil voters away. Not surprisingly, a small minority of eligible voters elected a proslavery territorial legislature. Free-Soilers, meanwhile, staged their own constitutional convention in Lawrence and created a Free-Soil government at Topeka. It banned blacks from the state. The proslavery legislature settled in Lecompton, giving Kansas two governments.

Neither President Pierce nor Congress could do anything except send an investigating committee, which further inflamed passions. Throughout 1855, the call to arms grew more strident. One proslavery newspaper invited southerners to bring their weapons and "send the scoundrels" from the North "back to whence they came, or . . . to hell, it matters not which." At Yale University, the noted minister Henry Ward Beecher presented Bibles and rifles to young men who would go fight for the Lord in Kansas. Missourians dubbed the rifles "Beecher's Bibles" and vowed, as one newspaper put it, "Blood for Blood! . . . for each drop spilled, we shall require one hundred fold!"

"Bleeding Kansas"

Inevitably, blood flowed in Kansas. In May 1856, supported by a prosouthern federal marshall, a mob entered Lawrence, smashed the offices and presses of a Free-Soil newspaper, fired several cannonballs into the Free State Hotel, and destroyed homes and shops. Three

"Bleeding Kansas"

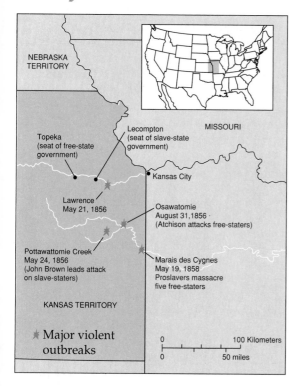

NEBRASKA TERRITORY

MISSOURI

Topeka (seat of free-state government)

Lecompton (seat of slave-state government)

Kansas City

Lawrence May 21, 1856

Osawatomie August 31, 1856 (Atchison attacks free-staters)

Pottawattomie Creek May 24, 1856 (John Brown leads attack on slave-staters)

Marais des Cygnes May 19, 1858 Proslavers massacre five free-staters

KANSAS TERRITORY

✳ Major violent outbreaks

0   100 Kilometers
0   50 miles

nights later, motivated by vengeance and a feeling that he was doing God's will, John Brown led a small New England band, including four of his sons, to a proslavery settlement near Pottawatomie Creek. There they dragged five men out of their cabins and despite the terrified entreaties of their wives, hacked them to death with swords.

Violence also entered the halls of Congress. That same week, abolitionist senator Charles Sumner accused proslavery Senate leaders, especially Atchison and Andrew Butler of South Carolina, of cavorting with "the harlot, Slavery." Two days later, Butler's nephew, Congressman Preston Brooks, avenged the honor of his colleague by beating Sumner senseless with his cane as he sat at his Senate desk.

The sack of Lawrence, the massacre at Pottawatomie Creek, and the caning of Sumner set off a minor civil war, which historians have

called "Bleeding Kansas." It lasted throughout the summer. Crops were burned, homes were destroyed, fights broke out in saloons and streets, and night raiders tortured and murdered their enemies. For residents like Charles Lines, who just wanted to farm his land in peace, it was impossible to remain neutral. Lines hoped his neighbors near Lawrence would avoid "involving themselves in trouble." But when proslavery forces seized a mild-mannered neighbor, bound him, tortured him, and left him to die, Lines joined the battle. He wrote to a friend that "blood must end in the triumph of the right."

Even before the bleeding of Kansas began, the New York *Tribune* warned, "We are two peoples. We are a people for Freedom and a people for Slavery. Between the two, conflict is inevitable." The competing visions of two separate cultures for the future destiny of the United States were at stake.

Northern Views and Visions

The North saw itself as a prosperous land of bustling commerce and expanding, independent agriculture. Northern farmers and workers were self-made men who believed that individualism, equality of opportunity, and government support for free labor and industrial growth would lead to economic progress. Although the North contained many growing cities, northerners revered the values of the small towns that spread from New England across the Upper Midwest. These values included a respect for the rights of the people, tempered by the rule of law; individual enterprise, balanced by a concern for one's neighbors; and a fierce morality rooted in Calvinist Protestantism. Many northerners would regulate morality — by persuasion if possible but by legislation if necessary — to remove the sins of irreligion, illiteracy, and intemperance from American society. It was no accident that the ideas of universal public education and laws against the sale and consumption of alcohol both began in New England.

Northerners also believed that only free men could achieve economic progress and moral society. Therefore, the worst sin in the northerner's view was the loss of one's freedom. Slavery was the root of all evil, and for many, the South represented the antithesis of everything that northerners saw as good. Northern migrants to Kansas described southerners as subhuman, unclean, and uncivilized. They were, as one put it, "drunken ourang-outans," "wild beasts" who drank whiskey, ate dirt, uttered oaths, raped slave women, and fought or dueled at the slightest excuse. In the popular language of the day, they were known as "Pukes."

The Southern Perspective

Epithets aside, southerners were a diverse people who, like northerners, shared certain broad values, generally those of the planter class. If in the North the values of economic enterprise were most important, southerners revered social values most. Like the English gentry they sought to emulate, they saw themselves as courteous, refined, hospitable, and chivalrous. By contrast, they saw northerners as coarse, ill-mannered, aggressive, materialistic "Yankees." In a society where one person in three was a black slave, racial distinctions and paternalistic relationships were crucial in maintaining order and white supremacy. Fear of slave revolt was ever present. The South had five times more military schools than the North. Northerners educated the many for economic utility, but southerners educated the few for grace and character. In short, the South saw itself as a genteel, ordered society guided by the aristocratic code of the gentleman planter.

Southerners believed that the democratic principle of self-government was best preserved in local political units such as the state. They cherished the Union, but preferred the loose confederacy of the Jeffersonian past to the centralized nationalism New York senator William Seward kept invoking.

Two images dominated the South's view of northerners: either they were stingy, hypocritical, moralizing Puritans, or they were grubby, slum-dwelling, Catholic immigrants.

Each side, then, saw the other threatening its freedom and infringing on its view of a proper republican society. As hostilities increased, the views each section had of the other grew steadily more rigid and conspiratorial. Northerners saw the South as a "slave power," determined to foist the slave system on free labor throughout the land. Southerners saw the North as full of "black Republicanism," determined to destory the southern way of life.

Polarization and the Road to War

Because of the national constituencies of the two major political parties, northern and southern cultural stereotypes and conspiratorial accusations had been largely held in check. But events in Kansas solidified the image of the Republicans as a northern party and seriously weakened the Democrats. Further events, still involving the question of slavery in the territories, soon split the Democratic party irrevocably into sectional halves: the Dred Scott decision of the Supreme Court (1857), the constitutional crisis in Kansas (1857), the Lincoln-Douglas debates in Illinois (1858), John Brown's raid in Virginia (1859), and Lincoln's election (1860). These incidents also further polarized the two cultures and set the nation on the final road to civil war.

The Dred Scott Case, Kansas, and the Democrats

The events of 1857 reinforced the arguments of those who believed in a slave power conspiracy. Two days after James Buchanan's inauguration, the Supreme Court finally ruled in *Dred Scott* v. *Sandford*. The case had been pending before the Court for nearly three years, but the slave family of Dred Scott had been waiting longer for the decision. In 1846, Dred and Harriet Scott had filed suit in Missouri for their freedom. They argued that their master had taken them into Minnesota, Wisconsin, and other territories where the Missouri Compromise prohibited slavery, and therefore they should be freed.

When the Court, which had a majority of southern judges, issued its decision, by a vote of 7 to 2, it made three rulings. First, since blacks were, as Chief Justice Roger Taney put it, "beings of an inferior order [who] had no rights which white men were bound to respect," Dred Scott was not a citizen and had no right to sue in federal courts. The second ruling stated that the Missouri Compromise was unconstitutional because Congress did not have the power to ban slavery in a territory. And third, the fact that the Scotts had been taken in and out of free states did not affect their status. Despite two eloquent dissenting opinions, Dred and Harriet Scott remained slaves.

The implications of these decisions went far beyond the Scotts' personal freedom. The arguments about black citizenship insulted and infuriated many northerners. Even more troublesome was the possibility hinted at in the decision that slavery might be permitted in the free states of the North, where it had long been banned. One issue that remained unresolved by the Court was whether or not a territorial legislature could write a constitution that permitted the introduction of new slaves.

The Dred Scott decision, endorsed by Buchanan, fed northern suspicions of a slave power conspiracy to impose slavery everywhere. Events in Kansas, which still had two governments, heightened these fears. In the summer of 1857, Kansas had still another election, with so many irregularities that only 2,000 out of a possible 24,000 voters participated. They elected a proslavery slate of delegates to a constitutional convention meeting at Lecompton as a preparation for statehood. The convention decided to exclude free blacks from the state, to guarantee the property rights of the few slaveholders in Kansas, and to ask voters to decide in a referendum whether to permit more slaves.

The proslavery Lecompton constitution, clearly unrepresentative of the wishes of the majority of the people of Kansas, was sent to Con-

gress for approval. Eager to retain the support of southern Democrats, Buchanan endorsed it. Stephen Douglas, a northern Democrat, opposed it. Congress sent the Lecompton constitution back to the people of Kansas for another referendum. This time they defeated it, which meant that Kansas remained a territory rather than becoming a slave state. While Kansas was left in an uncertain status, the larger political effect of the struggle was to split the Democratic party almost beyond repair.

Lincoln and the Illinois Debates

No sooner had Douglas settled the Lecompton question than he faced reelection in Illinois in 1858. Opposing him was Abraham Lincoln, who had emerged to challenge William Seward for leadership of the Republican party. Lincoln's character was shaped on the midwestern frontier, where he had educated himself, developed antislavery views, and dreamed of America's greatness.

Since Douglas was clearly the leading Democrat, the Senate election in Illinois appeared to be a preview of the presidential election of 1860. The Illinois campaign featured a series of seven debates between Lincoln and Douglas in different cities. With a national as well as a local audience, the debates provided a remarkable opportunity for the two men to state their views on the heated racial issues before the nation.

Lincoln set a solemn tone when he accepted the Republican senatorial nomination in Chicago in June. The American nation, he said, was in a "crisis" and building toward a worse one : "A House divided against itself cannot stand. I believe this government cannot endure, permanently half *slave* and half *free*." Lincoln said he did not expect the Union "to be dissolved" or "the house to fall" but rather that "it will become *all* one thing, or *all* the other." In the ensuing debates with Douglas, Lincoln skillfully staked out a moral position not only in advance of Douglas but well ahead of his time.

Lincoln was also very much a part of his time. He believed that whites were superior to

As he revealed in the debates with Stephen Douglas in 1858, Abraham Lincoln's views on slavery and black equality were at once more progressive than those of most Americans and sufficiently mainstream to win him the Republican party's presidential nomination in 1860.

blacks and opposed equal rights for free blacks. He believed, furthermore, that the physical and moral differences between whites and blacks would "forever forbid the two races from living together on terms of social and political equality." However, he not only believed that blacks were "entitled to all the natural rights . . . in the Declaration of Independence" but also that they had many specific economic rights as well, like "the right to put into his mouth the bread that his own hands have earned." In these rights, blacks were, Lincoln said, "my equal and the equal of Judge Douglas, and the equal of every living man."

Unlike Douglas, Lincoln hated slavery. At Galesburg, he said, "I contemplate slavery as a moral, social, and political evil." In Quincy, he said that the difference between a Republican and a Democrat was quite simply whether one thought slavery wrong or right. Douglas's moral indifference to slavery was clear in his admission that he did not care if a territorial legislature voted it "up or down." Republicans did care, Lincoln affirmed, sounding a warning that by stopping the expansion of slavery, the course toward its "ultimate extinction" had begun.

Douglas won the election. When he and Lincoln met again two years later, the order of their finish would be reversed. Elsewhere in 1858, however, Democrats did poorly, losing 18 congressional seats to the Republicans.

John Brown's Raid

The slavery issue grew more heated on October 16, 1859, when John Brown and a band of 22 men attacked a federal arsenal at Harpers Ferry, Virginia (now West Virginia). He hoped that the action might provoke a general uprising of slaves throughout the Upper South or at least provide the arms by which slaves could make their way to freedom. Although he seized the arsenal, federal troops soon overcame him. Nearly half his men were killed, including two sons. Brown himself was captured, tried, and hanged for treason. So ended a lifetime of failures.

In death, however, he was not a failure. Brown's daring if foolhardy raid, and his impressively dignified behavior during his trial and speedy execution, unleashed powerful passions, further widening the gap between North and South. Northerners responded to his death with an outpouring of admiration and sympathy, for both the man and his cause. But many southerners concluded that northerners would stop at nothing, including armed force, to free the slaves. Brown's raid stimulated a wave of fear and suspicion. In response to the Brown raid, southerners also became more convinced, as the governor of South Carolina put it, that a "black Republican" plot in the North was "arrayed against the slaveholders."

The Election of 1860

The conflict between Buchanan and Douglas took its toll on the Democratic party. When the

• • •

nominating convention met in Charleston, South Carolina, a hotbed of secessionist sentiments, it met for a record ten days without being able to name a presidential candidate. The Democrats went through 59 ballots, adjourned, and then met again, acknowledging their irreparable division by naming two candidates. Douglas represented northern Democrats, and John C. Breckenridge, Buchanan's vice-president, carried the banner of the proslavery South. The Constitutional Union party, made up of former southern Whigs and border-state nativists, claimed the middle ground of compromise and nominated John Bell, a slaveholder from Tennessee with mild views.

With Democrats split in two and a new party in contention, the Republican strategy aimed at keeping the states carried by Frémont in 1856 and adding Pennsylvania, Illinois, and Indiana. Lincoln, a moderate midwesterner with widespread appeal, won his party's nomination.

The Republican platform also reflected moderation, reducing attacks on slavery to oppose only its extension. Most of the platform spoke to the concerns of the several elements of the party: tariff protection, subsidized internal improvements, free labor, and a homestead bill. Above all, the Republicans, like southern Democrats, defended their view of what republican values meant for America's future. It did not include the kind of society of equal rights envisioned by Frederick Douglass. An English traveler in 1860 observed that in American "we see, in effect, two nations — one white and another black — growing up together within the same political circle, but never mingling on a principle of equality."

The Republican strategy for electoral victory worked exactly as planned, as Lincoln swept the entire Northeast and Midwest. Although receiving less than 40 percent of the popular vote nationwide, his triumph in the North was decisive. Even a united Democratic party could not have defeated him. With victory assured, Lincoln prepared for the consequences and awesome responsibilities of his election. They came even before his inauguration.

The Divided House Falls

The Republicans overestimated the extent of Unionist sentiment in the South. They could not believe that the secessionists would prevail after Lincoln's victory. A year earlier, some southern congressmen had walked out in protest of the selection of an antislavery speaker of the House. A Republican leader, Carl Schurz, recalling this act, said that the southerners had taken a drink and then come back. After Lincoln's election, Schurz predicted, they would walk out, take two drinks, and come back again. He was wrong.

Secession and Uncertainty

On December 20, 1860, South Carolina seceded from the Union, declaring the "experiment" of putting people with "different pursuits and institutions" under one government a failure. By February 1, the other six Deep South states (Mississippi, Florida, Alabama, Georgia, Louisiana, and Texas) had seceded. A week later, delegates met in Montgomery, Alabama, created the Confederate States of America, adopted a constitution, and elected Jefferson Davis, a Mississippi senator and cotton planter, its provisional president. The divided house had fallen, as Lincoln had predicted it would.

The nation waited and watched, wondering what Virginia and the border states would do, what outgoing President Buchanan would do, and what Congress would do. Buchanan did nothing, and so the entire nation waited for Abraham Lincoln.

Frederick Douglass waited too, without much hope. Seeing northern politicians and businessmen "granting the most demoralizing concessions to the Slave Power," Douglass began to explore possibilities for emigration and colonization in Haiti, an idea he had long opposed. In February, Douglass said, "Let the conflict come." He opposed all compromises, hoping that with Lincoln's inauguration in March it would "be decided, and decided forever, which

Major Causes and Events Leading to the Civil War

Date	Event	Impact or Effect as Cause of Civil War
1600s-1860s	Slavery in the South	Major underlying pervasive cause
1700s-1860s	Development of two distinct socioeconomic systems and cultures	Further reinforced slavery as fundamental socioeconomic, cultural, moral issue
1787-1860s	States' rights, nullification doctrine	Ongoing political issue, less fundamental as cause
1820	Missouri Compromise (36°30′)	Background for conflict over slavery in territories
1828-1833	South Carolina tariff nullification crisis	Background for secession leadership in South Carolina
1831-1860s	Antislavery movements, southern justification	30 years of emotional preparation for conflict
1846-1848	Mexican War (Wilmot Proviso, Calhoun, popular sovereignty)	Options for slavery in territories issue
1850	Compromise of 1850	Temporary and unsatisfactory "settlement" of divisive issue
1851-1854	Fugitive slaves returned and rescued in North; personal liberty laws passed in North; Harriet Beecher Stowe's *Uncle Tom's Cabin*	Heightened northern emotional reactions against the South and slavery
1852-1856	Breakdown of Whig party and national Democratic party; creation of a new party system with sectional basis	Made national politics an arena where sectional and cultural differences over slavery were fought
1854	Ostend Manifesto and other expansionist efforts in Central America	Reinforced image of Democratic party as favoring slavery
	Formation of Republican party	Major party identified as opposing the expansion of slavery
	Kansas-Nebraska Act	Reopened "settled" issue of slavery in the territories
1856	"Bleeding Kansas"; Senator Sumner physically attacked in Senate	Foretaste of civil war (200 killed, $2 million in property lost) inflamed emotions and polarized North and South
1857	Dred Scott decision; proslavery Lecompton constitution in Kansas	Made North fear a "slave power conspiracy," supported by President Buchanan and the Supreme Court
1858	Lincoln-Douglas debates in Illinois; Democrats lose 18 seats in Congress	Set stage for election of 1860
1859	John Brown's raid and reactions in North and South	Made South fear a "black Republican" plot against slavery; further polarization and irrationality
1860	Democratic party splits in half; Lincoln elected president; South Carolina secedes from Union	Final breakdown of national parties and election of "northern" president; no more compromises
1861	Six more southern states secede by February 1; Confederate Constitution adopted February 4; Lincoln inaugurated March 4; Fort Sumter attacked April 12	Civil War begins

of the two, Freedom or Slavery, shall give law to this Republic."

Lincoln and Fort Sumter

As Douglass penned these thoughts, Lincoln began a long, slow train ride from Springfield, Illinois, to Washington, writing and rewriting his inaugural address. Lincoln was firmly opposed to secession and to any compromises with the principle of stopping the extension of slavery. He would neither conciliate secessionist southern states nor force their return.

But Lincoln believed in his constitutional responsibility to uphold the laws of the land, and on this significant point he would not yield. The focus of his attention was a federal fort in the harbor of Charleston, South Carolina. Major Robert Anderson, the commander of Fort Sumter, was running out of provisions and had requested new supplies from Washington. Lincoln would enforce the laws and protect federal property at Fort Sumter.

As the new president rose to deliver his inaugural address on March 4, he faced a tense and divided nation. Federal troops, fearing a Confederate attack on the nation's capital, were everywhere. Lincoln asserted his unequivocal intention to enforce the laws of the land, arguing that the Union was constitutionally "perpetual" and indissoluble. He reminded the nation that the "only substantial dispute" was that "one section of our country believes slavery is *right*, and ought to be extended, while the other believes it is *wrong*, and ought not to be extended." Still hoping to appeal to Unionist strength among southern moderates, Lincoln indicated that he

would make no attempts to interfere with existing slavery or the law to return fugitive slaves. He urged against rash actions and put the burden of initiating a civil war on the "dissatisfied fellow-countrymen" who had seceded. His deepest hope was that

> the mystic chords of memory, stretching from every battlefield, and patriot grave, to every living heart and hearthstone, all over this broad land, will yet swell the chorus of the Union, when again touched, as surely they will be, by the better angels of our nature.

On April 6, Lincoln notified the governor of South Carolina that he was sending "provisions only" to Fort Sumter. No effort would be made "to throw in men, arms, or ammunition" unless the fort were attacked. On April 10, Jefferson Davis directed General P. G. T. Beauregard to demand the surrender of Fort Sumter. Davis told Beauregard to reduce the fort if Major Anderson refused.

On April 12, as Lincoln's relief expedition neared Charleston, Beauregard's batteries began shelling Fort Sumter, and the Civil War began. Frederick Douglass was about to leave for Haiti when he heard the news. He immediately changed his plans: "This is no time . . . to leave the country." He announced his readiness to help end the war by aiding the Union to organize freed slaves "into a liberating army" to "make war upon . . . the savage barbarism of slavery." Benjamin Allston, who was in Charleston, described the events to his father. On April 14, he reported exuberantly "the glorious, and astonishing news that Sumter has fallen." With it fell America's divided house.

CONCLUSION:
The "Irrepressible Conflict"

Lincoln had been right. The nation could no longer endure half slave and half free. The collision between North and South, William Seward said, was not an

"accidental, unnecessary" event but "an irrepressible conflict between opposing and enduring forces." Those forces had been at work for many decades but developed with increasing intensity after 1848 in the conflict over the question of the extension of slavery into the territories. Although economic, cultural, political, constitutional, and emotional forces all con-tributed to the developing opposition between North and South, slavery was the fundamental, enduring force that underlay all others, causing what poet Walt Whitman called "the red blood of civil war."

RECOMMENDED READING

Easily the finest overall account of the political history of the 1850s is David Potter's superb narrative, *The Impending Crisis, 1848–1861* (1976), completed by Donald Fehrenbacher after Potter's death. See also James McPherson, *Ordeal by Fire : The Civil War and Reconstruction* (1982). Essay collections on recent Civil War scholarship are Eric Foner, ed., *Politics and Ideology in the Age of the Civil War* (1980); and William E. Gienapp, Thomas B. Alexander, Michael F. Holt, Stephen E. Mazlish, and Joel H. Silbey, *Essays on American Antebellum Politics, 1840–1860* (1982). Kenneth Stampp has compiled the most useful combination of primary and secondary sources representing differences of opinion, *The Causes of the Civil War*, rev. ed. (1974), a good book in which to explore various historical interpretations.

Michael F. Holt, *The Political Crisis of the 1850s* (1978), is the best overall work of "new politics" showing the breakdown of political parties as a major cause of the Civil War. On ethnic and religious politics and the effects of nativism on political behavior, see Paul Kleppner, *The Third Electoral System, 1853–1892 : Parties, Voters, and Political Cultures* (1979). For a monumental new synthesis and interpretation, see William E. Gienapp, *The Origins of the Republican Party, 1852–1856* (1987). Specialized works on the effects of the issue of slavery in the territories on sectional rivalry and political parties are William J. Cooper, *The South and the Politics of Slavery* (1978); and Richard Sewell, *Ballots for Freedom : Antislavery Politics in the United States, 1837–1865* (1976).

On racism in the West, see James Rawley, *Race and Politics : "Bleeding Kansas" and the Coming of the Civil War* (1969). The definitive work on the Dred Scott case is Donald Fehrenbacher, *Slavery, Law, and Politics : The Dred Scott Case in Historical Perspective* (1981). The final road to war after Lincoln's election in 1860 is detailed in William Barney, *The Road to Secession* (1972); and Steven Channing, *Crisis of Fear : Secession in South Carolina* (1970).

Among biographies of major figures see Robert Johannsen, *Stephen Douglas* (1973); Stephen Oates, *To Purge This Land with Blood : A Biography of John Brown* (1970) and *With Malice Toward None : The Life of Abraham Lincoln* (1982). The emotional flavor of the decade is captured in Harriet Beecher Stowe's novel, *Uncle Tom's Cabin* (1852); and Walt Whitman's poetry in *Leaves of Grass* (any edition).

Time Line

1832	Nullification crisis	**1855**	Walt Whitman publishes *Leaves of Grass*
1835– 1840	Intensification of abolitionist attacks on slavery Violent retaliatory attacks on abolitionists	**1855– 1856**	Thousands pour into Kansas, creating months of turmoil and violence
1840	Liberty party formed	**1856**	John Brown's massacre in Kansas Summer-Brooks incident in Senate James Buchanan elected president
1846	Wilmot Proviso		
1848	Free-Soil party founded Zachary Taylor elected president	**1857**	Dred Scott decision legalizes slavery in territories Lecompton constitution in Kansas
1850	Compromise of 1850, including Fugitive Slave Act	**1858**	Lincoln-Douglas debates
1850– 1854	"Young America" movement	**1859**	John Brown's raid at Harpers Ferry
1851	Women's rights convention in Akron, Ohio	**1860**	Democratic party splits Four-party campaign Abraham Lincoln elected president
1852	Harriet Beecher Stowe publishes *Uncle Tom's Cabin* Franklin Pierce elected president	**1860– 1861**	Seven southern states secede
1854	Ostend Manifesto Kansas-Nebraska Act nullifies Missouri Compromise Republican and Know-Nothing parties formed	**1861**	Confederate States of America founded Attack on Fort Sumter begins Civil War

16

The Union Severed

W e cannot escape history," Abraham Lincoln reminded Congress in 1862. "We of this Congress and this administration will be remembered in spite of ourselves." Lincoln's conviction that Americans would long remember him and other major actors of the Civil War — Jefferson Davis, Robert E. Lee, Ulysses S. Grant — was correct. Whether seen as heroes or villains, these great men have dominated the story of the Civil War.

Yet from the earliest days, the war touched the lives of even the most uncelebrated Americans. From Indianapolis, 20-year-old Arthur Carpenter wrote to his parents in Massachusetts begging for permission to enlist in the volunteer army: "I have always longed for the time to come when I could enter the army and be a military man, and when this war broke out, I thought the time had come, but you would not permit me to enter the service . . . now I make one more appeal to you." The pleas worked, and Carpenter enlisted, spending most of the war fighting in Kentucky and Tennessee.

In that same year, in Tennessee, George and Ethie Eagleton faced anguishing decisions. Though not an abolitionist, George, a 30-year-old Presbyterian preacher, was unsympathetic to slavery and opposed to secession. But when his native state left the Union, George felt compelled to follow and enlisted in the 44th Tennessee Infantry. Ethie, his 26-year-old wife, despaired over the war, George's decision, and her own forlorn situation:

> Pres. Lincoln has done what no other Pres. ever dared to do — he has divided these once peaceful and happy United States. And Oh! the dreadful dark cloud that is now hanging over our country — 'tis enough to sicken the heart of any one. . . . Mr. E. is gone. . . . What will become of me, left here without a home and relatives, a babe just nine months old and no George?

Both Carpenter and the Eagletons survived the war, but the conflict transformed all of their lives. Carpenter had difficulty settling down to civilian life. Filled with bitter memories of the war years in Tennessee, the Eagletons moved to Arkansas.

• • •

For thousands of Americans, from Lincoln and Davis to Carpenter and the Eagletons, war was both a profoundly personal and a major national event. Its impact reached far beyond the four years of hostilities. The war that was fought to conserve two political, social, and economic visions ended by changing familiar ways of political, social, and economic life in both North and South. War was a transforming force, both destructive and creative in its effect on the structure and social dynamics of society and on the lives of ordinary people. This theme underlies this chapter's analysis of the war's three stages: the initial months of preparation, the years of military stalemate between 1861 and 1865, and, finally, resolution.

Organizing for War

The Confederate bombardment of Fort Sumter on April 12, 1861, and the surrender of Union troops the next day ended the uncertainty of the secession winter. The North's response to Fort Sumter was a virtual declaration of war as President Lincoln called for state militia volunteers to crush southern "insurrection." His action pushed several slave states (Virginia, North Carolina, Tennessee, Arkansas) off the fence and into the southern camp. Other states (Maryland, Kentucky, and Missouri) agonizingly debated which way to go. The "War Between the States" was now a reality.

Many Americans were unenthusiastic about the course of events. Southerners like George Eagleton only reluctantly followed Tennessee out of the Union. Robert E. Lee of Virginia was initially hesitant to resign his federal commission. Many southern whites and residents of border states were dismayed at secession and war. Many would eventually join the Union forces.

Secession of the Southern States

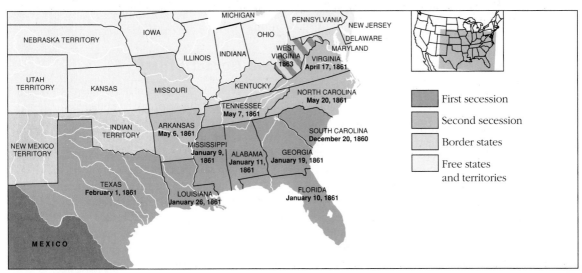

In the North, large numbers had supported neither the Republican party nor Lincoln. Nevertheless, the days following Fort Sumter and Lincoln's call for troops saw an outpouring of support on both sides, fueled in part by relief at decisive action, in part by patriotism and love of adventure, in part by unemployment. Sisters, wives, and mothers set to work making uniforms. A New Yorker, Jane Woolsey, described the drama of those early days "of terrible excitement."

> Outside the parlor windows the city is gay and brilliant with excited crowds, the incessant movement and music of marching regiments and all the thousands of flags, big and little, which suddenly came fluttering out of every window and door.

The war fever produced so many volunteers that neither northern nor southern officials could handle the throng. Northern authorities turned aside offers from blacks to serve. Both sides sent thousands of white would-be soldiers home. The conviction that the conflict would rapidly come to a glorious conclusion fueled the eagerness to enlist. Lincoln's call for 75,000 state militiamen for only 90 days of service and a similar enlistment term for Confederate soldiers supported the notion that the war would be short.

The Balance of Resources

Despite the bands, parades, cheers, and confidence, the outcome of the approaching civil conflict was much in doubt. The military stalemate in 1861 and 1862 proved that in the short term, North and South were not unevenly matched. Almost 187,000 Union troops bore arms in July 1861, while just over 112,000 men marched under Confederate colors.

The Union, however, enjoyed impressive economic advantages. In the North, one million workers in 110,000 manufacturing concerns produced goods valued at $1.5 billion annually, while 110,000 southern workers in 18,000 man-

ufacturing concerns produced goods valued at only $155 million a year. The North had one factory for every southern industrial worker, and 70 percent of the nation's railroad tracks were in the North. Producing 17 times as much cotton cloth and woolen goods, 32 times as many firearms, and 20 times as much pig iron as the South, the North could clothe and arm troops and move them and their supplies on a scale that the South could not match. But to be effective, northern industrial resources had to be mobilized for war. Furthermore, the depleted northern treasury made the government's first task the raising of funds to pay for military necessities.

The South traditionally depended on imported manufactured goods from the North and from Europe. If Lincoln cut off that trade, the South would face the enormous task of creating its industry almost from scratch. Moreover, its railroad system was organized to move cotton, not armies and supplies. Yet the agricultural South did have important resources of food, draft animals, and, of course, cotton, which southerners believed would secure British and French support. Finally, in choosing to wage a defensive war, the South could tap regional loyalty and would enjoy protected lines of supply and support, while Union forces, embarked on an expensive war of conquest, would have extended supply lines vulnerable to attack.

The Border States

When the seven states of the Deep South seceded during the winter of 1860–1861, the strategically important border states adopted a wait-and-see attitude. Delaware identified with the Union camp, but the others vacillated. Lincoln's call for troops precipitated decisions in several states, however. Between April 17 and May 20, 1861, Virginia, Arkansas, Tennessee, and North Carolina joined the Confederacy.

In Maryland, sympathies were divided, but Confederate enthusiasts abounded in Baltimore. On April 19, the 6th Massachusetts Regiment arrived in Baltimore headed for Washington. Because the regiment had to change railroad lines, the soldiers set out across the city on foot and in horsecars. As they marched through the streets, a mob of some 10,000 southern sympathizers, flying Confederate flags, attacked them with paving stones, then bayonets and bullets. The soldiers fought back, but would-be secessionists burned the railroad bridges connecting Baltimore to the North and to the South. Washington found itself cut off from the rest of the Union, an island in the middle of hostile territory.

Lincoln took stern measures to secure Maryland. Hundreds of southern sympathizers, including 19 state legislators and Baltimore's mayor, were arrested and languished in prison without trial. Although the chief justice of the United States, Roger B. Taney, challenged the legality of the president's action, Lincoln ignored him. A month later, Taney ruled in *Ex parte Merryman* that if the public's safety was endangered, only Congress had the right to suspend a writ of habeas corpus. By then, Lincoln had secured Maryland for the Union.

Though Lincoln's quick and harsh response ensured Maryland's loyalty, he was more cautious elsewhere, for any hasty action would push border states into the waiting arms of the Confederacy. In the end, after some fighting and much maneuvering, Kentucky and Missouri, like Maryland, stayed in the union.

Challenges of War

During the tense weeks after Fort Sumter, both the North and the South faced enormous organizational problems as they readied for war. The South had to create everything from a constitution and governmental departments to a flag and postage stamps.

In February 1861, the original seceding states sent delegates to Montgomery, Alabama, to begin work on a provisional framework and to select a provisional president and vice-president. The delegates swiftly wrote a constitution, much like the federal constitution of 1787 except in its emphasis on the "sovereign and independent character" of the states and its explicit rec-

ognition of slavery. The provisional president, Jefferson Davis of Mississippi, put together a geographically and politically balanced cabinet, but it had few men of political stature. As time passed, it turned out to be unstable as well. In a four-year period, 14 men held six positions.

Davis's cabinet appointees faced the formidable challenge of creating government departments from scratch. The president's office was in a hotel parlor. The Confederate Treasury Department was housed in a room in an Alabama bank "without furniture of any kind." Treasury Secretary Christopher G. Memminger bought furniture with his own money; operations lurched forward in fits and starts. Other departments faced similar difficulties.

Lincoln never had to set up a postal system or decide whether laws passed before 1861 were valid, but the new president also faced organizational problems. The treasury was empty. The Republicans had won their first presidential election, and floods of office seekers who had worked for Lincoln now thronged into the White House looking for rewards.

Not knowing many of the "prominent men of the day," Lincoln appointed important Republicans from different factions of the party to cabinet posts whether they agreed with him or not. Most were almost strangers to the president. Several scorned him as a bumbling backwoods politician.

Lincoln and Davis

A number of Lincoln's early actions illustrated that he was no malleable backcountry bumbler. After Sumter, he swiftly called up the state militias, expanded the navy, and suspended habeas corpus. He ordered a naval blockade of the South and approved the expenditure of funds for military purposes, all without congressional sanction, since Congress was not in session. As Lincoln told legislators later, "The dogmas of the quiet past are inadequate to the stormy present. . . . As our case is new, so must we think anew, and act anew . . . and then we shall save our country." This willingness to "think anew" was a valuable personal asset, even though some critics called his expansion of presidential power despotic.

By coincidence, Lincoln and his rival, Jefferson Davis, were born only 100 miles apart in Kentucky. However, the course of their lives diverged radically. Lincoln's father had migrated north and eked out a simple existence as a farmer in Indiana and Illinois. Abraham had only a rudimentary formal education and was largely self-taught. Davis's family, however, had moved south to Mississippi and become cotton planters. Davis grew up in comfortable circumstances, went to Transylvania University and West Point, fought in the Mexican War before his election to the U.S. Senate, and served as secretary of war under Franklin Pierce (1853–1857). Tall and distinguished-looking, he appeared every inch the aristocratic southerner.

Davis reassured southerners in his inaugural address that his aims were conservative, "to preserve the Government of our fathers in spirit." Yet under the pressure of events, he moved toward creating a new kind of South.

Clashing on the Battlefield, 1861–1862

The Civil War was the most brutal and destructive conflict in American history. Much of the bloodshed resulted from the application of the theories of Henri Jomini, a French military historian, to the battlefield. Jomini argued that an army seized victory by concentrating its infantry attack at the weakest point in the enemy's defenses. At the time Jomini wrote, this offensive strategy made military sense. The artillery, stationed well outside the range of enemy fire, could prepare the way for the infantry attack by bombarding enemy lines. By 1861, however, the range of rifles had increased from 100 yards to 500 yards. It was no longer possible to position the artillery close enough to the enemy to allow it to soften up the opposing line in preparation for the infantry charge. During the Civil War, then, enemy fire mowed down attacking infantry soldiers as they ran the 500 fatal yards to the front lines. Battles based on Jomini's theories produced a ghastly crop of dead men.

War in the East

The war's brutal character only gradually revealed itself. The Union commanding general, 70-year-old Winfield Scott, at first pressed for a cautious, long-term strategy, known as the Anaconda Plan. Scott proposed weakening the South gradually through blockades on land and at sea. The excited public, however, hungered for action and quick victory. So did Lincoln, who knew that the longer the war lasted, the more embittered the South and the North would both become, making reunion ever more difficult. Under the cry of "Forward to Richmond!" 35,000 partially trained men led by General Irwin McDowell headed out from Washington in sweltering July weather.

On July 21, 1861, only 25 miles from the capital at Manassas Creek, or Bull Run, as it is also called, inexperienced northern troops confronted 25,000 raw Confederate soldiers commanded by Brigadier General P. G. T. Beauregard, a West Point classmate of McDowell's. Although sightseers, journalists, and politicians accompanied the Union troops, expecting only a Sunday outing, the encounter at Bull Run was no picnic. The course of battle swayed back and forth before the arrival of 2,300 fresh Confederate troops, brought by trains, decided the day. Union soldiers and sightseers fled toward Washington in terror and confusion.

Yet inexperienced Confederate troops failed to turn the rout into the quick and decisive victory they sought. As General Joseph E. Johnston pointed out, his men were disorganized, confused by victory, and not well enough supplied with food to chase the Union army back toward Washington.

In many ways, the Battle of Bull Run was prophetic. Victory would be neither quick nor easy. As the disorganization and confusion of both sides suggested, the armies were unprofessional.

Eastern Theater of the Civil War, 1861–1862

For the Union the loss at Bull Run was sobering. Replacing McDowell with 34-year-old General George McClellan, Lincoln began his search for a northern commander capable of winning the war. McClellan, formerly an army engineer, confronted the task of transforming the Army of the Potomac into a fighting force. Short-term militias went home. When Scott retired in the fall of 1861, McClellan became general in chief of the Union armies.

McClellan had considerable organizational ability but no desire to be a daring leader on the battlefield. Convinced that the North must combine military victory with efforts to persuade the South to return to the Union, he sought to avoid unnecessary and embittering loss of life and property. He intended to win the war "by maneuvering rather than fighting."

Pushed by an impatient Lincoln, in June 1862 McClellan advanced with 130,000 troops toward Richmond, now the Confederate capital, but failed to take it. Other Union defeats fol-

lowed in 1862 as commanders came and went. In September, the South boldly invaded Maryland, but suffered a costly defeat at Antietam, in which more than 5,000 soldiers were slaughtered and another 17,000 wounded on the grisliest day of the war. Lee withdrew to Virginia, and the war in the East was stalemated.

War in the West

The East was only one of three theaters of actions. Between the Appalachian Mountains and the Mississippi lay the western theater, the states of Kentucky, Tennessee, Mississippi, and Alabama. At its edge lay the Mississippi, with its vital river trade and its great port, New Orleans. Here both George Eagleton and Arthur Carpenter served. Beyond lay the trans-Mississippi West — Louisiana, Arkansas, Missouri, Texas, and the Great Plains — where Native American tribes joined the conflict on both sides.

In the western theater, the Union had two strategic objectives: the domination of Kentucky and eastern Tennessee, the avenues to the South and West, and control of the Mississippi River in order to split the South in two. Major campaigns sought strategic points along rivers and railroads.

It was in the western theater that Ulysses S. Grant rose to prominence. He had attended West Point and served creditably in the Mexican War. Soon after Fort Sumter, Grant enlisted as a colonel in an Illinois militia regiment. Within two months, he was a brigadier general.

Grant realized that the Tennessee and Cumberland rivers were the paths for the successful invasion of Tennessee. Assisted by gunboats, he was largely responsible for the capture of Fort Henry and Fort Donelson, key points on the rivers, in February 1862. His army was nearly destroyed, however, by a surprise Confederate attack at Shiloh Church in Tennessee. The North won this battle, but suffered over 13,000 casualties, while 10,000 Confederates lay dead or wounded. More men fell in this single battle than in the American Revolution, the War of 1812, and the Mexican War combined. Because neither army offered sufficient care on the battlefield, many men died of untreated wounds and exposure.

The war in the trans-Mississippi West was a sporadic, far-flung struggle for the control of this vast area. California was one prize that lured both armies into the Southwest. Confederate troops from Texas held Albuquerque and Santa Fe briefly in 1862. Volunteer soldiers from the Colorado mining fields, joined by Mexican-Americans and other soldiers, drove the Texas Confederates from New Mexico. A Union force recruited in California arrived after the Confederates were gone. They spent the remainder of the Civil War years fighting the Apache and the Navajo and with brutal competence crushed both Native American nations.

Farther east was another prize, the Missouri River, which flowed into the Mississippi River, bordered Illinois, and affected military campaigns in Kentucky and Tennessee. Initially,

Confederate troops were successful here, but in March 1862, at Pea Ridge in northern Arkansas, the Union forces defeated a Confederate army of 16,000 that included a brigade of Native Americans from the Five Civilized Nations. Missouri entered the Union camp for the first time in the war, and fierce guerrilla warfare continued in the region.

Naval Warfare

Lincoln's naval blockade of southern ports was not immediately effective. With no more than 33 ships, the Union navy tried to close up 189 ports along a 3,500-mile coastline. In 1861, the navy intercepted only about one blockade runner in ten and in 1862, one in eight. In the short run, the blockade did little damage to the South.

More successful were operations to gain footholds along the southern coast. In November 1861, a Union expedition took Port Royal Sound, where it freed the first slaves, and the nearby South Carolina sea islands. A few months later, the navy defeated a Confederate force on Roanoke Island. But the Union's greatest naval triumph in the early war years was the capture of New Orleans, the South's greatest port, in 1862.

The Confederate leadership, recognizing that the South could not match the Union fleet, concentrated on developing new weapons like torpedoes and formidable ironclad vessels. They raised the *Merrimac*, a sunken U.S. warship, and covered it with heavy iron armor. Rechristened the *Virginia*, the ship steamed out of Norfolk in March 1862, heading directly for the Union ships blocking the harbor. Using its 1,500-pound ram and guns, the *Virginia* drove a third of the ships aground and destroyed the squadron's largest ships. Victory was short-lived. The next day, the *Virginia* confronted the *Monitor*, a newly completed Union iron vessel. Their duel was inconclusive, and the *Virginia* withdrew. It was burned during the evacuation of Norfolk that May.

The Confederate navy's policy of harming northern commerce was moderately successful.

Trans-Mississippi Campaign of the Civil War

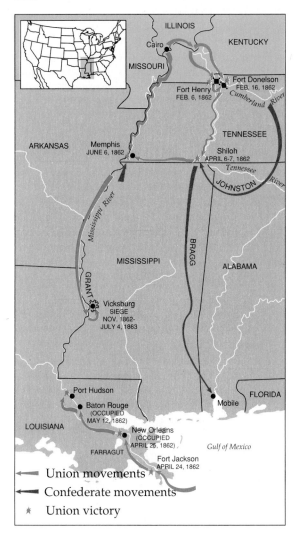

ILLINOIS
Cairo
KENTUCKY
MISSOURI
Fort Donelson
FEB. 16, 1862
Fort Henry
FEB. 6, 1862
Cumberland River
TENNESSEE
ARKANSAS
Memphis
JUNE 6, 1862
Shiloh
APRIL 6-7, 1862
Tennessee River
JOHNSTON
Mississippi River
GRANT
BRAGG
MISSISSIPPI
ALABAMA
Vicksburg
SIEGE
NOV. 1862–
JULY 4, 1863
Port Hudson
Baton Rouge
(OCCUPIED
MAY 12, 1862)
New Orleans
(OCCUPIED
APRIL 25, 1862)
FLORIDA
Mobile
LOUISIANA
FARRAGUT
Gulf of Mexico
Fort Jackson
APRIL 24, 1862

⟵ Union movements
⟵ Confederate movements
✳ Union victory

Confederate raiders wreaked havoc on northern shipping. In its two-year career, the raider *Alabama* destroyed 69 Union merchant vessels valued at more than $6 million.

Throughout the first two years of conflict, both sides achieved victories, but the war remained deadlocked. The costs in manpower and supplies far exceeded what either side had anticipated. The need to replace lost men and supplies thus loomed ever more serious at the end of 1862.

Cotton Diplomacy

Both sides in the Civil War realized that attitudes in Europe could be critical. The Confederacy hoped to gain European diplomatic recognition and European loans and assistance. The European powers, however, consulted their own national interests, and one by one declared a policy of neutrality.

Southerners were sure that the need of English and French textile mills for cotton would eventually force recognition of the Confederacy and an end to the North's blockade. But European industrialists found new sources for cotton in India and Egypt, and Southern hopes were dashed.

Union Secretary of State Seward sought above all else to prevent diplomatic recognition of the Confederacy. He daringly threatened Great Britain with war if it interfered in what he insisted was an internal matter. Some called his boldness reckless, even mad. Nevertheless, his policy succeeded. Even though England allowed the construction of Confederate raiders in its ports, it did not intervene in American affairs in 1861 or 1862. Nor did the other European powers.

Common Problems, Novel Solutions

As the conflict dragged on into 1863, unanticipated problems appeared in both the Union and the Confederacy, and leaders devised novel approaches to solve them.

Both treasuries had been empty initially, and the war was proving extraordinarily expensive. Eventually both sides initiated taxation on a small scale. Ultimately taxes financed 21 percent of the North's war expenses (but only one percent of southern expenses). Both treasuries also tried borrowing. Northerners bought over $2 billion worth of bonds, but southerners proved reluctant to buy their government's bonds.

Finally, both sides resorted to printing paper money. In August 1861, the Confederacy put into circulation $100 million in crudely engraved bills. Millions more followed the next year. Five months later, the Union issued $150 million in paper money, soon nicknamed "greenbacks" because of their color. The resulting inflation was particularly troublesome in the Confederacy, but it also caused an 80 percent increase in food prices for Union city families.

Both sides confronted manpower problems as initial enthusiasm for the war evaporated. Young men were shocked at the deadliness of diseases that accompanied the army wherever it went, and they were unprepared for the boredom of camp life. Those in the service longed to go home. The swarm of volunteers disappeared. Rather than fill their military quotas from within, rich northern communities began offering bounties of $800 to $1,000 to outsiders who would join up.

Arthur Carpenter's letters reveal growing disillusionment with the war as his regiment moved into Kentucky and Tennessee in the winter of 1862. "Soldiering in Kentucky and Tennessee," he complained, "is not so pretty as it was in Indianapolis. . . . We have been half starved, half frozen, and half drowned." Soldiering often meant marching over rutted roads carrying 50 or 60 pounds of equipment with insufficient food, water, or supplies. One blanket was not enough in the winter. In the summer, stifling woolen uniforms attracted lice and other vermin. Poor food, bugs, inadequate sanitation, and exposure invited disease. Carpenter marched through Tennessee suffering from diarrhea and then fever. His regiment left him behind in a convalescent barracks in Louisville, which he fled as soon as he could. He feared the hospital at least as much as the sickness. "[Ninety-nine] Surgeons out of a hundred," he wrote his parents, "would not know whether his patient had the horse distemper, lame toe, or any other disease."

Confederate soldiers, even less well supplied than their northern counterparts, complained similarly. In 1862, a Virginia captain wrote :

> During our forced marches and hard fights, the soldiers have been compelled to throw away their knapsacks . . . Hundreds of men are perfectly barefooted and there is no telling when they can be supplied with shoes.

Desertion was common, and as the manpower problems became critical, both governments resorted to the draft. Ultimately, over 30 percent of the Confederate army and six percent of the Union forces were draftees.

The Confederacy relied more heavily on the draft than the Union did because the North's initial manpower pool was larger and growing. During the war, 180,000 foreigners of military age poured into the northern states. Some came specifically to claim bounties and fight. Immigrants made up at least 20 percent of the Union army.

The draft laws were very unpopular. The first Confederate conscription declared all able-bodied men between 18 and 35 eligible for military service but allowed numerous exemptions and the purchase of substitutes. Critics complained that the provision entitling every planter with more than 20 slaves to one exemption from

Many deaths resulted from inadequate care for the wounded and sick soldiers of both armies. This wounded soldier receives water from a canteen rather than medical attention.

military service favored rich slave owners. The legislation fed class tension and encouraged disloyalty and desertion among the poorer classes, particularly among southern mountaineers. One woman shouted after her husband as he was dragged off to the army, "You desert again, quick as you kin. . . . Desert, Jake!"

The northern draft law of 1863 also allowed the hiring of substitutes and $300 bought exemption from military service. Workers resented the ease with which moneyed citizens could avoid army duty. In July 1863, the resentment boiled over in New York City in the largest civil disturbance of the nineteenth century. Several Irish draftees destroyed draft records and the Enrollment Office. Events then spun out of control as a mob also burned the armory, plundered the houses of the rich, and looted jewelry stores. Blacks, whom the Irish hated as economic competitors and the cause of the war, became special targets. Mobs beat and lynched blacks and even burned the Colored Orphan Asylum. More than 100 people died in the three days of rioting. There was much truth in the accusation that the war on both sides was a rich man's war but a poor man's fight.

Political Dissension, 1862

As the war continued, rumbles of dissension grew louder. In the South, criticism of Confederate leaders mounted. Wrote one southerner to a friend, "Impeach Jeff Davis for incompetency & call a convention of the States. . . . West Point is death to us & sick Presidents & Generals are equally fatal." Because the South had no party system, dissatisfaction with Davis and his handling of the war tended to be factional, petty, and personal.

Although Lincoln has since become a folk hero, at the time many northerners derided his performance and hoped for a new president in 1864. Peace Democrats, called Copperheads, claimed that Lincoln betrayed the Constitution and that working-class Americans bore the brunt of his policy of conscription. Immigrant workers had little sympathy for abolitionism or

blacks, and they supported the antiwar stance of the Copperheads. Even Democrats favoring the war effort found Lincoln arbitrary and tyrannical, while some Republicans judged him indecisive and inept.

Republicans split gradually into two factions. The moderates favored a cautious approach toward winning the war and feared the possible consequences of emancipating the slaves, confiscating Confederate property, or arming blacks. The radicals, however, urged Lincoln to make emancipation a wartime objective. The reduction of the congressional Republican majority in the fall elections of 1862 made it imperative that Lincoln not only listen to both factions but also to the Democratic opposition.

The Tide Turns, 1863–1865

Hard political realities made Lincoln delay an emancipation proclamation until 1863. Like congressional Democrats, many northerners supported a war for the Union but not one for emancipation. Many, if not most, whites saw blacks as inferior. They also suspected that emancipation would trigger a massive influx of former slaves who would steal white men's jobs and political rights. Race riots in New York, Brooklyn, Philadelphia, Buffalo, and Cincinnati dramatized white attitudes.

The Emancipation Proclamation, 1863

If the president moved too fast on emancipation, he risked losing the allegiance of people like Carpenter, offending the border states, and increasing the Democrats' chances for political victory. But if he did not move at all, he would alienate abolitionists and lose the support of radical Republicans, which he could ill afford.

For these reasons, Lincoln proceeded cautiously. In the early spring of 1862, he urged Congress to pass a joint resolution offering federal compensation to states beginning a "gradual abolishment of slavery." Border-state opposition killed the idea. Abolitionists and northern blacks, however, greeted Lincoln's proposal with "a thrill of joy."

That summer, Lincoln told his cabinet he intended to emancipate the slaves. Secretary of State Seward urged the president to delay any general proclamation until the North won a decisive military victory. Otherwise, he warned, Lincoln would appear to be urging racial insurrection behind the Confederate lines to compensate for northern military bungling.

Lincoln followed Seward's advice, using that summer and fall to prepare the North for the shift in the war's purpose. In August, Horace Greeley, the influential abolitionist editor of the New York *Tribune*, printed an open letter to Lincoln attacking him for failing to act on slavery. In his reply, Lincoln linked the idea of emancipation to military necessity. His primary goal, he wrote, was to save the Union:

> If I could save the Union without freeing *any* slave, I would do it; and if I could save it by freeing *all* the slaves, I would do it; and if I could do it by freeing some and leaving others alone, I would also do that. What I do about Slavery and the colored race, I do because I believe it helps to save this Union.

In September 1862, the Union victory at Antietam gave Lincoln the opportunity to issue a preliminary emancipation proclamation. It stated that unless rebellious states (or parts of states in rebellion) returned to the Union by January 1, 1863, the president would declare their slaves "forever free." Although supposedly aimed at bringing the southern states back into the Union, Lincoln never expected the South to lay down arms after two years of bloodshed. Rather, he was preparing northerners to accept the eventuality of emancipation on the grounds of necessity. Frederick Douglass greeted the president's action with jubilation. "We shout for joy," he wrote, "that we live to record this righteous decree."

Cautious cabinet members begged Lincoln to forget about emancipation, but on New Year's Day, 1863, he issued the final Emancipation Proclamation. It was "an act of justice, warranted by the Constitution upon military necessity." Thus what had started as a war to save the Union now also became a struggle that, if victorious, would free the slaves. Yet the proclamation had no immediate impact on slavery. It affected only slaves living in the unconquered portions of the Confederacy. It was silent about slaves in the border states and in parts of the South already in northern hands. These limitations led Elizabeth Cady Stanton and Susan B. Anthony to establish the woman's Loyal National League to lobby Congress to emancipate all southern slaves.

Though the Emancipation Proclamation did not immediately liberate southern slaves from their masters, it had a tremendous symbolic importance. Blacks realized that the proclamation had changed the nature of the war. For the first time, the government had committed itself to freeing slaves. Jubilant blacks could only believe that the president's action heralded a new era for their race. More immediately, the proclamation sanctioned the policy of accepting blacks as soldiers into the military.

Black soldiers, some from southern states, were accepted for combat duty in the Union army as the war progressed. Here the First Carolina Volunteers gather to celebrate emancipation on January 1, 1863.

Diplomatic concerns also lay behind the Emancipation Proclamation. Lincoln and his advisers anticipated that the commitment to abolish slavery would favorably impress foreign powers. European statesmen, however, did not abandon their cautious stance toward the Union. The English prime minister called the proclamation "trash." But important segments of the English public who opposed slavery now came to regard any attempt to help the South as immoral.

Unanticipated Consequences of War

The Emancipation Proclamation was but one example of the war's surprising consequences. Innovation was necessary for victory, and one of the Union's experiments involved using black troops for combat duty. Blacks had offered themselves as soldiers in 1861 but had been turned away. They were serving as cooks, laborers, teamsters, and carpenters in the army, however, and composed as much as a quarter of the navy. But as white casualties mounted, so did the interest in black service on the battlefield. The Union government allowed states to escape draft quotas if they enlisted enough volunteers and allowed them to count southern black enlistees on their state rosters.

Black leaders like Frederick Douglass pressed for military service. "Once let the black man get upon his person the brass letter, U.S., let him get an eagle on his button, and a musket on his shoulder and bullets in his pocket," Douglass believed, "there is no power on earth that can deny that he has earned the right to citizenship." By the war's end, 186,000 blacks (10 percent of the army) had served the Union cause, 134,111 of them escapees from slave states.

Enrolling blacks in the Union army was an important step toward citizenship and acceptance of blacks by white society. But the black experience in the army highlighted some of the obstacles to racial acceptance. Black soldiers, usually led by white officers, were second-class soldiers for most of the war, receiving lower pay ($10 a month as compared to $13), poorer food, often more menial work, and fewer benefits than whites. "If we are good enough to fill up white men's places and fight, we should be treated then, in all respects, the same as the white man," one black soldier protested.

The faith in Jomini's military tactics was another wartime casualty. The infantry charge, so valued at the war's beginning, resulted in horrible carnage. Military leaders came to realize the importance of the strong defensive position. Although Confederate soldiers criticized General Lee as "King of Spades" when he first ordered them to construct earthworks, the epithet evolved into one of affection as it became obvious that earthworks saved lives. By the end of 1862, both sides were digging defensive earthworks and trenches.

Gone, too, was the courtly idea that war involved only armies. Early in the war, many officers tried to protect civilians and their property, but such restraint soon vanished, and along with it went chickens, corn, livestock, and, as George Eagleton noted with disgust, even the furnishings of churches. War touched all of society, not just the battlefield participants.

Changing Military Strategies, 1863–1865

In the early war years, the South's military strategy combined defense with selective maneuvers. This policy, however, did not change the course of the war, and Lee concluded that the South had to win victories in the North in order to gain the peace it so desperately needed and European recognition.

In the summer of 1863, Lee led the Confederate Army of Northern Virginia across the Potomac into Maryland and southern Pennsylvania. His goal was a victory that would threaten both Philadelphia and Washington.

At Gettysburg on a hot and humid July 1, Lee came abruptly face to face with a Union army led by General George Meade. During three days of fighting, the fatal obsession with the infantry charge returned as Lee ordered costly assaults that probably lost him the battle. On July 3, Lee sent three divisions, about 15,000 men in all, against the Union center. The assault, known as Pickett's Charge, was as futile as it was gallant. At 700 yards, the Union artillery opened fire. One southern officer described the scene: "Pickett's division just seemed to melt away in the blue musketry smoke which now covered the hill. Nothing but stragglers came back."

Lee's dreams of victory died that hot week, with grave consequences for the southern cause. Gettysburg marked the turn of the military tide in the East.

Despite the Gettysburg victory, Lincoln was dissatisfied with General Meade, who had failed to finish off Lee's demoralized and exhausted army as it retreated. His disappointment soon faded with news of a great victory at Vicksburg in the western theater on July 4. The com-

mander, Ulysses S. Grant, completed the Union campaign to gain control of the Mississippi River and to divide the South.

Grant's successful capture of Vicksburg illustrated the boldness and flexibility that Lincoln sought in a commander, and in March 1864, Lincoln appointed him general in chief of the Union armies. Grant planned for victory within a year. "The art of war is simple enough," he reasoned. "Find out where your enemy is. Get at him as soon as you can. Strike at him as hard as you can, and keep moving on."

Grant proposed a grim campaign of annihilation, using the North's superior resources of men and supplies to wear down and defeat the South. He aimed "to consume everything that could be used to support or supply armies." Following this new policy of "total war," he set out after Lee's army in Virginia. General William Tecumseh Sherman, who pursued Confederate General Joseph Johnston from Tennessee toward Atlanta, further refined this plan.

The Tide Turns, 1863–1865

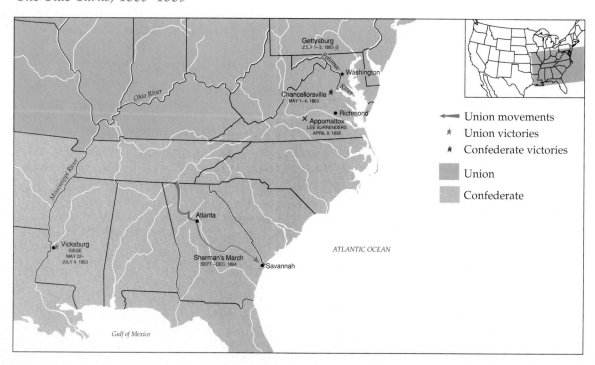

• • •

Sherman wanted to make southerners "fear and dread" their foes. Therefore, his campaign to seize Atlanta and his march to Savannah spread destruction and terror. A Georgia woman described in her diary the impact of Sherman's march :

> There was hardly a fence left standing all the way from Sparta to Gordon. The fields were trampled down and the road was lined with carcasses of horses, hogs and cattle that the invaders, unable either to consume or to carry away with them, had wantonly shot down, to starve out the people.... The dwellings that were standing all showed signs of pillage, and on every plantation we saw ... charred remains.

This destruction, with its goal of total victory, showed once more how conflict produced the unexpected. The war that both North and South had hoped would be quick and relatively painless was ending after four long years with great cost to both sides.

Changes Wrought by War

As bold new tactics emerged both on and off the battlefield, both governments took steps that changed their societies in surprising ways. Of the two, the South, which had left the Union to conserve a traditional way of life, experienced the more radical transformation.

A New South

The expansion of the central government's power in the South, starting with the passage of the 1862 Conscription Act, continued in the last years of the war. Secession grew out of the concept of states' rights, but, ironically, winning the war depended on central direction and control. Many southerners denounced Davis as a tyrant and a despot because he recognized the need for the central government to take the lead. Despite the accusations, the Confederate Congress cooperated with him and established important precedents. In 1863, it enacted a comprehensive

tax law and an impressment act that allowed government agents to requisition food, horses, wagons, and other necessary war materials, often for only about half their market price. These were prime examples of the central government's power to interfere with private property. Government impressment of slaves for war work in 1863 affected the very form of private property that had originally driven the South from the Union.

The Conscription Act of 1862 was followed in 1864 by an expanded conscription measure which made all white males between the ages 17 and 50 subject to the draft. By 1865, the necessities of war had led to the unthinkable : arming slaves as soldiers. Black companies were recruited in Richmond and other southern towns. However, because the war soon ended, no blacks actually fought for the Confederacy.

Southern agriculture also changed under the pressure of war. Earlier, the South had imported food from the North, concentrating on the production of staples such as cotton and tobacco for market. Now, more and more land was turned over to food crops. Cotton production declined from 4.5 million bales in 1861 to 300,000 bales in 1864, but food remained in short supply.

The war also triggered the expansion of military-related industries in the South. The war and navy offices directed industrial development, awarding contracts to private manufacturing firms like Richmond's Tredegar Iron Works and operating other factories themselves. The number of southerners working in industry rose dramatically. In 1861, the Tredegar Iron Works employed 700 workers ; two years later, it employed 2,500, more than half of them black. At the end of the war, the soldiers were better supplied with arms and munitions than with food.

Although the war did not transform the southern class structure, relations between the classes began to change. Draft resistance and desertion reflected growing alienation from a war perceived as serving only the interests of upper-class plantation owners. More and more yeoman families suffered grinding poverty as the men went off to war and government officials and armies requisitioned needed resources. This new poverty was an ominous hint of the decline of the yeoman farming class in postwar years.

The Victorious North

Although changes in the South were more noticeable, the Union's government and economy also responded to the demands of war. Like Davis, Lincoln was accused of being a dictator. Although he rarely tried to control Congress, veto its legislation, or direct government departments, Lincoln did use executive power freely. He violated the writ of habeas corpus by suspending the civil rights of over 13,000 northerners, who languished in prison without trials; curbed the freedom of the press because of supposedly disloyal and inflammatory articles; established conscription; issued the Emancipation Proclamation; and removed army generals. Lincoln argued that this vast extension of presidential power was temporarily justified because, as president, he was responsible for defending and preserving the Constitution.

Many of the wartime changes in government proved more permanent than Lincoln had imagined. The financial necessities of war helped to revolutionize the country's banking system. Ever since Andrew Jackson's destruction of the Bank of the United States, state banks had served American financial needs. Treasury Secretary Chase found this banking system inadequate and chaotic and proposed to replace it. In 1863 and 1864, Congress passed banking acts that established a national currency issued by federally chartered banks and backed by government bonds. The country had a federal banking system once again.

The northern economy also changed under wartime demands. Agriculture expanded, as did investment in farm machinery, notably McCormick reapers, which performed the work of four to six men. During the war, McCormick sold 165,000 of his machines. Northern farmers not only grew enough grain to feed civilians and soldiers but gathered a surplus to export as well.

The war also selectively stimulated manufacturing, although it retarded overall economic growth. Industries that produced for the war machine, especially those with advantages of scale, expanded and made large profits. Each year, the Union army required 1.5 million uniforms and 3 million pairs of shoes; the woolen and leather industries grew accordingly. Meatpackers and producers of iron, steel, and pocket watches all profited from wartime opportunities. Cincinnati was one city that flourished from supplying soldiers with everything from pork to soap and candles.

On the Home Front, 1861–1865

In numerous, less tangible ways, the war transformed northern and southern society. Civilians read newspapers and national weekly magazines with a new eagerness. The use of the mails increased dramatically as they corresponded with faraway relatives and friends. The war helped to make Americans less parochial, integrating them into the larger world.

For some Americans, like John D. Rockefeller and Andrew Carnegie, war brought army contracts and profits. In the South, blockade runners made fortunes slipping luxury goods past Union ships. For the majority of Americans, however, war meant deprivation. To be sure, the demand for workers ended unemployment. Large numbers of women and blacks entered the work force, a phenomenon that would be repeated in all future American wars. But while work was easy to get and wages appeared to increase, real income actually declined. Inflation, especially destructive in the South, was largely to blame. By 1864, eggs sold in Richmond for $6 a dozen; butter brought $25 a pound. Strikes and union organizing pointed to working-class discontent.

Low wages particularly harmed women workers. As more women entered the work force, employers cut costs by slashing wages. In 1861, the Union government paid Philadelphia seamstresses 17 cents per shirt. At the height of inflation, three years later, the government reduced the piecework rate to 15 cents. Private employers paid even less, about eight cents a shirt. Working women in the South fared no better. War may have brought prosperity to a few Americans, North and South, but for most it meant trying to survive on an inadequate income.

Shortages and hardships were severe in the South, especially in cities, where carts brought in vital supplies since trains were reserved for military use. Hunger was rampant. Food riots erupted in Richmond and other cities ; crowds of hungry whites broke into stores to steal food. The very cleanliness of southern cities pointed to urban hunger. As one Richmond resident noted, everything was so "cleanly consumed that no garbage or filth can accumulate."

Thousands of southerners who fled as Union armies advanced suddenly found themselves homeless. "The country for miles around is filled with refugees," noted an army officer in 1862. "Every house is crowded and hundreds are living in churches, in barns and tents."

One slave described the upsetting arrival of the Yankees at his plantation in Arkansas : "Them folks stood round there all day. Killed hogs . . . killed cows. . . . Took all kinds of sugar

Ruined buildings and mourning women were common sights in Richmond as the war came to an end. This photograph gives a vivid sense of the devastation of the South in 1865.

and preserves. . . . Tore all the feathers out of the mattresses looking for money. Then they put Old Miss and her daughter in the kitchen to cooking." So frightened was this slave's mother that she hid in her bed, only to be roused by the lieutenant, who told her, "We ain't a-going to do you no hurt. . . . We are freeing you." But the next day, the Yanks were gone and the Confederates back. "Pa was 'fraid of both" and resolved the problem by hiding out in the cotton patch.

Wartime Race Relations

The journal kept by Emily Harris in South Carolina conveys some of the character of life behind the lines. Emily and her husband David lived on a 500-acre farm with their seven young children and ten slaves. When David went to war, Emily had to manage the farm, even though David worried that she would be "much at a loss with the . . . farm and the negroes."

Indeed, Emily's relations with her slaves proved a major problem. As so many southerners discovered, war transformed the master-slave relationship. Because Emily was not the master David had been, her slaves gradually began to take unaccustomed liberties. At Christmas in 1864, several left the farm without her permission ; others stayed away longer than she allowed. "Old Will" boldly requested his freedom. Worse yet, she discovered that her slaves had helped three Yankees who had escaped from prison camp.

The master-slave relationship was crumbling, and Emily reported in her journal, "It seems people are getting afraid of negroes." In March she wrote, "The Negroes are all expecting to be set free very soon and it causes them to be very troublesom."

Such scenes, which occurred throughout the South, and the thousands of blacks (probably 20 percent of all slaves) who fled toward Union lines after the early months of the war were proof of the changing nature of race relations and the harm slaves could do to the southern cause.

Women and the War

Emily Harris's journal illustrates how the war affected women's lives. So many men on both sides had gone off to fight that women had to find jobs and had to carry on farming operations. During the war years, southern women who had no slaves to help with the farmwork and northern farm wives who labored without the assistance of husbands or sons carried new physical and emotional burdens.

Women also participated in numerous war-related activities. In the North, hundreds of women became military nurses. Under the supervision of Drs. Emily and Elizabeth Blackwell; Dorothea Dix, superintendent of army nurses; and Clara Barton, northern women nursed the wounded and dying for low pay or even for none at all. They also attempted to improve hospital conditions by attacking red tape and bureaucracy. The diary of a volunteer, Harriet Whetten, revealed the activist attitude of many others:

> I have never seen such a dirty disorganized place as the Hospital. The neglect of cleanliness is inexcusable. All sorts of filth, standing water, and the embalming house near the Hospital. . . . No time had to be lost. Miss Gill and I set the contrabands at work making beds & cleaning.

Although men largely staffed southern military hospitals, Confederate women also played an important part in caring for the sick and wounded in their homes and in makeshift hospitals behind the battle lines. Women also worked as volunteers in soldiers' aid societies and in the United States Sanitary Commission. Many others made bandages and clothes, put together packages for soldiers at the front, helped army wives and disabled soldiers find jobs, and joined in war-related fund-raising activities.

Many of the changes women experienced during war years ended when peace returned and the men came home. But for women whose men came home maimed or not at all, the work had not ended.

The Election of 1864

In the North, the election of 1864 brought some of the transformations of wartime into the political arena. The Democrats, capitalizing on war weariness, nominated General George McClellan for president and demanded an armistice with the South. They accused Lincoln of arbitrarily expanding executive power and insinuated that if the Republicans won, a fusion of blacks and whites would result.

Although Lincoln easily gained the Republican renomination because of his tight control over party machinery and patronage, his party did not unite behind him. His veto of the radical reconstruction plan for the South, the Wade-Davis bill, led to cries of "usurpation." The Emancipation Proclamation did not sit well with conservatives. But Sherman's capture of Atlanta in September 1864 and the march through Georgia to Savannah helped swing voters to Lincoln. He won 55 percent of the popular vote and swept the electoral college.

Why the North Won

In the months after Lincoln's reelection, the war drew to an agonizing conclusion. Sherman moved north from Atlanta to North Carolina, while Grant pummeled Lee's forces in Virginia. The losses Grant would sustain were staggering: 18,000 in the Battle of the Wilderness, over 8,000 at Spotsylvania, and another 12,000 at Cold Harbor. On April 9, 1865, Grant accepted Lee's surrender at Appomattox, and the war was finally over.

Grant's military strategy succeeded because the Union could survive staggering losses of men and equipment while the Confederacy could not. As Union armies pushed back the borders of the Confederacy, the South lost control of territories essential for their war effort. Finally, naval strategy eventually paid off because the North could build enough ships to make its blockade work. In 1861, fully 90 percent of the blockade runners were slipping through the naval cordon. By the war's end, only half made it.

The South had taken tremendous steps toward meeting war needs. But, as one civilian realized, "The question of bread and meat. . . . is beginning to be regarded as a more serious one even than that of War." Women farming alone or with disgruntled slaves and worn-out farm equipment could not produce enough food. The government's impressment of slaves and animals cut production. The half million blacks who fled to Union lines also played their part in pulling the South down in defeat.

Advancing Union forces destroyed many industries. A Confederate officer in northern Virginia observed, "Many of our soldiers are thinly clothed and without shoes and in addition to this, very few of the infantry have tents. With this freezing weather, their sufferings are indescribable." By 1864, the Union armies were so well supplied that soldiers often threw away heavy blankets and coats as they advanced.

The South's woefully inadequate transportation system also contributed to defeat. Primitive roads became all but impassable without repairs. The railroad system, geared to the needs of cotton, not war, was inefficient. When tracks wore out or were destroyed, they were not replaced. Thus food intended for the army rotted awaiting shipment. Food riots in southern cities pointed to the hunger, anger, and growing demoralization of civilians.

Ironically, measures the Confederacy took to win the war undermined its own war effort. Conscription, impressment, and taxes all contributed to resentment and sometimes open resistance. The many southern governors who refused to contribute men, money, and supplies on the scale Davis requested implicitly condoned disloyalty to the cause. The belief in states' rights and the sanctity of private property that gave birth to the Confederacy also helped kill it.

It is tempting to compare Lincoln and Davis as war leaders. There is no doubt that Lincoln's humanity, eloquence, and determination to save the Union set him apart as one of this country's most extraordinary presidents. Yet the men's personal characteristics were probably less important than the differences between the political and social systems of the two regions. Without the support of a party behind him, Davis failed to engender enthusiasm or loyalty. Lincoln, commanding considerable resources of patronage, was able to line up federal, state, and local officials behind his party and administration.

Just as the northern political system provided Lincoln with more flexibility and support, its social system also proved more able to meet the war's extraordinary demands. Northerners were more cooperative, disciplined, and aggressive in meeting the organizational and production challenges of wartime. In the southern states, old attitudes, habits, and values impeded the war effort. Southern governors, wedded to states' rights, refused to cooperate with the Confederate government. North Carolina, the center of the southern textile industry, actually kept back most uniforms for its own regiments. At the war's end, 92,000 uniforms and thousands of blankets, shoes, and tents still lay in its warehouses. Even slaveholders whose property had been the cause for secession resisted the impressment of their slaves for war work.

One northerner described southerners as they surrendered at Appomattox:

> Before us in proud humiliation stood the embodiment of manhood : men whom neither toils and sufferings, nor the fact of death, nor disaster, nor hopelessness could bend from their resolve ; standing before us now, thin, worn, and famished, but erect, and with eyes looking level into ours, waking memories that bound us together as no other bond.

The Costs of War

In the end, the Confederacy collapsed, exhausted and bleeding. The long war was over, but the memories of that event would fester for years to come. About three million American men, a third of all free males between the ages of 15 and 59, had served in the army. Each would remember his own personal history of the war. For George Eagleton, who had worked in army field hospitals, the history was one of "Death and destruction! Blood! Blood! Agony! Death! Gaping flesh wounds, broken bones, amputations, bullet and bomb fragment extractions." Of all wars Americans have fought, none has been more deadly. The death rate during this war was over five times as great as the death rate during World War II. About 360,000 Union soldiers and another 258,000 Confederate soldiers died, about a third of them because their wounds were either improperly treated or not treated at all. Disease claimed more lives than combat.

Many men would be reminded of the war by the missing limbs that marked them as Civil War veterans. About 275,000 on each side were maimed. Another 410,000 (195,000 northerners and 215,000 southerners) would recall their time in wretchedly overcrowded and unsanitary prison camps, such as Andersonville in Georgia, where 31,000 Union soldiers were confined. At the war's end, over 12,000 graves were counted there.

Some Americans found it hard to throw off wartime experiences and return to civilian routines. Even those who adjusted successfully discovered that they looked at life from a different perspective. The experience of fighting, of mixing with all sorts of people from many places, of traveling far from home had lifted former soldiers out of their familiar local world and widened their vision. Fighting the war made the concept of national union real.

An Uncertain Future

What, then, had the war accomplished? On the one hand, death and destruction. The South suffered an estimated 43 percent decline in wealth during the war years, exclusive of the value of slaves. Great cities like Atlanta, Columbia, and Richmond lay in ruins. Fields lay uncultivated, much livestock had disappeared, and two-thirds of the railroads had been destroyed. Thousands were hungry, homeless, and bitter, and over three million slaves, a vast financial investment, were free.

On the other hand, the war had resolved the question of union and ended the debate over the relationship of the states to the federal government. During the war, Republicans seized the opportunity to pass legislation that would foster national union and economic growth: the Pacific Railroad Act of 1862, which set aside huge tracts of public land to finance the transcontinental railroad; the Homestead Act of 1862, which was to provide yeoman farmers cheaper and easier access to the public domain; the Morrill Act of 1862, which established support for agricultural (land-grant) colleges; and the banking acts of 1863 and 1864.

The war had also resolved the issue of slavery, but new questions had to be faced. What would happen to the former slaves? Were blacks to have the same civil and political rights as whites? Would they be given land, the means for economic independence? What would be their relations with their former owners?

What, indeed, would be the status of the conquered South in the nation? Should it be punished for the rebellion? Some people thought so. But Lincoln, as early as December 1863, had announced a generous plan of reconciliation. He was willing to recognize the government of former Confederate states established by a group of citizens equal to 10 percent of those voting in 1860, as long as the group swore to support the Constitution and to accept the abolition of slavery. He began to restore state governments in three former Confederate states on that basis. But not all northerners agreed with his leniency, and the debate continued.

In his 1865 inaugural address, Lincoln urged Americans to harbor "malice towards none . . . and charity for all." "Let us strive," he urged, "to finish the work we are in; to bind up the nation's wounds . . . to do all which may achieve a just and lasting peace." Generosity and goodwill would pave the way for reconciliation. On April 14, he pressed the point home to his cabinet. His wish was to avoid persecution and bloodshed.

That same evening, only five days after the surrender at Appomattox, the president attended a play at Ford's Theater. There, as one horrified eyewitness reported,

> a pistol was heard and a man ... dressed in a black suit of clothes leaped onto the stage apparently from the President's box. He held in his right hand a dagger whose blade appeared about 10 inches long. ... Every one leaped to his feet, and the cry of 'the President is assassinated' was heard — Getting where I could see into the President's box, I saw Mrs. Lincoln ... in apparent anguish.

John Wilkes Booth, a southern sympathizer, had killed the president.

CONCLUSION
An Uncertain Future

As the war ended, many Americans grieved for the man whose decisions had so marked their lives for five years. "Strong men have wept tonight & the nation will mourn tomorrow," wrote one eyewitness to the assassination. Many more wept for friends and relations who had not survived the war but whose actions had in one way or another contributed to its outcome. Perhaps not all Americans realized how drastically the war had altered their lives, their futures, their nation. It was only as time passed that the war's impact became clear to them. And it was only with time that they recognized how many problems the war had left unsolved. It is to these years of Reconstruction that we turn next.

RECOMMENDED READING

Good general introductions are Peter J. Parrish, *The American Civil War* (1985); and James McPherson, *Battle Cry of Freedom: The Civil War Era* (1988). Careful studies of the Confederacy include Emory M. Thomas, *The Confederate Nation, 1861–1865* (1979); and Paul D. Escott, *After Secession: Jefferson Davis and the Failure of Confederate Nationalism* (1978). For economic matters, consult David Gilchrist and W. David Lewis, eds., *Economic Change in the Civil War Era* (1965).

The military aspects of the war can be followed in Richard E. Beringer, Herman Hattaway, Archer Jones, and William N. Still, Jr., *Why the South Lost the Civil War* (1986); and Henry S. Commager, ed., *The Blue and the Gray: The Story of the Civil War as Told by Participants*, 2 vols. (1950).

Eric Foner's essays, collected in *Politics and Ideology in the Age of Civil War* (1980), are valuable for understanding the political context of the Civil War. Also helpful is John L. Thomas, ed., *Abraham Lincoln and the American Political Tradition* (1986). For a biography, see Stephen B. Oates, *With Malice Towards None: The Life of Abraham Lincoln* (1977).

Benjamin Quarles studies southern blacks in *The Negro in the Civil War* (1968 ed.), while Leon F. Litwack illuminates changing race relations in *Been in the Storm So Long: The Aftermath of Slavery* (1979). A good primary source is James M. McPherson, ed., *The Negro's Civil War* (1965). The strength of white racism is portrayed in George M. Frederickson, *The Black Image in the White Mind* (1971); and in C. Vann Woodward, *American Counterpoint: Slavery and Racism in the North-South Dialogue* (1971).

The experience of women is treated in Mary E. Massey's *Bonnet Brigades* (1966). Although Mary Boykin Chesnut's diary was actually written after the war, her vivid account, *Mary Chesnut's Civil War* (1981), is well worth consulting. Southern Unionists are explored in Phillip Shaw Paludan's *Victims: A True Story of the Civil War* (1981).

Novels about the Civil War include Stephen Crane, *The Red Badge of Courage* (any ed.), and MacKinlay Kantor, *Andersonville* (1955).

Time Line

1861	Lincoln calls up state militia and suspends habeas corpus First Battle of Bull Run Union blockades the South
1862	Battles at Shiloh, Bull Run, and Antietam *Monitor* and *Virginia* battle First black regiment authorized by Union Union issues greenbacks South institutes military draft Pacific Railroad Act Homestead Act Morrill Land-Grant College Act
1863	Lincoln issues Emancipation Proclamation

Congress adopts military draft
Battles of Gettysburg and Vicksburg
Union Banking Act
Southern tax laws and impressment act
New York draft riots
Southern food riots

1864	Sherman's march through Georgia Lincoln reelected Union Banking Act
1865	Lee surrenders at Appomattox Lincoln assassinated; Andrew Johnson becomes president Congress passes Thirteenth Amendment, abolishing slavery

17

The Union
Reconstructed

*I*n April 1864, one year before Lincoln's assassination, Robert Allston died of pneumonia. His wife, Adele, and daughter, Elizabeth, took over the affairs of their many rice plantations. With Yankee troops moving through coastal South Carolina in the late winter of 1864–1865, Elizabeth's sorrow over the loss of her father turned to "terror" as Union soldiers arrived seeking liquor, firearms, and hidden valuables. The Allston women endured an insulting search and then fled. In a later raid, Yankee troops encouraged the Allston slaves to take furniture and other household goods from the Big Houses, some of which the blacks returned when the Yankees were gone. But before they left, the Union soldiers, in their role as liberators, gave the keys to the crop barns to the semifree slaves.

When the war was over, Adele Allston took an oath of allegiance to the United States and secured a written order commanding the blacks to relinquish these keys. She and Elizabeth made plans to return in the early summer of 1865 to resume control of the family plantations, thereby reestablishing white authority. Possession of the keys to the barns, Elizabeth wrote, would be the "test case" of whether former masters or their former slaves would control land and labor.

Not without some fear, Adele and Elizabeth Allston rode up in a carriage to their former home, Nightingale Hall, to confront their ex-slaves. To their surprise, a pleasant reunion took place. A trusted black foreman handed over the keys to the barns. This harmonious scene was repeated elsewhere.

But at Guendalos, a plantation owned by a son absent during most of the war fighting with the Confederate army, the Allston women met a very different situation. As their carriage arrived, a defiant group of armed ex-slaves lined both sides of the road, following the carriage as it passed by. Tension grew when the carriage stopped. A former black driver, Uncle Jacob, was unsure whether to yield the keys to the barns full of rice and corn, put there by black labor. An angry young man shouted out: "Ef yu gie up de key, blood'll flow." Uncle Jacob slowly slipped the keys back into his pocket.

The tension increased as the blacks sang freedom songs and brandished hoes, pitchforks, and guns in an effort to discourage anyone from going to town for help.

The Allstons spent the night safely, if restlessly, in their house. Early the next morning, they were awakened by a knock at the unlocked front door. Adele slowly opened the door, and there stood Uncle Jacob. Without a word, he gave her the keys.

• • •

The story of the keys reveals most of the essential human ingredients of the Reconstruction era. Despite defeat and surrender, southern whites were determined to resume control of both land and labor. Rebellion aside, the law, property titles, and federal enforcement were generally on the side of the original owners of the land.

In this encounter between former slaves and the Allston women, the role of the northern federal officials is most revealing. The Union soldiers, literally and symbolically, gave the keys of freedom to the blacks but did not stay around long enough to guarantee that freedom. Understanding the limits of northern help, Uncle Jacob handed the keys to land and liberty back to his former owner. The blacks at Guendalos knew that if they wanted to ensure their freedom, they had to do it themselves.

The goals of the groups at the Allston plantations were in conflict. The theme of this chapter is the story of what happened to people's various dreams as they sought to form new social, economic, and political relationships during Reconstruction.

For much of the twentieth century, Reconstruction was seen as a disgraceful period in which vindictive northern Radical Republicans imposed a harsh rule of evil carpetbaggers, scalawags, and illiterate blacks on the helpless, defeated South. *Gone with the Wind* reflects this view. In 1935, the black scholar, W. E. B. Du Bois, challenged this interpretation, suggesting instead that an economic struggle over land and the exploitation of black workers was the crucial focus of Reconstruction. Other historians have shown the beginnings of biracial cooperation and political participation in some southern states and the eventual violent repression of the freedmen's dreams of land, schooling, and votes. This chapter reflects this later interpretation, enriched by an awareness of the ambiguity of human motives and the devastation and divisions of class and race in pursuit of conflicting goals.

The Bittersweet Aftermath of War

"There are sad changes in store for both races," the daughter of a Georgia planter wrote in her diary early in the summer of 1865, adding, "I wonder the Yankees do not shudder to behold their work." In order to understand the bittersweet nature of Reconstruction, we must look at the state of the nation in the spring of 1865, shortly after the assassination of President Lincoln.

The United States in 1865

The "Union" was in a state of constitutional crisis in April 1865. The status of the 11 states of the former Confederate States of America was unclear. Lincoln's official position had been that the southern states had never left the Union, which was "constitutionally indestructible." As a result of their rebellion, they were only "out of their proper relation" with the United States. The president, therefore, as commander in chief, had the authority to decide on the basis for setting relations right and proper again.

The United States in 1865 : Crisis at the End of the Civil War

- Military casualties
  360,000 Union soldiers dead
  260,000 Confederate soldiers dead
  620,000 Total dead
  375,000 seriously wounded and maimed
  995,000 casualties nationwide in a total
  　　　　 male population of 15 million
  　　　　 (nearly 1 in 15)
- Physical and economic crisis
  The South devastated, its railroads, industry, and some major cities in ruins, its fields and livestock wasted
- Constitutional crisis
  Eleven ex-Confederate states not a part of the Union, their status unclear and uncertain
- Political crisis
  Republican party (entirely of the North) dominant in Congress ; a former Democratic slaveholder from Tennessee, Andrew Johnson, in the presidency
- Social crisis
  Nearly 4 million black freedmen throughout the South face challenges of survival and freedom, along with thousands of hungry demobilized white southern soldiers and displaced white families
- Psychological crisis
  Incalculable resentment, bitterness, anger, and despair throughout North and South

Lincoln's congressional opponents argued that by declaring war on the Union, the Confederate states had broken their constitutional ties and reverted to a kind of prestatehood status like territories or "conquered provinces." Congress, therefore, which decided on the admission of new states, should resolve the constitutional issues and assert its authority over the reconstruction process. This conflict between Congress and the president reflected the fact that the president had taken on broad powers necessary for rapid mobilization of resources and domestic security during the war. As soon as the war was over, Congress sought to reassert its authority, as it would do after every subsequent war.

In April 1865, the Republican party ruled victorious and virtually alone. Although less than a dozen years old, the Republicans had won the war, preserved the Union, and enacted a program for economic growth. The Democratic party, by contrast, was in shambles. Nevertheless, it had been politically important in 1864 for the Republicans to show that the war was a bipartisan effort. A Jacksonian Democrat and Unionist from Tennessee, the tactless Andrew Johnson, had therefore been nominated as Lincoln's vice-president. In April 1865, he headed the government.

The United States in the spring of 1865 was a picture of stark economic contrasts. Northern cities hummed with productive activity while southern cities lay in ruins. Roadways and railroad tracks laced the North, while in the South railroads and roads lay in ruins. Southern financial institutions were bankrupt, while northern banks flourished. Northern farms, under increasing mechanization, were more productive than ever before. Southern farms and plantations, especially those that had lain in the path of Sherman's march, were like a "howling waste."

Despite pockets of relative wealth, the South was largely devastated as soldiers demobilized and returned home in April 1865. Yet, as a later southern writer, Wilbur Cash, explained, "If this war had smashed the Southern world, it had left the essential Southern mind and will . . .

entirely unshaken." Many southerners wanted nothing less than to resist Reconstruction and restore their old world.

The dominant social reality in the spring of 1865, however, was that nearly four million former slaves were on their own, facing the challenges of freedom. After an initial reaction of joy and celebration, the freedmen quickly became aware of their continuing dependence on former owners.

Hopes Among Freedmen

Throughout the South in the summer of 1865, there were optimistic expectations in the old slave quarters. As Union soldiers marched through Richmond, prisoners in slave-trade jails chanted: "Slavery chain done broke at last! Gonna praise God till I die!" The slavery chain, however, was not broken all at once but link by link. After Union soldiers swept through an area, Confederate troops would follow, or master and overseer would return, and the slaves learned not to rejoice too quickly or openly. "Every time a bunch of No'thern sojers would come through," recalled one slave, "they would tell us we was free and we'd begin celebratin'. Before we would get through somebody else would tell us to go back to work, and we would go." So former slaves became cautious about what freedom meant.

Gradually, the freedmen began to test their new freedom. The first thing they did was to leave the plantation, if only for a few hours or days. Some former slaves cut their ties entirely, leaving cruel and kindly masters alike.

Many freedmen left the plantation in search of members of their families. For some, freedom meant getting married legally. Legal marriage was important morally, but it also served such practical purposes as establishing the legitimacy of children and gaining access to land titles and other economic opportunities. Marriage also meant special burdens for black women who took on the now familiar double role as housekeeper and breadwinner. For many newly married blacks, however, the initial goal was to create a traditional family life, resulting in the widespread withdrawal of women from plantation field labor.

Another way in which freedmen demonstrated their new status was by choosing surnames; names associated with the concept of independence, such as Washington, were common. Emancipation changed black manners around whites as well. Masks were dropped, and old expressions of humility — tipping a hat, stepping aside, feigning happiness, addressing whites with titles of deference — were discarded. For the blacks, these were necessary symbolic expressions of selfhood; they proved that things were now different. To whites, these behaviors were seen as acts of "insolence," "insubordination," and "puttin' on airs."

However important were choosing names, dropping masks, moving around, getting married, and testing new rights, the primary goal for most freedmen was the acquisition of their own land. During the war, some Union generals had placed liberated slaves in charge of confiscated and abandoned lands. In the Sea Islands off the coast of South Carolina and Georgia, blacks had been working 40-acre plots of land and harvesting their own crops for several years. Some blacks held title to these lands. Northern philanthropists had organized others to grow cotton for the Treasury Department to prove the superiority of free labor over slavery.

Many freedmen expected a new economic order as fair payment for their years of involuntary work on the land. As one freedman put it, "Gib us our own land and we take care ourselves; but widout land, de ole massas can hire us or starve us, as dey please." However cautiously expressed, the freedmen had every expectation, fed by the intensity of their dreams, that "forty acres and a mule" would be provided.

The White South's Fearful Response

White southerners had mixed goals at the war's end. Yeoman farmers and poor whites stood side by side with rich planters in bread lines as together they looked forward to the restoration of their land and livelihood. Suffering from "extreme want and destitution," as a Georgia resident put it, white southerners responded with feelings of outrage, loss, and injustice. "I tell you it is mighty hard," said one man, "for my pa paid his own money for our niggers; and that's not all they've robbed us of. They have taken our horses and cattle and sheep *and everything*."

A more dominant emotion, however, was fear. The entire structure of southern society was shaken, and the semblance of racial peace and order that slavery had provided was shattered. Many white southerners could hardly imagine a society without blacks in bondage. Having lost control of all that was familiar and revered, whites feared everything from losing their cheap labor supply to having to sit next to blacks on trains.

The mildest of their fears was the inconvenience of doing various jobs and chores they had rarely done before, like housework. The worst fears of southern whites were rape and revenge.

Both white southerners and their former slaves suffered in the immediate aftermath of the Civil War, as illustrated by this engraving from Frank Leslie's Illustrated Newspaper.

The presence of black soldiers touched off fears of violence. Although demobilization occurred rapidly after Appomattox, a few black militia units remained in uniform, parading with guns in southern cities. Acts of violence by black soldiers against whites, however, were rare.

Believing that their world was turned upside down, the former planter aristocracy set out to restore the old plantation order and appropriate racial relationships. The key to reestablishing white dominance were the "black codes" that state legislatures passed in the first year after the end of the war. Many of the codes granted freedmen the right to marry, sue and be sued, testify in court, and hold property. But these rights were qualified. Complicated passages in the codes explained under exactly what circumstances blacks could testify against whites or own property (mostly they could not) or exercise other rights of free persons. Some rights were denied, including racial intermarriage and the right to bear arms, possess alcoholic beverages, sit on trains except in baggage compartments, be on city streets at night, or congregate in large groups.

Many of the alleged rights guaranteed by the black codes — testimony in court, for example — were passed to induce the federal government to withdraw its remaining troops from the South. This was a crucial issue, for in many places marauding groups of whites were assaulting and terrorizing virtually defenseless freedmen, who clearly needed protection and the right to testify in court against whites.

Because white planters needed the freedmen's labor, the crucial provisions of the black codes were intended to regulate the freedmen's economic status. "Vagrancy" laws provided that any blacks not "lawfully employed," which usually meant by a white employer, could be arrested, jailed, fined, or hired out to a man who would assume responsibility for their debts and future behavior. The codes regulated the work contracts by which black laborers worked in the fields for white landowners, including severe penalties for leaving before the yearly contract was fulfilled and rules for proper behavior, attitude, and manners. Thus southern leaders sought to reestablish their dominance. A Kentucky newspaper commented: "The tune . . . will not be 'forty acres and a mule,' but . . . 'work nigger or starve.'"

National Reconstruction

The question facing the national government in 1865 was whether it would use its power to support the black codes and the reimposition of racial intimidation in the South or to uphold the newly sought rights of the freedmen. Would the federal government side with the democratic reform impulse in American history, which stressed human rights and liberty, or with the forces emphasizing property, order, and self-interest? Although the primary drama of Reconstruction took place in the conflict between white landowners and black freedmen over land and labor in the South, the struggle over Reconstruction policy among politicians in Washington played a significant role in the local drama, as well as the next century of American history.

The Presidential Plan

After initially calling for punishment of the defeated Confederates for "treason," President Johnson soon adopted a more lenient policy. On May 29, 1865, he issued two proclamations setting forth his reconstruction program. Like Lincoln, he maintained that the southern states had never left the Union. His first proclamation continued Lincoln's policies by offering "amnesty and pardon, with restoration of all rights of property" to all former Confederates who would take an oath of allegiance to the Constitution and the Union of the United States. The old Jacksonian made exceptions: ex-Confederate government leaders and rich rebels whose taxable property was valued at over $20,000. Any southerners not covered by the amnesty proclamation could, however, apply for special individual pardons, which Johnson granted to

nearly all applicants. By the fall of 1865, only a handful remained unpardoned.

Johnson's second proclamation laid out the steps by which southern states could reestablish state governments. First, the president would appoint a provisional governor, who would call a state convention representing "that portion of the people of said State who are loyal to the United States." This included those who took the oath of allegiance or were otherwise pardoned. The convention should ratify the Thirteenth Amendment, which abolished slavery, void secession, repudiate all Confederate debts, and then elect new state officials and members of Congress.

Under this lenient plan, each of the southern states successfully completed reconstruction and sent newly elected members to the Congress that convened in December 1865. Southern voters defiantly elected dozens of former officers and legislators of the Confederacy, including a few not yet pardoned. Some state conventions hedged on ratifying the Thirteenth Amendment, and some asserted their right to compensation for the loss of slave property. No state provided for black suffrage, and most did nothing to guarantee civil rights, schooling, or economic protection for the freedmen. Less than eight months after Appomattox, Reconstruction seemed to be over.

Congressional Reconstruction

As they looked at the situation late in 1865, northern leaders painfully saw that almost none of their postwar goals were being fulfilled. The South was taking advantage of the president's program to restore the power of the prewar planter aristocracy. The freedmen were receiving neither equal citizenship nor economic independence. And the Republicans were not likely to maintain their political power and stay in office. Would the Democratic party and the South gain by postwar politics what they had been unable to achieve by civil war?

Congressional Republicans, led by Congressman Thaddeus Stevens of Pennsylvania and Senator Charles Sumner of Massachusetts, decided to assert their own policies for reconstructing the nation. Although branded as "radicals," only for a brief period in 1866 and 1867 did "radical" rule prevail. Rejecting Johnson's notion that the South had already been reconstructed, Congress asserted its constitutional authority to decide on its own membership and refused seats to the newly elected senators and representatives from the old Confederate states. Congress then established the Joint Committee on Reconstruction to investigate conditions in the South. Its report documented disorder and resistance and the appalling treatment and conditions of the freedmen. Even before the report was made final in 1866, Congress passed a civil rights bill to protect the fragile rights of the blacks and extended for two more years the Freedmen's Bureau, an agency providing emergency assistance at the end of the war. President Johnson vetoed both bills, arguing that they were unconstitutional and calling his congressional opponents "traitors."

Johnson's growing anger forced moderates into the radical camp, and Congress passed both bills over his veto. Both, however, were watered down by weakening the power of enforcement. Southern civil courts, therefore, regularly disallowed black testimony against whites, acquitted whites charged with violence against blacks, sentenced blacks to compulsory labor, and generally made discriminatory sentences for the same crimes. In this judicial climate, racial violence erupted with discouraging frequency.

In Memphis, for example, a race riot occurred in May 1866 that typified race relations during the Reconstruction period. A street brawl erupted between the police and some recently discharged but armed black soldiers. After some fighting and an exchange of gunfire, the soldiers went back to their fort. That night, white mobs, led by prominent local officials, invaded the black section of the city. With the encouragement of the Memphis police, the mobs engaged in over 40 hours of terror, killing, beating, robbing, and raping virtually helpless residents and burning houses, schools, and churches. When it

was over, 48 persons, all but two of them black, had died in the riot. The local Union army commander took his time intervening to restore order, arguing that his troops had "a large amount of public property to guard [and] hated Negroes too." A congressional inquiry found that in Memphis, blacks had "no protection from the law whatever."

A month later, Congress proposed to the states the ratification of the Fourteenth Amendment, the single most significant act of the Reconstruction era. The first section of the amendment sought to provide permanent constitutional protection of the civil rights of freedmen by defining them as citizens. States were prohibited from depriving "any person of life, liberty, or property, without due process of law," and all persons were guaranteed "the equal protection of the laws." In section 2, Congress paved the way for black male suffrage in the South by declaring that states not enfranchising black males would have their "basis of representation reduced" proportionally. Other sections of the amendment denied leaders of the Confederacy the right to hold national or state political office (except by act of Congress), repudiated the Confederate debt, and denied claims of compensation by former slave owners for their lost property.

President Johnson urged the southern states not to ratify the Fourteenth Amendment, and ten states immediately rejected it. Johnson then went on the campaign trail in the midterm election of 1866 to ask voters to throw out the radical Republicans. Vicious name calling and other low forms of electioneering marked this first political campaign since the war's end. The result of the election was an overwhelming victory for the Republicans and a repudiation of Andrew Johnson and his policies.

Therefore, early in 1867, Reconstruction Acts were passed dividing the southern states into five military districts to maintain order and protect the rights of property and persons and defining a new process for readmitting a state. Qualified voters, which included blacks and excluded unreconstructed rebels, would elect delegates to state constitutional conventions, which then would write new constitutions guaranteeing black suffrage. After the new voters of the states had ratified the constitutions, elections would be held to choose governors and state legislatures. When a state ratified the Fourteenth Amendment, its representatives to Congress would be accepted, thus completing readmission to the Union.

The President Impeached

At the same time as it passed the Reconstruction Acts, Congress also approved bills to restrict the powers of the president and to establish the dominance of the legislative branch over the executive. The Tenure of Office Act, designed to protect the outspoken secretary of war, Edwin Stanton, from removal by Johnson, limited the president's appointment powers. Other measures restricted his power as commander in chief. Johnson behaved exactly as congressional Republicans had anticipated, vetoing the Reconstruction Acts, issuing orders to limit military commanders in the South, and removing cabinet and other government officials sympathetic to Congress's program. The House Judiciary Committee investigated, charging the president with "usurpations of power," but moderate House Republicans defeated impeachment resolutions to remove Johnson from office.

In August 1867, Johnson finally dismissed Stanton and asked for Senate consent. When the Senate refused, the president ordered Stanton to surrender his office, which he refused, barricading himself inside. This time the House rushed impeachment resolutions to a vote, charging the president with "high crimes and misdemeanors" as detailed in 11 offenses while in office, mostly focusing on alleged violations of the Tenure of Office Act. The three-month trial in the Senate early in 1868 featured impassioned oratory, but in the end, seven moderate Republicans joined Democrats against conviction, and the effort to find the

president guilty as charged fell short of the two-thirds majority required by a single vote.

As the moderate or regular Republicans gained strength in 1868 through their support of the presidential election winner, Ulysses S. Grant, radicalism lost much of its power within Republican ranks. Not for another 100 years would a president again face removal from office through impeachment.

Congressional Moderation

The impeachment crisis revealed that most Republicans were more interested in protecting themselves than the freedmen and in punishing Johnson rather than the South. It is revealing to look not only at what Congress did during Reconstruction but also at what it did not do.

With the exception of Jefferson Davis, Congress did not imprison Confederate leaders, and only one person, the commander of the infamous Andersonville prison camp, was put to death. Congress did not insist on a long-term probationary period before southern states could be readmitted to the Union. It did not reorganize southern local governments. It did not mandate a national program of education for the four million ex-slaves. It did not confiscate and redistribute land to the freedmen, nor did it prevent President Johnson from taking land away from freedmen who had gained possessory titles during the war. It did not, except indirectly, provide economic help to black citizens.

What Congress did do, and that only reluctantly, was grant citizenship and suffrage to the freedmen. Black suffrage gained support after the election of 1868, when General Grant, a military hero regarded as invincible, barely won the popular vote in several states. Congressional Republicans, who had twice rejected a suffrage amendment, took another look at the idea as a way of adding grateful black votes to party rolls. After a bitterly contested fight, repeated in several state ratification contests, the Fifteenth Amendment, forbidding all states to deny the vote to anyone "on account of race, color, or previous condition of servitude," became part of the Constitution in 1870. A black preacher from Pittsburgh observed that "the Republican party had done the Negro good, but they were doing themselves good at the same time."

For political reasons, therefore, Congress gave blacks the vote but not the land, the opposite priority of what the freedmen wanted. Almost alone, Thaddeus Stevens argued that "forty acres . . . and a hut would be more valuable . . . than the . . . right to vote." But Congress never seriously considered his plan to confiscate the land of the "chief rebels" and to give a small portion of it, divided into 40-acre plots, to the freedmen.

Although most Americans, in the North as well as the South, opposed confiscation and black independent landownership, Congress passed an alternative measure. Proposed by George Julian of Indiana, the Southern Homestead Act of 1866 made public lands available to blacks and loyal whites in five southern states. But the land was of poor quality and inaccessible, and claimants had only until January 1, 1867, to claim their land. But that was nearly impossible for most blacks because they were under contract with white employers until that date. Only about 4,000 black families even applied for the Homestead Act lands, and fewer than 20 percent of them saw their claims completed. The record of white claimants was not much better. Congressional moderation, therefore, left the freedmen economically weak as they faced the challenges of freedom.

Reconstruction Amendments

Amendment	Substance	Date of Congressional Passage	Outcome of Ratification Process	Finally Implemented and Enforced
Thirteenth	Prohibited slavery in the United States	January 1865	Ratified by 27 states, including 8 southern states, by December 1865	Immediately, although economic freedom came by degrees
Fourteenth	1. Defined equal national citizenship 2. Reduced state representation in Congress proportional to number of disfranchised voters 3. Denied former Confederates the right to hold office	June 1866	Rejected by 12 southern and border states by February 1867; radicals made readmission depend on ratification; ratified in July 1868	Civil Rights Act of 1964
Fifteenth	Prohibited denial of vote because of race, color, or previous servitude	February 1869	Ratification by Virginia, Texas, Mississippi, and Georgia required for readmission; ratified in March 1870	Voting Rights Act of 1965

Women and the Reconstruction Amendments

One casualty of the Fourteenth and Fifteenth amendments was the goodwill of the women who had been petitioning and campaigning for suffrage for two decades. They had hoped that grateful male legislators would recognize their support for the Union effort during the war and the suspension of their own demands in the interests of the more immediate concerns of preserving the Union, nursing the wounded, and emancipating the slaves. They were therefore shocked to see the wording of the Fourteenth Amendment, which for the first time inserted the word *male* in the Constitution in referring to a citizen's right to vote. Stanton and Anthony campaigned actively against the Fourteenth Amendment, and when the Fifteenth Amendment was proposed, they wondered why the word *sex* could not have been added to the "conditions" no longer a basis for denial of the vote.

Disappointment over the suffrage issue was one of several reasons that led to a split in the women's movement in 1869. Anthony and Stanton continued their fight for a national amendment for woman suffrage and a long list of other rights, while other women concentrated their hopes on securing the vote on a state-by-state basis.

Life After Slavery

Clinton Fisk, a well-meaning white who helped to found a black college in Tennessee, told freedmen in 1866 that they could be "as free and as happy" working again for their "old master . . . as any where else in the world." For many blacks such pronouncements sounded familiar, reminding them of white preachers' exhortations during slavery to work hard and obey their masters. Ironically, though, Fisk was an agent of the Freedmen's Bureau, the crucial agency intended to ease the transition from slavery to freedom for the four million ex-slaves.

The Freedmen's Bureau

Never in American history has one small agency — underfinanced, understaffed, and undersupported — been given a harder task than was the Bureau of Freedmen, Refugees and Abandoned Lands. Its purposes and mixed successes illustrate the tortuous course of Reconstruction.

The activities of the Freedmen's Bureau included issuing emergency rations of food and providing clothing and shelter to the homeless, hungry victims of the war; establishing medical care and hospital facilities; providing funds for transportation for the thousands of freedmen and white refugees dislocated by the war; helping blacks search for and put their families back together; and arranging for legal marriage ceremonies. The bureau also served as a friend in local civil courts to ensure that the freedmen got fair trials. Although not initially empowered to do so, the agency was responsible for the education of the ex-slaves. To bureau schools came many idealistic teachers from various northern Freedmen's Aid societies.

In addition, the largest task of the Freedmen's Bureau was to serve as an employment agency, tending to the economic well-being of the blacks. This included settling them on abandoned lands and getting them started with tools, seed, and draft animals, as well as arranging work contracts with white landowners. In the area of work contracts, the Freedmen's Bureau served more to "reenslave" the freedmen as impoverished fieldworkers than to set them on their way as independent farmers.

Although some agents were idealistic young New Englanders eager to help slaves adjust to freedom, others were Union army officers more concerned with social order than social transformation. On a typical day, these overworked and underpaid agents would visit courts and schools in their district, supervise the signing of work contracts, and handle numerous complaints, most involving contract violations between whites and blacks or property and domestic disputes among blacks. Although helpful in finding work for the freedmen, more often than not the agents found themselves defending white landowners by telling the blacks to obey orders, to trust their employers, and to sign and live by disadvantageous contracts.

Despite mounting pressures to support white landowners, personal frustrations, and even threats on their lives, the agents accomplished a great deal. In little more than two years, the Freedmen's Bureau issued 20 million rations (nearly one-third to poor whites), reunited families and resettled some 30,000 displaced war refugees, treated some 450,000 cases of illness and injury, built 40 hospitals and hundreds of schools, provided books, tools, and furnishings — and even some land — to the freedmen, and occasionally protected their economic and civil rights. Historian W. E. B. Du Bois wrote an epitaph for the bureau that might stand for the whole of Reconstruction: "In a time of perfect calm, amid willing neighbors and streaming wealth," he wrote, it "would have been a herculean task" for the bureau to fulfill its many purposes. But in the midst of hunger, sorrow, spite, suspicion, hate, and cruelty, "the work of any instrument of social regeneration was . . . foredoomed to failure."

Economic Freedom by Degrees

The economic failures of the Freedmen's Bureau forced the freedmen into a new economic dependency on their former masters, and both were affected by the changing character of southern agriculture in the postwar years. First, land ownership was concentrated into fewer and even larger holdings than before the Civil War. From South Carolina to Louisiana, the wealthiest tenth of the population owned about 60 percent of the real estate in the 1870s. Second, these large planters increasingly concentrated on one crop, usually cotton, and were tied into the international market. This resulted in a steady drop in food production in the postwar period. Third, reliance on one-crop farming meant that a new credit system emerged whereby most farmers, black and white, depended on local merchants for renting seed, farm implements and animals, provisions, housing, and land. These changes affected race relations and class tensions among whites.

This new system, however, took a few years to develop after emancipation. At first, most freedmen signed contracts with white landowners and worked in gangs in the fields as farm laborers very much as during slavery. But what the freedmen wanted, a Georgia planter correctly observed, was "to get away from all overseers, to hire or purchase land, and work for themselves."

Many blacks therefore broke contracts, ran away, engaged in work slowdowns or strikes, burned barns, and otherwise expressed their displeasure with the contract labor system. Blacks' insistence on autonomy and land of their own was the major impetus for the change from the contract system to tenancy and sharecropping. As a South Carolina freedman put it, "If I can't own de land, I'll hire or lease land, but I won't contract." The sharecroppers were given seed, fertilizer, farm implements, and all necessary food and clothing to take care of their families. In return, the landlord (or a local merchant) told them what to grow and how much and took a share — usually half — of the harvest. The half retained by the cropper, however, was usually needed to pay for goods bought on credit (at huge interest rates) at the landlord's store. Thus the sharecroppers were semiautonomous but remained tied to the landlord's will for economic survival.

Under the tenant system, farmers had only slightly more independence. In advance of the harvest, a tenant farmer promised to sell his crop to a local merchant in return for renting land, tools, and other necessities. He was also obligated to purchase goods on credit (at higher prices than whites paid) against the harvest from the merchant's store. At "settling up" time, the income from the sale of the crop was matched with debts accumulated at the store. But tenants usually remained in debt at the end of each year and were then compelled to pledge the next year's crop. Thus a system of debt peonage replaced slavery. Only a very few blacks became independent landowners — about 2 to 5 percent by 1880, but closer to 20 percent in some states by 1900.

These changes in southern agriculture affected yeoman and poor white farmers as well as the freedmen, especially as cotton production doubled between the Civil War and 1880. Like the freedmen, whites, too, were forced to concentrate on growing staples, to pledge their crops against high-interest credit from local merchants, and to face perpetual indebtedness.

Larger planters' reliance on cotton meant fewer food crops, which led to greater dependence on local merchants for provisions and a poorer diet. Poor whites thus faced diminishing fortunes throughout the South. Some became farmhands, earning $6 a month (with board) from other farmers. Other fled to low-paying jobs in urban cotton mills.

In part because their lives were so hard, poor whites persisted in their belief in white superiority. As a federal officer reported in 1866, "The poorer classes of white people . . . have a most intense hatred of the Negro, and swear he shall never be reckoned as part of the population." Many poor whites, therefore, joined the Ku Klux Klan and other southern white terror groups that emerged between 1866 and 1868. But however hard life was for poor whites, blacks were far more often sentenced to chain gangs for the slightest crimes and were bound to a life of debt, degradation, and dependency. The high hopes with which the freedmen had greeted emancipation turned slowly to resignation and disillusionment. Felix Haywood, a former Texas slave, recalled:

We thought we was goin' to be richer than white folks, 'cause we was stronger and knowed how to work, and the whites . . . didn't have us to work for them anymore. But it didn't turn out that way. We soon found out that freedom could make folks proud but it didn't make 'em rich.

Black Self-Help Institutions

It was clear to many black leaders that since white institutions could not fulfill the promises of emancipation, black freedmen would have to do it themselves. Fortunately, the tradition of black community self-help survived in the organized churches and schools of the antebellum free Negro communities and in the "invisible" cultural institutions of the slave quarters. Religion, as usual, was vital. Emancipation brought an explosion in the growth of membership in black churches. The Negro Baptist church grew from 150,000 members in 1850 to 500,000 in 1870. The various branches of the African Methodist Episcopal church increased fourfold in the decade after the Civil War, from 100,000 to over 400,000 members.

Black ministers continued their tradition of community leadership and revivalist preaching. An English visitor to the South in 1867 and 1868, after observing a preacher in Savannah arouse nearly 1,000 people to "sway, and cry, and groan," noted the intensity of black "devoutness."

The freedmen's desire for education was as strong as for religion. A school official in Virginia echoed the observation of many when he said that the freedmen were "down right crazy to learn." This enthusiasm was dampened by the demands of fieldwork and scarce resources for black schools. The first teachers of the black children in the South were unmarried northern women, the legendary "Yankee schoolmarms," sent by groups such as the American Missionary Association. But blacks increasingly preferred their own teachers, who could better understand former slaves. To ensure the training of black preachers and teachers, northern philanthropists founded Howard, Atlanta, Fisk, Morehouse, and other black universities in the South between 1865 and 1867.

Black schools, like churches, became community centers. They published newspapers, provided training in trades and farming, and promoted political participation and land ownership. These efforts made black schools objects

Along with equal civil rights and land of their own, what the freedmen most wanted was education. Despite white opposition and limited facilities for black schools, one of the most positive outcomes of the Reconstruction era was education in freedmen's schools.

of local white hostility. In 1869, in Tennessee alone, 37 black schools were burned to the ground.

White opposition to black education and land ownership stimulated the rise of black nationalism and separatism. In the late 1860s, Benjamin "Pap" Singleton, a former Tennessee slave who had escaped to Canada, organized a land company in 1869, and promoted relocation of blacks to separatist communities in Kansas. When these schemes failed, Singleton and other nationalists urged emigration to Canada and Liberia. Other black leaders, notably Frederick Douglass, continued to assert that suffrage would eventually lead to full citizenship rights within the United States.

Reconstruction in the States

Douglass's confidence in the power of the ballot seemed warranted in the enthusiastic early months under the Reconstruction Acts of 1867. With President Johnson neutralized,

national Republican leaders were finally in a position to accomplish their political goals. Local Republicans, taking advantage of the inability or refusal of many southern whites to vote, overwhelmingly elected their delegates to state constitutional conventions in the fall of 1867. With guarded optimism and a sense of the "sacred importance" of their work, black and white Republicans turned to the task of creating new state governments.

Republican Rule

Despite popular belief, the southern state governments under Republican rule were not dominated by illiterate black majorities intent on "Africanizing" the South by passing compulsory racial intermarriage laws, as many whites feared. Nor were these governments unusually corrupt or financially extravagant. Nor did they use massive numbers of federal troops to enforce their will. Rather, they tried to do their work in a climate of economic distress and increasingly violent harassment.

A diverse combination of political groups made up the new governments elected under congressional Reconstruction. Labeled the "black and tan" governments by their opponents to suggest domination by former slaves and mulattoes, they were actually predominantly white, with the one exception of the lower house of the South Carolina legislature. The new leadership included an old Whiggish elite class of bankers, industrialists, and others interested far more in economic growth than in radical social reforms; northern Republican capitalists seeking investment opportunities; retired Union veterans; and missionaries and teachers. Such people were unfairly labeled "carpetbaggers."

Moderate blacks also participated in the Republican state governments. A large percentage of black officeholders were mulattoes, many of them well-educated preachers, teachers, and soldiers from the North. Others, such as John Lynch of Mississippi, were self-educated tradesmen or representatives of the small landed class of southern blacks. This class composition meant that black leaders often supported land policies that largely ignored the economic needs of the black masses.

These black politicians were more interested in pursuing political influence and education than land redistribution or state aid to black peasants. They sought no revenge or reversal of power, only, as an 1865 petition said, "that the same laws which govern white men shall govern black men [and that] we be dealt with as others are — in equity and justice."

The primary accomplishment of Republican rule in the South was in eliminating the undemocratic features of earlier state constitutions. All states provided universal men's suffrage and loosened requirements for holding office. The basis of state representation was made fairer by apportioning more legislative seats to the interior regions of southern states. Social and penal laws were also modernized.

Republican governments undertook the task of financially and physically reconstructing the South, overhauling tax systems, and approving generous railroad and other capital investment bonds. Most important, the Republican governments provided for a state-supported system of public schools, absent before in most of the South. As in the North, these schools were largely segregated, but for the first time, rich and poor, black and white alike had access to education. As a result, black school attendance increased from 5 to over 40 percent and white from 20 to over 60 percent by the 1880s. All of this cost money, and the Republicans did indeed greatly increase tax rates and state debts. All in all, the Republican governments "dragged the South, screaming and crying, into the modern world."

Despite its effectiveness in modernizing southern state governments, the Republican coalition did not last very long. In fact, as the map indicates, Republican rule lasted for different periods of time in different states. In some states, Virginia, for example, the Republicans ruled hardly at all. In South Carolina, the unwillingness of black leaders to use their power to help black laborers contributed to their loss of political control to the Democrats. Class tensions and divisions among blacks in Louisiana helped to weaken that Republican regime as well. Republican rule lasted the longest in the black-belt states of the Deep South, where the black population was equal to or greater than the white.

Violence and "Redemption"

Democrats used racial violence, intimidation, and coercion to restore their power. The Ku Klux Klan was only one of several secret organizations that used force and violence against black and white Republicans. The cases of North Carolina and Mississippi are representative in showing how conservative Democrats were able to regain control.

After losing a close election in North Carolina in 1868, conservatives waged a concentrated campaign of terror in several counties in the piedmont area. If the Democrats could win these counties in 1870, they would most likely win statewide. In the year prior to the election, several prominent Republicans were killed, including a white state senator, whose throat was

Return to the Union During Reconstruction

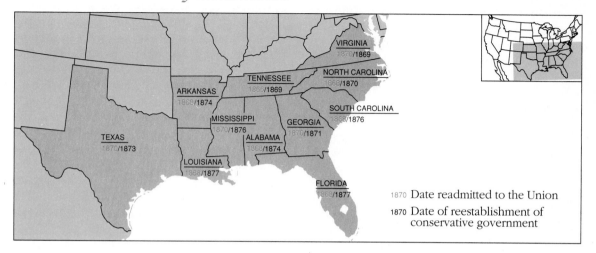

1870 Date readmitted to the Union

1870 Date of reestablishment of conservative government

cut, and a leading black Union League organizer, who was hanged in the courthouse square with a sign pinned to his breast: "Bewar, ye guilty, both white and black." Scores of citizens were flogged, tortured, fired from their jobs, or forced to flee in the middle of the night from burning homes and barns. The courts consistently refused to prosecute anyone for these crimes. Local papers, in fact, charged that "disgusting negroes and white Radicals" had committed the crimes. The conservative campaign worked. In the election of 1870, some 12,000 fewer Republicans voted in the two crucial counties than had voted two years earlier, and the Democrats swept back into power.

In the state election in Mississippi in 1875, Democrats used similar tactics. In what was called the Mississippi Plan, local Democratic clubs organized themselves into armed militias, marching defiantly through black areas, breaking up Republican meetings, and provoking riots to justify the killing of hundreds of blacks. Armed men were posted during voter registration to intimidate Republicans. At the election itself, anyone still bold enough to attempt to vote was either helped by gun-toting whites to cast a Democratic ballot or driven away from the polls with cannon and clubs. Counties that had earlier given Republican candidates majorities in the

thousands, in 1875 managed a total of less than a dozen votes!

Democrats called their victory "redemption." As conservative Democratic administrations resumed control of each state government, Reconstruction came to an end. Redemption resulted from a combination of the persistence of white southern resistance, including violence and other coercive measures, and a loss of will to persist in the North.

Congress and President Grant did not totally ignore the violence in the South. Three Force Acts, passed in 1870 and 1871, gave the president strong powers to use federal supervisors to make sure that citizens were not prevented from voting by force or fraud. The third act, known as the Ku Klux Klan Act, declared illegal secret organizations that used disguise and coercion to deprive others of equal protection of the laws. Congress created a joint committee to investigate Klan violence, which reported in 1872 in 13 huge volumes of horrifying testimony. Grant issued proclamations condemning lawlessness, and sent some additional troops to South Carolina. However, as reform Republicans realized that black voters supported Grant, they lost interest in defending those voters. Regular Republicans were also not very supportive, since many felt that they could do without black voters. In 1875, Grant's advisers told him that Republicans might lose important Ohio elections if he continued to protect blacks. Thus he decided that year to reject appeals by Mississippi blacks that troops be stationed in their state to guarantee free elections. Grant declared instead that he and the nation "had tired of these annual autumnal outbreaks."

The federal government did little to stop the reign of terror against black and white Republicans throughout the South. The Force Acts were wholly inadequate and were themselves weakly enforced. Although the Ku Klux Klan's power was officially ended, the attitudes (and tactics) of Klansmen would continue long into the next century.

Reconstruction, Northern Style

The American people, like their leaders, were tired of battles over the freedmen and were shifting their attention to other matters. Frustrated with the difficulties of trying to transform an unwilling South and seemingly ungrateful blacks, the easiest course was to give blacks their citizenship and the vote and move on to something else. After the interruptions of civil war and its aftermath, most Americans were primarily interested in starting families, finding work, and making money. This meant firing furnaces in the new steel plant in Wheeling, West Virginia, pounding in railroad ties for the Central Pacific in the Nevada desert, struggling to teach in a one-room schoolhouse in Vermont for $23 a month, or battling heat, locusts, and railroad rates on a family homestead in Kansas.

At both the individual and national levels, Reconstruction, northern style, meant the continuation of the enormous economic revolution of the nineteenth century. Although failing to effect a smooth transition from slavery to freedom for ex-slaves, Republican northerners were able to accelerate and solidify their program of economic growth and industrial and territorial expansion.

The years between 1865 and 1875 featured not only the rise (and fall) of Republican govern-

ments in the South but also the spectacular rise of working-class activity and organization. Stimulated by the Civil War to improve working conditions in northern factories, such groups as trade unions, labor reform associations, and labor parties flourished, culminating in the founding of the National Labor Union in 1866. Before the depression of 1873, an estimated 300,000 to 500,000 American workers had enrolled in some 1,500 trade unions, the largest such increase in the nineteenth century. This growth would inevitably affect class tensions. In 1876, hundreds of freedmen in the rice region along the Combahee River in South Carolina went on strike to protest a 40-cent-per-day wage cut, clashing with local sheriffs and white Democratic rifle clubs. A year later, also over wage cuts, thousands of railroad workers in Pittsburgh, St. Louis, Omaha, and other northern cities went out in a nationwide wave of strikes, clashing with local police and the National Guard.

As economic relations changed, so did the Republican party. It changed from the party of moral reform to one of material interest. In the continuing struggle in American politics between "virtue and commerce," self-interest was again winning. No longer willing to support an agency like the Freedmen's Bureau, Republican politicians had no difficulty backing huge grants of money and land to the railroads. As blacks were told to go to work and help themselves, the Union Pacific was being given subsidies of between $16,000 and $48,000 for each mile of track laid across western plains and mountains.

By 1869, the year financier Jay Gould almost succeeded in cornering the gold market, the nation was increasingly defined by materialistic "go-getters" and by sordid grasping for wealth and power. Ulysses Grant himself was an honest man, but his judgment of others was flawed. His administration featured a series of scandals that touched several cabinet officers and relatives and even two vice-presidents. Under Grant's appointments, outright graft flourished in a half dozen departments. Most scandals involved large sums of public money.

As early as 1868, three white groups — here stereotyped as apelike northern Irish workers, unrepentant ex-Confederates, and rich northern capitalists — joined hands to bring Republican Reconstruction to an end almost before it began. The immigrant's vote, the Kluxer's knife, and the capitalist's dollars would restore "a white man's government" on the back of the freedman, still clutching the Union flag and reaching in vain for the ballot box. No single image better captures the story of the end of Reconstruction than this Thomas Nast cartoon.

panies for transcontinental railroads (in this case a dummy company) received generous bonds and work contracts in exchange for giving congressmen gifts of money, stocks, and railroad lands. Henry Adams spoke for many Americans when he said that Grant's administration "outraged every rule of decency."

The election of 1872 marked the decline of public interest in moral issues. A "liberal" faction of the Republican party, unable to dislodge Grant and disgusted with his administration, formed a third party with a reform platform and nominated Horace Greeley, editor of the New York *Tribune*, for president. Democrats, lacking notable presidential candidates, also nominated Greeley, even though he had spent much of his earlier career assailing Democrats as "rascals." Despite his wretched record, Grant easily won a second term.

The End of Reconstruction

Soon after Grant's second inauguration, a financial panic, caused by overconstruction of railroads and the collapse of some crucial eastern banks, created a terrible depression that lasted throughout the mid-1870s. In times of hardship, economic issues dominated politics, further pulling attention away from the plight of the freedmen. As Democrats took control of the House of Representatives in 1874 and looked toward winning the White House in 1876, politicians talked about such issues as new scandals in the Grant administration, unemployment and various proposals for public works expenditures for relief.

As their nominee for president in 1876, the Republicans turned to a former governor of Ohio, Rutherford B. Hayes, partly because of his reputation for honesty, partly because he had been an officer in the Union army (a necessity for post–Civil War candidates), and partly because, as Henry Adams put it, he was "obnoxious to no one." The Democrats chose Governor Samuel J. Tilden of New York, who achieved national recognition as a civil service reformer in breaking up the corrupt Tweed Ring.

The Whiskey Ring affair, for example, cost the public millions of dollars in lost tax revenues siphoned off to government officials. Gould's gold scam received the unwitting aid of Grant's Treasury Department and the knowing help of his brother-in-law.

Nor was Congress pure in these various schemes. Crédit Mobilier figured in the largest of several scandals in which construction com-

Tilden won a majority of the popular vote and appeared to have enough electoral votes for victory. Of 20 disputed electoral votes, all but one came from states in the Deep South, where Democrats had applied various versions of the Mississippi Plan to intimidate voters. To resolve the disputed votes, Congress created a special electoral commission, which awarded Hayes all 20 votes, enough to win, 185 to 184.

Outraged Democrats threatened to stop the Senate from officially counting the electoral votes, thus preventing Hayes's inauguration. The country was in a state of crisis, and some Americans wondered if civil war might break out again.

As the inauguration date approached and newspapers echoed outgoing President Grant's call for "peace at any price," the forces of mutual self-interest concluded the "compromise of 1877." The Democrats agreed to suspend resistance to the counting of the electoral votes, and on March 2, Rutherford B. Hayes was declared president. In exchange for the presidency, Hayes ordered the last remaining troops out of the South, appointed a former Confederate general to his cabinet, supported federal aid to bolster economic and railroad development in the South, and announced his intentions to let southerners handle race relations themselves. Hayes let it be known that he would not enforce the Fourteenth and Fifteenth amendments, thus initiating a pattern of executive inaction not broken until the middle of the twentieth century. But the immediate crisis was averted, officially ending the era of Reconstruction.

CONCLUSION
A Mixed Legacy

In the 12 years between Appomattox and Hayes's inauguration, the diverse dreams of victorious northern Republicans, defeated white southerners, and hopeful black freedmen conflicted. There was little chance that all could be realized, yet each group could point to a modest fulfillment of its goals. The compromise of 1877 cemented the reunion of South and North, thus providing new opportunities for economic development in both regions. The Republican party achieved its economic goals and preserved its political hold on the White House, though not Congress, with two exceptions, until 1932. The ex-Confederate states were brought back into the Union, and southerners retained their firm control of southern lands and black labor, though not without struggle and some changes. To the extent that the peace of 1877 was preserved "at any price," that price was paid by the freedmen.

In 1880, Frederick Douglass summarized Reconstruction for the freedmen, saying that it was a wonder to him "not that freedmen have made so little progress, but, rather, that they have made so much ; not that they have been standing still, but that they have been able to stand at all." Indeed, despite their liabilities, the freedmen had made admirable gains in education and in economic and family survival. Although sharecropping and tenancy were harsh systems, black laborers organized themselves to achieve a measure of autonomy and opportunity in their lives that could never be diminished. Moreover, the three great Reconstruction amendments to the Constitution, despite flagrant violation over the next 100 years, held out the promise that the rights of equal citizenship and political participation would yet be fulfilled.

RECOMMENDED READING

The best overviews of the Reconstruction era are John Hope Franklin, *Reconstruction After the Civil War* (1961); Kenneth Stampp, *The Era of Reconstruction, 1865–1877* (1965); and the brilliant new work by Eric Foner, *Reconstruction: America's Unfinished Revolution, 1863–1877* (1988).

The fullest, most moving account of the black experience in the transition from slavery to freedom is Leon Litwack's massive and sensitive work, *Been in the Storm So Long: The Aftermath of Slavery* (1980). The southern white response to emancipation is described in Dan T. Carter, *When the War Was Over: The Failure of Self-reconstruction in the South, 1865–1867* (1985).

The economy of the South and the freedmen's experience with land and labor are described in Roger Ransom and Richard Sutch, *One Kind of Freedom: The Economic Consequences of Emancipation* (1977); and Eric Foner, *Nothing but Freedom: Emancipation and Its Legacy* (1983). An excellent work showing the white experience with tenancy in the changing economy of the South is Stephen Hahn, *The Roots of Southern Populism* (1983). The Freedmen's Bureau is the subject of Donald Nieman, *To Set the Law in Motion: The Freedmen's Bureau and the Legal Rights of Blacks, 1865–1868* (1979). Continuing racial prejudice in the South and North is the subject of C. Vann

Woodward, *The Strange Career of Jim Crow*, 3d rev. ed. (1974). See also W. E. B. Du Bois's *Black Reconstruction* (1935) and *The Souls of Black Folk* (1903).

Northern politics during Reconstruction have been widely discussed. See David Donald, *The Politics of Reconstruction* (1965); and Michael Les Benedict, *A Compromise of Principle: Congressional Republicans and Reconstruction, 1963–1869* (1974). Southern politics is best seen in Michael Perman, *The Road to Redemption: Southern Politics, 1869–1879* (1984). Grant's presidency and the abandonment of the freedmen by northern Republicans can be traced in William McFeeley, *Grant: A Biography* (1981); and William Gillette, *Retreat from Reconstruction, 1969–1879* (1979). The campaign of violence that ended the Republican governments in the South is told with gripping horror in George C. Rable, *But There was No Peace: The Role of Violence in the Politics of Reconstruction* (1984).

Five novels written at different times and representing different interpretations of the story of Reconstruction are Albion Tourgée, *A Fool's Errand* (1879); Thomas Dixon, *The Clansman* (1905); W. E. B. Du Bois, *The Quest of the Silver Fleece* (1911); Howard Fast, *Freedom Road* (1944); and Ernest Gaines, *The Autobiography of Miss Jane Pittman* (1971).

Time Line

1865	Civil War ends
	Lincoln assassinated; Andrew Johnson becomes president
	Johnson proposes general amnesty and reconstruction plan
	Racial confusion, widespread hunger, and demobilization
	Thirteenth Amendment ratified
	Freedmen's Bureau established
1865– 1866	Black codes
	Repossession of land by whites and freedmen's contracts
1866	Freedmen's Bureau renewed and Civil Rights Act passed over Johnson's veto
	Southern Homestead Act
	Ku Klux Klan formed
	Tennessee readmitted to Union
1867	Reconstruction Acts passed over Johnson's veto
	Impeachment controversy
	Freedmen's Bureau ends
1868	Fourteenth Amendment ratified
	Impeachment of Johnson fails
	Ulysses Grant elected president
1868– 1870	Ten states readmitted under congressional plan
1869	Georgia and Virginia reestablish Democratic party control

1870	Fifteenth Amendment ratified
1870s– 1880s	Black "exodusters" migrate to Kansas
1870– 1871	Force Acts
	North Carolina and Georgia reestablish Democratic control
1872	General Amnesty Act
	Grant reelected president
1873	Crédit Mobilier scandal
	Panic causes depression
1874	Alabama and Arkansas reestablish Democratic control
1875	Civil Rights Act
	Mississippi reestablishes Democratic control
1876	Hayes-Tilden election
1876– 1877	South Carolina, Louisiana, and Florida reestablish Democratic control
1877	Compromise of 1877; Rutherford B. Hayes assumes presidency and ends Reconstruction
1880s	Tenancy and sharecropping prevail in the South
	Disfranchisement and segregation of southern blacks begins

Appendix

DECLARATION OF INDEPENDENCE IN CONGRESS, JULY 4, 1776

The Unanimous Declaration of the Thirteen United States of America

When, in the course of human events, it becomes necessary for one people to dissolve the political bonds which have connected them with another, and to assume, among the powers of the earth, the separate and equal station to which the laws of nature and of nature's God entitle them, a decent respect to the opinions of mankind requires that they should declare the causes which impel them to the separation.

We hold these truths to be self-evident: That all men are created equal, that they are endowed by their Creator with certain unalienable rights; that among these are life, liberty, and the pursuit of happiness; that, to secure these rights, governments are instituted among men, deriving their just powers from the consent of the governed; that whenever any form of government becomes destructive of these ends, it is the right of the people to alter or to abolish it, and to institute new government, laying its foundation on such principles, and organizing its powers in such form, as to them shall seem most likely to effect their safety and happiness. Prudence, indeed, will dictate that governments long estab-lished should not be changed for light and transient causes; and accordingly all experience hath shown that mankind are more disposed to suffer, which evils are sufferable, than to right themselves by abolishing the forms to which they are accustomed. But when a long train of abuses and usurpations, pursuing invariably the same object, evinces a design to reduce them under absolute despotism, it is their right, it is their duty, to throw off such government, and to provide new guards for their future security. Such has been the patient sufferance of these colonies; and such is now the necessity which constrains them to alter their former systems of government. The history of the present King of Great Britain is a history of repeated injuries and usurpations, all having in direct object the establishment of an absolute tyranny over these states. To prove this, let facts be submitted to a candid world.

He has refused his assent to laws the most wholesome and necessary for the public good.

He has forbidden his governors to pass laws of immediate and pressing importance, unless suspended in their operation till his assent should be obtained; and, when so suspended, he has utterly neglected to attend to them.

He has refused to pass other laws for the accommodation of large districts of people, unless those people would relinquish the right of representation in the legislature, a right inestimable to them, and formidable to tyrants only.

He has called together legislative bodies at places unusual, uncomfortable, and distant from the depository of their public records, for the sole purpose of fatiguing them into compliance with his measures.

He has dissolved representative houses repeatedly, for opposing, with manly firmness, his invasions on the rights of the people.

He has refused for a long time, after such dissolutions, to cause others to be elected; whereby the legislative powers, incapable of annihilation, have returned to the people at large for their exercise; the state remaining, in the mean time, exposed to all the dangers of invasions from without and convulsions within.

He has endeavored to prevent the population of these states; for that purpose obstructing the laws for naturalization of foreigners; refusing to pass others to encourage their migration hither, and raising the conditions of new appropriations of lands.

He has obstructed the administration of justice, by refusing his assent to laws for establishing judiciary powers.

He has made judges dependent on his will alone, for the tenure of their offices, and the amount and payment of their salaries.

He has erected a multitude of new offices, and sent hither swarms of officers to harass our people and eat out their substance.

He has kept among us, in times of peace, standing armies, without the consent of our legislatures.

He has affected to render the military independent of, and superior to, the civil power.

He has combined with others to subject us to a jurisdiction foreign to our constitution, and unacknowledged by our laws, giving his assent to their acts of pretended legislation:

For quartering large bodies of armed troops among us;

For protecting them, by a mock trial, from punishment for any murders which they should commit on the inhabitants of these states;

For cutting off our trade with all parts of the world;

For imposing taxes on us without our consent;

For depriving us, in many cases, of the benefits of trial by jury;

For transporting us beyond seas, to be tried for pretended offenses;

For abolishing the free system of English laws in a neighboring province, establishing therein an arbitrary government, and enlarging its boundaries, so as to render it at once an example and fit instrument for introducing the same absolute rule into these colonies;

For taking away our charters, abolishing our most valuable laws, and altering fundamentally the forms of our governments;

For suspending our own legislatures, and declaring themselves invested with power to legislate for us in all cases whatsoever.

He has abdicated government here, by declaring us out of his protection and waging war against us.

He has plundered our seas, ravaged our coasts, burned our towns, and destroyed the lives of our people.

He is at this time transporting large armies of foreign mercenaries to complete the works of death, desolation, and tyranny already begun with circumstances of cruelty and perfidy scarcely paralleled in the most barbarous ages, and totally unworthy the head of a civilized nation.

He has constrained our fellow-citizens, taken captive on the high seas, to bear arms against their country, to become the executioners of their friends and brethren, or to fall themselves by their hands.

He has excited domestic insurrection among us, and has endeavored to bring on the inhabitants of our frontiers the merciless Indian savages, whose known rule of warfare is an undistinguished destruction of all ages, sexes, and conditions.

In every stage of these oppressions we have petitioned for redress in the most humble terms; our repeated petitions have been answered only by repeated injury. A prince, whose character is thus marked by every act which may define a tyrant, is unfit to be the ruler of a free people.

Nor have we been wanting in our attentions to our British brethren. We have warned them, from time to time, of attempts by their legislature to extend an unwarrantable jurisdiction over us. We have reminded them of the circumstances of our emigration and settlement here. We have appealed to their native justice and magnanimity; and we have conjured them, by the ties of our common kindred, to disavow these usurpations, which would inevitably interrupt our connections and correspondence. They, too, have been deaf to the voice of justice and of consanguinity. We must, therefore, acquiesce in the necessity which denounces our separation, and hold them, as we hold the rest of mankind, enemies in war, in peace friends.

We, therefore, the representatives of the United States of America, in General Congress assembled, appealing to the Supreme Judge of the world for the rectitude of our intentions, do, in the name and by the authority of the good people of these colonies, solemnly publish and declare, that these United Colonies are, and of right ought to be, FREE AND INDEPENDENT STATES; that they are absolved from all allegiance to the British crown, and that all political connection between them and the state of Great Britain is, and ought to be, totally dissolved; and that, as free and independent states, they have full power to levy war, conclude peace, contract alliances, establish commerce, and do all other acts and things which independent states may of right do. And for the support of this declaration, with a firm reliance on the protection of Divine Providence, we mutually pledge to each other our lives, our fortunes, and our sacred honor.

CONSTITUTION OF THE UNITED STATES OF AMERICA*

Preamble

We the people of the United States, in order to form a more perfect union, establish justice, insure domestic tranquillity, provide for the common defense, promote the general welfare, and secure the blessings of liberty to ourselves and our posterity, do ordain and establish this Constitution for the United States of America.

Article 1

Section 1 All legislative powers herein granted shall be vested in a Congress of the United States, which shall consist of a Senate and a House of Representatives.

*The Constitution became effective March 4, 1789.

NOTE: Any portion of the text that had been amended appears in italics.

Section 2 The House of Representatives shall be composed of members chosen every second year by the people of the several States, and the electors in each State shall have the qualifications requisite for electors of the most numerous branch of the State Legislature.

No person shall be a Representative who shall not have attained to the age of twenty-five years, and been seven years a citizen of the United States, and who shall not, when elected, be an inhabitant of that State in which he shall be chosen.

Representatives and direct taxes shall be apportioned among the several States which may be included within this Union, according to their respective numbers, *which shall be determined by adding to the whole number of free persons, including those bonded in service for a term of years and excluding Indians not taxed, three-fifths of all other persons.* The actual enumeration shall be made within three years after the first meeting of the

Congress of the United States, and within every subsequent term of ten years, in such manner as they shall by law direct. The number of Representatives shall not exceed one for every thirty thousand, but each State shall have at least one Representative ; *and until such enumeration shall be made, the State of New Hampshire shall be entitled to choose three, Massachusetts eight, Rhode Island and Providence Plantations one, Connecticut five, New York six, New Jersey four, Pennsylvania eight, Delaware one, Maryland six, Virginia ten, North Carolina five, South Carolina five, and Georgia three.*

When vacancies happen in the representation from any State, the Executive authority thereof shall issue writs of election to fill such vacancies.

The House of Representatives shall choose their Speaker and other officers ; and shall have the sole power of impeachment.

Section 3   The Senate of the United States shall be composed of two Senators from each State, *chosen by the legislature thereof,* for six years ; and each Senator shall have one vote.

Immediately after they shall be assembled in consequence of the first election, they shall be divided as equally as may be into three classes. The seats of the Senators of the first class shall be vacated at the expiration of the second year, of the second class at the expiration of the fourth year, and of the third class at the expiration of the sixth year, so that one-third may be chosen every second year ; *and if vacancies happen by resignation or otherwise, during the recess of the legislature of any State, the Executive thereof may make temporary appointments until the next meeting of the legislature, which shall then fill such vacancies.*

No person shall be a Senator who shall not have attained to the age of thirty years, and been nine years a citizen of the United States, and who shall not, when elected, be an inhabitant of that State for which he shall be chosen.

The Vice-President of the United States shall be President of the Senate, but shall have no vote, unless they be equally divided.

The Senate shall choose their other officers, and also a President *pro tempore,* in the absence of the Vice-President, or when he shall exercise the office of President of the United States.

The Senate shall have the sole power to try all impeachments. When sitting for that purpose, they shall be on oath or affirmation. When the President of the United States is tried, the Chief Justice shall preside ; and no person shall be convicted without the concurrence of two-thirds of the members present.

Judgment in cases of impeachment shall not extend further than to removal from the office, and disqualification to hold and enjoy any office of honor, trust or profit under the United States : but the party convicted shall nevertheless be liable and subject to indictment, trial, judgment and punishment, according to law.

Section 4   The times, places and manner of holding elections for Senators and Representatives shall be prescribed in each State by the legislature thereof ; but the Congress may at any time by law make or alter such regulations, except as to the places of choosing Senators.

The Congress shall assemble at least once in every year, and such meeting *shall be on the first Monday in December, unless they shall by law appoint a different day.*

Section 5   Each house shall be the judge of the elections, returns and qualifications of its own members, and a majority of each shall constitute a quorum to do business ; but a smaller number may adjourn from day to day, and may be authorized to compel the attendance of absent members, in such manner, and under such penalties, as each house may provide.

Each house may determine the rules of its proceedings, punish its members for disorderly behavior, and with the concurrence of two-thirds, expel a member.

Each house shall keep a journal of its proceedings, and from time to time publish the same, excepting such parts as may in their judgment require secrecy ; and the yeas and nays of the members of either house on any question shall, at the desire of one-fifth of those present, be entered on the journal.

Neither house, during the session of Congress, shall, without the consent of the other, adjourn for more than three days, nor to any other place than that in which the two houses shall be sitting.

Section 6 The Senators and Representatives shall receive a compensation for their services, to be ascertained by law and paid out of the treasury of the United States. They shall in all cases except treason, felony and breach of the peace be privileged from arrest during their attendance at the session of their respective houses, and in going to and returning from the same; and for any speech or debate in either house, they shall not be questioned in any other place.

No Senator or Representative shall, during the time for which he was elected, be appointed to any civil office under the authority of the United States, which shall have been created, or the emoluments whereof shall have been increased, during such time; and no person holding any office under the United States shall be a member of either house during his continuance in office.

Section 7 All bills for raising revenue shall originate in the House of Representatives; but the Senate may propose or concur with amendments as on other bills.

Every bill which shall have passed the House of Representatives and the Senate, shall, before it becomes a law, be presented to the President of the United States; if he approve he shall sign it, but if not he shall return it with objections to that house in which it originated, who shall enter the objections at large on their journal, and proceed to reconsider it. If after such reconsideration two-thirds of that house shall agree to pass the bill, it shall be sent, together with the objections, to the other house, by which it shall likewise be reconsidered, and, if approved by two-thirds of that house, it shall become a law. But in all such cases the votes of both houses shall be determined by yeas and nays, and the names of the persons voting for and against the bill shall be entered on the journal of each house respectively. If any bill shall not be returned by the President within ten days (Sundays excepted) after it shall have been pre-

sented to him, the same shall be a law, in like manner as if he had signed it, unless the Congress by their adjournment prevent its return, in which case it shall not be a law.

Every order, resolution, or vote to which the concurrence of the Senate and House of Representatives may be necessary (except on a question of adjournment) shall be presented to the President of the United States; and before the same shall take effect, shall be approved by him, or being disapproved by him, shall be repassed by two-thirds of the Senate and House of Representatives, according to the rules and limitations prescribed in the case of a bill.

Section 8 The Congress shall have power:

To lay and collect taxes, duties, imposts, and excises, to pay the debts and provide for the common defense and general welfare of the United States; but all duties, imposts and excises shall be uniform throughout the United States;

To borrow money on the credit of the United States;

To regulate commerce with foreign nations, and among the several States, and with the Indian tribes;

To establish an uniform rule of naturalization, and uniform laws on the subject of bankruptcies throughout the United States;

To coin money, regulate the value thereof, and of foreign coin, and fix the standard of weights and measures;

To provide for the punishment of counterfeiting the securities and current coin of the United States;

To establish post offices and post roads;

To promote the progress of science and useful arts by securing for limited times to authors and inventors the exclusive right to their respective writings and discoveries;

To constitute tribunals inferior to the Supreme Court;

To define and punish piracies and felonies committed on the high seas and offenses against the law of nations;

To declare war, grant letters of marque and reprisal, and make rules concerning captures on land and water;

To raise and support armies, but no appropriation of money to that use shall be for a longer term than two years ;

To provide and maintain a navy ;

To make rules for the government and regulation of the land and naval forces ;

To provide for calling forth the militia to execute the laws of the Union, suppress insurrections, and repel invasions ;

To provide for organizing, arming, and disciplining the militia, and for governing such part of them as may be employed in the service of the United States, reserving to the States respectively the appointment of the officers, and the authority of training the militia according to the discipline prescribed by Congress ;

To exercise exclusive legislation in all cases whatsoever, over such district (not exceeding ten miles square) as may, by cession of particular States, and the acceptance of Congress, become the seat of government of the United States, and to exercise like authority over all places purchased by the consent of the legislature of the State, in which the same shall be, for erection of forts, magazines, arsenals, dockyards, and other needful buildings ; — and

To make all laws which shall be necessary and proper for carrying into execution the foregoing powers, and all other powers vested by this Constitution in the government of the United States, or in any department or officer thereof.

Section 9 *The migration or importation of such persons as any of the States now existing shall think proper to admit shall not be prohibited by the Congress prior to the year 1808 ; but a tax or duty may be imposed on such importation, not exceeding $10 for each person.*

The privilege of the writ of habeas corpus shall not be suspended, unless when in cases of rebellion or invasion the public safety may require it.

No bill of attainder or ex post facto law shall be passed.

No capitation or other direct tax shall be laid, unless in proportion to the census or enumeration herein before directed to be taken.

No tax or duty shall be laid on articles exported from any State.

No preference shall be given by any regulation of commerce or revenue to the ports of one State over those of another ; nor shall vessels bound to, or from, one State be obliged to enter, clear, or pay duties in another.

No money shall be drawn from the treasury, but in consequence of appropriations made by law ; and a regular statement and account of the receipts and expenditures of all public money shall be published from time to time.

No title of nobility shall be granted by the United States : and no person holding any office of profit or trust under them, shall, without the consent of the Congress, accept of any present, emolument, office, or title, of any kind whatever, from any king, prince, or foreign state.

Section 10 No State shall enter into any treaty, alliance, or confederation ; grant letters of marque and reprisal ; coin money ; emit bills of credit ; make anything but gold and silver coin a tender in payment of debts ; pass any bill of attainder, ex post facto law, or law impairing the obligation of contracts, or grant any title of nobility.

No States shall, without the consent of Congress, lay any imposts or duties on imports or exports, except what may be absolutely necessary for executing its inspection laws : and the net produce of all duties and imposts, laid by any State on imports or exports, shall be for the use of the treasury of the United States ; and all such laws shall be subject to the revision and control of the Congress.

No State shall, without the consent of Congress, lay any duty of tonnage, keep troops or ships of war in time of peace, enter into any agreement or compact with another State, or with a foreign power, or engage in war, unless actually invaded, or in such imminent danger as will not admit of delay.

Article II

Section 1 The executive power shall be vested in a President of the United States of America. He shall hold his office during the term of four years, and, together with the Vice-President, chosen for the same term, be elected as follows:

Each State shall appoint, in such manner as the legislature thereof may direct, a number of electors, equal to the whole number of Senators and Representatives to which the State may be entitled in the Congress; but no Senator or Representative, or person holding an office of trust or profit under the United States, shall be appointed an elector.

The electors shall meet in their respective States, and vote by ballot for two persons, of whom one at least shall not be an inhabitant of the same State with themselves. And they shall make a list of all the persons voted for, and of the number of votes for each, which list they shall sign and certify, and transmit sealed to the seat of government of the United States, directed to the President of the Senate. The President of the Senate shall, in the presence of the Senate and House of Representatives, open all the certificates, and the votes shall then be counted. The person having the greatest number of votes shall be the President, if such number be a majority of the whole number of electors appointed; and if there be more than one who have such majority, and have an equal number of votes, then the House of Representatives shall immediately choose by ballot one of them for President; and if no person have a majority, then from the five highest on the list said house shall in like manner choose the President. But in choosing the President the votes shall be taken by States, the representation from each State having one vote; a quorum for this purpose shall consist of a member or members from two-thirds of the States, and a majority of all the States shall be necessary to a choice. In every case, after the choice of the President, the person having the greatest number of votes of the electors shall be the Vice-President. But if there should remain two or more who have equal votes, the Senate shall choose from them by ballot the Vice-President.

The Congress may determine the time of choosing the electors and the day on which they shall give their votes; which day shall be the same throughout the United States.

No person except a natural-born citizen, *or a citizen of the United States at the time of the adoption of this Constitution*, shall be eligible to the office of President; neither shall any person be eligible to that office who shall not have attained to the age of thirty-five years, and been fourteen years a resident within the United States.

In case of the removal of the President from office or of his death, resignation, or inability to discharge the powers and duties of the said office, the same shall devolve on the Vice-President, and the Congress may by law provide for the case of removal, death, resignation, or inability, both of the President and Vice-President, declaring what officer shall then act as President, and such officer shall act accordingly, until the disability be removed, or a President shall be elected.

The President shall, at stated times, receive for his services a compensation, which shall neither be increased nor diminished during the period for which he shall have been elected, and he shall not receive within that period any other emolument from the United States, or any of them.

Before he enter on the execution of his office, he shall take the following oath or affirmation: — "I do solemnly swear (or affirm) that I will faithfully execute the office of the President of the United States, and will to the best of my ability preserve, protect and defend the Constitution of the United States."

Section 2 The President shall be commander in chief of the army and navy of the United States, and of the militia of the several States, when called into the actual service of the United States; he may require the opinion, in writing, of the principal officer in each of the executive departments, upon any subject relating to the duties of their respective offices, and he shall have power to grant reprieves and pardons for offenses against the United States, except in cases of impeachment.

He shall have power, by and with the advice and consent of the Senate, to make treaties, provided two-thirds of the Senators present concur ; and he shall nominate, and by and with the advice and consent of the Senate, shall appoint ambassadors, other public ministers and consuls, judges of the Supreme Court, and all other officers of the United States, whose appointments are not herein otherwise provided for, and which shall be established by law : but Congress may by law vest the appointment of such inferior officers, as they think proper, in the President alone, in the courts of law, or in the heads of departments.

The President shall have power to fill up all vacancies that may happen during the recess of the Senate, by granting commissions which shall expire at the end of their next session.

Section 3 He shall from time to time give to the Congress information of the state of the Union, and recommend to their consideration such measures as he shall judge necessary and expedient ; he may, on extraordinary occasions, convene both houses, or either of them, and in case of disagreement between them, with respect to the time of adjournment, he may adjourn them to such time as he shall think proper ; he shall receive ambassadors and other public ministers ; he shall take care that the laws be faithfully executed, and shall commission all the officers of the United States.

Section 4 The President, Vice-President and all civil officers of the United States shall be removed from office on impeachment for, and on conviction of, treason, bribery, or other high crimes and misdemeanors.

Article III

Section 1 The judicial power of the United States shall be vested in one Supreme Court, and in such inferior courts as the Congress may from time to time ordain and es-

tablish. The judges, both of the Supreme and inferior courts, shall hold their offices during good behavior, and shall, at stated times, receive for their services a compensation which shall not be diminished during their continuance in office.

Section 2 The judicial power shall extend to all cases, in law and equity, arising under this Constitution, the laws of the United States, and treaties made, or which shall be made, under their authority — to all cases affecting ambassadors, other public ministers and consuls ; — to all cases of admiralty and maritime jurisdiction ; — to controversies to which the United States shall be a party ; — to controversies between two or more States ; — *between a State and citizens of another State* ; — between citizens of different States ; — between citizens of the same State claiming lands under grants of different States, and between a State, or the citizens thereof, and foreign states, citizens or subjects.

In all cases affecting ambassadors, other public ministers and consuls, and those in which a State shall be party, the Supreme Court shall have original jurisdiction. In all the other cases before mentioned, the Supreme Court shall have appellate jurisdiction, both as to law and fact, with such exceptions, and under such regulations, as the Congress shall make.

The trial of all crimes, except in cases of impeachment, shall be by jury ; and such trial shall be held in the State where said crimes shall have been committed : but when not committed within any State, the trial shall be at such place or places as the Congress may by law have directed.

Section 3 Treason against the United States shall consist only in levying war against them, or in adhering to their enemies, giving them aid and comfort. No person shall be convicted of treason unless on the testimony of two witnesses to the same overt act, or on confession in open court.

The Congress shall have power to declare the punishment of treason, but no attainder of treason shall work corruption of blood, or forfeiture except during the life of the person attainted.

Article IV

Section 1 Full faith and credit shall be given in each State to the public acts, records, and judicial proceedings of every other State. And the Congress may by general laws prescribe the manner in which such acts, records, and proceedings shall be proved, and the effect thereof.

Section 2 The citizens of each State shall be entitled to all privileges and immunities of citizens in the several States.

A person charged in any State with treason, felony, or other crime, who shall flee from justice, and be found in another State, shall on demand of the executive authority of the State from which he fled, be delivered up, to be removed to the State having jurisdiction of the crime.

No person held to service or labor in one State, under the laws thereof, escaping into another, shall, in consequence of any law or regulation therein, be discharged from such service or labor, but shall be delivered up on claim of the party to whom such service or labor may be due.

Section 3 New States may be admitted by the Congress into this Union; but no new State shall be formed or erected within the jurisdiction of any other State; nor any State be formed by the junction of two or more States, or parts of States, without the consent of the legislatures of the States concerned as well as of the Congress.

The Congress shall have power to dispose of and make all needful rules and regulations respecting the territory or other property belonging to the United States; and nothing in this Constitution shall be so construed as to prejudice any claims of the United States, or of any particular State.

Section 4 The United States shall guarantee to every State in this Union a republican form of government, and shall protect each of them against invasion; and on application of the legislature, or of the executive (when the legislature cannot be convened), against domestic violence.

Article V

The Congress, whenever two-thirds of both houses shall deem it necessary, shall propose amendments to this Constitution, or, on the application of the legislatures of two-thirds of the several States, shall call a convention for proposing amendments, which, in either case, shall be valid to all intents and purposes, as part of this Constitution, when ratified by the legislatures of three-fourths of the several States, or by conventions in three-fourths thereof, as the one or the other mode of ratification may be proposed by the Congress; provided *that no amendments which may be made prior to the year one thousand eight hundred and eight shall in any manner affect the first and fourth classes in the ninth section of the first article; and* that no State, without its consent, shall be deprived of its equal suffrage in the Senate.

Article VI

All debts contracted and engagements entered into, before the adoption of this Constitution, shall be as valid against the United States under this Constitution, as under the Confederation.

This Constitution, and the laws of the United States which shall be made in pursuance thereof; and all treaties made, or which shall be made, under the authority of the United States, shall be the supreme law of the land; and the judges in every State shall be bound thereby, anything in the Constitution or laws of any State to the contrary notwithstanding.

The Senators and Representatives before mentioned, and the members of the several State legislatures, and all executive and judicial officers, both of the United States and of the several States, shall be bound by oath or affirmation to support this Constitution; but no religious test shall ever be required as a qualification to any office or public trust under the United States.

Article VII

The ratification of the conventions of nine States shall be sufficient for the establishment of this Constitution between the States so ratifying the same.

Done in Convention by the unanimous consent of the States present, the seventeenth day of September in the year of our Lord one thousand seven hundred and eighty-seven and of the Independence of the United States of America the twelfth. In witness whereof we have hereunto subscribed our names.

AMENDMENTS TO THE CONSTITUTION*

Amendment I [1791]

Congress shall make no law respecting an establishment of religion, or prohibiting the free exercise thereof ; or abridging the freedom of speech, or of the press ; or the right of the people peaceably to assemble, and to petition the government for a redress of grievances.

Amendment II [1791]

A well-regulated militia being necessary to the security of a free State, the right of the people to keep and bear arms shall not be infringed.

Amendment III [1791]

No soldier shall, in time of peace, be quartered in any house without the consent of the owner, nor in time of war, but in a manner to be prescribed by law.

Amendment IV [1791]

The right of the people to be secure in their persons, houses, papers, and effects, against unreasonable searches and seizures, shall not be violated, and no warrants shall issue but upon probable cause, supported by oath or affirmation, and particularly describing the place to be searched, and the persons or things to be seized.

Amendment V [1791]

No person shall be held to answer for a capital or otherwise infamous crime, unless on a presentment or indictment of a grand jury, except in cases arising in the land or naval forces, or in the militia, when in actual service in time of war or public danger ; nor shall any person be subject for the same offense to be twice put in jeopardy of life or limb ; nor shall be compelled in any criminal case to be a witness against himself, nor be deprived of life, liberty or property, without due process of law ; nor shall private property be taken for public use without just compensation.

Amendment VI [1791]

In all criminal prosecutions, the accused shall enjoy the right to a speedy and public trial, by an impartial jury of the State and district wherein the crime shall have been committed, which district shall have been previously ascertained by law, and to be informed of the nature and cause of the accusation ; to be confronted with the witnesses against him ; to have compulsory process for obtaining witnesses in his favor, and to have the assistance of counsel for his defense.

Amendment VII [1791]

In suits at common law, where the value in controversy shall exceed twenty dollars, the right of trial by jury shall be preserved, and no fact tried by a jury shall be otherwise reexamined in any court of the United States, than according to the rules of the common law.

Amendment VIII [1791]

Excessive bail shall not be required, nor excessive fines imposed, nor cruel and unusual punishments inflicted.

*The first ten amendments are known as the Bill of Rights.

Amendment IX [1791]

The enumeration in the Constitution, of certain rights, shall not be construed to deny or disparage others retained by the people.

Amendment X [1791]

The powers not delegated to the United States by the Constitution, nor prohibited by it to the States, are reserved to the States respectively, or to the people.

Amendment XI [1798]

The judicial power of the United States shall not be construed to extend to any suit in law or equity, commenced or prosecuted against one of the United States by citizens of another State, or by citizens or subjects of any foreign state.

Amendment XII [1804]

The electors shall meet in their respective States, and vote by ballot for President and Vice-President, one of whom, at least, shall not be an inhabitant of the same State with themselves; they shall name in their ballots the person voted for as President, and in distinct ballots the person voted for as Vice-President, and they shall make distinct lists of all persons voted for as President, and of all persons voted for as Vice-President, and of the number of votes for each, which lists they shall sign and certify, and transmit sealed to the seat of government of the United States, directed to the President of the Senate; — the President of the Senate shall, in the presence of the Senate and House of Representatives, open all the certificates and the votes shall then be counted; — the person having the greatest number of votes for President shall be the President, if such number be a majority of the whole number of electors appointed; and if no person have such majority, then from the persons having the highest numbers not exceeding three on the list of those voted for as President, the House of Representatives shall choose immediately, by ballot, the President. But in choosing the President, the votes shall be taken by States, the representation from each State having one vote; a quorum for this purpose shall consist of a member or members from two-thirds of the States, and a majority of all the States shall be necessary to a choice. And if the House of Representatives shall not choose a President whenever the right of choice shall devolve upon them, before *the fourth day of March* next following, then the Vice-President shall act as President, as in the case of the death or other constitutional disability of the President.

The person having the greatest number of votes as Vice-President shall be the Vice-President, if such number be a majority of the whole number of electors appointed; and if no person have a majority, then from the two highest numbers on the list the Senate shall choose the Vice-President; a quorum for the purpose shall consist of two-thirds of the whole number of Senators, and a majority of the whole number shall be necessary to a choice. But no person constitutionally ineligible to the office of President shall be eligible to that of Vice-President of the United States.

Amendment XIII [1865]

Section 1 Neither slavery nor involuntary servitude, except as a punishment for crime whereof the party shall have been duly convicted, shall exist within the United States, or any place subject to their jurisdiction.

Section 2 Congress shall have power to enforce this article by appropriate legislation.

Amendment XIV [1868]

Section 1 All persons born or naturalized in the United States, and subject to the jurisdiction thereof, are citizens of the United States and of the State wherein they reside. No State shall make or enforce any law which shall abridge the privileges or immunities of citizens of the United States; nor shall any State deprive any person of life, liberty, or property, without due process of law; nor deny to any person within its jurisdiction the equal protection of the laws.

Section 2   Representatives shall be apportioned among the several States according to their respective numbers, counting the whole number of persons in each State, excluding Indians not taxed. But when the right to vote at any election for the choice of Electors for President and Vice-President of the United States, Representatives in Congress, the executive and judicial officers of a State, or the members of the legislature thereof, is denied to any of the male inhabitants of such State, being twenty-one years of age and citizens of the United States, or in any way abridged, except for participation in rebellion, or other crime, the basis of representation therein shall be reduced in the proportion which the number of such male citizens shall bear to the whole number of male citizens twenty-one years of age in such State.

Section 3   No person shall be a Senator or Representative in Congress, or Elector of President and Vice-President, or hold any office, civil or military, under the United States, or under any State, who, having previously taken an oath, as a member of Congress, or as an officer of the United States, or as a member of any State legislature, or as an executive or judicial officer of any State, to support the Constitution of the United States, shall have engaged in insurrection or rebellion against the same, or given aid or comfort to the enemies thereof. Congress may, by a vote of two-thirds of each house, remove such disability.

Section 4   The validity of the public debt of the United States, authorized by law, including debts incurred for payment of pensions and bounties for services in suppressing insurrection or rebellion, shall not be questioned. But neither the United States nor any State shall assume or pay any debt or obligation incurred in aid of insurrection or rebellion against the United States, or any claim for the loss of emancipation of any slave ; but all such debts, obligations, and claims shall be held illegal and void.

Section 5   The Congress shall have power to enforce, by appropriate legislation, the provisions of this article.

Amendment XV [1870]

Section 1   The right of citizens of the United States to vote shall not be denied or abridged by the United States or by any State on account of race, color, or previous condition of servitude.

Section 2   The Congress shall have power to enforce this article by appropriate legislation.

Amendment XVI [1913]

The Congress shall have power to lay and collect taxes on incomes, from whatever source derived, without apportionment among the several States, and without regard to any census or enumeration.

Amendment XVII [1913]

Section 1   The Senate of the United States shall be composed of two Senators from each State, elected by the people thereof, for six years ; and each Senator shall have one vote. The electors in each State shall have the qualifications requisite for electors of [voters for] the most numerous branch of the State legislatures.

Section 2   When vacancies happen in the representation of any State in the Senate, the executive authority of such State shall issue writs of election to fill such vacancies : Provided that the legislature of any State may empower the executive thereof to make temporary appointments until the people fill the vacancies by election as the legislature may direct.

Section 3   The amendment shall not be so construed as to affect the election or term of any Senator chosen before it becomes valid as part of the Constitution.

Amendment XVIII [1919]

Section 1   After one year from the ratification of this article the manufacture, sale, or transportation of intoxicating liquors within, the importation thereof into, or the exportation thereof from the United States and all territory subject to the jurisdiction thereof, for beverage purposes, is hereby prohibited.

Section 2   The Congress and the several States shall have concurrent power to enforce this article by appropriate legislation.

Section 3   This article shall be inoperative unless it shall have been ratified as an amendment to the Constitution by the legislatures of the several States, as provided by the Constitution, within seven years from the date of the submission thereof to the States by the Congress.

Amendment XIX [1920]

Section 1   The right of citizens of the United States to vote shall not be denied or abridged by the United States or by any State on account of sex.

Section 2   The Congress shall have power to enforce this article by appropriate legislation.

Amendment XX [1933]

Section 1   The terms of the President and Vice-President shall end at noon on the 20th day of January, and the terms of Senators and Representatives at noon on the 3d day of January, of the years in which such terms would have ended if this article had not been ratified; and the terms of their successors shall then begin.

Section 2   The Congress shall assemble at least once in every year, and such meeting shall begin at noon on the 3d day of January, unless they shall by law appoint a different day.

Section 3   If, at the time fixed for the beginning of the term of the President, the President-elect shall have died, the Vice-President-elect shall become President. If a President shall not have been chosen before the time fixed for the beginning of his term, or if the President-elect shall have failed to qualify, then the President-elect shall act as President until a President shall have qualified, and the Congress may by law provide for the case wherein neither a President-elect nor a Vice-President-elect shall have

qualified, declaring who shall then act as President, or the manner in which one who is to act shall be selected, and such persons shall act accordingly until a President or Vice-President shall have qualified.

Section 4   The Congress may by law provide for the case of the death of any of the persons from whom the House of Representatives may choose a President whenever the right of choice shall have devolved upon them, and for the case of the death of any of the persons from whom the Senate may choose a Vice-President whenever the right of choice shall have devolved upon them.

Section 5   Sections 1 and 2 shall take effect on the 15th day of October following the ratification of this article.

Section 6   This article shall be inoperative unless it shall have been ratified as an amendment to the Constitution by the legislatures of three-fourths of the several States within seven years from the date of its submission.

Amendment XXI [1933]

Section 1   The eighteenth article of amendment to the Constitution of the United States is hereby repealed.

Section 2   The transportation or importation into any State, Territory, or Possession of the United States for delivery or use therein of intoxicating liquors, in violation of the laws thereof, is hereby prohibited.

Section 3   This article shall be inoperative unless it shall have been ratified as an amendment to the Constitution by conventions in the several States, as provided in the Constitution, within seven years from the date of submission thereof to the States by the Congress.

Amendment XXII [1951]

Section 1   No person shall be elected to the office of President more than twice, and no person who has held the office of President, or acted as President, for more than two years of a term to which some other person was elected President shall be elected to the office of President more than once. But this article shall not apply to any person holding the office of President when this article was proposed by the Congress, and shall not prevent any person who may be holding the office of President, or acting as President, during the term within which this article becomes operative from holding the office of President or acting as President during the remainder of such term.

Section 2   This article shall be inoperative unless it shall have been ratified as an amendment to the Constitution by the legislatures of three-fourths of the several States within seven years from the date of its submission to the States by the Congress.

Amendment XXIII [1961]

Section 1   The District constituting the seat of Government of the United States shall appoint in such manner as the Congress may direct:

A number of electors of President and Vice-President equal to the whole number of Senators and Representatives in Congress to which the District would be entitled if it were a State, but in no event more than the least populous State; they shall be in addition to those appointed by the States, but they shall be considered for the purposes of the election of President and Vice-President, to be electors appointed by a State; and they shall meet in the District and perform such duties as provided by the twelfth article of amendment.

Section 2   The Congress shall have the power to enforce this article by appropriate legislation.

Amendment XXIV [1964]

Section 1   The right of citizens of the United States to vote in any primary or other election for President or Vice-President, for electors for President or Vice-President, or for Senator or Representative in Congress, shall not be denied or abridged by the United States or any State by reason of failure to pay any poll tax or other tax.

Section 2   The Congress shall have the power to enforce this article by appropriate legislation.

Amendment XXV [1967]

Section 1   In case of the removal of the President from office or of his death or resignation, the Vice-President shall become President.

Section 2   Whenever there is a vacancy in the office of the Vice-President, the President shall nominate a Vice-President who shall take office upon confirmation by a majority vote of both houses of Congress.

Section 3   Whenever the President transmits to the President pro tempore of the Senate and the Speaker of the House of Representatives his written declaration that he is unable to discharge the powers and duties of his office, and until he transmits to them a written declaration to the contrary, such powers and duties shall be discharged by the Vice-President as Acting President.

Section 4   Whenever the Vice-President and a majority of either the principal officers of the executive departments or of such other body as Congress may by law provide, transmit to the President pro tempore of the Senate and the Speaker of the House of Representatives their written declaration that the President is unable to discharge the powers and duties of his office, the Vice-President shall immediately assume the powers and duties of the office as Acting President.

Thereafter, when the President transmits to the President pro tempore of the Senate and the Speaker of the House of Representatives his written declaration that no inability exists, he shall resume the powers and duties of his office unless the Vice-President and a majority of either the principal officers of the executive department[s] or of such other body as Congress may by law provide, transmit within four days to the President pro tempore of the Senate and the Speaker of the House of Representatives their written declaration that the President is unable to discharge the powers and duties of his office. Thereupon Congress shall decide the issue, assembling within forty-eight hours for that purpose if not in session. If the Congress, within twenty-one days after receipt of the latter written declaration, or, if Congress is not in session, within twenty-one days after Congress is required to assemble, determines by two-thirds vote of both Houses that the President is unable to discharge the powers and duties of his office, the Vice-President shall continue to discharge

the same as Acting President; otherwise, the President shall resume the powers and duties of his office.

Amendment XXVI [1971]

Section 1 The right of citizens of the United States, who are eighteen years of age or older, to vote shall not be denied or abridged by the United States or by any State on account of age.

    Section 2 The Congress shall have power to enforce this article by appropriate legislation.

PRESIDENTIAL ELECTIONS

Year	Candidates	Parties	% of Popular Vote*†	Electoral Vote‡	% Voter Participation†
1789	GEORGE WASHINGTON	No party designations		69	
	John Adams			34	
	Other candidates			35	
1792	GEORGE WASHINGTON	No party designations		132	
	John Adams			77	
	George Clinton			50	
	Other candidates			5	
1796	JOHN ADAMS	Federalist		71	
	Thomas Jefferson	Democratic-Republican		68	
	Thomas Pinckney	Federalist		59	
	Aaron Burr	Democratic-Republican		30	
	Other candidates			48	
1800	THOMAS JEFFERSON	Democratic-Republican		73	
	Aaron Burr	Democratic-Republican		73	
	John Adams	Federalist		65	
	Charles C. Pinckney	Federalist		64	
	John Jay	Federalist		1	
1804	THOMAS JEFFERSON	Democratic-Republican		162	
	Charles C. Pinckney	Federalist		14	
1808	JAMES MADISON	Democratic-Republican		122	
	Charles C. Pinckney	Federalist		47	
	George Clinton	Democratic-Republican		6	
1812	JAMES MADISON	Democratic-Republican		128	
	DeWitt Clinton	Federalist		89	
1816	JAMES MONROE	Democratic-Republican		183	
	Rufus King	Federalist		34	
1820	JAMES MONROE	Democratic-Republican		231	
	John Quincy Adams	Independent Republican		1	

Year	Candidates	Parties	% of Popular Vote*†	Electoral Vote‡	% Voter Participation†
1824	JOHN QUINCY ADAMS	Democratic-Republican	30.5	84	26.9
	Andrew Jackson	Democratic-Republican	43.1	99	
	Henry Clay	Democratic-Republican	13.2	37	
	William H. Crawford	Democratic-Republican	13.1	41	
1828	ANDREW JACKSON	Democratic	56.0	178	57.6
	John Quincy Adams	National Republican	44.0	83	
1832	ANDREW JACKSON	Democratic	54.5	219	55.4
	Henry Clay	National Republican	37.5	49	
	William Wirt	Anti-Masonic	8.0	7	
	John Floyd	Democratic		11	
1836	MARTIN VAN BUREN	Democratic	50.9	170	57.8
	William H. Harrison	Whig		73	
	Hugh L. White	Whig		26	
	Daniel Webster	Whig	49.1	14	
	W. P. Mangum	Whig		11	
1840	WILLIAM H. HARRISON	Whig	53.1	234	80.2
	Martin Van Buren	Democratic	46.9	60	
1844	JAMES K. POLK	Democratic	49.6	170	78.9
	Henry Clay	Whig	48.1	105	
	James G. Birney	Liberty	2.3	0	
1848	ZACHARY TAYLOR	Whig	47.4	163	72.7
	Lewis Cass	Democratic	42.5	127	
	Martin Van Buren	Free-Soil	10.1	0	
1852	FRANKLIN PIERCE	Democratic	50.9	254	69.6
	Winfield Scott	Whig	44.1	42	
	John P. Hale	Free-Soil	5.0	0	
1856	JAMES BUCHANAN	Democratic	45.3	174	78.9
	John C. Frémont	Republican	33.1	114	
	Millard Fillmore	American	21.6	8	
1860	ABRAHAM LINCOLN	Republican	39.8	180	81.2
	Stephen A. Douglas	Democratic	29.5	12	
	John C. Breckinridge	Democratic	18.1	72	
	John Bell	Constitutional Union	12.6	39	
1864	ABRAHAM LINCOLN	Republican	55.0	212	73.8
	George B. McClellan	Democratic	45.0	21	
1868	ULYSSES S. GRANT	Republican	52.7	214	78.1
	Horatio Seymour	Democratic	47.3	80	
1872	ULYSSES S. GRANT	Republican	55.6	286	71.3
	Horace Greeley	Democratic	44.0	0§	
1876	RUTHERFORD B. HAYES	Republican	48.0	185	81.8
	Samuel J. Tilden	Democratic	51.0	184	
1880	JAMES A. GARFIELD	Republican	48.5	214	79.4
	Winfield S. Hancock	Democratic	48.1	155	
	James B. Weaver	Greenback-Labor	3.4	0	
1884	GROVER CLEVELAND	Democratic	48.5	219	77.5
	James G. Blaine	Republican	48.2	182	

Year	Candidates	Parties	% of Popular Vote*†	Electoral Vote‡	% Voter Participation†
1888	BENJAMIN HARRISON	Republican	47.9	233	79.3
	Grover Cleveland	Democratic	48.6	168	
1892	GROVER CLEVELAND	Democratic	46.0	277	74.7
	Benjamin Harrison	Republican	43.0	145	
	James B. Weaver	Populist	8.5	22	
1896	WILLIAM McKINLEY	Republican	51.1	271	79.3
	William J. Bryan	Democratic	46.7	176	
1900	WILLIAM McKINLEY	Republican	51.7	292	73.2
	William J. Bryan	Democratic; Populist	45.5	155	
1904	THEODORE ROOSEVELT	Republican	56.4	336	65.2
	Alton B. Parker	Democratic	37.6	140	
	Eugene V. Debs	Socialist	3.0	0	
1908	WILLIAM H. TAFT	Republican	51.6	321	65.4
	William J. Bryan	Democratic	43.1	162	
	Eugene V. Debs	Socialist	2.8	0	
1912	WOODROW WILSON	Democratic	41.9	435	58.8
	Theodore Roosevelt	Progressive	27.4	88	
	William H. Taft	Republican	23.2	8	
	Eugene V. Debs	Socialist	6.0	0	
1916	WOODROW WILSON	Democratic	49.4	277	61.6
	Charles E. Hughes	Republican	46.2	254	
	Allan L. Benson	Socialist	3.2	0	
1920	WARREN G. HARDING	Republican	60.4	404	49.2
	James M. Cox	Democratic	34.2	127	
	Eugene V. Debs	Socialist	3.4	0	
1924	CALVIN COOLIDGE	Republican	54.0	382	48.9
	John W. Davis	Democratic	28.8	136	
	Robert M. La Follette	Progressive	16.6	13	
1928	HERBERT C. HOOVER	Republican	58.2	444	56.9
	Alfred E. Smith	Democratic	40.9	87	
1932	FRANKLIN D. ROOSEVELT	Democratic	57.4	472	56.9
	Herbert C. Hoover	Republican	39.7	59	
1936	FRANKLIN D. ROOSEVELT	Democratic	60.8	523	61.0
	Alfred M. Landon	Republican	36.5	8	
1940	FRANKLIN D. ROOSEVELT	Democratic	54.8	449	62.5
	Wendell L. Willkie	Republican	44.8	82	
1944	FRANKLIN D. ROOSEVELT	Democratic	53.5	432	55.9
	Thomas E. Dewey	Republican	46.0	99	
1948	HARRY S. TRUMAN	Democratic	49.5	303	53.0
	Thomas E. Dewey	Republican	45.1	189	
	J. Strom Thurmond	States' Rights	2.4	39	
	Henry A. Wallace	Progressive	2.4	0	
1952	DWIGHT D. EISENHOWER	Republican	55.1	442	63.3
	Adlai E. Stevenson	Democratic	44.4	89	
1956	DWIGHT D. EISENHOWER	Republican	57.4	457	60.6
	Adlai E. Stevenson	Democratic	42.0	73	

Year	Candidates	Parties	% of Popular Vote*†	Electoral Vote‡	% Voter Participation†
1960	JOHN F. KENNEDY	Democratic	49.7	303	64.0
	Richard M. Nixon	Republican	49.6	219	
	Harry F. Byrd	Independent	0.7	15	
1964	LYNDON B. JOHNSON	Democratic	61.1	486	61.7
	Barry M. Goldwater	Republican	38.5	52	
1968	RICHARD M. NIXON	Republican	43.4	301	60.6
	Hubert H. Humphrey	Democratic	42.7	191	
	George C. Wallace	American Independent	13.5	46	
1972	RICHARD M. NIXON	Republican	60.7	520	55.5
	George S. McGovern	Democratic	37.5	17	
1976	JIMMY CARTER	Democratic	50.0	297	54.3
	Gerald R. Ford	Republican	48.0	240	
1980	RONALD REAGAN	Republican	50.8	489	53.0
	Jimmy Carter	Democratic	41.0	49	
	John B. Anderson	Independent	6.6	0	
1984	RONALD REAGAN	Republican	58.7	525	52.9
	Walter F. Mondale	Democratic	40.6	13	
1988	GEORGE BUSH	Republican	54.0	426	50.1
	Michael Dukakis	Democratic	46.0	111	

*Candidates receiving less than 2.5 percent of the popular vote have been omitted. Hence the percentage of popular vote may not total 100 percent.
†Prior to 1824, most presidential electors were chosen by state legislators rather than by popular vote.
‡Before the Twelfth Amendment was passed in 1804, the electoral college voted for two presidential candidates; the runner-up became the vice-president.
§Greeley died before the electoral college met. His votes were divided among four other candidates.

Credits

Index

Abolitionism, 65, 134–135, 226–227, 247, 265–268
Abortion, 225
Adams, Abigail, 130
Adams, Charles, 192
Adams, Henry, 347
Adams, John, 94–96, 98–99, 101, 128, 133, 163–166
Adams, John Quincy, 165–166, 185–186, 188–189, 253
Adams, Samuel, 96–99, 127
Adams-Onis treaty (1819), 176, 274–275
Africa, 8, 10, 16–17, 45–52
Afro-American culture, 49–50
Agriculture
    antebellum, 227–229, 233–234
    Civil War changes to the, 323–324
    colonial, 69–70, 72–73, 104–106
    depression and, 125–126, 144–146
    early evolution of, 3–4, 9
    family farms, 32, 69–70
    on the frontier, 282–283
    improved productivity, 194–195
    in the North, 69–70, 194–196
    preindustrial, 194–196
    in pre-Revolutionary era, 104–106
    protest movements, 144–146
    in the Reconstruction era, 341–342
    in the Revolutionary era, 104–106, 125–126, 144–146
    sharecropping and tenancy, 341–342
    in the South, 72–73, 195–196, 233–234, 341–342
    technology, 227–229
    tobacco, 19, 23–27, 72–73, 125–126
Alabama, 234–236, 305, 311
Alabama (the ship), 317
Albany, New York, 35
Alcohol, 202, 263–264
Alcott, Bronson, 262
Algonquian, 34
Alien Act of 1798, 164–165, 174
Alien Enemies Act, 165
Allen, Ethan, 100
Allen, Richard, 208
Allston, Adele Petigru, 240–241, 331–332
Allston, Elizabeth, 331–332
Allston, Robert Francis Withers, 239–240, 243, 331–332

Almshouses, 76, 203–204
American Anti-Slavery Society, 266
American Colonization Society, 208
American Slavery As It Is (Weld), 266
American Temperance Society, 263
Ames, Fisher, 160–161, 163
Amherst, Jeffrey, 91
Anaconda Plan, 314
Anderson, Robert, 307
Andros, Sir Edmund, 55
Anthony, Susan B., 269, 320, 340
Antietam, Battle of, 315, 320
Anti-Federalists, 149–151, 167–168
Archaic era, 3–4
Argentina, 185–186
Arkansas, 234–236, 311–312, 316
Armed forces
    Civil War, 320
        casualties, 315–316, 326, 328, 333
        military strategies, 314–316, 321–323, 326–327
        naval warfare, 316–317, 326
        recruitment of, 312–313, 318–319
    Confederate army, 312, 318–319, 321–323
    Confederate navy, 316–317
    draft, 318–319
    in Jefferson's administration, 174
    militia, 119–120, 139–140, 145–146
    Navy, 126, 316–317, 326
    Revolutionary War, 119, 126
        casualties, 120–121
        grievances of, 139–140
        military operations in the, 113–117
    in the west, 6, 69
Arms, right to bear, 156
Arnold, Benedict, 121
Art, 9
Articles of Confederation, 112–113, 139, 146, 148
Artisans, 75–76, 103–104, 201
Assembly, 83–85, 132–133
Astor, John Jacob, 193
Asylums, 264–265
Atchison, David, 300–301
Atlantic basin trading system, 75
Austin, Stephen F., 275
Austrian Succession, War of, 90
Aztec empire, 14–16

Backus, Isaac, 133–134
Bacon, Nathaniel, 53–54, 57
Bacon's Rebellion, 53–54
Ballou, Adin, 261
Baltimore, Maryland, 184–185
Bank(s)
    Civil War changes to the, 324
    during depressions, 197
    foreign, national debt held by, 142
    Jackson's opposition to, 256–258
    land, 80
    of North America, 144
    preindustrial, 193–194
    during the Reconstruction era, 347
    silver, 80
    state, 197
    of the United States, 158–159, 187, 197, 256–258
Banking Act(s), 324, 328
Barlow, Joel, 187
Barton, Clara, 326
Beauregard, P. G. T., 307, 314
Beecher, Catharine, 224, 268
Beecher, Henry Ward, 300
Beecher, Lyman, 265
Belcher, Andrew, 60, 76–77
Bell, John, 305
Berkeley, Sir William, 53
Berlin, 183
Berlin Decree, 183
Bernard, Francis, 94
Biddle, Nicholas, 256–257
Bill of Rights, 156
Birth control, 225, 268
Birthrate, 202
Black(s)
    in the armed forces
        in the Civil War, 320–321, 323
        in the Revolutionary War, 123–124
    citizenship for, 129–130, 337–338
    culture, 245–246
    education, 227, 342–343
    emancipation and, 319–321
    free
        black codes, 335–336
        Freedmen's Bureau and, 340–341
        in Philadelphia, 226–227
        poverty among, 248–249
        in Revolutionary era, 129–130, 134–135

Black(s) (continued)
    in the Spanish colonies, 67–68
    in Virginia, 44–45
    Great Compromise and, 148–149
    in politics, 343–344
    population increase, 63
    property ownership by, 203, 334–
        343
    in Reconstruction era, 334–343
    refuge among the Indians, 124
    religion, 51–52, 208, 244–245, 342–
        343
    self-help institutions for, 342–343
    social structure, 51–52, 208
    westward expansion by, 280
Black Christianity, 244–245
Black Hawk, 289
Black Pioneers, 124
Blackwell, Elizabeth, 326
Blackwell, Emily, 326
Bloodworth, Timothy, 138–139
Boardinghouses, company, 219
Board of Trade, 89
Bolivia, 16
Booth, John Wilkes, 328–329
Boston, Massachusetts
    colonial, 70, 75–76, 79–80, 96–97,
        99
    impressment riot of 1747 in, 83
    Revolutionary War and, 113–
        114
Boston massacre, 96
Boston radicals, 97
Boston Tea Party, 96, 98
Boucher, Jonathan, 128
Bowdoin, James, 145
Bowie, Jim, 276
Braddock, Edward, 90–91
Brant, Joseph (Tayadaneega), 117–
    118
Brazil, 14, 16–17
Breck, Samuel, 218, 223–224
Breckenridge, John, 173, 305
Bronson, Arthur, 215, 228
Brook Farm, 262
Brooks, Preston, 301
Brown, David, 154–155
Brown, John, 301, 304
Buchanan, James, 297, 299–300,
    303
Burgoyne, John, 114, 121
Burke, Edmund, 96
Burke, Thomas, 204–205
Burr, Aaron, 166
Butler, Andrew, 301
Butler, Charles, 215, 228

Cahokia, 4–5
Calhoun, John C., 184, 188–189, 241
    Free-Soiler(s) opposition by, 293–
        294
California, 68–69, 277–278, 284, 289–
    290, 294–295, 316
California Trail, 280–282
Calvert, George, 26
Calvin, John, 13
Calvinist concept, 77
Canning, George, 185
Cannon, James, 104
Capital investments, 215
Capitalism, merchant, 196–199
Carnegie, Andrew, 324
Carolina colonies, 35–40, 180. See
    also South Carolina
Carpenter, Arthur, 310–311, 318
Cartier, Jacques, 18
Cash, Wilbur, 333–334
Cass, Lewis, 272–273, 276, 294, 297
Catholic immigrants, 299
Catholic Reformation, 13–14
Champlain, Samuel de, 34
Charles I, King of England, 28, 33
Charles II, King of England, 55
Charleston, South Carolina, 115, 307
Chase, Salmon P., 324
Chase, Samuel, 173
Cherokee, 177, 179–181
    Andrew Jackson and, 254–255
    changes in tribal organization, 66–
        67
    in the Revolutionary War, 117–118
    Seven Years' War and, 91
Chesapeake Bay, 2–3, 23–27, 72–73,
    117. See also Virginia
Chesapeake-Leopard affair, 183
Chesnut, Mary Boykin, 240–241
Cheves, Langdon, 184
Chickasaw, 177
Childbirth, 71–72
Children, 64–65, 72, 131, 224–225
    mixed-race, 51–52, 67
Chile, 185–186
Chippewa, 140
Choctaw, 177
Cincinnati, Ohio, 221–222
Cities
    class structure in, 223
    colonial, 74–77, 103–104
    family life in, 223–227
    on the frontier, 286
    growth of, 222–223, 236, 238
    housing in, 224
    in pre-Revolutionary era, 103–104

Civil Rights Act of 1964, 339
Civil rights movement
    school desegregation, 267
Civil War. See also Reconstruction
    era
    accomplishments of, 328–329
    balance of resources in the, 312
    battles of, 314–316, 320–322, 326.
        See also specific battle
    casualties, 315–316, 326–328, 333
    causes and events leading to, 302–
        307
    crisis at the end of the, 333–336
    in the East, 314–315
    economy and the, 317–318, 324–
        325
    Fort Sumter attack, 306–307
    Illinois debates and, 303–304, 306
    impressment during, 323, 327
    life on the home front, 324–325
    military strategies, 314–316, 321–
        323, 326–327
    Native Americans in the, 315–316
    naval warfare, 316–317, 326
    northern victory, 324, 326–327
    organizing for the, 311–313
    political dissension during the, 319
    race relations and the, 325
    Southern reconstruction, 328
    troops, 312–313, 318–321, 323
    in the West, 315–317
    women and the, 324–326
Clark, Williams, 176
Clay, Henry, 184, 188–189, 253, 256–
    257, 294–295
Clay's Omnibus Bill, 294–295
Clinton, George, 147
Clocks, 201, 218
Clothing, 218
Coercive Acts, 98–99
Colleges and universities
    in the preindustrial era, 206–207
Colombia, 185–186
Colonies. See also Revolutionary War
    agriculture in, 69–70, 72–73, 104–
        106
    artisan's of the, 75–76, 103–104
    Colonies, 93, 95–98
    currency dispute in, 80
    Dutch, 34–35
    economy, 76–77, 80, 92–93, 125–
        127
    English, 18–19, 54–55, 84, 89–91,
        95–96
    factional conflict in, 102–103
    family life in, 24, 26–27, 71–74

government in, 81–83, 102–103
immigrants, 64–65
industry, in the southern, 72–73
Native Americans and the, 5–6, 8,
     23–24, 35–37, 180
New England, 27–32, 69–70
nonimportation movement, 96,
     103–104
period of colonization, 34–43
politics, 56–57, 81–85, 103, 131–134
Quaker, 38–41
Revolutionary War and, 100–106
Seven Years' War and, 91–93
slavery in the
     English colonies, 45–52, 72–73
     French colonies, 67–68
     Revolutionary era, 134–135
     Spanish colonies, 67–68
social structure in, 54, 56, 72–77
suffrage in, 82–83, 129
trade in the, 75
urban society, 74–77, 103–104
women in, 6, 8, 26–27, 30, 70–72
Colorado, 176
Columbus, Christopher, 11–12
Committee of Correspondence, 97
Common Sense (Paine), 100–102
Commonwealth period, 33
Communications
     newspapers, 127
     in preindustrial America, 200
Compromise of 1850, 294–297, 306
Compromise of 1877, 348
Concord, Massachusetts, 99
Condict, John, 130
Confederate States of America, 305–
     307, 313, 317–319
Confederation Congress, 139–143
Confederation of New England, 33
Congress, 140–141, 148–149
Congressional reconstruction, 336–
     340
Connecticut, 29, 31, 35, 52–53, 79–
     80, 131, 133, 152
Conscription Act (1862), 323
Constitution
     confederate, 303, 306
     federal
          amendments to, 166, 269
               Fifteenth, 338–340, 348
               First, 135
               Fourteenth, 337, 339–340, 348
               Nineteenth, 269
               Thirteenth, 336, 339
               Twelfth, 166
          Grand Convention and, 146–149

Great Compromise and, 148–149
     ratification of, 149–152
Lecompton, 303, 306
state, 131–133
Continental Congress, 98–100, 112–
     113
Convention of 1818, 273
Copperheads, 319
Corn production, 234
Cornwallis, Charles, 112, 116–117
Coronado, Francisco Vásquez de, 17
Corporations, 193–194
Cortés, Hernando, 14–16
Cosby, William, 85
Cotton gin, 195, 234
Cotton production, 195–196, 233–
     236, 317, 323, 342
Cowpens, South Carolina, 116
Crady, Timothy, 204–205
Crandall, Prudence, 227
Crawford, William, 188–189
Credit, 142, 144, 156–159
Creek, 66–67, 117–118, 140–141, 177,
     181–182
Crockett, Davy, 276
Cuba, 298–299
Currency, 127, 318
     Specie Circular of 1836, 257
Currency Act, 93

Daughters of Liberty, 131
Davis, Jefferson, 305, 313–314, 319,
     323, 327, 338
Davis, John, 154
Debt
     national, 142, 157–159, 174–175
     Revolutionary War, 135–136, 142,
          157
     state, federal assumption of, 157
Declaration of Independence, 100
Declaration of Sentiments, 268–269
Deerfield, Massachusetts, 59
De Grasse, Comte, 117
Delancy, James, 104
Delaney, Martin, 249, 267
Delaware, 35, 133, 152, 177, 312
Delaware tribes, 39–41, 140–141
Democratic-Republican societies,
     Citizen Genêt and the, 162–
     163
Depression
     agriculture and, 144–146
     in the antebellum South, 236
     of 1819, 197, 199, 204
     of 1893–1897
          banks and, 197

of 1837, 257–258, 264
post-Seven Years' War, 92–93
in Reconstruction era, 347
Van Buren and, 256–258
Derby, E. H., 193
Desegregation
     in schools, 267
De Soto, Hernando, 17
Dickinson, John, 112
Diet, 202, 242–243
Disease, 2, 15–16, 24, 26–27, 37–38,
     67, 120, 122, 202–203
Divorce, 207
Dix, Dorothea, 264–265, 326
Douglas, Stephen, 276, 295, 297–298,
     303–306
Douglass, Frederick, 232–234, 300
     abolitionism and, 248–249, 266–267
     election of 1860 and, 292
     Fugitive Slave Act and, 296
     on land ownership, 248–249, 266–
          267
     on the life of slaves, 243, 245–246,
          248–249
     Lincoln and, 304–305, 307, 320
     in Reconstruction era, 343, 348
     Revolutionary War and, 321
Draft, 318–319
Dragging Canoe, 117
Drake, Francis, 18
Dred Scott v. *Sanford*, 302–303, 306
Duane, James, 98–99
Due process of law, right to, 156
Dunmore, Lord, 124
Dutch, 18, 34–35, 56
Dwight, Timothy, 187, 207

Eagleton, George and Ethie, 310–
     311, 321, 327–328
East India Company, 97–98
Economy and economics
     Alexander Hamilton's policy of,
          156–159
     Civil War, 312, 317–318, 323–325,
          327
     colonial, 76–77, 80, 92–93, 125–127
     credit crisis with England, 144
     development of, 186–187, 213, 216,
          234
     government promotion of, 215
     impact of slavery on, 236, 238
     preindustrial, 192–194
     under President Jackson, 256–258
     under President Lincoln, 312, 317–
          318, 324
     under President Madison, 157

• • •

Economy and economics (continued)
  under President Washington, 158–159
  Revolutionary War and, 125–127, 135–136
  Seven Years' War effect on, 92–93
Education
  blacks and, 227, 342–343
  desegregation in schools, 267
  economic growth and, 216
  Native Americans and, 179
  in the preindustrial era, 206–207
  public schools, 206, 216, 267, 344
  Puritan, 30, 33
  reforms, 264–265
  social values and, 216
  women and, 207
Edwards, Jonathan, 79
Elbridge, Gerry, 164
Electoral process, 149
Eliot, John, 32
Elizabeth I, Queen of England, 18
Elskwatawa, 181
Emancipation Proclamation (1863), 319–321
Embargo Act of 1807, 183–184, 196
Emerson, Ralph Waldo, 260, 262, 296
Emigrants' Guide to Oregon and California (Hastings), 274
Emlen, Anne, 130
Environment, 5–6
Erie Canal, 214–215, 222
Essay Concerning Human Understanding (Locke), 77
Europe and Europeans, 5–6, 10–11
  investors, 215
  wars in, 58–60, 192–194
Exposition and Protest (Calhoun), 255

Factories, 217–218, 221–222, 265
Fallen Timbers, Battle of, 181–182
Family life
  Africans, 8–9
  colonial, 71–74
  frontier, 282–284
  Mormon, 284–286
  Native American, 6, 8
  plantation, 74
  in preindustrial communities, 201–204
  urban, 223–227
Federal Indian policy, 177–179
Federalist Papers, 150
Federal-Republican, 184–185

Ferdinand, King of Spain, 11
Feudal system, in Europe, 10–11
Fillmore, Millard, 295, 299–300
Finney, Charles G., 259–260
Fishing industry, 125
Florida, 305, 311
  Spain and, 17, 68–69, 141–142, 176
Forbes, John, 91
Force Acts, 345–346
Force Bill of 1833, 256
Foreign policy
  of Jeffersonians, 182–183
Fort Atkinson, 176
Fort Donelson, 316
Fort Duquesne, 91
Fort Henry, 316
Fort Laramie Council, 289
Fort Laramie Treaty, 289
Fort Nelson, 182
Fort Orange, 35
Fort Snelling, 176
Fort Sumter, 306–307
Fort Ticonderoga, 91, 100
France, 11–12
  fur trade, 34
  inland empire, 67–68
  Louisiana Purchase and, 175–176
  at Peace of Utrecht, 59–61
  in Revolutionary War, 117
  Revolution in, 161–166
  Seven Year War and, 89–93
  slavery in colonies, 67–68
  wars with England, 58–60, 161, 192–193
  XYZ affair in, 164
Franklin, Benjamin, 70, 77–78, 99–101, 146–149
Freedmen's Bureau, 337, 340–341
Free-Soiler(s), 293–294, 299–301
Frelinghuysen, Theodore, 79
Frémont, John C., 299–300, 305
French and Indian War, 89–93
French Revolution, 161–166
Frontier, 140–142, 228–229
Fugitive Slave Act of 1793, 294–296
Fulton, Robert, 200–201
Furman, Gabriel, 204–205
Fur trade, 34, 66–67, 179, 273

Gadsden, James, 298
Gadsden Purchase (1853), 274
Gage, Thomas, 98–99
Gag rule, 267
Galloway, Joseph, 98–99
Gama, Vasco da, 11–12
Gardiner, John, 207

Garnet, Henry Highland, 266
Garrison, William Lloyd, 243, 266–267
Gaspee, 97
Genêt, Citizen Edmund, 162–163
George III, King of England, 95–96, 114
Georgia, 133, 135, 152, 180, 234–236, 305, 311
German(s), 63–64, 114, 121–123, 213–214
Gerry, Elbridge, 146–149
Gettysburg, Battle of, 321–322
Gibson, Thomas and Mary, 272–273
Giles, William Branch, 159, 173
Girard, Stephen, 193
Gleaner, The (Murray), 207
Glorious Revolution, 55–56
Gold, 280, 283–284, 288–290
Gordon, William, 129
Gould, Jay, 346–347
Government
  colonial, 81–83, 102–103
  credit, 142, 144
  in District of Colombia, 157–158, 171
  national, 148–149
  post-Revolutionary War, 131–133
  power, 102–103, 131–132, 148–151
  reform, 146–149
Governors, 83–84
Graft, 346–347
Graham, Sylvester, 264
Grand Convention, 146–149
Grant, Ulysses S., 316, 322, 326, 338, 345–347
Great Awakening, 77, 79–81, 205–206, 259–260
Great Britain (England)
  colonies, 54–55, 89–91, 93, 95–98
  corn laws, 196
  credit crisis with, 144
  Dutch colonies defeated by, 35
  Dutch Protestants, aid to, 18
  explorations of, 11, 17–18
  first colonization by, 18–19
  French Revolution and, 161
  Jay's Treaty and, 163
  navy, 161–163, 183–184
  occupation in America, 96, 99, 114–115, 121–122, 163, 183–184, 273, 279
  Peace of Utrecht and, 59–61
  post-Revolutionary possessions, 142–143
  Protestant-Catholic conflict in, 18

in Revolutionary War, 96, 99, 113–119, 123
Seven Years' War and, 91–93
slave trade and, 48
Spanish Armada defeated by, 18
War of 1812 and, 184–185
wars with France, 58–60, 161, 192–193
wars with Spain, 90
Great Compromise, 146, 148
Greeley, Horace, 320, 347
Green, Nathanael, 116, 119
Greenbacks, 318
Green Mountain boys, 100
Grenville, George, 93
Grimké, Sarah, 268–269
Grundy, Felix, 184
Gulf Coast, 141–142
Gwin Land Law (1851), 290

Haiti, 208
Hakluyt, Richard (nephew and uncle), 18
Haldeman, H. R., 86
Hale, Sarah, 224
Hamilton, Alexander, 146–150, 156–159
Hamilton, Andrew, 85
Hamiltonians, 166
Hancock, John, 96–97, 99–100
Handsome Lake, 177
Harmonists, 261
Harpers Ferry, (West) Virginia, 304
Harris, Emily and David, 325–326
Harrison, William Henry, 182, 258–259
Hartford Convention, 185
Harvard College, 30, 81
Hastings, Lanford, 274
Hawthorne, Nathaniel, 260
Hayes, Rutherford B., 347–348
Health, sexuality and, 264
Henry, Patrick, 94–95, 98–99, 101, 147
Henry the Navigator, Prince, 11
Henry VIII, King of England, 14
Hispanic-Americans, 289–290
Hispaniola, 12, 15–16
Hog production, 238–239
Holland Land Company, 199
Holy Alliance, 185
Homespun, 126
Homestead Act, 280, 328
Hopedale, Massachusetts, 261
Hopi, 4
Hopkins, Lemuel, 187

Hopkins, Samuel, 135
Horseshoe Bend, Battle of, 182
Hospitals, Civil War, 326–328
House of Representatives, 149
Housing
    in Chesapeake Bay colonies, 27
    in the middle 1800s, 224
    in preindustrial America, 202
    in Puritan villages, 33
    for slaves, 242
    urban middle class, 224
Houston, Sam, 276
Howe, William, 114
Hudson Bay territory, 59
Hudson river valley, 35
Humphries, David, 187
Huron, 34
Hutchinson, Anne, 30
Hutchinson, Thomas, 96

Immigrants and immigration
    in Colonial period, classes of, 64–65
    1820–1860, 213–214
    westward expansion by, 279–282
    in the work force, 222
Impressment, 83, 323, 327
Incas, 14–16
Indentured servants, 24–25, 47–48, 64–65
Indiana, 181–182
Indigo production, 73, 125–126
Individualism, 205
Industry
    advance of, 217–218
    in the colonies, 72–73
    education and, 216
    impact of, 218–219
    military related, 323–324
    in the South, 72–73, 236, 238
Inflation
    Civil War and, 317–318, 324–325
Insurrection, pre-Revolutionary, 123–124
Interracial relationships, 48, 51
Intolerable Acts, 98–99
Investment, 196–199, 215
Irish-Americans, 213–214, 277
Iroquois, 6, 34–35, 66–67, 90–91, 117–118, 140
Isabella, Queen of Spain, 11–12

Jackson, Andrew, 185, 188–189
    abolition and, 267
    campaign against the Creeks, 182
    distrust of banks by, 256–258

election of, 252–254, 257
Indian policy of, 254–255
James II, King of England, 55
Jamestown, Virginia, 24
James VI, King of England, 28
Jarratt, Devereaux, 62, 73, 79–80
Jay, John, 142, 146–150, 163
Jay-Gardoqui affair, 141–142, 144
Jay's Treaty, 163
Jefferson, Thomas, 147, 164
    Bill for Religious Freedom, 135
    Declaration of Independence and, 100
    election of (1800), 166–167
    Federalist party eliminated by, 172–175
    inauguration of, 171–173
    national bank and, 158–159
    at the Second Continental Congress, 99–100
Jeffersonian Republicans, 156
    decline of, 187
    election of 1800 and the, 166–168
    versus Federalists, 163–168
    foreign policy of, 182–183
    land policies of the, 174–177
    territorial expansion by the, 174–177
John Brown's Raid, 304, 306
Johnson, Andrew, 333, 336–338, 343
Johnson, Anthony, 44–45
Johnson, Richard, 184
Johnston, Joseph, 322
Johnston, Joseph E., 314
Jolliet, Louis, 58
Jomini, Henri, 314, 321
Jones, Absalom, 208
Judah, Henry, 272–273
Judiciary Act, 173
Julian, George, 339

Kansas, slavery conflict in, 300–303
Kansas-Nebraska Act (1854), 297–298, 300, 306
Kearny, Stephen W., 278
Kelly, Abby, 267–269
Kennedy, John F.
    assassination of, 200
Kentucky, in the Civil War, 313, 316
Kentucky Resolutions of 1798, 165
Keteltas, William, 205
King, Rufus, 146–149, 184
King George's War, 90
King Philip's War, 52–53
King William's War, 58–60
Kithtippecanoe, Battle of, 181–182

Knowles, Charles, 83
Know-Nothing party, 298–300
Knox, Henry, 178
Ku Klux Klan, 342, 344–346
Ku Klux Klan Act, 345

Labor unions
    in frontier factories, 222
    in the 1970s and 1980s, 168
    in the Reconstruction era, 346–347
    social reform and, 265
    women in the, 220
Lafayette, James Armistead, 124
Land. See also Property
    ordinances, 140
    ownership
        blacks and, 248–249, 266–267
        in the Reconstruction era, 334–
            336, 339, 341–342
    survey of, 140
    treaties with Native Americans,
        140–141, 177–180
    western, ceded by the states, 112–
        113
Land Act of 1801, 176
Lane Seminary, 265
Latin America
    slavery and slaves in, 248
    United States' relation with, 185–
        186
Laud, William, 28
Lawrence, Kansas, 300–301
League of Armed Neutrality, 118
Lecompton constitution, 303, 306
Lee, Richard Henry, 98–99
Lee, Robert E., 311, 315, 321, 326
Leisler, Jacob, 55–57
Leisler's Rebellion, 55–56
Lewis, Meriwether, 176
Liberator, The, 266
Liberty, 131, 134
Life expectancy, 243
Lincoln, Abraham, 310–311
    assassination of, 328–329
    call for troops by, 312–313
    Civil War and, 314–315, 319, 322,
        324, 328
    election of, 304–305, 326
    Emancipation Proclamation and,
        319–321
    Fort Sumter and, 307
    Illinois debates and, 303–304, 306
    Jefferson Davis compared to, 313–
        314, 327
Lines, Charles, 301
Literacy rate, 218

Livestock production, 238–239
Locke, John, 77
Louisiana, 59, 234–236, 305, 311
Louisiana Purchase (1803), 174–177
Louis XIV, King of France, 58–59
Louis XVI, King of France, 161
Lovejoy, Elijah, 267
Lowell, Francis Cabot, 217–218
Lowell, Massachusetts, 218–221
Lowell system, 217–218
Loyalists, 114, 118–123, 134
Loyal National League, 320
Luther, Martin, 13
Lynch, John, 344
Lynn, Massachusetts, 196–197

McClellan, George, 315, 326
McCormick Reaper Works, 324
McCulloch v. Maryland (1819), 173
McDowell, Irwin, 314
MacIntosh, Ebenezer, 88–89, 94
McPherson, William, 160
Madison, James, 150, 157, 184
    at the Grand Convention, 146–149
    national bank and, 158–159
    War of 1812 and, 184
Maine, 59, 263–264
Malthus, Thomas, 175
Manhattan, New York, 114
Manifest Destiny, 274, 276
Mann, Horace, 216, 264
Manufacturing
    colonial, 126, 196
    effect of factories on, 217–218
    New England, 126, 217–219
    preindustrial, 196–197
    Revolutionary era, 125–127
    textile, 217–219
Marbury v. Madison (1803), 173
Marcy, William, 298–299
Maroons, 247
Marquette, Jacques, 58
Marshall, John, 164, 171, 173
Maryland, 26, 72, 135, 152, 184–185,
    312–313
Mason, George, 146–149
Mason, John, 22–23
Masonic order, 257
Massachusetts, 28–29, 83, 152
    colonial, 27–32, 70, 75–76, 80, 96,
        99
    European Wars, losses in, 60
    Farmers' Rebellion, 144–146
    politics, revolutionary in, 132–134
    public education in, 216
    Revolutionary War in, 113–114

shoe industry in, 196–197
state constitution, 129, 133
suffrage in, 129
textile industry in, 218–221
witchcraft trials in, 57–58
Massachusetts Emigrant Aid society,
    300
Mather, Cotton, 70, 72
Matlack, Timothy, 104, 132
Meade, George, 321–322
Melville, Herman, 260
Memminger, Christopher G., 313
Memphis, Tennessee, 337
Merchants, 75, 196–199, 215
Merrimac, 316
Metacomet, 52–53
Mexicans
    westward expansion and, 289–290
Mexican War, 276–278, 293–294, 306
Mexico, 15–16, 176
    Gadsden Purchase and, 279
    Spanish conquest of, 14–17
    in Texas, 275–278
    United States relations with, 185–
        186
Miami Indians, 141, 177
Middle class, 224
Midwives, 71–72
Migration, 3
    population, 121–122, 234, 236
Miller, William, 262
Millerites, 262
Mining, 16–17, 280, 283–284, 288
Minorca, 59
Minutemen, 99
Mississippi, 234–236, 305, 311
Mississippi Plan, 345, 348
Mississippi River, 58, 140–142, 176
Missouri, in the Civil War, 313, 316
Missouri Compromise, 187–188, 293–
    294, 297–298, 303, 306
Missouri River, 58, 176
Moby Dick (Melville), 260
Mohawk, 117–118
Molasses Act of 1733, 90
Monitor, 316
Monroe, James, 175, 186
Monroe Doctrine (1823), 186
Montezuma's Aztec empire, 14–16
Montgomery, Richard, 114
Montreal, 91
Moody, Paul, 217–218
Morgan, Daniel, 116
Mormons, 262–263, 284–286
Morrill Act of 1862, 328
Morris, Gouverneur, 173

Morris, Robert, 126, 146–149
Mortality rate, 202–203
Mott, Lucretia, 268–269
Mound-building societies, 4
Music, 245–246
Muslims, North African, 8, 11

Napoleon, 175, 183
National Labor Union, 346
National Negro Convention Movement, 267
National Republicans, 187
National Trades Union, 265
Native Americans, 3–8, 19–20, 31–32, 65–66, 124, 285
  civil rights for, 53, 129–130
  in Civil War, 315–316
  colonies and, 5–6, 8, 23–26, 35–37, 180
  culture of, 66–67, 179–181
  education and, 179
  fur trade with, 66–67, 179
  land treaties with, 177–179
  missionaries and, 179–181
  President Jackson's and, 254–255
  Removal Act of 1830 and, 254–255
  in Revolutionary War, 117–118
  settlers relations with, 177–182
  in Seven Years' War, 90–91
  Spanish and, 68–69
  trans-Mississippi settlement by, 274
  Treaty of Fort Stanwix and, 140
  Treaty of Paris and, 92, 140
  tribal warfare of, 287–288
  westward expansion and, 140–142, 281–282, 286–289
  women, 6, 8, 129, 142
Nativism, 299–300
Nat Turner's revolt, 236, 243, 248
Naturalization Act of 1798, 165
Navigation Acts, 89
Navy Department, creation of, 164–165
New Amsterdam, Dutch in, 35
New England
  agriculture, 227–228
  colonial, 27–32, 69–70
  Confederation of, 33
  Glorious Revolution in, 55
  King Philip's War in, 52–53
  manufacturing, 126, 217–219
  New France conflict, 58–60
  Puritans in, 29–34
  town meetings, 85
  in War of 1812, 185

Newfoundland, 19, 118
New France, 34, 58–60
New Hampshire, 133, 152
New Harmony, Indiana, 261–262
New Jersey, 79–80, 114, 133, 152
New Jersey Plan, 148
New Light Presbyterianism, 80–81
New Mexico, 68–69, 277–278, 289, 294–295, 316
New Netherland, 34–35
New Orleans, 67–68, 141–142, 185, 316
Newton, Isaac, 77
New York, 55, 60, 75, 106, 129, 152
New York City, New York, 35, 50, 114, 121–122, 155–156
Non-Importation Act of 1806, 183
Norfolk, Virginia, 100
North, Lord, 98, 112
North Carolina, 129, 152, 180, 311–312
North Carolina Regulators, 105–106
Northwest, 176, 228–229
Northwest Ordinance, 140, 187
Noyes, John Humphrey, 261

Oberlin College, 265
Occupation Treaty of 1827, 273
Ohio, 90, 181–182, 221–222, 296
Olive Branch Petition, 99–100
Oneida, New York, 261
Opechancanough, 2–3, 25–26
Ordinance of Nullification (1828), 256, 306
Oregon Territory, 273, 279
Oregon Trail, 280–282
Ostend Manifesto, 298–299, 306
Ottawa Indians, 140
Owen, Robert, 261–262

Pacific Railroad Act of 1862, 328
Pacifism, Quaker, 39–41
Paine, Thomas, 100–102, 104, 129, 132
Palmer v. *Mulligan*, 215
Paterson, William, 148
Patriots, 119–120
Peace of Utrecht, 59–60
Pea Ridge, Battle of, 316
Penn, William, 39–41
Pennsylvania, 39–41, 79–80, 114, 129, 131–133, 135, 152
Pennsylvania Blues, 160
Pequot, 22–23, 32
Perry, Oliver-Hazard, 185
Peru, 14–16
Peters, Thomas, 124

Philadelphia, Pennsylvania, 75, 114, 121–122, 157–158, 225–227
Philadelphia Gazette, 225–226
Philip II, King of Spain, 18
Phillips, Wendell, 266
Phips, William, 57, 60
Pickering, John, 173
Pickering, Timothy, 165
Pickett's Charge, 322
Pierce, Franklin, 297–298
Pike, Zebulon, 176
Pilgrims, 28–29
Pinckney, C. C., 184
Pinckney, Charles, 146–149, 164
Pinckney, Eliza Lucas, 73
Pinckney, Thomas, 163
Piracy, English, 162–163, 183–184
Pitt, William, 91
Pitt-Grafton ministry, 95–96
Pizarro, Francisco, 14–15
Plains of Abraham, 91
Plantation life, 72–74, 239–246
Plymouth, Massachusetts, 28–29
Pocahontas, 25
Police, 226
Political parties
  Anti-Mason, 257
  Democratic, 258–259, 306
    during the Civil War, 319
    formation of, 253
    during Jackson's presidency, 253–256
    in Kansas, 302–303
    during the Reconstruction era, 344–345, 347–348
    weakening of, 297–299, 302–303
  Federalist
    versus Anti-Federalist, 149–151, 167–168
    decline of, 171–173, 187
    in the election of 1800, 166–168
    during Jefferson's administration, 163–168, 171–172
    Judiciary Act and, 173
    rise of, 146
  Federalist-Jeffersonian system, 187
  Free-Soil, 294, 299–301
  Know-Nothing, 298–300
  National Republican, 187
  Republican, 298–300, 306
    during the Civil War, 319
    Jeffersonian, 156
    in Kansas, 302–303
    in the Reconstruction era, 344–348
    in the Revolutionary era, 129

Political parties (continued)
  second party system, 258–259, 294
  Whig, 85, 100–102, 257–259
Politics, 83
  blacks in, 343–344
  Catholic immigrants and, 299
  colonial, 56–57, 81–85, 103
  the Great Awakening and, 79–81
  Jeffersonian policies of, 174–175
  patterns of, 186–189
  reform and, 260
  religion and, 127–128, 299
  Revolutionary era, 127–136
  slavery and, 293–295, 297
Polk, James, 276–279
Polygamy, 284–286
Pontiac, Chief, 92
Poor Richard's Almanack, 70
Popé's revolt, 17
Popular sovereignty, 294, 306
Population
  America's first explosion, 63–66
  decline from disease, 15–16
  growth of, 1820–1860, 213–214
  migration, 121–122, 234, 236
  mixed-race, 51–52, 67
  slave, 63, 72–73, 236
  in the southern colonies, 72–73
  urban, 222
Porter, Peter, 184
Port Royal, Acadia, 58–59, 316
Portugal, 11–12, 14, 16–17
Potawatomi, 177
Potomac River, 157–158, 171
Pottawatomie Creek massacre, 301
Poverty
  black, 248–249
  in colonial Boston, 76
  following the Seven Years' War,
    92–93
  in preindustrial America, 203–204
  in the Reconstruction era, 334–336
  social reform and, 206
  in southern whites, 238–239
Powhatan, 2–3, 24–26, 53–54
Pre-Columbus era, 3–8
Preindustrial
  agriculture, 194–196
  birthrate, 202
  commerce, 192–194
  death rate, 202–203
  economy, 192–194
  education, 206–207
  family life, 201–204
  manufacturing, 196–197
  poverty, 203–204

roads, 200
social reform, 204–208
society, 199–208
westward settlement, 198–
  200
work force, 196–197, 201
Prendergast, William, 106
Presidential elections
  1789, 155–156
  1792, 163–164
  1796, 163–164
  1800, 166–167
  1808, 184
  1824, 188–189, 253
  1828, 252–254
  1832, 257
  1836, 257
  1840, 258–259
  1844, 276
  1848, 294
  1852, 297
  1856, 299–300
  1860, 304–305
  1864, 326
  1868, 338
  1872, 347
  1876, 347–348
Press, 127, 156
Price controls, 136
Printing industries, 218
Prison reform, 264–265
Proclamation of 1763, 92
Profiteering, 120, 126, 135
Prohibition, 263–264
Property, 5–6. See also Land
  ownership, 69–71, 82–83, 203–204,
    334–343
  Revolutionary War and, 121–122,
    127
Prosser, Gabriel, 208, 248
Prostitution, 283–284
Providence, Rhode Island, 30
Publishing industry, 218, 225
Pueblo, 4, 17
Puritans, 28–34, 38, 70, 72
Putting-out system, 196–197

Quakers, 38–41, 65–66, 72
Quartering Act of 1765, 96
Quebec, 34, 91
Queen Anne's War, 58–60
Quincy, Josiah, Jr., 96

Railroads
  abolitionist organized, 247
  construction of, 214–215

in the Reconstruction era, 346–347
  westward expansion of, 297–298
Raleigh, Walter, 19, 23
Reconstruction Acts (1867), 337–338,
  343
Reconstruction Amendments, 336–
  340
Reconstruction era, 332, 347–348. See
  also Civil War
  agriculture in, 341–342
  blacks in, 334–343
  congressional reconstruction, 336–
    340
  economy in, 334–336, 347
  graft during, 346–347
  labor unions in, 346–347
  land ownership in, 334–336, 339,
    341–342
  in the North, 333–334, 346–347
  political parties in, 343–348
  racial violence in, 335–337, 344–346
  railroads in, 346–347
  in the South, 333–336, 341–342
  suffrage in, 337–339
Red Eagle, 182
Red Sticks, 182
Reed, Esther DeBerdt, 130
Religion
  African Methodist Episcopal
    church, 342
  Anglican Church, 33, 77, 79, 133
  Baptists, 80, 135, 205
  of blacks, 51–52, 208, 244–245,
    342–343
  Catholicism, 18, 55, 299
  Christianity, 13–14, 162, 179, 224–
    225
  churches, 77, 79, 208
  Church of England, 28, 38
  clergy, 77, 79–81
  communitarianism, 260–262
  conflicts, 8, 13–14, 18
  Congregationalists, 133–134
  English Protestant church, 28, 38
  evangelicalism, 79–80
  freedom of, 156
  Glorious Revolution and, 55
  Great Awakening and, 77, 79–81,
    205
  Methodists, 205
  missionaries, 12–13, 179–181, 342
  Mormons, 284–286
  Negro Baptist church, 342
  Protestant, 13–14, 18, 55, 135
  Puritans and, 30
  Quakers and, 38

Revolutionary politics and, 127–128
separation of church and state, 30, 81, 133–134, 285
of West Africans, 9
Removal Act of 1830, 254–255
Report on Manufactures (1791), 159
Reports on the Public Credit, 156–159
Republicans, 129–133, 144, 156, 302–303, 319, 343–344
Republican Society, preindustrial, 204–208
Republic of Sonora, 298
Restoration colonies, 35–37
Revenue Act of 1764, 93
Revolutionary era
abolitionism, 134–135
agriculture, 104–106, 125–126, 144–146
blacks in, 129–130, 134–135
cities, 103–104
frontier in, 140–142
manufacturing, 125–127
Native Americans in, 129–130
politics, 127–136
slavery and slaves in, 120, 134–135
speculators, 120, 135
suffrage, 130–131
women in, 104, 130–131
Revolutionary War. *See also* Colonies
blacks and the, 123–124
British defeat in, 118–119
casualties in the, 120–121
civilians and the, 121–122
debt, 135–136, 142, 157
economy and, 125–127
events leading to, 93–99, 105–106
foreign relations following the, 142–143
international effects of, 118
military operations in the, 113–117
in the North, 113–115
peace negotiations, 118
politics during, 127–134
recruiting an army for the, 119–120
in the South, 114–117
Treaty of Paris, 118
Rhode Island, 29–30, 97, 131, 133, 152
Rice production, 37–38, 73, 125–126
Richmond, Virginia, 208
Ripley, George, 262
Roads, 174, 200
Robinson, Emily, 251–252, 269

Robinson, Marius, 251–252
Rochester, New York, 259–260
Rockefeller, John D., 324
Rolfe, John, 25
Rural America, 80–81, 104–106
Rush, Benjamin, 104, 207
Rutledge, John, 146–149

Sacajawea, 176
Salem, Massachusetts, 57–58
Salt Lake City, Utah, 284–286
San Antonio, Texas, 276
San Francisco, California, 284
Santa Anna, Antonio López de, 276
Santa Fe, New Mexico, 274, 278
Santa Fe Trail, 280–282
Saratoga, New York, 114
Savannah, Georgia, 115
Scarlet Letter, The (Hawthorne), 260
Schenectady, New York, 59
Schurz, Carl, 305
Schuyler, Elizabeth, 147
Scots-Irish settlements, 63–64
Scott, Dred and Harriet, 302–303
Scott, William, 110–111
Scott, Winfield, 297, 314
Secession, 305, 307
Secessionism, 295–296
Secotan, 23
Sectionalism, 187–188
Sedition Act of 1798, 164–165, 174
Segregation
in public schools, 267
Seizure, unreasonable, 156
Self-incrimination, 156
Seminole, 177
Seneca Falls Convention, 268–269
Seneca Indians, 177
Sentiments of an American Women, The, 130
Separation of church and state, 30, 81, 133–134, 285
Separatists, 29
Servants, 24–25, 47–48, 64–65
Seven Years' War, 89–93
Sewall, Samuel, 70
Seward, William, 303, 317, 320
Sewing machine, 221
Sex ratios, 51, 283, 286
Sexuality
abuse of women, 243–244
birth control, 225, 268
health and, 264
social reform and, 261, 264
women's rights and, 268
Shakers, 261

Sharecropping, 341–342
Shattuck, Jacob, 144–146
Shawnee, 141, 177, 181–182
Shays's Rebellion, 144–146
Sherman, Roger, 146–149
Sherman, William Tecumseh, 322–323, 326
Shiloh Church, Battle of, 316
Shipbuilding, New England, 126
Shipping, European War and, 192–193
Sierra Leone, 124
Silver, 16–17
Singleton, Benjamin "Pap," 343
Sit-ins, 267
Slavery and slaves. *See also* Abolitionism
in Africa, 9
in American colonies, 45–52
the bondage system, 48–49
in the Carolinas, 35, 37–40, 135
in the Cherokee nation, 181
Civil War and, 320–321, 323, 327–328
Compromise of 1850 and, 294–297
concentration of, 236–237
cotton production and, 195–196
culture, 49–50, 246
daily life of, 239–246
Dred Scott decision and, 302–303, 306
economic impact of, 236, 238
emancipation of, 334
expansion of, 50–51
field slaves, 242
in the French colonies, 67–68
in Georgia, 135
Great Compromise and, 149
house slaves, 242
Illinois debates and, 303–304, 306
indentured servants and, 47–48
John Brown's raid and, 304
justifying, 241
in Kansas, 297–298, 300–303, 306
in Latin American, 248
laws governing, 243–244
life after, 340–343
master-slave relationship, 325–326
Missouri Compromise and, 187–188, 293–294, 297–298, 303, 306
in Northern colonies, 48
Northwest Ordinance and, 140, 187
overseer, 242
on the plantation, 239–246

Slavery and slaves (continued)
    popular sovereignty and, 294, 306
    population, 63, 72–73, 236
    rebellions by, 50–51, 208
    in a republican society, 134–135
    Revolutionary War and, 124, 134–135
    rice production and, 37–38, 73, 125–126
    runaway, 247, 296
    secession and, 285, 296, 305, 307, 311–312
    sexual abuse of women, 243–244
    slaveholders, burdens of, 239–246
    slave trade, 8, 46–48, 134–135, 195–196, 236
    social reform and, 207–208
    southern social structure and, 238–239
    in Spanish colonies, 67–68
    sugar production with, 16–17, 45–47
    in Texas, 276
    tobacco production and, 23–27, 72–73
    treatment of, 46–47, 243–244
    westward expansion and, 293–297
    Wilmot Proviso and, 293–294, 306
Slidell, John L., 277
Smith, Adam, 198
Smith, John, 2, 24
Smith, Joseph, 284
Smith, Mrs. Samuel Harrison, 171
Social reform
    education and, 206–207, 216
    in factories, 265
    Great Awakening and, 79–81
        Second, 205–206, 259–260
    poverty and, 206
    preindustrial, 204–208
    in public institutions, 264–265
    racism and, 207–208
    sexuality and, 261, 264
    slavery and, 207–208
    women and, 262–264
    working-class, 265
Social structure
    black, 51–52, 208
    colonial, 54, 72–77
    in the South, 72–73, 238–239, 323–324
Society of Friends, 38–41
Sons of Liberty, 94
Sort Smith, 176
Soulé, Pierre, 298
South, nonslaveholding, 238–239

South America, 14–16, 19
South Carolina, 115, 152. See also
        Carolina colonies
    cotton production in, 234–236
    Fort Sumter attack, 306–307
    Nullification Ordinance of, 256, 306
    secession of, 305–306, 311
    slavery in, 135
    Tariff of Abomination and, 255–256, 306
Southern Homestead Act of 1866, 339
Southern social structure, 238–239
Spain, 16–17
    in colonial America, 68–69
    East Florida ceded by, 176
    Louisiana ceded to France by, 175
    New World Empire of, 14–17, 68–69, 141–143, 176, 273
    ocean explorations of, 11–12
    Ostend Manifesto and, 298–299
    Peace of Utrecht and, 59–61
    trans-Mississippi holdings, 273
    Treaty of San Lorenzo and, 163
    war with England 1739, 90
Spanish Armada, 18
Specie Circular, 257
Speculators, 120, 126, 135
Speech, freedom of, 156
Stamp Act Congress, 94
Stamp Act of 1765, 93–95
Stamp Act Riots, 94–95
Stanton, Edwin, 338
Stanton, Elizabeth Cady, 268–269, 320, 340
Steamboats, 200–201
Stevens, Thaddeus, 336–337, 339
Stewart, John, 179
Stowe, Harriet Beecher, 296–297
Strikes
    frontier factory, 222
    women and, 219–220
Stuart, Archibald, 129
Suffrage
    amendment for, 269, 340
    black, 129
        in the middle 1800s, 226–227
        in the Reconstruction era, 337–339
    in the colonial era, 82–83, 129
    female
        colonial era, 82–83
        Reconstruction Amendments and, 340

    in the Revolutionary era, 130–131
    property ownership and, 82–83
Sugar Act of 1764, 93
Sugar production, 16–17, 45–47
Sullivan, John, 117–118
Sumner, Charles, 301, 306, 336–337
Susquehannocks, 53

Talleyrand, 164–166, 175
Taney, Roger, 257, 303
Tariffs, 187
    of Abominations, 255–256, 306
Taxes
    Civil War and, 317–318
    on colonies, 93–95, 97–98
    in post-Revolutionary era, 135–136
    power of taxation, 157
    Whiskey, 159–161
Taylor, Zachary, 277, 294
Tea Act, 97–98
Technology, 4, 77
Tecumseh, 181–182, 184
Temperance movement, 263–264
Tenancy, 341–342
Tennent, Gilbert, 79
Tennessee, 180, 311–312, 316, 337
Tenochtitlán, 14–16
Tenure of Office Act, 338
Texas
    annexation of, 275–276
    in the Civil War, 316
    cotton production in, 234–236
    Hispanics-Americans in, 289
    Mexico in, 275–278
    New Mexico border dispute, 294–295
    secession of, 305, 311
    settlement of, 273–276
    Spanish military posts in, 68–69
Textile industry, 217–218
Thames, Battle of the, 182
Thayer, Eli, 300
Thoreau, Henry David, 260
Tilden, Samuel J., 347–348
Tippecanoe, Battle of, 181–182
Tobacco production, 19, 23–27, 72–73, 125–126
Toombs, Robert, 294
Tories, 114, 118–123, 134
Townshend Acts, 95–96
Trade
    with England, 144, 161
    the European war and, 192–193
    foreign, 143, 196
    with France, 161

fur, 34, 66–67, 179, 273
  with Native Americans, 177–179
  networks, 4, 10
  post-Revolutionary, 125
  slave. *See under* Slavery and slaves
Trail of Tears, 255
Transcendentalists, 260
Transportation, 214–215
Travel
  canals, 214–215, 222
  in preindustrial America, 200–201
  steamboats, 200–201
Traveling preachers, 80–81
Treaty of Ghent, 185
Treaty of Guadalupe Hidalgo (1848),
      279, 285, 289
Treaty of Paris (1783), 118
Treaty of Paris (1763), 91–93
Treaty of San Lorenzo, 163
Treaty of 1778, 164–165
Treaty of Tordesillas, 14
Tredegar Iron Company, 236, 323
Trial by jury, right of, 156
Trist, Nicholas, 278–279
Trumbull, Jonathan, 187
Truth, Sojourner, 296
Tryon, William, 106
Tsenacommacah, 2
Tubman, Harriet, 247
Turner, Nat, 236, 248
Tweed Ring, 347
Tyler, John, 258–259, 276

Uncle Tom's Cabin (Stowe), 296–297,
      306

Valley Forge, 119–120
Van Buren, Martin, 294
  abolition and, 267
  depression and, 257–258
  in the election of 1840, 258–259
  election of (1836), 257
Varick, Mayor, 205
Vásquez, Tiburcio, 290
Vergennes, Charles, 118
Vermont, 131, 133
Verrazano, Giovanni da, 18
Vesey, Denmark, 248
Vicksburg, Battle of, 322
Virginia, 19, 25–26, 72, 80–81, 152.
      See also Chesapeake Bay
  Bacon's Rebellion in, 53–54
  blacks in, 44–45, 208
  revolutionary politics in, 131, 134
  secession of, 311–312
  slavery in, 135, 248

Virginia Company of London, 24
Virginia House of Burgesses, 94–95
Virginia Plan, 147–148
Virginia Resolutions, 165
Virginia (the ship), 316
Voting Rights Act of 1965, 339

Wages
  during the Civil War, 324
Wage slavery, 220–221
Walden (Thoreau), 260
Walker, David, 266
Walker, Robert, 276
Walker, William, 298
Wampanoags, 52–53
War Hawks, 184
War of Austrian Succession, 90
War of 1812, 181–182, 184–185
Washington, George, 139–140, 155–
      156, 181, 200
  at Continental Congress, 99–100
  election of, 163–164
  the European war and, 161–162
  at Fort Duquesne, 90
  French Revolution and, 162–163
  at Grand Convention, 146–149
  national bank and, 158–159
  Revolutionary War and, 113–114,
      119
  Whiskey Rebellion and, 159–161
Washington D. C., 157–158, 171, 184
Washington Temperance Society,
      263
Wayne, Anthony, 181
Way to Wealth, The, 70
Wealth, distribution of, 203–204,
      238–239
Wealth of Nations (Smith), 198
Webster, Daniel, 256
Webster, Noah, 187, 206
Weld, Theodore Dwight, 263, 265–
      268
Wells, Maine, 59
Wells, Rachel, 104
West Indies, 19
West Jersey, Quakers in, 39
Westward expansion, 140–142, 272–
      290
  by blacks, 280
  California, 278
  commercial reasons for, 273
  frontier life, 282–287
  fur trade and, 34, 66–67, 179, 273
  Gadsden Purchase (1853), 274, 279
  gold mining and, 280, 283–284,
      288

Hispanic-Americans and, 289–290
immigration routes, 279–282
Jeffersonians and, 174–177
Louisiana Purchase, 174–177
Manifest Destiny and, 274
Mexicans and, 289–290
Mexican War (1846–1848), 276–278
Mormons and, 284–286
Native Americans and, 140–142,
      281, 286–289
New Mexico, 278
Oregon, 279–280
overland trails, 281–282
in the post-Revolutionary era,
      140–142
preindustrial, 198–200
of railroads, 297–298
slavery and, 293–297
into Texas, 275–276
Whetten, Harriet, 326
Whig party, 85, 100–102, 258–259
Whiskey Rebellion, 159–161
Whiskey Ring, 347
Whiskey Tax (1791), 159–161
Whitefield, George, 79–81
Whitney, Eli, 195, 234
William of Orange, 55
Williams, Roger, 30
Wilmot, David, 293
Wilmot Proviso, 293–294, 306
Wilson, James, 146–149
Winthrop, John, 19, 29–32
Wirt, William, 257
Witchcraft, 57–58
Wolfe, James, 91
Women
  alcohol consumption by, 202
  birth control and, 268
  black, 51, 243–244, 334
  childbirth and, 71–72
  child-rearing, 224–225
  Civil War and, 324–326
  colonial, 6, 8, 26–27, 30, 70–72
  divorce and, 207
  education and, 207
  European, colonial, 6, 8, 70, 72
  farm, 125
  frontier life for, 71, 283–284
  Mormon, 284–286
  Native American, 6, 8, 129, 142
  plantation life, 51–52, 240–241
  property ownership by, 203–
      204
  Puritan, 33
  Quaker, 38
  Republican, 130–131

Women (continued)
   in the Revolutionary era, 104, 130–131
   as servants, 25
   slaves, 242–244
   social reform and, 262–264
   southern white, 240–241
Women's rights
   abolitionism and, 265–266, 268
   abortion, 225
   Anne Hutchinson and, 30
   birth control and, 268
   conventions, 268–269, 296
   property rights of, 71
   Reconstruction Amendments and, 340
   sexuality and, 268
Woolman, John, 65
Worcester v. Georgia, 255

Work force
   blacks in the
      during the Civil War, 324–325
      job competition for, 208, 227, 236
   ethnic composition of, 220–222
   in factories, 221–222
   gender composition of, 220–221
   Germans in the, 222
   immigrants in the, 222
   Irish in the, 222
   outworkers, 221
   preindustrial, 196–197, 201
   transition from indentured white, to black slaves, 47–48
   women in the, 324–325
      responses to work, 219–220
      in the textile industry, 218–221
      work stoppages by, 219–220

Working class
   in the cities, 223
   development of in England, 11
   in the Reconstruction era, 346–347
   social reform and, 265
World Anti-Slavery Convention, 268
Wyandotte, 140–141

XYZ affair, 164

Yale College, 81
Yellow fever epidemics, 203
Yorktown, Virginia, Cornwallis's surrender at, 117
Young, Brigham, 284–286
Young, Thomas, 104, 132–133

Zenger, John Peter, 85
Zuni, 4